JESUS AND DIVINE CHRISTOLOGY

Jesus and Divine Christology

Brant Pitre

William B. Eerdmans Publishing Company
Grand Rapids, Michigan

Wm. B. Eerdmans Publishing Co.
4035 Park East Court SE, Grand Rapids, Michigan 49546
www.eerdmans.com

Published 2024

Book design by Leah Luyk

Printed in the United States of America

30 29 28 27 26 25 24 1 2 3 4 5 6 7

ISBN 978-0-8028-7512-9

Library of Congress Cataloging-in-Publication Data

A catalog record for this book is available from the Library of Congress.

IN MEMORIAM

John P. Meier

Requiem aeternam dona ei, Domine,
et lux perpetua luceat ei
(cf. 4 Ezra 2:34–35)

God could sooner change into a human
than a human into God.

—Philo of Alexandria, *Embassy to Gaius* 118

Contents

CHAPTER 1

The Quest and Jesus's Divinity

> We should hold a funeral for the view that Jesus entertained no exalted thoughts about himself.
>
> —Dale C. Allison Jr.[1]

> It is possible to understand the Gospel only if both Jesus and the Jews around him held to a high Christology whereby the claim to Messiahship was also a claim to being a divine man.
>
> —Daniel Boyarin[2]

The Historical Jesus

In his watershed book, *The Quest of the Historical Jesus*, written at the dawn of the twentieth century, Albert Schweitzer points out that the modern quest was motivated from its very beginnings by more than just the historical aim of discovering what Jesus of Nazareth really did and said. The quest was also explicitly directed against the idea that the historical Jesus claimed to be more than merely human. In his opening chapter on the "problem" of the historical Jesus, Schweitzer writes:

> The historical investigation of the life of Jesus did not take its rise from a purely historical interest; it turned to the Jesus of history as an ally in the struggle against the tyranny of dogma. . . . For hate as well as love can write a Life of Jesus, and the greatest of them are written with hate. . . . It was hate not so much of the person of Jesus as of the supernatural nimbus with

1. Dale C. Allison Jr., *Constructing Jesus: Memory, Imagination, and History* (Grand Rapids: Baker Academic, 2010), 227, 304.

2. Daniel Boyarin, *The Jewish Gospels: The Story of the Jewish Christ* (New York: New Press, 2012), 55.

> which it was so easy to surround him, and with which he had in fact been surrounded. They were eager to picture him as an ordinary person, to strip from him the robes of splendor with which he had been appareled, and clothe him once more with the coarse garments in which he had walked in Galilee.[3]

In other words, the modern historical quest for Jesus—at least in the eighteenth and nineteenth centuries—was often explicitly driven by the theological aim of liberating readers from the ancient Christian doctrine, formulated above all at the ecumenical councils of Nicaea (325 CE) and Chalcedon (451 CE), that Jesus of Nazareth was both fully human and fully divine—what Schweitzer calls "the dogma of the two natures."[4] According to Schweitzer, "This dogma had first to be shattered before people could once more go out in quest of the historical Jesus, before they could even grasp the thought of his existence."[5]

Since Schweitzer first penned these words in 1906, historical Jesus research has come a long way. On the one hand, a strong case can be made that the most important works on the historical Jesus are no longer written with "hate." In my view, most contributors to contemporary Jesus research are sincerely seeking the historical truth about who Jesus of Nazareth was, how he fit into his first-century Jewish context, and the relationship between his public ministry and the birth of early Christianity. Moreover, in contrast to the eighteenth and nineteenth centuries, in which the quest for the historical Jesus was dominated almost exclusively by European Protestant scholars, contemporary Jesus research involves contributions from multiple continents, multiple languages, and multiple perspectives, including Jewish, Christian, and nonreligious scholars alike.[6]

At the same time, a case can be made that the contemporary quest has inherited from its early forebears an almost reflexive reluctance to explore the question of whether the historical Jesus ever claimed to be anything more than merely human. For example, in his presidential address to the Cambridge Theological Society, John A. T. Robinson once described the question

3. Albert Schweitzer, *The Quest of the Historical Jesus*, trans. William Montgomery, J. R. Coates, Susan Cupitt, and John Bowden (Minneapolis: Fortress, 2001), 5–6.

4. Schweitzer, *Quest of the Historical Jesus*, 5.

5. Schweitzer, *Quest of the Historical Jesus*, 5.

6. See Jens Schröter and Christine Jacobi, eds., *The Jesus Handbook*, trans. Robert L. Brawley (Grand Rapids: Eerdmans, 2022), 1–121, for an up-to-date overview of the contemporary quest.

of whether Jesus claimed to be more than human as one of several "'no-go' areas" around which twentieth-century scholarship had erected warning signs and which "it would not be intelligent or respectable to question."[7] He goes on to depict the situation as follows:

> What lay at the centre of Jesus' life has been left a blank, and indeed been regarded as forbidden territory. We can say what the church said about him, but we cannot say—or apparently be allowed to care—what he thought about himself.[8]

Four decades after Robinson penned these words, the situation remains largely unchanged. Though a growing number of scholars agree that Jesus spoke and acted as if he were a messianic figure, the possibility that he saw himself as divine (in some sense) is still often treated as a "no-go area." For example, in his recent study of the origins of early divine Christology, Bart Ehrman emphasizes that the "one thing" contemporary studies of the historical Jesus "all agree on" is this:

> Jesus did not spend his ministry declaring himself to be divine. . . . One of the enduring findings of modern scholarship on the New Testament and early Christianity over the past two centuries is that the followers of Jesus, during his life, understood him to be human through and through, not God.[9]

As we will see momentarily, Ehrman's assessment of the modern quest as a whole is quite accurate. As I hope to demonstrate over the course of this study, however, when one takes a closer look at recent research on Second Temple Jewish messianism, the evidence in the first-century gospels, and the practice and belief of the early church, one finds serious reasons for reopening the question of whether Jesus himself ever claimed to be more than merely human. In particular, several key historical questions emerge that deserve thorough answers:

7. John A. T. Robinson, "The Last Tabu? The Self-Consciousness of Jesus," in *The Historical Jesus in Recent Research*, ed. James D. G. Dunn and Scot McKnight, Sources for Biblical and Theological Study 10 (Winona Lake, IN: Eisenbrauns, 2005), 553.

8. Robinson, "The Last Tabu?," 555.

9. Bart D. Ehrman, *How Jesus Became God: The Exaltation of a Jewish Preacher from Galilee* (San Francisco: HarperOne, 2014), 88, 44.

- Did Jesus of Nazareth ever speak and act as if he were divine? If so, in what sense?[10]
- How did Jesus's self-claims fit into his first-century Jewish context, especially the context of early Jewish monotheism?[11]
- How did Jesus's self-claims relate to the Christology of the earliest Jewish believers?

In order to see clearly why these questions are worth asking and answering, we will need to take a few moments to explore the contemporary problem of the historical Jesus and the origins of early "high" Christology.

Early High Christology

When we compare the results of the modern quest for the historical Jesus with recent research on the earliest Christology—that is, the earliest beliefs about Jesus's identity and mission as the Jewish "messiah" (Greek: *christos*)—we discover something of a paradox.

10. Here I use the word *divine* according to the general definition of "superhuman," "godlike," or "partaking of the nature of God or a god." See Angus J. Stevenson, ed., *Shorter Oxford English Dictionary*, 2 vols. (Oxford: Oxford University Press, 2007), 1:726. Over the course of this study, I will take pains to examine each text on a case-by-case basis and be as precise as possible in describing *what kind of divinity* is in view. See Ruben A. Bühner, *Messianic High Christology: New Testament Variants of Second Temple Judaism* (Waco, TX: Baylor University Press, 2021), 10–20, for a discussion of the terminological issue.

11. Here I use the expression "early Jewish monotheism" to refer to the ancient Jewish faith in and worship of "one" (*monos*) "God" (*theos*) (cf. Deut 6:4–6 LXX). In recent years, some have argued that the expression *monotheism* should be abandoned or replaced with *henotheism* (adherence to one particular deity out of several) or *monolatry* (the exclusive worship of one particular deity without denying the existence of other deities). However, given the fact that one important early Jewish writing explicitly speaks about the distinctively Jewish practice of worshiping "the only God" (*ton monon theon*) in contrast to the Gentile belief in "many gods" (*pollous theous*) (*Letter of Aristeas* 134, 139), it is not anachronistic to speak of early Jewish "monotheism" as long as one emphasizes that it did not, as a rule, deny the *existence* of other heavenly beings, who could be called "gods" (*theoi*) (cf. Deut 32:8, 17–18 LXX). For discussion, see Kevin P. Sullivan, "Monotheism," in *Encyclopedia of Second Temple Judaism*, 2 vols., ed. Daniel M. Gurtner and Loren T. Stuckenbruck (London: T&T Clark, 2020), 2:513–15; Larry W. Hurtado, "Monotheism," in *The Eerdmans Dictionary of Early Judaism*, ed. John J. Collins and Daniel C. Harlow (Grand Rapids: Eerdmans, 2010), 961–64; R. W. L. Moberly, "How Appropriate Is 'Monotheism' as a Category for Biblical Interpretation?," in *Early Jewish and Christian Monotheism*, ed. Loren T. Stuckenbruck and Wendy E. S. North (London: T&T Clark, 2004), 216–34.

The Historical Jesus Did Not Claim to Be Divine

On the one hand, when it comes to contemporary Jesus research, the vast majority of modern scholars agree that Jesus of Nazareth himself did not think, speak, or act as if he was in any way "divine"—that is, more than human. Consider, for example, the following statements of prominent contributors to the quest for the historical Jesus:

> Jesus did not declare himself to be God.[12]

> There is no indication that Jesus thought or spoke of himself as having preexisted with God. . . . We cannot claim that Jesus believed himself to be the incarnate Son of God.[13]

> The religion proclaimed by Jesus was a wholly theocentric one in which he played the role of the man of God . . . without being himself in any sense the object of worship as he later became.[14]

> There is no evidence whatever that [Jesus] spoke or acted as if he believed himself to be "a god" or "divine."[15]

Notice here that the view that Jesus did not claim to be divine can be found in the works of Jewish, Christian, and nonreligious scholars alike.[16] It has even found its way into the writings of prominent contemporary systematic theologians.[17]

12. Ehrman, *How Jesus Became God*, 128.

13. James D. G. Dunn, *Christology in the Making: A New Testament Inquiry into the Origins of the Doctrine of the Incarnation*, 2nd ed. (Grand Rapids: Eerdmans, 1989), 254. For a similar point, see James D. G. Dunn, *Jesus Remembered*, vol. 1 of *Christianity in the Making* (Grand Rapids: Eerdmans, 2003), 761–62.

14. Geza Vermes, *Christian Beginnings: From Nazareth to Nicaea* (New Haven: Yale University Press, 2013), 60.

15. A. E. Harvey, *Jesus and the Constraints of History* (Philadelphia: Westminster, 1982), 168.

16. See also Maurice Casey, *Jesus of Nazareth: An Independent Historian's Account of His Life and Teaching* (London: T&T Clark, 2010), 399, 506; Marcus Borg, "Jesus and God," in Marcus J. Borg and N. T. Wright, *The Meaning of Jesus: Two Visions* (San Francisco: HarperOne, 1999), 145.

17. See Gerald O'Collins, SJ, *Christology: A Biblical, Historical, and Systematic Study of Jesus*, 2nd ed. (Oxford: Oxford University Press, 2009), 66–67: "The earthly Jesus . . . did not

Significantly, this view goes back to the earliest days of the modern quest for Jesus. For example, three of its most influential figures—Herman Samuel Reimarus (1778), David Friedrich Strauss (1836), and Ernst Renan (1863)—are at one in the assertion that Jesus never claimed to be divine:

> It was not his [Jesus's] intention to present a triune God or to make himself God's equal, no matter how much he makes of himself.[18]

> Jesus had indeed an intimate communion of thought and will with God, but . . . the boundary line between divine and human was strictly preserved.[19]

> That Jesus never dreamt of making himself pass for an incarnation of God is a matter about which there can be no doubt. Such an idea was totally foreign to the Jewish mind; and there is no trace of it in the Synoptical Gospels: we only find it indicated in portions of the Gospel of John, which cannot be accepted as expressing the thoughts of Jesus.[20]

Notice that the confidence with which these figures assert that Jesus never made divine claims rests on two key pillars: (1) The notion that Jesus thought himself divine is deemed impossible because it would "deviate from Judaism" and be "totally foreign to the Jewish mind."[21] In other words, any kind of divine claim on Jesus's part would be incompatible with early Jewish monotheism. (2) Although Jesus does claim to be divine in the Gospel of John (e.g., John 8:58–59; 10:30–33), there is "no trace" of a divine self-claim in the Synoptic Gospels.[22]

To this day, the assertion that Jesus never speaks or acts as if he is divine in the Synoptic Gospels continues to play a decisive role in the view that the historical Jesus did not claim to be more than human. Consider, for example, the argument of Bart Ehrman:

---

present himself as the pre-existent Creator of the world. . . . Such claims surface in John's Gospel (e.g., John 5:17; 8:58), but these are later theological reflections rather than historical traditions that reach back to Jesus himself."

18. Herman Samuel Reimarus, *Fragments*, ed. Charles H. Talbert, trans. Ralph Fraser (Philadelphia: Fortress, 1970 [orig. 1774–1778]), 96.

19. David Friedrich Strauss, *The Life of Jesus Critically Examined*, trans. George Eliot (Philadelphia: Fortress, 1972 [orig. 1835–1836]), 289; cf. Strauss, *Life of Jesus*, 29–91.

20. Ernest Renan, *The Life of Jesus* (London: Watts & Co., 1935 [orig. 1863]), 132 (emphasis added).

21. Reimarus, *Fragments*, 96; Renan, *Life of Jesus*, 132.

22. Renan, *Life of Jesus*, 132.

> If Jesus went around Galilee proclaiming himself to be a divine being sent from God—one who existed before the creation of the world, who was in fact equal with God—could anything *else* that he might say be so breath-taking and thunderously important? And yet none of these earlier sources [i.e., the Synoptic material] says any such thing about him. Did they (all of them!) just decide not to mention the one thing that was most significant about Jesus? Almost certainly the divine self-claims in John are not historical.[23]

According to this view, when it comes to the four first-century biographies of Jesus that we possess, the "score" is three against one: three earlier gospels in which Jesus does not claim to be divine (Matthew, Mark, and Luke) and only one later gospel in which Jesus makes divine self-claims (John). In light of such data, the weight of evidence clearly falls in favor of a historical Jesus who never claimed to be more than human.

In sum, it is no overstatement to conclude that "the overwhelming majority" of contemporary scholars agree "that Jesus did not think of, or present, himself in divine terms."[24] To be sure, there are some exceptions, from both Jewish and Christian scholars alike.[25] However, a brief glance at Jesus research in the last century or so shows that the vast majority render a negative verdict. Indeed, one searches most major monographs on the historical Jesus in vain for any mention of the possibility that Jesus may have made divine claims during his lifetime. Perhaps the most striking example of this is the massive four-volume, 3,600-page *Handbook for the Study of the Historical Jesus* (2011), which contains no discussion of whether the historical Jesus ever made divine claims.[26] The implication of such a gaping lacuna is clear: it is so self-evident that Jesus did not claim to be divine that the topic is not even worthy of dis-

23. Ehrman, *How Jesus Became God*, 125.

24. Crispin Fletcher-Louis, *Christological Origins: The Emerging Consensus and Beyond*, vol. 1 of *Jesus Monotheism* (Eugene, OR: Cascade, 2015), 27.

25. See Boyarin, *Jewish Gospels*, 56–70; Sigurd Grindheim, *God's Equal: What Can We Know about Jesus' Self-Understanding in the Synoptic Gospels?*, Library of New Testament Studies 446 (London: T&T Clark, 2011); Peter Stuhlmacher, "The Messianic Son of Man: Jesus' Claim to Deity," in Dunn and McKnight, *Historical Jesus in Recent Research*, 325–44.

26. Edwin K. Broadhead, "Implicit Christology and the Historical Jesus," and Matthias Kreplin, "The Self-Understanding of Jesus," in *Handbook for the Study of the Historical Jesus*, 4 vols., ed. Tom Holmén and Stanley E. Porter (Leiden: Brill, 2011), 2:1169–82, 3:2473–2517, deal exclusively with Jesus's messianic claims.

cussion. For contemporary Jesus research taken as a whole, the answer to the question, Did Jesus claim to be divine? is a resounding no.

The Earliest Christology Was High Christology

On the other hand, when we turn from contemporary Jesus research to recent studies in early Christology—or early Christologies[27]—we discover that a remarkable number of scholars agree that the earliest Jewish believers in Jesus held what might be described as a "high" Christology, in which Jesus is regarded as divine in some sense.

In recent decades, it has become popular to use the expression *high Christology* to describe beliefs about Jesus in which he originates as a heavenly being who becomes human. Conversely, the expression *low Christology* is often used to describe beliefs about Jesus in which he originates as an earthly human being who is later exalted (at some point) to the status of divine.[28] To be sure, there are problems with this terminology—not the least of which is a tendency to oversimplify matters. Nevertheless, with these common definitions in mind, consider the following statements of major contributors to the study of early Christology:

> I have been a member of the Early High Christology Club (EHCC) for quite a few years now.[29]

> The idea that Jesus is God . . . was the view of the very earliest Christians soon after Jesus' death.[30]

> A Christology that portrays Christ as divine emerges very early, in distinctively Jewish terminology and within a Jewish context.[31]

27. Michael F. Bird, *Jesus the Eternal Son: Answering Adoptionist Christology* (Grand Rapids: Eerdmans, 2017), 1, 5, rightly cautions against speaking of "a single monolithic Christology of the early church."

28. See Francesca Aran Murphy, ed., *The Oxford Handbook of Christology* (Oxford: Oxford University Press, 2015), 300, 306, 350–51, 564, for examples of the similar expressions of "Christology from above" and "Christology from below."

29. Paula Fredriksen, "How High Can Early High Christology Be?," in *Monotheism and Christology in Greco-Roman Antiquity*, ed. Matthew V. Novenson, Supplements to Novum Testamentum 180 (Leiden: Brill, 2020), 293.

30. Ehrman, *How Jesus Became God*, 3.

31. Andrew Chester, "High Christology—Whence, When, and Why?," *Early Christianity* 2 (2011): 38.

> No follower of Jesus, to our knowledge, ever called Paul divine or reckoned him a god. Christians did, however, say astounding things about Jesus, and that from the very beginning.[32]

> The earliest Christology was already the highest Christology.[33]

> Devotion to Jesus as divine erupted suddenly and quickly, not gradually and late, among first-century circles of followers.[34]

It is worth noting that the existence of early high Christology is agreed upon by Jewish, Christian, and nonreligious scholars alike. It should also be stressed that the scholars quoted above have different opinions regarding *in what sense* the earliest Jewish believers viewed Jesus as divine: for example, as an exalted human being, an angelic figure, equal with the Creator, and/or God incarnate.[35] They also have different explanations for exactly how the belief in Jesus's divinity arose so quickly: for example, as a by-product of Jesus's execution as "king of the Jews," a result of the resurrection appearances, or the effect of revelatory experiences of the exalted Jesus in heaven. Despite these differences, however, they all agree on one thing: after the death of Jesus, his earliest Jewish followers did not begin with a low Christology in which Jesus was regarded as merely human and then slowly develop a high Christology in which Jesus was regarded as in some sense divine. Rather, Jesus was regarded as "Divine from the Beginning."[36]

32. Allison, *Constructing Jesus*, 304.

33. Richard Bauckham, *Jesus and the God of Israel: God Crucified and Other Studies on the New Testament's Christology of Divine Identity* (Grand Rapids: Eerdmans, 2008), x.

34. Larry Hurtado, *Lord Jesus Christ: Devotion to Jesus in Earliest Christianity* (Grand Rapids: Eerdmans, 2003), 650. Cf. Michael Peppard, *The Son of God in the Roman World: Divine Sonship in Its Social and Political Context* (Oxford: Oxford University Press, 2011), 26: "I agree with Hurtado that Jesus came to be regarded quickly as a divine human son of God."

35. Cf. Michael F. Bird, *Jesus Among the Gods: Early Christology in the Greco-Roman World* (Waco, TX: Baylor University Press, 2022), 11–12.

36. Andrew Chester, *Messiah and Exaltation: Jewish Messianic and Visionary Traditions and New Testament Christology*, Wissenschaftliche Untersuchungen zum Neuen Testament 207 (Tübingen: Mohr Siebeck, 2007), 17. See also Andrew Ter Ern Loke, *The Origin of Divine Christology*, Society for New Testament Studies Monograph Series 169 (Cambridge: Cambridge University Press, 2017), 24–48; Fletcher-Louis, *Jesus Monotheism*, 3–30; Martin Hengel, *Between Jesus and Paul: Studies in the Earliest History of Christianity*, trans. John Bowden (Philadelphia: Fortress, 1983), 31, 39.

The Problem of Jesus and Early High Christology

To sum up what we've seen so far: although the vast majority of contributions to the modern quest agree that the historical Jesus never claimed to be divine, recent studies of the early church also agree that Jesus was regarded as divine in some sense from the very beginning. This somewhat paradoxical pair of hypotheses raises an important historical question: *If Jesus himself never claimed to be divine in any sense, then how do we explain the origins of early high Christology?* Again, Bart Ehrman puts the point well when he asks:

> How did an apocalyptic prophet from the backwaters of rural Galilee, crucified for crimes against the state, come to be thought of as equal to the One God Almighty, maker of all things? How did Jesus—in the minds and hearts of his later followers—come to be God?[37]

The question of the genesis of early high Christology is particularly pressing when we recall that the earliest believers in Jesus—including the apostle Paul—were *Jewish* believers, who believed in and exclusively worshiped the "one" God of Israel (cf. Deut 6:4–6).[38] How did early believers in Jesus, who were also Jewish monotheists, come to regard Jesus as in some sense equal with the one God?[39] In other words, how do we solve "the riddle of the origin of the christology of the early church"?[40] Recent studies of early Christology have given a variety answers.

For example, some contend that the origins of Christology lie in the mistaken identification of Jesus as a messiah by the Jewish crowds at his final Passover.[41] According to this hypothesis, although Jesus and his disciples did not think he was the messiah, it was the messianic fervor of the Jerusalem crowds that led Jesus to be wrongly crucified by Pontius Pilate under the

37. Ehrman, *How Jesus Became God*, 45.

38. See Paula Fredriksen, *When Christians Were Jews: The First Generation* (New Haven: Yale University Press, 2018).

39. See, e.g., Matthew Novenson, "Did Paul Abandon Either Judaism or Monotheism?," in *The New Cambridge Companion to St. Paul*, ed. Bruce W. Longenecker (Cambridge: Cambridge University Press, 2020), 239–59.

40. Martin Hengel, *The Son of God: The Origin of Christology and the History of Jewish-Hellenistic Religion* (Philadelphia: Fortress, 1976), 1.

41. See Paula Fredriksen, *Jesus of Nazareth, King of the Jews* (New York: Vintage Books, 1999), 235–59. Cf. Gerd Lüdemann, *Jesus after Two Thousand Years: What He Really Said and Did*, trans. John Bowden (London: SCM; Amherst: Prometheus Books, 2001), 691.

messianic title "King of the Jews" (Matt 27:37; Mark 15:26; Luke 23:38; John 19:19). Now, it is theoretically possible that the origins of Christology lay with a mob-induced case of mistaken identity. However, this explanation is very difficult to square with the historical evidence that, before he was crucified, Jesus (1) placed himself above the twelve apostles, who represented the heads of the restored twelve tribes of Israel (e.g., Matt 19:28; Luke 22:29–30; Mark 6:7; John 6:67) and (2) publicly rode a donkey into Jerusalem, just like the Jewish Scriptures said the future "king" would do (Matt 21:1–11; Mark 11:1–10; Luke 19:29–38; John 12:12–16; cf. Zech 9:9). As E. P. Sanders argues, taken together, these prophetic signs show that Jesus "thought he was in some sense 'king'" of the coming kingdom of God.[42] In a first-century Jewish context, another name for the long-awaited king was, of course, "messiah." In the words of Martin Hengel: "The origin of christology appears unthinkable without the assumption of a messianic claim of Jesus."[43]

Others argue that it was early beliefs about the bodily resurrection of Jesus that led his followers to not only proclaim him to be the messiah, but also (in some sense) divine.[44] One problem with this hypothesis is that it assumes that belief in the bodily resurrection would necessarily lead to a belief in Jesus's divinity. However, there were other first-century Jews—such as John the Baptist (Matt 14:1–2; Mark 6:14–16; Luke 9:7–9), Jairus's daughter (Matt 9:18–26; Mark 5:21–43; Luke 9:40–56), the widow of Nain's son (Luke 7:11–17), and Lazarus of Bethany (John 11:1–45; 12:9–11)—who were also believed by some of their Jewish contemporaries to have been raised from the dead. Yet, there is no evidence that any of them were ever considered to be divine beings as a result. As Dale Allison rightly points out: "The resurrection alone cannot account for Christology, and Easter did not turn Jesus into someone or something altogether different than he was before."[45]

Still others argue that it was the experience of "revelatory experiences" in the early church, during which early Jewish believers in Jesus saw him alive and exalted into heaven, that led them to think Jesus could be worshiped as a divine being.[46] One weakness of this hypothesis is that there were other prom-

42. E. P. Sanders, *The Historical Figure of Jesus* (London: Penguin, 1993), 248.

43. Martin Hengel, *Studies in Early Christology* (London: T&T Clark, 1995), 217.

44. Gerd Theissen and Annete Merz, *The Historical Jesus: A Comprehensive Guide*, trans. John Bowden (Minneapolis: Fortress, 1998), 464, 560.

45. Allison, *Constructing Jesus*, 243.

46. Larry W. Hurtado, *How on Earth Did Jesus Become a God? Historical Questions about Earliest Devotion to Jesus* (Grand Rapids: Eerdmans, 2005), 13–30 (here 13). For the fullest exposition of his position, see Hurtado, *Lord Jesus Christ*.

inent figures in early Jewish belief—most notably, Moses and Elijah—who were also widely regarded as having been exalted into heaven (cf. Deut 34:1–6; 2 Kgs 2:1–12; Josephus, *Antiquities* 4.323–326; Lives of the Prophets 21:1–15). Both figures were also believed to have appeared to some first century Jews in powerful revelatory experiences—most notably, to the disciples of Jesus himself during the transfiguration (Matt 17:1–8; Mark 9:2–10; Luke 9:28–36). Yet, as far as we know, there is no evidence that Jesus's disciples—or any other Jews in the Second Temple period—ever offered Moses or Elijah the kind of worship given to God. And this is just one of several difficulties faced by this hypothesis.[47]

What then are we to say? How do we solve the problem of the relationship between Jesus and early high Christology? In this study, I will argue that *the best explanation for why the earliest Jewish followers of Jesus believed he was divine shortly after his death is because Jesus himself spoke and acted as if he were divine during his lifetime.* Indeed, when we interpret the words and deeds attributed to Jesus in a first-century Jewish context, a strong case can be made that *the historical Jesus claimed to be divine, but he did so in a very Jewish way*—using riddles, questions, and allusions to Jewish Scripture to both reveal and conceal the apocalyptic secret of his divinity. As we will see, it is precisely the riddle-like and scripturally allusive nature of Jesus's divine claims that gave birth to an early Christology that was simultaneously both very "high" (i.e., divine) and very "low" (i.e., human).

Four Historical Warrants

It will take the rest of this book for me to test this hypothesis regarding Jesus and the origins of early high Christology. However, given the fact that even asking the question of whether the historical Jesus claimed to be divine has been for some time regarded as a "no-go area,"[48] it will be helpful before we begin to briefly outline several reasons for even undertaking such an investigation.

In the last two decades, twenty-first-century scholarship on Second Temple Judaism, the historical Jesus, and earliest Christianity has provided us with at least four historical warrants for exploring whether the early high Christology of the first Jewish believers in Jesus might indeed have its origins in the words

47. See Loke, *Origin of Divine Christology*, 119–30.

48. Robinson, "The Last Tabu," in Dunn and McKnight, *Historical Jesus in Recent Research*, 553.

and actions of Jesus himself: (1) early Jewish evidence for divine messiahs, (2) the emerging agreement regarding Jesus's messianic self-identification, (3) a growing recognition that Jesus makes divine self-claims in the Synoptic Gospels as well as the Gospel of John, and (4) often-overlooked evidence that other figures in the Second Temple period made divine claims. In this section, we will take a few moments to examine each of these.

1. The Divinity of the Messiah in Second Temple Judaism

The first reason for reopening the question of whether the historical Jesus claimed to be divine flows from the now-widespread recognition that some early Jewish texts do in fact describe expected messianic figures as superhuman. Consider, for example, the following conclusions of recent scholarship on early Jewish messianism:

> The several types of messiahs attested in ancient Jewish texts are commonly classified, not unreasonably, under the headings "royal," "priestly," "prophetic," and "heavenly."[49]

> Not all messianic figures . . . were human.[50]

> The ruler anointed by God is not a mere mortal; he is a divine being who has always existed, who sits beside God on his throne. . . . The Son of Man figure . . . would be one such divine figure.[51]

> The idea of the divinity of the messiah has its roots in the royal ideology of ancient Judah. . . . In the Hellenistic period, . . . hopes for deliverance often focused on supernatural, heavenly, mediator figures.[52]

49. Matthew Novenson, "Messiah," in *T&T Clark Encyclopedia of Second Temple Judaism*, ed. Daniel M. Gurtner and Loren T. Stuckenbruck, 2 vols. (London: T&T Clark, 2020), 2:493; Novenson, *The Grammar of Messianism: An Ancient Jewish Political Idiom and Its Users* (Oxford: Oxford University Press, 2017), 10.

50. David B. Levenson, "Messianic Movements," in *The Jewish Annotated New Testament*, 2nd ed., ed. Amy-Jill Levine and Marc Zvi Brettler (Oxford: Oxford University Press, 2017), 623.

51. Ehrman, *How Jesus Became God*, 67, 68.

52. Adela Yarbro Collins and John J. Collins, *King and Messiah as Son of God: Divine,*

> The term "messiah" did have great interpretive range in Jesus' period. This figure could be a priest, a prophet, a royal warrior, perhaps even an angelic, nonhuman figure.[53]

Notice that this conclusion regarding the divinity of the messiah in early Judaism can be found in the works of Jewish, Christian, and nonreligious scholars alike.[54] Notice also that it is not just any figure, but the Danielic "one like a son of man" who is often singled out as an example of a heavenly or divine messiah (cf. Dan 7:13–14). We will take a closer look at the precise relationship between the heavenly and human character of the "one like a son of man" in the book of Daniel later. For now, the upshot of these statements is simple: in contrast to the age-old assumption that at the time of Jesus, most Jewish people were waiting for a merely human messiah, recent scholarship suggests that "*the divinity of the messiah*" was a significant part of the early Jewish messianic landscape.[55] Indeed, it is quite telling that several recent surveys of early Jewish messianism add the category of "heavenly" messiah to the now-standard paradigms of royal, priestly, and prophetic messianic claimants.[56] Hence, the popular notion that all Jewish messianic expectation involved a merely human (and often military) figure needs to be abandoned once and for all. As we will see, in the diverse world of Second Temple Judaism, there is ample evidence for both human and heavenly messiahs—especially when those messianic figures are based in some way on the heavenly son of man in the book of Daniel.[57]

Human, and Angelic Messianic Figures in Biblical and Related Literature (Grand Rapids: Eerdmans, 2008), xi, xii.

53. Fredriksen, *Jesus of Nazareth*, 212–13. Curiously, when it comes to Jesus's self-understanding, Fredriksen insists "we can rule out the hazy figure of the nonhuman heavenly or angelic messiah at once."

54. See also Bühner, *Messianic High Christology*, 190 and throughout; Boyarin, *Jewish Gospels*, 56: "The reasons that many Jews came to believe that Jesus was divine was because they were already expecting that the Messiah/Christ would be a god-man. This expectation was part and parcel of Jewish tradition."

55. Yarbro Collins and Collins, *King and Messiah*, xi (emphasis added).

56. Novenson, "Messiah," 493; Kenneth E. Pomykala, "Messianism," in Collins and Harlow, *Eerdmans Dictionary of Early Judaism*, 942; John J. Collins, *The Scepter and the Star: Messianism in Light of the Dead Sea Scrolls*, 2nd ed. (Grand Rapids: Eerdmans, 2010), 18.

57. See Bühner, *Messianic High Christology*, for a full-length study.

2. *The Historical Jesus Saw Himself as a Messianic Figure*

Another reason for revisiting the possibility that the historical Jesus claimed to be more than human is the increasing support in recent scholarship for the conclusion that Jesus spoke and acted as if he was the Jewish messiah. Consider, for example, the following conclusions of contributors to the contemporary quest:

> I think . . . that the usual criteria of historicity invoked in Jesus research favor the view that the picture of Jesus as Son of David or royal Davidic Messiah goes back to the historical Jesus.[58]

> I think there are excellent reasons for thinking that Jesus imagined himself as the messiah.[59]

> Taking his ministry as a whole, it is evident that [Jesus] saw himself as the kind of figure who was later to be hailed as "the Messiah," though he did not use this term of himself.[60]

> The ever so popular "unmessianic Jesus" never existed. . . . the emergence of the earliest Christology . . . has its ultimate foundation in Jesus' activity and way.[61]

> It is quite certain that in his own lifetime Jesus became accepted by many—not just Peter—as the Messiah. Had it not been so, Pilate would not have written above the cross of Jesus, "King of the Jews."[62]

Notice once again that the hypothesis that Jesus saw himself as the messiah is present in the works of Jewish, Christian, and nonreligious scholars alike.[63]

58. John P. Meier, "From Elijah-Like Prophet to Royal Davidic Messiah," in *Jesus: A Colloquium in the Holy Land*, ed. Doris Donnely (New York: Continuum, 2001), 48, 71.

59. Ehrman, *How Jesus Became God*, 118, 119.

60. Casey, *Jesus of Nazareth*, 399.

61. Martin Hengel and Anna Maria Schwemer, *Jesus and Judaism*, trans. Wayne Coppins (Waco, TX: Baylor University Press, 2019 [orig. 2007]), xix.

62. David Flusser with R. Steven Notley, *The Sage from Galilee: Rediscovering Jesus' Genius* (Grand Rapids: Eerdmans, 2007), 115.

63. See also Bühner, *Messianic High Christology*, 190–91; Gerhard Lohfink, *Jesus of Nazareth: What He Wanted, Who He Was*, trans. Linda M. Maloney (Collegeville: Liturgical Press,

To be sure, some disagree.[64] Others qualify the conclusion somewhat by suggesting that Jesus saw himself as a messiah "in waiting,"[65] or by emphasizing that though Jesus did not explicitly refer to himself as messiah, he "did not reject his being designated this way either."[66] Nevertheless, many scholars of the historical Jesus agree that if Jesus identified himself with *any* messianic figure, it was with the "son of man" in the book of Daniel[67]—who does indeed appear to be a "superearthly" figure and a "heavenly being."[68] If Jesus of Nazareth saw himself as not just any kind of anointed leader, but as the *heavenly* figure of Daniel 7, then there is ample reason for taking a fresh look at exactly what kind of messiah Jesus may have claimed to be.

3. *Jesus Makes Divine Claims in the Synoptic Gospels—Not Just John*

A third historical warrant for venturing into the "no-go area" of whether the historical Jesus made divine claims is a growing recognition among contemporary commentators that Jesus is depicted as speaking and acting as if he is divine in all four first-century gospels—not just in the Gospel of John. This may come as something of a shock to readers familiar with the commonplace assertion that Jesus only claims to be divine in the Fourth Gospel. Consider, however, the following sampling of conclusions of recent scholarship on Mark:

> *Even in Mark*, where the Christology can be seen as low, *some aspects of Jesus' divine nature appear*. For example, in Mk 6.48, Jesus walks on the

---

2012), 314; Armand Puig i Tàrrech, *Jesus: A Biography*, trans. Jenny Read-Heimerdinger (Waco, TX: Baylor University Press, 2011), 449; Michael F. Bird, *Are You the One Who Is to Come? The Historical Jesus and the Messianic Question* (Grand Rapids: Baker Academic, 2009); Sanders, *Historical Figure of Jesus*, 248.

64. Fredriksen, *Jesus of Nazareth*, 235–59; Jürgen Becker, *Jesus of Nazareth*, trans. James E. Crouch (New York: Walter de Gruyter, 1998), 197; Geza Vermes, *Jesus the Jew: A Historian's Readings of the Gospels* (Philadelphia: Fortress, 1973), 223.

65. Allison, *Constructing Jesus*, 290, 291.

66. Jens Schröter, *Jesus of Nazareth: Jew From Galilee, Savior of the World*, trans. Wayne Coppins and S. Brian Pounds (Waco, TX: Baylor University Press, 2014), 175.

67. See Larry W. Hurtado and Paul L. Owen, eds., *"Who Is This Son of Man?" The Latest Scholarship on a Puzzling Expression of the Historical Jesus*, Library of New Testament Studies 390 (London: Bloomsbury T&T Clark, 2011), for an overview of recent scholarship on the historical Jesus and the Son of Man.

68. Schröter, *Jesus of Nazareth*, 175. See Puig i Tàrrech, *Jesus: A Biography*, 454, 55.

water (cf. Mt 14.25; Jn 6.19); the Transfiguration (Mt 17.2; Mk 9.2) as well hints at Jesus' divine nature.[69]

> [Regarding Jesus's words in Mark 12:35–36:] A seated position at the right hand of a deity implies co-regency with him. . . . The imagery of the quoted portion of the psalm, then, implies that "my lord" stands in *a relation of near equality with God.*[70]

> In this saying [Mark 14:62], Jesus claims to be a messiah of the heavenly type, who will be exalted to the right hand of God (Ps 110:1). *Being seated at the right hand of God implies being equal to God*, at least in terms of authority and power.[71]

Once again, some disagree.[72] For this reason, I will spend the rest of this book examining key episodes in the Synoptic Gospels in which Jesus appears to speak and act as if he is divine.

For the purposes of this introduction, however, it may be helpful to highlight one important example: the recurrent accusations of blasphemy levied against Jesus. Consider the following evidence, taken from all four first-century gospels:

> Then some of the scribes said to themselves, "This man is *blaspheming*." (Matt 9:3)[73]

> Then the high priest tore his clothes and said, "He has *blasphemed*! Why do we still need witnesses? You have now heard his *blasphemy*. What is your verdict?" They answered, "He deserves death." (Matt 26:65–66)

69. Randi Rashkover, "Christology," in Levine and Brettler, *Jewish Annotated New Testament*, 754 (emphasis added).

70. Joel Marcus, *Mark*, 2 vols., Anchor Yale Bible 27–27A (New Haven: Yale University Press, 2000, 2009), 2:850 (emphasis added).

71. Adela Yarbro Collins, *Mark: A Commentary*, Hermeneia (Minneapolis: Fortress, 2007), 706 (emphasis added).

72. See especially J. R. Daniel Kirk, *A Man Attested by God: The Human Jesus of the Synoptic Gospels* (Grand Rapids: Eerdmans, 2016), for a comprehensive (though in my view unconvincing) case for a merely human Jesus in the Synoptic Gospels.

73. Unless otherwise noted, all scriptural translations herein are from the NRSV, and all emphases appearing in quotations from ancient sources (such as Scripture, the Dead Sea Scrolls, Josephus, Philo, etc.) are added by the author.

> "Why does this fellow speak in this way? It is *blasphemy*! Who can forgive sins but God alone?" (Mark 2:7)

> Then the high priest tore his clothes and said, "Why do we still need witnesses? You have heard his *blasphemy*! What is your decision?" All of them condemned him as deserving death. (Mark 14:63–64)

> Then the scribes and the Pharisees began to question, "Who is this who is speaking *blasphemies*? Who can forgive sins but God alone?" (Luke 5:21)

> The Jews answered, "It is not for a good work that we are going to stone you, but *for blasphemy*, because *you*, though only a human being, *are making yourself God*." (John 10:33)

> The Jews answered him, "We have a law, and *according to that law he ought to die* because he has claimed to be the Son of God." (John 19:7)[74]

Notice the prominence of the question "who?" in virtually every one of these passages (Matt 26:63; Mark 2:7; 14:61; Luke 5:21; John 10:24; 18:33, 37; 19:9). Hence, in both the Synoptics and the Gospel of John, Jesus is accused of blasphemy in the context of questions about "who" he claims to be. This raises an important question: *If Jesus never claims to be divine in the Synoptic Gospels, then why is he accused of blasphemy in the context of questions about his identity?*

In this regard, it is crucial to recall that, in a Second Temple Jewish context, it was not blasphemy to claim to be the messiah.[75] After all, if it were, how would anyone identify the long-awaited deliverer when he finally arrived? On the other hand, it *was* blasphemy to claim to be divine.[76] For example, one early Jewish writing describes the Seleucid king Antiochus IV Epiphanes (second century BCE) as a "blasphemer" (*blasphēmos*) (2 Macc 9:8) precisely

74. See Adele Reinhartz, "The Gospel according to John," in Levine and Brettler, *Jewish Annotated New Testament*, 214, for the view the "law" spoken of here is "the prohibition against blasphemy" (cf. Lev 24:16; m. Sanhedrin 7:4).

75. See Sven-Olav Black, "The Trials of Jesus," in *The Jesus Handbook*, ed. Jens Schröter and Christine Jacobi, trans. Robert L. Brawley (Grand Rapids: Eerdmans, 2022), 474–81 (here 478); E. P. Sanders, *Jewish Law from Jesus to the Mishnah: Five Studies* (London: SCM; Philadelphia: Trinity Press International, 1990), 57–67.

76. See Adela Yarbro Collins, "Blasphemy," in Collins and Harlow, *Eerdmans Dictionary of Early Judaism*, 445.

because he refused to recognize the following truth: "It is right to be subject to God, and no mortal should think he is equal to God" (*isothea*) (2 Macc 9:12). Along similar lines, Philo of Alexandria, a contemporary of Jesus, describes the words of anyone who "has dared to compare himself to the all blessed God" as "blaspheming" (*blasphēmeō*) (Philo, *On Dreams* 2.130).[77] Finally, in the context of affirming Jewish belief in one God, the first-century Jewish historian Josephus makes clear that people who blaspheme against the God of Israel are guilty of a capital crime:

> God is one and the Hebrew race is one. Let him that blasphemes God [*blasphēmēsas theon*] be stoned, then hung for a day, and buried ignominiously and in obscurity. (Josephus, *Antiquities* 4.202)[78]

In light of such texts, the question before us is this: Did Jesus of Nazareth make claims about himself that could be regarded by some of his Jewish contemporaries as blasphemy against the one God of Israel? Did Jesus speak or act as if he too were in some sense "equal to God" (cf. 2 Macc 9:12)?

Of course, one could contend that all the accusations of blasphemy against Jesus cited above are unhistorical. And some do.[79] But this cannot simply be asserted; it needs to be convincingly argued. Yet, as we will see, a surprising number of major works on the historical Jesus and early Christology simply *ignore* the accusations of blasphemy as if they did not exist.[80] However, the charges of blasphemy levied against Jesus pose serious problems for the now-commonplace assertion that there is no trace of Jesus making divine claims in the Synoptic Gospels. Even if one concludes that they are all unhistorical, what cannot be said is that Jesus makes no divine claims in the Synoptic Gospels or that Jesus only makes such claims in the Gospel of John. As we will see, when all of the evidence is taken into account, *Jesus speaks and acts as if he is more than human in all four first-century gospels—not just one.* Indeed, when

77. Unless otherwise noted, all translations of Philo are from the Loeb Classical Library edition. See also Philo, *Embassy to Gaius* 45.367–368.

78. Unless otherwise noted, all translations of Josephus are from the Loeb Classical Library edition.

79. E.g., Casey, *Jesus of Nazareth*, 440; Lüdemann, *Jesus after Two Thousand Years*, 102.

80. E.g., Schröter, *Jesus of Nazareth*; Ehrman, *How Jesus Became God*; Joachim Gnilka, *Jesus of Nazareth. Message and History*, trans. Siegfried S. Schatzmann (Peabody, MA: Hendrickson, 1997). Contrast Scot McKnight and Joseph B. Modica, eds., *Who Do My Opponents Say That I Am? An Investigation of the Accusations against Jesus*, Library of New Testament Studies 327 (London: T&T Clark, 2008), 76–94.

it comes to the Four Gospels, the "score" is not three against one, but four against *zero*: four first-century gospels in which Jesus speaks and acts as if he is divine and none in which he is merely human.[81]

4. Other Historical Figures Who Claimed to Be Divine

The fourth and final warrant for exploring whether the historical Jesus claimed to be divine is the often-overlooked fact that other prominent historical figures from the Second Temple period also made divine self-claims.

Although the fact is almost universally ignored in contemporary Jesus research, there is abundant evidence that Alexander the Great (fourth century BCE), Antiochus IV Epiphanes (second century BCE), King Herod Agrippa I (first century CE), and the Roman emperor Gaius Caligula (first century CE) all spoke and acted as if they were divine *during their lifetimes*, and did so in a variety of different ways. Consider the following data:

1. **Alexander the Great** (356–323 BCE)
   - wore the "horns of Ammon, as if he had been the god" (Ephippus, *Fragments of Greek Historians* 126 F5)[82]
   - accepted being greeted as "son" of the "god" (*theos*) Ammon and as having had a "divine birth" (*ek tou theou geneseōs*) (Diodorus Siculus, *The Library* 17.51.1, 3)
   - demanded to be "believed a god" (*deus credi*) (Quintus Curtius, *History of Alexander* 6.11.24)
   - wished "not only to be called" but "believed to be the son of Jupiter" (*Iovis filium*) and "ordered" the Macedonians "to salute him by prostrating themselves" (Quintus Curtius, *History of Alexander* 8.5.5–6)
   - accepted "worship" (*proskynēsis*) as if he were "a god" (*theos*) (Arrian, *Anabasis* 4.10.5–6)[83]
   - acted "like one fully persuaded of his divine birth and parentage" (*tēs ek theō*

81. See Richard B. Hays, *Echoes of Scripture in the Gospels* (Waco, TX: Baylor University Press, 2016), 363–64 and throughout; Hays, *Reading Backwards: Figural Christology and the Fourfold Gospel Witness* (Waco, TX: Baylor University Press, 2014), for a study of this on the narrative level of the four evangelists.

82. Quoted in Ian Worthington, *Alexander the Great: Man and God* (London: Pearson/Longman, 2004), 273. Other quotations in this list are from the Loeb Classical Library editions.

83. See also *Anabasis* 4.10.7–11.7; 7.20.1; 7.27.3.

geneseōs kai teknōseōs) and "assumed his own divinity" (*heauton exetheiaze*) (Plutarch, *Alexander* 28.1).[84]

2. **Antiochus IV Epiphanes** (215–164 BCE)
   - displayed "superhuman arrogance" (*hyper anthrōpon alazoneian*) (2 Macc 9:8)
   - acted as if he was "equal to God" (*isothea*) (2 Macc 9:12)
   - minted coins with "King Antiochus, God Manifest" (*theou epiphanous*) (Josephus, *Antiquities* 12.258)
   - regarded by some as "the Madman" (*epimanēs*) instead of "Epiphanes" (Polybius, *Histories* 26.1)

3. **Herod Agrippa I** (11 BCE–44 CE)
   - hailed as a "god" (*theos*), not a "human" (*anthrōpos*) (Acts 12:22)
   - accepted being addressed as "a god" (*theon*) and as "more than mortal in nature" (*kreittona thnētēs physeōs*) (Josephus, *Antiquities* 19.344–345)
   - "did not rebuke" this divine acclamation (Josephus, *Antiquities* 19.346).

4. **Gaius Caligula** (12–41 CE)
   - was guilty of "not only saying but thinking he was god" (*ou legōn monon alla kai oiomenos einai theos*) (Philo, *Embassy to Gaius* 162)
   - "wished to be considered a god" (*theon*) (Josephus, *War* 2.184)
   - "ceased to think of himself as a man" (*anthrōpinōs*) and "imagined himself a god" (*ektheiazōn heauton*) (Josephus, *Antiquities* 18.256)
   - displayed "madness" (*manias*) when he "deified himself" (*exetheiazen heauton*) and demanded honors not given to "man" (*anthrōpos*) (Josephus, *Antiquities* 19.1, 4)
   - crossed the waters of a bay on a chariot, "as befitted his godhead" (*theō*) (Josephus, *Antiquities* 19.5–6)
   - "worshiped" (*adorandum*) by supplicants and set up a temple to "his own godhead" (*numini suo*) (Suetonius, *Lives of the Caesars* 4.22.3).

In light of such evidence, prominent contemporary historians and biographers agree that Alexander the Great embraced "belief in his own divinity,"[85]

84. Cf. *Alexander* 27.3–6; 33.1.

85. A. E. Fredricksmeyer, "Alexander's Religion and Divinity," in *Brill's Companion to Alexander the Great*, ed. Joseph Roisman (Leiden: Brill, 2003), 253–78 (here 253). See also F. S. Naiden, *Soldier, Priest, and God: A Life of Alexander the Great* (Oxford: Oxford Uni-

that Antiochus IV took "the epithets *Theos* (God) and *Epiphanēs* (Manifest)" because he saw himself as divine,[86] that Herod Agrippa "gradually" came to "[see] himself as a god" and performed "a kind of self-apotheosis,"[87] and that Gaius Caligula did indeed make a "claim to divinity" during his lifetime.[88] Notice also that all four of these divine claimants are *royal figures*. Though three of the four are gentiles, one of them—King Herod Agrippa—was of mixed Jewish descent and known for his "enthusiasm and zeal for Judaism."[89] This fact presses us to take seriously the possibility that another first-century Jew who saw himself as a royal figure—Jesus of Nazareth—may likewise have spoken and acted as if he were divine, albeit in a distinctively Jewish way.

One reason it is necessary to emphasize the fact that other historical figures in the Second Temple period made divine claims is because some scholars contend the question of whether Jesus made divine claims is not accessible to historical inquiry. For example, in her important study of the historical Jesus, Paula Fredriksen states:

> I suggest that [the crucifixion] is where we should look for the explanation of Jesus' death. . . . Not to Jesus' psyche or to his innermost convictions about himself and his identity, to which we have no access in any case. Even if for some reason Jesus had been convinced that he were the messiah, but in some radically new and unanticipated way, his self-image would not

versity Press, 2019), 175–76; Peter Green, *Alexander of Macedon, 356–323 B.C.: A Historical Biography* (Berkeley: University of California Press, 2013), 372–74; Worthington, *Alexander the Great: Man and God*, 274, 280, 283.

86. Robert Doran, "Antiochus IV Epiphanes," in *Eerdmans Dictionary of Early Judaism*, ed. John J. Collins and Daniel C. Harlow (Grand Rapids: Eerdmans, 2010), 338–39. See also Peter Franz Mittag, *Antiochos IV. Epiphanes: Eine politische Biographie*, *Klio* 11 (Berline: Akademie Verlag, 2006), 128–39.

87. Nikos Kokkinos, *The Herodian Dynasty: Origins, Role in Society, and Eclipse* (London: Spinck, 2010), 302–3. See also Bruce Chilton, *The Herods: Murder, Politics, and the Art of Succession* (Minneapolis: Fortress, 2021), 199–200; Daniel R. Schwartz, *Agrippa I: The Last King of Judaea*, Texte und Studien zum antiken Judentum 23 (Tübingen: Mohr Siebeck, 1990), 145–49.

88. Anthony A. Barrett, *Caligula: The Abuse of Power*, 2nd ed. (London: Routledge, 2015), 190–222 (here 192). See also Aloys Winterling, *Caligula: A Biography*, trans. Deborah Lucas Schneider, Glenn W. Most, and Paul Psoinos (Berkeley: University of California Press, 2011), 1; Peter Herz, "Emperors: Caring for the Empire and Their Successors," in *A Companion to Roman Religion* (Oxford: Wiley-Blackwell, 2011), 308, for an inscription that describes the people hurrying "to see the face of a god" on the day of Caligula's coronation in 37 CE.

89. Adam Marshak, "Herodian Dynasty," in Collins and Harlow, *Eerdmans Dictionary of Early Judaism*, 738.

> have mattered to anybody in power, and would scarcely have made sense to anybody outside himself.[90]

Now, Fredriksen is of course right to insist that we have no direct access to Jesus's "psyche." But I am aware of no reputable scholar who claims we do. At the same time, she goes too far when she insists we have "no access" to what an ancient public figure like Jesus of Nazareth claimed about "himself and his identity." If historians can investigate what other historical figures from the Second Temple period believed about themselves and their identities, then why not Jesus of Nazareth? Even more puzzling is her claim that even if Jesus spoke and acted as if he were divine, it would "not have mattered" to anyone in power. As even a cursory study of Alexander, Agrippa, and Caligula shows, it was *precisely* people in power who were often scandalized by the divine pretensions of living kings.[91] As one of Alexander's biographers wrote: it is one thing for a king to be deified after he was dead; it is quite another for him to act as if he were divine while still alive.[92] As we will see by the end of this study, according to the extant evidence, Jesus's divine claims did indeed matter very much—especially to the people in power.

In summary, if there were other Second Temple Jews who believed that the messiah would be a heavenly or divine figure, and if Jesus of Nazareth claimed to be a heavenly (and not merely human) messiah, and if Jesus, like other figures from the Second Temple period, spoke and acted as if he were divine, then this would provide a plausible historical explanation for how it was that the first Jewish followers of Jesus came to regard him as more than merely human. In particular, it would provide a plausible historical explanation for why some of his Jewish contemporaries—most notably, some members of the Jerusalem Sanhedrin—accused him of blasphemy and handed him (and *not* his disciples) over to the Roman authorities for execution. In the words of the contemporary Jewish scholar Daniel Boyarin:

90. Fredriksen, *Jesus of Nazareth*, 234.

91. See, e.g., Philotas, Callisthenes, and the Macedonians' opposition to Alexander's acceptance of *proskynesis* in Quintus Curtius, *History of Alexander* 4.7.30–31; 6.9.23–26; 8.5.5–7; Arrian, *Anabasis* 4.10.5–11.7. James Romm refers to this as "the *proskynesis* crisis" in Romm, *Alexander the Great: Selections from Arrian, Diodorus, Plutarch, and Quintus Curtius* (Indianapolis: Hackett, 2005), 103–4.

92. See Arrian, *Anabasis* 4.11.7: "Even Heracles himself did not receive divine honours [*theiai timai*] from the Greeks in his own lifetime [*zōnti eti*], no even after his death till the god of Delphi gave his sanction to honouring him as a god [*hōs theon*]" (translation from the Loeb Classical Library edition).

> I submit that it is possible to understand the Gospel only if both Jesus and the Jews around him held to a high Christology whereby the claim to Messiahship was also a claim to being a divine man. Were it not the case, we would be very hard-pressed to understand the extremely hostile reaction to Jesus on the part of the Jewish leaders who did not accept his claim. . . . Jesus saw himself as the divine Son of Man.[93]

If this idea of a "divine Son of Man" was indeed already present in the Judaism of Jesus's day, and if Jesus was accused of blasphemy in the context of questions about his divine self-claims, then this provides ample justification for reexamining the widespread assumption that the historical Jesus never claimed to be anything more than merely human. Before we turn to the evidence itself, however, we need to bring this chapter to a close with a few words about the method by which this investigation will proceed.

Method of Proceeding

If there is any aspect of the contemporary quest for the historical Jesus that is currently in a state of flux, it is the question of method.[94] In recent decades, methodology in Jesus research has become a field of study in its own right.[95] Indeed, a whole host of fundamental issues—such as the literary genre of the Gospels, their relationship to the living memories of eyewitnesses to Jesus, the Synoptic problem and the existence of the "Q" source, the literary relationship between the Gospel of John and the Synoptics, just to mention a few—can no longer be treated as settled but are the subject of ongoing debate.[96]

93. Boyarin, *Jewish Gospels*, 55, 56 (emphasis added).

94. See Brant Pitre, *Jesus and the Last Supper* (Grand Rapids: Eerdmans, 2015), 28–52; Jordan Ryan, "The Historian's Craft and the Future of Historical Jesus Research: Engaging Brant Pitre's *Jesus and the Last Supper* as a Work of History," *Journal for the Study of the Historical Jesus* 15 (2017): 60–87.

95. See James H. Charlesworth, Brian Rhea, and Petr Pokorny, eds., *Jesus Research: New Methodologies and Perceptions; The Second Princeton-Prague Symposium on Jesus Research* (Grand Rapids: Eerdmans, 2014); Tom Holmén and Stanley E. Porter, eds., *How to Study the Historical Jesus*, vol. 1 of *Handbook for the Study of the Historical Jesus* (Leiden: Brill, 2011), 1–851.

96. See M. David Litwa, *How the Gospels Became History: Jesus and Mediterranean Myths* (New Haven: Yale University Press, 2019); Craig S. Keener, *Christobiography: Memory, History, and the Reliability of the Gospels* (Grand Rapids: Eerdmans, 2019); Richard A. Burridge, *What Are the Gospels? A Comparison with Graeco-Roman Biography*, 25th anniv.

Above all, there is the current debate over the validity of the form-critical criteria of historical authenticity. To be sure, several prominent scholars continue to employ the criteria of authenticity that grew out of twentieth-century form, source, and redaction criticism—that is, multiple attestation, embarrassment, coherence, and dissimilarity—in their reconstructions of the life of Jesus.[97] On the other hand, a growing number of other scholars have levied serious (if not devastating) critiques of some or all of the "traditional" criteria of authenticity.[98] These studies call for the now-standard methods of historical authentication to be either radically revised or, in some cases, abandoned altogether.

In the midst of so much disagreement about fundamentals, modesty and caution seem called for on several counts. In light of the compelling critiques

---

ed. (Waco: Baylor University Press, 2018); Alan Kirk, *Memory and the Jesus Tradition*, The Reception of Jesus in the First Three Centuries 2 (London: T&T Clark, 2018); Richard Bauckham, *Jesus and the Eyewitnesses: The Gospels as Eyewitness Testimony*, 2nd ed. (Grand Rapids: Eerdmans, 2017); Eric Eve, *Behind the Gospels: Understanding the Oral Tradition* (Minneapolis: Fortress, 2014); Chris Keith, *Jesus' Literacy: Scribal Culture and the Teacher from Galilee*, Library of New Testament Studies 413, Library of Historical Jesus Studies 8 (London: Bloomsbury T&T Clark, 2011); Anthony LeDonne, *The Historiographical Jesus: Memory, Typology, and the Son of David* (Waco, TX: Baylor University Press, 2009), 1–64; Eric Eve, *Writing the Gospels: Composition and Memory* (London: SPCK, 2016); Paul Foster, A. Gregory, J. S. Kloppenborg, and J. Verheyden, eds., *New Studies in the Synoptic Problem: Oxford Conference, April 2008; Essays in Honor of Christopher M. Tuckett*, Bibliotheca Ephemeridum Theologicarum Lovaniensium 239 (Leuven: Peeters, 2011); Mark Goodacre, *The Case against Q: Studies in Markan Priority and the Synoptic Problem* (Harrisburg: Trinity Press International, 2002); Eve-Marie Becker, Helen K. Bond, and Catrin H. Williams, eds., *John's Transformation of Mark* (London: T&T Clark, 2021); Harold W. Attridge, "John and Other Gospels," in *The Oxford Handbook of Johannine Studies*, ed. Judith M. Lieu and Martinus C. de Boer (Oxford: Oxford University Press, 2018), 44–62; James W. Barker, *John's Use of Matthew* (Minneapolis: Fortress, 2015); D. Moody Smith, *John among the Gospels*, 2nd ed. (Columbia: University of South Carolina Press, 2001).

97. See John P. Meier, "Basic Methodology in the Quest for the Historical Jesus," in Holmén and Porter, *Handbook for the Study of the Historical Jesus*, 1:155–58; Darrell L. Bock and Robert L. Webb, eds., *Key Events in the Life of the Historical Jesus*, Wissenschaftliche Untersuchungen zum Neuen Testament 247 (Tübingen: Mohr Siebeck; Grand Rapids: Eerdmans, 2009).

98. See Helen K. Bond, *The Historical Jesus: A Guide for the Perplexed* (London: Bloomsbury, 2014), 15–19; Chris Keith and Anthony Le Donne, eds., *Jesus, Criteria, and the Demise of Authenticity* (London: T&T Clark, 2012); Dale C. Allison Jr., "How To Marginalize the Traditional Criteria of Authenticity," in Holmén and Porter, *Handbook for the Study of the Historical Jesus*, 1:3–30; Rafael Rodríguez, "Authenticating Criteria: the Use and Misuse of a Critical Method," *Journal for the Study of the Historical Jesus* 7 (2009): 152–67.

of the form-critical criteria of authenticity, it seems unwise to simply continue using them as if there were no serious problems. Likewise, given the recent debates over the Synoptic problem and the existence of "Q," it also seems imprudent to base any historical conclusions about Jesus on a particular source-critical solution to the question of the literary relationship between the Gospels. This is especially true when we consider that E. P. Sanders himself once drew the rather shocking conclusion that the two-source hypothesis is in fact "the least satisfactory" of "all the solutions" to the Synoptic problem![99] As Albert Schweitzer pointed out over a century ago, in the final analysis, the Synoptic problem is "a *literary* question" that is methodologically incapable of answering "the *historical* problem" of whether Jesus did or said any of the things reported in the Gospels.[100] Whatever solution one adopts to the question of the literary relationship between the Gospels, we are still left with the historical plausibility or implausibility of any given saying or action attributed to Jesus, which must be evaluated on other grounds.

The Triple-Context Approach of E. P. Sanders

With all these caveats in mind, how then should one proceed? Given the current state of affairs, I have chosen to model my approach herein on the method laid out by E. P. Sanders in his rightly famous work *Jesus and Judaism*.[101] Although Sanders's study is not without its own methodological inconsistencies, it remains to my mind one of the most brilliant and enduring contributions to the historical study of Jesus.[102] In an important formulation of his method, Sanders not only anticipates the recent criticisms of the criteria approach, but, unlike some recent studies, suggests a reasonable alternative:

> No matter what criteria for testing the sayings are used, scholars still need to move beyond the sayings themselves to a broader *context* than a summary of their contents if they are to address historical questions about Jesus. . . . The only way to proceed in the search for the historical Jesus is to offer hypotheses based on the evidence and to evaluate them in light of how

99. E. P. Sanders and Margaret Davies, *Studying the Synoptic Gospels* (London: SCM; Philadelphia: Trinity Press International, 1989), 117.

100. Schweitzer, *Quest of the Historical Jesus*, xli.

101. E. P. Sanders, *Jesus and Judaism* (Minneapolis: Fortress, 1985).

102. Cf. Casey, *Jesus of Nazareth*, 499: "E. P. Sanders . . . has written the best life of Jesus so far."

> satisfactorily they account for [1] the material in the Gospels, while also making Jesus [2] a believable figure in first-century Palestine and [3] the founder of a movement that eventuated in the Church.[103]

In Sanders's descriptions of his method of proceeding, there are three implicit arguments for historicity, which I would define as follows:

1. Contextual plausibility within first-century Judaism
2. Coherence with other evidence about Jesus
3. Consequences in the early church

This "triple-context" approach is, in my opinion, one of the main reasons that Sanders's *Jesus and Judaism* has been so influential and, on many points, has stood the test of time. In fact, I would contend that these three arguments are implicitly at work in virtually all studies of the historical Jesus, including those penned by critics of the criteria of authenticity.[104] As we will see through this study, when the historical reasoning of scholars is closely analyzed, one or more of these three arguments often constitute the actual *reasons* scholars conclude for or against the historicity of particular saying or action attributed to Jesus. In order to see this clearly, however, we will need to take a few moments to examine each of Sanders's implicit arguments, flesh out their implications, and see how they are in fact endorsed by and implicitly at work in a diverse body of recent Jesus research.

1. Contextual Plausibility within Judaism

According to Sanders, any hypothesis must first make Jesus "a believable figure in first century Palestine."[105] This can be described as an argument from contextual plausibility within first-century Judaism. In this view, if evidence about

103. Sanders, *Jesus and Judaism*, 17, 166–67 (enumeration added).

104. For example, Dale Allison implicitly appeals to all three of these contextual arguments when he contends that Jesus should be regarded as an eschatological prophet because this reconstruction is (1) compatible with "whatever knowledge we have of his first-century Jewish world," (2) coheres with "whatever circumstances about his life we can recover with assurance," and (3) because a non-eschatological Jesus entails "discontinuity with the movement out of which he came as well as with the movement that came out of him." See Allison, "How to Marginalize," 26–27.

105. Sanders, *Jesus and Judaism*, 167.

Jesus is compatible with or credible within his first-century Jewish context, then it works in favor of its historicity.

Although the argument from contextual plausibility takes different forms, it is easy to demonstrate its presence in almost all recent works on the historical Jesus. Consider the following statements from major contributions to the quest for Jesus:

> The criterion of double dissimilarity . . . has been replaced by a procedure according to which Jesus tradition that can plausibly be traced back to first-century Palestinian Judaism should be considered authentic.[106]

> I concur [with Sanders] that we should proceed by abduction—that is, by inference to the best explanation, always looking for a Jesus who makes the most sense of the available facts and what we otherwise know of Judaism.[107]

> No saying of Jesus can be reckoned authentic unless it was intelligible to first-century Jews in a Palestinian/Galilean setting.[108]

> What is plausibly "Jewish" enjoys a high degree of historical plausibility in being traced back to the historical Jesus. . . . That is what we call "Jewish contextual plausibility."[109]

Such statements could easily be multiplied.[110] For our purposes here, what matters is that the argument from contextual plausibility within first-century Judaism is a major determining factor in the way much contemporary scholarship on Jesus evaluates the historicity of sayings and actions attributed to Jesus in the Gospels—including scholars who are critical of the traditional form-critical criteria.

106. David du Toit, "The Third Quest for the Historical Jesus," in Schröter and Jacboi, *Jesus Handbook*, 93–108 (here 105).

107. Allison, *Constructing Jesus*, 22.

108. Geza Vermes, *The Authentic Gospel of Jesus* (London: Penguin, 2003), 375.

109. Gerd Theissen and Dagmar Winter, *The Quest for the Plausible Jesus: The Question of Criteria*, trans. M. Eugene Boring (Louisville: Westminster, 2002), 206.

110. See Hengel and Schwemer, *Jesus and Judaism*, 275–76; Schröter, *Jesus of Nazareth*, 65; Puig i Tàrrech, *Jesus: A Biography*, 4; Casey, *Jesus of Nazareth*, 106; Sean Freyne, *Jesus, a Jewish Galilean: A New Reading of the Jesus-Story* (repr., London: T&T Clark, 2005), 22–23, 171; Graham Stanton, *The Gospels and Jesus*, 2nd ed. (Oxford: Oxford University Press, 2002), 175; Craig A. Evans, *Jesus and His Contemporaries: Comparative Studies*, Arbeiten zur Geschichte des antiken Judentums und des Urchristentums 25 (Leiden: Brill, 1995), 13.

With that said, it is important to stress that contextual plausibility is not sufficient in itself to make a historical argument (e.g., "if it's Jewish, then it's from Jesus"). Rather, it should be used in tandem with the other two sets of information: other evidence about Jesus and consequences in the early church.

2. *Coherence with Other Evidence about Jesus*

According to Sanders, any hypothesis about Jesus must also provide a "satisfactory account of the material in the Gospels."[111] This can be described as the argument from coherence with other evidence about Jesus. If a particular saying or deed attributed to Jesus is both contextually plausible and congruent with other first-century evidence about Jesus, then this too is an important argument in favor of its historicity.

It is, of course, a standard principle of historiography to aim at constructing a basically coherent account of the words and deeds of any given historical figure. Consequently, it comes as no surprise that the argument from coherence is easily documented in recent works on the historical Jesus. Consider the following examples:

> Coherence is a necessary and inevitable principle. . . . coherence will continue to be employed in all kinds of historical research, including Jesus studies.[112]

> Establishing genuine doctrines with the help of the criterion of coherence will form the second stage of the forthcoming quest.[113]

> The question again and again will be not simply "Is this detail or that detail historically plausible/reliable?" but "Does this particular story or teaching build into a coherent and consistent picture of the person who made the impact evident in the broader picture?"[114]

111. Sanders, *Jesus and Judaism*, 167

112. Anthony Le Donne, "The Criterion of Coherence: Its Development, Inevitability, and Historiographical Limitations," in *Jesus, Criteria, and the Demise of Authenticity*, ed. Chris Keith and Anthony Le Donne (London: T&T Clark, 2012), 113.

113. Vermes, *Authentic Gospel of Jesus*, 375.

114. Dunn, *Jesus Remembered*, 334.

Once again, such examples could easily be multiplied.[115] Indeed, even a cursory reading of recent Jesus research reveals that scholars consistently accept or reject a given piece of evidence based on whether it coheres with other data about Jesus that they accept as substantially historical. In this study, I will treat the argument from coherence as particularly forceful when it also demonstrates explanatory power for data that may seem otherwise obscure or difficult.[116]

With that said, when it comes to a case of coherence, I will always try to explain *how* I think one piece of evidence coheres with another, rather than just asserting that it does. Again, this will make for somewhat longer discussions of historicity than is found in other works on Jesus—something I consider a strength, since the reader will be free to evaluate the historical arguments that lead to my conclusions. In the final analysis, as Sanders points out, "the reader will have to judge how good the evidence is."[117]

3. Consequences in the Early Church

Third and finally, according to Sanders, any sound historical hypothesis must also depict Jesus as "the founder of a movement that eventuated in the Church."[118] This can be described as an argument from the plausibility of effects in the early church. In this view, if a saying or deed attributed to Jesus is contextually plausible, coherent with other evidence about Jesus, and has the power to explain why the early church acted and believed as it did, then it is reasonable to conclude that the saying or deed goes back to Jesus himself.

The first thing that needs to be said about the argument from plausibility of effects is that it stands in direct opposition to the form-critical criterion of "dissimilarity" with the early church.[119] In principle, the criterion of dis-

115. See also Hengel and Schwemer, *Jesus and Judaism*, 279; Ernst Baasland, "Fourth Quest? What Did Jesus Really Want?," in Holmén and Porter, *Handbook for the Study of the Historical Jesus*, 49; Casey, *Jesus of Nazareth*, 107; Keener, *Historical Jesus*, 155–56; Vermes, *Authentic Gospel of Jesus*, 375; Lüdemann, *Jesus after Two Thousand Years*, 5; Evans, *Jesus and His Contemporaries*, 13.

116. See Brant Pitre, *Jesus, the Tribulation, and the End of the Exile: Restoration Eschatology and the Origin of the Atonement*, Wissenschaftliche Untersuchungen zum Neuen Testament 2.204 (Tübingen: Mohr Siebeck; Grand Rapids: Baker Academic, 2005), 27.

117. Sanders, *Jesus and Judaism*, 22.

118. Sanders, *Jesus and Judaism*, 167.

119. See Chris Keith, "The Indebtedness of the Criteria Approach to Form Criticism and Recent Attempts to Rehabilitate the Search for an Authentic Jesus," in *Jesus, Criteria, and*

similarity was only supposed to be used to argue in favor of the historicity of evidence unlikely to have been created by the early church.[120] It was, however, frequently used as a criterion of inauthenticity: any evidence even remotely similar to the practice and belief of the early church was often deemed unhistorical.[121] As recent scholarship has recognized, this drives far too strong of a wedge between Jesus and the movement that followed him.[122] As a result, more and more scholars are emphasizing the importance of plausible consequences in the early church:

> The final and perhaps most important consideration of all is the *aftermath* of Jesus.[123]

> We must be able to see the connections between the historical Jesus and the subsequent movement which regarded him as its central figure.[124]

> What we know of Jesus as a whole must allow him to be recognized within his contemporary Jewish context and must be compatible with the Christian (canonical and noncanonical) history of his effects.[125]

Perhaps the strongest formulation comes from Sanders himself:

> In the first place, a good hypothesis with regard to Jesus' intention and his relationship to Judaism should meet [Joseph] Klausner's test: it should situate Jesus believably in Judaism and yet explain why the movement initiated by him eventually broke with Judaism. . . . I propose that a hypothesis which does offer a reasonable and well-grounded connection between Jesus and

the Demise of Authenticity, ed. Chris Keith and Anthony Le Donne (London: T&T Clark, 2012), 25–48.

120. See Theissen and Winter, *Quest for the Plausible Jesus*, 1–171.

121. See, e.g., Lüdemann, *Jesus after Two Thousand Years*, 4.

122. See Dagmar Winter, "Saving the Quest for Authenticity from the Criterion of Dissimilarity: History and Plausibility," in *Jesus, Criteria, and the Demise of Authenticity*, ed. Chris Keith and Anthony Le Donne (London: T&T Clark, 2012), 115–31; Dunn, *Jesus Remembered*, 92–97, 191–92; Tom Holmén, "Doubts about Double Dissimilarity: Restructuring the Main Criterion of Jesus-of-History Research," in *Authenticating the Words of Jesus*, ed. Bruce Chilton and Craig A. Evans (Leiden: Brill, 1999), 47–80.

123. Stanton, *Gospels and Jesus*, 176.

124. Casey, *Jesus of Nazareth*, 107.

125. Theissen and Winter, *Quest for the Plausible Jesus*, 211–12.

> the Christian movement is better than one which offers no connection, but which appeals, finally, to accident.[126]

As we will see later, the hypothesis that Jesus claimed to be divine provides a historically compelling (yet often unexplored) explanation for "why the movement initiated by him eventually broke with Judaism."[127] For now, however, I simply want to emphasize that there is growing scholarly support for the argument from consequences in the early church.[128] The reason for this is simple. As Sanders puts it, "That there is no causal thread between [Jesus's] life, his death, and the Christian movement . . . is possible, but is not satisfying historically."[129]

The Triple-Context Approach: Weaknesses and Strengths

Before moving on, it is important to note that the triple-context approach is not without its weaknesses.[130]

For one thing, when it comes to contextual plausibility, it is important to emphasize that there are now and will always be major gaps in our knowledge about early Judaism at the time of Jesus. Indeed, the force of the argument is directly dependent on how familiar any given scholar is with early Jewish practice and belief. What seems implausible to someone who is ignorant of some aspect of Second Temple Judaism may appear eminently probable to a scholar who is better versed in the subject. For this reason, in this study, I will take pains to quote and analyze key passages from Jewish Scripture and other early Jewish sources. Moreover, the argument from coherence with other evidence about Jesus is more or less contingent on the historical veracity of the other evidence cited. If the corroborative evidence is substantially unhistorical or distorted enough to be misleading, then it obviously loses its force. In order to offset this weakness as much as possible, in what follows, I will always try

126. Sanders, *Jesus and Judaism*, 18, 22. He is following Klausner, *Jesus of Nazareth*, 369.

127. Sanders, *Jesus and Judaism*, 22.

128. See Baasland, "Fourth Quest?," 49; Keener, *Historical Jesus*, 144, 157; Tom Holmén, "An Introduction to the Continuum Approach," in *Jesus from Judaism to Christianity: Continuum Approaches to the Historical Jesus*, ed. Tom Holmén, Library of New Testament Studies 352 (London: T&T Clark, 2007), 4; Becker, *Jesus of Nazareth*, 14.

129. Sanders, *Jesus and Judaism*, 22.

130. See Pitre, *Jesus and the Last Supper*, 31–46, for a longer discussion of these potential weaknesses.

to give a judicious sampling of evidence about Jesus when making a case from coherence so that it does not hang upon the historicity of any one word or deed. As Sanders says,

> The method which is being followed more and more, and the one which it seems necessary to follow in writing about Jesus, is to construct hypotheses which, on the one hand, do rest on material generally considered reliable without, on the other hand, being totally dependent on the authenticity of any given pericope.[131]

Along similar lines, the argument from plausibility of effects is also limited by the fact that we simply do not know everything there is to know about the early church.[132] Not only was the movement that came from Jesus characterized by a remarkable diversity, but many of its early practices and beliefs are shrouded in mystery. Hence, in any given case, I will try to explain (insofar as possible) a plausible trajectory of development.[133]

Despite these weaknesses, however, one strength of the triple-context approach is that these three arguments can also be inverted and used as reasons *against* the historicity of words and actions attributed to Jesus, as follows:

1. Contextual implausibility within first-century Judaism
2. Incoherence with other evidence about Jesus
3. Implausibility of effects in the early church

In other words, if evidence about Jesus cannot be plausibly situated within a first-century Jewish context (contextual implausibility), is irreconcilable with other data about him (incoherence), and cannot be plausibly situated at the origins of the movement which he initiated (implausibility of effects), then it is reasonable to conclude that the evidence in question is unhistorical.[134]

It is important to stress that the triple-context approach I am employing in this study also works in reverse, since one of the most important criticisms of the form-critical criteria of multiple attestation, embarrassment,

131. Sanders, *Jesus and Judaism*, 3.

132. Allison, *Jesus of Nazareth*, 5.

133. See Holmén, "Introduction to the Continuum Approach," 2–3.

134. On criteria of inauthenticity, see Casey, *Jesus of Nazareth*, 107–8; Keener, *Historical*, 157; Lüdemann, *Jesus after Two Thousand Years*, 4; Sanders, *Jesus and Judaism*, 22. For the whole issue, see Allison, "How to Marginalize," 3–30.

and dissimilarity is that they only work in one direction—to authenticate evidence.[135] More sound historical tools should be able to be used both for and against any given piece of data. Of course, this will necessitate weighing the arguments *both for and against* the historicity of any given saying or deed of Jesus; but this is what studies of the historical Jesus should be doing anyway.

Historicity and the **Substantia Verborum Jesu**

When it comes to drawing conclusions about particular sayings attributed to Jesus, it is important to be precise about what I mean when I speak about "historicity."

Some readers of the Gospels come to them looking for the *ipsissima verba Jesu* (the "exact words of Jesus"). As contemporary scholarship rightly insists, rarely, if ever, is it possible for us to reconstruct the precise words of Jesus.[136] Even a cursory comparison of the sayings of Jesus in a Gospel synopsis shows, on many occasions, the authors of the Gospels themselves do not seem bent on giving us anything like the exact words of Jesus.[137] In light of such differences, the Four Gospels should not be treated as stenographs of Jesus's teachings but as ancient Greco-Roman biographies, in which the historical veracity of Jesus's sayings cannot be equated with exactitude in form and detail.

For this reason, some scholars suggest we should rather be seeking the *ipsissima vox Jesu*, sometimes identified as "the basic message of Jesus."[138] At first glance this may seem more reasonable, but the expression "the exact voice of Jesus" (*ipsissima vox Jesu*) actually reflects a peculiarly modern preoccupation with exactitude (*ipse*), one that smacks of historical positivism. Moreover, the image of the "voice" (*vox*) of Jesus places too much emphasis on the *form* of Jesus's words (how he sounds) rather than the *content* (what he says). However, in the quest for the historical Jesus, it

135. See Robert L. Webb, "The Historical Enterprise and Historical Jesus Research," in Brock and Webb, *Key Events*, 54–75.

136. See Geza Vermes, *Jesus in His Jewish Context* (Minneapolis: Fortress, 2003), 74; Meier, *A Marginal Jew*, 1:174.

137. The most obvious example is the words of Jesus at the Last Supper (see Matt 26:28; Mark 14:24; Luke 22:19–20; 1 Cor 11:23–25). See Pitre, *Jesus and the Last Supper*, for a full study.

138. John P. Meier, *A Marginal Jew: Rethinking the Historical Jesus*, 5 vols., Anchor Yale Bible Reference Library (New Haven: Yale University Press, 1991–2016), 1:174.

is not so much the form of Jesus's teaching that is most important, but the "content" or "substance."[139] Once again, even a quick glance at the Gospels reveals a remarkable diversity of precise forms. By contrast, parallel traditions in the Gospels are identified as such precisely because there is often a substantial amount of overlap in the substance of the words (*verba*).[140] This is of course because in human discourse, content is inextricably tied to words.

In light of such considerations, I suggest a third way. In this study, when dealing with the sayings attributed Jesus, I will be pursuing the *substantia verborum Jesu*—that is, the "substance of the words of Jesus." In other words, I am interested in *what* he said and did and what it might have meant in a first-century Jewish context. Hence, whenever I conclude that a particular saying or action is "historical," I am not saying that Jesus said exactly these words (*ipsissima verba*), nor am I just saying the text "sounds exactly like Jesus" (*ipsissima vox*). Instead, I am claiming that the basic *substance* of the teaching or action can be reasonably understood as having originated with him. That is what I mean by historical—no more and no less.[141] Unlike the *ipsissima verba* and *ipsissima vox* approaches, I am not looking for the *ipsissima* anything.

This focus on the substance of the sayings of Jesus in the Gospels has important practical implications. For one thing, I will make no attempt to reconstruct an "original form" of any of Jesus's sayings.[142] Modern scholarly reconstructions of such primitive forms, for all their ingenuity and display of learning, manifest precisely the concern for exactitude and detail that the first-century evangelists do not seem concerned about and that I wish to avoid. Moreover, I will also not spend much time evaluating differences in form and detail between various accounts of Jesus's words or actions in the Gospels. Such differences in detail are often quite significant for redaction-critical analyses of the Gospels but are of far less importance for historical Jesus research. Obviously, this will entail a certain amount of reductionism, as well as judgments about what is substantial and major and what is incidental and minor with reference to any given data. I leave it to the reader to decide to what extent I have succeeded.

139. Meier, *A Marginal Jew*, 1:43.

140. See, e.g., the synoptic charts throughout Dunn, *Jesus Remembered*.

141. See Theissen and Winter, *Quest for the Plausible Jesus*, 197–99.

142. Cf. Dunn, *Jesus Remembered*, 332.

The Gospel of John in Contemporary Jesus Research

With that said, I want to stress that this methodological focus on the substance of Jesus's sayings will both enable us and require us to pay close attention to key pieces of evidence in the Gospel of John. For most of the twentieth century, it was standard practice in the quest for the historical Jesus to ignore most (if not all) of the evidence in the Fourth Gospel. However, in recent decades, more scholars are calling for future research to not ignore *any* first-century data about Jesus, including that which is found in the Gospel of John:[143]

> With regard to individual aspects of the history of Jesus, the Gospel of John provides historical details that should be taken seriously.[144]

> John's Gospel is . . . of immense value to students inquiring about the historical Jesus.[145]

> Before the [Dead Sea] Scrolls' recovery . . . many scholars regarded the Gospel of John as . . . both late and intrinsically nonhistorical. . . . The discovery of the Scrolls—whose place, date, and completely Jewish context is very secure—undermined this view of the Fourth Gospel. . . . The Scrolls incontrovertibly show that early first-century Judean Jews spoke and thought in similar ways. An earlier, Jewish context of composition for John's Gospel then reopens the question of its historical value for reconstructing Jesus' life.[146]

> John's Gospel, in my opinion, is not to be rejected en masse and a priori as a source for the historical Jesus. . . . Each case must be judged on its own merits; the "tyranny of the Synoptic Jesus" should be consigned to the dustbin of the post-Bultmannians.[147]

143. See James H. Charlesworth and Jolyon G. R. Pruszinski, eds., *Jesus Research: The Gospel of John in Historical Inquiry*, Jewish and Christian Texts 26 (London: T&T Clark, 2019), xvii: "John should be used in Jesus Research."

144. Jörg Frey, "The Gospel of John as a Historical Source," in Schröter and Jacboi, *Jesus Handbook*, 138–40 (here 139).

145. James D. G. Dunn, "John and the Historical Jesus: A Response," in Paul N. Anderson, Felix Just, SJ, and Tom Thatcher, eds., *Glimpses of Jesus Through the Johannine Lens*, vol. 3 of *John, Jesus, and History* (Atlanta: Society of Biblical Literature, 2016), 504.

146. Fredriksen, *Jesus of Nazareth*, 5.

147. Meier, *A Marginal Jew*, 1:45.

Once again, these examples could be multiplied, and some disagree.[148] For now, I simply want to emphasize that I will be following John Meier's (surely unassailable) principle that each piece of evidence in the Gospel of John must be judged on a case-by-case basis. At the same time, I must insist that by examining some of the sayings of Jesus in John's Gospel, I am *not* implying that it provides the *ipsissima verba Jesu*, or even the *ipsissima vox Jesu*—though I anticipate some readers will assume I am doing just that. Rather, what I am saying is that if scholars are going to be methodologically consistent, then we need to be able to apply the same arguments for historicity to the words and deeds attributed to Jesus in the Gospel of John as we do to the Synoptics, Paul, or any other source.

In this way, I hope to offer an important corrective to the widespread tendency of Jesus research to ignore the Gospel of John, which John Meier has rightly referred to as "the tyranny of the Synoptic Jesus."[149] Indeed, one cannot help but wonder if this tyranny of the Synoptics in Jesus research is due to the fact that, in the final analysis, many scholars really *are* searching for the *exact* words of Jesus. As a result, they continue to focus almost exclusively on the forms found in the Synoptic Gospels.[150]

Interpretation and Historicity

Finally, in contrast to some studies on Jesus, I contend that a scholar must first interpret the evidence in the Gospels *before* drawing any conclusions about

148. See Paul N. Anderson, "Why the Gospel of John is Fundamental to Jesus Research," in *Jesus Research: the Gospel of John in Historical Inquiry*, ed. James H. Charlesworth and Jolyon G. R. Pruszinski, Jewish and Christian Texts 26 (London: T&T Clark, 2019), 7–46; Paul N. Anderson, Felix Just, SJ, and Tom Thatcher, eds., *John, Jesus, and History*, 3 vols. (Atlanta: Society of Biblical Literature, 2007–2016); Dwight Moody Smith, "Jesus Tradition in the Gospel of John," in Holmén and Porter, *Handbook for the Study of the Historical Jesus*, 3:1997–2040. For criticisms of the way the Gospel of John is sometimes used in Jesus research (some of which I share), see Harold W. Attridge, "Some Methodological Considerations regarding John, Jesus, and History," in Charlesworth and Pruszinski, *Jesus Research*, 71–84; Jörg Frey, *Theology and History in the Fourth Gospel: Tradition and Narration* (Waco, TX: Baylor University Press, 2018), 59–142; Paul Foster, "Memory, Orality, and the Fourth Gospel: Three Dead Ends in Historical Jesus Research," *Journal for the Study of the Historical Jesus* 10 (2012): 191–227.

149. Meier, *A Marginal Jew*, 1:45.

150. Consider, for example, Paul Foster's repeated emphasis on the "distinctive language," the "distinctive voice of Jesus," and "Jesus' language" in John's Gospel as decisive in declaring the use of John a "dead-end in historical Jesus research." See Foster, "Memory," 224–25.

the historicity of a saying or deed attributed to Jesus.[151] As Gerd Theissen and Dagmar Winter rightly note, interpretation and historical plausibility are inextricably tied to one another:

> The question of the authenticity is bound up with the understanding of the meaning of the saying, and vice versa. . . . Since the time that the historicity of the Jesus traditions has been disputed, whether or not they have been considered historical has depended largely on their interpretation.[152]

The same point holds true for the historicity of "events" in the life of Jesus.[153] Yet, as we will see over and over again, many contributors to the quest for the historical Jesus will reject a particular episode from the Gospels as unhistorical or implausible *before they have even attempted to interpret the evidence in its first-century Jewish context.* In this way, historical conclusions are drawn based on presuppositions and prejudgments that are often unstated, apart from any detailed analysis of the passage in question. But how can one decide whether or not an episode from the Gospels is historically plausible without first attempting to situate it in Jesus's historical context to see whether it fits? Failure to do so would be to put the historical "cart" before the exegetical "horse" and, in my opinion, constitutes one of the most serious weaknesses of the twentieth-century quest for the historical Jesus.

As we will also see, many interpreters will often conclude that simply because a passage from the Gospels can be given plausible interpretation within an early Christian context (*Sitz im Leben*), then the saying or action attributed to Jesus must not be historical. As Theissen and Winter also point out:

> It is possible for a saying that has a plausible Christian sense to receive a different plausible meaning if it can be traced back to Jesus. Thus, in declaring a tradition to be inauthentic, we must always also test whether the saying, in a different meaning, cannot also be understood as a saying of the historical Jesus. Fitting well into the context of post-Easter Christianity *does not exclude* the possibility that it also fits well into the context of Jesus' ministry.[154]

151. See Pitre, *Jesus and the Last Supper*, and *Jesus, the Tribulation*, throughout.

152. Theissen and Winter, *Quest for the Plausible Jesus*, 193; see also the same work, p. 197 (regarding events).

153. Theissen and Winter, *Quest for the Plausible Jesus*, 197.

154. Theissen and Winter, *Quest for the Plausible Jesus*, 207.

This is quite true and why it is so important that historical exegesis must be carried out prior to any conclusions being drawn about historical plausibility. Hence, in what follows, my first step will always be to attempt to offer a contextually anchored interpretation of any given saying or deed of Jesus before weighing the arguments for or against historicity. And even when historical judgments are rendered, it is important to keep in mind that all such conclusions are contingent matters of greater or lesser probability and do not constitute incontrovertible "proofs."

With all of this in mind, let us now turn to the evidence that suggests—to use Joseph Klausner's image—that the "smoke" of early high Christology had its origins in the "fire" of the words and deeds of Jesus.[155]

155. Cf. Klausner, *Jesus of Nazareth*, 369.

CHAPTER 2

The Epiphany Miracles

> At this time, there appeared Jesus, a wise man, if indeed one should call him a man. For he was a doer of startling deeds.
>
> —Josephus[1]

> Whatever you think about the philosophical possibility of miracles, it's clear that Jesus was widely reputed to have done them.
>
> —Bart Ehrman[2]

> All of Jesus' miracles have a certain "epiphanic" quality about them. In one way or another all of them reveal something of a divine presence and power suddenly appearing and acting in the earthly realm.
>
> —John Meier[3]

The Miracles of Jesus

The primary purpose of this chapter is to demolish the modern scholarly myth—which goes back at least as far as the time of Ernst Renan—that Jesus is not depicted as divine in the Synoptic Gospels, but only in the Gospel of John.[4] For it is this myth that is one of the principal barriers to recognizing that Jesus speaks and acts as if he is more than merely human in all four of his first-century biographies. In saying this, I want to emphasize that my main goal is *not* to persuade readers of the historicity of the miracles attributed

1. Josephus, *Antiquities* 18.63, translation in John P. Meier, *A Marginal Jew: Rethinking the Historical Jesus*, 5 vols., Anchor Yale Bible Reference Library (New Haven: Yale University Press, 1991–2016), 1:60.

2. Bart D. Ehrman, *Jesus: Apocalyptic Prophet of the New Millennium* (Oxford: Oxford University Press, 1999), 199.

3. Meier, *A Marginal Jew*, 2:928.

4. See Ernest Renan, *The Life of Jesus* (London: Watts & Co., 1935 [orig. 1863]), 132.

to Jesus. I am well aware that some (perhaps many) readers have *a priori* philosophical commitments that prohibit them from even entertaining the possibility that Jesus of Nazareth could have performed the "startling deeds" attributed to him by first-century writers like Josephus or the authors of the Four Gospels. This study is not the place to adjudicate these kinds of philosophical commitments.

Instead, I ask my readers for patience. In the next chapter, we will turn to teachings of Jesus that are almost universally regarded as historical and which have a direct bearing on the question of whether he made divine claims during his lifetime. But before doing so, we must first consider how the contemporary quest for Jesus presents us with something of a paradox when it comes to the so-called epiphany miracles.

Jesus Was Regarded as a Miracle Worker

On the one hand, contemporary scholars across a wide spectrum of religious and philosophical perspectives are virtually unanimous in agreeing that Jesus was regarded by his fellow first-century Jews as a worker of miracles. Consider, for example, the following statements:

> That Jesus healed the sick and exorcised demons in a way that struck onlookers as miraculous is virtually certain.[5]

> Whatever we may think of the events which might have occasioned these stories, the most obvious conclusion to draw is that there were various incidents during Jesus' mission which were experienced/witnessed as miracles.[6]

> Jesus as exorcist, healer (even to the point of raising the dead), and miracle worker is one of the strongest, most ubiquitous, and most variously attested depictions in the Gospels. . . . Yes, I think that Jesus probably did perform deeds that contemporaries viewed as miracles.[7]

5. Helen K. Bond, *The Historical Jesus: A Guide for the Perplexed* (London: T&T Clark, 2012), 102.

6. James D. G. Dunn, *Jesus Remembered*, vol. 1 of *Christianity in the Making* (Grand Rapids: Eerdmans, 2003), 683.

7. Paula Fredriksen, *Jesus of Nazareth, King of the Jews* (New York: Vintage Books, 1999), 114.

> Put dramatically but with not too much exaggeration: if the miracle tradition from Jesus' public ministry were to be rejected *in toto* as unhistorical, so should every other Gospel tradition about him.[8]

Such quotes could easily be multiplied.[9] In light of such statements, in a significant study of the historical Jesus and early Jewish miracles, Eric Eve speaks of a "growing consensus" that "this miraculous activity formed an integral part of Jesus's ministry and should not be brushed aside to leave room for a Jesus who was almost entirely a teacher."[10]

The reason for this virtual consensus is simple. Without prejudice to the historicity of any single account, in all four first-century biographies of Jesus, there is abundant evidence that he was remembered as having performed "deeds of power" (*dynameis*),[11] extraordinary "works" (*erga*),[12] "signs" (*sēmeia*),[13] "wonders" (*terata*),[14] and "startling deeds" (*paradoxa*).[15] Moreover, we also have the testimony of the first-century Jewish historian Josephus, who describes Jesus as both a teacher and a worker of miracles: "At this time there appeared Jesus, a wise man, if indeed one should call him a man. For *he was a doer of startling deeds*, a teacher of the people who receive the truth with pleasure" (Josephus, *Antiquities* 18.63).[16] Although many scholars consider the line "if indeed one should call him a man" to be a later Christian interpolation, Josephus's assertion that Jesus was a doer of "startling deeds" (*paradoxōn*)—later translated into Latin as "miracles" (*mirabilium*)[17]—is widely regarded

8. Meier, *A Marginal Jew*, 2:630.

9. See Gerhard Lohfink, *Jesus of Nazareth: What He Wanted, Who He Was*, trans. Linda M. Maloney (Collegeville: Liturgical Press, 2012), 132; Armand Puig i Tàrrech, *Jesus: A Biography*, trans. Jenny Read-Heimerdinger (Waco, TX: Baylor University Press, 2011), 363; Gerd Theissen and Annette Merz, *The Historical Jesus: A Comprehensive Guide*, trans. John Bowden (Minneapolis: Fortress, 1998), 281; Geza Vermes, *Jesus the Jew: A Historian's Reading of the Gospels* (Philadelphia: Fortress, 1973), 223.

10. Eric Eve, *The Jewish Context of Jesus' Miracles*, Library of New Testament Studies 172, Journal for the Study of the New Testament Supplement Series 231 (London: Sheffield Academic Press, 2002), 17. See also Graham H. Twelftree, "The Message of Jesus I: Miracles, Continuing Controversies," in *Handbook for the Study of the Historical Jesus*, 4 vols., ed. Tom Holmén and Stanley E. Porter (Leiden: Brill, 2011), 3:2517–48.

11. Matt 11:20–21, 23; 13:54–58; 14:2; Mark 6:2, 5, 14; Luke 10:13, 19:37; cf. 5:17.

12. Matt 11:2; John 4:34; 5:20, 36; 7:3; 9:3–4; 10:25, 32–38; 14:10–12; 15:24; 17:4.

13. Luke 23:8; John 2:11, 23; 3:2; 4:48, 54; 6:2, 14, 26; 7:31; 9:16; 11:47; 12:18, 37; 20:30.

14. John 4:48.

15. Luke 5:26.

16. Translation in Meier, *A Marginal Jew*, 1:60 (emphasis added).

17. For an ancient Latin translation of Josephus's *Testimonium*, see Jerome, *Lives of Illustrious Men* 13.

as authentic.[18] If this is correct, then we have five first-century sources, all written within the living memory of Jesus, that testify with one voice that he was known as a miracle worker.

The Divinity of Jesus and the Epiphany Miracles

On the other hand, when it comes to the question of whether Jesus spoke or acted as if he was divine, many contemporary Jesus researchers are equally emphatic that the miracles attributed to Jesus did not lead anyone to believe in his divinity. Consider, for example, the words of E. P. Sanders:

> Like other ancient people, Jews believed in miracles but did not think that the ability to perform them proved exalted status. . . . in the first century Jesus' miracles were not decisive in deciding whether or not to accept his message and . . . they did not "prove" to his contemporaries that he was superhuman. . . . Historically, it is an error to think that . . . in Jesus' own day his miracles were taken as proving partial or full divinity.[19]

Notice here that Sanders agrees that Jesus was believed to have performed miracles. However, he insists there is no evidence that any of these purported miracles led Jesus's contemporaries to believe that he had any kind of "exalted status" or that he was "superhuman." Instead, Jesus was no different than other miracle workers in Jewish Scripture, such as Moses or Elijah, or among his contemporaries, such as Honi the Circle Drawer. According to this view, the miracles attributed to Jesus have nothing to do with whether or not he believed himself to be (or was considered by others to be) divine. When it comes to the question of his divinity, the miracles of Jesus are irrelevant.

There are several major problems with this point of view. For one thing, it ignores the fact that, in antiquity, *not all miracles were created equal.* Instead, some miracles were believed to be so far beyond human power that they *did* in fact point to the divinity of the one who performed them. Consider, for

18. See Jan Willem van Henten, "*Testimonium Flavianum*," in *From Paul to Josephus: Literary Receptions of Jesus in the First Century CE*, ed. Helen K. Bond, vol. 1 of *The Reception of Jesus in the First Three Centuries* (London: T&T Clark, 2020), 365–70; Alice Whealey, "The *Testimonium Flavianum*," in *A Companion to Josephus*, ed. Honora Howell Chapman and Zuleika Rodgers (London: Wiley Blackwell, 2016), 345–55; Meier, *A Marginal Jew*, 2:621–22.

19. E. P. Sanders, *The Historical Figure of Jesus* (London: Penguin, 1993), 133, 134, 135. For a similar view, see Ehrman, *Jesus: Apocalyptic Prophet*, 199.

example, Plutarch's account of Alexander the Great's interaction with an ancient sage of India:

> One [wise man] was asked [by Alexander] how a man [*tis ex anthrōpōn*] might become a god [*genoito theos*]. He answered: 'By doing something that a man cannot do' [*ei ti praxeien ho praxai dynaton anthrōpō mē estin*]. (Plutarch, *Life of Alexander* 64.4)[20]

Moreover, according to contemporary historical Jesus scholarship, *certain* miracles attributed to Jesus can be described as "epiphanies,"[21] or "epiphany miracles,"[22] precisely because their main function is to "show" or "make visible" (*epiphainō*) the invisible mystery of "his identity."[23] As John Meier writes:

> All of Jesus' miracles have a certain "epiphanic" quality about them. In one way or another all of them reveal something of a divine presence and power suddenly appearing and acting in the earthly realm. . . . What, then, is required for an epiphany miracle in the strict sense? . . . in my view the essential elements must include the absence (or invisibility) of the divine or heavenly figure at the beginning of the story, his or her sudden and frightening appearance in great power and majesty at a certain moment in the story, and usually some statement by the figure that reveals his or her true identity.[24]

As we will see, all of these elements are present in several episodes in the Gospels. Should, however, there be any concern that the language of "epiph-

20. In Plutarch, *Hellenistic Lives, Including Alexander the Great*, trans. Robin Waterfield (Oxford: Oxford University Press, 2016), 67. Cited in Ian Worthington, *Alexander the Great: Man and God* (Harlow: Longman Pearson, 2004), 273.

21. Bernd Kollmann, "Resuscitations of the Dead and Nature Miracles," in *The Jesus Handbook*, ed. Jens Schröter and Christine Jacobi, trans. Robert L. Brawley (Grand Rapids: Eerdmans, 2022), 315–22 (here 321, 320).

22. Joachim Gnilka, *Jesus of Nazareth: Message and History*, trans. Siegfried S. Schatzmann (Peabody, MA: Hendrickson, 1997), 133.

23. Bond, *Historical Jesus*, 121. See also Eve, *Healer from Nazareth*, 113–16; Theissen and Merz, *Historical Jesus*, 285–313. Bond uses the category of "nature miracle" to refer to these epiphany miracles, which I will avoid herein because of its anachronistic and philosophically freighted connotations. See the essays in Graham H. Twelftree, ed., *The Nature Miracles of Jesus: Problems, Perspectives, and Prospects* (Eugene, OR: Cascade, 2017), for further discussion.

24. Meier, *A Marginal Jew*, 2:928–29.

any" miracle might be anachronistic, it is important to recall that the ancient Seleucid king Antiochus IV took the name "King Antiochus, God Manifest" (*theou epiphanous*) precisely because he was publicly claiming to be divine.[25] In a similar fashion, a case can be made that three key "epiphany miracles" attributed to Jesus likewise describe him as being more than merely human:

1. Stilling of the storm (Matt 8:23–27; Mark 4:35–41; Luke 8:22–25)
2. Walking on the sea (Matt 14:22–27; Mark 6:45–52; John 6:16–21)
3. The transfiguration (Matt 17:1–9; Mark 9:2–9; Luke 9:28–36)

As I will show, when each of these episodes is interpreted in a first-century Jewish context, a strong case can be made that in all three, Jesus is acting and speaking as if he is not just *any* kind of deity or heavenly being, but in some sense equal with the one God of Israel.

The Historicity of Miracles and the Divinity of Jesus in the Synoptics

Once again, I realize that many readers of this volume may object to even considering the historical plausibility of the epiphany miracles—or any other miracles, for that matter—due to *a priori* philosophical commitments.[26] Indeed, entire books devoted to the self-understanding of the historical Jesus have been written without any reference whatsoever to the epiphanic actions attributed to him.[27] For such readers, I have three brief suggestions.

First, as a matter of principle, the *historical* question of whether any of the actions attributed to Jesus goes back to an incident in his life cannot be decided on the grounds of a *philosophical* assumption that miracles are impossible. Rather, like every other episode in the Gospels, the epiphany

25. See Josephus, *Antiquities* 12.258. Robert Doran, "Antiochus IV Epiphanes," in *Eerdmans Dictionary of Early Judaism*, ed. John J. Collins and Daniel C. Harlow (Grand Rapids: Eerdmans, 2010), 338–39; Peter Franz Mittag, *Antiochos IV. Epiphanes: Eine politische Biographie, Klio* 11 (Berline: Akademie Verlag, 2006), 128–39.

26. See James Crossley, "The Nature Miracles as Pure Myth," and Ruben Zimmerman, "Re-counting the Impossible," in *The Nature Miracles of Jesus: Problems, Perspectives, and Prospects*, ed. Graham H. Twelftree (Eugene, OR: Cascade, 2017), 86–106, 107–27. Cf. also Ehrman, *How Jesus Became God*, 147–51; Fredriksen, *Jesus of Nazareth*, 114.

27. See Ben Witherington III, *The Christology of Jesus* (Minneapolis: Fortress, 1990), 162, who dispenses with them in a single sentence: "We will not study the epiphanic miracles because most scholars believe they reflect later church interests."

miracles attributed to Jesus must be evaluated on the basis of contextual plausibility within first-century Judaism, coherence with other evidence about Jesus, and plausibility of effects within the early church. As John Meier rightly states:

> Any claims for or against historicity must proceed not by invoking a philosophical bias but by using the same criteria of historicity by which the rest of the Jesus material (e.g., sayings, parables) is judged. . . . Such early material cannot be dismissed out of hand without a serious examination, which is what I have tried to provide.[28]

Second, whenever I take up the question of the historicity of a particular account of Jesus performing some extraordinary deed, I am asking a very modest and circumscribed historical question: namely, whether Jesus performed actions that he himself and his Jewish followers regarded as miracles. Here again I follow Meier's approach:

> I do not claim to be able to decide the theological question of whether particular extraordinary deeds done by Jesus were actually miracles, i.e., direct acts of God accomplishing what no ordinary human being could accomplish. . . . Rather, my quest seeks to remain within the realm of what, at least in principle, is verifiable by historical research. Hence I ask: Given the fact of the many miracle stories present in the Four Gospels, are there reasons for thinking that at least the core of some of these stories go back to the time and ministry of Jesus himself? In other words, did the historical Jesus actually perform certain startling, extraordinary deeds (e.g., supposed healings or exorcisms) that were considered by himself and his audience to be miracles? Or did such reports come entirely from the creative imagination of the early church?[29]

Finally, I want to state very clearly up front that I recognize the fact that some readers will not be able to go even this far with me. Hence, if for philosophical or other reasons, the reader cannot take seriously the arguments for or against the historicity of any miracle attributed to Jesus, this chapter nevertheless still has historical value. For in it I hope to do away with the now widespread assumption that Jesus is not depicted as divine in the Synoptic

28. Meier, *A Marginal Jew*, 2:919–20 (emphasis added).
29. Meier, *A Marginal Jew*, 2:617.

Gospels, but only in the Gospel of John. As we will see by the end of this chapter, even if one regards all three of the epiphanic acts attributed to Jesus as unhistorical products of the early church, nevertheless, when interpreted in their first-century Jewish context, it is quite clear from these examples that *Jesus speaks and acts as if he is divine in all three Synoptic Gospels*. Moreover, I will show that the depiction of Jesus as divine in the Synoptics is supported by a wide range of contemporary exegetes, including Jewish, Christian, and nonreligious scholars alike.

In order to see all this clearly, however, we will need to turn to the evidence itself and interpret it in its first-century context.

Stilling the Storm

The first episode in which Jesus acts as if he is more than merely human is the well-known account of the stilling of the storm on the sea of Galilee. This episode is recounted in all three of the Synoptic Gospels and (notably for our purposes) climaxes with the disciples raising the question of Jesus's identity. Consider the following (I have italicized the most salient features):

> And when he got into the boat, his disciples followed him. A windstorm arose on the sea, so great that the boat was being swamped by the waves; but he was asleep. And they went and woke him up, saying, "Lord, save us! We are perishing!" And he said to them, "*Why are you afraid, you of little faith?*" *Then he got up and rebuked the winds and the sea; and there was a dead calm*. They were amazed, saying, "*What sort of man is this, that even the winds and the sea obey him?*" (Matt 8:23–27)

> On that day, when evening had come, he said to them, "Let us go across to the other side." And leaving the crowd behind, they took him with them in the boat, just as he was. Other boats were with him. A great windstorm arose, and the waves beat into the boat, so that the boat was already being swamped. But he was in the stern, asleep on the cushion; and they woke him up and said to him, "Teacher, do you not care that we are perishing?" *He woke up and rebuked the wind, and said to the sea, "Peace! Be still!" Then the wind ceased, and there was a dead calm*. He said to them, "*Why are you afraid? Have you still no faith?*" And they were filled with great awe and said to one another, "*Who then is this, that even the wind and the sea obey him?*" (Mark 4:35–41)

> One day he got into a boat with his disciples, and he said to them, "Let us go across to the other side of the lake." So they put out, and while they were sailing he fell asleep. A windstorm swept down on the lake, and the boat was filling with water, and they were in danger. They went to him and woke him up, shouting, "Master, Master, we are perishing!" *And he woke up and rebuked the wind and the raging waves; they ceased, and there was a calm.* He said to them, "*Where is your faith?*" They were afraid and amazed, and said to one another, "*Who then is this, that he commands even the winds and the water, and they obey him?*" (Luke 8:22–25)

Given the modern history of rationalistic interpretations of this episode, I want to begin by emphasizing what the Gospels do *not* say. As David Friedrich Strauss pointed out a long time ago, the accounts of Jesus stilling the storm say nothing about his "intelligent observation of the state of the weather" or his "exalted courage in the presence of real peril."[30] Nor do they suggest the disciples mistook the coincidence of Jesus's words and actions with the quelling of the wind and sea for a miracle because they were "simple-minded."[31] Most certain of all, they do not say that Jesus walked on "ice floes" (!)—a theory that was seriously suggested back in 2006 by scientists claiming that "Palestine had at least two extended cold periods in ancient times, which would have made it possible for water to freeze near the shore."[32] Instead, as more sober scholarship attests, all three accounts depict an "epiphany miracle."[33] That is, they depict Jesus and the disciples speaking and acting as if the cessation of the storm is the *result* of Jesus's rebuke of the wind and waves. In the words of Strauss himself: "Taking the incident as it is narrated by the Evangelists, we must regard it as a miracle."[34]

With that said, despite some differences in detail, the basic substance of the accounts of Jesus stilling the storm can be summarized as follows: (1) when a sudden storm arises on the sea of Galilee, Jesus's disciples awaken him while

30. David Friedrich Strauss, *The Life of Jesus Critically Examined*, trans. George Eliot (Philadelphia: Fortress, 1972 [orig. 1835–1836]), 497.

31. Joseph Klausner, *Jesus of Nazareth: His Life, Times, and Teaching* (New York: Macmillan, 1926), 269.

32. Kollmann, "Resuscitations of the Dead," 315–22 (here 321). Kollmann himself rightly describes this theory as "bizarre."

33. See Hengel and Schwemer, *Jesus and Judaism*, 489; Gnilka, *Jesus of Nazareth*, 133. See also Dunn, *Jesus Remembered*, 683; Theissen and Merz, *The Historical Jesus*, 295; Meier, *A Marginal Jew*, 2:928.

34. Strauss, *Jesus of Nazareth*, 497.

he is sleeping in the boat; (2) Jesus responds by rebuking the wind and the sea, which immediately grow still; (3) Jesus upbraids the disciples for their lack of faith; and (4) the disciples respond to Jesus's actions by raising the question of his identity.[35] With this content in mind, several key observations are important to make.

Jesus Is Asleep in a Fishing Boat on the Sea of Galilee

The episode begins with Jesus and his disciples sailing across the Sea of Galilee (Matt 8:23; Mark 4:35–36; Luke 8:22). While Jesus is asleep in the boat, a sudden storm arises so that the boat is in peril of sinking, and, in a state of panic, Jesus's disciples waken him from sleep to tell him of the danger (Matt 8:24–25; Mark 4:37–38; Luke 8:23–24). In order to situate these initial elements in a first-century context, a few observations are in order.

If the boat that Jesus and his disciples are in is at all similar to the first-century fishing boat discovered in the Sea of Galilee in 1986 and later restored by archaeologists, then what the Gospels may be describing here is a relatively small, flat-bottomed, wooden fishing vessel, about twenty-seven feet long by seven-and-a-half feet wide.[36] If it is anything like the two-hundred and thirty boats that Josephus describes as being commandeered for a military action on the Sea of Galilee in the midst of the Jewish revolt, then it may have held, on average, "no more than four sailors" (Josephus, *War* 2.635).[37] In sum, if these estimates are similar to the kind of fishing vessel described by the Gospels, it is easy to see how Jesus could be depicted as sleeping on the flat bottom of the boat during travel.

To this day, the Sea of Galilee is also known for both its fishing industry and for its sudden storms. According to Jerome Murphy O'Connor, even in contemporary times, "small boats have still to watch for the sudden gusts

35. Cf. Dunn, *Jesus Remembered*, 217; Meier, *A Marginal Jew*, 2:925–27.

36. See Jens Schröter, *Jesus of Nazareth: Jew From Galilee, Savior of the World*, trans. Wayne Coppins and S. Brian Pounds (Waco, TX: Baylor University Press, 2014), 21; Jodi Magness, *The Archaeology of the Holy Land: From the Destruction of Solomon's Temple to the Muslim Conquest* (Cambridge: Cambridge University Press, 2012), 203; John Dominic Cross and Jonathan L. Reed, *Excavating Jesus: Beneath the Stones, Behind the Texts* (San Francisco: HarperCollins, 2001), 85–87. For a full study, see Shelley Wachsmann, *The Sea of Galilee Boat* (College Station, TX: Texas A&M University Press, 2000).

37. See Jerome Murphy-O'Connor, *The Holy Land: An Oxford Archaeological Guide*, 5th ed. (Oxford: Oxford University Press, 2008), 239.

from the surrounding wadis which can whip the normally tranquil surface in a matter of minutes" (Matt 8:23–27; 14:24–33).[38] Apparently, this is the kind of thing being described when the Gospels say that a "gust of wind" (Mark 4:37; Luke 8:23) or a "great storm" (Matt 8:24) arose so that the boat of Jesus and his disciples is in danger of sinking beneath the waves.

All three accounts also emphasize that, when the windstorm arises on the Sea of Galilee, Jesus is "asleep" in the boat (Matt 8:24; Mark 4:38; Luke 8:23). On the basis of archaeological indications, what may be envisaged here is Jesus sleeping beneath a "large stern platform, which was the helmsman's station, underneath which there was an area protected from the elements."[39] In any case, for our purposes, it is also worth pointing out that in all three gospels, Jesus is clearly described as *human*: that is, he is "subject" to the kind of "human fatigue" that is an ordinary part of travel—especially sailing at night (cf. Mark 4:35).[40]

Jesus Rebukes the Wind and Waves as If He Is Divine

With that said, Jesus does not respond to the danger faced by him and his disciples in the boat in anything like an ordinary human way. Instead, he gets up and "rebukes" the wind and the waves, so that the storm ceases and the sea becomes "calm" (Matt 8:26; Mark 4:39; Luke 8:24). What are we to make of Jesus's response?

Some suggest that Jesus is simply acting like the anointed Davidic king in the book of Psalms, which says that God "set his [the king's] hand on the sea and his right hand on the rivers" (Ps 89:26).[41] According to this view, he is an exalted (or "idealized") human being, but nothing more.

Others suggest that Jesus is acting like the prophet Jonah, who, when threatened with the danger of a similar storm at sea, rises and asks the gentiles sailing with him to throw him into the sea so that it will "quiet down" for them (cf. Jonah 1:4–15).[42] This suggestion, however, runs up against the fact

38. Murphy O'Connor, *Holy Land*, 464.

39. See Joel Marcus, *Mark*, 2 vols., Anchor Yale Bible 27–27A (New Haven: Yale University Press, 2000, 2009), 1:333.

40. Joseph A. Fitzmyer, SJ, *The Gospel according to Luke*, 2 vols., Anchor Yale Bible 28–28A (New Haven: Yale University Press, 1983, 1985), 1:729.

41. J. Daniel Kirk, *A Man Attested by God: The Human Jesus of the Synoptic Gospels* (Grand Rapids: Eerdmans, 2016), 435–44.

42. Roger David Aus, *The Stilling of the Storm: Studies in Early Palestinian Judaic Traditions* (Binghamton: Binghamton University, 2000), 3–55.

that the differences between what Jonah does and what Jesus does far outweigh the similarities, the most notable of which is that Jonah never commands the wind or the waves to do anything.[43]

The best explanation, therefore, is that Jesus is speaking and acting as if he possesses *divine power* which Jewish Scripture attributes to God. On several occasions in the Hebrew Bible, the one God is described as having the power to control the wind and the waves of the sea. For example, in the book of Job, the creator God is described as having the "power" to "rebuke" the pillars of "heaven" and "still the Sea" (Job 26:11–12). Along similar lines, in the book of Psalms, the "Lord" (YHWH), the "God" of Israel, is said to "rebuke" the "waters" of the sea and control "the winds" (Ps 104:1, 4–7). Significantly, in both of these passages, God manifests his divine power over wind and sea precisely as *creator*.[44] In other words, God has power over these forces of nature because he is the one who made them. Finally, and most significantly, the book of Psalms also describes the God of Israel as able to save sailors from death by commanding the wind and waves of the sea:

> Some went down to the sea in ships,
> doing business on the mighty waters;
> they saw *the deeds of the Lord*,
> his wondrous works in the deep.
> For he commanded and raised the stormy wind,
> which lifted up the waves of the sea.
> They mounted up to heaven, they went down to the depths;
> *their courage melted away in their calamity*;
> they reeled and staggered like drunkards,
> and were at their wits' end.
> *Then they cried to the Lord in their trouble,*
> *and he brought them out from their distress;*
> *he made the storm be still,*

43. See Eric Eve, "The Growth of the Nature Miracles," in *The Nature Miracles of Jesus*, ed. Graham H. Twelftree (Eugene, OR: Cascade, 2017), 66–85 (here 77–78). Other major differences are (1) Jonah is in a boat because he is fleeing from "the presence of the Lord" (Jonah 1:1–3), while Jesus is simply crossing the sea of Galilee; (2) Jonah's act of disobedience is what brings about the storm (Jonah 1:4, 12), while Jesus has done nothing wrong; (3) Jonah does not say or do anything directly to make the storm cease; it is the gentiles who cry out to God and cast Jonah into the sea (Jonah 1:14–15), while Jesus himself commands the wind and waves to cease as if he has authority over them.

44. See Frank Lothar Hossfeld and Eric Zenger, *Psalms 3: A Commentary on Psalms 101–150*, trans. Linda M. Maloney, Hermeneia (Minneapolis: Fortress, 2011), 49.

> *and the waves of the sea were hushed.*
> Then they were glad because they had quiet,
> and he brought them to their desired haven. (Ps 107:23–30)

Notice here that the God of Israel is explicitly described as stilling a "storm" and "the waves of the sea" in the context of his identity as savior: that is, as the God who has the power to "rescue human beings" who cry out to him when their courage melts away in the face of a storm on the sea.[45]

In light of such passages from Jewish Scripture, studies of the historical Jesus recognize that when Jesus commands both the winds and the waves to be still, he is acting as if he is divine. Consider the following:

> In Jewish traditions of stilling storms (Jon. 1; Ps. 107:23–32; T. Naph. 6:1–10 . . .), the appeasement of the forces of nature is accomplished as the work of God alone.[46]

> Jesus is in the place of and acting as Yhwh, the Lord of creation.[47]

> A Jesus who has the power to calm the seas and still the wind puts him in a category with the other gods—with Yhwh, with Zeus, with Poseidon.[48]

In other words, when Jesus presumes to command both the winds and the waves of the sea with a mere word—especially in an ancient Jewish context—he is speaking and acting as if he himself possesses divine power equal with that of the Creator. He is speaking as if he is on par with the God of the Psalms.

In support of this point, it is worth pointing out that *unlike* other figures in Jewish Scripture who find themselves in the face of danger at sea—again, most famously, Jonah and his gentile sailing companions—"Jesus does not pray to God but directly addresses the storm" (cf. Jonah 1:6).[49] Hence, despite some similarities between the account of Jonah and Jesus's act of stilling of the storm,

45. Hossfeld and Zenger, *Psalms 3*, 108.
46. Kollmann, "Resuscitations of the Dead," 320.
47. Meier, *A Marginal Jew*, 2:932 (slightly adapted).
48. Robert W. Funk and the Jesus Seminar, *The Acts of Jesus: The Search for the Authentic Deeds of Jesus* (San Francisco: HarperSanFrancisco/Polebridge, 1998), 76 (slightly adapted).
49. W. D. Davies and Dale C. Allison Jr., *A Critical and Exegetical Commentary on the Gospel according to Saint Matthew*, 3 vols., International Critical Commentaries (Edinburgh: T&T Clark, 1988–1997), 2:70.

in the final analysis, Jesus is far "more like God than like Jonah."[50] Indeed, whereas Jonah must submit himself to divine judgment in order to quell the storm, Jesus acts as if he has immediate and direct authority over some of the most powerful elements in creation—the wind and the waves—which Jewish Scripture explicitly and repeatedly places under the creative and salvific power of the creator God.

The Disciples' Reaction: The Question of Jesus's Identity

In case there is any doubt about the divine implications of Jesus's rebuking the wind and commanding the sea in an ancient Jewish context, it is important to emphasize how the disciples respond to Jesus's action. In all three Synoptic accounts, Jesus's stilling of the storm climaxes with the disciples asking a question:

> They were amazed, saying, "*What sort of man is this*, that even the winds and the sea obey him?" (Matt 8:27)

> And they were filled with great awe and said to one another, "*Who then is this*, that even the wind and the sea obey him?" (Mark 4:41)

> They were afraid and amazed, and said to one another, "*Who then is this*, that he commands even the winds and the water, and they obey him?" (Luke 8:25)

Notice here that the disciples' initial response to Jesus's act of commanding the wind and waves is one of fear and awe. In Jewish Scripture, such fear is a standard human response to a theophany, that is, an appearance of God to figures such as Adam, Abraham, Jacob, Moses, Isaiah, and Daniel (see Gen 3:10; 15:1; 28:17; Exod 3:6; 20:18–20; Isa 6:5; Dan 10:11–12).[51] Notice also that this awe in the face of Jesus's implicitly divine power prompts the disciples to "ask about the *identity* of Jesus."[52] Taken together, their fear and their question about his identity imply that the disciples recognize that Jesus has done

50. Marcus, *Mark*, 1:338.

51. See Theodore Hiebert, "Theophany in the Old Testament," in *The Anchor Bible Dictionary*, 6 vols., ed. David Noel Freedman (New York: Doubleday, 1992), 6:505–11. Curiously, there is no corresponding article on theophanies in the New Testament.

52. François Bovon, *Luke: A Commentary*, trans. Christine M. Thomas, Donald S. Deer, and James E. Crouch, 3 vols., Hermeneia (Minneapolis: Fortress, 2002–2013), 1:321.

something no ordinary human being is able to do. As François Bovon rightly states: "They know from Scripture that only God has a word that is effective to this extent."[53] In other words, the disciples' question about Jesus's *identity* is implicitly a question about his *divinity*.

The Stilling of the Storm and the Divinity of Jesus

In light of such considerations, on the level of exegesis, a remarkable number of commentators on the Synoptic Gospels agree that, in the accounts of stilling the storm, Jesus does indeed speak and act as if he is divine. Consider the following statements from Jewish and Christian commentators alike:

> Matthew portrays Jesus, like God, as lord over nature, thus surpassing Jonah.[54]
>
> The image is not that of the superior human being . . . but of the lord of nature who is master over its onslaught. The ancient church correctly spoke here of the deity of Jesus.[55]
>
> Jesus rebuked the wind and sea, which follows the ancient near eastern and Israelite image of the god who conquers the sea.[56]
>
> Jesus is more than a prophet . . . because in rebuking the roaring waves he exercises the power of Yahweh himself.[57]
>
> Jesus is portrayed not so much as a human being who has trust in God's power to save, but as a divine being.[58]

53. Bovon, *Luke*, 1:321.

54. Aaron M. Gale, "The Gospel according to Matthew," in *The Jewish Annotated New Testament*, 2nd ed., ed. Amy-Jill Levine and Mark Zvi Brettler (Oxford: Oxford University Press, 2017), 27 (emphasis added).

55. Ulrich Luz, *Matthew: A Commentary*, trans. James E. Crouch, 3 vols., Hermeneia (Minneapolis: Fortress, 2001–2007), 2:20.

56. Lawrence M. Wills, "The Gospel according to Mark," in Levine and Brettler, *Jewish Annotated New Testament*, 79 (emphasis added).

57. Davies and Allison, *Matthew*, 2:70; cf. also 2:74.

58. Adela Yarbro Collins, *Mark: A Commentary*, Hermeneia (Minneapolis: Fortress, 2007), 260.

> [This episode] also perhaps reflects . . . a high Christology that goes a long way toward equating Jesus with the OT God. . . . The one so acknowledged is not just a human but a cosmic figure; if he is the Messiah, he is a Messiah who bears the marks of divinity.[59]

> Jesus achieves victory without praying. Thus he is exalted into the sphere of God himself.[60]

Note well that these commentators see in the stilling of the storm a revelation of Jesus's *equality with the one God of Israel*, and not merely his superhuman status.[61] Now, if even one of these scholars is correct—and that they are all wrong is, shall we say, less than probable—then the shopworn idea that Jesus never speaks or acts as if he is divine in the Synoptic Gospels needs to be consigned once and for all to the dustbin of history, where it has always belonged. On the level of exegesis, all three Synoptic Gospels—Matthew, Mark, and Luke—depict Jesus in the stilling of the storm as somehow both a human being (who gets tired and needs sleep) and equal with the one creator God (who has absolute power over the wind and waves of the sea).

Arguments against Historical Plausibility

With these exegetical considerations in mind, we can now ask: Are the reports about Jesus stilling the storm on the Sea of Galilee inventions of the early church, or do they go back to an event in the life of Jesus himself? Once again, I want to stress that I am not making a philosophical argument for the possibility of the miraculous. Nor do I think that the historian has to explain precisely *how* reportedly extraordinary events may have taken place. Rather, I simply want to ask the question, What are the *historical* (not philosophical) arguments for and against Jesus performing the startling act of commanding the wind and waves of the sea to be still?

In this regard, the overwhelming majority of contemporary works on the historical Jesus render a negative verdict. Most studies of the historical Jesus—even some focused on the origins of high Christology—simply ig-

59. Marcus, *Mark*, 1:339, 340.

60. Bovon, *Luke*, 1:319; cf. Fitzmyer, *Gospel according to Luke*, 1:728.

61. Cf. Ruben A. Bühner, *Messianic High Christology: New Testament Variants of Second Temple Judaism* (Waco, TX: Baylor University Press, 2021), 11–12.

nore the episode as if it did not exist.[62] Others mention it in passing, but without any discussion of whether it goes back to an event in the life of Jesus.[63] Still others think that there may have been some incident of a storm coming up quickly on the Sea of Galilee and then growing quiet, but they reject miraculous interpretation as a delusion of "simple-minded people."[64] Many, however, conclude that it is a fabrication of the early church that does not reflect an event from the life of Jesus.[65] In support of this verdict, three arguments stand out.

The first reason many hold that the accounts of Jesus stilling the storm are unhistorical is not a historical argument but a *philosophical assumption* regarding the impossibility of miracles. According to this view, since miracles are by definition impossible; the miraculous stilling of the storm recounted in the first-century biographies of Jesus cannot be rooted in a historical event. Consider, for example, the words of Gerd Lüdemann and Adolf von Harnack:

62. For example, the stilling of the storm receives no discussion in Bart D. Ehrman, *How Jesus Became God: The Exaltation of a Jewish Preacher from Galilee* (San Francisco: HarperOne, 2014); Sigurd Grindheim, *God's Equal: What Can We Know about Jesus' Self-Understanding in the Synoptic Gospels?*, Library of New Testament Studies 446 (London: T&T Clark, 2011); Richard Bauckham, *Jesus: A Very Short Introduction* (Oxford: Oxford University Press, 2011); Dale C. Allison Jr., *Constructing Jesus: Memory, Imagination, and History* (Grand Rapids: Baker Academic, 2010); Maurice Casey, *Jesus of Nazareth: An Independent Historian's Account of His Life and Teaching* (London: T&T Clark, 2010); Craig S. Keener, *The Historical Jesus of the Gospels* (Grand Rapids: Eerdmans, 2009); Darrell L. Bock and Robert L. Webb, eds., *Key Events in the Life of the Historical Jesus*, Wissenschaftliche Untersuchungen zum Neuen Testament 247 (Tübingen: Mohr Siebeck, 2009); David Flusser with R. Steven Notley, *The Sage from Galilee: Rediscovering Jesus' Genius* (Grand Rapids: Eerdmans, 2007); Ehrman, *Jesus: Apocalyptic Prophet*; Jürgen Becker, *Jesus of Nazareth*, trans. James E. Crouch (New York: Walter de Gruyter, 1998); Geza Vermes, *The Religion of Jesus the Jew* (Minneapolis: Fortress, 1993); Witherington, *Christology of Jesus*; E. P. Sanders, *Jesus and Judaism* (Minneapolis: Fortress, 1985).

63. E.g., Schröter, *Jesus of Nazareth*, 21; N. T. Wright, *Jesus and the Victory of God*, vol. 2 of *Christian Origins and the Question of God* (Minneapolis: Fortress, 1996), 193.

64. Klausner, *Jesus of Nazareth*, 269.

65. See Paula Fredriksen, *Jesus of Nazareth, King of the Jews* (New York: Vintage Books, 1999), 115; Theissen and Merz, *The Historical Jesus*, 295; Meier, *A Marginal Jew*, 2:920–23, 933; Funk and the Jesus Seminar, *Acts of Jesus*, 77; Joachim Jeremias, *The Proclamation of Jesus*, trans. John Bowden, New Testament Theology 1 (New York: Charles Scribner's Sons, 1971), 88; Rudolf Bultmann, *History of the Synoptic Tradition*, trans. John Marsh, rev. ed. (Oxford: Basil Blackwell, 1963), 235.

> The historical yield is nil as . . . not even magicians can break the laws of nature.[66]

> Miracles, it is true, do not happen. . . . that a storm was quieted by a word, we do not believe, and we shall never again believe.[67]

Notice the appeal here to the modern philosophical categories of "the laws of nature," as well as to language of "belief." Both statements are manifestly philosophical objections rooted in a particular worldview, not historical evaluations of the evidence in light of arguments from contextual plausibility, coherence, or the aftermath of Jesus's life. In light of such statements, it seems pretty clear that the philosophical assumption that miracles are impossible constitutes the principal reason most modern scholars either reject the stilling of the storm as unhistorical or decide that the episode is unworthy of mention in historical reconstructions of the life of Jesus.[68]

The second major argument against historicity is from incoherence with other evidence about Jesus. According to this view, the stilling of the storm is incongruent with other evidence in which Jesus performs miracles focused on helping others, rather than revealing his divinity.[69] Consider, for example, the words of the Jesus Seminar:

> The stories of Jesus as an exorcist ([Mark] 1:21–28) and Jesus as a healer of Peter's mother-in-law (1:29–31), of the leper (1:40–45), of the paralytic (2:1–2), of the man with a crippled hand (3:1–6) identify Jesus as simply another charismatic sage with healing powers; but a Jesus who has the power to calm the seas and still the wind puts him in a category with the other gods—with Yhwh, with Zeus, with Poseidon. In other words, the "christology" of this story is that of the early Christian community. For this reason alone, many scholars have concluded that the tale is the fictional product of the believing community. The Fellows of the Jesus Seminar were unanimous in their judgment that the stilling of the storm is not based on an event in the life of Jesus.[70]

66. Gerd Lüdemann, *Jesus after Two Thousand Years: What He Really Said and Did*, trans. John Bowden (London: SCM; Amherst: Prometheus Books, 2001), 34.

67. Adolf von Harnack, *What Is Christianity?*, trans. Thomas Bailey Saunders (Philadelphia: Fortress, 1986 [orig. 1901]), 28.

68. Cf. Dunn, *Jesus Remembered*, 688.

69. Meier, *A Marginal Jew*, 2:933.

70. Funk and the Jesus Seminar, *Acts of Jesus*, 76–77 (slightly adapted).

Notice that the Jesus Seminar recognizes that the Gospels depict Jesus as in the same "category" as YHWH, Zeus, and Poseidon; this alone suffices to conclude that the stilling of the storm does not go back to Jesus's public ministry. The implicit assumption here is that since the historical Jesus never spoke or acted as if he were divine, any evidence in which he does so must be regarded as unhistorical. In the words of Gerd Theissen and Annette Merz: "to attribute to [Jesus] divine power over the wind and waves" was "only possible after Easter."[71]

A third major argument against historicity is from the implausibility of effects in the early church. According to E. P. Sanders, if the stilling of the storm (or any of the other so-called nature miracles) is historical, then it is difficult to explain why more of Jesus's contemporaries did not believe in him:

> The stilling of the storm, the first nature miracle in Matthew and Mark, provoked only wonder: "What sort of man is this, that even winds and sea obey him?" (Mark 4.41; Matt. 8.27). . . . But if he really performed miracles, and if miracles were proof, then more people should have believed. . . . The modern reader is inclined to think that this curious situation arises in part from a tension between actual history and the evangelists reporting of it.[72]

According to this logic, if Jesus had really done anything as stupendous as stilling the wind and waves of the sea, then far more people should have come to believe in him than actually did. This is an excellent example of an argument from the implausibility of effects in the aftermath of Jesus's life.

In light of such considerations, the vast majority of works on the historical Jesus either ignore the stilling of the storm or conclude, along with John Meier, that "the walking on the water is most likely from start to finish a creation of the early church, a christological confession in narrative form."[73]

Contextual Plausibility: The Messiah, Antiochus, and Divine Power over Wind and Sea

Despite this negative verdict, some works on the historical Jesus do argue that there are good historical reasons to think the accounts of the stilling of

71. Theissen and Merz, *Historical Jesus*, 295.
72. Sanders, *Historical Figure of Jesus*, 156–57.
73. Cf. Meier, *A Marginal Jew*, 2:921.

the storm are based on an event from the life of the historical Jesus. Some take a very cautious view and are only willing to affirm that "historical reminiscences" of some sort have been "incorporated" in the gospel accounts.[74] Others are more confident, affirming that the stilling of the storm is not "mere fiction" but rather has "a concrete basis in the actions of Jesus."[75] Still others insist on the substantial "historical validity" of the episode.[76] If we bracket the philosophical and theological issues involved in any attempt to explain *how* such a miracle could take place and focus rather on analyzing the episode from a triple-context approach, the first argument in favor of the substantial historicity of the gospel accounts of Jesus stilling the storm is from contextual plausibility within first-century Judaism, on several counts.

For one thing, it is contextually quite plausible that Jesus and his disciples were once caught in a sudden windstorm while sailing on the sea of Galilee. As I have already noted, even in our own day, such fast-forming windstorms over the waters of the lake are a common occurrence.[77] For this reason, the early twentieth-century Jewish scholar Joseph Klausner had no doubts about the historicity of this aspect of the gospel accounts: "This [sudden windstorm] is unquestionably what happened: the Sea of Galilee frequently becomes rough suddenly and as suddenly becomes calm again. The present writer witnessed such a change while sailing on the Sea in the spring of 1912."[78] Others confirm this basic observation, including Josephus, who writes of an extraordinarily sudden and powerful windstorm arising in the Golan Heights during the Roman siege of the city of Gamala (Josephus, *War* 4.75–77).

Second, it is also plausible within a first-century Jewish context that Jesus would respond to the rise of the storm by verbally rebuking the wind and the sea, as if they could respond to commands. In Jewish literature, there is a widespread belief that visible meteorological phenomena were governed by invisible angelic powers. For example, Jewish Scripture describes the "winds" as God's "messengers" or "angels" (*mal'akayw*) (Ps 104:4), and several early Jewish apocalypses identify the "water" and "winds" as governed by "angels" (1 Enoch 69:21–22; Jubilees 2:2; 2 Enoch 19:1, 4 [J]).[79] Seen in this light, Jesus's

74. Dunn, *Jesus Remembered*, 687.

75. Martin Hengel and Anna Maria Schwemer, *Jesus and Judaism*, trans. Wayne Coppins (Waco, TX: Baylor University Press, 2019 [orig. 2007]), 525.

76. Puig i Tàrrech, *Jesus: A Biography*, 383–84.

77. Murphy O'Connor, *Holy Land*, 464.

78. Klausner, *Jesus of Nazareth*, 269.

79. See George W. E. Nickelsburg and James C. VanderKam, *1 Enoch 2*, Hermeneia (Minneapolis: Fortress, 2012), 304; James C. VanderKam, *Jubilees: A Commentary*, 2 vols.,

act of rebuking the wind and waves appears to be a kind of "exorcism" of the invisible angelic powers stirring up the wind and the sea.[80] This is especially plausible if Jesus considered himself to be the messiah. For there is clear evidence in the Dead Sea Scrolls that the "anointed one" or "messiah" (Hebrew *mashiakh)* has just this kind of power:

> [For *the heav*]*ens and the earth will listen to his messiah* [*lmshykh*], [and all th]at is in them will not turn away from the precepts of the holy ones. . . . For he [the Lord] will honour the pious upon the throne of an eternal kingdom, freeing prisoners, giving sight to the blind, straightening out the twi[sted]. . . . And the Lord will perform marvelous acts such as have not existed, just as he sa[id], [for] he will heal the badly wounded and will make the dead live. (4QMessianic Apocalypse [4Q521] 2, II, 1–2, 7–8, 11–12)[81]

Due to the fragmentary nature of the scroll, there is debate about exactly what the text means.[82] However, given its overarching emphasis on the miraculous acts God will perform at the time of the messiah's coming, the suggestion of Joel Marcus seems reasonable: "obedience is rendered to the Messiah not only by human beings but also by inanimate powers. The one so acknowledged is not just a human but a cosmic figure; if he is the Messiah, he is *a Messiah who bears the marks of divinity*."[83] If this is correct, and if Jesus of Nazareth saw himself as a *divine* messiah, then it is even more contextually plausible that he would speak and act as if he had power over inanimate elements.

Perhaps most striking of all, if Jesus spoke as if he had power over the wind and sea, then it is contextually plausible that he would be perceived by his Jewish disciples to be acting as if he were *equal with God*. As we have already seen, Jewish Scripture describes the power to control the wind and sea as a prerogative of the Creator (e.g., Job 26:11–12; Pss 104:1–7; 107:23–30).

Hermeneia (Minneapolis: Fortress, 2018), 167; James H. Charlesworth, ed., *Old Testament Pseudepigrapha*, 2 vols., Anchor Bible Reference Library (New York: Doubleday, 1983, 1985), 1:132.

80. Gnilka, *Jesus of Nazareth*, 133.

81. In Florentino García Martínez and Eibert J. C. Tigchelaar, *The Dead Sea Scrolls Study Edition*, 2 vols. (Grand Rapids: Eerdmans, 2000), 2:1045 (adapted). Brackets represent portions of the text that are damaged or missing.

82. See John J. Collins, *The Scepter and the Star: Messianism in Light of the Dead Sea Scrolls*, 2nd ed. (Grand Rapids: Eerdmans, 2010), 131–41; Émile Puech, "Messianic Apocalypse," in *Encyclopedia of the Dead Sea Scrolls*, 2 vols., ed. Lawrence H. Schiffman and James C. VanderKam (Oxford: Oxford University Press, 2002), 1:543–44.

83. Marcus, *Mark*, 1:339, 340 (emphasis added).

Along similar lines, one early Jewish writing tells us that the Seleucid King Antiochus IV Epiphanes claimed to have power over the wind and sea precisely because he thought he was equal with God.[84] Consider this early Jewish account of Antiochus's death:

> The all-seeing Lord, the God of Israel, struck [Antiochus] with an incurable and invisible blow. As soon as he stopped speaking he was seized with a pain in his bowels, for which there was no relief, and with sharp internal tortures—and that very justly, for he had tortured the bowels of others with many and strange inflictions. Yet he did not in any way stop his insolence, but was even more filled with arrogance, breathing fire in his rage against the Jews, and giving orders to drive even faster. And so it came about that he fell out of his chariot as it was rushing along, and the fall was so hard as to torture every limb of his body. *Thus he who only a little while before had thought in his superhuman arrogance that he could command the waves of the sea, and had imagined that he could weigh the high mountains in a balance, was brought down to earth and carried in a litter, making the power of God manifest to all.* And so the ungodly man's body swarmed with worms, and while he was still living in anguish and pain, his flesh rotted away, and because of the stench the whole army felt revulsion at his decay. Because of his intolerable stench no one was able to carry the man who a little while before had thought that he could touch the stars of heaven. Then it was that, broken in spirit, he began to lose much of his arrogance and to come to his senses under the scourge of God, for he was tortured with pain every moment. And when he could not endure his own stench, he uttered these words, "*It is right to be subject to God; mortals should not think that they are equal to God.*" (2 Macc 9:5–12)

Notice here that the "superhuman arrogance" (*tēn hyper anthrōpon alazoneian*) of Antiochus's divine claim lies specifically in the fact that "he thought . . . he could command the waves of the sea" (2 Macc 9:8). Notice also that Antiochus's claim to have power over the sea implies that he is "equal to God" (*isothea*) (2 Macc 9:12). In short, by claiming power over the sea, "Antiochus makes himself out to be a God."[85] This is of course why, as other sources make clear, Antiochus had coins minted with the title: "King Antiochus, God Man-

84. Cf. Kollman, "Resuscitations of the Dead," 321.

85. Eyal Regev, "2 Maccabees," in *The Jewish Annotated Apocrypha*, ed. Jonathan Klawans and Lawrence M. Wills (Oxford: Oxford University Press, 2020), 272.

ifest" (*Theou Epiphanous*) (Josephus, *Antiquities* 12.258).[86] The upshot of the this parallel is straightforward but momentous: if Jesus, like Antiochus, spoke and acted as if he had power over the wind and the sea, then it is contextually plausible that he not only regarded himself as a divine messiah, but also as *equal with God*. This at least would explain why Jesus's Jewish disciples respond to his stilling of the storm by raising the question of his identity (Matt 8:27; Mark 4:41; Luke 8:25).

Coherence: The Sea of Galilee, Jesus the Exorcist, and the Call to Faith

Another important argument in favor of the historical plausibility of Jesus stilling the storm is from its multiple counts of coherence with other evidence about Jesus.

For one thing, the basic account of Jesus and the disciples sailing on the sea of Galilee coheres with other evidence that some of Jesus's disciples—namely, Peter, Andrew, James, and John—were Galilean fishermen, who would have been accustomed to travel by boat on the Sea of Galilee (Matt 4:18–20; Mark 1:16–20; Luke 5:1–11).[87]

Moreover, Jesus's act of rebuking his disciples for their lack of "faith" (Matt 8:26; Mark 4:40; Luke 8:22–25) coheres remarkably well with other evidence that he is more than willing to upbraid his disciples for their "little faith" (Matt 6:30; Luke 12:28), which is apparently even smaller than "the size of a mustard seed" (Matt 17:20; Luke 17:6)! In light of such evidence, Geza Vermes rightly concludes that the importance of faith was "one of the chief doctrines of Jesus"; therefore, a "lack of faith" was likewise one of the chief impediments to recognizing the divine authorization of Jesus's actions.[88]

Finally, as several scholars have recognized, even Jesus's striking act of commanding the wind and the waters as if they were animated by angelic powers also coheres with other evidence that Jesus spoke and acted as if he had power over invisible spiritual forces.[89] Consider, for example, the

86. On this point, see Robert Doran, "Antiochus IV Epiphanes," in Collins and Harlow, *Eerdmans Dictionary of Early Judaism*, 338; Martin Hengel, *Judaism and Hellenism: Studies in Their Encounter in Palestine During the Early Hellenistic Period*, trans. John Bowden, 2 vols. (Philadelphia: Fortress, 1974), 1:285, 2:189–90.

87. See Meier, *A Marginal Jew*, 3:159–63, on the disciples who were fishermen.

88. Geza Vermes, *The Authentic Gospel of Jesus* (London: Penguin, 2003), 7.

89. See Puig i Tàrrech, *Jesus: A Biography*, 383; Vermes, *Authentic Gospel of Jesus*, 7; Lüde-

words of Gerhard Lohfink: "Jesus acts like an exorcist. He 'shouts at the wind' and commands it as if it were a demon: 'Peace! Be still!' (cf. Mark 1:25). . . . Jesus' action was altogether plausible to people in antiquity: water, especially deep water, was regarded as the residence of demons, just as the desert was."[90]

In light of such parallels, there is good reason to conclude that the way in which Jesus goes about stilling the storm is perfectly congruent with the abundant evidence that he saw himself as an exorcist who had power over unclean spirits and other demonic forces at work in the world. This is particularly important to stress since some reject the historicity of the episode (in large part) because of the modern categorization of it as a "nature miracle," when in fact it is much closer to the kind of exorcisms that Jesus is widely regarded as having engaged in during his public ministry.

Consequences: Early Belief in Jesus as Creator

A final argument for the historicity of the stilling of the storm is from consequences in the early church. According to this argument, if Jesus stilled the wind and waves during a storm on the sea of Galilee, then this extraordinary deed would provide a plausible explanation for why the early church went on to describe Jesus not only as the Jewish messiah but as the Creator of the cosmos.[91] Consider the following passages:

> For us there is one God, the Father, from whom are all things and for whom we exist, and *one Lord, Jesus Christ, through whom are all things* and through whom we exist. (1 Cor 8:6)

> He is the image of the invisible God, the firstborn of all creation; for *in him all things in heaven and on earth were created*, things visible and invisible, whether thrones or dominions or rulers or powers—*all things have been created through him and for him*. (Col 1:15–16)

---

mann, *Jesus after Two Thousand Years*, 33; Gnilka, *Jesus of Nazareth*, 133; Meier, *A Marginal Jew*, 2:926. Curiously, neither Vermes, nor Meier, nor Lüdemann uses this point of coherence as an argument for historicity.

90. Lohfink, *Jesus of Nazareth*, 133.

91. See Sean M. McDonough, *Christ as Creator: Origins of a New Testament Doctrine* (Oxford: Oxford University Press, 2009), for a full study.

> In these last days [God] has spoken to us by a Son, whom he appointed heir of all things, *through whom he also created the worlds*. He is the reflection of God's glory and the exact imprint of God's very being, and *he sustains all things by his powerful word*. (Heb 1:2–3)

In each of these passages, Jesus is repeatedly described as the one through whom "all things" (*ta panta*) were created and as the one who has divine power over "all things" (*ta panta*)—meaning *all of creation*.[92] How do we explain such a widespread identification of Jesus with the Creator in the early church? One plausible explanation is that, during his public ministry, Jesus spoke and acted in the presence of his disciples as if he had power over two of the most powerful elements in creation: the wind and sea.

In fact, in light of this evidence, the argument of E. P. Sanders cited above can be turned on its head. If Jesus did *not* perform extraordinary deeds such as the stilling of the storm, then it is difficult to explain why *anyone* went on to believe that he was not only the messiah but also the creator of the universe. In other words, the stilling of the storm provides a plausible point of origin for the otherwise inexplicable early Christian belief that Jesus of Nazareth was not just the messiah but also the one through whom the world was made.[93]

Weighing the Arguments for and against Historicity

Having surveyed the major reasons given by scholars for and against the historical plausibility of the accounts of Jesus stilling the storm, we can now step back and evaluate the comparative weight of the arguments.

Somewhat surprisingly, when subjected to critical scrutiny, the most popular arguments against historicity are remarkably weak. For one thing, the

92. See Brant Pitre, Michael P. Barber, and John A. Kincaid, *Paul, a New Covenant Jew: Rethinking Pauline Theology* (Grand Rapids: Eerdmans, 2019), 116–20; Joseph A. Fitzmyer, *First Corinthians*, Anchor Yale Bible 32 (New Haven: Yale University Press, 2008), 343; Johannes Beutler, SJ, *A Commentary on the Gospel of John*, trans. Michael Tait (Grand Rapids: Eerdmans, 2017), 37; Markus Barth and Helmut Blanke, *Colossians*, Anchor Bible 34B (New York: Doubleday, 1994), 199; Richard Bauckham, *Jesus and the God of Israel: God Crucified and Other Studies on the New Testament's Christology of Divine Identity* (Grand Rapids: Eerdmans, 2008), 233–44; Harold Attridge, *Hebrews: A Commentary*, Hermeneia (Minneapolis: Fortress, 1989), 40.

93. Cf. McDonough, *Christ as Creator*, 25–26.

primary reason given by scholars for concluding the accounts are unhistorical is the *philosophical* claim that miracles are impossible. Whatever one may think about this claim, it cannot bear the *historical* weight often assigned to it. Indeed, its continued use in historical Jesus research is a good example of philosophy masquerading as history. Apart from this philosophical objection, the remaining historical arguments are far from compelling. For one thing, the claim that the stilling must have originated after Easter because in it Jesus speaks and acts as if he is divine is a classic case of begging the question. How can the historian know in advance that Jesus never spoke or acted as if he were divine unless she or he has prejudged the issue? Moreover, the argument that if Jesus had in fact performed anything as stupendous as the stilling of the storm, then more of his contemporaries would have believed in him fails to note that the event is only described as being witnessed by a handful of Jesus's followers. In this instance, the obvious explanation for why "not many people" are "convinced" by the "dramatic miracle" attributed to Jesus is because not many people are even present to witness it.[94]

On the other hand, if we bracket the philosophical question and approach the accounts of Jesus stilling the storm from a triple-context perspective, they fare remarkably well. When it comes to contextual plausibility within a first-century Jewish context, it goes without saying that the depiction of Jesus and his disciples (some of whom are Galilean fishermen) getting caught in a quick-rising storm on the sea of Galilee is completely credible. Moreover, however shocking it may have been, even Jesus's act of commanding the wind and waves would be comprehensible if he thought the messiah would have divine power over creation (4QMessianic Apocalypse [4Q521] 2, II), or if he, like Antiochus IV Epiphanes, saw himself as "equal with God" (2 Macc 9:8, 12). Indeed, when it comes to plausibility of effects in the early church, such an action would provide a compelling explanation for why the early church went on to believe that Jesus was not just the Jewish messiah, but the one through whom "all things" were made (1 Cor 8:6; Col 1:15–16; Heb 1:2–3).

In sum, when it comes to the gospel accounts of Jesus stilling the storm, a close investigation reveals that when the philosophical argument from the impossibility of miracles is taken off the table, the actual historical arguments in favor of its historicity are much stronger than those against it.[95] When

94. Cf. Sanders, *Historical Figure of Jesus*, 156–57.
95. See Puig i Tàrrech, *Jesus: A Biography*, 384.

examined closely, the episode is contextually credible, strongly coheres with other evidence about Jesus, and provides a plausible explanation for the origins of the early Christian belief in Jesus as both Jewish messiah and creator of the cosmos.

Walking on the Sea

The second extraordinary deed of Jesus in which he speaks and acts as if he is more than merely human involves the well-known account of him walking on the Sea of Galilee. Like the stilling of the storm, Jesus's act of walking on the sea is widely identified by scholars as an "epiphany miracle."[96] In this instance, the episode is recounted in two of the Synoptic Gospels and the Gospel of John:

> Immediately he made the disciples get into the boat and go on ahead to the other side, while he dismissed the crowds. And after he had dismissed the crowds, he went up the mountain by himself to pray. When evening came, he was there alone, but *by this time the boat*, battered by the waves, *was far from the land*, for the wind was against them. And early in the morning he came *walking toward them on the sea. But when the disciples saw him walking on the sea, they were terrified*, saying, "It is a ghost!" And they cried out in fear. But immediately Jesus spoke to them and said, "*Take heart, it is I; do not be afraid*." (Matt 14:22–27)

> Immediately he made his disciples get into the boat and go on ahead to the other side, to Bethsaida, while he dismissed the crowd. After saying farewell to them, he went up on the mountain to pray. When evening came, *the boat was out on the sea*, and he was alone on the land. When he saw that they were straining at the oars against an adverse wind, he came towards them early in the morning, *walking on the sea*. He intended to pass them by. *But when they saw him walking on the sea*, they thought it was a ghost and cried out; *for they all saw him and were terrified*. But immediately he spoke to them and said, "*Take heart, it is I; do not be afraid*." Then he got into the boat with them and the wind ceased. And *they were utterly astounded*. (Mark 6:45–51)

96. Hengel and Schwemer, *Jesus and Judaism*, 489; Lohfink, *Jesus of Nazareth*, 132; Lüdemann, *Jesus after Two Thousand Years*, 46; Gnilka, *Jesus of Nazareth*, 133; Meier, *A Marginal Jew*, 2:907, 914.

> When evening came, his disciples went down to the sea, got into a boat, and started across the sea to Capernaum. It was now dark, and Jesus had not yet come to them. The sea became rough because a strong wind was blowing. *When they had rowed about three or four miles, they saw Jesus walking on the sea and coming near the boat, and they were terrified.* But he said to them, "*It is I; do not be afraid.*" Then they wanted to take him into the boat, and immediately the boat reached the land toward which they were going. (John 6:16–21)

Given the fascinating history of rationalistic approaches to this episode,[97] it is once again important to begin by emphasizing what the Gospels *do not say*. They do not say anything about Jesus walking on "a great floating raft,"[98] or "wading through the surf near the hidden shore,"[99] or "walking on the very edge of the sea (or in the shallows)."[100] Nor do they give the slightest hint that Jesus "was on the land but the surface was obscured by a low mist that looked like the sea," much less that "perhaps he knew where there were submerged rocks"![101] As Eric Eve has recently argued, all such "rationalizing explanations" that postulate Jesus "walking on a log or concealed sandbar" do exegetical "violence" to the gospel accounts.[102] I for one can think of no greater examples of blatant eisegesis anywhere in the Gospels.

Instead, the basic substance of all three accounts of Jesus walking on the sea is relatively clear and can be summarized as follows: (1) the disciples attempt to cross the Sea of Galilee in a boat while Jesus remains on shore; (2) after rowing for some miles into the middle of the sea, they see Jesus

97. For excellent overviews of the history of exegesis, see Patrick J. Madden, *Jesus' Walking on the Sea*, Beihefte zur Zeitschrift für die neutestamentliche Wissenschaft 81 (Berlin: Walter de Gruyter, 1997), 1–41; and Hendrik van der Loos, *The Miracles of Jesus*, Supplements to Novum Testamentum 9 (Leiden: Brill, 1965), 558–61.

98. Albert Schweitzer, *The Quest of the Historical Jesus: A Critical Study of Its Progress from Reimarus to Wrede*, trans. William Montgomery, rev. ed. (New York: Macmillan, 1968), 41, describes the interpretation of the eighteenth-century writer Karl Friedrich Bahrdt.

99. Vincent Taylor, *The Gospel according to St. Mark* (London: Macmillan, 1957), 327.

100. J. Duncan M. Derrett, "Why and How Jesus Walked on the Sea," *NovT* 23 (1981): 340–48, as described by Graham H. Twelftree, *Jesus the Miracle Worker: A Historical and Theological Study* (Downers Grove: IVP Academic, 1999), 322.

101. Sanders, *Historical Figure of Jesus*, 158, recounting "rational explanations" of the episode.

102. Eve, "The Growth of the Nature Miracles," 82. Cf. Strauss, *Life of Jesus*, 500.

walking toward them on the surface; (3) the disciples are frightened, but Jesus says, "It is I [*egō eimi*], do not be afraid." With this basic summary in mind, several key exegetical points need to be made before turning to and weighing the arguments for and against the historicity of this episode in the life of Jesus.

Location: The Disciples Are Miles from the Shore

The first observation involves a geographical point of clarification regarding the size of the lake and the location of the event. Although some contemporary readers might imagine the Sea of Galilee as little more than a small body of water, when it comes to its being traversed by an ancient fishing boat, it is actually quite large. According to contemporary measurements, the Sea of Galilee is about thirteen miles (or twenty-one kilometers) long from north to south, and seven and a half miles (or twelve kilometers) wide from east to west.[103]

With these distances in mind, the evidence in the Gospels clearly depicts the disciples as being a few miles from shore when Jesus comes to them walking on the sea.[104] For example, one account states that the boat is "in the middle of the sea" (*en mesō tēs thalassēs*) (Mark 6:47). Taken at face value, this would place the disciples about three or four miles from the shore.[105] Another account states that when Jesus comes to the disciples, the boat is already "far from the land"—or, more literally, "many stadia from the land" (*stadious pollous apo tēs gēs*) (Matt 14:24). Since a Greek *stadion* is about 607 feet (or 185 meters), this easily places the disciples more than a mile from the shore. Still another account states more precisely that the disciples are "about three or four miles," that is, "twenty-five or thirty stadia" (*hōs stadious eikosi pente ē triakonta*) away from the shore (John 6:19).

Taken together, the upshot of this data is striking: according to the Gospels, *Jesus walks on the surface of the sea for several miles before coming to the disciples*. When they encounter him, they are in the middle of the miles-wide Sea of Galilee, and not anywhere near the shore where they left Jesus.

103. Jerome Murphy-O'Connor, *The Holy Land: An Oxford Archaeological Guide*, 5th ed. (Oxford: Oxford University Press, 2008), 465.

104.Hengel and Schwemer, *Jesus and Judaism*, 366; Meier, *A Marginal Jew*, 2:911.

105. Marcus, *Mark*, 1:423.

The Book of Job: God Alone Walks on the Waves

Even more significantly, in all three accounts, Jesus does something which the Jewish Scriptures say God alone can do: he walks on the surface of the sea. Consider, for example, the description of the creator God in the book of Job, in both its Hebrew and ancient Greek versions:

> *[God] alone* stretched out the heavens
> *and trampled the waves of the Sea;*
> who made the Bear and Orion,
> the Pleiades and the chambers of the south;
> who does great things beyond understanding,
> and marvelous things without number. (Job 9:8–10 MT)

> *[God] alone* stretched out the sky
> *and walks on the sea as on dry ground,*
> who makes Pleiades and Venus
> and Arcturus and the chambers of the south,
> who does great and inscrutable things,
> things both glorious and extraordinary without number.
> (Job 9:8–10 LXX)[106]

Notice here that the surrounding context in Job is a hymn of praise to God as creator of the universe: the one who made the sea, the mountains, the sun and the stars (Job 9:1–13).[107] Notice also that both versions emphasize that the creator God "alone" is able to walk upon the waves of the sea (Job 9:8).[108] In the Septuagint, the description of God's unique ability is even more explicit: God alone "walks on the sea as on dry ground" (*peripatōn hōs ep' edaphous epi thalassēs*) (Job 9:8 LXX).

In light of such passages, scholars from a variety of religious perspectives agree that by walking on the surface of the sea, Jesus is doing what the book of Job says only God can do:

106. Translation in *A New English Translation of the Septuagint*, ed. Albert Pietersma and Benjamin G. Wright (Oxford: Oxford University Press, 2007), 675.

107. Carol A. Newsom, "The Book of Job," in *The New Interpreter's Bible*, vol. 4 (Nashville: Abingdon, 1996), 410.

108. MT *bad*; LXX *monos*.

> [Jesus is depicted] as enacting or embodying the Creator's mastery over the elements . . . God "walks on the water."[109]

> In antiquity the capacity to walk on water was regarded as divine power. . . . Old Testament parallels are to be noted here, according to which God can walk on the water or on the waves of the sea (cf. Job 9.8; Ps. 77).[110]

> Only a divine being can walk on water.[111]

> On almost any reckoning, walking on the water is an epiphany story. An epiphany is the appearance of God, a god, or a divine being such as an angel, to mortals, often suddenly and unexpectedly. . . . In this scene Jesus is not an ordinary Galilean sage; he is the manifestation of a divine being.[112]

> This passage in Job is especially significant for the story of Jesus walking on the water. . . . the image of God the Creator walking on the sea as on dry ground conveys his unlimited power over the sea and indeed over all the forces of creation—a power humans do not have.[113]

When we interpret Jesus's act of walking on the sea in the light of Jewish Scripture, a strong case can be made that it is *epiphanic*: that is, it reveals that Jesus is equal in divine power to the Creator. For without assistance from anyone, Jesus does something that only the creator God can do.

In support of this point, it is important to emphasize that in all three gospels, the disciples respond to Jesus walking on the sea with the ordinary human reaction to a theophany or appearance of God: they are completely "terrified" (Matt 14:26; Mark 6:50; John 6:19). As with the stilling of the storm, this kind of fearful response is a typical feature of how human beings react to an epiphany or theophany (see Gen 3:10; 15:1; 28:17; Exod 3:6; 20:18–20; Isa 6:5; Dan 10:11–12).[114]

109. Dunn, *Jesus Remembered*, 687n331.

110. Lüdemann, *Jesus after Two Thousand Years*, 46.

111. Theissen and Merz, *Historical Jesus*, 303.

112. Funk and the Jesus Seminar, *Acts of Jesus*, 93.

113. Meier, *A Marginal Jew*, 2:914, 915.

114. Funk and the Jesus Seminar, *Acts of Jesus*, 93; Meier, *A Marginal Jew*, 2:907, 910. Cf. Hiebert, "Theophany in the Old Testament," in *ABD*, 6:505–11.

Jesus Identifies Himself by Using the Divine "I Am"

Perhaps most important of all, when the disciples react with fear to the appearance of Jesus walking on the sea, in all three accounts, he responds to them by declaring: "It is I [*egō eimi*]; do not be afraid" (Matt 14:27; Mark 6:50; John 6:20). How should we interpret these words?

Some commentators insist that Jesus is merely identifying himself.[115] In support of this interpretation, elsewhere in the Gospel of John, the man born blind likewise identifies himself in response to questions about whether he is the same man who used to sit and beg by saying: "I am the man" (*egō eimi*) (John 9:9). According to this view, the English translation "It's me" captures "exactly the nuance of Jesus's words."[116]

To be sure, when Jesus says, "It is I" (*egō eimi*), there is no doubt that he *is* identifying himself for the disciples.[117] On the other hand, when his words are interpreted in their early Jewish context, there are three good reasons for agreeing with Rudolf Schnackenburg that Jesus's "sovereign 'It is I' (in the Greek, 'I am') is not *merely* a formula of identification, but *divine self-revelation*, in the same way that Yhwh so often presents himself in the Old Testament."[118]

For one thing, contrary to the impression created by the common English translation "It is I," Jesus's expression is absolute; there is no predicate. Compare, for example, the accounts of him walking on the sea with the way he identifies himself after the resurrection:

115. Kirk, *A Man Attested by God*, 251. See also C. K. Barrett, *The Gospel according to John*, 2nd ed. (London: SPCK, 1978), 281.

116. Kirk, *A Man Attested by God*, 251. Kirk is right to insist that, in isolation, "I am" is "not a magical phrase" that "entails a claim to being Israel's God." His translation of *egō eimi* as merely "It's me" fails to take into account the fact that (1) Jesus says it while he is *walking on the sea*—something Jewish Scripture says only God can do (Job 9:3), and (2) the juxtaposition "I am" with the standard theophanic command "do not fear" (Matt 14:27; Mark 6:50; John 6:20) suggests the appearance of a heavenly being (cf. Gen 15:1; 26:24; 28:13; Exod 20:20; Judg 6:23; Dan 10:12; Isa 43:1; 44:2). In other words, Kirk is right in what he affirms, but wrong in what he denies: by saying "I am; do not fear," Jesus is *both* identifying himself to the disciples *and* revealing his divine status and power. This is especially clear in the Gospel of Matthew, in which the disciples respond by "worshiping" (*proskyneō*) Jesus, an act which Jesus elsewhere says is to be given "only" to "the Lord your God" (Matt 14:33; cf. 4:10). So rightly Richard B. Hays, *Echoes of Scripture in the Gospels* (Waco, TX: Baylor University Press, 2016), 167–68.

117. Luz, *Matthew*, 2:320; Yarbro Collins, *Mark*, 335.

118. Rudolf Schnackenburg, *The Gospel of Matthew*, trans. Robert R. Barr (Grand Rapids: Eerdmans, 2002), 144–45 (slightly adapted; emphasis added).

> Take heart, I am [*egō eimi*]; do not be afraid. (Matt 14:27)
>
> Take heart, I am [*egō eimi*]; do not be afraid. (Mark 6:50)
>
> I am [*egō eimi*]; do not be afraid. (John 6:20)
>
> See that . . . it is I myself [*egō eimi autos*]. (Luke 24:39)[119]

As is widely noted, the absolute form of Jesus's self-identification echoes the divine self-designation given by God to Moses on Mount Sinai.[120] Compare the following:

> God said to Moses, "*I Am Who I Am*." He said further, "Thus you shall say to the Israelites, '*I Am* has sent me to you.'" God also said to Moses, "Thus you shall say to the Israelites, 'The LORD, the God of your ancestors, the God of Abraham, the God of Isaac, and the God of Jacob, has sent me to you': This is my name forever, and this my title for all generations." (Exod 3:14–15)

In the passage from Exodus, the absolute "I am" (*'ehyeh*) is a divine self-designation.[121] In context, it appears to function almost as another name for "the LORD God" (*YHWH 'elohim*), the one God of Israel (Exod 3:15). This divine "I am" also seems to suggest that the God who appears to Moses is eternal; this God has no beginning and no end; he simply "is."[122] Indeed, some suggest that the name YHWH is best translated as "He Who Is."[123]

Moreover, though the point is often overlooked by those who contend Jesus is merely identifying himself, Jesus does not only say "I am"; he also says "do not fear" (Matt 14:27; Mark 6:50; John 6:20). Strikingly, the combination of these two declarations takes place in two of the most exalted

119. Author's translations.

120. See Matthias Konradt, *The Gospel according to Matthew: A Commentary*, trans. M. Eugene Boring (Waco, TX: Baylor University Press, 2020), 229; Hays, *Echoes of Scripture*, 72–73; Yarbro Collins, *Mark*, 335; Francis J. Moloney, SDB, *The Gospel of John*, Sacra Pagina 4 (Collegeville: Liturgical Press, 1998), 203.

121. William H. C. Propp, *Exodus*, 2 vols., Anchor Yale Bible 2–2A (New Haven: Yale University Press, 1999, 2006), 1:204–5, 223–25.

122. James Kugel, *Traditions of the Bible: A Guide to the Bible As It Was at the Start of the Common Era* (Cambridge, MA: Harvard University Press, 1997), 516–17.

123. David Noel Freedman, "Yhwh," in *Theological Dictionary of the Old Testament*, ed. G. J. Botterweck et al., 15 vols. (Grand Rapids: Eerdmans, 1974–2006), 5:501–11.

and decidedly monotheistic descriptions of the one God of Israel in all of Jewish Scripture:

> But now thus says the LORD,
> he who created you, O Jacob,
> he who formed you, O Israel:
> *Do not fear*, for I have redeemed you . . .
> so that you may know and believe me
> and understand that *I am he.*
> Before me no god was formed,
> nor shall there be any after me. (Isa 43:1, 10)

> *I, I am He*,
> who blots out your transgressions for my own sake,
> I will not remember your sins . . .
> Thus says the LORD who made you,
> who formed you in the womb and will help you:
> *Do not fear*, O Jacob my servant. (Isa 43:25; 44:2)

As Joseph Blenkinsopp points out, the divine self-designation "I Am He" (Isa 43:10)[124] functions as "a self-predication" of YHWH that is "reminiscent" of "the equally enigmatic *'ehyeh* ('I am'? 'I will be'?) heard by Moses from the burning thornbush (Exod 3:14; cf. Hos 1:9)."[125] Hence, it is only by ignoring the numinous combination of "I am" and "Do not fear" that one can maintain Jesus is merely identifying himself ("It's me").

Perhaps most important of all, when Jesus says "I am," he does not do so in just any context. Rather, he says "I am; do not fear" *while he is walking on the sea*—something Jewish Scripture says only God can do:

> *[God] alone* stretched out the heavens
> and *trampled the waves of the Sea.* (Job 9:8)

Once again, interpreters who insist that Jesus is merely identifying himself fail to take seriously the extraordinary context in which he uses this particular self-designation. It is only by ignoring the echoes of Job in the description of

124. MT *'ani hu'*; LXX *egō eimi.*

125. Joseph Blenkinsopp, *Isaiah*, 3 vols., Anchor Yale Bible 19, 19A, 19B (New Haven: Yale University Press, 2000, 2002, 2003), 2:224.

Jesus walking on the sea that one can seriously maintain that Jesus is simply saying "It's me."[126]

In light of such considerations, scholars of very different perspectives agree that Jesus's response to the disciples on the Sea of Galilee is not merely a self-identification but a "self-revelation" in which Jesus uses the divine "I am" to refer to himself.[127] On this point, John Meier and the Jesus Seminar agree:

> While the "surface meaning" of *egō eimi* in the Gospel narrative is "It is I," the many OT allusions in the story (especially to the Creator God's domination of the waters of chaos in a context of theophany) intimate a secondary, solemn meaning: *the divine "I am."* Ultimately this solemn utterance goes all the way back to Yahweh's revelation of himself to Moses in the burning bush. (Exod 3:14–15).[128]

> In this scene Jesus is not an ordinary Galilean sage; he is the manifestation of a divine being . . . , until he reassures them that it is he. In so doing he uses a Greek formula *ego eimi*, "It's me!" *that is reminiscent of . . . the "I am" saying of God in the Hebrew bible* (Exod 3:14: "I am" is the name of God, which in Hebrew is Yhwh).[129]

In addition to works on the historical Jesus, major commentators on the gospel accounts of Jesus walking on the sea come to the same conclusion.[130] As Ulrich Luz writes:

> Now the divine being begins to speak. Ἐγώ εἰμι has no predicate. Jesus does not say that he is this or that but simply: "It is I." On the surface that is a simple reference of the speaker to himself. . . . Beneath the surface, however, his "It is I" is reminiscent of Yhwh's self-introduction in the Bible. Jesus presents himself here . . . with the language of the Old Testament God.[131]

126. For example, Kirk (*Man Attested by God*) completely ignores Job 9:8 in his study.

127. Meier, *A Marginal Jew*, 2:908.

128. Meier, *A Marginal Jew*, 2:918 (emphasis added).

129. Funk and the Jesus Seminar, *Acts of Jesus*, 93 (adapted; emphasis added).

130. See Konradt, *Gospel according to Matthew*, 229; Hays, *Echoes of Scripture*, 72–73; Yarbro Collins, *Mark*, 335; Moloney, *Gospel of John*, 203.

131. Luz, *Matthew*, 2:320.

If this interpretation is correct, the implications are enormous. Just as the God of Israel reveals the divine "I am" to Moses while displaying his power over the bush that burns but is not consumed, so now Jesus uses the divine "I am" while displaying his power over creation by walking on the sea. *Though the divine "I am" is the exclusive and unique self-designation of the one God of Israel, in the context of an epiphany miracle, Jesus uses it to refer to himself.*

The Walking on the Water and the Divinity of Jesus

In light of these exegetical observations, scholars across a wide spectrum of perspectives agree that Jesus's act of walking on the sea indicates that he is more than merely human; he is also divine. Consider the following quotations from Jewish, Christian, and nonreligious commentators alike:

> Even in Mark . . . some aspects of Jesus' divine nature appear. For example, in Mark 6:48, Jesus walks on the water (cf. Mt 15:25; Jn 6:19).[132]

> *Egō eimi* is the vehicle whereby [Jesus] makes himself manifest as the one exercising power that the Hebrew Bible attributes to God alone (cf. Job 9:8; 38:16; Hab. 3:15).[133]

> Jesus here exhibits an authority which the Jewish Scriptures associate exclusively with the deity. . . . Jesus is bold enough to refer to himself with the loaded and numinous "I am." . . . The step towards the later ecumenical creeds, which affirm Christ's deity, appears undeniable.[134]

> Like its counterpart in the Gospel of Mark, John's version of walking on the water is also an epiphany or a theophany. . . . the author [portrays] Jesus as a divine being in this sea story.[135]

132. Randi Rashkover, "Christology," in Levine and Brettler, *Jewish Annotated New Testament*, 754.

133. Catrin H. Williams, "'I Am' or 'I Am He': Self Declaratory Pronouncements in the Fourth Gospel and Rabbinic Tradition," in *Jesus in the Johannine Tradition*, ed. Robert T. Fortna and Tom Thatcher (Louisville: Westminster John Knox, 2001), 346.

134. Davies and Allison, *Matthew*, 2:512.

135. Funk and the Jesus Seminar, *Acts of Jesus*, 389.

Other examples of similar conclusions could easily be given.[136] For our purposes here, the upshot is when Jesus's act of walking on the sea is situated in its ancient Jewish context, it is far from a mere "ghost story."[137] Instead, when the words and actions of Jesus are interpreted in their first-century Jewish context, a solid case can be made that the episode is a *theophany* in which Jesus reveals his divinity by manifesting divine power over creation and by taking the divine name of the one God of Israel as his own.

Arguments against Historical Plausibility

With these exegetical conclusions in mind, we can now ask: Do the accounts of Jesus walking on the sea of Galilee and taking the divine "I am" as his own go back to an event in the life of Jesus? Or are they fabrications or distortions created by the early church? Once again, I recognize that many readers will dismiss the account due to *a priori* philosophical commitments. Nevertheless, it is incumbent upon me as a historian to survey and evaluate the actual *historical* arguments for and against Jesus making divine claims in the manner described in this episode.

As with the accounts of the stilling of the storm, so it is with the accounts of Jesus walking on the sea: the overwhelming majority of contemporary works on the historical Jesus simply ignore the evidence, as if it did not exist.[138] Curiously, this tendency to ignore the episode can even be found in

136. See, e.g., Jörg Frey, *Theology and History in the Fourth Gospel: Tradition and Narration* (Waco, TX: Baylor University Press, 2018), 51 ("When the ["I am"] formula is used absolutely, the issue is not a mere recognition but the comforting and terrifying insight that in Jesus God himself is encountered"); Lawrence Wills, "The Gospel according to Matthew," in Levine and Brettler, *Jewish Annotated New Testament*, 38 ("Like God, Jesus has power over the sea"); Lüdemann, *Jesus after Two Thousand Years*, 46 ("In antiquity the capacity to walk on water was regarded as divine power"). See also Yarbro Collins, *Mark*, 335: "Jesus is being portrayed here as divine in a functional, not necessarily in a metaphysical sense." It is hard to know what to make of such a distinction, especially since the Septuagint translation of God's declaration to Moses "I am the one who is" (*Egō eimi ho ōn*) (Exod 3:14 LXX) is the most explicitly *onto*logical (i.e., metaphysical) description of God in all of Jewish Scripture. Cf. Kugel, *Traditions of the Bible*, 515–17.

137. Dunn, *Jesus Remembered*, 688.

138. The accounts of Jesus walking on the sea and declaring "I am" receive no discussion in Allison, *Constructing Jesus*; Bauckham, *Jesus: A Very Short Introduction*; Keener, *Historical Jesus of the Gospels*; Casey, *Jesus of Nazareth*; Flusser with Notley, *Sage from Galilee*; Bock and Webb, *Key Events*; Maurice Casey, *Is John's Gospel True?* (London: Routledge, 1996);

works explicitly devoted to explaining the origins of early Christian belief in Jesus's divinity.[139] Some reconstructions do mention it in passing, but never discuss the question of its historicity.[140] But the vast majority of Jesus researchers who actually deign to mention the episode either assume or assert that the accounts are substantially unhistorical. For example, Geza Vermes (without argumentation) deems the episode a "folk legend" generated by "exhausted disciples" who "imagined they saw a ghost walking on the water."[141] Along similar lines, the Jesus Seminar declares the words attributed to Jesus about his identity to be "the invention of a storyteller."[142] Paula Fredriksen asserts (also without any argumentation) that the account of Jesus walking on the sea is not even intended by the gospel authors to be historical; it functions like other "wonders attributed to Jesus," as "ways of proclaiming Jesus' power" rather than as "reports of remembered events."[143] Still others suggest the account of Jesus walking on water were created on the basis of the account of the stilling of the storm.[144]

When historical Jesus scholars take time to discuss reasons against the historicity of the accounts of Jesus walking on the sea of Galilee, three major arguments stand out.

The first and most decisive reason given is not a historical argument at all, but a philosophical assumption that miracles and supernatural appearances of a divine being are simply not possible. As John Meier rightly points out:

> Some critics will think this exploration of the historicity of the walking on the water a waste of time. Their judgement is made, however, not on strictly historical grounds but on the basis of a philosophical or theological a priori, a version of Bultmann's incantation that "modern man cannot believe in miracles."[145]

Becker, *Jesus of Nazareth*; Wright, *Jesus and the Victory of God*; Vermes, *Religion of Jesus*; Witherington, *Christology of Jesus*; Sanders, *Jesus and Judaism*; Klausner, *Jesus of Nazareth*.

139. E.g., Ehrman, *How Jesus Became God*; Grindheim, *God's Equal*.

140. E.g., Lohfink, *Jesus of Nazareth*, 132; Puig i Tàrrech, *Jesus: A Biography*, 363–64; Ehrman, *Jesus of Nazareth*, 199.

141. E.g., Vermes, *Authentic Gospel of Jesus*, 13. Cf. Vermes, *Jesus the Jew*, 26. For a similar explanation, see Klausner, *Jesus of Nazareth*, 269.

142. Robert W. Funk, Roy Hoover, and the Jesus Seminar, *The Five Gospels: The Search for the Authentic Words of Jesus* (New York: Macmillan, 1993), 66.

143. Fredriksen, *Jesus of Nazareth*, 115.

144. Jeremias, *Proclamation of Jesus*, 87; Bultmann, *History of the Synoptic Tradition*, 216.

145. Meier, *A Marginal Jew*, 2:919.

Meier is right about this. As a case in point, the Jesus Seminar contends that the "historical reliability" of Jesus walking on the sea can be determined simply by a recognition of "*the kind of story* involved"—that is, "an epiphany story" involving the "appearance of God, a god, or a divine being."[146] The implicit logic of the seminar's position is that since divine beings cannot appear in human forms in epiphanies, any accounts of epiphanies are by definition not based on historical events. For this reason alone, "almost to a person, the Fellows doubted that Jesus actually walked on the water" and deemed the episode "improbable," if not "largely or entirely fictive."[147]

The second major argument against historicity is from a lack of coherence with other evidence about Jesus. According to John Meier:

> Almost all the miracles that have some claim to go back to an event in Jesus' life . . . seek to help a person in dire need or mortal danger. . . . [They] do not focus on Jesus' person and status or seek his self-glorification. . . . In contrast, the walking on the water fails to cohere with this tendency; indeed, it is diametrically opposed to it.[148]

In other words, because the walking on the sea primarily reveals Jesus's divinity and only secondarily rescues the disciples from danger, it is too incongruent with other miracles of Jesus to be historical.

The third major argument against the historicity—and the one that is perhaps most important for our study—is from the implicit Christology of the account. According to this argument, in the account of Jesus walking on the sea, he speaks and acts as if he is divine; therefore, the story must be unhistorical, since we know that Jesus could not be regarded as divine by himself (or anyone else) until the "post-Easter period."[149] In the words of the Jesus Seminar and Gerd Theissen with Annette Merz:

> In virtually every case [where Jesus states "I am"], the reader is being confronted with the language of the evangelist and not the language of Jesus.[150]

> In the walking on the water . . . poetic fantasy has caught hold of historical reminiscences. . . . In antiquity the capacity to walk on water was regarded

146. Funk and the Jesus Seminar, *Acts of Jesus*, 93.
147. Funk and the Jesus Seminar, *Acts of Jesus*, 93; cf. the same work, p. 37.
148. Meier, *A Marginal Jew*, 2:920; cf. Meyer, 2:921.
149. Schröter, *Jesus of Nazareth*, 99.
150. Funk, Hoover, the Jesus Seminar, *Five Gospels*, 199, 419.

> as a sign of divine power. . . . the story as a whole already presupposes a belief in the divine character of Jesus which was possible only after and on the basis of Easter.[151]

According to this view, Jesus of Nazareth—unlike Alexander the Great, Antiochus Epiphanes, Herod Agrippa, or Caligula—could not have spoken or acted in ways that led anyone to believe that he was divine or equal with God during his lifetime. Hence, what we have here is a negative use of the old criterion of discontinuity: because Jesus speaks and acts in a way that is strongly continuous with beliefs about his identity in the early church, the episode must be substantially unhistorical.[152] In light of such considerations, some conclude that "the walking on the water is most likely from start to finish a creation of the early church,"[153] that it "cannot be traced back to the time of the historical Jesus."[154]

Contextual Plausibility: The Divine "I Am," Antiochus IV, and Caligula's Sea-Crossing

With this in mind, if we approach the evidence without appealing to philosophical assumptions, but instead ask the simple question of whether the historical Jesus performed an extraordinary deed in which his disciples believed him to have walked on the Sea of Galilee and identified himself with the divine name, several arguments emerge in favor of historical plausibility. The first is from contextual plausibility within Judaism, on two fronts.

For one thing, if the historical Jesus considered himself to be more than merely human, then it is contextually credible that he would do so in *a distinctively Jewish way*, by taking the divine "I am" used in the Second Temple period as an epithet for the one God of Israel as his own.[155] Consider, for example, the following early Jewish texts:

151. Theissen and Merz, *Historical Jesus*, 295; cf. also 303, 310.

152. For similar views, see Hengel and Schwemer, *Jesus and Judaism*, 366; Lüdemann, *Jesus after Two Thousand Years*, 46; Jeremias, *New Testament Theology*, 87; Bultmann, *History of the Synoptic Tradition*, 216, 230.

153. Meier, *A Marginal Jew*, 2:921.

154. Schröter, *Jesus of Nazareth*, 99.

155. For a full study, see Catrin H. Williams, *I Am He: The Interpretation of 'Anî Hû' in Jewish and Early Christian Literature*, Wissenschaftliche Untersuchungen zum Neuen Testament 113 (Tübingen: Mohr Siebeck, 2000).

> And Moses said to God, "Look, I shall come to the sons of Israel and shall say to them, 'The God of your fathers has sent me to you'; they will ask me, 'What is his name?' What shall I say to them?" And God said to Moses, "*I am the One Who Is.*" And he said, "Thus shall you say to the sons of Israel, "The One Who Is has sent me to you." (Exod 3:13–14 LXX)[156]

> See, see that *I am*,
> and *there is no god except me.* (Deut 32:39 LXX)[157]

> *I, God, am first,*
> and for the things that are coming, *I am.* (Isa 41:4 LXX)[158]

> The servant whom I have chosen
> so that you may know and believe
> and understand that *I am.*
> *Before me there was no other god,*
> nor shall there be any after me.
> *I am God,*
> and besides me there is none who saves. (Isa 43:10–11 LXX)[159]

> Then a voice came speaking to me twice, "Abraham, Abraham!" And I said, "Here I am." And he said, "*Behold, it is I. Fear not, for I am Before-the-World and Mighty,* before the light of the age." (Apoc. Ab. 9:1)[160]

Notice the explicitly ontological character of the first revelation of the divine name to Moses on Mount Sinai: "I am the One Who Is" (*egō eimi ho ōn*) (Exod 3:14 LXX).[161] This emphasis presents a real challenge to those who insist Jesus is only using the divine "I am" in a merely "functional" way.[162] Notice also

156. Pietersma and Wright, *New English Translation of the Septuagint*, 53 (slightly adapted).

157. Pietersma and Wright, *New English Translation of the Septuagint*, 171.

158. Pietersma and Wright, *New English Translation of the Septuagint*, 854.

159. Pietersma and Wright, *New English Translation of the Septuagint*, 857.

160. In Charlesworth, *Old Testament Pseudepigrapha*, 1:693.

161. Cf. J. W. Wevers, *Notes on the Greek Text of Exodus*, Septuagint and Cognate Studies 30 (Atlanta: Scholars Press, 1990), 33–34. See Kugel, *Traditions of the Bible*, 514–16, citing Philo, *On the Change of Names* 11; *The Worse Attacks the Better* 160.

162. E.g., Yarbro Collins, *Mark*, 335; Raymond E. Brown, *The Gospel according to John*, 2 vols., Anchor Yale Bible Commentary 29–29A (New Haven: Yale University Press, 1966, 1970), 1:408.

that the absolute form of "I am" (with no predicate) repeatedly occurs in the context of *monotheistic* declarations that there is "no other god" except the God of Israel, the one who declares "I am" (*egō eimi*) (Deut 32:39; Isa 41:4; 43:10 LXX). Finally, in the first-century Apocalypse of Abraham, the divine "It is I" is juxtaposed with the exhortation "Fear not," just as in all three accounts Jesus says to the disciples: "I am; do not be afraid" (Matt 14:27; Mark 6:50; John 6:20). Taken together, these early Jewish parallels suggest that, however shocking it may be, Jesus's use of the divine "I am" is comprehensible within a first-century Jewish context.[163]

Second, Jesus of Nazareth is not the only figure from the Second Temple period who reputedly acted as if he had power over the sea in order to manifest his divinity. For example, according to 2 Maccabees, the Seleucid king Antiochus IV Epiphanes, who claimed to be a god "manifest" in the flesh, also acted as if he could walk on the sea:

> So Antiochus carried off eighteen hundred talents from the temple, and hurried away to Antioch, *thinking in his arrogance that he could sail on the land and walk on the sea*, because his mind was elated. (2 Macc 5:21)

Notice here that the "arrogance" that led Antiochus to believe that he could "walk on the sea" was the same "superhuman arrogance" (*tēn hyper anthrōpon alazoneian*) that led him to be deemed a "blasphemer" who thought he was "equal to God" (*isothea*) (cf. 2 Macc 9:8, 12, 28).[164]

Along similar lines, the first-century Roman emperor, Gaius Caligula, not only made divine claims during his lifetime (Josephus, *Antiquities* 18.256; Sue-

163. Indeed, a case could be made that using the divine "I am" would be the only way for Jesus to make a fully divine claim without violating early Jewish belief in the oneness of God (cf. Deut 6:4). For example, it is worth noting that these "I am [he]" passages from Jewish Scripture are the very texts cited in early rabbinic literature against the idea that the vision of the Ancient of Days and the son of man in Daniel 7 justified belief in "two powers" in heaven. For example, the Mekilta states: "And it says, 'As I watched thrones [were set in place, and the Ancient of Days took his throne]' (Dan. 7:9).... So as not to give an opportunity for the nations of the world to say: 'There are two powers', but [rather Scripture says]: (1) 'The Lord is a man of war; the Lord is his name.'... He is the one who was in the past, he is the one who will be in the future to come.... As it is said: 'See now that I, I am he etc.' (Deut. 32:39).... And it is written: 'Thus says the Lord... I am the first and the last' (Isa. 44:6).... 'I, the Lord, am the first and with the last, I am he' (Isa. 41:4)" (Mekilta Shirta 4 on Exod 15:3). Translation in Williams, *I Am He*, 118.

164. Jonathan A. Goldstein, *2 Maccabees*, Anchor Yale Bible 41A (New Haven: Yale University Press, 1983), 354, speaks of "the king's arrogant aspirations to godlike feats."

tonius, *Lives of the Caesars* 4.22.2).[165] He also linked his divinity to his ability to cross the waters of the sea without the aid of a ship. In order to manifest his divine power, he had an imperial bridge built over the Bay of Baiae and traversed it riding a chariot. Here are the accounts of Josephus and Suetonius:

> His other actions too did not fall short of madness. For instance, it was insufferable, he thought, to cross the bay from the city of Dicaearchia in Campania to Misenum, another maritime city, in a trireme. Then, too, *he considered it his privilege as lord of the sea to require the same service from the sea as he received from the land.* So the thirty furlongs of sea from headland to headland were connected by pontoons, which cut off the whole bay, and over this bridge, he drove in his chariot. *That way of travelling, said he, befitted his godhead.* (Josephus, *Antiquities* 19.4)[166]

> Besides this, he [Caligula] devised a novel and unheard of kind of pageant; for he bridged the gap between Baiae and the mole at Puteoli, a distance of about thirty-six hundred paces [= over three and a half Roman miles], by bringing together merchant ships from all sides and anchoring them in a double line, after which a mound of earth was heaped upon them in the manner of the Appian Way. *Over this bridge he rode across and back on two successive days.* (Suetonius, *Lives of the Caesars* 4.19.1–2)[167]

Notice here that the reason Caligula engages in this unique form of travel is because it "befitted his godhead" (*theō gar onti*). Notice also that in both accounts the distance he traveled over the water—some three and a half miles—is emphasized.[168] In light of such considerations, Wendy Cotter rightly concludes that at "the time of Jesus himself, the image of a man riding over the waves was already used as a metaphor for what is impossible for a human being."[169]

165. See Anthony A. Barrett, *Caligula: The Abuse of Power*, 2nd ed. (London: Routledge, 2015), 240–43.

166. On the madness of Gaius Caligula, see also Suetonius, *Life of Caligula* 22; Philo, *Legate to Gaius* 34; Cassius Dio, *Roman History* 59.29.1; Tacitus, *Annals* 11.3.

167. Loeb Classical Library translation.

168. Barrett, *Caligula*, 242–43.

169. Wendy Cotter, CSJ, *Miracles in Greco-Roman Antiquity: A Sourcebook* (London: Routledge, 1999), 159. Along similar lines, Dio Chrysostom says Socrates taught that "of all men under the sun that man is most powerful and in might no whit inferior to the gods themselves who is able to accomplish the seemingly impossible—if it should be his will, to

If this is true of Antiochus IV and Caligula, then the accounts of Jesus walking on the sea for some miles in order to manifest his divinity are also contextually plausible in a first-century setting.

Coherence: Exhortations, Miracles, and the Identity of Jesus

The next major argument in favor of historicity is from coherence with other evidence about Jesus, in at least two key ways.

For one thing, in all three accounts of Jesus walking on the sea, he responds to the fear experienced by his disciples in the face of his extraordinary deed by declaring: "Do not be afraid" (Matt 14:27; Mark 6:50; John 6:20). This exhortation coheres perfectly with other evidence in which Jesus says "Do not fear" or "Do not be afraid" in the wake of his performing extraordinary deeds of power (see Matt 17:17; Mark 5:36; Luke 5:10; 8:50).

Moreover, the accounts of Jesus walking on the sea also strongly cohere with other evidence in which Jesus uses his miracles to reveal his hidden identity. For example, when asked by John the Baptist whether he is "the one who is to come" (Matt 11:2; Luke 7:18–19), Jesus points directly to his miracles:

> *Go and tell John what you hear and see:* the blind receive their sight, the lame walk, the lepers are cleansed, the deaf hear, the dead are raised, and the poor have good news brought to them. (Matt 11:2–6)

> *Go and tell John what you have seen and heard*: the blind receive their sight, the lame walk, the lepers are cleansed, the deaf hear, the dead are raised, the poor have good news brought to them. (Luke 7:18–23)

We will look at this saying in more detail in chapter 4. For now, the main point is that this episode demonstrates that the claim that the miracles "do not focus on Jesus' person and status" is overstated.[170] According to Jesus himself, his extraordinary acts of giving sight to the blind, healing lepers, and raising the dead are *precisely* where one ought to look in order to answer the question of his identity.

---

have men walk dryshod over the sea [*pezeuesthai men tēn thalattan*]" (Dio Chrysostom, *Discourses* 3.30 [Loeb Classical Library translation]).

170. Meier, *A Marginal Jew*, 2:920–21.

Consequences: Christ as the Eternal "I Am"

Last, but certainly not least, if the evidence that Jesus performed the deed of traversing the Sea of Galilee and using the divine "I am" goes back to an episode that took place during his public ministry, then it would provide a plausible explanation for early Christian writings in which the divine "I am" is used both for the one eternal creator God and for the risen Christ. Consider, for example, the following passage from the Apocalypse of John:

> [God:] "*I am* the Alpha and the Omega," says the Lord God, who is and who was and who is to come, the Almighty. (Rev 1:8)
>
> [Christ:] "Do not be afraid; *I am* the first and the last, and the living one." (Rev 1:17)
>
> [God:] "*I am* the Alpha and the Omega, the beginning and the end." (Rev 21:6)
>
> [Christ:] "*I am* the Alpha and the Omega, the first and the last, the beginning and the end." (Rev 22:13)

Notice here that both the one eternal God and the risen Christ repeatedly use the divine "I am" (*egō eimi*) in the context of affirming their eternal nature. As Craig Koester observes, in these passages from the Apocalypse,

> Christ's role is fused with that of God. . . . These expressions identify him as the one who precedes all things as their Creator and the one who brings all things to their fulfillment. . . . Revelation uses language for Christ that was typically reserved for God alone: "I am the first and I am the last; besides me there is no God" (Isa 44:6). *Revelation extends this language to Jesus, while retaining a monotheistic perspective*. Christ is not worshiped as a second deity alongside God, but within the worship of the one true God.[171]

How does one explain the origin of this combination of monotheistic belief in one eternal creator God and divine Christology? One plausible historical

171. Craig R. Koester, *Revelation*, Anchor Yale Bible 38A (New Haven: Yale University Press, 2014), 854 (emphasis added). See likewise Bauckham, *Jesus and the God of Israel*, 38–39.

explanation is that, already during his ministry, Jesus *himself* was perceived as acting as if he were equal with the one God who alone "trampled the waves of the sea" (Job 9:8) and as speaking as if he were the same God who revealed himself to Moses in the burning bush and was known by the divine "I am" (Exod 3:14; Isa 43:10). In other words, the account of Jesus walking on the sea in particular gives a plausible point of origin for the rise of what some have called the "christological monotheism" of early Jewish Christianity.[172]

Weighing the Arguments for and against Historicity

Now that we have completed our survey of major arguments for and against the historicity of the accounts of Jesus walking on the sea, we can step back for a moment and evaluate the weight of the different positions.

Perhaps surprisingly, when we subject the arguments against historicity to critical scrutiny, we discover that they are remarkably thin. For one thing, the primary reason for concluding the episode is unhistorical seems once again to be the philosophical *a priori* that supernatural phenomena are impossible. Whether or not readers find this philosophical outlook personally convincing, it has no weight as a historical argument. Likewise, the argument from a lack of coherence with other miracles attributed to Jesus because Jesus reveals his identity rather than rescues his disciples assumes (without justification) all of the miracles attributed to Jesus must function in the same way. It also completely ignores the fact that Jesus himself points to his miracles precisely in order to reveal his identity to John the Baptist (Matt 11:2–6; Luke 7:18–23). Finally—and this is important—the argument that Jesus's use of the divine "I am" to identify himself must be unhistorical because its implicit "Christology" is "too high" is yet another example of begging the very historical question that is at the heart of this study. That Jesus never took the divine "I am" as his own must be demonstrated; it cannot simply be assumed.

On the other hand, if we leave the philosophical question of the miraculous to one side and focus on the arguments from contextual plausibility, coherence, and consequences in the early church, the accounts of Jesus walking on the sea fare remarkably well. For one thing, as we saw above, however

172. See, e.g., Carey C. Newman, James R. Davila, Gladys S. Lews, eds., *The Jewish Roots of Christological Monotheism: Papers from the St. Andrews Conference on the Historical Origins of the Worship of Jesus* (Leiden: Brill, 1999; Waco, TX: Baylor University Press, 2017).

extraordinary and inexplicable the accounts of Jesus walking on the sea may be, they are contextually plausible given the fact that Gaius Caligula performed a similar act of crossing the waters of the Bay of Baiae precisely because he wanted to manifest "his godhead" (Josephus, *Antiquities* 19.4; Suetonius, *Lives of the Caesars* 4.19.1–2; 4.22.2). Moreover, as we will see in chapter 5, even Jesus's use of the divine "I am" to identify himself (Matt 14:27; Mark 6:50; John 6:20) coheres with other evidence in which he refers to himself using the divine "I am" (John 8:58; cf. Exod 3:13–14; Isa 41:4; 43:10). Indeed, if Jesus thought he was divine and wanted to reveal his divinity to his Jewish disciples without undermining the Jewish belief in one God, the use of this mysterious self-designation would be a comprehensible way in which to do so. It would also provide a compelling explanation for the early Christian use of the divine "I am" to identify Christ with the one God of early Jewish monotheism (cf. Rev 1:8, 17; 21:6; 22:13; cf. Isa 44:6).

In light of such considerations, it is difficult to avoid the conclusion that the historical arguments in favor of the episode are much stronger than the arguments against it.[173] From a historical perspective, the accounts of Jesus walking on the sea and identifying himself by using the divine "I am" are contextually plausible, cohere with other evidence about Jesus, and make good sense of the aftermath of his life in the early church.

The Transfiguration

The third and final episode that demands our attention involves Jesus taking Peter, James, and John up a mountain with him to be transfigured before them in the presence of Moses and Elijah. Like the stilling of the storm and the walking on the sea, the transfiguration of Jesus is often classified as one of the "epiphany miracles," which focus in a particular way on "his *identity*."[174] This particular episode is recounted in all three Synoptic Gospels:

> Six days later, *Jesus took with him Peter and James and his brother John and led them up a high mountain, by themselves. And he was transfigured before*

173. Cf. Bruce J. Malina, "Assessing the Historicity of Jesus' Walking on the Sea," in *Authenticating the Activities of Jesus*, ed. Bruce Chilton and Craig A. Evans (Leiden: Brill, 1999), 369: "As reported in the Gospels, the incident has all the hallmarks of historical verisimilitude and should be ranked as a historically authentic episode."

174. See Bond, *Historical Jesus*, 121; Theissen and Merz, *Historical Jesus*, 295–96.

them, and his face shone like the sun, and his clothes became dazzling white. Suddenly there appeared to them Moses and Elijah, talking with him. Then Peter said to Jesus, "Lord, it is good for us to be here; if you wish, *I will make three dwellings here*, one for you, one for Moses, and one for Elijah." While he was still speaking, suddenly *a bright cloud overshadowed them, and from the cloud a voice said, "This is my Son, the Beloved; with him I am well pleased; listen to him!" When the disciples heard this, they fell to the ground and were overcome by fear*. But Jesus came and touched them, saying, "Get up and do not be afraid." And when they looked up, they saw no one except Jesus himself alone. *As they were coming down the mountain, Jesus ordered them, "Tell no one about the vision* until after the Son of Man has been raised from the dead." (Matt 17:1–9)

Six days later, *Jesus took with him Peter and James and John, and led them up a high mountain apart, by themselves. And he was transfigured before them, and his clothes became dazzling white*, such as no one on earth could bleach them. *And there appeared to them Elijah with Moses*, who were talking with Jesus. Then Peter said to Jesus, "Rabbi, it is good for us to be here; *let us make three dwellings, one for you, one for Moses, and one for Elijah*." He did not know what to say, *for they were terrified. Then a cloud overshadowed them, and from the cloud there came a voice, "This is my Son, the Beloved; listen to him!"* Suddenly when they looked around, they saw no one with them any more, but only Jesus. *As they were coming down the mountain, he ordered them to tell no one about what they had seen*, until after the Son of Man had risen from the dead. (Mark 9:2–9)

Now about eight days after these sayings *Jesus took with him Peter and John and James, and went up on the mountain to pray*. And while he was praying, *the appearance of his face changed, and his clothes became dazzling white. Suddenly they saw two men, Moses and Elijah, talking to him*. They appeared in glory and were speaking of his departure, which he was about to accomplish at Jerusalem. Now Peter and his companions were weighed down with sleep; but since they had stayed awake, they saw his glory and the two men who stood with him. Just as they were leaving him, Peter said to Jesus, *"Master, it is good for us to be here; let us make three dwellings, one for you, one for Moses, and one for Elijah"—not knowing what he said. While he was saying this, a cloud came and overshadowed them; and they were terrified as they entered the cloud. Then from the cloud came a voice that said, "This is my Son, my Chosen; listen to him!"* When the voice had spoken, Jesus was

> found alone. *And they kept silent and in those days told no one any of the things they had seen.* (Luke 9:28–36)

As with the other epiphanic acts of Jesus, the transfiguration has a remarkable history of rationalistic exegesis that makes it necessary to begin by emphasizing what the gospel accounts do *not* say. For example, they do not say that Peter, James, and John fell asleep and (somehow collectively) "dreamed that Moses and Elijah were present and that Jesus conversed with them" until the "illusion" was dispelled by "the first confused moments after their awakening."[175] Nor do they say that the three disciples awoke and saw Jesus talking with "two strangers" who were "illuminated by the beams of the rising sun," so that "their drowsiness, and the clouds which in an autumnal sunrise float to and fro over those mountains," left them with "the vague undefined impression of having been in contact with apparitions from a higher sphere."[176] Finally, the Gospels certainly do not say anything about Jesus's face being "lit up" when, "in a flash of insight," he suddenly realized his death was going to be salvific.[177]

Instead, despite a number of differences in detail, the substance of all three accounts can be summed up as follows: (1) Jesus takes his inner circle of three disciples up to the top of an unidentified mountain; (2) the disciples witness the transfiguration of Jesus's appearance and clothing and the appearance of Moses and Elijah; (3) Peter responds by suggesting the disciples build three "tabernacles"—one for Jesus, Moses, and Elijah; (4) a cloud overshadows the disciples, and a heavenly voice from the cloud identifies Jesus as his "Son"; (5) after coming down from the mountain, the disciples do not tell anyone about what they have witnessed. Let us take a few moments here to interpret each of these basic features in an early Jewish context.

Jesus Takes Peter, James, and John to the Top of a Mountain

The episode begins when Jesus takes three of the twelve disciples—Peter, James, and John—alone with him to the top of a mountain in Galilee. Al-

175. Strauss, *Life of Jesus*, 538.

176. Schweitzer, *Quest of the Historical Jesus*, 52–53, summarizing the views of the early nineteenth-century rationalist Heinrich Eberhard Gottlob Paulus, *Philologisch-kritische und historische Commentar über die drey ersten Evangelien*, 4 vols. (Lübeck: Bohn, 1800–1808), 2:539–43.

177. Jerome Murphy-O'Connor, "What Really Happened at the Transfiguration?," *Bible Review* 3 (1987): 8–21.

though the exact location is not specified, the mountain is usually identified either as Mount Hermon, which stands over 9,000 feet and is the highest point in Syria,[178] or as Mount Tabor, which stands over 1,800 feet and is the highest peak in Lower Galilee.[179]

Whatever location is in view, in context, it is Jesus's act of choosing three of the twelve disciples to ascend the mountaintop with him to experience a heavenly vision that is most striking. For according to Jewish Scripture, Moses does something remarkably similar when he ascends to the top of Mount Sinai with the three figures of Aaron, Nadab, and Abihu:

> Then [God] said to Moses, "*Come up to the Lord, you and Aaron, Nadab, and Abihu*, and seventy of the elders of Israel, and worship at a distance. . . ." *Then Moses and Aaron, Nadab, and Abihu*, and seventy of the elders of Israel *went up, and they saw the God of Israel*. Under his feet there was something like a pavement of sapphire stone, like the very heaven for clearness. God did not lay his hand on the chief men of the people of Israel; also *they beheld God*, and they ate and drank. (Exod 24:1, 9–11)

Note well that Moses's act of bringing Aaron, Nadab, and Abihu, along with the seventy "elders," to the top of Sinai takes place in the context of a *theophany*: they "beheld God" (Exod 24:11).[180] As David Strauss pointed out long ago, the purpose of Moses's actions on Mount Sinai and Jesus's actions on the mountain of transfiguration are strikingly similar:

> Moses, on an earlier ascent of the mountain . . . , had taken with him, besides the seventy elders, three confidential friends, Aaron, Nadab, and Abihu, to participate in the vision of Jehovah (Exod. xxiv. 1, 9–11); so Jesus takes with him his three most confidential disciples, that, so far as their powers are adequate, they might be witnesses of the sublime spectacle.[181]

In other words, just as Moses took the three priestly figures of Aaron, Nadab, and Abihu (two brothers) with him to the top of Mount Sinai in order to see

178. So Yarbro Collins, *Mark*, 421; Klausner, *Jesus of Nazareth*, 303.

179. So Puig i Tàrrech, *Jesus: A Biography*, 303. See Frédéric Manns, "Mount Tabor," in *Jesus and Archaeology*, ed. James H. Charlesworth (Grand Rapids: Eerdmans, 2006), 167–77.

180. George Savran, *Encountering the Divine: Theophany in Biblical Narrative*, Journal for the Study of the Old Testament Supplement 420 (London: T&T Clark, 2005), 75–76; see also Propp, *Exodus*, 2:293–94; Yarbro Collins, *Mark*, 416–17.

181. Strauss, *Jesus of Nazareth*, 544. See also Luz, *Matthew*, 2:395–96.

the God of Israel, so now Jesus takes Peter, James, and John (two brothers) with him to the top of the mountain in Galilee in order to see Jesus transfigured.

The Three Disciples See Jesus Dressed like a Heavenly Being

Given these parallels with the theophany at Mount Sinai, it is not surprising that, after reaching the top of the mountain, Peter, James, and John experience a kind of heavenly vision in which the appearance of Jesus is altered so that his clothing becomes luminously "white" (Matt 17:2; Mark 9:3; Luke 9:3). The luminosity of Jesus's garments is extremely significant: in both Jewish Scripture and early Jewish apocalypses, luminously white garments are often worn by *heavenly beings.*[182]

For example, in the book of Psalms, "the LORD" is described as being "wrapped in light as with a garment" (Ps 104:2)—something that is "part of the imagery of appearances of ancient Near East divinities."[183] Even more striking, both the book of Daniel and the early Jewish apocalypse of Enoch describe God in heaven as wearing dazzlingly white garments:

> As I [Daniel] watched,
> *thrones were set in place,*
> *and an Ancient of Days took his throne,*
> *his clothing was white as snow,*
> and the hair of his head like pure wool. (Dan 7:9)[184]

> And I [Enoch] was looking,
> And I saw a lofty throne . . .
> *And the Great Glory sat upon it;*
> *his raiment was like the appearance of the sun*
> *and whiter than much snow.*
> And no angel could enter into this house and behold his face
> because of the splendor and glory;
> and no flesh could behold him. (1 Enoch 14:18, 20–21)[185]

182. M. David Litwa, *Iesous Deus: The Early Christian Depiction of Jesus as a Mediterranean God* (Minneapolis: Fortress, 2014), 121.

183. Hossfeld and Zenger, *Psalms 3*, 49. Compare the Septuagint: "throwing off light like a garment" (*anaballomenos phōs hōs imation*) (Ps 103:2 LXX [104:2]).

184. NRSV, adapted.

185. In George W. E. Nickelsburg, *1 Enoch 1*, Hermeneia (Minneapolis: Fortress, 2001), 257.

In both passages, Daniel and Enoch are described as seeing the luminous garments of God in the context of an apocalyptic theophany in which they (somehow) "see" God (cf. Dan 7:1–8; 1 Enoch 14:1–17).[186] This strongly suggests that Peter, James, and John's vision of the transfiguration of Jesus's clothing is likewise both apocalyptic and theophanic.[187] Just as Daniel and Enoch experience an apocalyptic vision in which the God of Israel appears in heaven dressed in supernaturally white clothing, so now Peter, James, and John have an apocalyptic vision in which Jesus appears on the mountaintop dressed in luminously white garments.

If this assessment is correct, then the Synoptic accounts of the transfiguration suggest that *Jesus is not merely a human being; he is also a heavenly being*—one who temporarily lifts the visible appearance of his humanity to give his disciples a glimpse of his invisible heavenly glory. In this regard, it is significant that other human figures in early Jewish literature only become luminous after death, once they have been raised from the dead (Dan 12:6–7) or are exalted into heaven (Testament of Abraham 11:4–9). By contrast, Jesus appears dressed in luminous garments during his earthly life.[188] In other words, Jesus is being depicted as *a human who is already a heavenly being*, but whose heavenly identity is currently hidden under his ordinary human appearance.[189]

The Three Disciples See Moses and Elijah on the Mountaintop

In order to feel the full force of this point, it is important to emphasize that it is not merely the luminosity of Jesus's garments that suggests his heavenly iden-

186. See John J. Collins, *Daniel: A Commentary*, Hermeneia (Minneapolis: Fortress, 1993), 294; Nickelsburg, *1 Enoch 1*, 261.

187. Michael F. Bird, *Jesus the Eternal Son: Answering Adoptionist Christology* (Grand Rapids: Eerdmans, 2017), 94, aptly describes it as a "Theophanic Episode."

188. Cf. Luz, *Matthew*, 2:397, who lists 1 Enoch 62:15–16; 4 Ezra 7:97; and 2 Baruch 51:3 as examples of the luminous garments and appearances of the righteous in the new creation in early Jewish apocalypses.

189. *Contra* Kirk, *Man Attested by God*, 75, who uses a description of Adam "in glory" as having an appearance like "the Lord's" (Testament of Abraham 11:4, 9) to argue that because a human being can "be depicted as looking like God, particularly 'in glory,'" the "physical appearance that embodies heavenly luminosity (e.g., in the transfiguration story, Mark 9:2–8), is no indication that a figure is either divine per se or angelic." This argument fails to note the significant difference between being a heavenly being who has come down to earth and an earthly being who has been exalted into heaven. Along similar lines, Kirk (*Man Attested by God*, 195) is right to affirm that the transfiguration is "a glimpse of the future" but fails to reckon with the fact that Jesus *already* possesses this glory during his life on earth.

tity, but the context in which his garments are transfigured: the appearance of Moses and Elijah on a mountaintop (Matt 17:3; Mark 9:4; Luke 9:30).

Why Moses and Elijah? The answer, once again, appears to lie in the Jewish Scriptures.[190] For one thing, both Moses and Elijah end their lives in unique ways. After his death, Moses appears to be buried by God himself (Deut 34:5–6), while Elijah is taken up into heaven in a chariot of fire (2 Kgs 2:9–12). As we will see below, in later Jewish writings, the tradition arises that both Elijah and Moses were assumed into heaven (e.g., Josephus, *Antiquities* 4.325–326; 9.28).[191] Even more significantly, out of all of the figures in Jewish Scripture, it is Moses and Elijah alone who are described as experiencing *theophanies* on Mount Sinai in which they talk with God but cannot see his face.[192] Compare the following:

> Moses said, "*Show me your glory, I pray.*" And [the LORD] said, "I will make all my goodness pass before you, and will proclaim before you the name, 'The LORD'; and I will be gracious to whom I will be gracious, and will show mercy on whom I will show mercy. *But," he said, "you cannot see my face; for no one shall see me and live.*" And the LORD continued, "See, there is a place by me where you shall stand on the rock; and while my glory passes by I will put you in a cleft of the rock, and I will cover you with my hand until I have passed by; *then I will take away my hand, and you shall see my back; but my face shall not be seen.*" (Exod 33:18–23)

> At that place [Elijah] came to a cave, and spent the night there. Then the word of the LORD came to him. . . . He said, "*Go out and stand on the mountain before the Lord, for the LORD is about to pass by.*" Now there was a great wind, so strong that it was splitting mountains and breaking rocks in pieces before the LORD, but the LORD was not in the wind; and after the wind an earthquake, but the LORD was not in the earthquake; and after the earthquake a fire, but the LORD was not in the fire; and after the fire a sound of sheer silence. *When Elijah heard it, he wrapped his face in his mantle and went out and stood at the entrance of the cave. Then there came a voice to him that said,* "What are you doing here, Elijah?" (1 Kgs 19:9, 11–14)

190. As Ulrich Luz rightly points out, the old view that Moses and Elijah "represent the Law and Prophets" is inadequate on several counts. See Luz, *Matthew*, 2:398.

191. Puig i Tàrrech, *Jesus: A Biography*, 460.

192. Dunn, *Jesus Remembered*, 665. Davies and Allison, *Saint Matthew*, 2:697: "Why are Moses and Elijah mentioned? Probably because they are the two OT figures who encountered God on Sinai/Horeb."

Notice here that the theophanies experienced by Moses and Elijah take place on the very same mountain: Mount Sinai (cf. Exod 34:2–3; 1 Kgs 19:8). Notice also that while Moses and Elijah are both able to speak with God, neither is able to see God's face. As the text makes clear, Moses asks to see God's "glory," but he is refused and is only permitted to see God's "back" (Exod 33:23). The latter expression means that "the divine Face may not be experienced," but only "the divine *back*," that "part of God's essence . . . less fraught with his dangerous aura than his Face or front side."[193] Likewise, before going out of the cave to speak with God, Elijah wraps his "face" in his mantle (1 Kgs 19:13) because he wants to avoid "viewing YHWH."[194]

Once we give due emphasis to the fact that both Moses and Elijah are allowed to encounter the God of Israel on Mount Sinai but not to see his face, the transfiguration of Jesus takes on a startling new significance: *on the mountain of transfiguration, Moses and Elijah are finally allowed to see the unveiled face of God*. In the transfiguration, Jesus is not only being revealed as a heavenly being who has come to earth. He is also implicitly identified as the same heavenly being whose face Moses and Elijah were once unable to see but upon whom they can now gaze. How is this possible? Because the heavenly being who once appeared to them on Mount Sinai has now become a human being. *In Jesus, the God of Mount Sinai now has a human face.*

Peter Responds by Offering to Build Three Tabernacles

Further support for the theophanic character of the transfiguration of Jesus can be found in Peter's offer to build three "dwellings" or "tabernacles" (*skēnas*)—one for Jesus, one for Moses, and one for Elijah (Matt 17:4; Mark 9:4; Luke 9:33). At first glance, the reason for Peter's response is somewhat puzzling. However, it can be plausibly explained when we recall that, in Jewish Scripture, after God appears to Moses on Mount Sinai (Exod 24:1–11), the Israelites respond by building a sanctuary or "tabernacle" for God to dwell in:

> The Lord said to Moses: "Tell the Israelites to take for me an offering. . . . *And have them make me a sanctuary, so that I may dwell among them.* In

193. Propp, *Exodus*, 2:608.

194. Mordechai Cogan, *1 Kings*, Anchor Yale Bible 10A (New Haven: Yale University Press, 2001), 453.

> accordance with all that I show you concerning *the pattern of the tabernacle* and of all its furniture, so you shall make it." (Exod 25:1–2, 8–9)

The portable sanctuary referred to here as the "tabernacle" (Exod 25:9)[195] will later become the principle dwelling place of God on earth and the portable sanctuary, as well as the place where Moses himself goes to speak to God "face to face."[196] Indeed, the rest of the book of Exodus is given over to painstakingly detailed instructions for and descriptions of the construction of the tabernacle (cf. Exod 25–40).

Once this scriptural background is clear, the logic of Peter's response makes more sense: just as the Israelites responded to the appearance of God on Mount Sinai by building a "tabernacle" for the heavenly deity, so too Peter responds to the apocalyptic revelation of Jesus, Moses, and Elijah by offering to build three "tabernacles"—one for each of the heavenly humans standing before him.[197] Clearly, Peter does not grasp the difference between Jesus on the one hand and Moses and Elijah on the other. He seems to place them on par with one another.

The Apocalyptic Secret of Jesus's Divinity

After Peter suggests building the tabernacles, he and the two other disciples see and hear something perhaps even more remarkable. They see a "cloud" come down from heaven and hear "a voice" from the cloud identifying Jesus—and not Moses or Elijah—as his "Son" and commanding the disciples to "listen" to him (Matt 17:5; Mark 9:7; Luke 9:35). After this, Moses, Elijah, and the cloud itself vanish from their sight, and the disciples find themselves alone with Jesus (Matt 17:8; Mark 9:8; Luke 9:36).

Of all the features of the transfiguration, the appearance of the cloud and the hearing of the voice are perhaps the most explicitly apocalyptic and theophanic.[198] As Rudolf Bultmann rightly noted: "The cloud is known to be

195. MT *mishkan*; LXX *skēnē*.

196. See Exod 33:7–11; Deut 31:14–15; Lev 16:2.

197. See Yarbro Collins, *Mark*, 418–19; Davies and Allison, *Matthew*, 2:700: "It is tempting to infer that Peter wanted to build booths because he wanted to recreate the conditions which obtained at Sinai."

198. See Yarbro Collins, *Mark*, 425, who lists 1 Enoch 13:8 (Greek); 65:4; 2 Baruch 13:1; 22:1 as examples of heavenly voices in early Jewish apocalypses. See also Bovon, *Luke*, 1:372.

the traditional form of a theophany."[199] For in Jewish Scripture, the way God visibly and audibly manifests himself to the Israelites during their time at Mount Sinai is by descending from heaven under the appearance of a "dense cloud" and speaking to Moses and the Israelites from the cloud (Exod 19:9). Consider just one example:

> *Then Moses went up on the mountain, and the cloud covered the mountain. The glory of the* Lord *settled on Mount Sinai, and the cloud covered it for six days; on the seventh day he called to Moses out of the cloud.* Now the appearance of the glory of the Lord was like a devouring fire on the top of the mountain in the sight of the people of Israel. Moses entered the cloud, and went up on the mountain. (Exod 24:15–18)

What we have here are descriptions of what would later come to be known as the Shekinah, or "glory cloud."[200] The function of this numinous cloud is to provide a visible and audible sign of God's presence to the people of Israel, one that both reveals and conceals the divine presence. In light of such scriptural background, it seems quite clear that "the cloud" that is seen by the disciples on the mountain of transfiguration is likewise "a theophanic element, signifying the presence of God."[201]

For this reason, it is equally clear that the voice the disciples hear coming from the cloud is the voice of the heavenly Father, who explicitly identifies Jesus as his "Son" (Matt 17:6; Mark 9:7; Luke 9:35). In short, the theophany of the glory cloud on the mountain of transfiguration reveals that Jesus is not just *any* heavenly being; he is *the heavenly Son of God*. In the words of Armand Puig i Tàrrech:

> The cloud and voice are traditional instruments for divine revelation, for the mysterious and glorious presence of God. When Moses received the tablets with the Law on Mount Sinai, a cloud covered the mountains and he went inside it (Exod 24:12, 24:15–18). As with Moses, the disciples were covered by the cloud and received a new revelation directly from God: he revealed Jesus' definitive identity, which could be revealed only in this way. Jesus was his beloved Son. . . . However, the great revelation that the three disciples experienced had to remain a secret, as Jesus' identity in relation to

199. Bultmann, *History of the Synoptic Tradition*, 260.

200. Bovon, *Luke*, 1:378; Propp, *Exodus*, 1:549–50; cf. Isa 4:5; Ezek 10:4; 2 Macc 2:8; Josephus, *Antiquities* 4.326.

201. Yarbro Collins, *Mark*, 425.

> the Father was to be made clear to everyone only once God had freed him from the bonds of death.[202]

Just as the glory cloud appears on Mount Sinai so that the Israelites can hear the voice of God and believe Moses when he speaks to them (Exod 19:9), so now the glory cloud appears on the mountain of transfiguration so that Peter, James, and John can hear the voice of God and believe Jesus when he speaks to them. At this point, only Peter, James, and John are privy to the apocalyptic revelation that Jesus their teacher is both a human being and the heavenly Son of God; they are to tell no one about it until later (cf. Matt 17:9; Mark 9:9). As Adela Yarbo Collins puts it: because "the identity of Jesus is revealed in a special way to three selected disciples," his true identity "is still to some degree a secret."[203] And what is this secret of his identity? That "Jesus was *a divine being walking the earth*."[204]

The Transfiguration and the Divinity of Jesus

In light of such observations, a remarkably wide array of New Testament scholars agree that in the accounts of the transfiguration, Jesus is being depicted as a human being who is also (in some sense) divine. Consider the following conclusions of Jewish, Protestant, Catholic, and nonreligious scholars alike:

> Even in Mark, where the Christology can be seen as low, some aspects of Jesus' divine nature appear. For example . . . the Transfiguration (Mt 17.2; Mk 9.2) . . . hints at Jesus' divine nature.[205]

> The story of Jesus' transfiguration . . . would have indicated that Jesus was a divine being—indeed, a god clothed in human flesh. The metamorphosis of Jesus is an epiphany of a divine being.[206]

> The fact that Jesus took on a radically different aspect as he appeared with bright glistening clothes indicates that he was more than a man, that his definitive identity was divine.[207]

202. Puig i Tàrrech, *Jesus: A Biography*, 461.
203. Yarbro Collins, *Mark*, 426.
204. Yarbro Collins, *Mark*, 426 (emphasis added).
205. Randi Rashkover, "Christology," 754.
206. Litwa, *Iesus Deus*, 112, 113.
207. Puig i Tàrrech, *Jesus: A Biography*, 460.

> The narrator's statement that "he was transfigured . . ." [suggests] that Jesus walked the earth as a divine being, whose true nature is momentarily revealed in the transfiguration.[208]

> Jesus is not taking on an alien nature provisionally, but rather uncovering his true identity. . . . Jesus belongs to the divine realm.[209]

> The transfiguration on the mountain . . . [describes] the revelation of a superhuman being.[210]

> Jesus is a divine being come down from heaven who on earth has assumed human form and once before a small circle of intimate disciples reveals his original divinity through his transformation.[211]

These are not the words of Christian apologists defending the divinity of Jesus; they are the exegetical conclusions of a wide array of Gospel experts. And this is only a sampling; similar statements could be multiplied.[212] For our purposes here, these conclusions demonstrate once again that *the widespread notion that Jesus is merely human in the Synoptic Gospels is simply wrong*. Among other things, it does not take seriously the evidence of the accounts of his transfiguration on the mountain, in which he clearly appears as a heavenly being who is also human.

Arguments against Historical Plausibility

With these exegetical conclusions in mind, we can now ask: What are the major arguments for and against the historicity of the accounts of the transfiguration of Jesus?

As with the other epiphany miracles we have covered in this chapter, most major works on the historical Jesus imply a negative historical verdict by sim-

208. Yarbro Collins, *Mark*, 421.

209. Bovon, *Luke*, 1:372, 373, 375.

210. Theissen and Merz, *Historical Jesus*, 296–97.

211. Ernst Lohmeyer, "Die Verklärung Jesu nach dem Markus-Evangelium," *Zeitschrift für die Neutestamentliche Wissenschaft* 21 (1922): 185–215 (here 203). Translation in Litwa, *Iesus Deus*, 116.

212. See also Bird, *The Eternal Son*, 96–97; Lüdemann, *Jesus after Two Thousand Years*, 61; Davies and Allison, *Matthew*, 2:699.

ply ignoring this episode.[213] Others mention the transfiguration in passing, but they give no discussion of its historicity, and it plays no role in their overall reconstructions.[214] Finally, still others explicitly deny the historicity of the episode.[215] The principal reasons for arriving at a negative verdict are several.

The primary argument against historicity is once again based on the philosophical assumption that patently supernatural events like the transfiguration of Jesus are impossible. For example, well over a century ago, David Friedrich Strauss wrote: "The text forbids a natural interpretation, . . . [and] it is impossible to maintain as historical the supernatural interpretation which it sanctions. . . . I do not, it is true, see in the evangelical narrative any real event."[216] More recent versions of this argument are somewhat more nuanced: though the possibility of miracles taking place is not necessarily denied, the presence of the miraculous element *does* mean that the evidence cannot be included in a historical reconstruction of the life of Jesus. For example, James Dunn states that the question of whether any "historical reminiscence" lies behind the transfiguration accounts can be "posed" but not "answered with any confidence." [217] In the end, it is "more likely" that later perceptions about Jesus "gave rise to the story," rather than "vice versa."[218]

The second popular argument against the historicity of the transfiguration accounts is more of a literary observation. According to this view, because the gospel accounts contain such strong parallels with the accounts of Moses in the Jewish Scriptures, it follows that they must have been created by the early church on the basis of the Scriptures. Consider, once again, the words of David

213. For example, the accounts of the transfiguration are never discussed in Ehrman, *How Jesus Became God*; Lohfink, *Jesus of Nazareth*; Grindheim, *God's Equal*; Bauckham, *Jesus: A Very Short Introduction*; Allison, *Constructing Jesus*; Keener, *Historical Jesus of the Gospels*; Bock and Webb, *Key Events*; Becker, *Jesus of Nazareth*; Vermes, *Religion of Jesus the Jew*; Witherington, *Christology of Jesus*; Jeremias, *New Testament Theology*.

214. See Hengel and Schwemer, *Jesus and Judaism*, 337; Schröter, *Jesus of Nazareth*, 213; Vermes, *Authentic Gospel of Jesus*, 282; Sanders, *Historical Figure of Jesus*, 245; Gnilka, *Jesus of Nazareth*, 133, 249; Meier, *A Marginal Jew*, 2:342, 900; Sanders, *Jesus and Judaism*, 328.

215. See Günther Bornkamm, *Jesus of Nazareth*, trans. Irene McLuskey and Fraser McLuskey, with James M. Robinson (New York: Harper, 1960), 171, 173; Bultmann, *History of the Synoptic Tradition*, 259, 261. Casey (*Jesus of Nazareth*, 382, 457) describes "the historicity" of "the Transfiguration" as "doubtful" in one place, but elsewhere seems to entertain its possible historicity (p. 489).

216. Strauss, *Jesus of Nazareth*, 541, 545, 546.

217. Dunn, *Jesus Remembered*, 666.

218. Dunn, *Jesus Remembered*, 666, following Barbara E. Reid, *The Transfiguration: A Source- and Redaction-Critical Study of Luke 9:28–36* (Paris: Gabalda, 1993), 147.

Friedrich Strauss: "[There was] in the early church a tendency to introduce into the life of Jesus an imitation of . . . the life of Moses. . . . *We have here a mythus*, the tendency of which is . . . to exhibit in the life of Jesus an enhanced repetition of the glorification of Moses."[219] According to this view, the fact that Jesus acts like Moses by going up a mountain to pray, bringing three chosen disciples with him, and experiencing the appearance of a heavenly cloud can only be explained in one way: the evangelists have created the accounts of the transfiguration out of whole cloth (cf. Exod 24:1–2, 9–11, 15–18). As W. D. Davies and Dale Allison put the point: "How can a factual episode exhibit so many similarities to an event in the life of Moses?"[220]

The third major argument against the historicity of the transfiguration revolves its ostensible links with the resurrection of Jesus. According to this view, the parallels with appearances of the risen Jesus suggest that the accounts of the transfiguration must have originally been accounts of the resurrection. Likewise, Jesus's command to the disciples to keep quiet until after the resurrection suggests that the episode did not take place during the public ministry of Jesus. As Gerd Lüdemann, Gerd Theissen, and Annette Merz state:

> Because of the inventory, namely the motif of light and the mountain, the tradition can with good reason be designated an Easter story. . . . Since the tradition is an original Easter story, its historicity is *a priori* ruled out.[221]

> The commandment to keep silent after the Transfiguration until Jesus has risen from the dead shows . . . this Easter character of the story.[222]

Here Lüdemann appears to be under the influence of Rudolf Bultmann, who deemed the transfiguration account a "legend" about Jesus that was "originally a resurrection story."[223] According to this position, the fact that the transfiguration takes place on a mountain, like one of the resurrection appearances (Matt 28:16), and Jesus is wearing luminous garments, like the later angels at the tomb (Matt 28:3; Mark 16:5; Luke 24:4), can mean only one thing: the account is an early Christian "invention" that "originated as a story of an appear-

219. Strauss, *Life of Jesus*, 544, 545 (emphasis added).

220. Davies and Allison, *Matthew*, 2:689.

221. Lüdemann, *Jesus after Two Thousand Years*, 61.

222. Theissen and Merz, *Historical Jesus*, 304.

223. Bultmann, *History of the Synoptic Tradition*, 259, 261. We will leave to one side Bultmann's suggestion that "the disciples' sleep perhaps goes back to the fairy-tale motif of magic sleep."

ance of the risen Jesus."[224] Along similar lines, Jesus's command to keep silence "so obviously presupposes the experience of Good Friday and Easter" that "it is impossible to treat it forthwith as a teaching of the historical Jesus."[225]

Context: Sign Prophets, the Appearance of Moses and Elijah, and Tabernacles

If we bracket the philosophical question about the possibility of supernatural phenomena and simply apply the triple-context approach to the transfiguration accounts, a somewhat different picture emerges.

For one thing, in a first-century Jewish context, it is quite credible that an apocalyptic prophet like Jesus would recapitulate the actions of Moses by taking his disciples to a special place in order to experience a miraculous theophany. That is, after all, precisely what was done by two other first-century prophets: Theudas (active in the mid-40s CE) and "the Egyptian" (active in the mid-50s CE). Consider Josephus's description of these two figures:

> During the period when Fadus was procurator of Judaea, a certain impostor named Theudas persuaded the majority of the masses to take up their possessions and to follow him to the Jordan River. He stated that he was a prophet and that at his command the river would be parted and would provide them an easy passage. (Josephus, *Antiquities* 20.97)

> At this time there came to Jerusalem from Egypt a man who declared that he was a prophet and advised the masses of the common people to go out with him to the mountain called the Mount of Olives, which lies opposite the city at a distance of five furlongs. For he asserted that he wished to demonstrate from there that at his command Jerusalem's walls would fall down, through which he promised to provide them entry into the city. (Josephus, *Antiquities* 20.169–170)

The historical upshot of these parallels should be obvious. If the first-century prophet Theudas could take his followers to the Jordan River to experience a miracle like that of Moses and Joshua (cf. Exod 14; Josh 4–5), and the first-century Egyptian prophet could take his followers up the scripturally charged

224. Funk and the Jesus Seminar, *Acts of Jesus*, 166.
225. Bornkamm, *Jesus of Nazareth*, 171.

Mount of Olives to experience a miracle like the biblical figures of Joshua and the Israelites (cf. Josh 6), then it is completely plausible that a first-century prophet like Jesus could take three of his followers up to the top of a mountain in Galilee in order to experience a theophany like that of Moses and the Israelites at Mount Sinai (cf. Exod 24–25). In this regard, it is important to underscore that the mere presence of literary parallels between Theudas and the Egyptians' actions and the scriptural accounts of Moses crossing the Red Sea, Joshua crossing the Jordan river, or the miraculous siege of Jericho do not mean Josephus constructed fictional accounts on the basis of the Jewish Scriptures. Instead, *these Jewish prophets deliberately modeled their actions on well-known figures from Jewish Scripture.* They did this precisely in order to reveal that they saw themselves as (somehow) fulfilling or recapitulating the Scriptures in their own actions.[226]

Moreover, in a first-century Jewish context, it is also quite plausible that the experience of a heavenly vision on a mountaintop by Jesus and his disciples would involve the figures of Moses and Elijah, since both men were believed in Second Temple Judaism to possess bodily immortality.[227] In Jewish Scripture, Moses is explicitly said to have died and been buried (Deut 34:5–6), while Elijah is said to have been taken up into heaven in a chariot of fire (2 Kgs 2:11). By the first century, however, the belief had spread that both Elijah and Moses had been assumed into heaven and that they were now alive with God.[228] Once again, it is Josephus who gives testimony to this effect:

> When [Moses] arrived on the mountain called Abaris—a lofty eminence . . . affording to those on its summit a wide view beneath of the best of the land of the Canaanites—he dismissed the elders. And, while [Moses] bid farewell to Eleazar and Joshua and was yet communing with them, a cloud of a sudden descended upon him and he disappeared in a ravine. (Josephus, *Antiquities* 4.325–326)

> Now about that time Elijah disappeared from among men, and to this day no one knows his end. (Josephus, *Antiquities* 9.28)

226. See Rebecca Gray, *Prophetic Figures in Late Second Temple Jewish Palestine: The Evidence from Josephus* (Oxford: Oxford University Press, 1993), 112–43; and Craig A. Evans, *Jesus and His Contemporaries: Comparative Studies* (Leiden: Brill, 1995), 74–76.

227. Cf. Schröter, *Jesus of Nazareth*, 212; and Lüdemann, *Jesus after Two Thousand Years*, 61.

228. See Daniel K. Falk, "Moses," in Collins and Harlow, *Eerdmans Dictionary of Early Judaism*, 967–70; and Christine E. Joynes, "Elijah," in Collins and Harlow, *Eerdmans Dictionary of Early Judaism*, 577–78.

In light of such parallels, the description of Jesus and his three disciples experiencing the appearance of Moses and Elijah in particular—out of all the many figures in Jewish Scripture—makes perfect sense in a Second Temple Jewish context.

Even Peter's otherwise puzzling offer of making three tabernacles for Jesus, Moses, and Elijah is contextually plausible in a Jewish setting. After all, several key figures in Jewish Scripture respond to heavenly theophanies by building a sanctuary of some sort. To take just two examples: after Jacob has a vision of "the LORD" standing above the ladder upon which the angels are ascending and descending, he consecrates a stone and names the place "Bethel," meaning "House of God" (Gen 28:10–18). Along similar lines, after king David has a vision of the destroying angel at the threshing floor of Araunah, he consecrates the place by building "an altar to the LORD" and offering sacrifices to God to avert the plague (2 Sam 24:15–25). Indeed, as the book of Chronicles makes explicit, it is on this very site of the apparition to David that the temple of Jerusalem will later be built (1 Chron 21:14–22:1). Now, if a first-century Galilean Jew like Simon Peter experienced what he believed to be a vision of heavenly beings—especially one in which Jesus appears dressed like the heavenly Ancient of Days—it is eminently plausible that he would respond by suggesting some kind of sanctuaries or tabernacles be built in response.

Coherence: The Three Disciples, the New Moses, and the Secret of Jesus's Sonship

The second major argument for the historicity of the transfiguration accounts can be made from multiple points of coherence with other evidence about Jesus. For one thing, Jesus's act of choosing Peter, James, and John to accompany him to the top of the mountain and experience the transfiguration coheres perfectly with other evidence that Jesus chose these three disciples to accompany him during key private moments of his public ministry, such as the raising of Jairus's daughter (Mark 5:37; Luke 8:51) and his agony and prayers in Gethsemane on the Mount of Olives (Matt 26:37, 41; Mark 14:33, 37–38).[229] This act of choosing Peter, James, and John is particularly striking when we recall that other evidence exists that suggests Jesus saw himself as a new Moses and deliberately arranged the circles of his disciples according to

229. Puig i Tàrrech, *Jesus: A Biography*, 263.

the priestly hierarchy of Moses and the Israelites at Mount Sinai.[230] Consider the following parallels:

Moses and the Priestly Hierarchy	*Jesus and His Disciples*
Moses	Jesus
The 1: the high priest Aaron	The 1: Peter, head of the apostles[231]
The 3: Aaron, Nadab, Abihu	The 3: Peter, James, and John[232]
The 12: Twelve pillars / "young men" of the twelve tribes	The 12: Twelve apostles of the twelve tribes[233]
The 70: Priestly elders of Israel[234]	The 70: Appointed and sent out[235]

In light of such parallels, there is really no compelling reason to doubt that if Jesus saw himself as a new Moses, he could easily have partially reenacted the theophany at Mount Sinai by choosing to bring a select group with him up the mountain of transfiguration. This is especially plausible if Jesus and his disciples were *apocalyptic* Jews who on occasion had visionary experiences, such as when Jesus claimed to have "watched Satan fall from heaven like a flash of lightning" (Luke 10:18).[236]

Last, but certainly not least, the claim that Peter, James, and John did not speak about what they had seen in their vision of Jesus's heavenly identity during Jesus's public ministry coheres perfectly with the other evidence that Jesus treated his heavenly sonship as a kind of apocalyptic "secret" during his public ministry:

> All things have been handed over to me by my Father; and *no one knows the Son except the Father*, and no one knows the Father except the Son and *anyone to whom the Son chooses to reveal him.* (Matt 11:27)

230. See Brant Pitre, *Jesus and the Last Supper* (Grand Rapids: Eerdmans, 2015), 139–41.

231. Matt 10:2; 16:17–19; Mark 1:36; 3:16; 16:7; Luke 6:14; 9:32; 12:41; 22:31–32; John 1:42; 6:66–69.

232. Mark 3:16–17; 9:2–8; 14:32–42.

233. See Matt 10:1–2; 19:28; Mark 3:13–15; Luke 9:1; 22:30; John 6:67.

234. See Exod 24:1–11.

235. Luke 10:1–20.

236. Hengel and Schwemer, *Jesus and Judaism*, 337; Casey, *Jesus of Nazareth*, 489.

> All things have been handed over to me by my Father; and *no one knows who the Son is except the Father*, or who the Father is except the Son and *anyone to whom the Son chooses to reveal him*. (Luke 10:22)

We will look at this saying in more detail in chapter 4. For now, the main point is that just as Jesus declares the identity of "the Son" hidden from everyone except "the Father" (Matt 11:27; Luke 10:22), so too on the mountain of transfiguration the Father reveals the identity of his "Son" to Peter, James, and John in an apocalyptic revelation (Matt 17:5; Mark 9:7; Luke 9:35). And just as Jesus says that the identity of the Father is only "revealed" (*apokalyptō*) to those "whom the Son chooses" (Matt 11:27; Luke 10:22), so too the voice of the Father on the mountaintop is only heard by the three disciples chosen by Jesus to accompany him: Peter, James, and John (Matt 17:1; Mark 9:2; Luke 9:28).

Consequences: The Three "Pillars" as Witnesses to the Transfiguration

Last, an argument for the historicity of the transfiguration accounts can also be made from the aftermath of Jesus's life in the early church. After all, if Jesus did indeed choose Peter, James, and John to accompany him to the top of the mountain and experience an apocalyptic vision of his divinity and his identity as Son, this would provide a compelling explanation for the remarkable prominence of these three members of the twelve in the early Jerusalem church.[237] Consider, for example, the apostle Paul's testimony that these three disciples in particular were acknowledged as "pillars" of the church:

> *When James and Cephas and John, who were acknowledged pillars*, recognized the grace that had been given to me, they gave to Barnabas and me the right hand of fellowship, agreeing that we should go to the Gentiles and they to the circumcised. (Gal 2:9)

It is not exactly clear why Peter, James, and John as described as "pillars" (*styloi*), though some connection with the apocalyptic expectation of an "eschatological temple" seems likely.[238] For our purposes here, what matters is that Paul is striving to put some distance between himself and the Jerusalem

237. Puig i Tàrrech, *Jesus: A Biography*, 263.
238. J. Louis Martyn, *Galatians*, Anchor Bible 33A (New York: Doubleday, 1997), 205.

leaders and to establish his own apostolic credentials (cf. Gal 1:18–20, 2:6–7); nevertheless, he is forced to admit that he sought the fellowship of these three apostles while he was in Jerusalem. One plausible historical explanation for the prominence of Peter, James, and John in the early Jerusalem church is that Jesus himself had already singled them out among the twelve during his public ministry.

In addition, if Peter, James, and John did in fact experience a vision of Jesus transfigured on the mountaintop, then this would provide an explanation for why the apostle Peter is described as having written a letter in which he claims to have been an "eyewitness" to the "majesty" of Jesus and to have heard the heavenly Father identify Jesus as his "Son."[239] Consider the following:

> For we did not follow cleverly devised myths when we made known to you the power and coming of our Lord Jesus Christ, but *we had been eyewitnesses of his majesty*. For he received honor and glory from God the Father when that voice was conveyed to him by the Majestic Glory, saying, "This is my Son, my Beloved, with whom I am well pleased." *We ourselves heard this voice come from heaven, while we were with him on the holy mountain.* (2 Pet 1:16–17)

As is well known, the authorship of the two Petrine epistles is debated, with most contemporary scholars arguing against the Petrine authorship of 2 Peter.[240] For our purposes here, apart from the issue of authorship, the letter nevertheless provides explicit early Christian evidence that Peter was believed to have seen the transfiguration of Jesus with his own eyes and heard the voice identifying him as the heavenly Son of God with his own ears. How does one explain the origin of this early Christian belief? One plausible explanation is that the reason Peter, James, and John were believed by some in the early church to have witnessed the transfiguration of Jesus on the mountain is because that is what happened.

239. Cf. Strauss, *Jesus of Nazareth*, 541.

240. For arguments against Petrine authorship, see Jörg Frey, *The Letter of Jude and the Second Letter of Peter: A Theological Commentary*, trans. Kathleen Ess (Waco, TX: Baylor University Press, 2018), 213–20; Bart D. Ehrman, *Forgery and Counterforgery: The Use of Literary Deceit in Early Christian Polemics* (Oxford: Oxford University Press, 2013), 222–29. For arguments in favor of Petrine authorship, see Gene L. Green, *Jude and 2 Peter*, Baker Exegetical Commentary on the New Testament (Grand Rapids: Baker Academic, 2008), 139–50.

Weighing the Arguments for and against Historicity

Once more, we need to step back from the particular reasons that have been advanced for or against the historicity of the accounts of Jesus's transfiguration on the mountain and evaluate which set of arguments is more cogent and compelling.

It should come as no surprise at this point in our investigation that the decisive consideration for many is the philosophical supposition that supernatural events simply do not take place. Once this supposition is taken off the table of historical reconstruction (as it should be), the remaining arguments against historicity are shockingly weak. For example, the claim that there are too many parallels between the actions of Jesus and the life of Moses for the episode to be historical completely fails to reckon with the fact that other first-century Jewish figures like Theudas and the Egyptian not only modelled their action on figures from Jewish Scripture but also expected supernatural events to take place when they did so (Josephus, *Antiquities* 20.97, 169–170). Likewise, the argument that the parallels between the accounts of the transfiguration and later appearances of the risen Jesus mean that they must have originated in the post-Easter period is a total non sequitur. Apart from positive evidence situating the transfiguration in the post-Easter period (of which there is none), such a claim is pure speculation. Finally, the contention that the transfiguration accounts must have been fabricated by the early church because the disciples are told to say nothing until after the resurrection fails to reckon with evidence that Jesus, as an apocalyptic prophet, gave certain teachings to his disciples that were not (at least initially) given to the general public (cf. Matt 13:10–13; Mark 4:10–12; Luke 8:9–10).[241]

By contrast, the positive arguments from contextual plausibility, coherence with other evidence about Jesus, and consequences in the early church are remarkably strong. As we've already noted, given the fact that Theudas and the Egyptian modeled their actions on those of Moses and Joshua, it is completely plausible that Jesus would imitate Moses by taking Peter, James, and John with him to the top of a mountain to experience an apocalyptic revelation (cf. Exod 24:1–11). Indeed, if the historical Jesus never experienced the kind of revelation described in the accounts of the transfiguration, he would present us with the rather odd case of a Jewish apocalyptic prophet who did not actually experience

241. On this point, Ben F. Meyer, *The Aims of Jesus* (London: SCM, 1979), 202–19, remains instructive.

any apocalyptic visions![242] Moreover, Jesus's selection of these three disciples also coheres perfectly with other evidence that Jesus chose Peter, James, and John to be the privileged witnesses to certain other actions of Jesus (Matt 26:37, 41; Mark 5:37; 14:33–38; Luke 8:51). Even the requirement that the disciples tell no one about Jesus's identity as "Son" of God is congruent with the evidence that Jesus declared that his identity as the unique "Son" of the Father is something that would be "hidden" from some but "revealed" to others (Matt 11:25–27; Luke 10:21–22). Last, the account of Jesus taking Peter, James, and John with him to experience this particular revelation provides a very plausible point of origin for their later identification as "pillars" in the early church (cf. Gal 2:9).

In light of such observations, it seems clear to me the arguments in favor of the historicity of the transfiguration are much stronger than those against it. In this regard, it is perhaps worth noting that two of the most prominent Jewish scholars of the historical Jesus in the twentieth century—Joseph Klausner and David Flusser—both regarded the accounts of the "vision" of Jesus's transfiguration as "authentic."[243] If they are correct, the implications are momentous. For this would mean that, at some point during his public ministry, Jesus of Nazareth took Peter, James, and John with him to the top of a mountain to reveal to them "that he was more than a man, that his definitive identity was divine."[244]

The Epiphany Miracles and the Divinity of Jesus

Where then do we find ourselves at the end of this survey of the stilling of the storm, the walking on the sea, and the transfiguration? Perhaps it will be helpful to bring our chapter to a close with the programmatic statement of Bart Ehrman, who has this to say about the implication of Jesus's miracles in his study of the origins of divine Christology:

> Whatever you think about the philosophical possibility of miracles, it's clear that Jesus was widely reputed to have done them. . . . *Interestingly enough, these activities were not taken in our earliest sources to be signs that Jesus himself was God.* They were the sorts of things Jewish prophets did. Jesus simply did them better than anyone else.[245]

242. See chapter 4 for a fuller discussion of Jesus as an apocalyptic prophet.
243. Flusser with Notley, *Sage from Galilee*, 103; cf. Klausner, *Jesus of Nazareth*, 303.
244. Puig i Tàrrech, *Jesus: A Biography*, 460; cf. 360–61.
245. Ehrman, *Jesus: Apocalyptic Prophet*, 199 (emphasis added).

As I think I have shown in some detail, when it comes to the epiphanic miracles of Jesus, Ehrman is simply wrong. Although not *all* of Jesus's miracles were taken as signs of his divinity, in context, the epiphany miracles certainly *were* taken as signs that he was more than merely human.

Indeed, in all three cases, it is precisely when we interpret the gospel accounts in their first-century Jewish context that we discover Jesus speaking and acting as if he is a divine being: the heavenly Son of God, who is equal with the one God of Israel who appeared on Mount Sinai. In the stilling of the storm, Jesus demonstrates the divine power of the Creator when he commands the wind and the waves, something which Jewish Scripture says God alone possesses. When Jesus walks on the sea and identifies himself with the divine self-designation "I am," he is also doing something that Jewish Scripture says only God can do—walk on the sea. Finally, in the transfiguration on the mountain, not only do the disciples see Jesus's appearance changed into that of a heavenly being come down to earth, but the reason Moses and Elijah appear is because they were the two great figures who experienced theophanies on Mount Sinai but were not able to see the face of God. In the transfiguration of Jesus, however, the one God who appeared to Moses and Elijah on Mount Sinai now has a human face. In sum, *a close study of the epiphany miracles demolishes the modern myth that Jesus only speaks and acts as if he is divine in the Fourth Gospel.* As these three episodes demonstrate, even just on the narrative level, *Jesus is depicted as divine in all four first-century gospels—the Synoptics included.*

Of course, I realize that, due to philosophical commitments, many readers may not be able to accept the historical plausibility of any of the epiphanic miracles attributed to Jesus. For this reason, in the next chapter, we will look at three "riddles" of Jesus's divinity that are almost universally accepted as historical.

CHAPTER 3

The Riddles of Jesus's Divinity

> An important source for Jesus' understanding of himself is also his *parables*.
>
> —Michael Wolter[1]

> Jesus used riddles both to establish his authority as a teacher and to communicate his message.
>
> —Tom Thatcher[2]

The Teacher of Parables

If there is anything about which historical Jesus scholars of the widest possible array of perspectives agree, it is that Jesus of Nazareth taught in parables.[3] Indeed, even scholars who are often quite reserved in what historical claims

1. Michael Wolter, "Jesus's Understanding of Himself," in *The Jesus Handbook*, ed. Jens Schröter and Christine Jacobi, trans. Robert L. Brawley (Grand Rapids: Eerdmans, 2022), 422–29 (here 424).

2. Tom Thatcher, *Jesus the Riddler: The Power of Ambiguity in the Gospels* (Louisville: Westminster John Knox, 2006), xi.

3. The secondary literature on the parables of Jesus is, to put it lightly, enormous. For a representative sampling with bibliography, see Gerhard Lohfink, *The Forty Parables of Jesus*, trans. Linda M. Maloney (Collegeville: Liturgical Press, 2021); Klyne R. Snodgrass, *Stories with Intent: A Comprehensive Guide to the Parables of Jesus*, 2nd ed. (Grand Rapids: Eerdmans, 2018); John P. Meier, *A Marginal Jew: Rethinking the Historical Jesus*, 5 vols., Anchor Yale Bible Reference Library (New Haven: Yale University Press, 1991–2016); Levine, *Short Stories by Jesus*; Arland J. Hultgren, "The Message of Jesus II: Parables," in *Handbook for the Study of the Historical Jesus*, 4 vols., ed. Tom Holmén and Stanley E. Porter (Leiden: Brill, 2011), 3:2549–71; Michael Wolter, "Jesus as a Teller of Parables: On Jesus' Self-Interpretation in His Parables," in *Jesus Research: An International Perspective, The First Princeton-Prague Symposium on Jesus Research*, ed. James H. Charlesworth and Petr Pokorny (Grand Rapids: Eerdmans, 2009), 123–39; Geza Vermes, *The Authentic Gospel of Jesus* (London: Penguin, 2003), 114–72; Arland J. Hultgren, *The Parables of Jesus: A Commentary* (Grand Rapids: Eerdmans, 2000).

they are willing to make about Jesus of Nazareth are remarkably categorical in their claims that the historical Jesus taught using parables. Consider, for example, the following quotations from major contributors to the contemporary quest:

> There are . . . very good reasons for thinking that Jesus taught in parables.[4]

> Scholars of various ideologies and faith commitments (or lack thereof) have been united in one unshakable article of faith: the parables provide the most secure way, the royal road, the easiest and most reliable access to the historical Jesus.[5]

> Jesus was . . . the greatest Jewish artist in parables, though not the inventor of this form.[6]

> It is beyond dispute that Jesus told many parables.[7]

Such quotations could easily be multiplied.[8] Indeed, it is not uncommon to find experts describing the parables as "the surest bedrock we have of Jesus's teaching" and declaring that there is virtually no "parallel to the remarkable art of his parables."[9]

Jesus and Jewish Riddles

With that said, it is crucial to emphasize that in Jesus's first-century Jewish context, the word "parable" (Hebrew *mashal*; Greek *parabolē*) was not

4. Amy-Jill Levine, *Short Stories by Jesus: The Enigmatic Parables of a Controversial Rabbi* (San Francisco: HarperOne, 2014), 13.

5. Meier, *A Marginal Jew*, 5:48, 49.

6. Vermes, *Authentic Gospel of Jesus*, 114.

7. James D. G. Dunn, *Jesus Remembered*, vol. 1 of *Christianity in the Making* (Grand Rapids: Eerdmans, 2003), 698.

8. See Hultgren, "Message of Jesus II," 2549; Joachim Jeremias, *The Parables of Jesus*, 2nd rev. ed. (Upper Saddle River, NJ: Prentice Hall, 1972), 11–12; C. H. Dodd, *The Parables of the Kingdom*, rev. ed. (New York: Charles Scribner's Sons, 1961), 13; Adolf Jülicher, *Die Gleichnisreden Jesu*, 2nd ed., 2 vols. (Tübingen: J. C. B. Mohr [Paul Siebeck], 1899), 1:11.

9. Snodgrass, *Stories with Intent*, 31; Joseph Klausner, *Jesus of Nazareth: His Life, Times, and Teaching* (New York: Macmillan, 1926), 414.

only used to refer to the kind of intriguing stories Jesus is so well-known for telling—what scholars nowadays refer to as "narrative parables." In early Judaism, the word "parable" was *also* used to refer a wide range of thought-provoking sayings, from brief maxims to puzzling questions, including *riddles*. Consider the statements of Geza Vermes and James Dunn:

> Known as *mashal* in Hebrew, the parable is a well-established literary category both in the Bible and in rabbinic writings. *Mashal* has a broader meaning in the Old Testament than in the Gospels, and covers all things sapiential from a brief maxim in the strict sense (the biblical book of Proverbs is called *Meshalim*, the plural of *mashal*) to a riddle or fable.[10]

> Jesus would need no telling that the word he most probably used, *mašal*, had a range of meaning. Typically it denoted proverbial wisdom, as in ben Sira. *But in wider usage it often referred to an obscure or puzzling saying*. . . . If Jesus referred to his teaching (in whole or in part) as *m^eshalim*, then double entendre lay close to hand. He could hardly have been unaware that his teaching, while bringing light to some, came across to others as obscure and puzzling.[11]

Though this broader meaning of the word "parable" is widely agreed upon among scholars, it is less well known in popular parlance.[12] One reason for this is likely because even the most comprehensive studies of the parables of Jesus invariably focus exclusively on the narrative *meshalim* and ignore Jesus's *other* parables—that is, his riddles and puzzling sayings.[13]

However, when we speak about Jesus as a teacher of parables, this does not mean that he only used narrative parables. It also means that Jesus was known for utilizing *meshalim* that took the form of riddles, puzzling sayings, and/or questions that were deliberately intended to be both ambiguous and thought-provoking. Consider, for example, the following sayings attributed to Jesus in the Gospels, all of which are explicitly identified as "parables" (*parabolai*):

10. Vermes, *Authentic Gospel of Jesus*, 114.

11. Dunn, *Jesus Remembered*, 494 (emphasis added).

12. See Hultgren, *Parables of Jesus*, 5.

13. For example, Snodgrass, *Stories with Intent*; Levine, *Short-Stories by Jesus*; Meier, *A Marginal Jew*. All focus exclusively on the narrative parables of Jesus.

Riddle-Like Parables of Jesus

1. The "parable" of the divided kingdom and the strong man (Matt 12:25–29; Mark 3:23–27; Luke 11:17–22)
2. The "parable" of the fig tree (Matt 24:32–35; Mark 13:28–31; Luke 21:29–33)
3. The "parable" of what defiles a person (Matt 15:10–20; Mark 7:14–23)
4. The "parable" of the new garments and new wineskins (Luke 5:36–38; cf. Matt 9:16–17; Mark 2:21–22).
5. The "parable" of the blind leading the blind (Luke 6:39)
6. The "parable" of the householder and the thief (Luke 12:39–41)

Notice here that none of these *parabolai* is a story or narrative. Nor do any of them draw a comparison with the kingdom of God. Instead, they are all *riddles* that deal with the question of the identity of Jesus, eschatology, ritual and moral purity, and the relationship between the present age and the age to come.

Jesus Used Riddles to Reveal (and Conceal) His Identity

In this chapter, I will argue that there are good reasons to believe that Jesus not only used these riddle-like parables to both reveal and conceal the mystery of the kingdom of God; he also used them to reveal and conceal the mystery of his *divinity*. As Michael Wolter has argued, the parables of Jesus are "crucial for Jesus' self-interpretation" precisely because they manifest a "distinctive implicit Christology."[14] Wolter makes this claim about the narrative parables; I will suggest that the same is true for three of Jesus's more riddle-like *meshalim*:

1. More than father or mother (Matt 10:37–39; Luke 14:25–27)
2. No one is good but God (Matt 19:16–22; Mark 10:17–22; Luke 18:18–23)
3. The riddle of David's "Lord" (Matt 22:41–46; Mark 12:35–37; Luke 20:41–43)

As we will see, each of these sayings is widely recognized as posing a riddle-like question or puzzle. In each of them, Jesus uses the deliberate ambiguity so common to parables to provoke his audience to ask: Who exactly is Jesus claiming to be? And what is he implying about the identity of the messiah?

14. Wolter, "Jesus as a Teller of Parables," 139.

Moreover, I will also argue that in each case, the full force of what the riddle reveals about who Jesus is claiming himself and/or the messiah to be can only be felt when due attention is given to *the Jewish Scriptures* to which each riddle alludes. As the contemporary Jewish scholar Amy-Jill Levine writes in her important study of Jesus's parables:

> In listening to parables and appreciating them within their initial context, we also do well to listen for echoes of Israel's scriptures, since the parables evoke earlier stories and then comment on them.[15]

Sure enough, each of the parables we will examine in this chapter alludes to Jewish Scripture: (1) the riddle about loving Jesus "more than father or mother" echoes the command in the Decalogue (cf. Exod 20:14); (2) the declaration that "no one is good except the one God" harks back to the Shema (cf. Deut 6:4–6); and (3) the question about David's "son" and David's "Lord" alludes to both the Prophets and the Psalms (cf. 2 Sam 7; Ps 110:1–4). As I will argue, when these three riddles are interpreted in the light of Jewish Scripture, each of them will lead to the conclusion that Jesus sees both himself and the Jewish messiah as more than merely human. In order to see all this clearly, however, we need to turn our attention to the riddles themselves.

Greater than Father or Mother

The first riddle-like parable of Jesus in which he implies that he is more than merely human is his shocking demand that, in order to be one of his disciples, his followers must love him more than they love their own fathers and mothers:

> *Whoever loves father or mother more than me is not worthy of me*; and whoever loves son or daughter more than me is not worthy of me. (Matt 10:37)
>
> Now large crowds were traveling with him; and he turned and said to them, "*Whoever comes to me and does not hate father and mother*, wife and children, brothers and sisters, yes, and even life itself, *cannot be my disciple*." (Luke 14:25–27)

15. Levine, *Short Stories by Jesus*, 9.

Despite the curious proclivity of some interpreters to shift the emphasis of this parable away from the person of Jesus, in point of fact, Jesus says absolutely *nothing* about "the coming Kingdom,"[16] or "the Kingdom of God,"[17] or "God's imperial rule."[18] Instead, the entire focus of the saying is on Jesus's disciples' relationship to *himself.* It is also helpful to note right from the start that these passages provide us an excellent example of the problem of trying to reconstruct the exact words of Jesus (the so-called *ipsissima verba Jesu*), rather than focusing on the substance of Jesus's teachings (the *substantia verborum Jesu*).[19] Although many scholars suggest that in this case the Gospel of Luke has preserved the "more original" form of Jesus's words, I for one see no way to know this for certain.[20] Indeed, in the case of a short aphorism such as this, it is entirely possible that Jesus made the same basic demand of his disciples in more than one form and on different occasions.

Hence, for our purposes here, we will follow our standard procedure and focus on the basic substance of the saying, which can be summed up in this case by one basic point: whoever loves his or her parents or family *more than Jesus* is not worthy to be his disciple. In order to see this basic meaning clearly, we will need to take a few moments to interpret both forms of Jesus's logion in his first-century Jewish context.

Jesus Demands to Be Loved above Father and Mother

Despite their differences, in both versions of the saying, Jesus is demanding that anyone who wishes to be one of his followers must love Jesus more than his or her father, mother, or other immediate family.

This focus on loving Jesus is explicit in Matthew's version of the logion and implicit in Luke's version. For in Jewish Scripture, the verb *to hate* can be used

16. Bart D. Ehrman, *Jesus: Apocalyptic Prophet of the New Millennium* (Oxford: Oxford University Press, 1999), 170.

17. Jürgen Becker, *Jesus of Nazareth*, trans. James E. Crouch (New York: Walter de Gruyter, 1998), 310.

18. Robert W. Funk, Roy Hoover, and the Jesus Seminar, *The Five Gospels: The Search for the Authentic Words of Jesus* (New York: Macmillan, 1993), 353.

19. See chapter 1 for discussion.

20. So Craig S. Keener, *The Historical Jesus of the Gospels* (Grand Rapids: Eerdmans, 2009), 204; Gerd Lüdemann, *Jesus after Two Thousand Years: What He Really Said and Did*, trans. John Bowden (London: SCM; Amherst: Prometheus Books, 2001), 361; Becker, *Jesus of Nazareth*, 309–10.

hyperbolically and idiomatically to mean "love less" or "not love."[21] Consider, for example, the following two passages:

> So Jacob went in to Rachel also, and *he loved Rachel more than Leah*. He served Laban for another seven years. When the LORD saw that *Leah was unloved* [literally, "hated"], he opened her womb; but Rachel was barren. Leah conceived and bore a son, and she named him Reuben; for she said, "Because the LORD has looked on my affliction; surely *now my husband will love me*." She conceived again and bore a son, and said, "Because the LORD has heard that *I am hated*, he has given me this son also"; and she named him Simeon. (Gen 29:30–33)

> Those who spare the rod *hate* their children,
> but *those who love them* are diligent to discipline them. (Prov 13:24)

In context, when Leah says that she is "hated"[22] by Jacob (Gen 29:33), it clearly means that she is "unloved" or "loved less," because Jacob "loved" Rachel "more than Leah" (Gen 29:30–31).[23] Likewise, the saying from Proverbs—which, not inconsequentially, is a *mashal*—does not mean that parents who do not discipline their children literally "hate"[24] them or wish to harm them (Prov 13:24). Rather, as the second half of the proverb makes clear, it simply means that they do not "love" them.[25] In the same way, when Jesus declares that anyone who does not "hate" (*miseō*) their families cannot be his disciple (Luke 14:26), he does not mean that they must *actually* hate their families—in the sense of wishing them evil. Rather, he is using a hyperbolic biblical expression to emphasize that anyone who comes to him and loves his or her earthly families more than him cannot be his disciple.[26] In other words, in this logion, *Jesus demands of his disciples an exclusive, super-*

21. Maurice Casey, *Jesus of Nazareth: An Independent Historian's Account of His Life and Teaching* (London: T&T Clark, 2010), 299; Dunn, *Jesus Remembered*, 594; T. W. Manson, *The Sayings of Jesus* (London: SCM, 1949), 131.

22. MT *sane'*; LXX *miseō*.

23. See Claus Westermann, *Genesis 12–36*, trans. John J. Scullion, SJ (Minneapolis: Fortress, 1995), 469–70, who actually translates the verb as "unloved."

24. MT *sane'*; LXX *miseō*.

25. Michael V. Fox, *Proverbs 10–31*, Anchor Yale Bible 18B (New Haven: Yale University Press, 2009), 570: "Though the lax father does not really *hate* his son, his laxity will have disastrous consequences."

26. Cf. Vermes, *Authentic Gospel of Jesus*, 272.

parental love. He wants his followers to prefer him to all others, even their closest family members.[27]

The Decalogue and Jesus's Demand of Super-Parental Love

One reason Jesus's demand of super-parental love is so striking is because it places his disciples' obligations to him above their obligations to their fathers and mothers. As is well known, in the Decalogue, the first commandment oriented toward love of neighbor is the commandment to honor one's father and mother:

> *Honor your father and your mother*, so that your days may be long in the land that the LORD your God is giving you. (Exod 20:12)
>
> *Honor your father and your mother*, as the LORD your God commanded you, so that your days may be long and that it may go well with you in the land that the LORD your God is giving you. (Deut 5:16)

Although the Decalogue does not use the language of "love" to describe one's relationship with one's parents, it nevertheless clearly places a "supreme value" on "filial piety."[28] Given the supremacy of this duty to one's parents and Jesus's insistence on putting himself before his followers' parents, Dale Allison rightly contends that Jesus's declaration "daringly inverts the commandment to honor father and mother, seemingly raising a question mark over a Mosaic commandment, or at least its applicability to those literally following Jesus."[29]

27. Cf. David Flusser with R. Steven Notley, *The Sage from Galilee: Rediscovering Jesus' Genius* (Grand Rapids: Eerdmans, 2007), 15–16n37; Joachim Gnilka, *Jesus of Nazareth: Message and History*, trans. Siegfried S. Schatzmann (Peabody, MA: Hendrickson, 1997), 166.

28. William H. C. Propp, *Exodus 19–40*, Anchor Bible 2A (New York: Doubleday, 2006), 178; Moshe Weinfeld, *Deuteronomy 1–11*, Anchor Bible 5 (New York: Doubleday, 1991), 311. Cf. Lev 19:3; Deut 21:18–21; 27:16; Prov 1:8–9; 6:20–21; 10:1; 15:20; Sirach 7:27–30.

29. Dale C. Allison Jr., *Constructing Jesus: Memory, Imagination, and History* (Grand Rapids: Baker Academic, 2010), 272. Contrast this with the suggestion of Martin Hengel, *The Charismatic Leader and His Followers*, trans. James Greig (New York: Crossroad, 1981), 13n31, who goes too far when he claims that Jesus's declaration means "the annulment of the Fourth Commandment."

The Decalogue and the Status of Parents: "Second Only to God"

One reason this apparent challenge to the Decalogue is so striking—if not "outrageous"[30]—is because in a first-century Jewish context, the biblical obligation to honor one's father and mother had come to be regarded as second only to the obligation to honor God himself.[31] This belief is strongly witnessed in a number of Jewish writings from the Second Temple period and the time of Jesus and his disciples:

> Honor *God foremost*, and *afterward your parents.* (Pseudo-Phocylides 8)[32]

> *The duty of honoring parents . . . stands on the border-line between the human and the divine. For parents are midway between the natures of God and man, and partake of both*; the human obviously because they have been born and will perish, the divine because they have brought others to the birth and have raised not-being to being. . . . Honor therefore, [Moses] says, next to God, your father and your mother, who are crowned with a laurel of the second rank assigned to them by nature. (Philo of Alexandria, *Special Laws* 2.224–225, 235–236)[33]

> Honor to parents the Law ranks *second only to honor to God*, and if a son does not respond to the benefits received from them—for the slightest failure in his duty towards them—it hands him over to be stoned. (Josephus, *Against Apion* 2.206)[34]

In this remarkable series of early Jewish texts, the honor given to one's parents is, as Josephus states, "second only to honor to God" (*tēn pros theon deuteron etaxe*). Astonishingly, Philo even goes so far as stating that the biblical obliga-

30. Allison, *Constructing Jesus*, 93.

31. Sigurd Grindheim, *God's Equal: What Can We Know about Jesus' Self-Understanding in the Synoptic Gospels?*, Library of New Testament Studies 446 (London: T&T Clark, 2011), 122; Keener, *Historical Jesus*, 204.

32. Translation in James H. Charlesworth, ed., *Old Testament Pseudepigrapha*, 2 vols., Anchor Bible Reference Library (New York: Doubleday, 1983, 1985), 2:574.

33. Loeb Classical Library translation adapted. For a similar statement, see also Philo, *On the Decalogue* 106–7: "Parents by their nature stand on the border-line between the mortal and immortal side of existence, the mortal because of their kinship with men and other animals through the perishableness of the body; the immortal because the act of generation assimilates them to God, the generator of All."

34. Loeb Classical Library translation adapted.

tion to honor parents stands on "the border-line between the human and the divine" (*methorion anthrōpeiōn te kai theiōn*). Indeed, because of parents' role in giving life to their children, father and mother are midway between "the natures of God and man, and partake of both" (*metaxu theias kai anthrōpinēs physeōs eis metechontes amphoin*). That is why they must be honored "next to God," with the status of "second rank" to the Creator alone.

It is difficult to overestimate the significance of these early Jewish parallels for interpreting Jesus's demand of super-parental love from his followers. If the honor due to one's parents is second only to God himself because of their role in the creation of their children, and Jesus insists that his disciples love him above their father and mother, then who exactly is he claiming to be? In a Second Temple Jewish context, the answer is inescapable: Jesus is implying that he is (somehow) worthy of honor on a level that is equal with *the God of the Decalogue*.

The Demand of Love and the Divinity of Jesus

In light of such considerations, a number of works on the historical Jesus agree that, with his demand to be loved more than parents, Jesus is making an implicitly divine self-claim. Consider the following:

> [Jesus] dares to act as God himself.[35]

> The explanation for Jesus' demand is rather that he saw himself as the rightful recipient of the honor due to God. . . . Where the law prescribed dedication to God, he demanded dedication to himself.[36]

> Some radical philosophers demanded such loyalty to philosophy and some rabbis to Torah, but few teachers demanded such loyalty to themselves. Jesus told disciples that whoever loved parents or children more than him were unworthy of him (Matt 10:37//Luke 14:26). . . . Many viewed honoring one's parents as the highest social obligation; even if some spoke of honoring one's teacher more, no Jewish teacher would speak of "hating" one's parents by comparison. God alone was worthy of that role.[37]

35. Martin Hengel and Anna Maria Schwemer, *Jesus and Judaism*, trans. Wayne Coppins (Waco, TX: Baylor University Press, 2019 [orig. 2007]), 382.

36. Grindheim, *God's Equal*, 123.

37. Keener, *Historical Jesus of the Gospels*, 204.

Perhaps the most striking of these statements comes from the prolific American Jewish scholar Jacob Neusner. In his best-selling book, *A Rabbi Talks with Jesus*, Rabbi Neusner singled out Jesus's demand of love in particular as implying a divine claim:

> Now we see what is truly at stake: honor of parents forms a this-worldly analogy to honor of God. So the issue is not discipleship alone, but the comparison between and among relationships: relationship of disciple to master, relationship of child to parent, relationship of human being to God. . . . For, I now realize, only God can demand of me what Jesus is asking. . . . In the end the master, Jesus, makes a demand that only God makes.[38]

In short, when Jesus's riddle-like demand that his disciples place him above their parents and families is interpreted in a first-century Jewish context, it shockingly implies that Jesus sees himself as somehow equal with the one God of Israel.

Arguments against Historical Plausibility

When we turn to the historical plausibility of Jesus's demand that his disciples place him above and before their parents and family (Matt 10:37–39; Luke 14:25–27), we find ourselves in the relatively rare situation of dealing with a logion that virtually no major Jesus researchers consider to be unhistorical. To be sure, some works simply ignore the passage, and so their verdict on its historicity cannot be ascertained.[39] Nevertheless, very few argue that the saying does not go back to Jesus. For this reason, and in keeping with our triple-context approach, we will take a just few moments to catalogue some possible arguments against its historicity.[40]

38. Jacob Neusner, *A Rabbi Talks with Jesus* (New York: Doubleday, 1993), 53. For the revised edition, see Jacob Neusner, *A Rabbi Talks with Jesus*, rev. ed. (Montreal: McGill-Queen's University Press, 2000), 67–68.

39. For example, Jesus's demand for super-parental love is not discussed in Bart D. Ehrman, *How Jesus Became God: The Exaltation of a Jewish Preacher from Galilee* (San Francisco: HarperOne, 2014); Gerhard Lohfink, *Jesus of Nazareth: What He Wanted, Who He Was*, trans. Linda M. Maloney (Collegeville: Liturgical Press, 2012); E. P. Sanders, *The Historical Figure of Jesus* (London: Penguin, 1993); Ben Witherington III, *The Christology of Jesus* (Minneapolis: Fortress, 1990); E. P. Sanders, *Jesus and Judaism* (Minneapolis: Fortress, 1985); Joachim Jeremias, *The Proclamation of Jesus*, trans. John Bowden, New Testament Theology 1 (New York: Charles Scribner's Sons, 1971).

40. See, e.g., A. D. Jacobson, "Jesus against the Family: The Dissolution of Family Ties

For one thing, if one interprets Jesus's command to hate one's parents *literally*, one could argue, on the basis of Jewish contextual implausibility, that Jesus would never have taught his disciples to "hate" their parents (Luke 14:25). Not only would such a demand go directly against the commandment to "honor" one's father and mother (Exod 20:12; Deut 5:16), but it would also violate the command in Jewish Scripture to "love" one's "neighbor" as oneself (Lev 19:16).

Along similar lines, one could also argue the demand to hate one's parents displays a lack of coherence with other evidence about Jesus. For Jesus elsewhere explicitly states that the two greatest commandments in Jewish Scripture are the commands to love God with all one's heart, soul, and strength (Deut 6:4) and to love one's neighbor as oneself (Lev 19:16; cf. Matt 22:34–40; Mark 12:28–34; Luke 10:25–28). By contrast, Jesus's demand that his disciples "hate" their parents and family flies full in the face of his distinctive emphasis on the necessity and primacy of the love of neighbor.

Finally, one could also argue from implausibility of effects in the early church that if Jesus actually taught his disciples to hate their relatives, we would expect to see some evidence of strife between the followers of Jesus and their family members. However, our earliest accounts of life in the church provide ample evidence that followers of Jesus did not consider hatred for parents or family members to be a requirement for believing in him. For example, in the so-called Pauline "Household Codes," children who are believers in Christ are explicitly commanded to honor and obey their fathers and mothers:

> Children, obey your parents in the Lord, for this is right. "Honor your father and mother"—this is the first commandment with a promise: "so that it may be well with you and you may live long on the earth." (Eph 6:1–3)

> Children, obey your parents in everything, for this is your acceptable duty in the Lord. (Col 3:20)

Such evidence strongly suggests that the earliest Christian communities were not "anti-family" and did not, as a rule, display animus toward parents or other family members.[41] Hence, according to some scholars, it seems unlikely that

---

in the Gospel Tradition," in *From Quest to Q: Festschrift for James M. Robinson*, ed. J. M. Asgeirsson et al., Bibliotheca Ephemeridum Theologicarum Lovaniensium 146 (Leuven: Leuven University Press, 2000), 189–218 (esp. 191–99).

41. See Carolyn Osiek and David L. Balch, *Families in the New Testament World: Households and House Churches* (Louisville: Westminster John Knox, 1997), 103–55.

Jesus ever demanded that his disciples show antipathy toward their families or choose him over and against their families.

Contextual Plausibility: The God of the Decalogue and the Shema

Despite these possible arguments against historicity, when it comes to Jesus's demand that his disciples love him more than their parents, the logion has been rightly described as "all but universally credited to Jesus."[42] The overwhelming majority of historical Jesus scholars—including some of the most cautious regarding historical claims—conclude that the demand to place devotion to Jesus above one's father and mother has its origins with Jesus himself.[43] In fact, it is so widely accepted that many works on the historical Jesus simply assume its historicity without any argumentation whatsoever. The reasons for this virtual unanimity can be outlined according to a triple-context approach.

First, Jesus's demand that his disciples love him more than their own parents and children presents us with a powerful example of contextual plausibility within Judaism. If Jesus wanted to teach his disciples that he was divine, then it is contextually plausible that he would do so by demanding that they love him even more than the honor that the Decalogue commanded them to give to their parents. For in an early Jewish context, the Decalogue was not only perhaps the most well-known passage of Jewish Scripture; it was also closely connected the commandment to "love" the "one Lord" with all one's heart, soul, and strength (Deut 6:4–6)—a passage later known as the Shema. As both literary and archaeological evidence suggests, there is good reason to believe that at the time of Jesus, both the Decalogue and the Shema were recited together in certain liturgical contexts.[44] Consider, for example, an ancient

42. W. D. Davies and Dale C. Allison Jr., *A Critical and Exegetical Commentary on the Gospel according to Saint Matthew*, 3 vols., International Critical Commentaries (Edinburgh: T&T Clark, 1988–1997), 2:221.

43. For example, the demand for super-parental love is regarded as historical by Hengel and Schwemer, *Jesus and Judaism*, 380–81; Jens Schröter, *Jesus of Nazareth, Jew from Galilee, Savior of the World*, trans. Wayne Coppins (Waco, TX: Baylor University Press, 2014), 47; Puig i Tàrrech, *Jesus, A Biography*, 237; Helen K. Bond, *The Historical Jesus: A Guide for the Perplexed* (London: T&T Clark, 2012), 115; Allison, *Constructing Jesus*, 272; Casey, *Jesus of Nazareth*, 299 (though he rejects the hatred of one's "wife" as an inauthentic element "added" by Luke); Flusser with Notley, *Sage from Galilee*, 15–16; Lüdemann, *Jesus after Two Thousand Years*, 362; Becker, *Jesus of Nazareth*, 309–10; Gnilka, *Jesus of Nazareth*, 166; Klausner, *Jesus of Nazareth*, 383. Even Funk, Hoover, and the Jesus Seminar, *Five Gospels*, 174–75, 353, give the Luke 14:26 a "pink" vote, meaning "Jesus probably said something like this."

44. See Kim Huat Tan, "Jesus and the Shema," in Holmén and Porter, *Handbook for the*

Hebrew text from the second century BCE which juxtaposes the Decalogue with the beginning of the Shema, along with a first-century description of daily Jewish prayer:

> [I am the Lo]RD your God who [brought] you out of
> the land of E[gypt:]
> [you shall not hav]e other gods be[fore] me. . . .
> *Honor your father and your moth[er,* so that]
> it may be well with you and your days may be long
> upon the ground [that]
> the LORD your God gives you. . . .
> [And these are the statute]s and the judgments that
> Moses commanded the [sons of]
> [Israel] in the wilderness, when they went forth from
> the land of Egypt. "*Hea[r]*
> *[O Isra]el: the LORD our God, the LORD is one; and you*
> *shall l[ove]*
> *[the LORD your G]o[d with al]l y[our heart . . .]*
> (Nash Papyrus, lines 1–2, 16–18, 22–25)[45]

> At dawn, they [the Jews] lift up holy arms
> toward heaven, from their beds . . .
> and *they honor only the Immortal who always rules,*
> *and then their parents.* (Sibylline Oracles 3:590–94)[46]

In the first passage, we have an ancient papyrus that seems to preserve the sacred words of the Decalogue first, followed by the Shema, perhaps for recitation. In the second passage, the early Jewish author seems to be alluding to the daily recitation of the Shema ("they honor *only* the Immortal"), as well as to the Decalogue ("and then their parents"). In light of such evidence, experts in early Judaism have argued that the Decalogue was not only "part of the Jewish liturgical tradition already in the Second Temple period," but that it "was

Study of the Historical Jesus, 3:2677–707; Armin Lange, "The Shema Israel in Second Temple Judaism," *Journal of Ancient Judaism* 1.2 (2010): 207–14; E. P. Sanders, *Judaism: Practice and Belief 63 BCE–66 CE* (Minneapolis: Fortress, 2016), 338–39, 387.

45. Translation in F. C. Burkitt, "The Hebrew Papyrus of the Ten Commandments," *Jewish Quarterly Review* 15 (1903): 392–408 (here 395–96, slightly adapted).

46. In Charlesworth, *Old Testament Pseudepigrapha*, 1:375.

performed by the community along with the Shema."[47] If this is correct, and the Decalogue and Shema were recited together at the time of Jesus, then it is plausible that Jesus drew on the language of the Decalogue and the Shema to reveal to his disciples that he saw himself as in some sense equal with the God of Israel. Indeed, one might even go so far to suggest that the only way Jesus could reveal that he saw himself as divine *without* compromising early Jewish belief in one God would be to identify himself with *the God of the Decalogue and of the Shema.*

Coherence: Jesus Placed Himself above Parents and Family

Second, and equally important, Jesus's demand for his disciples to place him above all other human obligations and loves, including love of parents, coheres remarkably well with other evidence about Jesus in several ways.

For one thing, the demand to put Jesus ahead of one's familial ties coheres quite well with Jesus's own act of leaving his family in Nazareth behind (Matt 13:53–58; Mark 6:1–6; Luke 4:16–30) and calling his disciples—such as Peter, Andrew, James, and John—to do the same (Matt 4:18–22; Mark 1:16–20; Luke 5:1–11; cf. John 1:35–42).[48] Moreover, it also fits well with other evidence that Jesus promised eternal life to those who chose to leave their parents and families behind and become his followers:[49]

> And everyone who has left houses or brothers or sisters *or father or mother or children* or fields, *for my name's sake*, will receive a hundredfold, and will inherit eternal life. (Matt 19:29)

> Jesus said, "Truly I tell you, there is *no one who has left* house or brothers or sisters or *mother or father or children* or fields, *for my sake* and for the sake of the good news, who will not receive a hundredfold now in this age—houses, brothers and sisters, mothers and children, and fields, with persecutions—and in the age to come eternal life. (Mark 10:29–30)

47. Hindy Najman, "Decalogue," in *The Eerdmans Dictionary of Early Judaism*, ed. John J. Collins and Daniel C. Harlow (Grand Rapids: Eerdmans, 2010), 527.

48. Keener, *Historical Jesus of the Gospels*, 204; Gnilka, *Jesus of Nazareth*, 166.

49. Dunn, *Jesus Remembered*, 593; Gerd Theissen and Annette Merz, *The Historical Jesus: A Comprehensive Guide*, trans. John Bowden (Minneapolis: Fortress, 1998), 218–19.

> And he said to them, "Truly I tell you, *there is no one who has left* house or wife or brothers *or parents or children, for the sake of the kingdom of God,* who will not get back very much more in this age, and in the age to come eternal life." (Luke 18:29–30)

Perhaps most striking of all, Jesus's demand that his disciples love him more than their parents in particular coheres perfectly with one equally shocking passage in which Jesus places himself even before the duty to bury one's deceased parent:[50]

> Another of his disciples said to him, "*Lord, first let me go and bury my father.*" But Jesus said to him, "*Follow me,* and let the dead bury their own dead." (Matt 8:21–22)

> To another he said, "*Follow me.*" But he said, "*Lord, first let me go and bury my father.*" But Jesus said to him, "Let the dead bury their own dead; but as for you, go and proclaim the kingdom of God." (Luke 9:59–60)

This is an excellent example of how a saying of Jesus can be both perfectly intelligible and deeply shocking in a first-century Jewish context. For in the Second Temple period and beyond, the responsibility to bury one's parents was considered a grave obligation (see Tobit 4:3; 6:13–15; Sirach 38:16).[51] Hence, by declaring that discipleship to him comes even before the duty to bury one's parent, "at least once Jesus was willing to say that following him superseded the requirements of piety and the Torah."[52] In this way, he gives us yet "another example of how he takes the place that belongs to God alone."[53]

50. Lüdemann, *Jesus after Two Thousand Years*, 362; Funk, Hoover, and the Jesus Seminar, *Five Gospels*, 175.

51.See Sanders, *Jesus and Judaism*, 252–55. For Jewish burial practices, see Steven Fine, "Death, Burial, and Afterlife," in *The Oxford Handbook of Jewish Daily Life in Roman Palestine*, ed. Catherine Hezser (Oxford: Oxford University Press, 2010), 440–62. Given our focus on Deut 6:4–6, it is worth noting that the Mishnah says the obligation to bury dead relatives overrides even the obligation to recite the Shema. See m. Berakot 3:1.

52. Sanders, *Jesus and Judaism*, 255.

53. Grindheim, *God's Equal*, 122.

Consequences in the Early Church: "Love" for Jesus and Devotion to Christ

Last, Jesus's demand that his disciples love him more than their parents and other immediate family members provides a plausible explanation for why early Christians not only believed that Jesus was divine but also used the particular language of "love" (*agapaō*) to express their devotion to him. Consider just two examples:

> Peace be to the whole community, and love with faith, from God the Father and the Lord Jesus Christ. Grace be with all who have *an undying love for our Lord Jesus Christ.* (Eph 6:24)

> So that the genuineness of your faith—being more precious than gold that, though perishable, is tested by fire—may be found to result in praise and glory and honor when Jesus Christ is revealed. *Although you have not seen him, you love him.* (1 Pet 1:7–8)

Although the notion of "loving" Jesus has become so familiar over the centuries that it is easy to take it for granted, it is worth pausing to emphasize that just because early Christians believed Jesus was more than merely human, this would not necessarily lead them to speak about loving him. In the ancient world, divine beings of all sorts were honored, feared, worshiped, and served—but not necessarily *loved.*[54] However, if the historical Jesus spoke and acted as if he were somehow equal with the one God of the Decalogue—the God whose Ten Commandments pronounced blessings for "those who love" him (Exod 20:6) and whose Torah taught Israel to "love" him with all their heart, soul, mind, and strength (Deut 6:4–6)—then it would provide a perfectly plausible point of origin for the fact that early Christians not only *believed* in Jesus but also *loved* him.

54. For example, one searches in vain for discussions of the importance of humans loving the gods in the wide-ranging essays collected in *The Oxford Handbook of Ancient Greek Religion*, ed. Esther Eidinow and Julia Kindt (Oxford: Oxford University Press, 2015), or *A Companion to Roman Religion*, ed. Jörg Rüpke (Oxford: Wiley-Blackwell, 2011). Contrast this with the absolute centrality of loving God in early Judaism (e.g., Deut 6:4–6) and the importance of loving Christ in early Christianity (e.g., Eph 6:24; 1 Pet 1:7–8). The question of to what degree Judaism and Christianity differed from other ancient religions on this point is a question worthy of further research.

Weighing the Arguments for and against Historical Plausibility

In sum, when we evaluate the arguments for and against the historical plausibility of Jesus's demand that his followers love him more than their own families—including their mothers and fathers—the weight of the evidence easily tips the scale in favor of substantial historicity.

For one thing, all three of the arguments against the historicity of the logion surveyed above are based on a faulty exegesis of Jesus's saying that takes the command to "hate" literally rather than hyperbolically or parabolically (cf. Gen 29:30–33; Prov 13:24). This is an excellent example of how conclusions about historical plausibility are directly dependent on exegesis, and why Jesus researchers should not draw historical conclusions about any saying or action attributed to Jesus without first attempting to interpret it correctly within a first-century Jewish context. In this case, it is faulty exegesis that leads to a faulty verdict against historicity.

By contrast, when the saying is interpreted correctly as a kind of riddle or parable implying Jesus's divine status, multiple lines of arguments converge toward the conclusion that Jesus's demand of super-parental love is contextually plausible within a first-century Jewish context in which the command to love God above all and honor one's parents as second only to God was well known (Deut 6:4–6; Nash Papyrus; Sibylline Oracles 3:590–594; Pseudo-Phocylides 8; Philo, *Special Laws* 2.224–236; Josephus, *Against Apion* 2.206), coherent with other evidence that Jesus demanded his disciples place him above even their closest family members (Matt 19:29; Mark 10:29–30; Luke 18:29–30; Matt 8:21–22; Luke 9:59–60), and a plausible origin of the early Christian emphasis on not just serving or obeying Jesus, but loving him (Eph 6:24; 1 Pet 1:7–8).

Given the cumulative strength of these arguments from contextual plausibility, coherence, and consequences in the early church, it is perhaps not surprising that contemporary scholars strongly affirm that the demand to put Jesus before one's parents and families goes back to the man from Nazareth himself:

> There is no reason . . . to suppose that Jesus did not demand total allegiance from followers.[55]

> There can be little doubt that Jesus said something like Luke 14.26.[56]

55. Bond, *Historical Jesus*, 115.
56. Dunn, *Jesus Remembered*, 592.

The content of this harsh saying can hardly be denied to Jesus.[57]

Perhaps the most remarkable expression of this comes once again from the pen of Rabbi Jacob Neusner, who says of Jesus's demand to be loved more than father and mother:

> Some Christians maintain that the historical Jesus, the man who really lived and taught, would not have recognized the faith that the Christian Church formulated later on. They identify with the "authentic" teachings of Jesus the man, but not with the added-on doctrines in the name of Christ, formulated, they allege, by the Church. . . . The distinction between the one and the other . . . strikes me as not well founded. . . . For in these observations about what is at stake in a very humble matter, honor of parents as against "He who loves father or mother more than me is not worthy of me" [Matt 10:37], I find myself unable to recognize that abyss between the man, Jesus, and the Christ of faith. . . . When we compare what he says on the commandment to honor parents with what other sages have to say . . . we see in the Jesus of history precisely that Christ of faith.[58]

To put the point somewhat differently: if Jesus's demand to be loved more than one's parents is authentic, then Jesus is, quite simply, claiming to be equal with the God of Israel. For, as Neusner rightly notes, "*only God can demand of me what Jesus is asking*."[59]

No One Is Good but God

The second major episode in which Jesus uses a riddle to both reveal and conceal the mystery of his identity is the famous story of his encounter with the rich man. This particular episode has the unique position of being perhaps the most frequently cited evidence that Jesus explicitly *denied* that he is in any way divine. It is recounted in all three Synoptic Gospels:

> Then someone came to him and said, "Teacher, what good deed must I do to have eternal life?" And he said to him, "*Why do you ask me about what*

57. Becker, *Jesus of Nazareth*, 309.
58. Neusner, *Rabbi Talks with Jesus*, 54.
59. Neusner, *Rabbi Talks with Jesus*, 53 (emphasis added).

> *is good? There is only one who is good. If you wish to enter into life, keep the commandments.*" He said to him, "Which ones?" And Jesus said, "You shall not murder; You shall not commit adultery; You shall not steal; You shall not bear false witness; Honor your father and mother; also, You shall love your neighbor as yourself." The young man said to him, "I have kept all these; what do I still lack?" Jesus said to him, "*If you wish to be perfect, go, sell your possessions*, and give the money to the poor, and you will have treasure in heaven; *then come, follow me*." When the young man heard this word, he went away grieving, for he had many possessions. (Matt 19:16–22)

> As he was setting out on a journey, a man ran up and knelt before him, and asked him, "*Good Teacher, what must I do to inherit eternal life?*" Jesus said to him, "*Why do you call me good? No one is good but God alone. You know the commandments*: 'You shall not murder; You shall not commit adultery; You shall not steal; You shall not bear false witness; You shall not defraud; Honor your father and mother.'" He said to him, "Teacher, I have kept all these since my youth." Jesus, looking at him, loved him and said, "*You lack one thing; go, sell what you own*, and give the money to the poor, and you will have treasure in heaven; *then come, follow me*." When he heard this, he was shocked and went away grieving, for he had many possessions. (Mark 10:17–22)

> A certain ruler asked him, "*Good Teacher, what must I do to inherit eternal life?*" Jesus said to him, "*Why do you call me good? No one is good but God alone. You know the commandments*: 'You shall not commit adultery; You shall not murder; You shall not steal; You shall not bear false witness; Honor your father and mother.'" He replied, "I have kept all these since my youth." When Jesus heard this, he said to him, "*There is still one thing lacking. Sell all that you own* and distribute the money to the poor, and you will have treasure in heaven; *then come, follow me*." But when he heard this, he became sad; for he was very rich. (Luke 18:18–23)

Unlike some of the other episodes we have examined, these accounts are notably different from one another. The most obvious difference is that in Matthew, the rich man asks about what "good deed" he must do to inherit eternal life (Matt 19:16), but in Mark and Luke, he addresses Jesus as "good Teacher" (Mark 10:17; Luke 18:18). Likewise, in Matthew, Jesus responds by saying, "Why do you ask me about what is good?" (Matt 18:17), but in Mark and Luke, Jesus responds by asking, "Why do you call me good?" (Mark 10:18;

Luke 18:19). Despite these differences in the form of the question and answer, the gist of the episode is substantially the same: (1) a rich man addresses Jesus as teacher and asks what he must do in order to have eternal life; (2) Jesus responds by insisting on the exclusive goodness of God and the necessity of keeping the commandments; (3) Jesus also requires the rich man to sell his possessions, give to the poor, and follow him; (4) the rich man responds with sorrow because of his many possessions. In what follows, we will take a few moments to interpret these basic points in an early Jewish context.

The Rich Man Asks Jesus How to Obtain "Eternal Life"

In all three accounts, a rich man asks Jesus what he must do in order to have "eternal life" (Matt 19:16; Mark 10:17; Luke 10:18). If we want to interpret this expression in its first-century Jewish context, it is important to recall that it only occurs once in all of Jewish Scripture—in a prophecy from the book of Daniel about the final bodily resurrection:

> But at that time your people shall be delivered, everyone who is found written in the book. Many of those who sleep in the dust of the earth shall awake, some to *everlasting life*, and some to shame and everlasting contempt. Those who are wise shall shine like the brightness of the sky, and those who lead many to righteousness, like the stars forever and ever. (Dan 12:1–3)

In this passage, the phrase "everlasting life," or "eternal life,"[60] clearly refers to the unending life of those who will be raised from the dead at the final judgment (Dan 12:2).[61] The opposite of "eternal life" is "everlasting contempt," or "eternal shame,"[62] which the unrighteous will likewise experience after the judgment (Dan 12:2). Hence, when the rich man asks Jesus about how to obtain "eternal life," he is not asking about how his soul might "go to heaven" after he dies, but rather how to participate in the bodily resurrection of the righteous

60. MT *khayey ʿolam*; LXX *zōēn aiōnion*.

61. John J. Collins, *Daniel: A Commentary*, Hermeneia (Minneapolis: Fortress, 1993), 392. For similar uses in the Second Temple period, see 2 Maccabees 7:9; Psalms of Solomon 3:12; 9:5; 13:11; 14:4, 7–10; 1 Enoch 37:4; 40:9; 58:3. For a full study, see C. D. Elledge, *Resurrection of the Dead in Early Judaism* (Oxford: Oxford University Press, 2017).

62. MT *dir'on ʿolam*; LXX *aischynēn aiōnion*.

on the last day. In other words, he is not just asking Jesus a legal or ethical question; he is asking a question about eschatological salvation.

Jesus Responds by Alluding to the Shema and the Ten Commandments

In response to the rich man's question, Jesus insists on two points: that there is only "one" who is "good," and that it is necessary to keep "the commandments" in order to have eternal life (Matt 19:17; Mark 10:17; Luke 18:20).

In a first-century Jewish context, Jesus's declaration that there is only "one" (*heis*) who is "good" (*agathos*) (Matt 19:17; Mark 10:17; Luke 18:20) would easily be recognized as an allusion to Moses's famous exhortation to Israel, later known as the Shema (cf. Deut 6:4–9).[63] In this instance, however, Jesus combines it with a well-known refrain from the book of Psalms. Compare the following:

> Hear, O Israel: *The* LORD *is our God, the* LORD *is one.* You shall love the LORD your God with all your heart, and with all your soul, and with all your might. (Deut 6:4–5)
>
> O give thanks to *the* LORD, for *he is good*;
> for his steadfast love endures forever. (Ps 106:1; cf. Ps 100:5)

Moses immediately goes on to command the Israelites to "recite" his words about the "God" who is "one" when they "lie down" and when they "rise" (Deut 6:4–7).[64] Because of this, the recitation of these verses eventually became part of common Jewish daily prayer during the Second Temple period.[65] Along similar lines, the book of Ezra says that the confession of God's goodness found in the refrain from Psalm 106 was already being sung "responsively" by the people of Israel during liturgical worship (Ezra 3:11; cf. 1 Chron 16:34).[66] Hence, when Jesus insists that there is only "one" who is "good," he is clearly referring to *the one God of Israel* who was confessed as "one" in the daily Shema and praised as "good" in the temple and synagogues.

63. Meier, *A Marginal Jew*, 3:587; Casey, *Jesus of Nazareth*, 287.

64. "God": MT *'elohim*; LXX *theos*. "One": MT *'ekhad*; LXX *heis*.

65. See Tan, "Jesus and the Shema," 3:2677–708.

66. See Judith H. Newman, "Psalms, Book of," in *The Eerdmans Dictionary of Early Judaism*, ed. John J. Collins and Daniel C. Harlow (Grand Rapids: Eerdmans, 2010), 1105–7.

In a first-century Jewish context, Jesus's insistence on the necessity of keeping "the commandments" would also easily be recognized as a reference to the Ten Commandments, or, as Jewish Scripture calls them, the "ten words" of Moses (Exod 34:28; cf. Exod 20:1–21; Deut 5:1–22).[67] Although there are a variety of ways to order and enumerate the Ten Commandments, by the first century they were already being distinguished into two major groupings: (1) laws regarding love of God (the first "tablet"), and (2) laws regarding relations with one's neighbor (the second "tablet"):[68]

The "Ten Words"

First "Tablet" (Love of God)	**Second "Tablet" (Love of Neighbor)**
You shall have no other gods before me . . .	*Honor your father and mother . . .*
You shall not make a graven image . . .	*You shall not kill.*
You shall not take the name	*You shall not commit adultery.*
of the Lord your God in vain . . .	*You shall not steal.*
Remember the Sabbath day . . .	*You shall not bear false witness*
	against your neighbor.
	You shall not covet . . .
	anything that is your neighbor's.
(Exod 20:3, 4, 7, 8)	(Exod 20:12–17)

Notice here that the reason for linking the first tablet with "love" of God is because in the Decalogue itself, God describes humans who do not practice idolatry as "those who *love me*" (Exod 20:6; Deut 5:10).[69] Likewise, the reason

67. Armand Puig i Tàrrech, *Jesus: A Biography*, trans. Jenny Read-Heimerdinger (Waco, TX: Baylor University Press, 2011), 430; Cf. Philo *Special Laws* 4.137; Josephus, *Antiquities* 4.213.

68. See E. P. Sanders, *Judaism: Practice and Belief, 63 BCE–66 CE* (Minneapolis: Fortress, 2016), 311–96 (here 314); David Flusser, "The Ten Commandments and the New Testament," in *The Ten Commandments in History and Tradition*, ed. Ben-Zion Segal, trans. Gershon Levi (Jerusalem: Magnes, 1990), 219–46. Cf. also Philo, *Special Laws* 2.63. Philo enumerates the law's two main principles as "piety" (*eusebeia*) (= first tablet) and "justice/righteousness" (*dikaiosynē*) (= second tablet).

69. See Propp, *Exodus*, 2:173; Weinfeld, *Deuteronomy 1–11*, 299–300, 338.

for linking the second tablet with love of "neighbor" comes from the repeated references to "your neighbor" (Exod 20:16, 17 [2×], 18) in the text of the Decalogue. Intriguingly, in his reply to the rich man, Jesus only gives specific examples of commandments from the second tablet of the Decalogue, those involving love of neighbor (italicized in the chart above).[70]

In sum, when all of Jesus's allusions to Jewish Scripture are taken together, the upshot of his answer to the rich man is this: in order to have the eternal life of the resurrection, it is necessary both to profess the goodness of the one God of Israel and to live according to the Decalogue, especially the commandments focused on love of neighbor. However, Jesus does not stop with this otherwise unsurprising answer. Instead, after affirming the necessity of keeping the Decalogue to obtain eternal life, Jesus immediately goes on to add a requirement to it.

Jesus Adds to the Decalogue: Give to the Poor and Follow Him as a Disciple

Perhaps the most striking feature of Jesus's encounter with the rich man comes at the end of the episode, when Jesus *adds* a requirement to keeping the Ten Commandments. In all three gospel accounts, Jesus says that the rich man must *also* "sell" his possessions, give "the money to the poor," and then "come, follow" Jesus (Matt 19:21; Mark 10:21; Luke 18:22).

Jesus's requirement that the rich man give his money to the poor is by no means unprecedented. Like the other aspects of Jesus's reply, it too is deeply rooted in Jewish Scripture. In the book of Deuteronomy, Moses commands the people of Israel to be generous in giving to those in need: "Since the poor will never cease from the land, I therefore command you, 'You shall open wide your hand to the poor and needy neighbor in your land'" (Deut 15:11).[71] Notice that this is not a suggestion; it is a "commandment" (*mitzvah*) (Deut 15:5)—the same word used for the ten "commandments" (*mitzvoth*) (Exod 20:6). Notice also that the Israelites are instructed to be generous, giving to anyone in need.

With that said, Jesus does not merely require the rich man to give some of his money away. Jesus demands that the man sell everything he has, give the proceeds to the poor, and—even more radical—come and "follow" (*akoloutheō*) Jesus (Matt 19:21; Mark 10:21; Luke 18:22). In an ancient Jewish

70. Meier, *A Marginal Jew*, 3:587.
71. NRSV, adapted.

context, the command to follow Jesus does not just mean accepting his teachings. Rather, it means leaving behind his former life and becoming a disciple.[72] Consider, for example, the use of the same language in the scriptural account of the prophet Elijah calling Elisha to be his follower:

> So he set out from there, and found Elisha son of Shaphat, who was plowing. There were twelve yoke of oxen ahead of him, and he was with the twelfth. Elijah passed by him and threw his mantle over him. He left the oxen, ran after Elijah, and said, "*Let me kiss my father and my mother, and then I will follow you.*" Then Elijah said to him, "Go back again; for what have I done to you?" He returned from following him, took the yoke of oxen, and slaughtered them; using the equipment from the oxen, he boiled their flesh, and gave it to the people, and they ate. *Then he set out and followed Elijah, and became his servant.* (1 Kgs 19:19–21)

In this passage, Elisha's decision to "walk after," or "follow,"[73] the prophet Elijah is technical terminology for him being summoned to "a call that involves literal following and service to the prophet."[74] It means that Elisha will leave his family and former life behind and take up the life of Elijah, his new master.

With all of this in mind, the radical nature of Jesus's response to the rich man is arresting. In the context of answering the rich man's question about how to obtain eternal life, Jesus clearly implies that it is not enough for the man to simply recognize the goodness of the one God, keep the Decalogue, and give to the poor. If he wants to have the fullness of eternal life, he must also leave everything behind and become a disciple of Jesus.[75] Indeed, it is precisely this final demand of discipleship that proves to be too much for the man. When Jesus declares that God alone is good, the rich man raises no objection. Nor does he balk in the slightest at Jesus's insistence on the necessity of keeping the Decalogue. It is only when he requires the rich man to sell what he owns and follow Jesus that the latter responds with dismay. As the gospel accounts tell us: he became sorrowful, because he "had many possessions" (Matt 19:22; Mark 10:22; cf. Luke 18:23).

With these basic exegetical points in mind, we can now ask the question: What are the implications of Jesus's responses to the rich man for who Jesus

72. Meier, *A Marginal Jew*, 3:72.

73. MT *halak akhar*; LXX *akoloutheō*.

74. Meier, *A Marginal Jew*, 3:49. See also Mordechai Cogan, *1 Kings*, Anchor Bible 10 (New York: Doubleday, 2000), 455.

75. Meier, *A Marginal Jew*, 515.

thinks he is? In particular, what light does Jesus's response shed on whether he saw himself as more than merely human? In this regard, there are two major interpretive options.

Option #1: Jesus Denies That He Is God (and That He Is Good)

On the one hand, for many scholars, the obvious implication of Jesus's insistence that the "one" God alone is "good" is that Jesus is denying that he is God. From the nineteenth century right up to the present day, Jesus's declaration of the exclusive goodness of God has frequently been interpreted as clear evidence that Jesus did not consider himself to be divine in any sense. Consider the following statements:

> Here Jesus so tenaciously maintains the distinction between himself and God, that he renounces the predicate of (perfect) goodness, and insists on its appropriation to God alone.[76]

> So far was Jesus from teaching the dogma which later arose—that he was the Son of God and one of the three persons in the Godhead—that when someone hailed him as "Good master," Jesus replied, "Why callest thou me good? There is none good save one: God."[77]

> "Why do you call me good? None is good, except the one God." (Mk 10.18). . . . [This] does not mean that Jesus was really a liar or a thief: it simply means that faced with the One God himself, Jesus did not feel perfectly good. . . . This is what Christian commentators have been unable to cope with, because of their belief in Jesus' sinlessness. . . . Jesus did not feel that he was perfectly good, and it is long past time that his sinful modern followers noticed that.[78]

Note well that, according to this view, when Jesus insists on the exclusive goodness of God, he is not merely implying that he is not divine—*he is also implying that he is not good.* Hence, Jesus's response to the rich man's question seems to draw a clear dividing line between the good God and sinful human

76. Strauss, *Jesus of Nazareth*, 289.
77. Klausner, *Jesus of Nazareth*, 364–65.
78. Casey, *Jesus of Nazareth*, 286–87.

beings and to place Jesus himself squarely on the sinful human side of the line. Indeed, for some, this single passage alone settles the issue of Jesus's self-understanding: Jesus's declaration that no one is "good" except God provides conclusive evidence that he does not see himself as equal with God, but rather as a sinful human being.[79]

Option #2: Jesus Uses the Shema and the Decalogue to Imply He Is Equal with God

According to other scholars, however, Jesus is not denying that he is divine. Instead, he is actually using the allusions to the Shema and the Decalogue to invite the rich man to realize that Jesus is much more than just a merely human "teacher" (Matt 19:16; Mark 10:17; Luke 18:18). In order to see this clearly, two key observations need to be made.

First and foremost: despite what is often claimed, *Jesus does not actually deny that he is good—much less that he is God.* A closer look at the evidence shows that Jesus never says, "I am not good," or "I am not God." In fact, he does not say anything explicit about himself one way or the other. Instead, he simply responds to the rich man's question about how to obtain eternal life by insisting that the one God alone is good and that it is necessary to keep the commandments. In other words, Jesus begins his response to the rich man with an "affirmation of monotheism."[80] This affirmation is particularly important, given what Jesus does next.

Second, *Jesus adds a commandment to the Decalogue that is entirely focused on following him.* In a first-century Jewish context, it is difficult to overestimate just how striking Jesus's act of adding a requirement to the Decalogue would have been. In Jewish Scripture, the Ten Commandments alone are written by the very "finger of God" (Exod 31:18). As such, they have a unique and supreme place in the Mosaic Torah.[81] Hence, for Jesus to presume to add *anything* to the Decalogue raises the question: Who does Jesus think he is? It is difficult to overestimate just how problematic "the extreme nature" of Jesus adding a requirement to the Decalogue is for those who argue that Jesus is denying both that he is good (and that he is God).[82] If Jesus is actually denying that

79. Cf. Lüdemann, *Jesus after Two Thousand Years*, 70.

80. Witherington, *Christology of Jesus*, 276.

81. See Najman, "Decalogue," 526–27.

82. Casey, *Jesus of Nazareth*, 287.

he is good, then how can he possibly make "following" him as a disciple a condition for obtaining "eternal life"? How could it be necessary for salvation to follow a sinful human teacher who insists that he is not even "good," much less that he is not God?

In light of such observations, a strong case can be made that, far from denying his equality with God, Jesus's response to the rich man is actually a *riddle* meant to lead the man to the realization of who Jesus really is:

> When Jesus adds that no one is good but God alone, he does not make a direct statement about himself. What this statement means regarding Jesus' identity is merely implied. . . . Jesus' answer was intended to tease out the implications that Jesus was indeed equal with God . . . Jesus thus takes the place of God in giving absolute commandments. . . . He does not make a statement about himself, but provokes the audience to make their own judgment.[83]

> If God alone is good and able to give commandments, then Jesus does so as well. By implication, then, he is also good. And he is good not in the sense implied by the rich man, but in the absolute, divine sense, used by Jesus himself.[84]

In other words, when it comes to the question of eternal life, following Jesus is essential. Indeed—and this is important—the only way to take Jesus's declaration that no one is good but God alone as a denial of his divinity is to wrench his words completely out of context by separating his initial response from his final demand. Taken as a whole, Jesus's response to the rich man functions as a riddle-like invitation to discover the truth about Jesus's identity. As Richard Hays points out, when Jesus's allusions to the Shema and the Decalogue are given due weight, we discover that "the rich inquirer has spoken more truly than he realizes."[85]

In sum, when the account of Jesus and the rich man is interpreted in its first-century Jewish context, we come to a significant conclusion. *Upon closer inspection, the episode perhaps most frequently cited to argue that Jesus sees him-*

83. Grindheim, *God's Equal*, 187.

84. Simon J. Gathercole, *The Preexistent Son: Recovering the Christologies of Matthew, Mark, and Luke* (Grand Rapids: Eerdmans, 2006), 74.

85. Richard B. Hays, *Echoes of Scripture in the Gospels* (Waco, TX: Baylor University Press, 2016), 384n99.

self as merely human turns out to be powerful evidence that Jesus puts himself on par with the God of the Decalogue. With that said, it is important to emphasize that Jesus implies his divinity in a way that is both deeply Jewish—by alluding to the Shema and the Commandments—and very consistent with his identity as a teacher of parables and riddles. In this episode, Jesus wants the rich man to ask for himself: Who is Jesus? And what is his relationship with the one God of Israel? To this end, Jesus uses allusions to the Shema, combined with his addition of a requirement to the Decalogue, to lead the rich man to discover for himself the mystery of Jesus's equality with the one God of Israel.

Arguments against Historical Plausibility

When we turn from exegesis to the question of historicity, we find ourselves with one of the other few episodes in the Gospels in which there is a virtual consensus in favor of its historicity. As James Dunn writes: "Most accept that an episode from Jesus' life is here recalled."[86]

In fact, one searches the pages of major works on the historical Jesus in vain for *any* arguments against the historicity of Jesus's exchange with the rich man. To be sure, some works on Jesus either ignore the episode or express doubt about whether a historical verdict is possible.[87] However, the vast majority of Jesus researchers either seem to assume that the episode is historical or give positive arguments in favor of historicity.[88] In particular, scholars are quite confident that Jesus's declaration that the "one" God alone is "good"—interpreted as a denial that Jesus himself is good—is true to history. Consider the following:

86. Dunn, *Jesus Remembered*, 520n155.

87. Jesus's encounter with the rich man receives no discussion in Schröter, *Jesus of Nazareth*; Ehrman, *How Jesus Became God*; Flusser with Notley, *Sage from Galilee*; Becker, *Jesus of Nazareth*; Vermes, *Jesus the Jew*. Sanders (*Jesus and Judaism*, 255) holds that "we can by no means be sure that the story of the rich man is authentic," but he gives no reasons why.

88. For the assumption that it is historical, see Hengel and Schwemer, *Jesus and Judaism*, 380; Lohfink, *Jesus of Nazareth*, 98–99; Allison, *Constructing Jesus*, 200–201; Puig i Tàrrech, *Jesus: A Biography*, 325, 349; Fredriksen, *Jesus of Nazareth*, 117; Ehrman, *Jesus: Apocalyptic Prophet*, 165–66; Gnilka, *Jesus of Nazareth*, 201; Jeremias, *Proclamation of Jesus*, 153, 174; Günther Bornkamm, *Jesus of Nazareth*, 60. For positive arguments favoring historicity, see Dunn, *Jesus Remembered*, 520–21; Vermes, *Authentic Gospel of Jesus*, 287–88; Davies and Allison, *Matthew*, 3:40; Bultmann, *History of the Synoptic Tradition*, 21. Even Funk, Hoover, and the Jesus Seminar (*The Five Gospels*, 91) give it a "gray" designation, meaning "Jesus did not say this, but the ideas contained in it are close to his own."

> [Jesus] rejected even being addressed as "good teacher," since in his view only God is good (Mark 10.17). This rejection of an overestimation of him is certainly historical.[89]

> Probably the historical Jesus spoke of God as good and rejected this divine predicate for himself.[90]

> Jesus brusquely rejects the adulation. . . . It is difficult to imagine the post-Easter church, as it sought to win converts to its faith that the risen Jesus was Lord, Messiah, and Son of God, went out of its way to create this particular answer.[91]

Note well that in each of these examples, the verdict in favor of historicity is directly based on the view that Jesus is rejecting the implication that he is good like God. This is an excellent example of how exegesis has a direct impact on conclusions about historicity.[92] Notice also that in each case, the argument in favor of historicity is a form of the form-critical "criterion of embarrassment": namely, that a saying or deed of Jesus is more likely to be historical if it is difficult to reconcile with or is potentially embarrassing to the practice and belief of the early church.[93] Since, however, the criterion of embarrassment has been subject to incisive criticism (with which I largely agree), and because I do not agree that Jesus is denying that he is good, I do not think this is a valid argument against historicity.[94] Instead, I will follow our standard procedure and evaluate the historical plausibility of the accounts of Jesus and the rich man from a triple-context approach. When we do so, we discover that there are in fact other, better arguments in favor of the substantial historicity of the episode.

89. Theissen and Merz, *Historical Jesus*, 557–58.

90. Lüdemann, *Jesus after Two Thousand Years*, 70.

91. Meier, *A Marginal Jew*, 3:516.

92. See chapter 1 herein, and Gerd Theissen and Dagmar Winter, *The Quest for the Plausible Jesus: The Question of Criteria*, trans. M. Eugene Boring (Louisville: Westminster, 2002), 193, 197.

93. See Meier, *A Marginal Jew*, 1:168–71.

94. For problems with the criterion of embarrassment, see Rafael Rodriguez, "The Embarrassing Truth about Jesus: The Criterion of Embarrassment and the Failure of Historical Authenticity," in *Jesus, Criteria, and the Demise of Authenticity*, ed. Chris Keith and Anthony Le Donne (London: T&T Clark, 2012), 132–51; Dale C. Allison Jr., "How to Marginalize the Traditional Criteria of Authenticity," in Holmén and Porter, *Handbook for the Study of the Historical Jesus*, 1:3–30.

Contextual Plausibility within Judaism

The first reason there is such widespread unanimity about the historical plausibility of Jesus's exchange with the rich man is because virtually every aspect of the episode fits quite squarely into a first-century Jewish context.

For example, it is eminently plausible that the rich man would ask a Jewish "teacher" like Jesus a question about how to inherit "eternal life" (Matt 19:16; Mark 10:17; Luke 18:18). Although the expression "eternal life" is only used once in Jewish Scripture (Dan 12:2–3), by the first century, the concept was quite at home in early Jewish literature focused on eschatology.[95] To take just one example:

> The destruction of the sinner is forever,
> and he will not be remembered when (God) looks after the righteous . . .
> but those who fear the Lord shall rise up to *eternal life*,
> and their life shall be in the Lord's light, and it shall never end.
> (Psalms of Solomon 3:11–12)[96]

Given the possibility of experiencing eternal punishment due to sin, it is quite credible that someone would ask a Jewish teacher like Jesus what they must do to avoid such a fate and instead inherit eternal life.

Moreover, it is equally plausible that, as a Jew, Jesus would respond to a question about eternal life by alluding to the Shema and the Decalogue and insisting on the necessity of keeping the Ten Commandments (Matt 19:17; Mark 10:17; Luke 18:18).[97] As we have already seen above, the discovery of the Nash Papyrus in the early twentieth century provided evidence that the Shema and the Ten Commandments were already being juxtaposed in the Second Temple period.[98] This found further support in the late 1940s with the discovery of the Dead Sea Scrolls, among which were found ancient Jewish phylacteries—the box-like leather containers worn on the forehead and arms—containing texts of the Decalogue (Deut 5:6–18) along with the words of the Shema

95. Meier, *A Marginal Jew*, 3:586; George W. E. Nickelsburg, *Resurrection, Immortality, and Eternal Life in Intertestamental Judaism and Early Christianity*, exp. ed., Harvard Theological Studies 56 (Cambridge, MA: Harvard University Press, 2006), remains a classic study.

96. In Charlesworth, *Old Testament Pseudepigrapha*, 2:655. For other examples, see 2 Macc 7:9; Psalms of Solomon 9:5; 13:11; 14:4, 7–10; 1 Enoch 37:4; 40:9; 58:3.

97. Funk, Hoover, and the Jesus Seminar, *Five Gospels*, 91.

98. See Najman, "Decalogue," 527.

(Deut 6:4–9).[99] This discovery is particularly important given positive evidence for the use of phylacteries in Jewish daily prayer, as in Josephus:

> Twice each day, at the dawn thereof and when the hour comes for turning to repose, let all acknowledge before God the bounties which He has bestowed on them through their deliverance from the land of Egypt. . . . They shall inscribe also on their doors the greatest of all the benefits which they have received from God and each shall display them on his arms . . . let them bear a record thereof written on the head and on the arm. (Josephus, *Antiquities* 4.213)[100]

When the evidence for the use of phylacteries from Josephus is combined with the phylacteries found among the Dead Sea Scrolls, a strong case can be made that, at the time of Jesus, because of their role in daily prayer, the texts of the Shema and the Decalogue would have been perhaps *the two most familiar passages in all of Jewish Scripture*. Hence, it is completely credible that Jesus would respond to a question about how to inherit eternal life by alluding to the centrality of upholding the Shema and keeping the Ten Commandments.

Finally, if Jesus's declaration that no one is "good" except the "one" God is in fact not a rejection of his own goodness, but a riddle meant to lead the rich man into a realization of Jesus's divinity, then even Jesus's act of adding a requirement to the Decalogue is contextually plausible. For by the time of Jesus, it was widely recognized that the Ten Commandments were unique among the laws of God, because they alone were written with "the finger of God" (Exod 31:18). That is, they were given by God himself. Consider, for example, the words of Jesus's Jewish contemporary Philo of Alexandria:

> *The ten oracles . . . God gave forth Himself as well befitted his holiness.* For it was in accordance with his nature that the pronouncements in which the special laws were summed up *should be given by Him in His own person . . . He was God* [*theos ēn*], *and it follows at once that as Lord He was good*, the cause of good only and of nothing ill. (Philo, *Decalogue* 33.175–176)

Notice here that Philo, like Jesus, insists that the God who gave the "ten oracles" to Israel was "good" (*agathos*), and "the cause of good only" (*monōn*

99. See David Rothstein, "Phylacteries and Mezuzoth," in Collins and Harlow, *Eerdmans Dictionary of Early Judaism*, 1086–88.

100. See also *Letter of Aristeas* 159; Philo, *Special Laws* 4.137.

agathōn aitios). Notice also that Philo affirms that the Ten Commandments, unlike other laws, were given by God "in his own person" (*autoprosōpōs*), rather than through the mediation of a prophet. Hence, if a first-century Jewish teacher like Jesus wanted to lead the rich man to discover for himself that Jesus was God come *in person*, then one contextually intelligible way to do so would be for Jesus to both affirm the truth of the Shema that there is only one God and to add a requirement to the Decalogue that had been given directly by God—a requirement that necessitated following *him*.

Coherence with Other Evidence about Jesus

The accounts of Jesus's encounter with the rich man also present a powerful case from coherence with other evidence about Jesus.

For example, Jesus's act of responding to the rich man's calling him "Teacher" and asking him about "eternal life" with a riddle-like question and an allusion to the Shema (Matt 19:17; Mark 10:18; Luke 18:19) coheres perfectly with the abundant evidence that "Jesus used riddles both to establish his authority as a teacher and to communicate his message."[101] As we will see in more detail in chapter 4, when it comes to the question of Jesus's identity, the evidence strongly suggests that, when speaking about his identity, Jesus preferred to utilize indirect, riddle-like speech rather than direct, explicit statements.[102] For now, consider the episode in which Jesus implies that he is "greater" than Jonah or Solomon:

> The people of Nineveh will rise up at the judgment with this generation and condemn it, because they repented at the proclamation of Jonah, and see, *something greater than Jonah is here!* The queen of the South will rise up at the judgment with this generation and condemn it, because she came from the ends of the earth to listen to the wisdom of Solomon, and see, *something greater than Solomon is here!* (Matt 12:41–42)

> The queen of the South will rise at the judgment with the people of this generation and condemn them, because she came from the ends of the earth to listen to the wisdom of Solomon, and see, *something greater than Solomon is here!* The people of Nineveh will rise up at the judgment with

101. Thatcher, *Jesus the Riddler*, xi.
102. Bauckham, *Jesus: A Very Short Introduction*, 58.

> this generation and condemn it, because they repented at the proclamation of Jonah, and see, *something greater than Jonah is here!* (Luke 11:31–32)

Note well that in this saying—which a variety of scholars regard as substantially historical[103]—Jesus does not explicitly say who he is. Instead, he uses allusions to Jewish Scripture to imply that he is someone far greater than the wise king Solomon or the prophet Jonah (cf. 1 Kgs 4:29–34; Jonah 3:1–10). In the same way, when Jesus responds to the rich man with an allusion to the Shema (Deut 6:4–6), he is not denying that he is more than merely human. Rather, he is using a riddle-like question to lead the rich man to recognize for himself who Jesus really is and why he should leave everything to follow him.

In addition, Jesus's allusion to the Shema and his insistence on the necessity of keeping the second "tablet" of the Decalogue (Matt 19:17–19; Mark 10:18–19; Luke 18:19–20) coheres perfectly with other evidence that Jesus combined the Shema (Deut 6:4–6) with the Mosaic command to love one's neighbor (Lev 19:18):

> One of them, a lawyer, asked him a question to test him. "Teacher, which commandment in the law is the greatest?" He said to him, "'*You shall love the Lord your God with all your heart, and with all your soul, and with all your mind.*' This is the greatest and first commandment. And a second is like it: 'You shall love your neighbor as yourself.' On these two commandments hang all the law and the prophets." (Matt 22:35–40)

> One of the scribes came near and heard them disputing with one another, and seeing that he answered them well, he asked him, "Which commandment is the first of all?" Jesus answered, "*The first is, 'Hear, O Israel: the Lord our God, the Lord is one; you shall love the Lord your God with all your heart, and with all your soul, and with all your mind, and with all your strength.'* The second is this, 'You shall love your neighbor as yourself.' There is no other commandment greater than these." (Mark 12:28–31)

> Just then a lawyer stood up to test Jesus. "Teacher," he said, "what must I do to inherit eternal life?" He said to him, "What is written in the law? What do you read there?" He answered, "*You shall love the Lord your God with all your heart, and with all your soul, and with all your strength, and with all*

103. See Dunn, *Jesus Remembered*, 440–41; Lüdemann, *Jesus after Two Thousand Years*, 331.

> *your mind;* and your neighbor as yourself." And he said to him, "You have given the right answer; do this, and you will live." (Luke 10:25–28)

In light of Jesus's emphasis on the utter centrality of the commandments to love God and neighbor—which is also widely regarded as substantially historical[104]—it makes perfect sense that he would answer the rich man's question about how to have eternal life by (implicitly) pointing to the requirement to love God in the Shema and to the requirement to love one's neighbor in the commandments from the second tablet of the Decalogue.

Moreover, Jesus's demand that the rich man sell his possessions, give the money to the poor, and come follow him (Matt 19:21; Mark 10:21; Luke 18:22) also coheres remarkably well with abundant other evidence in which Jesus emphasizes "the danger of wealth" and invites his disciples to "give up their resources" to follow him.[105] One thinks here of the evidence that Jesus instructed his disciples to store up "treasure[s] in heaven" rather than on earth (Matt 6:19–21; Luke 12:33), his warnings about "the lure of wealth" and "riches" in his explanation of the parable of the sower (Matt 13:22; Mark 4:19; Luke 8:14), and his explicit commands for his disciples to "sell" their possessions and "give alms" (Luke 12:33; Matt 6:2–3).[106] Particularly noteworthy in this regard is Jesus's shocking declaration that a person who loves money cannot love God:

> No one can serve two masters; for a slave will either *hate* the one and *love* the other, or be devoted to the one and despise the other. *You cannot serve God and wealth.* (Matt 6:24)

> No slave can serve two masters; for a slave will either *hate* the one and *love* the other, or be devoted to the one and despise the other. *You cannot serve God and wealth.* (Luke 16:13)

This saying, which is also widely regarded as historical, provides a solid case of coherence with Jesus's response to the rich man.[107] When we recall that the

104. See Hengel and Schwemer, *Jesus and Judaism*, 456–59; Meier, *A Marginal Jew*, 4:481–582; Dunn, *Jesus Remembered*, 584–86.

105. Dunn, *Jesus Remembered*, 521; Hengel and Schwemer, *Jesus and Judaism*, 380; Puig i Tàrrech, *Jesus: A Biography*, 430–31; Keener, *Historical Jesus of the Gospels*, 206–7; Lüdemann, *Jesus after Two Thousand Years*, 70; Funk, Hoover, and the Jesus Seminar, *Five Gospels*, 91.

106. Funk and the Jesus Seminar, *Five Gospels*, 91.

107. E.g., Lüdemann, *Jesus after Two Thousand Years*, 148: "The saying [in Matt 6:24; Luke 16:13] is authentic."

first tablet of the Ten Commandments is focused on "love" of God (Exod 20:6; Deut 5:10) and that Jesus only lists commandments from the second tablet, involving love of neighbor, one cannot help but wonder if perhaps Jesus's injunction for the rich man to divest himself of his wealth implies that though the man has kept the commandment to love his neighbor, his attachment to wealth has kept him from fulfilling the commandment to love God.[108] If this is correct, then Jesus gives a stunningly "self-centered" solution to the problem: *if the rich man truly wants to love God, then he will give up his money and follow Jesus.* Seen in this light, Jesus seems to be putting himself in the place of God.

Last, Jesus's act of adding a requirement to the Decalogue (Matt 19:21; Mark 10:21; Luke 18:22) also coheres with other evidence in which he appears to place following him above the ordinary obligations of the Torah. We have already looked at Jesus's shocking demand that his disciples place him above their duties to their parents (Matt 10:37–39; Luke 14:25–27), as well as his equally shocking response to a potential disciple who wished to first bury his father: "Let the dead bury their own dead" (Matt 8:21–22; Luke 9:59–60). In both passages, Jesus appears to say that "following him superseded the requirements of piety and the Torah."[109] This is exactly what Jesus is doing when he not only requires the rich man to keep the Ten Commandments of the God of Israel, but to sell all that he has and come follow Jesus.

Consequences in the Early Church

Finally, if the gospel accounts of Jesus's encounter with the rich man are substantially historical, they would also provide a plausible origin for several aspects of practice and belief in the early church.

For one thing, Jesus's insistence that the rich man keep the Ten Commandments in order to have eternal life (Matt 19:17–19; Mark 10:19; Luke 18:20) provides a plausible explanation for why the early church continued to insist that its members follow the Decalogue, even though it taught that other commandments of Moses—such as the law of circumcision—were not necessary for salvation.[110] Here are just a few key examples:

108. Dunn, *Jesus Remembered*, 521.

109. Sanders, *Jesus and Judaism*, 255.

110. See R. A. Freund, "The Decalogue in Early Judaism and Christianity," in *The Function of Scripture in Early Judaism and Christian Tradition*, ed. Craig A. Evans and James A.

> Circumcision is nothing, and uncircumcision is nothing; but *obeying the commandments of God is everything.* (1 Cor 7:19)

> Owe no one anything, except to love one another; for the one who loves another has fulfilled the law. *The commandments,* "You shall not commit adultery; You shall not murder; You shall not steal; You shall not covet"; and any other commandment, *are summed up in this word, "Love your neighbor as yourself."* Love does no wrong to a neighbor; therefore, love is the fulfilling of the law. (Rom 13:8–10)

> By this we know that we love the children of God, when we love God and obey his commandments. *For the love of God is this, that we obey his commandments.* (1 John 5:2–3)

> Here is a call for the endurance of the saints, *those who keep the commandments of God* and hold fast to the faith of Jesus. (Rev 14:12; cf. 12:17)

As these passages make clear, though certain commandments of Moses may have been considered by some in the early church to be nonbinding (cf. Acts 15:1–21), by contrast, the Ten Commandments—insofar as they focused on love of God and love of neighbor—were widely regarded as binding. One plausible explanation for the widespread affirmation of keeping the Decalogue in the early church is that Jesus himself had insisted that love of God and love of neighbor were necessary for salvation.

Moreover, Jesus's demand that the rich man sell everything, give his money to the poor, and then come follow Jesus (Matt 19:21–22; Mark 10:21–22; Luke 18:22–23) provides a plausible genesis for why members of the early Jerusalem church divested themselves of all their wealth and held everything in common: "All who believed were together and had all things in common; they would sell their possessions and goods and distribute the proceeds to all, as any had need" (Acts 2:44–45). Although some scholars question the historical veracity of this description, it seems quite reasonable to suggest that the reason many early Jewish Christians voluntarily sold their possessions and gave the proceeds to the poor is because Jesus himself made these kinds of demands on those he called to be his disciples.[111]

Sanders (Sheffield: Sheffield Academic Press, 1998), 124–41; Flusser, "Ten Commandments," 219–46.

111. Cf. Meier, *A Marginal Jew*, 3:517, 588n87.

Last, but certainly not least, if Jesus did use his riddle-like allusion to the Shema and his demand for the rich man to leave everything and follow him as a way of putting himself on par with the "one" God of Israel (Matt 19:17; Mark 10:18; Luke 18:19), this would provide a plausible genesis for why someone like the apostle Paul would likewise use an allusion to the Shema to uphold both the unity of the one God and the divinity of Christ:

> Indeed, even though there may be so-called gods in heaven or on earth—as in fact there are many gods and many lords—yet *for us there is one God, the Father*, from whom are all things and for whom we exist, *and one Lord, Jesus Christ*, through whom are all things and through whom we exist. (1 Cor 8:5–6)

As I have argued elsewhere in more depth, with these words, *Paul affirms the divinity of Jesus by including him in the Shema.*[112] For the "one" (*heis*) God and the "one" (*heis*) Lord spoken of by Paul is undoubtedly an allusion to the "Lord God" (*kyrios ho theos*) of the Shema, who is likewise "one" (*heis*) (1 Cor 8:6; cf. Deut 6:4 LXX).[113] How then do we explain Paul's remarkable inclusion of a fully human being such as Jesus in the central Jewish confession of the one God? The most reasonable explanation is that Paul was not the first to do so. In his encounter with the rich man, Jesus himself had already implied that he was in some way equal with the one good God who gave the Shema and the Decalogue to the people of Israel. Like Paul after him, Jesus used the Shema both to safeguard the oneness of God and to make clear that he was not another deity, but somehow the same God who gave the Decalogue to the people of Israel and commanded them to love him with all their heart, soul, and strength.

Weighing the Arguments for and against Historical Plausibility

With all of this in mind, what then do we make of the arguments for and against the historical plausibility of Jesus's encounter with the rich man—

112. See Brant Pitre, Michael P. Barber, and John A. Kincaid, *Paul, a New Covenant Jew: Rethinking Pauline Theology* (Grand Rapids: Eerdmans, 2019), 116–18.

113. See Chris Tilling, *Paul's Divine Christology* (Grand Rapids: Eerdmans, 2015), 90–92; N. T. Wright, *Paul and the Faithfulness of God*, vol. 4 of *Christian Origins and the Question of God* (Minneapolis: Fortress, 2013), 661–70; Joseph A. Fitzmyer, *First Corinthians*, Anchor Yale Bible 32 (New Haven: Yale University Press, 2008), 342; Richard Bauckham, *Jesus and the God of Israel* (Grand Rapids: Eerdmans, 2008), 27–28, 210–18.

especially his declaration that no one is good but God and his act of adding the requirement of following him to the Decalogue?

As I noted above, this is one of the few cases in which there is virtual unanimity among scholars—a unanimity that goes back to the very beginnings of the modern quest—that Jesus's response to the rich man's question is indeed historical. For this reason, there are not really any major arguments against historicity from major works on Jesus with which to engage. Of course, as I also noted above, this widespread affirmation of historicity is ordinarily based on the erroneous view that, in this exchange, Jesus both denies that he is God and that he is good, as well as the form-critical criterion of embarrassment. However convincing such an appeal to the criterion of embarrassment might seem at first glance, it is actually quite problematic. After all, if Jesus is in fact denying that he is God, and if his insistence that God alone is good was actually embarrassing to the authors of the Gospels, then why did none of them exclude it from their accounts (Matt 19:17; Mark 10:18; Luke 18:19)?

Hence, better reasons in support of historical plausibility can be found by employing a triple-context approach. When Jesus's declaration that no one is good but God is interpreted correctly as a riddle-like invitation to the rich man to realize the implications of his own words and give up everything to follow Jesus—a strong case can be made that Jesus's exchange with the rich man is contextually plausible within a first-century Jewish context, coherent with other evidence about Jesus, and provides a plausible explanation for early Christian practice and belief. In particular, if Jesus wanted to imply that he was divine without infringing on early Jewish belief in the one God of Israel, it makes sense that he would do so by alluding both to the Shema (Deut 6:4–6) and to the Decalogue (Exod 20:1–18). Moreover, his use of such indirect language is perfectly in keeping with other sayings in which Jesus does not explicitly say who he is, but uses allusions to Jewish Scripture to imply that he is greater than even the greatest figures in biblical history (Matt 12:41–42; Luke 11:31–32). Finally, even his emphasis on the truth of the Shema and the necessity of keeping the commandments provides a plausible explanation for the emphasis on keeping the Decalogue in the early church (1 Cor 7:19; Rom 13:8–10; 1 John 5:2–3; Rev 14:1), as well as one key passage in which Paul affirms the divinity of Christ by including Jesus in the Shema's confession of "one God" and "one Lord" (1 Cor 8:5–6).

In short, when we interpret the account of Jesus and the rich man in its first-century context, we discover that the passage most frequently used to argue that Jesus does not claim to be divine, upon closer inspection, turns out to be powerful evidence that Jesus does speak and act as if he is equal with God. However, the only way to see this clearly is to interpret the exchange in its first-century Jewish context. Seen in this light, Jesus implies that he is more than human, but he does so in a way that is both deeply Jewish (by alluding to the Shema and the Decalogue) and consistent with his tendency elsewhere to speak about his identity in implicit ways. During his public ministry, Jesus wants his interlocutors to ask for themselves: Who is this man? And what is his relationship with the one God of Israel?

The Riddle of David's Lord

The third episode in which Jesus uses riddle-like questions and allusions to Jewish Scripture to both reveal and conceal his divinity also happens to be the only passage in the Four Gospels in which Jesus explicitly describes the figure of "the messiah" (*ho christos*). This episode, which has been aptly described as "a riddle,"[114] and even as a "christological riddle,"[115] occurs in all three Synoptic Gospels:

> Now while the Pharisees were gathered together, Jesus asked them this question: "*What do you think of the Messiah? Whose son is he?*" They said to him, "The son of David." He said to them, "*How is it then that David by the Spirit calls him Lord*, saying,
>
> '*The Lord said to my Lord,*
> *"Sit at my right hand,*
> until I put your enemies under your feet"'?
>
> *If David thus calls him Lord, how can he be his son?*" No one was able to give him an answer, nor from that day did anyone dare to ask him any more questions. (Matt 22:41–46)

> While Jesus was teaching in the temple, he said, "*How can the scribes say that the Messiah is the son of David?* David himself, by the Holy Spirit, declared,
>
> '*The Lord said to my Lord,*
> *"Sit at my right hand,*
> until I put your enemies under your feet."'

114. Matthew V. Novenson, *The Grammar of Messianism: An Ancient Jewish Political Idiom and Its Users* (Oxford: Oxford University Press, 2017), 16.

115. Hengel and Schwemer, *Jesus and Judaism*, 846; cf. Dunn, *Jesus Remembered*, 635.

> *David himself calls him Lord; so how can he be his son?*" And the large crowd was listening to him with delight. (Mark 12:35–37)

> Then he said to them, "*How can they say that the Messiah is David's son?* For David himself says in the book of Psalms,
> *'The Lord said to my Lord,*
> *"Sit at my right hand,*
> until I make your enemies your footstool."'
> *David thus calls him Lord; so how can he be his son?*" (Luke 20:41–43)

While there are a few differences in detail, the substance of the three accounts can be summarized as follows: (1) Jesus asks an initial question about the filial identity of the messiah; (2) Jesus quotes the first line of Psalm 110 to show that King David himself referred to the messiah as "lord"; (3) Jesus poses a riddle: if David himself calls the messiah his "lord," then how can the messiah be David's "son"? In keeping with the other riddles we've examined in this chapter, in all three accounts, Jesus does not answer the question, but invites his audience to figure out how to reconcile the messiah being both descended from David and yet superior to David.

Jesus Does Not "Reject" the Davidic Identity of the Messiah

When it comes to exegesis, despite what some interpreters have claimed, Jesus neither "refutes" the teaching of Jewish Scripture that the future anointed king would be descended from King David,[116] nor does he assert that "the Messiah cannot be the Son of David."[117] Such a suggestion is quite wrong, on two counts.

To begin with, Jesus quite simply does not "refute" or "reject" anything. He merely *asks a question* about the filial identity of the messiah. Look again at the texts in question:

> What do you think of the Messiah? Whose son is he? (Matt 22:42)

> How can the scribes say that the Messiah is the son of David? (Mark 12:35)

> How can they say that the Messiah is David's son? (Luke 20:41)

116. Schröter, *Jesus of Nazareth*, 46; cf. 173.
117. Theissen and Merz, *Historical Jesus*, 194–95.

As anyone familiar with Jewish Scripture knows, this kind of riddle is amply attested in the wisdom literature (cf. Prov 1:6). Consider, for example, a remarkably similar question-shaped *mashal* from the book of Proverbs:

> Who has ascended to heaven and come down? . . .
> Who has wrapped up the waters in a garment?
> Who has established all the ends of the earth?
> *What is his name, and what is his son's name?*
> Surely you know! (Prov 30:4)[118]

In this passage from Proverbs and in Jesus's riddle about the messiah, the question about the identity of the "son" does not function as a *refutation*, but as an *invitation* to the audience to answer the question for themselves.[119] As James Dunn rightly states regarding Jesus's question: "the passage's riddling quality puts the onus on the hearer to draw out its significance."[120]

Even more important, Jewish Scripture repeatedly and unequivocally testifies that the future king of Israel *would* in fact be descended from King David. As John Collins writes: "The Hebrew Scriptures provided a clear basis for the expectation of a royal messiah from the line of David."[121] In support of this point, consider the following oracles about the future Davidic king:

> When your days are fulfilled and you lie down with your fathers, *I will raise up your offspring after you, who shall come forth from your body, and I will establish his kingdom.* He shall build a house for my name, and *I will establish the throne of his kingdom forever.* I will be his father, and *he shall be my son.* (2 Sam 7:12–14)

118. NRSV, slightly adapted.

119. See Michael V. Fox, *Proverbs*, Anchor Yale Bible 18A–18B (New Haven: Yale University Press, 2000, 2009), 1:65. Fox specifically cites Prov 30:4 in particular as an example of one of the riddle-like "enigmas" in the book.

120. Dunn, *Jesus Remembered*, 651.

121. John J. Collins, *The Scepter and the Star: Messianism in Light of the Dead Sea Scrolls*, 2nd ed. (Grand Rapids: Eerdmans, 2010), 24. See also Shirley Lucass, *The Concept of the Messiah in the Scriptures of Judaism and Christianity*, Library of Second Temple Studies 78 (London: Bloomsbury, 2011), 66–121; Adela Yarbro Collins and John J. Collins, *King and Messiah as Son of God: Divine, Human, and Angelic Messianic Figures in Biblical and Related Literature* (Grand Rapids: Eerdmans, 2008), 1–47; Antii Laato, *A Star Is Rising: The Historical Development of the Old Testament Royal Ideology and the Rise of the Jewish Messianic Expectations* (Atlanta: Scholars Press, 1997).

> *For a child has been born for us,*
> *a son given to us;*
> authority rests upon his shoulders;
> and he is named
> Wonderful Counselor, Mighty God,
> Everlasting Father, Prince of Peace.
> His authority shall grow continually,
> and there shall be endless peace
> *for the throne of David and his kingdom.*
> He will establish and uphold it
> with justice and with righteousness
> from this time onward and forevermore. (Isa 9:6–7; cf. 11:1–9)

> The days are surely coming, says the Lord, *when I will raise up for David a righteous Branch, and he shall reign as king* and deal wisely, and shall execute justice and righteousness in the land. (Jer 23:5)

In light of such passages—and they could easily be multiplied—it is highly implausible to suggest that Jesus is outright rejecting the scriptural teaching that the future king would be a Davidide simply because he poses a question about it.[122] Ben Witherington puts the point very well when he writes:

> The Davidic origin of the messiah was too well established for Jesus to dispute such a matter. Nowhere else in the Gospel tradition do we have any evidence that he did so. Rather, Jesus is showing the inadequacy, not the inaccuracy, of such an interpretation of the messiah. The point is that the messiah is more than a Son of David, not that he is other than a Son of David.[123]

In other words, Jesus questions the adequacy of describing "the Messiah" merely as the "son" of David (Matt 22:42; Mark 12:35; Luke 20:41), when in fact, he is much more. Such a qualification is especially plausible when we

122. See also 1 Chron 17:11–14; Isa 11:1–9; Jer 30:9; 33:15, 22; Ezek 34:23–24; 37:24; Hos 3:5; Amos 9:11; Vermes, *Authentic Gospel of Jesus*, 62; Witherington, *Christology of Jesus*, 189; Cf. Wright, *Jesus and the Victory of God*, 509: "Davidic sonship, however, is so clearly a part of the messianic profile in Jewish tradition, going back to 2 Samuel 7, that it seems unlikely that anyone, even Jesus, would have attempted to overturn it with a single counter-text."

123. Witherington, *Christology of Jesus*, 190. On the messianic character of Psalm 110, see Bond, *Historical Jesus*, 63; Dunn, *Jesus Remembered*, 634–35.

recall that the title "Son of David" never occurs in Jewish Scripture.[124] In other words, Jesus is not saying that the messiah will be non-Davidic; he is implying that the messiah will be *super-Davidic*.[125]

Psalm 110, David's "Lord," and the Divine Son of God

In order to illustrate the super-Davidic character of the messiah, Jesus quotes Psalm 110, in which King David himself refers to a royal figure who will take the throne as his "lord" (*kyrios*) (Matt 22:42–43; Mark 12:35–36; Luke 20:41–42). In order to feel the full force of Jesus's quotation, it is important to recall the contents of the opening lines of the psalm:

> A Psalm of David.
> *The* LORD *says to my lord,*
> *"Sit at my right hand,*
> *until I make your enemies your footstool."*
> The LORD sends out from Zion
> your mighty scepter.
> Rule in the midst of your foes.
> Yours is princely power in the day of your birth, in holy splendor;
> *From the womb of the dawn, like the dew, I have begotten you.*
> The LORD has sworn and will not change his mind,
> "You are a priest forever
> according to the order of Melchizedek." (Ps 110:1–14)[126]

Since Jesus explicitly identifies the royal figure spoken of by David in Psalm 110 as "the messiah" (*ho christos*) (Matt 22:41; Mark 12:35; Luke 20:41), this psalm gives us a crucial window into what Jesus is implying about the messiah—on several key points.[127]

124. The earliest extant use of "Son of David" as a messianic title comes from the first-century Psalms of Solomon 17:23. Despite the prominence of priestly messianic figures in the Dead Sea Scrolls, even they bear witness to the belief that the future king will be a Davidide (4QFlorilegium [4Q174] I, 11–13; cf. Amos 9:11).

125. Or, as Matthew Novenson puts it, "a supra-Davidide Jesus." See Novenson, *Grammar of Messianism*, 86.

126. NRSV, adapted.

127. See Frank Lothar Hossfeld and Eric Zenger, *Psalms 3*, trans. Linda M. Maloney (Minneapolis: Fortress, 2011), 140–49.

(1) The messiah in Psalm 110 is not just a descendant of David who wields the royal scepter. He is a "'new' David,"[128] who is also *greater than David*, since David addresses him as "lord" (Ps 110:1).[129]

(2) The messiah in Psalm 110 is also described as a *divine figure*. For one thing, unlike David and Solomon, whose throne is located in the earthly city of Jerusalem (cf. 1 Kgs 10:18–19; 1 Chron 29:23)—the figure in Psalm 110 sits at the "right hand" of God in heaven.[130] As John Collins points out: "The invitation to the king to sit at the right of the deity . . . is not only one of honor, but bespeaks the very close association of the king and the deity."[131] This association between the king and God is so close that the king can be described as "the 'throne companion' of YHWH,"[132] and his enthronement as "the enthronement of the king/god/God."[133]

(3) Finally, the messiah in Psalm 110 is also described as a *son of God*. This filial identity is difficult to see in the standard translation of the Hebrew text as "From the womb of the morning, like dew, your youth will come to you" (Ps 110:3 NRSV). However, as Psalm experts have shown, the Masoretic vocalization of the consonants that lies behind this translation is "problematic," for the unpointed Hebrew text is more naturally construed as saying the king was "begotten" (*yalad*) by God himself "from the womb of the dawn" (*merekhem mishkhar*) (Ps 110:3).[134] In the words of Frank Hossfeld and Eric Zenger:

> "I have borne/begotten you" [Ps 110:3] (as in Ps 2:7); that form is even given in numerous manuscripts. This reading thus proclaims the enthronement as divine begetting or birth from the dawn. This formulation was evidently

128. Hossfeld and Zenger, *Psalms 3*, 146.

129. MT *'adon*; LXX *kyrios*. Hengel and Schwemer, *Jesus and Judaism*, 599; Puig i Tàrrech, *Jesus: A Biography*, 453.

130. Hossfeld and Zenger, *Psalms 3*, 148.

131. Yarbro Collins and Collins, *King and Messiah*, 16.

132. Hossfeld and Zenger, *Psalms 3*, 147–48.

133. Lucass, *Concept of the Messiah*, 74. For ancient images of this divine enthronement, see Hossfeld and Zenger, *Psalms 3*, 148; and Othmar Keel, *The Symbolism of the Biblical World: Ancient Near Eastern Iconography and the Book of Psalms*, trans. Timothy J. Hallett (Winona Lake, IN: Eisenbrauns, 1997), 256–64.

134. Hossfeld and Zenger, *Psalms 3*, 142. The issue here is the problematic vocalization of the medieval Masoretic text as *yalduteka* ("your youth") rather than *yelidtika* ("I have borne/begotten you"). The latter finds strong support in the parallel divine "begetting" of the Davidic king in Ps 2:7. For similar arguments that the unpointed Hebrew refers to the "begetting of the messianic king," see Robert R. Cargill, *Melchizedek, King of Sodom: How Scribes Invented the Biblical Priest-King* (Oxford: Oxford University Press, 2019), 87–89.

> too mythical for the hand responsible for the [Masoretic] text we now have, and it was altered.[135]

Should there be any doubt about this suggestion, it is worth noting that the image of being "begotten" (*yalad*) by God is used elsewhere to describe the royal son of God (Ps 2:7), while "son of the Dawn" (*ben shakhar*) is a divine epithet used to describe a human king (Isa 14:12).[136] Given Jesus's emphasis on the filial identity of the messiah, this may be the most direct point of contrast implied by Jesus's quotation of Psalm 110. While many say the messiah is begotten of David, David himself in Psalm 110 says the king is "begotten" by the LORD. If this is correct, then by choosing Psalm 110, Jesus seems to be implying that *the messiah is not merely the human descendent of David; he is also the divinely begotten son of God.*

Jesus Is Implying That He Is a Divine Messiah

The reason Jesus's reference to the messiah in Psalm 110 is important for our study is simple but of enormous significance: *if Jesus thinks he is the messiah, then he is using Psalm 110 to reveal what he thinks about his own identity.* Psalm 110, therefore, is a crucial key to what some scholars refer to as the "Christology" of Jesus.[137] Consider the following conclusions of both Jewish and Christian scholars:

> Jesus implicitly claims he is superior to David, since in his interpretation, David (the presumed author of the Psalm) calls the Messiah "Lord."[138]

> [Jesus] begins to imply a corresponding identity greater than that of David. . . . Jesus is no mere David redivivus, no mere warrior king like David, but one far greater than David.[139]

135. Hossfeld and Zenger, *Psalms 3*, 142. See likewise James Kugel, *Traditions of the Bible: A Guide to the Bible as It Was at the Start of the Common Era* (Cambridge: Harvard University Press, 1997), 280.

136. Joseph Blenkinsopp, *Isaiah*, 3 vols., Anchor Yale Bible 19, 19A, 19B (New Haven: Yale University Press, 2000–2003), 1:288.

137. Cf. Witherington, *Christology of Jesus*, throughout.

138. Aaron M. Gale, "Matthew," in *The Jewish Annotated New Testament*, ed. Amy-Jill Levine and Marc Zvi Brettler, 2nd ed. (Oxford: Oxford University Press, 2017), 52.

139. Keener, *Historical Jesus of the Gospels*, 270.

> Clearly, this text is a crucial one in Jesus' process of self-discernment and self-understanding. This text, when coupled with others, strongly suggests that Jesus did see himself in more than ordinary human categories.[140]

I agree with these suggestions, but I would go a bit further and press the question: *In what sense* is Jesus superior to David?

The answer comes from a close reading of Psalm 110. By quoting Psalm 110, Jesus is implying that he himself is not just a descendent of King David; he is David's "lord." Moreover, when the rest of the psalm is taken into account, Jesus also appears to be implying that he will be seated at "the right hand" of God in heaven (Ps 110:1) and even perhaps that he was "begotten" by the Lord God from "the womb of the dawn" (Ps 110:3)—that is, as a superhuman being (cf. the "son of Dawn" in Isa 14:12).[141] In other words, *Jesus uses Psalm 110 to imply that the messiah is not simply the heir of David, but the super-Davidic, divine Son of God.* And Jesus does all this not by shouting it from the rooftops or going around declaring, "I am the divine messiah." Instead, as a Jewish teacher of parables, he uses riddles, questions, and allusions to Scripture to lead his audience to ask for themselves: "Who is the messiah really? What does David himself say?" In the end, Jesus himself "provides no solution to this question," precisely because he wants his audience to draw their own conclusions.[142]

In sum, a strong case can be made that Jesus uses the riddle of the messiah in Psalm 110 to reveal the mystery of his divine messiahship. As the messiah of Jewish Scripture, Jesus is both a descendent of King David and the Lord of King David. He is both the long-awaited king of Israel and the super-Davidic Son of God. In other words, he is both human and divine. And he reveals all this without ever explicitly proclaiming, "I am the messiah," or "I am David's Lord," much less, "I existed from before the womb of the dawn." Instead, Jesus uses the riddle about the messiah in Psalm 110 to both reveal and conceal his divine messiahship—until the time is right for him to be more explicit. Indeed, as we will see in the chapter 5, there is good reason to believe that Jesus also uses Psalm 110 (along with Daniel 7) to reveal his identity in the presence of the

140. Witherington, *Christology of Jesus*, 191.

141. Some also see some kind of preexistent status here, though it is admittedly difficult to demonstrate. See Matthew W. Bates, *The Birth of the Trinity: Jesus, God, and Spirit in New Testament and Early Christian Interpretations of the Old Testament* (Oxford: Oxford University Press, 2015), 53–54; Aquila H. Lee, *From Messiah to Preexistent Son: Jesus' Self-Consciousness and Early Christian Exegesis of Messianic Psalms*, Wissenschaftliche Untersuchungen zum Neuen Testament 2.192 (Tübingen: Mohr Siebeck, 2005), 111–14, 225–38.

142. Hengel and Schwemer, *Jesus and Judaism*, 599.

Jerusalem Sanhedrin and that he is accused of blasphemy and handed over to the Romans for execution as a result (cf. Matt 26:63–64; Mark 14:61–62; Luke 22:67–68). But we will have to hold off on that topic until later. For now, we must take up the question of whether or not there are good reasons to think Jesus's riddle about the messiah even goes back to him at all.

Arguments against Historical Plausibility

When we turn from the interpretation of Jesus's riddle about the messiah to the question of its historicity, we find ourselves in a remarkable situation. Despite widespread contemporary interest in early Jewish messianism and early Christology, and despite the fact that it is the only passage in the four first-century gospels in which Jesus explicitly speaks about the figure of "the messiah" (*ho christos*) (Matt 22:42; Mark 12:35; Luke 20:41), many works on the historical Jesus simply ignore it.[143] This silence is astonishing, and its practical effect is to imply (in the absence of any real argumentation) that the episode is substantially unhistorical and therefore irrelevant to the quest for the historical Jesus.

With that said, some scholars do explicitly reject Jesus's riddle about the messiah as a creation of the early church, on several grounds.[144] The first argument against historicity is from a form of contextual implausibility. According to this view, it is difficult to imagine a "plausible context" within the Judaism of Jesus's day in which Jesus would suggest that "the messiah was not the son of David."[145] Here again exegesis determines conclusions about historicity. Moreover, since there is no early Jewish evidence from before the time of Jesus that Psalm 110 was interpreted as referring to the messiah, the gospel passage likely does not come from Jesus.[146]

143. For example, Jesus's riddle about the messiah receives no discussion in Ehrman, *How Jesus Became God*; Lohfink, *Jesus of Nazareth*; Bond, *Historical Jesus*; Grindheim, *God's Equal*; Bauckham, *Jesus, a Very Short Introduction*; Casey, *Jesus of Nazareth*; Flusser with Notley, *Sage from Galilee*; Ehrman, *Jesus: Apocalyptic Prophet*; Fredriksen, *Jesus of Nazareth*; Becker, *Jesus of Nazareth*; Gnilka, *Jesus of Nazareth*; Sanders, *Jesus and Judaism*.

144. See Lüdemann, *Jesus after Two Thousand Years*, 87; Becker, *Jesus of Nazareth*, 196; Funk, Hoover, and the Jesus Seminar, *Five Gospels*, 105; Günther Bornkamm, *Jesus of Nazareth*, trans. Irene McLuskey and Fraser McLuskey, with James M. Robinson (New York: Harper, 1960), 227–28.

145. Funk, Hoover, and the Jesus Seminar, *Five Gospels*, 105.

146. Witherington, *Christology of Jesus*, 190, summarizing the view of others.

A second argument is from a lack of coherence with other evidence. According to this view, the account of Jesus raising a question about the messiah is clearly "a secondary composition" because Jesus himself "initiates [the] dialogue," rather than his ordinary custom of simply reacting to other people's questions.[147] Other scholars argue that the riddle is uncharacteristic of Jesus because of the kind of scriptural interpretation at work in it. In the influential words of Rudolf Bultmann: "Since the proof offered in Mk. 12^{35-37} has the air of scribal sophistry about it . . . the more probable conclusion is that Mk. 12^{35-37} is a community product."[148] According to this view, the kind of "quibbling biblical exegesis" manifest in the riddle-like question about Psalm 110 is impossible to attribute to Jesus himself. [149]

Finally, there is the argument from continuity with the early church. According to this view, because Psalm 110 was "a favorite in early Christian Christological speculation (note Acts 2:34–35; Heb 1:13; 10:12–13)," and because Jesus uses Psalm 110 to reveal that the messiah is superior to David, the passage must be a creation of the early church.[150] As Gerd Lüdemann asserts: "The piece has been formed by the community, which in a learned scribal way wanted to demonstrate that Jesus is more than son of David, namely son of God. . . . The historical value of the pericope is nil, as it can be explained exclusively from discussions in the community."[151] The implicit logic of this argument seems to be that if a passage is too continuous with the practice and belief of the early church—in this case, the superiority of Jesus to David—then it must have been created by the early church. Once again, the exegesis of the episode is decisive, as when Rudolf Bultmann states that it "would not be impossible for Jesus to have spoken" the riddle—as long as he did *not* speak of "pre-existence" or "a heavenly Messiah" "with reference to himself."[152] According to this view, because we (somehow) know in advance that Jesus did not claim to be a heavenly messiah, then any evidence in which he appears to do so cannot, *de facto*, be considered historical.

147. Funk, Hoover, and the Jesus Seminar, *Five Gospels*, 105.

148. Bultmann, *History of the Synoptic Tradition*, 137.

149. Vermes, *Authentic Gospel of Jesus*, 62–63.

150. Funk, Hoover, and the Jesus Seminar, *Five Gospels*, 105.

151. Lüdemann, *Jesus after Two Thousand Years*, 87.

152. Bultmann, *History of the Synoptic Tradition*, 137. Once again, the christological tail is wagging the historical dog for Bultmann.

Context: The Divine Messiah, the Heavenly Throne, and the Preexistent Son

With that said, a number of scholars do contend that the account of Jesus's question about the messiah is substantially historical.[153] In keeping with our method of proceeding, the first major argument in favor of historicity is from contextual plausibility within early Judaism, in several ways.

First, Jesus's identification of the royal figure in Psalm 110 as a heavenly or divine "messiah" (Matt 22:42; Mark 12:35; Luke 20:41) is actually quite plausible in a Second Temple Jewish context—when due weight is given to the fact that the royal figure David addresses as "lord" in Psalm 110 is *also* explicitly described as "a priest forever, according to the order of Melchizedek" (Ps 110:4). For one of the Dead Sea Scrolls not only interprets the priest-king of Psalm 110 as an eschatological savior; it also explicitly and repeatedly calls this savior figure "God." Consider the following:

> [Its interpretation] for the last days refers to the captives . . . they are the inherita[nce of *Melchize*]*dek*, who will make them return. And liberty will be proclaimed for them, to free them from [the debt of] all their iniquities . . . atonement shall be made for all the sons of [light and] for the men [of] the lot of Melchizedek . . . accor[ding to] a[ll] their [wor]ks, for *it is the time for "the year of grace" of Melchizedek*, and of [his armies, the nat]ion of the holy ones of God, *as is written about him in the songs of David, who said: "God will [st]and in the assem[bly of God,] in the midst of the gods he judges"* (Psa 82:1). *And about him he sa[id:* "And] above [it,] to the heights, return: *God will judge the peoples*" (Psa 7:8–9). . . . Melchizedek will carry out the vengeance of Go[d's] judgments, [and on that day he will fr]e[e them from the hand of] Belial and from the hand of all the sp[irits of his lot.] To his aid (shall come) all the "gods of [justice"; and h]e is the one w[ho . . .] all the sons of God, and . . . [. . .] This [. . .] is the day of [peace about whi]ch he said [. . . through Isa]iah the prophet, who said: ["How] beautiful upon the mountains are the feet [of] the messen[ger who] announces peace, the mess[enger of good who announces salvati]on, [sa]ying to Zion: your God [reigns] (Isa 52:7)." . . . *And the messenger i[s] the messiah of the*

153. See Hengel and Schwemer, *Jesus and Judaism*, 306, 599; Puig i Tàrrech, *Jesus: A Biography*, 453; Allison, *Constructing Jesus*, 286; Keener, *Historical Jesus of the Gospels*, 270–71; Dunn, *Jesus Remembered*, 635; Theissen and Merz, *Historical Jesus*, 195; Wright, *Jesus and the Victory of God*, 507–10; Vermes, *Religion of Jesus the Jew*, 61n19; Vermes, *Jesus the Jew*, 141; Jeremias, *Proclamation of Jesus*, 259; Klausner, *Jesus of Nazareth*, 42; Schweitzer, *Quest of the Historical Jesus*, 395.

> *spir[it] as Dan[iel] said [about him: "Until a messiah, a prince*, it is seven weeks" (Dan 9:25). And the messenger of] good who announ[ces salvation] is the one about whom it is written that [. . .] "To comfort the afflicted" (11QMelchizedek [11Q13] II, 4–6, 8–11, 13–16, 18–20)[154]

Much could be said about this fascinating text.[155] For our purposes here, just a few points are necessary. A strong case can be made that the eschatological savior identified as "Melchizedek" in the Scroll is the same figure identified as the "anointed one" or "messiah" (*mshykh*) (11QMelch. II, 18). Experts in the Dead Sea Scrolls have identified him both as a "heavenly" and "messianic figure,"[156] and even as a "heavenly messiah."[157] The scroll interprets certain Psalms ("songs of David") as referring to this eschatological Melchizedek (11QMelch. II, 10–11). Precisely on the basis of these Psalms, the scroll depicts this messianic Melchizedek as a heavenly being explicitly referred to as "God" or "Elohim" (*'lwhym*) (11QMelch. II, 10, 11; cf. II, 25). In light of such observations, both Jewish and Christian scholars alike agree that the figure depicted in the scroll is a divine being:

> If Psalm 110 is interpreted as referring to the begetting of the king or Melchizedek by God, this too would lend itself to a messianic interpretation. . . . 11QMelchizedek is important . . . because it shows the growing interest in imagining a savior figure who was divine in some sense.[158]

> The Melchizedek described in the psalm [Psalm 110] seemed in some ways superhuman. . . . In fact, Melchizedek is apparently the "lord" referred to in the first line, who was commanded by God to "sit at my right hand" like some sort of angel or divine being.[159]

154. In Florentino García Martínez and Eibert J. C. Tigchelaar, *The Dead Sea Scrolls Study Edition*, 2 vols. (Grand Rapids: Eerdmans, 2000), 2:1207–9 (adapted).

155. See Annette Steudel, "Melchizedek," in *Encyclopedia of the Dead Sea Scrolls*, ed. Lawrence H. Schiffman and James C. VanderKam, 2 vols. (Oxford: Oxford University Press, 2000), 2:535–36; Paul Rainbow, "Melchizedek as a Messiah at Qumran," *Bulletin of Biblical Research* 7 (1997): 179–94.

156. Joseph A. Fitzmyer, *The One Who Is to Come* (Grand Rapids: Eerdmans, 2007), 98n68.

157. Florentino García Martínez, *Qumranica Minora II*, Studies in the Texts of the Desert of Judea 64 (Leiden: Brill, 2007), 20.

158. Yarbro Collins and Collins, *King and Messiah*, 86.

159. Kugel, *Traditions of the Bible*, 279.

It should be noted that the kind of divinity ascribed to the messianic figure in this Dead Sea Scroll does not appear to be equality with the one God, but rather a kind of superhuman or heavenly status.[160] Nevertheless, the implications of even this kind of divine messianism for the study of Jesus and early high Christology are enormous, for it would provide early Jewish evidence for a divine messiah directly based on Psalm 110. And if the early Jewish author of this Dead Sea Scroll could interpret Psalm 110 as a reference to a heavenly messiah who is in some way divine, then it is contextually plausible that the historical Jesus could do the same. Likewise, if the Dead Sea Scrolls can explicitly refer to this messiah as "God" (*'lwhym*), then there is no reason to doubt (and every reason to believe) that Jesus of Nazareth could use the very same psalm to imply that the messiah is not just human (David's "son") but also divine (David's "lord").

Second, Jesus's suggestion that "the messiah" would be exalted to "sit" at the "right hand" of God in heaven (Matt 22:44; Mark 12:36; Luke 20:42) is also contextually plausible within early Judaism. Consider, for example, the descriptions of the heavenly exaltation of an unidentified figure in the Dead Sea Scrolls and of the messianic "son of man" in the apocalypse of Enoch:

> [. . . et]ernal; *a mighty throne in the congregation of the gods* above which none of the kings of the East shall sit . . . *my glory is in{comparable} and besides me no-one is exalted*, nor comes to me, for *I reside in [. . .] the heavens*, and there is no [. . .] . . . *I am counted among the gods and my dwelling is in the holy congregation*. . . . Who bea[rs all] sorrows like me? And who [suffe]rs evil like me? There is no-one. I have been instructed, and there is no teaching comparable [to my teaching . . .] . . . *[f]or among the gods is [my] posi[tion, and] my glory is with the sons of the king*. To me (belongs) [pure] gold, and to me, the gold of Ophir . . . [. . . exult], just ones, in the God of [. . .] the holy dwelling, sing for h[im. . .] . . . in eternal happiness; and there is no . . . *to establish the horn of [his] Mess[iah. . .]* . . . to make known his power and strength. (4QSelf-Glorification Hymn^{b} [4Q491] frags. 11–12, lines 5–6, 9–14)[161]

> And the Lord of Spirits <seated him> upon *the throne of his glory*;
> and the spirit of righteousness was poured upon him. . . .

160. See especially Ruben A. Bühner, *Messianic High Christology: New Testament Variants of Second Temple Judaism* (Waco, TX: Baylor University Press, 2021), 58–60.

161. Translation in García Martínez and Tigchelaar, *The Dead Sea Scrolls Study Edition*, 2:981.

> and pain will seize them when they see *that Son of Man sitting on the throne of his glory* . . .
> *For from the beginning the Son of Man was hidden,*
> and the Most High preserved him in the presence of his might,
> and he revealed him to the chosen. (1 Enoch 61:2, 5, 7)[162]

Notice here that both texts envision the exaltation of a "human figure" to sit on a heavenly throne (cf. Ps 110:2).[163] Both texts also depict the figure in question as more than merely human. In the scroll, the exalted human figure explicitly describes himself as "reckoned among the gods" (*'lym*), so that he possesses "a status that is envisaged as divine and heavenly rather than human and mortal."[164] In 1 Enoch, the exalted son of man is explicitly described as having existed "from the beginning" (1 Enoch 62:7). In other words, he is a "transcendent figure" who possesses "preexistence."[165] Finally, both texts also describe a *messianic* figure. Although the fragmentary nature of the scroll makes definitive interpretation impossible, several scholars have suggested that the speaker is in fact a messianic figure—not least because the scroll explicitly mentions God's "messiah" (*mshykh*) (4QSelf-Glorification Hymn[b] [4Q491[c]] frag. 1, line 15).[166] As for 1 Enoch, we have already seen elsewhere that the apocalypse explicitly identifies the preexistent "son of man" as the "messiah" (cf. 1 Enoch 48:10; 52:4). Now, if the Jewish authors of the Dead Sea Scrolls and 1 Enoch could envision a human messianic figure who is also either preexistent or somehow a divine being exalted to a heavenly throne, then it is equally plausible that Jesus of Nazareth—whose followers actually went on to regard him as divine—could envision the same kind of heavenly enthronement for himself.

Last, it is also contextually plausible that Jesus would interpret Psalm 110 not only as a reference to the messiah in general, but to the "Son" of God in particular (cf. Matt 22:42; Mark 12:35; Luke 20:41). As we noted above, accord-

162. George W. E. Nickelsburg and James C. VanderKam, *1 Enoch 2*, Hermeneia (Minneapolis: Fortress, 2012), 254.

163. Collins, *Scepter and the Star*, 163.

164. Collins, *Scepter and the Star*, 164.

165. Nickelsburg and VanderKam, *1 Enoch 2*, 170, 259.

166. See Collins, *Scepter and the Star*, 163; Esther Eshel, "The Identification of the 'Speaker' in the Self-Glorification Hymn," in *The Provo International Conference on the Dead Sea Scrolls*, Studies on the Texts of the Desert of Judah 30 (Leiden: Brill, 1999), 619–35; Johannes Zimmerman, *Messianische Texte as Qumran*, Wissenschaftliche Untersuchungen zum Neuen Testament 2.104 (Tübingen: Mohr Siebeck, 1998), 310.

ing to the most ancient Jewish interpretation of Psalm 110 we possess—namely, the Septuagint—the psalm describes the divine "begetting" of the priest-king by God himself:

> From the womb, before the Morning-star, I have begotten you.
> The Lord swore and will not change his mind,
> "You are a priest forever according to the order of Melchisedek.
> (Ps 109:3–4 LXX [110:3–4])[167]

As several scholars have shown, the imagery of being "begotten" (*exegennēsa*) by God "before the morning star" (*ek gastros pro heōsphorou*) implies "the pre-existence" of the king,[168] who is "conceived before the earth itself."[169] Now, if the Jewish translator(s) of the Septuagint could interpret the Hebrew of Psalm 110 as referring to the divine begetting of the preexistent Melchizedek, then it is contextually plausible that the historical Jesus could interpret Psalm 110 as referring to the divine sonship of the messiah. Indeed, if this is correct, then it would provide a plausible explanation for why Jesus chooses Psalm 110 in particular to pose a riddle about the relationship between the humanity and divinity of the messiah. Given the fact that other early Jewish interpreters seem to have taken Psalm 110 as a reference to a messianic figure who was both preexistent and divine, if Jesus of Nazareth wanted to lead his audience to the conclusion that the messiah is more than merely human, then it is difficult to think of a more fitting and potent passage from Jewish Scripture.

Coherence: Unanswered Questions, Someone "Greater than" David, and Psalm 110

A second major reason in support of the historicity of Jesus's riddle of the messiah is from coherence with other evidence about Jesus.

167. Albert Pietersma and Benjamin G. Wright, eds., *A New English Translation of the Septuagint* (Oxford: Oxford University Press, 2007), 603, adapted.

168. Yarbro Collins and Collins, *King and Messiah as Son of God*, 84. See also Ruben A. Bühner, *Messianic High Christology: New Testament Variants of Second Temple Judaism* (Waco, TX: Baylor University Press, 2021), 90–92.

169. Fitzmyer, *One Who Is to Come*, 78. See also Kugel, *Traditions of the Bible*, 280; Joachim Schaper, *Eschatology in the Greek Psalter*, Wissenschaftliche Untersuchungen zum Neuen Testament 2.76 (Tübingen: Mohr Siebeck, 1995), 104.

For one thing, to the extent that Jesus's quotation of Psalm 110 implies that "the messiah" is greater than King David (Matt 22:41, 45; Mark 12:35, 37; Luke 20:41, 43), it also coheres with other evidence we've already examined in which Jesus implies that "the Son of Man" is "greater than" both the prophet Jonah and King Solomon (Matt 12:38–42; Luke 11:29–32). Indeed, just as Jesus speaks about the messianic "son of man" in the third person, without explicitly identifying himself as that figure (Matt 12:40; Luke 11:30), so too Jesus speaks about "the messiah" in the third person, without explicitly identifying himself as the long-awaited king (Matt 22:41; Mark 12:35; Luke 20:41). In both cases, he only poses a "hint" of self-identification.[170] And just as Jesus implies that the "Son of Man" is "greater than" the prophet Jonah and King Solomon (Matt 12:40–42; Luke 11:31–32), he also implies that "the messiah" is greater than David, insofar as he is David's "lord" (Matt 22:41; Mark 12:35; Luke 20:41). Hence, if Jesus taught that the son of man was a super-Solomonic figure—and there are good reasons to think he did[171]—then it is also reasonable to suggest that Jesus taught that the messiah was a super-Davidic figure.

With regard to his manner of teaching, Jesus's act of posing a "riddle" about the status of the messiah without giving an answer (Matt 22:42, 45; Mark 12:35, 37; Luke 20:41, 44) coheres quite well with other evidence in which Jesus poses a question about the status of John the Baptist without giving an answer.[172] After being asked about the source of his "authority' (Matt 21:23; Mark 11:27–28; Luke 20:1–2), Jesus answers the question with a question:

> Jesus said to them, "*I will also ask you one question*; if you tell me the answer, then I will also tell you by what authority I do these things. *Did the baptism of John come from heaven, or was it of human origin?*" (Matt 21:23–25)

> Jesus said to them, "*I will ask you one question*; answer me, and I will tell you by what authority I do these things. *Did the baptism of John come from heaven, or was it of human origin?* Answer me." (Mark 11:27–30)

> He answered them, "*I will also ask you a question,* and you tell me: *Did the baptism of John come from heaven, or was it of human origin?*" (Luke 20:3–4)

170. Witherington, *Christology of Jesus*, 190.

171. See Hengel and Schwemer, *Jesus and Judaism*, 407–8; Puig i Tàrrech, *Jesus: A Biography*, 338; Dunn, *Jesus Remembered*, 439–40.

172. Dunn, *Jesus Remembered*, 635.

This episode, which is widely held to be historical, illustrates how Jesus was "a master in the art of parables and oblique discourse."[173] By means of his question, Jesus invites his audience to answer for themselves whether John's baptism is "from heaven" or "of human origin" (Matt 21:25; Mark 11:30; Luke 20:4). Now, if Jesus did indeed pose the riddle-like question of whether the baptism of John was human or heavenly, then it seems quite plausible to suggest that Jesus also posed a similar question about whether the messiah would be human or heavenly. Indeed, as we will see in chapter 4, Jesus's riddle about David and the messiah of Psalm 110 will cohere remarkably well with other evidence in which Jesus is reticent to speak openly about his own identity during his public ministry—the so-called "Messianic Secret."[174]

Finally, Jesus's interpretation of Psalm 110 as referring to "the messiah" (*ho christos*) (Mark 22:42; Mark 12:35; Luke 20:41) coheres perfectly with the evidence that when Jesus is asked point blank in the presence of the Sanhedrin about whether he is "the messiah" (*ho christos*), he responds by quoting Daniel 7 ("you will see the Son of Man" coming "with the clouds") and Psalm 110 ("sitting at the right hand" of God) (Matt 26:63–64; Mark 14:61–62; Luke 22:67–68).[175] As James Dunn writes:

> How could the anointed king be both David's son and David's lord? Perhaps, then, the tradition originated with the memory of Jesus posing the conundrum in a day when the possible messianic significance of Ps. 110.1 was beginning to be discussed. That he was in the event (shortly after this) denounced to Pilate and then crucified as a messianic claimant makes it rather more credible that the issue of messiahship was in the air prior to Jesus' arrest.[176]

We will have to wait to treat the gospel accounts of Jesus and the Jerusalem Sanhedrin until chapter 5. Suffice it to say for now that Jesus's use of Psalm 110 in his riddle of the messiah will cohere quite well with the gospel accounts of his answer to the Jerusalem Sanhedrin.

173. Puig i Tàrrech, *Jesus: A Biography*, 512. See Dunn, *Jesus Remembered*, 698–700; Meier, *A Marginal Jew*, 2:163–67, for arguments in favor of its historicity.

174. Witherington, *Christology of Jesus*, 191.

175. Witherington, *Christology of Jesus*, 190.

176. Dunn, *Jesus Remembered*, 635.

Consequences: The Use of Psalm 110 in the Christology of the Early Church

The third major argument for the historicity of Jesus's question about the messiah is from consequences in the early church. If Jesus explicitly identified the royal figure in Psalm 110 as "the messiah" (Matt 22:42; Mark 12:35; Luke 20:41), this would provide a plausible explanation for why Psalm 110 not only "played a key role in the development of earliest christological understanding," but is *the* most frequently quoted passage from Jewish Scripture in the rest of the New Testament—some thirteen times.[177] Consider the following examples from Acts, the Pauline letters, Hebrews, and 1 Peter:

> *Being therefore exalted at the right hand of God*, and having received from the Father the promise of the Holy Spirit, he has poured out this that you both see and hear. *For David did not ascend into the heavens, but he himself says,*
>
> *'The Lord said to my Lord,*
> *"Sit at my right hand,*
> *until I make your enemies your footstool."'*
>
> Therefore let the entire house of Israel know with certainty that God has made him *both Lord and Messiah*, this Jesus whom you crucified. (Acts 2:33–35)

> Then comes the end, when he hands over the kingdom to God the Father, after he has destroyed every ruler and every authority and power. For he must reign *until he has put all his enemies under his feet.* (1 Cor 15:24–25)

> He [God] raised him [Christ] from the dead and *seated him at his right hand in the heavenly places*, far above all rule and authority and power and dominion, and above every name that is named, not only in this age but also in the age to come. And *he has put all things under his feet* . . . (Eph 1:20–22)

> In these last days he has spoken to us by a Son, whom he appointed heir of all things, *through whom he also created the worlds*. He is the reflection of God's glory and the exact imprint of God's very being, and he sustains all things by his powerful word. When he had made purification for sins, *he sat down at the right hand of the Majesty on high*, having become as much supe-

177. Dunn, *Jesus Remembered*, 634, citing Martin Hengel, *Studies in Early Christology* (London: T&T Clark, 1995), 118–225.

> rior to angels as the name he has inherited is more excellent than theirs. . . .
> But to which of the angels has he ever said,
> *"Sit at my right hand*
> *until I make your enemies a footstool for your feet"*? (Heb 1:2–3, 14)

> Jesus Christ . . . has gone into heaven and *is at the right hand of God*, with angels, authorities, and powers made *subject to him*. (1 Pet 3:21–22)

Much could be said about each of these passages.[178] For our purposes here, the main point is that, like Jesus's riddle about Psalm 110, all of these writings from the early church identify the royal figure in Psalm 110 as the "messiah" (*christos*) (Acts 2:36; 1 Cor 15:23, 25; Eph 1:20, 22; Col 3:1; Heb 1:13; 10:10–12; 1 Pet 3:21–22). However, whereas Jesus interprets Psalm 110 as a reference to the *messiah*, these early Christian writers explicitly interpret it as referring to *Jesus*. Likewise, whereas Jesus merely implies that the messiah is greater than David (he is David's "lord"), the letter to the Hebrews uses Psalm 110 to assert what Harold Attridge calls "a high or pre-existence christology," namely, that Christ is the preexistent "Son" through whom God "created the world" (Heb 1:2).[179] Finally, whereas Jesus says nothing explicit about the resurrection or ascension of the messiah in Psalm 110, all of the early Christian passages cited above explicitly apply Psalm 110 to the resurrection and ascension of Christ. In other words, these early Christian texts make explicit what is only implicit in the gospel accounts of Jesus's riddle; hence, they clearly reflect a post-Easter context. In sum, the most plausible explanation for why Psalm 110 is so frequently utilized in the explicit, post-Easter Christology of the early church is because Jesus himself used Psalm 110 in the implicit, pre-Easter messianic teaching of his public ministry.

178. See Bates, *Birth of the Trinity*, 60–62; Bauckham, *Jesus and the God of Israel*, 20–25, 152–81; Lee, *From Messiah to Preexistent Son*, 202–39, as well as the still-influential study by David M. Hay, *Glory at the Right Hand: Psalm 110 in Early Christianity*, Society of Biblical Literature Monograph Series 18 (Nashville: Abingdon, 1973).

179. Harold W. Attridge, *Hebrews*, Hermeneia (Minneapolis: Fortress, 1989), 40. See also Jared Compton, *Psalm 110 and the Logic of Hebrews*, Library of New Testament Studies 537 (London: T&T Clark, 2012), 19–37; Bauckham, *Jesus and the God of Israel*, 233–44.

Weighing the Arguments for and against Historical Plausibility

In light of everything we have seen, it seems clear to me that the arguments in favor of the historical plausibility of Jesus's exchange with the rich man regarding the goodness of God and the necessity of following Jesus solidly outweigh the arguments against it.

For one thing, the argument from the contextual implausibility of Jesus rejecting the Davidic ancestry of the messiah runs aground on the bare fact that Jesus does no such thing. He simply poses a question about how to reconcile the scribal designation of the messiah as "Son of David" with David's own description of him as "lord" (Ps 110:1). Moreover, claiming a lack of coherence because Jesus poses (rather than answers) a question is laughable. It completely fails to take seriously that Jesus was a teacher; like any other teacher, he was perfectly capable of both posing and answering questions. Finally, the argument that the episode is historically doubtful because Psalm 110 was one of the most popular passages from Jewish Scripture in the early church is, quite simply, a non sequitur. Logically speaking, it does not follow that just because a passage of scripture was popular in the early church that Jesus himself could not have employed it. Here faulty exegesis combines with faulty logic to make a very weak case against historicity.

On the other hand, despite the tendency of many major works on the historical Jesus to ignore Jesus's riddle about the messiah, the cumulative force of the arguments in favor of historicity is remarkably strong. In particular, a powerful argument from contextual plausibility can be made on the basis of early Jewish evidence for a preexistent, divine, and/or superhuman messiah, who was sometimes linked with Psalm 110:4 and could even be referred to as "God" or a "god" (cf. Ps 109:3–4 LXX [110:3–4]; 11QMelchizedek [11Q13] II, 5–20; 4QMessianic Apocalypse [4Q491] frags. 11–12; 1 Enoch 48:10; 52:4; 61:2–7). Along similar lines, Jesus's riddle-like question about the messiah coheres perfectly with his question about the baptism of John (Matt 21:23–25; Mark 11:28–30; Luke 20:1–4), as well as evidence that he implied he was greater than figures like Solomon and Jonah—all without explicitly revealing his identity (Matt 12:41–42; Luke 11:29–32). Finally, if there is any place where the force of the argument from consequences in the early church is on full display, it is in the case of the role of Psalm 110 in early Christian Christology. When the frequency with which Psalm 110 is quoted in early Christian writings is combined with the difference between Jesus's implicit, riddle-like use of the psalm and the early church's explicitly post-Easter interpretation (cf. Acts 2:33–35;

1 Cor 15:24–25; Eph 1:20–22; Col 3:1; Heb 1:2–3, 14; 1 Pet 3:21), the best explanation is that the reason Psalm 110 was so popular in early Christian writings was because Jesus himself used it to reveal his own identity as both Israel's "messiah" and King David's "lord."

In light of such considerations, it seems quite reasonable to conclude that, during his public ministry, Jesus himself used Psalm 110 to suggest to his followers that the long-awaited messiah was not merely the human descendant of David, but something much more: the preexistent divine son of God. In the words of David Friedrich Strauss and Albert Schweitzer:

> As it is thus evident that, immediately after the time of Jesus, the idea of a pre-existence of the Messiah was incorporated into higher Jewish theology, it is no far-fetched conjecture, that the same idea was afloat when the mind of Jesus was maturing, and that in his conception of himself as the Messiah, this attribute was included.[180]

> Hitherto the view has been that it was the primitive community which made the Lord into the Son of David because it held him to be the Messiah. It is time to consider seriously whether it was not rather Jesus who held himself to be the Messiah because he was descended from David.[181]

I agree. It is indeed time for us to seriously consider the evidence that Jesus believed himself to be divine because he regarded himself as the heavenly messiah of Psalm 110, who was begotten by God before the morning star and who would be exalted by God to sit beside him as his equal. In order to see this more clearly, however, we need to turn now to three sayings in which Jesus appears to both reveal and conceal what might be called the "apocalyptic secret" of his divinity.

180. Strauss, *Life of Jesus*, 293.
181. Schweitzer, *Quest of the Historical Jesus*, 319.

CHAPTER 4

The Apocalyptic Secret

> Jesus held very strongly to an apocalyptic worldview . . . in fact at the very core of his earthly proclamation was an apocalyptic message. This will be a key factor in seeing how he understood himself, whether as divine or otherwise.
>
> —Bart Ehrman[1]

> Our choice is not between an apocalyptic Jesus and some other Jesus; it is between an apocalyptic Jesus and no Jesus at all.
>
> —Dale C. Allison Jr.[2]

The Apocalyptic Jesus

If there is anything that is widely agreed upon in contemporary historical Jesus research, it is that Jesus of Nazareth was a first-century Jewish apocalyptic prophet. Many scholars agree that Jesus's words and actions—like those of John the Baptist before him—should be understood within the context of early Jewish apocalypticism.[3] Consider, for example, the following statements:

1. Bart D. Ehrman, *How Jesus Became God: The Exaltation of a Jewish Preacher from Galilee* (San Francisco: HarperOne, 2014), 99.

2. Dale C. Allison Jr., *Constructing Jesus: Memory, Imagination, and History* (Grand Rapids: Baker Academic, 2010), 47.

3. On early Jewish apocalypticism, see especially John J. Collins, *The Apocalyptic Imagination: An Introduction to Jewish Apocalyptic Literature*, 3rd ed. (Grand Rapids: Eerdmans, 2016), 1–320; John J. Collins, ed., *The Oxford Handbook of Apocalyptic Literature* (Oxford: Oxford University Press, 2014), 19–217; Frederick J. Murphy, *Apocalypticism in the Bible and Its World: A Comprehensive Introduction* (Grand Rapids: Baker Academic, 2012), 125–226; Crispin Fletcher-Louis, "Jewish Apocalyptic and Apocalypticism," in *Handbook for the Study of the Historical Jesus*, ed. Tom Holmén and Stanley E. Porter, 4 vols. (Leiden: Brill, 2011), 2:1569–1607.

> The view that Jesus was an apocalyptic prophet has a long pedigree. . . . There are strong reasons . . . for concluding that Jesus held an apocalyptic view in which God would intervene in human affairs and establish his kingdom on earth.[4]

> Jesus' ministry began with his association with John the Baptist, an apocalyptic prophet, and ended with the establishment of the Christian church, a community of apocalyptic Jews who believed in him. . . . How could both the beginning and the end be apocalyptic, if the middle was not as well? My conclusion is that Jesus himself must have been a Jewish apocalypticist.[5]

> A completely un-eschatological Jesus, a Jesus totally shorn of all apocalyptic traits, is simply not the historical Jesus.[6]

This is just a representative sample; other scholars of Jesus and Second Temple Judaism could be cited in support of this growing consensus.[7]

4. Helen K. Bond, *The Historical Jesus: A Guide for the Perplexed* (London: Bloomsbury T&T Clark, 2012), 90, 92.

5. Bart D. Ehrman, *Jesus: Apocalyptic Prophet of the New Millennium* (Oxford: Oxford University Press, 1999), 139.

6. John P. Meier, *A Marginal Jew: Rethinking the Historical Jesus*, 5 vols., Anchor Yale Bible Reference Library (New Haven: Yale University Press, 1991–2016), 2:317.

7. See Crispin Fletcher-Louis, "Jesus and Apocalypticism," in Holmén and Porter, *Handbook for the Study of the Historical Jesus*, 3:2877–909; Maurice Casey, *Jesus of Nazareth: An Independent Historian's Account of His Life and Teaching* (London: T&T Clark, 2010), 3; Collins, *Apocalyptic Imagination*, 325–26; Benedict T. Viviano, "Eschatology and the Quest for the Historical Jesus," in *The Oxford Handbook of Eschatology* (Oxford: Oxford University Press, 2008), 73–90; Jörg Frey, "Die Apokalyptik als Herausforderung der neutestamentlichen Wissenschaft. Zum Problem: Jesus und die Apokalyptik," in *Apokalyptik als Herausforderung neutestamentlicher Theologie*, ed. Michael Becker and Markus Öhler, Wissenschaftliche Untersuchungen zum Neuen Testament 2.214 (Tübingen: Mohr Siebeck, 2006), 23–94; Gerd Theissen and Annette Merz, *The Historical Jesus: A Comprehensive Guide*, trans. John Bowden (Minneapolis: Fortress, 1998), 249, 276; Meier, *A Marginal Jew*, 2:110. For the view that Jesus was not an apocalyptic prophet, along with a (compelling) rejoinder, see the essays by Dale C. Allison, Marcus J. Borg, John Dominic Crossan, and Stephen J. Patterson in Robert J. Miller, ed., *The Apocalyptic Jesus: A Debate* (Santa Rosa: Polebridge, 2001). Although the tally is three scholars arguing against an apocalyptic Jesus (Borg, Crossan, and Patterson) and one arguing for an apocalyptic Jesus (Allison), Allison wins the debate handily.

The Heavenly Dimension of Early Jewish Apocalypticism

With that said, ever since Albert Schweitzer published his classic work *The Quest of the Historical Jesus* (1906)—in which he vividly depicts Jesus as a Jewish prophet of the imminent end of the world—historical Jesus scholars have tended to focus almost entirely on the *eschatological* aspects of Jesus's apocalyptic worldview. More recent scholarship, however, has insisted that equal attention needs to be paid to the importance of the *heavenly* dimension of early Jewish apocalypticism. Consider, for example, the following influential definition of early Jewish apocalypses:

> [Apocalypse:] a genre of revelatory literature with a narrative framework, in which a revelation is mediated by an otherworldly being to a human recipient, disclosing a transcendent reality which is both temporal, insofar as it envisages eschatological salvation, and spatial insofar as it involves another, supernatural world.[8]

Once again, more examples could be given.[9] For our purposes here, what matters most is that contemporary experts on early Judaism largely agree that, generally speaking, early Jewish apocalypticism was not merely interested in the unveiling of hidden mysteries about the last days and the end of time. It was also very much focused on the revelation of heavenly mysteries involving transcendent realities and otherworldly beings.

If this is correct, and if Jesus shared such an outlook, then an important question arises: Did Jesus, like other Jewish apocalypticists, speak about both heavenly and eschatological mysteries? *If so, what heavenly mysteries did Jesus reveal to his disciples?*

8. Collins, *Apocalyptic Imagination*, 5.

9. See Benjamin E. Reynolds and Loren T. Stuckenbruck, introduction to *The Jewish Apocalyptic Tradition and the Shaping of New Testament Thought*, ed. Benjamin E. Reynolds and Loren T. Stuckenbruck (Minneapolis: Fortress, 2017), 6–7; Christopher Rowland and Christopher R. A. Morray-Jones, *The Mystery of God: Early Jewish Mysticism and the New Testament*, Compendia Rerum Iudaicarum ad Novum Testamentum 12 (Leiden: Brill, 2009), 13–27; Michael E. Stone, "Apocalyptic Literature," in *Jewish Writings of the Second Temple Period: Apocrypha, Pseudepigrapha, Qumran Sectarian Writings, Philo, Josephus*, ed. Michael E. Stone, Compendia Rerum Iudaicarum ad Novum Testamentum 2 (Assen, Netherlands: Van Gorcum, 1984), 383–441.

CHAPTER 4

The Apocalyptic Secret of Jesus's Identity

In this chapter, I will build on the widely accepted hypothesis that Jesus should be understood within the historical context of early Jewish apocalypticism. However, unlike most treatments of the apocalyptic Jesus, which focus exclusively on his apocalyptic eschatology, I want to explore the *heavenly* dimension of Jesus's apocalyptic worldview. In this regard, three passages in the Gospels stand out:

1. The healing of the paralytic and the heavenly son of man (Matt 9:2–7; Mark 2:1–2; Luke 5:17–26)
2. The question of John the Baptist about "the one who is to come" (Matt 11:2–6; Luke 7:18–23)
3. The "revelation" (*apokalyptō*) of the hidden Father and the Son (Matt 11:25–27; Luke 10:21–22)

As we will see, in all three of these episodes, Jesus uses the language of Jewish Scripture to reveal that he is both a human and heavenly figure: the heavenly son of man, the divine Messiah, and the omnipotent Son of the heavenly Father. When this evidence is analyzed from a triple-context perspective, a strong case can be made that one of the heavenly mysteries that Jesus saw himself as revealing to his disciples was the apocalyptic secret of his divinity.

In order to see this clearly, however, we will first need to interpret all three of these episodes in the light of their first-century Jewish context.

The Heavenly Son of Man

The first major episode in which Jesus reveals his identity using apocalyptic language and imagery also happens to be the first episode in the Synoptic Gospels in which Jesus is accused of blasphemy. I am speaking of the account of Jesus healing a paralytic, which is found in all three Synoptic Gospels:

> And just then some people were carrying a paralyzed man lying on a bed. When Jesus saw their faith, he said to the paralytic, "*Take heart, son; your sins are forgiven.*" Then some of the scribes said to themselves, "*This man is blaspheming.*" But Jesus, perceiving their thoughts, said, "Why do you think evil in your hearts? For which is easier, to say, 'Your sins are forgiven,' or to say, 'Stand up and walk'? *But so that you may know that the Son of Man has*

> *authority on earth to forgive sins*"—he then said to the paralytic—"Stand up, take your bed and go to your home." And he stood up and went to his home. When the crowds saw it, they were filled with awe, and they glorified God, who had given such authority to human beings. (Matt 9:2–8)

> When he returned to Capernaum after some days, it was reported that he was at home. So many gathered around that there was no longer room for them, not even in front of the door; and he was speaking the word to them. Then some people came, bringing to him a paralyzed man, carried by four of them. And when they could not bring him to Jesus because of the crowd, they removed the roof above him; and after having dug through it, they let down the mat on which the paralytic lay. When Jesus saw their faith, he said to the paralytic, "*Son, your sins are forgiven.*" Now some of the scribes were sitting there, questioning in their hearts, "Why does this fellow speak in this way? *It is blasphemy! Who can forgive sins but God alone?*" At once Jesus perceived in his spirit that they were discussing these questions among themselves; and he said to them, "Why do you raise such questions in your hearts? Which is easier, to say to the paralytic, 'Your sins are forgiven,' or to say, 'Stand up and take your mat and walk'? *But so that you may know that the Son of Man has authority on earth to forgive sins*"—he said to the paralytic—"I say to you, stand up, take your mat and go to your home." And he stood up, and immediately took the mat and went out before all of them; so that they were all amazed and glorified God, saying, "We have never seen anything like this!" (Mark 2:1–12)

> One day, while he was teaching, Pharisees and teachers of the law were sitting near by (they had come from every village of Galilee and Judea and from Jerusalem); and the power of the Lord was with him to heal. Just then some men came, carrying a paralyzed man on a bed. They were trying to bring him in and lay him before Jesus; but finding no way to bring him in because of the crowd, they went up on the roof and let him down with his bed through the tiles into the middle of the crowd in front of Jesus. When he saw their faith, he said, "*Friend, your sins are forgiven you.*" Then the scribes and the Pharisees began to question, "*Who is this who is speaking blasphemies? Who can forgive sins but God alone?*" When Jesus perceived their questionings, he answered them, "Why do you raise such questions in your hearts? Which is easier, to say, 'Your sins are forgiven you,' or to say, 'Stand up and walk'? *But so that you may know that the Son of Man has authority on earth to forgive sins*"—he said to the one who was par-

> alyzed—"I say to you, stand up and take your bed and go to your home." Immediately he stood up before them, took what he had been lying on, and went to his home, glorifying God. Amazement seized all of them, and they glorified God and were filled with awe, saying, "We have seen strange things today." (Luke 5:17–26)

When it comes to the common substance of this episode, four features of the Synoptic accounts of Jesus healing the paralytic stand out: (1) the declaration by Jesus that the paralyzed man's "sins" are "forgiven"; (2) the reaction to Jesus's declaration by Jewish scribes, who accuse him of "blasphemy"; (3) Jesus's response to the charge, in which he declares that "the Son of Man" has authority "to forgive sins" and heals the paralyzed man in order to demonstrate it; and (4) the reaction of the Jewish onlookers, who respond with amazement to what they have witnessed. Let's take a few moments to examine each of these basic points.

Jesus Declares the Paralytic's Sins to Be Forgiven

In all three accounts, the friends of a paralyzed man bring him to Jesus by letting him down through the roof of a house, and Jesus responds to their remarkable zeal by declaring the paralyzed man's "sins" to be "forgiven" (Matt 9:2; Mark 2:3–5; Luke 5:18–20). In order to properly interpret Jesus's declaration in a first-century Jewish context, it is important to recall two key points.

First, in Jewish Scripture, the word *sin* is regularly used to describe human actions that transgress the commandments of God—especially the Ten Commandments—and, in this way, stray from "the path" that leads to life (cf. Exod 20:1–20; Deut 5:33).[10] Although contemporary readers may think of sin as having only moral or spiritual consequences, Jewish Scripture often draws a causal connection between human sin and physical illness. For example, in the Pentateuch, God tells the Israelites through Moses that if they listen carefully to the "commandments" and obey them, he will not bring "any of the diseases of the Egyptians" upon them, because he is "the LORD" who "heals" (Exod 15:26; cf. Deut 7:15). Likewise, the book of Psalms describes "the LORD" as a God who "forgives" all the "iniquity" of Israel and "heals" all their "diseases" (Ps 103:2–3). To be sure, the book of Job demonstrates that not every illness

10. Hannah K. Harrington, "Sin," in *The Eerdmans Dictionary of Early Judaism*, ed. John J. Collins and Daniel C. Harlow (Grand Rapids: Eerdmans, 2010), 1230–31.

is the result of human sinfulness; sometimes, the righteous suffer as part of God's inexplicable providence (cf. Job 1–2). Nevertheless, in the Second Temple period—especially in writings affirming an "apocalyptic worldview," the "traditional etiology of sickness" continued to affirm that some human illness is the direct result of sin.[11] This explains why Jesus responds to his encounter with the paralytic not by focusing on the man's illness—about which Jesus initially says nothing—but on his sins.

Second, when Jesus declares the man's sins to be forgiven, he is describing an act which, in Jewish Scripture, is something only God does. For example, in the book of Exodus, when God appears on Mount Sinai and reveals the divine name "the LORD" (YHWH) to Israel, he describes himself as "a God merciful and gracious, slow to anger" and "forgiving iniquity and transgression and sin" (Exod 34:6–7). In this description, the power to forgive sin is not just a divine attribute; it is part of "one long divine name."[12] Likewise, when the book of Leviticus describes the forgiveness of human sins achieved by the offering of animal sacrifices in the sanctuary, it consistently uses the passive voice to emphasize that it is "the LORD" (YHWH) who forgives sins:

> The priest shall make atonement for them, and *they shall be forgiven*. . . . Thus the priest shall make atonement on his behalf for his sin, and *he shall be forgiven*. . . . Thus the priest shall make atonement on your behalf, and *you shall be forgiven*. . . .Thus the priest shall make atonement on your behalf for the sin that you have committed, and *you shall be forgiven*. (Lev 4:20, 26, 31, 35)

As Jacob Milgrom points out, this use of the divine passive is significant: "The Lord alone is the agent of forgiveness—hence, the verb is *niphʿal*, passive. The priest carries out the purgation rites but only God determines their efficacy. . . . *in the entire Bible only God dispenses* sālach *["forgiveness"], never humans*."[13] Along similar lines, in the book of Isaiah, in one of the most emphatically monotheistic passages in all of Jewish Scripture, we read:

11. Rebecca Raphael, "Sickness and Disease," in Collins and Harlow, *Eerdmans Dictionary of Early Judaism*, 1228–30, citing Dan 4; 1 Macc 6:8–13; 1QRule of the Community (1QS) IV, 6–14; 4QPrayer of Nabonidus ar (4Q242), frags. 1–4.

12. William H. C. Propp, *Exodus*, 2 vols., Anchor Yale Bible 2–2A (New Haven: Yale University Press, 1999, 2006), 2:611, 609.

13. Jacob Milgrom, *Leviticus*, 3 vols., Anchor Yale Bible 3, 3A, 3B (New Haven: Yale University Press, 1991–2001), 1:245 (emphasis added).

> Before me no god was formed,
> nor shall there be any after me.
> I, I am the Lord,
> and besides me there is no savior . . .
> I am God, and also henceforth I am He;
> there is no one who can deliver from my hand . . .
> *I, I am He*
> *who blots out your transgressions* for my own sake,
> and *I will not remember your sins.* (Isa 43:10–11, 13, 25)

As Joseph Blenkinsopp has pointed out, in this passage, the one God of Israel—the same God who revealed the divine name "I am" to Moses on Mount Sinai (cf. Exod 3:14)—makes clear that the "ability" to forgive sins is an exclusive "proof of divinity" and "test of divine status" (cf. Isa 45:20; 46:20; 47:13, 15).[14] In sum, in both the Torah and the Prophets, the power to forgive sins is an exclusively divine prerogative.

The Jewish Scribes React by Accusing Jesus of Blasphemy

Once this divine prerogative is clear, it comes as no surprise that, in all three Synoptic accounts, some of the Jewish "scribes" who hear Jesus's declaration of forgiveness react by accusing him of "blaspheming" (*blasphēmeō*) or committing "blasphemy" (*blasphēmia*) for claiming to do something only God can do (Matt 9:3; Mark 2:7; Luke 5:21). In order to understand this reaction, a couple of observations are necessary.

In an ancient Jewish context, the word "scribe" (Hebrew *sofer*; Greek *grammateus*) could be applied to a fairly wide variety of persons who were trained in the arts of reading and writing.[15] For example, the book of Jeremiah identifies Baruch, his secretary, as a "scribe" (*sofer*) (cf. Jer 36:26, 32). Later in the Second Temple period, the book of Sirach presents an idealized portrait of the "scribe" (*grammateus*) as an expert in and teacher of the

14. Joseph Blenkinsopp, *Isaiah*, Anchor Yale Bible 19, 19A, 19B (New Haven: Yale University Press, 2000–2003), 2:224.

15. See Chris Keith, "Scribes and Scribalism," in *T&T Clark Encyclopedia of Second Temple Judaism*, ed. Daniel M. Gurtner and Loren T. Stuckenbruck, 2 vols. (London: T&T Clark, 2020), 712–13; Meier, *A Marginal Jew*, 3:549–560; Christine Schams, *Jewish Scribes in the Second Temple Period*, Library of Hebrew Bible/Old Testament Studies 291 (Sheffield: Sheffield Academic Press, 1998).

Jewish Torah (cf. Sirach 38:24–39:11). It is this latter use of the term which seems to be at play in the Synoptic accounts of Jesus and the paralytic. The scribes in his audience who are trained readers of Jewish Scripture are the first to pick up on the divine implications of Jesus's declaration of forgiveness.

Equally important, at the time of Jesus, the word "blasphemy" (Greek *blasphēmeō*/*blasphēmia*) had a wide spectrum of meanings. The classic biblical description of blasphemy against God involves the illicit pronunciation of "the Name" of God by an unnamed man in the context of a quarrel—a capital crime for which he is punished with death (Lev 24:10–23).[16] By the Second Temple period, however, "blasphemy" could be used to refer to a variety of forms of sacrilegious speech or action:[17]

Various Kinds of "Blasphemy"

1. **Illicit pronunciation of the sacred name of God** (1QRule of the Community [1QS VI, 27–VII, 1; Philo, *Life of Moses* 2.199–206; Josephus, *Antiquities* 4.201–202 [cf. Lev 24:16; Deut 21:22–23 LXX])
2. **Derogatory speech against God** (2 Kgs 19:4–22; Ezek 24:12–13; 35:12; Isa 52:5; Dan 3:96 LXX; Tobit 1:18; 2 Maccabees 10:4; 12:14; Wisdom of Solomon 1:6; Philo, *Special Laws* 1.53; Josephus, *Antiquities* 6.183; 8.391)
3. **Derogatory speech against other deities** (cf. Exod 22:27; Dan 14:9 LXX; Philo, *Special Laws* 1.53; *Life of Moses* 2.205; *Questions on Exodus* 2.5; Josephus, *Antiquities* 4.207; *Against Apion* 2.237)
4. **Derogatory speech against sacred leaders or priests** (Exod 22:27 LXX; Josephus, *War* 2.145; *Antiquities* 4.215 [cf. Exod 22:27; Deut 16:18]; 13.293–295; cf. Sir 3:16)
5. **Sacrilegious acts against the Jerusalem temple** (including its vessels) (1 Macc 2:6; 2 Macc 8:4; 10:34–35; 15:24; Josephus, *Antiquities* 10.233, 242 [cf. Dan 5:2]; 20.108; *War* 2.223–236; cf. Isa 66:3 LXX)
6. **Speaking or acting as if one is divine or equal with God** (2 Macc 9:8, 28; cf. 5:21; Philo, *Decalogue* 61–65; *On Dreams* 2.130–133; *Embassy to Gaius* 45, 367–368)

16. See Milgrom, *Leviticus*, 3:2107–8.

17. See Adela Yarbro Collins, "Blasphemy," in Collins and Harlow, *Eerdmans Dictionary of Early Judaism*, 445; Darrell L. Bock, *Blasphemy and Exaltation in Judaism: The Charge against Jesus in Mark 14:53–65*, Wissenschaftliche Untersuchungen zum Neuen Testament 2.106 (Tübingen: Mohr Siebeck, 1998), 30–65; E. P. Sanders, *Jewish Law from Jesus to the Mishnah: Five Studies* (London: SCM; Harrisburg, PA: Trinity Press International, 1990), 57–63.

In the gospel accounts of the healing of the paralytic, there is no evidence that Jesus pronounces the name of God—much less that he uses derogatory language about the God of Israel, other deities, the Jewish priests, or the Jerusalem Temple (definitions 1–5). Therefore, in context, the only plausible explanation for the scribes' accusation of blasphemy is that Jesus is speaking or acting as if he is divine (definition 6). As Adela Yarbro Collins argues:

> The simple declaration "your sins are forgiven" . . . is unusual in the context of Jewish tradition. . . . Prophets and holy men of the past were credited with the ability to win forgiveness from God for the sins of others through their prayers. But there is no precedent for a human being making a simple declaration that God is at this moment forgiving another human being's sin.[18]

Other scholars agree.[19] It should however be noted that some suggest that because Jesus uses the passive voice ("your sins are forgiven") rather than the active voice ("I forgive your sins"), he is not in fact taking a divine prerogative upon himself.[20] This argument, however, fails to do justice to the fact that Jesus immediately goes on to declare that "the Son of Man" *himself* has "authority on earth *to forgive sins* [active voice]" (Matt 9:6; Mark 2:10; Luke 5:24). Others contend that because Jewish Scripture describes ordained priests as offering sacrifices and mediating divine forgiveness of sins (Lev 4:17–31), Jesus is only arrogating to himself a *priestly* prerogative—not a divine prerogative.[21] This view, however, runs up against the fact that the Jewish scribes do *not* say: "Who can forgive sins except the priests?" or "Who can forgive sins apart from the Temple?"[22] What the scribes say is: "Who can forgive sins except *the one God* [*heis ho theos*]?" (Mark 2:7), or "Who can forgive sins but *God alone* [*monos*

18. Adela Yarbro Collins, *Mark: A Commentary*, Hermeneia (Minneapolis: Fortress, 2007), 185.

19. So Jens Schröter, *Jesus of Nazareth: Jew from Galilee, Savior of the World*, trans. Wayne Coppins (Waco, TX: Baylor University Press, 2014), 147 ("Jesus himself possesses the authority to forgive sin that is actually reserved for God"); Armand Puig i Tàrrech, *Jesus: A Biography* (Waco, TX: Baylor University Press, 2011), 284 ("For [the scribes], Jesus was a blasphemer who dared to do what only God can do").

20. Geza Vermes, *The Authentic Gospel of Jesus* (London: Penguin, 2003), 40.

21. Ehrman, *How Jesus Became God*, 127; James D. G. Dunn, *Jesus Remembered*, vol. 1 of *Christianity in the Making* (Grand Rapids: Eerdmans, 2003), 786–87; E. P. Sanders, *Jesus and Judaism* (Philadelphia: Fortress, 1985), 273–74.

22. Tobias Hägerland, *Jesus and the Forgiveness of Sins: An Aspect of His Prophetic Mission*, Society for New Testament Studies Monograph Series 150 (Cambridge: Cambridge University Press, 2012), 140–41.

ho theos]?" (Luke 5:21).[23] Thus, the Jewish scribes consider Jesus's declaration of forgiveness to be blasphemous because it infringes on a *divine*—not a priestly—prerogative. According to the scribes, Jesus is claiming to do something only the one God of Israel can do.

Jesus Identifies Himself as the Heavenly "Son of Man"

Significantly, in all three accounts, Jesus does not "draw back" from the divine implications that give rise to the scribes' objection.[24] Instead, he responds to the accusation of blasphemy by implicitly identifying himself as "the Son of Man" (*ho huios tou anthrōpou*), who *does* in fact have "authority" (*exousia*) to "forgive sins" upon "the earth" (Matt 9:6; Mark 2:10; Luke 5:24; cf. Dan 7:13–14). Jesus then proceeds to demonstrate this authority by commanding the paralytic to stand up, take his mat, and go home—and he does (Matt 9:6–7; Mark 2:11–12; Luke 5:24–25). As John Meier insightfully states: Jesus performs the "visible" act of healing the paralytic to show that, as the son of man, he also has the power to perform the "invisible" act of forgiving the man's sin.[25]

In order to situate Jesus's response to the scribes in a first-century Jewish context, it is important to recall that that the expression "son of man" can be used in Jewish Scripture in a generic way to refer to a human being (cf. Ps 8:4–5). However, when Jesus uses the expression in the context of his interaction with the paralytic, he is alluding to a *specific* figure: "*the* Son of Man" who has "authority" (Matt 9:6; Mark 2:10; Luke 5:24).[26] As many scholars agree, Jesus is alluding to Daniel's famous apocalyptic vision of the coming of "one like a son of man" and the giving of "authority" to him (Dan 7:1–28).[27] Here is the key text:

23. Michael F. Bird, *Jesus the Eternal Son: Answering Adoptionist Christology* (Grand Rapids: Eerdmans, 2017), 92; Daniel Johannson, "Who Can Forgive Sins but God Alone? Human and Angelic Agents, and Divine Forgiveness in Early Judaism," *Journal for the Study of the New Testament* 33 (2011): 351–74.

24. Cf. Joel Marcus, *Mark*, 2 vols, Anchor Yale Bible 27–27A (New Haven: Yale University Press, 2000, 2009), 1:222.

25. Meier, *A Marginal Jew*, 2:679.

26. See John J. Collins, "The Son of Man in Ancient Judaism," in Holmén and Porter, *Handbook for the Study of the Historical Jesus*, 2:1545–68; Delbert Burkett, *The Son of Man Debate: A History and Evaluation*, Society for New Testament Studies Monograph Series 107 (Cambridge: Cambridge University Press, 2007).

27. See Hengel and Schwemer, *Jesus and Judaism*, 556–65; Schröter, *Jesus of Nazareth*, 166–68; Bond, *Historical Jesus*, 101; Allison, *Constructing Jesus*, 293–303; Dunn, *Jesus Remem-*

> *I saw one like a son of man*
> *coming with the clouds of heaven.*
> And he came to the Ancient of Days
> and was presented before him.
> *To him was given authority*
> and glory and kingdom,
> that all peoples, nations, and languages
> should serve him. (Dan 7:13–14)[28]

Although commentators on Daniel continue to debate whether the figure of "one like a son of man" is an angelic being,[29] a messianic figure, and/or a corporate or collective symbol of the people of God,[30] for the purpose of this study, three basic points are in order.

(1) However the modern exegete interprets Daniel 7 in its original context, the historian must reckon with how the passage was interpreted by Jews in the Second Temple period. As John Collins demonstrates, the oldest extant Jewish interpretations of this passage unanimously interpret the "one like a son of man" as a *messianic figure* and "assume that the phrase refers to an individual and is not a symbol for a collective identity" (e.g., 1 Enoch 46:1; 48:3, 10; 52:4; 4 Ezra 13:1–26).[31]

(2) The reason for this early Jewish messianic interpretation appears to be the implicit parallel between the "son of man" figure and the four beasts that precede his coming (cf. Dan 7:1–8). It cannot be overemphasized that in the angel's own interpretation of Daniel's vision, the "four beasts" are *ex-*

---

bered, 739–54; Paul Owen and David Shepherd, "Speaking Up for Qumran, Dalman, and the Son of Man: Was *Bar Enasha* a Common Term for 'Man' in the Time of Jesus?," *Journal for the Study of the New Testament* 81 (2001): 81–22.

28. Here I have employed the RSV to highlight the intertextual links obscured by the NRSV.

29. MT *bar 'enosh*; LXX *huios anthrōpou*.

30. For an overview of scholarly positions, see Carol A. Newsom, *Daniel: A Commentary*, with Brennan W. Breed (Louisville: Westminster John Knox, 2014), 234–43; John J. Collins, *Daniel: A Commentary*, Hermeneia (Minneapolis: Fortress, 1993), 304–10. For the angelic interpretation, see Collins, *Daniel*, 310. For the messianic interpretation, see Gerbern S. Oegema, *The Anointed and His People: Messianic Expectations from the Maccabees to Bar Kochba*, Journal for the Study of the Pseudepigrapha Supplement Series 27 (Sheffield: Sheffield Academic Press, 1998), 63–64. For the corporate or collective view, see Louis F. Hartman and Alexander A. DiLella, *The Book of Daniel*, Anchor Bible 23 (New York: Doubleday, 1978), 85–102.

31. Collins, *Daniel*, 306.

plicitly identified as "four *kings*" (*malkin*) (Dan 7:17). As John Collins points out, according to Daniel itself, "the beasts are not simply collective symbols but can also be understood to represent *the rulers*."[32] If this is correct, then it has direct "significance for the interpretation of the 'one like a human being.'"[33] For it suggests that the son of man figure is likewise an individual ruler who represents a collective kingdom. This point can be illustrated by the following chart:

The "Son of Man" and the "Four Kings" (Dan 7:14, 17)

Daniel's Dream	**Rulers**	**Collectives**	
1. Lion	1st king	1st kingdom	(Dan 7:4)
2. Bear	2nd king	2nd kingdom	(Dan 7:5)
3. Leopard	3rd king	3rd kingdom	(Dan 7:6)
4. Fourth Beast	4th king	4th kingdom	(Dan 7:7–8, 11–12, 19–26)
5. Son of man	5th king	5th kingdom/saints	(Dan 7:13–14, 18, 27)

Seen in this light, the royal "son of man" figure has the same symbolic function as the four royal beasts, but with a positive referent.[34]

(3) However one interprets the "one like a son of man," what matters most for our study is that he is indisputably a *heavenly* figure, who is described as if he is *divine*. For example, the son of man "comes on the clouds of heaven" (Dan 7:14)—something only God does in Jewish Scripture:

> Sing to God, sing praises to his name;
> lift up a song to *him who rides upon the clouds*—

32. Collins, *Daniel*, 312.

33. Collins, *Daniel*, 312.

34. See Brant Pitre, *Jesus, the Tribulation, and the End of the Exile: Restoration Eschatology and the Origin of the Atonement*, Wissenschaftliche Untersuchungen zum Neuen Testament 2.204 (Tübingen: Mohr Siebeck; Grand Rapids: Baker Academic, 2005), 53–55. I should emphasize here that my focus on the royal identification of the "one like a son of man" is in no way at odds with the possibility that he is also a priestly figure. Cf. Crispin Fletcher-Louis, *Christological Origins: The Emerging Consensus and Beyond*, vol. 1 of *Jesus Monotheism* (Eugene, OR: Cascade, 2015), 233–37. Note also that the fact that the "son of man" figure is royal does not negate his seemingly divine status, since the kings of the Babylonians, Medes, Persians, and Greeks were at various times and in various ways described as and considered to be divine figures.

> *his name is the* L*ORD*—
> be exultant before him. (Ps 68:4)

As multiple commentators have noted, "clouds are associated with the Deity,"[35] and "riding clouds" is something "beyond human ability."[36] Moreover, the description of the figure as "one *like* a son of man" (Dan 7:13) strongly suggests that though he *appears* to be a merely "human" figure, he is in fact "a heavenly being" (Dan 7:13; cf. 8:15; 10:5, 16, 18, 12:6–7).[37] Last, but certainly not least, after the Danielic "son of man" is presented to "the Ancient of Days" (Dan 7:13)—a title for God—all peoples, nations, and language will "serve" him (Dan 7:14).[38] The same verb is explicitly used elsewhere to describe how Daniel and his Jewish companions refused to "serve"[39] any "god"[40] except their own (Dan 3:28 MT; Dan 3:95 LXX). In other words, it is used to describe the cultic "service" offered to a "deity" (cf. Dan 3:12, 14, 18). In light of these points, both Jewish and Christian interpreters assert:

> What this text [Daniel 7] projects is a second divine figure to whom will be given eternal dominion of the entire world. . . . In other words, a simile, a God who looks like a human being (literally Son of Man) has become the name for that God, who is now called "son of man," a reference to his human-appearing divinity.[41]

> The Son of man is . . . a heavenly being whose home was with God, who already exists with God before creation; he is not a human being.[42]

Because the one like a son of man parallels the other human rulers (the four beasts), I would put this last point differently. Far from being a *merely* human

35. Collins, *Daniel*, 311.

36. Allison, *Constructing Jesus*, 296.

37. Theissen and Merz, *The Historical Jesus*, 553.

38. MT *pelakh*; LXX *latreuō*.

39. MT *pelahk*; LXX *latreuō*.

40. MT *'elohim*; LXX *theos*.

41. Daniel Boyarin, *The Jewish Gospels: The Story of the Jewish Christ* (New York: New Press, 2012), 32–33.

42. Joachim Gnilka, *Jesus of Nazareth: Message and History*, trans. Siegfried S. Schatzmann (Peabody, MA: Hendrickson, 1997), 249.

figure, in context, the Danielic "one like a son of man" is a "divine being" who appears in a human form.[43]

If we turn back to Jesus's healing of the paralytic with these points in mind, the meaning of Jesus's otherwise cryptic response to the scribes becomes clear. For one thing, it provides a plausible explanation of Jesus's puzzling declaration that "the Son of Man" has "authority" (*exousia*) to forgive sins "on earth" (Matt 9:6; Mark 2:10; Luke 5:24). This otherwise redundant addendum—where else would a human be except on earth?—makes perfect sense if Jesus is alluding to the *heavenly* "son of man" in Daniel, to whom "authority" (*exousia*) is given (Dan 7:13–14).[44] Moreover, it also explains why Jesus declares that the son of man has the authority to forgive sins immediately before he himself commands the paralyzed man to stand up, take his mat, and walk home. By means of this action, Jesus implicitly identifies *himself* as the heavenly "son of man" from the book of Daniel. In the words of Rudolf Bultmann: "When it is stated here that the *huios tou anthrōpou* ["son of man"] has the *exousia* ["authority"] to forgive sins, we are meant, without doubt to understand that the Son of Man is Jesus."[45]

Bultmann is by no means alone in this contention. More recent scholars agree that Jesus uses the son of man expression here (and elsewhere) as a "self-reference" and "a mysterious name for Jesus himself."[46] Significantly, Adela Yarbro Collins argues, the self-reference almost functions a kind of apocalyptic "riddle":

> There is great tension . . . between the revelation and the concealment of Jesus' identity. . . . the use of the epithet "the Son of Man" (*ho huios tou anthrōpou*) conceals as much as it reveals about who Jesus is. . . . the phrase alludes to Daniel 7:13, but in a very indirect and cryptic way. Its use by Jesus in his dialogue with the scribes is, in effect, a riddle. Jesus then issues them a challenge to discern his identity.[47]

43. Markus Zehnder, "Why the Danielic 'Son of Man' Is a Divine Being," *Bulletin of Biblical Research* 24.3 (2014): 331–47.

44. Ben Witherington III, *The Christology of Jesus* (Minneapolis: Fortress, 1990), 246–47.

45. Rudolf Bultmann, *History of the Synoptic Tradition*, trans. John Marsh, rev. ed. (Oxford: Basil Blackwell, 1963), 15.

46. Dunn, *Jesus Remembered*, 740; Gerhard Lohfink, *Jesus of Nazareth: What He Wanted, Who He Was*, trans. Linda M. Maloney (Collegeville: Liturgical Press, 2012), 315. See also Schröter, *Jesus of Nazareth*, 165–68; Allison, *Constructing Jesus*, 293–303; Theissen and Merz, *Historical Jesus*, 541–53; Meier, *A Marginal Jew*, 2:679.

47. Yarbro Collins, *Mark*, 186, 187.

In other words, when Jesus's somewhat cryptic self-references are interpreted in light of Jewish Scripture, they implicitly identify him both as a "human being" and as the heavenly "son of man" revealed in the apocalyptic book of Daniel.[48]

The Jewish Crowds' Reaction: Fear and Amazement

Should there be any doubt about the implicit divine claim present in both Jesus's words and actions, we need only note that, in all three Synoptic accounts, the Jewish crowds react to Jesus's words and actions by being utterly astounded:

> When the crowds saw it, they were filled with awe, and they glorified God, who had given such authority to human beings. (Matt 9:8)
>
> They were all amazed and glorified God, saying, "We have never seen anything like this!" (Mark 2:12)
>
> Amazement seized all of them, and they glorified God and were filled with awe, saying, "We have seen strange things today." (Luke 5:26)

Here we have a good example of how the gospel accounts can differ in details, but the substance is basically the same: the crowds react to what Jesus says and does with astonishment, and give glory to God. Notice here that the crowds do not say, "We've seen priests and prophets forgive sins before." Nor do they say, "We've seen other miracle workers do this kind of thing." Instead, they respond as if Jesus has spoken and acted in ways that are truly extraordinary, and they do not seem to know what to make of him.

The Apocalyptic Secret of Jesus's Divinity

In light of such observations, more than one scholar has concluded that, in the Synoptic accounts of the healing of the paralytic, Jesus both speaks and acts as if he is in some way more than merely human. Consider the following statements:

48. Compare Dunn, *Jesus Remembered*, 725: "Broadly speaking, for the last 150 years, the controversy has been between two principal interpretations—what might be characterized as the *human* son of man and the *heavenly* Son of man."

> What Jesus has said calls the unity of God into question.[49]

> Jesus emphasizes that "the Son of Man has authority to forgive sins." . . . Such an authorization exceeds the ability of a prophet. . . . Here too Jesus acts in the place of God.[50]

> The healing of the paralytic . . . provides a further clue about Jesus' divine identity.[51]

> When Jesus said, "Your sins are forgiven," he would no doubt be understood to be using a "divine passive," meaning "God forgives your sins." But this is not a prayer for God to forgive. It is an unequivocal declaration of God's forgiveness, as though Jesus claims the right to speak for God. . . . Jesus' practice of declaring God's forgiveness was perceived in his time as infringing on a divine prerogative.[52]

Other scholars could be cited to similar effect.[53] If this view is correct, then the account of the healing of the paralytic provides us with important evidence in which Jesus appears to claim that he is both a human being (a "son of man") and a heavenly being ("*the* Son of Man"). Indeed, by taking the divine prerogative to directly forgive sins as his own, and *by implicitly identifying himself as the heavenly "son of man" from the book of Daniel, Jesus both reveals and conceals the apocalyptic secret of his divinity*. If so, then the scribal accusation of blasphemy is understandable, for Jesus is indeed claiming to be more than merely human.

Arguments against Historical Plausibility

With these exegetical points in mind, we can now turn to the question of historicity. When it comes to the gospel accounts of Jesus healing the paralytic,

49. Yarbro Collins, *Mark*, 185.

50. Hengel and Schwemer, *Jesus and Judaism*, 493.

51. Richard B. Hays, *Echoes of Scripture in the Gospels* (Waco, TX: Baylor University Press, 2016), 64.

52. Richard Bauckham, *Jesus: A Very Short Introduction* (Oxford: Oxford University Press, 2011), 85.

53. See also Schröter, *Jesus of Nazareth*, 147; W. D. Davies and Dale C. Allison Jr., *A Critical and Exegetical Commentary on the Gospel according to Saint Matthew*, 3 vols., International Critical Commentaries (Edinburgh: T&T Clark, 1988–1997), 2:91.

many major works on the historical Jesus simply ignore it.[54] When explicit arguments against historicity are given, several in particular stand out.

Like the other miracles attributed to Jesus that we examined in chapter 3, the primary reason for concluding the episode is unhistorical is based on the *philosophical* assumption that miracles are impossible. This argument goes at least as far back as the nineteenth-century work of David Friedrich Strauss: "It is always incomparably more probable that histories of cures of the lame and paralytic in accordance with messianic expectation, should be formed by the legend, than that they should really have happened."[55] According to this view, because Jesus is described as able to both perceive the thoughts of the scribes and to heal paralysis (Matt 9:4–7; Mark 2:8–12; Luke 5:22–25)—that is, to perform miracles—the accounts are necessarily unhistorical.[56]

Another major argument against historicity is from contextual implausibility within early Judaism. According to this view, there is no corroborative first-century Jewish evidence that God alone was viewed as having the power to forgive sins. Instead, early Jewish writings outside the Bible suggest that human beings could also forgive sins.[57] In support of this position, scholars point to a Dead Sea Scroll in which the pagan King Nabonidus seems to say that a Jewish exorcist "forgave" (*shabaq*) his "sin" (4QPrayer of Nabonidus ar

54. For example, the healing of the paralytic and the accusation of blasphemy receives no discussion in Bond, *The Historical Jesus*; Allison, *Constructing Jesus*; Craig S. Keener, *The Historical Jesus of the Gospels* (Grand Rapids: Eerdmans, 2009); David Flusser, *The Sage from Galilee: Rediscovering Jesus' Genius*, with R. Steven Notley (Grand Rapids: Eerdmans, 2007); Ehrman, *Jesus: Apocalyptic Prophet*; Paula Fredriksen, *Jesus of Nazareth, King of the Jews* (New York: Vintage Books, 1999); Jürgen Becker, *Jesus of Nazareth*, trans. James E. Crouch (New York: Walter de Gruyter, 1998). This is true even of some books directly focused on the question of Jesus's divine identity, such as Ehrman, *How Jesus Became God*. Other reconstructions of the life of Jesus treat it so briefly that it might as well not exist. See, e.g., E. P. Sanders, *The Historical Figure of Jesus* (London: Penguin, 1993), 98. Others accept part of the episode as historical, but reject the accusation of blasphemy and Jesus's declaration that the "the Son of Man" *does* have authority to forgive sins (Matt 9:3, 6; Mark 2:6–8, 10; Luke 5:21, 24) as unhistorical. See Robert W. Funk and the Jesus Seminar, *The Acts of Jesus: The Search for the Authentic Deeds of Jesus* (San Francisco: HarperSanFrancisco/Polebridge, 1998), 63–65.

55. Strauss, *Jesus of Nazareth*, 457. Strauss is following David Hume, "Of Miracles," chapter 10 in *An Enquiry Concerning Human Understanding: And Other Writings*, ed. Stephen Buckle (Cambridge: Cambridge University Press, 2007), 96–116.

56. Casey, *Jesus of Nazareth*, 262; Gerd Lüdemann, *Jesus after Two Thousand Years: What He Really Said and Did*, trans. John Bowden (London: SCM; Amherst: Prometheus Books, 2001), 15.

57. See especially Hägerland, *Jesus and the Forgiveness of Sins*, 132–78.

[4Q242] frag. 1–3, 4) and a passage in Josephus where he seems to describe the prophet Samuel as being able "to forgive" (*aphiēmi*) the "sin" (*hamartia*) of the people (*Antiquities* 6.92).[58] On the basis of these two texts, both Geza Vermes and Tobias Hägerland contend that Jesus's declaration of forgiveness would not have been considered blasphemous by his Jewish contemporaries:

> Considered side by side with the Nabonidus story, there is nothing outstandingly novel or unique in the words of Jesus, "My son, your sins are forgiven." . . . The words are not disrespectful of God, nor do they imply that the speaker claimed for himself divine status.[59]

> The scribal accusation of blasphemy in [Mark] 2.6–7 is historically implausible. . . . In the light of . . . passage(s) predicating forgiveness of a prophet ([Josephus] *Ant* VI.92; 4Q242 1 1–3, 4?), the formula would have been heard as a claim to be a prophet more readily than as a blasphemous encroachment on the prerogatives of God.[60]

In other words, what the Jewish scribes should have said was, "Who can forgive sins but priests, exorcists, and prophets?" Because they say, "Who can forgive sins but God alone?" this aspect of the episode was likely composed by an early Christian writer who did not understand early Jewish practice and belief.[61]

A final major argument against historicity is from a lack of coherence with other evidence about Jesus. According to this view, Jesus's emphasis on the forgiveness of the paralyzed man's sins is out of step with the overall gospel tradition. In the words of Rudolf Bultmann: "There is no other reference in the tradition (apart from Lk. 7[47]) to Jesus pronouncing the forgiveness of sins."[62] Along similar lines, Jesus's declaration that he will heal the paralyzed man so that the Jewish scribes will "know" that, as "the Son of Man," he has authority to forgive sins, conflicts with other evidence in which Jesus refuses his audience's demand for a miraculous "sign" (Matt 16:1–4; Mark 8:11–12). For some

58. Hägerland, *Jesus and the Forgiveness of Sins*, 156, 146–49, respectively.

59. Vermes, *Jesus the Jew*, 68–69.

60. Hägerland, *Jesus and the Forgiveness of Sins*, 177.

61. See also Casey, *Jesus of Nazareth*, 262; Theissen and Merz, *Historical Jesus*, 527; Sanders, *Historical Figure of Jesus*, 213–14; Sanders, *Jewish Law*, 61–63; Sanders, *Jesus and Judaism*, 273–74.

62. Bultmann, *History of the Synoptic Tradition*, 15.

scholars, this conflict is irreconcilable; it "seals the verdict" on Jesus's declaration regarding the son of man "as fictitious."[63]

Context: John the Baptist, the Forgiveness of Sins, and the Divine Son of Man

With that said, there are a number of works on Jesus which conclude that the gospel accounts of the healing of the paralytic are substantially historical.[64] The first major argument for historicity is from contextual plausibility within Judaism, in several ways.

For one thing, Jesus's act of declaring the paralyzed man's sins to be "forgiven" (Matt 9:2; Mark 2:5; Luke 5:29) is quite plausible in the wake of the ministry of John the Baptist, who was famous for administering his baptism of repentance for "the forgiveness of sins" (Mark 1:4; Luke 3:3; cf. Matt 3:6, 11).[65] As we have already seen above, Jesus's act of linking the forgiveness of the paralyzed man's sins with his physical healing (Matt 9:2; Mark 2:5; Luke 5:29) fits perfectly into an early Jewish context, in which physical illness was often (though not always) described as being the result of sin (cf. Num 12:9–10; Deut 28:28–29; Job 4:7–8; 2 Kgs 6:18).[66]

Moreover, the reaction of the Jewish scribes to Jesus's declaration of forgiveness, in which they accuse him of blasphemy, is also contextually plausible. As we saw above, when describing the forgiveness of sins acquired through animal sacrifice, the book of Leviticus uses the divine passive to emphasize that it is God—not the priest—who forgives the sins of the penitent (cf. Lev 4:18–20, 25–26, 30–31). Likewise, the book of Isaiah makes crystal clear that it is the one God of Israel—whose name is "I am He"—who "blots out transgressions" and does not remember "sins" (Isa 43:25). But what about those two early Jewish texts from the Dead Sea Scrolls and Josephus that seem to describe human beings as having the power to directly forgive sins? Upon closer inspection, this argument has two serious problems. For one thing, even scholars who cite these texts admit that the Hebrew and Greek texts are ambiguous and

63. Hägerland, *Jesus and the Forgiveness of Sins*, 225.

64. See Hengel and Schwemer, *Jesus and Judaism*, 478n6, 492; Schröter, *Jesus of Nazareth*, 147; Grindheim, *God's Equal*, 60–71; Dunn, *Jesus Remembered*, 741; Theissen and Merz, *Historical Jesus*, 527–28; Gnilka, *Jesus of Nazareth*, 110, 116–17; Meier, *A Marginal Jew*, 2:679–80; Klausner, *Jesus of Nazareth*, 277–78.

65. Theissen and Merz, *Historical Jesus*, 527.

66. Funk and the Jesus Seminar, *Acts of Jesus*, 64.

can be translated in ways that do not support this conclusion.[67] Consider the following translations:

> [I, Nabonidus,] was smitten [with severe inflammation] lasting seven years. Beca[use] I was thus changed, [becoming like a beast, *I prayed to the Most High] and He forgave my sins.* An exorcist—a Jew, in fact, a mem[ber of the community of exiles—came to me and said,] "Declare and write down this story, and so ascribe glory and gre[at]ness to the name of G[od Most High." (4QPrayer of Nabonidus ar [4Q242] frags. 1–3, lines 2–5)[68]

> Astounded and terrified, they [the Israelites] confessed their sin, in which, they said, they had fallen through ignorance, and implored the prophet [Samuel], as a kind and gentle father, to render God gracious to them *that He might forgive this sin* which they had committed in addition to all their other insolences and transgressions. *And he promised that he would beseech God to pardon them in this thing* and would withal move Him thereto. (Josephus, *Antiquities* 6.92)

In this Dead Sea Scroll, the one who "forgives" the sin of Nabonidus is *not* the Jewish exorcists, but "the Most High" to whom Nabonidus prays. This translation makes better sense in context, since the Jewish exorcist instructs Nabonidus to "ascribe glory" for his healing to "God"—not himself (4QPrayer of Nabonidus ar [4Q242] frags. 1–3, line 5). Likewise, in Josephus, the Israelites ask the prophet Samuel to intercede for them so that "God" might "forgive" their "sin"—not Samuel himself (cf. 1 Sam 12:18). Again, this translation makes much better sense in context, since the sin for which they need forgiveness was the act of demanding a "king" for themselves, when "the LORD" was already their "king" (see 1 Sam 12:12, 19). In other words, they are not asking Samuel

67. See Hägerland, *Jesus and the Forgiveness of Sins*, 156. Hägerland admits that the grammatical subject of the Hebrew verb "forgive" (*shabaq*) is not clear. It could be the human "diviner," or it could be "God," depending on how one reconstructs the fragmentary text in line 3. The Hebrew of line 4 is ambiguous; it literally reads: ". . . my sin he forgave me a diviner and he . . . a Jew . . ." (*wkht'y shbq lh gzr whw' . . . yhwdy*) (4QPrayer of Nabonidus ar [4Q242] frags. 1–3, line 4). Likewise, Hägerland, *Jesus and the Forgiveness of Sins*, 146–49, admits that the subject of the verb in Josephus can also be understood as "God." The Greek text reads as follows: *iketeusen to prophētēn hōs patera chrēston kai epieikē ton theon autois eumenē katastēsai kai tauten apheinai tēn hamartian* (Josephus, *Antiquities* 6.92).

68. Michael O. Wise, Martin G. Abegg Jr., and Edward M. Cook, *The Dead Sea Scrolls: A New Translation*, rev. ed. (San Francisco: HarperOne, 2005), 342. The name of the document is from García Martínez and Tigchelaar, *Dead Sea Scrolls Study Edition*, 1:487.

to forgive them for sinning against him; they are asking him to intercede with God on their behalf (cf. Exod 32:30–32). In short, the (already slender) early Jewish evidence upon which scholars lean to claim that human beings could in fact forgive sins falls to the ground. For this reason, Adela Yarbro Collins rightly concludes: "The idea that God alone could forgive sins does not seem to have been a contested issue in Second Temple Judaism."[69]

Finally, though it may come as a surprise to some readers, even Jesus's implicit description of "the son of man" as a divine figure is eminently plausible within an early Jewish context. As we saw above, a case can be made that the book of Daniel itself describes the "one like a son of man" as "a second heavenly being" who appears in human form (Dan 7:13–14).[70] Should there be any doubt about this reading, our two earliest extant Jewish interpretations of the book of Daniel both identify the "son of man" as a heavenly messiah who existed before creation. Consider, for example, the following descriptions from two first-century Jewish apocalypses:[71]

> And in that hour, *that son of man* was named in the presence of the Lord of Spirits; and his name, before the Head of Days.
> *Even before the sun and the constellations were created*
> *his name was named before the Lord of Spirits . . .*
> He will be the light of the nations,
> and he will be a hope for those who grieve in their hearts.
> *All who dwell on the earth will fall down and worship before him*,
> and they will glorify and bless and sing hymns to the name of the Lord of Spirits.
> For this (reason) *he was chosen and hidden in his presence,*
> *before the world was created and forever*. (1 Enoch 48:2–7)[72]

> And I looked, and behold, this wind made *something like the figure of a man* come up out of the heart of the sea. And I looked, and behold, *that*

69. Yarbro Collins, *Mark*, 185n26.

70. Collins, *Daniel*, 301.

71. For compelling arguments for a first-century dating of the portion of 1 Enoch known as the Similitudes of Enoch (1 Enoch 37–71), see George W. E. Nickelsburg and James C. VanderKam, *1 Enoch* 2, Hermeneia (Minneapolis: Fortress, 2012), 58–69. Although 4 Ezra is dated to the late first century, it is still widely regarded as an important witness to early Jewish apocalypticism. See Collins, *Apocalyptic Imagination*, 240–63.

72. In Nickelsburg and VanderKam, *1 Enoch* 2, 166.

> *man flew with the clouds of heaven*; and wherever he turned his face to look, everything under his gaze trembled, and wherever the voice of his mouth issued forth, all who heard his voice melted as wax melts when it feels the fire. (4 Ezra 13:3–4)[73]

In light of these passages, experts in early Judaism agree that the Danielic son of man is being identified here as more than merely human. In the apocalypse of 1 Enoch, the son of man is not just the messiah; he is also a "heavenly being who existed before creation,"[74] a "transcendent figure" who possesses "preexistence."[75] Likewise, in the apocalypse of 4 Ezra, the son of man not only displays the "characteristics of God" when he flies on the clouds (cf. Ps 104:3; 97:5); he plays a "superhuman role" as a "transcendent redeemer."[76] In light of such evidence, recent scholars agree that at the time of Jesus, the messiah could be regarded as more than human:

> There is good evidence that the Davidic messiah was regarded as divine in a qualified sense (which certainly did not imply equality with the Almighty) not only in the Dead Sea Scrolls but also in Jewish tradition more generally.[77]

> The reason that many Jews came to believe that Jesus was divine was because they were already expecting that the Messiah/Christ would be a god-man. This expectation was part and parcel of Jewish tradition.[78]

If this is correct, then even Jesus's declaration that, as "son of man," he has the authority to do something only God can do—directly forgive human sins—is plausible, however extraordinary it might have been, within a first-century Jewish apocalyptic context. Indeed, if Jesus was claiming to be both a human and heavenly messiah, then the Jewish crowds react exactly as we would ex-

73. In Michael Edward Stone, *Fourth Ezra*, Hermeneia (Minneapolis: Fortress, 1990), 381.

74. Rebecca Lesses, "Supernatural Beings," in *The Jewish Annotated New Testament*, 2nd ed., ed. Amy-Jill Levine and Mark Zvi Brettler (Oxford: Oxford University Press, 2017), 686.

75. Nickelsburg and VanderKam, *1 Enoch* 2, 170, 259.

76. Stone, *Fourth Ezra*, 384. In this vein, compare also the parallels between the son of man and characteristics of God described elsewhere in the book (cf. 4 Ezra 8:19–36).

77. John J. Collins, "Powers in Heaven: God, Gods, and Angels in the Dead Sea Scrolls," in *Religion in the Dead Sea Scrolls*, ed. John J. Collins and Robert A. Kugler (Grand Rapids: Eerdmans, 2000), 22, quoted in Allison, *Constructing Jesus*, 304n349.

78. Boyarin, *Jewish Gospels*, 56.

pect them to react: with awe, amazement, and even fear (Matt 9:8; Mark 2:12; Luke 5:26).[79]

Coherence: The Divine Passive, the Son of Man, and the Forgiveness of Sins

The second major argument for the historicity of the accounts of Jesus and the paralytic is from coherence with other evidence about Jesus, in several ways.

As we've already discussed in chapter 3, the description of Jesus as performing an inexplicable healing coheres perfectly with the abundant evidence that Jesus was known for working miracles—especially healings (e.g., Matt 11:2–6; Luke 7:18–23; John 4:48; Josephus, *Antiquities* 18.63). As Helen Bond puts it: "That Jesus healed the sick . . . in a way that struck onlookers as miraculous is virtually certain."[80] Hence, whatever one thinks about the possibility of the miraculous, the account is perfectly congruous with the overall evidence that Jesus was regarded by his contemporaries as a wonder-worker.

Moreover, Jesus's initial use of the divine passive—"Your sins are forgiven" (Matt 9:2; Mark 2:5; Luke 5:20)—also coheres in striking fashion with abundant evidence elsewhere that Jesus frequently used the divine passive to speak about God (e.g., Matt 6:9–10; Luke 11:1–2; Matt 7:7; Luke 11:9; Matt 23:37; Luke 13:34).[81] It also coheres remarkably well with the petition for God to "forgive" human debts and sin in the Lord's Prayer (Matt 6:9–13; Luke 11:1–4), as well as parables of the unforgiving servant (Matt 18:23–35), the prodigal son (Luke 15:11–32), and the Pharisee and the tax collector (Luke 18:9–14).[82]

Likewise, Jesus's use of the peculiarly definite third-person expression "the Son of Man" (*ho huios tou anthrōpou*) to refer to himself and "to preserve his *incognito*" is superabundantly attested (see, e.g., Matt 10:23; 19:28; Mark 2:10; 8:38; 13:26; Luke 6:22; 17:22–24; 19:10; 21:36; John 1:51; 3:13–14; 5:27; 6:27; 8:28).[83] His declaration that the son of man has "authority" (*exousia*) to forgive sins

79. Hengel and Schwemer, *Jesus and Judaism*, 492–93n17.

80. Bond, *Historical Jesus*, 102.

81. Jeremias, *Proclamation of Jesus*, 11, notes that "the 'divine passive' occurs round about a hundred times in the sayings of Jesus."

82. Theissen and Merz, *Historical Jesus*, 527.

83. Flusser, *Sage from Galilee*, 115. On Jesus's use of this expression, see especially Allison, *Constructing Jesus*, 293–303; and Larry W. Hurtado and Paul L. Owen, eds., *"Who Is This Son of Man?" The Latest Scholarship on a Puzzling Expression of the Historical Jesus*, Library of New Testament Studies 390 (London: Bloomsbury T&T Clark, 2011).

(Matt 9:6; Mark 2:10; Luke 5:24), along with the awe and amazement expressed by the Jewish crowds, is likewise congruent with evidence that his onlookers were often impressed because he taught as "one having authority" (*exousia*) (Mark 1:22; Luke 4:36).[84]

Finally, Jesus's act of forgiving the paralyzed man coheres remarkably well with the famous account of Jesus declaring a woman who was a public "sinner" to be forgiven in the house of Simon the Pharisee (Luke 7:36–50). Although the question of how this episode relates to other passages in which Jesus is anointed is complex,[85] for our purposes here, the main parallel is Jesus's final declaration:

> Then he said to her, "*Your sins are forgiven.*" But those who were at the table with him began to say among themselves, "*Who is this who even forgives sins?*" And he said to the woman, "Your faith has saved you; go in peace" (Luke 7:44–50).

Just as Jesus says to the paralytic, "your sins are forgiven" (Matt 9:2; Mark 2:5; Luke 5:20), so too he says to the sinful woman, "Your sins are forgiven" (Luke 7:48). And just as the Jewish scribes react to Jesus's declaration of forgiveness by accusing Jesus of usurping a divine prerogative, so too those who are at table with Jesus raise the question of Jesus's identity: "Who is this who even forgives sins?" (Luke 7:49). In light of such parallels, even Gerd Lüdemann, who is not known for being overly credulous regarding the historicity of the Gospels, concludes: "The core of Jesus' claim to be able to forgive sins without having formal authority to do so must be historical (cf. also Luke 7.36–50)."[86]

Consequences: The Power to Forgive Sins and the Apocalyptic Son of Man

A third major argument for the historicity of Jesus's interaction with the paralytic can be made from the plausibility of its impact in the early church, in two ways.

84. Cf. Hengel and Schwemer, *Jesus and Judaism*, 492.

85. See Joseph A. Fitzmyer, SJ, *The Gospel according to Luke*, 2 vols., Anchor Yale Bible 28–28A (New Haven: Yale University Press, 1983, 1985), 1:684–86.

86. Lüdemann, *Jesus after Two Thousand Years*, 16 (cf. 308). See also Kathleen E. Corley, *Women and the Historical Jesus: Feminist Myths of Christian Origins* (Santa Rose: Polebridge, 2002), 90–92, who urges that the depiction of the woman "cannot be explained on the basis of Lukan theology alone."

For one thing, Jesus's arguably unprecedented declaration of his authority to directly forgive sins provides a plausible point of origin for the early Christian belief that the disciples of Jesus, and later the "elders" in the early church (Jas 5:14), had the power to declare the sins of penitent people forgiven. Consider, for example, the following:

> When he had said this, he [Jesus] breathed on them [the disciples] and said to them, "Receive the Holy Spirit. *If you forgive the sins of any, they are forgiven them; if you retain the sins of any, they are retained.*" (John 20:22–23)

> Are any among you sick? They should call for the elders of the church and have them pray over them, anointing them with oil in the name of the Lord. The prayer of faith will save the sick, and the Lord will raise them up; and *anyone who has committed sins will be forgiven.* (Jas 5:14–15)

Notice the use of the divine passive in both texts.[87] Notice also that both texts appear to reflect the fact that in the early church, the disciples of Jesus and later leaders did indeed claim the divine "prerogative" and "right to forgive sins."[88] Given the fact that in early Judaism, God alone had the prerogative to directly forgive human sins, how do we explain the origin of this practice in the early church? One plausible historical explanation is that Jesus himself not only claimed to possess divine authority to forgive sins; he was also believed to have delivered that same, unprecedented authority to his immediate circle of disciples, who then communicated it to later leaders.

Second, if Jesus implicitly identified himself as the heavenly "son of man" from the apocalypse of Daniel who has authority "on the earth" to forgive sins (Matt 9:6; Mark 2:10; Luke 5:24), then this would provide a plausible explanation for why early believers not only identified Jesus as the heavenly "Son of Man," but did so in ways that appear to suggest he is a divine being. Consider, for example, the apocalyptic visions of Stephen of Jerusalem and John, the author of the Apocalypse:

87. See Johannes Beutler, SJ, *A Commentary on the Gospel of John*, trans. Michael Tait (Grand Rapids: Eerdmans, 2013), 512–13; Dale C. Allison Jr., *A Critical and Exegetical Commentary on the Epistle of James*, International Critical Commentaries (London: Bloomsbury, 2013), 768.

88. Cf. Theissen and Merz, *Historical Jesus*, 527; Bultmann, *History of the Synoptic Tradition*, 16.

> But filled with the Holy Spirit, [Stephen] *gazed into heaven* and saw the glory of God and Jesus standing at the right hand of God. "Look," he said, "*I see the heavens opened and the Son of Man standing at the right hand of God!*" (Acts 7:55–56)

> Then *I turned to see* whose voice it was that spoke to me, and on turning I saw seven golden lampstands, and in the midst of the lampstands *I saw one like the Son of Man, clothed with a long robe and with a golden sash across his chest. His head and his hair were white as white wool, white as snow*; his eyes were like a flame of fire, his feet were like burnished bronze, refined as in a furnace, and his voice was like the sound of many waters. (Rev 1:12–15)

We will revisit both of these important texts later in our study. For now, the main point is that both passages identify Jesus as the heavenly "son of man" in the context of apocalyptic visions.[89] Moreover, in both visions, Jesus appears as the "heavenly Son of Man" and "a divine messianic figure."[90] In Stephen's vision, he stands at "the right hand of God" (Acts 7:55), and hence is a superhuman figure.[91] In John's vision, Jesus appears as the Ancient of Days himself—whose head and hair were like "white wool" (Rev 1:14; cf. Dan 7:9)—thereby suggesting "some kind of equal status" with "God."[92] How do we explain the origins of these apocalyptic visions of Jesus as the divine son of man among early Jewish believers? One plausible explanation is that Jesus himself used allusions to the apocalyptic "son of man" from the book of Daniel to both conceal and reveal the heavenly secret of his divinity.

Weighing the Arguments for and against Historicity

In light of all the evidence we have seen thus far, if we weigh the most prominent arguments for and against historicity, it seems clear to me that those in

89. See Kindalee Pfremmer De Long, "Angels and Visions in Luke-Acts," in *The Jewish Apocalyptic Tradition and the Shaping of New Testament Thought*, ed. Benjamin E. Reynolds and Loren T. Stuckenbruck (Minneapolis: Fortress, 2017), 100–101.

90. Richard I. Pervo, *Acts*, Hermeneia (Minneapolis: Fortress, 2009), 197; Francis J. Moloney, SDB, *The Apocalypse of John: A Commentary* (Grand Rapids: Baker Academic, 2020), 57.

91. I. Howard Marshall, "The Christology of Luke's Gospel and Acts," in *Contours of Christology in the New Testament*, ed. Richard N. Longenecker (Grand Rapids: Eerdmans, 2005), 133.

92. David Aune, "Stories of Jesus in the Apocalypse of John," in Longenecker, *Contours of Christology*, 312.

favor of the substantial historicity of Jesus's encounter with the paralytic greatly outweigh the arguments against it.

In this regard, it bears repeating that the principal argument against the historicity of this episode is not a historical argument at all, but a philosophical objection, based on personal belief about the impossibility of miracles. In my view, this kind of philosophical argument—or, better, assumption—has no place in a properly historical investigation of the life of Jesus. As I argued in chapter 3, when it comes to extraordinary or miraculous deeds attributed to Jesus, the historical Jesus scholar is under no burden to explain *how* such seemingly impossible actions may have taken place. Instead, the historian's job is to catalogue actual historical arguments for or against contextual plausibility, coherence, and consequences and evaluate which arguments are weightier.

With this in mind, when it comes to Jesus's encounter with the paralytic, the arguments from contextual implausibility and a lack of coherence are extremely weak. For one thing, the now-popular claim that Jesus's declaration of forgiveness of sins would not have been seen as blasphemous in a first-century Jewish context is based on dubious translations of two early Jewish texts (4QPrayer of Nabonidus ar [4Q242 frags. 1–3; Josephus, *Antiquities* 6.92). Upon closer inspection, these two texts actually support the idea that God alone could directly forgive human sin. And that is to say nothing about passages in Jewish Scripture itself which suggest that forgiveness of sins was a divine prerogative (see Lev 4:20–35; Isa 43:10–25). Moreover, the claim that Jesus's act of forgiving the paralytic's sin does not cohere with other evidence about him is simply untrue. Jesus was not only closely associated with John the Baptist—who was famous precisely because of his baptism of repentance for "the forgiveness of sins" (Mark 1:4; Luke 3:3; cf. Matt 3:6, 11). There is also good reason to believe that he once declared a woman who was a public "sinner" to be forgiven (Luke 7:44–50) and that he taught his disciples a prayer asking God the Father to "forgive" human sin (Matt 6:9–13; Luke 11:1–4).

Indeed, when it comes to the evidence that Jesus reacted to the Galilean scribes' accusation of blasphemy by declaring that, as "the Son of Man," he did indeed have authority "on earth" to forgive sins (Matt 9:2–8; Mark 2:1–12; Luke 5:17–26), we find ourselves faced with an extremely strong case of contextual plausibility within Judaism and coherence with other evidence about Jesus. For example, Jesus's implication that "the Son of Man" is a heavenly figure who has authority "on earth" to do what Scripture says God alone can fits quite squarely into a first-century Jewish apocalyptic context, in which the Danielic "one like a son of man" (Dan 7:13–14) was not only identified as the messiah, but described as a preexistent, heavenly being (1 Enoch 48:2–7; 4 Ezra 13:3–4). It also coheres remarkably well with a veritable mountain of other evidence in the Gospels in which Jesus uses the definite third-person expression "the Son of Man" to refer to himself (e.g., Matt 10:23; 19:28; Mark 8:38; 13:26; Luke 6:22; 17:22–24; 19:10; 21:36; John 1:51; 3:13–14; 5:27; 6:27; 8:28). Last, the account of Jesus forgiving the sins of the paralytic would provide a plausible point of origin for the remarkable early Christian practice of attributing the divine power to forgive sins to the apostles and leaders in the early church (John 20:22–23; Jas 5:14–15).

With all this in mind, when we evaluate the gospel accounts of Jesus's encounter with the paralytic from a triple-context perspective, I would concur with Joachim Gnilka that the episode is indeed "very plausible."[93] If this verdict is correct, then the implications for who Jesus thought himself to be are enormous. As Sigurd Grindheim writes:

> The best explanation for Jesus' acts is that he understood himself to have an authority that in a Jewish context was exclusively attributed to God. Jesus appears to have put himself in a role that was reserved for God and thus implicitly claimed to be God's equal.[94]

I think this is right. In the account of his encounter with a paralytic, Jesus implicitly identified himself as the heavenly son of man who had the authority to do what *God alone* was able to do—forgive human sin—and, as a result, some Jewish scribes in Galilee considered his words and actions to be blasphemous. And as we will see later, this is not the last time Jesus will be accused of blasphemy because of who he claims to be.

The Question of John the Baptist

Since John the Baptist is widely regarded as a Jewish apocalyptic prophet, it is quite fitting that the second episode that demands our attention involves John's question about the mystery of Jesus' identity. This exchange is recounted in the Gospels of Matthew and Luke:

93. Gnilka, *Jesus of Nazareth*, 110.

94. Sigurd Grindheim, *God's Equal: What Can We Know about Jesus' Self-Understanding in the Synoptic Gospels?*, Library of New Testament Studies 446 (London: T&T Clark, 2011), 76.

> When John heard in prison what the Messiah was doing, he sent word by his disciples and said to him, "*Are you the one who is to come*, or are we to wait for another?" Jesus answered them, "*Go and tell John what you hear and see: the blind receive their sight, the lame walk, the lepers are cleansed, the deaf hear, the dead are raised, and the poor have good news brought to them.* And *blessed is anyone who takes no offense at me.*" (Matt 11:2–6)

> The disciples of John reported all these things to him. So John summoned two of his disciples and sent them to the Lord to ask, "Are you the one who is to come, or are we to wait for another?" When the men had come to him, they said, "John the Baptist has sent us to you to ask, '*Are you the one who is to come*, or are we to wait for another?'" Jesus had just then cured many people of diseases, plagues, and evil spirits, and had given sight to many who were blind. And he answered them, "*Go and tell John what you have seen and heard: the blind receive their sight, the lame walk, the lepers are cleansed, the deaf hear, the dead are raised, the poor have good news brought to them. And blessed is anyone who takes no offense at me.*" (Luke 7:18–23)

Although there are several notable differences between these accounts, for our purposes here, their common substance can be summarized as follows: (1) John asks Jesus about his identity and whether or not he is "the one who is to come"; (2) Jesus responds to John's question by alluding to certain passages in Jewish Scripture (Isa 26:19; 35:5–6; 61:1) and pointing John to the miracles Jesus has performed; (3) Jesus also adds a final "beatitude" for anyone who is not scandalized or offended by him. In what follows we will take a few moments to interpret each of these features in their first-century Jewish context.

John's Question and the Coming of the Divine Messiah

It is important to begin by emphasizing that John does not ask Jesus, "Are you the Messiah?"[95] Instead, he asks him, "Are you *the one who is to come*?" (*ho erchomenos*) (Matt 11:3; Luke 7:20). Who is this mysterious figure?

On the one hand, there are several reasons to think that John the Baptist is referring to a *human figure* who is expected to come at some point in the future. For one thing, John elsewhere speaks of the "coming" of "one who is more powerful" (*ischyroteros*) than he as someone whose "sandals" he is not "worthy" to touch

95. Contra Klausner, *Jesus of Nazareth*, 249; Strauss, *Jesus of Nazareth*, 415.

(Matt 3:11; Luke 3:16).[96] It should go without saying that for John to describe God as being more powerful than himself would be a rather strange case of stating the obvious.[97] Likewise, although the Psalms sometimes speak metaphorically of God's "sandal" (e.g., Ps 60:8; 108:9), Jewish Scripture ordinarily depicts the one God as a transcendent being who has no body (cf. Exod 3:14–16). As James Dunn quips: "God does not wear sandals."[98] For this reason, many interpreters conclude that John is simply using a somewhat cryptic expression to refer to the coming of "the Messiah" or "the Son of Man-Messiah,"[99] perhaps alluding to the Danielic "son of man" who is described as "coming" on the clouds (cf. Dan 7:13–14).[100]

On the other hand, when John's question is examined in the light of the Jewish Scriptures, there are also reasons to think that he is speaking of *the God of Israel*.[101] For one thing, when John declares that the one who is to come will "baptize" with "fire" (Matt 3:11; Luke 3:16), he seems to be alluding to Daniel's vision of a "river of fire" flowing from the throne of "the Ancient of Days" (Dan 7:9–10). Likewise, when John describes the coming one as holding his "winnowing fork" and cleansing his "threshing floor" (Matt 3:12; Luke 3:17), he appears to be echoing Jewish Scriptures that describe the God of Israel as having a "winnowing fork" (Jer 15:7) with which he will "thresh" out his people on the day of judgment (Isa 27:12) and "scatter" the wicked "like chaff" (Jer 13:24).[102] Finally, when John says that the coming one will burn the wicked in "unquenchable fire" (Matt 3:11–12; Luke 3:16–17), he is clearly drawing on the book of Isaiah, which declares that "the LORD" will come and punish the wicked with "fire" that "shall not be quenched" (Isa 66:24).[103]

In light of such passages, a number of scholars argue that John is referring to the coming of God:

> The basic proclamation of John in Matt 3:7–10 par . . . provides a good argument for those who claim that John saw himself as the forerunner of God alone.[104]

96. See Meier, *A Marginal Jew*, 2:32–40.

97. See Davies and Allison, *Matthew*, 1:316–17.

98. Dunn, *Jesus Remembered*, 369n152, quoting E. Stauffer, "Jesus, Geschichte und Verkündigung," *Aufstieg und Niedergang der Römischen Welt* 25.1:3–130.

99. Amy-Jill Levine, "The Gospel according to Luke," in Levine and Brettler, *Jewish Annotated New Testament*, 128.

100. Hengel and Schwemer, *Jesus and Judaism*, 321; Flusser, *Sage from Galilee*, 26.

101. Theissen and Merz, *Historical Jesus*, 20.

102. Theissen and Merz, *Historical Jesus*, 201.

103. Cf. Fitzmyer, *Gospel according to Luke*, 1:474.

104. Meier, *A Marginal Jew*, 2:32.

> If the language here is metaphorical and anthropomorphic, the "coming one" could be God himself.[105]

> Whom did John expect? . . . God is a possibility not to be lightly discarded.[106]

> [John the Baptist] expected the coming judgment and the Stronger One, who at all events is a heavenly figure.[107]

Other examples could be given.[108] For our purposes here, what matters most is that John says nothing explicit about the messiah. Instead, he appears to be referring to the coming of a *divine* figure. To be sure, the fact that he is asking Jesus whether he is this figure "only makes sense if it was conceivable that a human being could fulfill this role."[109] However, this does not negate the fact that John's language cannot be explained fully if the figure he is asking about is merely human. Instead, when John's words are interpreted in light of Jewish Scripture and early Jewish evidence for the "divinity of the messiah,"[110] a case can be made that John is speaking about *a divine figure who comes as a human being.*

Jesus's Response and the Divinity of the Messiah

Should there be any doubt about this suggestion, it is important to emphasize that Jesus does *not* respond by explicitly affirming "I am the Messiah," or "I am the one who is to come."[111] Instead, he responds by alluding to several oracles in the book of Isaiah that appear to refer to both the coming of a human messianic figure and to the coming of God.[112]

105. Bond, *Historical Jesus*, 84.

106. Dunn, *Jesus Remembered*, 369.

107. Lüdemann, *Jesus after Two Thousand Years*, 306.

108. See also Knut Backhaus, "Jesus and John the Baptizer," in *The Jesus Handbook*, ed. Jens Schröter and Christine Jacobi, trans. Robert L. Brawley (Grand Rapids: Eerdmans, 2022), 241–48 (here 244); Grindheim, *God's Equal*, 49n31; Marius Reiser, *Jesus and Judgment: The Eschatological Proclamation in Its Jewish Context*, trans. Linda M. Maloney (Minneapolis: Fortress, 1997), 182, 185; Robert L. Webb, *John the Baptizer and Prophet: A Socio-Historical Study*, Journal for the Study of the New Testament Supplement Series 62 (Sheffield: JSOT Press, 1991), 282–88.

109. Bond, *Historical Jesus*, 84. So too Allison, *Constructing Jesus*, 275.

110. Yarbro Collins and Collins, *King and Messiah as Son of God*, xi.

111. Cf. Lohfink, *Jesus of Nazareth*, 313–14.

112. Cf. Schröter, *Jesus of Nazareth*, 99; Bond, *Historical Jesus*, 108; Puig i Tàrrech, *Jesus: A Biography*, 359.

For example, when Jesus answers John's question by declaring that "the poor" have "good news" preached to them (Matt 11:5; Luke 7:22), he is drawing on an Isaianic oracle about the coming of an anointed human figure:[113]

> The spirit of the Lord God is upon me,
> *because the* L*ORD has anointed me*;
> *he has sent me to bring good news* to the oppressed,
> to bind up the brokenhearted,
> to proclaim liberty to the captives,
> and release to the prisoners. (Isa 61:1)

Notice that the human figure in question is "anointed" (Hebrew *mashakh*) by God (Isa 61:1). In light of such language, it is unsurprising that commentators identify the speaker as "the Messiah-Servant."[114] Seen in this light, Jesus is implicitly identifying himself as a human messianic figure.

On the other hand, when Jesus responds to John's question about his identity by listing the wonders he has performed—the blind receiving their sight, the lame walking, the deaf hearing, and the dead being raised (Matt 11:4–5; Luke 7:22)—he is also alluding to oracles in Isaiah that describe the eschatological coming of God:[115]

> *Your dead shall live, their corpses shall rise.*
> O dwellers in the dust, awake and sing for joy!
> For your dew is a radiant dew,
> and *the earth will give birth to those long dead.*
> Come, my people, enter your chambers,
> and shut your doors behind you;
> hide yourselves for a little while
> until the wrath is past.
> *For the* L*ORD comes out from his place*
> to punish the inhabitants of the earth for their iniquity. (Isa 26:19–21)

> Say to those who are of a fearful heart,
> "Be strong, do not fear!

113. Puig i Tàrrech, *Jesus: A Biography*, 359; Dunn, *Jesus Remembered*, 516.

114. Blenkinsopp, *Isaiah*, 3:220. So too J. N. Oswalt, *The Book of Isaiah*, 2 vols., New International Commentary on the Old Testament (Grand Rapids: Eerdmans, 1986, 1998), 2:562–63.

115. Hengel and Schwemer, *Jesus and Judaism*, 493; Allison, *Constructing Jesus*, 275; Casey, *Jesus of Nazareth*, 182; Dunn, *Jesus Remembered*, 516.

Here is your God.
He will come with vengeance,
with terrible recompense.
He will come and save you."
Then the eyes of the blind shall be opened,
and the ears of the deaf unstopped;
then the lame shall leap like a deer,
and the tongue of the speechless sing for joy. (Isa 35:4–6)

Note well that neither oracle says anything about the coming of the messiah. Both are entirely focused on "the coming of God."[116] Notice also that not a word is said about the coming of "the Kingdom of God,"[117] or "the true spokesman for God"[118]—expressions some interpreters seem strangely inclined to substitute for what Isaiah actually says. Instead, Jesus's allusions to Isaiah show that his miracles are signs of "the coming of God."[119] In the words of Michael Wolter:

> Jesus applies the promises passed down through Isaiah to his own work in Israel: in this way he interprets his own activity as the fulfillment of these promises focused on *God's* action, and thereby raises no small claim that he himself acts in the place of God. What Israel expects from *God* is fulfilled through Jesus.[120]

Hence, when Jesus's response is interpreted in the light of Jewish Scripture, he appears to be fusing the coming of a human messiah and the coming of God into one event. In other words, he appears to be describing the advent of a *divine messiah.*

Jesus's Final Beatitude: The "Scandal" of His Identity

Should there be any doubt that Jesus is referring to a divine messiah, it is crucial to emphasize that this interpretation is strongly supported by Jesus's

116. Blenkinsopp, *Isaiah*, 2:186.
117. Bond, *Historical Jesus*, 108.
118. Sanders, *Historical Figure of Jesus*, 167.
119. Hengel and Schwemer, *Jesus and Judaism*, 346.
120. Michael Wolter, "Jesus's Understanding of Himself," in Schröter and Jacobi, *The Jesus Handbook*, 422–29 (here 422).

concluding beatitude: "And blessed is anyone who takes no offense"—literally, is not "scandalized" (*skandalizō*)—"at me" (Matt 11:6; Luke 7:23).

Once again, some interpreters seem to want to avoid the self-centered focus of Jesus's words and interpret his beatitude as a blessing for those who are not scandalized by his "mission."[121] But this is pure eisegesis. Jesus does not say "Blessed is anyone who takes no offense at my mission." He says, "Blessed is anyone who takes no offense *at me*" (*en emoi*) (Matt 11:6; Luke 7:23). As Dale Allison rightly notes: "The declaration, 'Blessed is anyone who takes no offense at me,' puts him at the center of things."[122] This point should be obvious, since Jesus pronounces this beatitude in the context of John's question about his *identity*. Moreover, there is no reason to think that the wonders performed by Jesus would have been considered scandalous. By contrast, if Jesus is identifying *himself* with the God whom the Jewish Scriptures say will one day come and "save" or "heal" his people by raising the dead, giving sight to the blind, and making the lame to walk, then that would be a very scandalous claim indeed.

In short, Jesus's final beatitude is not a blessing for those who might be scandalized by his actions, but for those who might be scandalized by his *self-claims*. When Jesus's response to John is interpreted in its ancient Jewish context, he is indeed making "a stupendous albeit implicit claim" about his identity.[123] This claim goes beyond the claim to mere messiahship, which is ultimately "inadequate" to explain why anyone would be "scandalized" by the person of Jesus.[124] After all, in a first-century Jewish context, there was nothing necessarily "scandalous" about claiming to be the messiah—unless the messiah in question is understood to be something more than just a human priest, prophet, or king.

Arguments against Historical Plausibility

With these exegetical points in mind, we can now ask: Can the exchange between John and Jesus be reasonably situated in the life of the historical Jesus himself, or should it rather be seen as a creation or distortion of the early church?

121. Dunn, *Jesus Remembered*, 450.
122. Allison, *Constructing Jesus*, 276.
123. Allison, *Constructing Jesus*, 278.
124. Lohfink, *Jesus of Nazareth*, 313.

When it comes to the historicity of this episode, a comparatively small number of Jesus researchers argue that the exchange between John the Baptist and Jesus is either mostly or completely unhistorical.[125] Several reasons are given in support of this conclusion.

The first argument is from contextual implausibility within a first-century Jewish context. According to this view, if John the Baptist was referring to God or a heavenly being when he spoke about "the one who is to come" (cf. Matt 3:11–12; Mark 1:7–8; Luke 3:15–18), then it is not believable that he would ask Jesus of Nazareth—who was obviously human—whether he was this superhuman figure. In the words of Gerd Lüdemann: "These verses are generally formulated from a post-Easter perspective and are therefore inauthentic. . . . John could not have put the question attributed to him to a historical person, for he expected the coming judgment and the Stronger One, who at all events is a heavenly figure."[126] Hence, Lüdemann rejects John's question as unhistorical on the grounds that, as a first-century Jew, John could not have believed that such a "heavenly figure"—much less God himself—could appear on earth as a human being.

A second argument against historical plausibility is from a lack of coherence with other evidence about Jesus. According to this view, the historical veracity of this exchange is doubtful because when Jesus answers the question about his identity, he makes no mention of the exorcisms for which he was well known (cf. Mark 1:34; Matt 9:32–34; Luke 11:14–20); nor does he refer to "the kingdom of God"—arguably the center of his message (cf. Matt 3:2; Mark 1:15; Luke 4:43).[127] Along similar lines, Jesus's allusions to prophecies from the book of Isaiah which he has fulfilled in his actions does not cohere with his tendency to make the kingdom of God (rather than himself) the center of his message. In the words of the Jesus Seminar: "The basic list is therefore taken from scripture, which means that [Jesus's] response is a piece of Christian apologetic, designated to demonstrate that these activities fulfill ancient prophecies."[128]

125. See Lüdemann, *Jesus after Two Thousand Years*, 306; Becker, *Jesus of Nazareth*, 11; Gnilka, *Jesus of Nazareth*, 131; Robert W. Funk, Roy Hoover, and the Jesus Seminar, *The Five Gospels: The Search for the Authentic Words of Jesus* (New York: Macmillan, 1993), 177–78; Bultmann, *History of the Synoptic Tradition*, 23; Klausner, *Jesus of Nazareth*, 249. In his earlier study, Sanders, *Jesus and Judaism*, 136–37 (somewhat uncharacteristically), follows Bultmann and seems doubtful about historicity. However, his later study (Sanders, *Historical Figure of Jesus*, 167–68) appears to reverse this verdict.

126. Lüdemann, *Jesus after Two Thousand Years*, 306.

127. Becker, *Jesus of Nazareth*, 112.

128. Funk, Hoover, and the Jesus Seminar, *Five Gospels*, 178.

The argument here seems to be that Jesus would not have taken a list of events from Jewish Scripture and identified it as being fulfilled in his own extraordinary deeds.

The third key argument against historicity is from the implausibility of effects within the early church. According to this view, the continued existence of followers of John the Baptist who did not acknowledge the messiahship or divinity of Jesus makes it unlikely that John the Baptist himself ever asked Jesus whether he was "the one who is to come." In the words of the early twentieth-century Jewish scholar Joseph Klausner:

> Even in the time of the Apostles, considerably after the crucifixion, there were to be found some who accepted John's teaching in such fashion as not to acknowledge Jesus' messiahship (and still less his divinity), and thought that the generation still needed preparation for the Messiah who was not yet to come. . . . It is obvious, therefore, that John had no personal acquaintance with Jesus and did not recognize his messiahship; hence there can be no historical foundation for the account, given by Matthew and Luke [Matt 11:2–5; Luke 7:18–35] but absent in Mark, which tells how John heard in prison (at Machaerus) of the wonderful works of Jesus, and sent to ask him whether he was the Messiah or not, and, in reply, Jesus pointed to the wonders that he was doing as a genuine proof of his messiahship.[129]

In support of this point, Klausner points to the evidence that, at the time of Paul, "a Jew named Apollos" of Alexandria was well known in the churches, but he "knew only the baptism of John" (Acts 18:24–25). Likewise, when Paul arrives in Ephesus, he discovers some twelve disciples who have only received "John's baptism" (cf. Acts 19:1–7). Klausner, like others, seems to interpret this data as suggesting that "the Baptist movement" was still alive and well during the mid- to late first century.[130] Here the implicit argument seems to be that if John the Baptist had in fact had such an exchange with Jesus, then all of his followers would have become believers in Jesus, and the community of John's disciples would have dissolved after his execution by Herod. Hence, Jesus's response can be deemed "a community product," created by the early church

129. Klausner, *Jesus of Nazareth*, 249.

130. See Joel Marcus, *John the Baptist in History and Theology* (Columbia: University of South Carolina Press, 2018), 164n10, following the classic study by Ernst Käsemann, "The Disciples of John the Baptist in Ephesus," in *Essays on New Testament Themes*, Studies in Biblical Theology 41 (London: SCM, 1964), 136–48.

in order to (falsely) call upon John the Baptist "as a witness to the Messiahship of Jesus."[131]

Context: Heavenly Visitors, Divine Miracles, and the One God Becoming Human

Despite these arguments against historicity, most contributors to the quest for Jesus conclude that the exchange between John the Baptist and Jesus is substantially historical.[132] For example, Maurice Casey—who is not known for being overly credulous—states: "John's question to Jesus and Jesus' answer are certainly authentic."[133] The first reason for such scholarly confidence is from several points of contextual plausibility within early Judaism.

For one thing, however strange it may seem to contemporary readers, even *if* John the Baptist saw "the one who is to come" as a heavenly being, or even as God himself, it is nevertheless quite plausible for John to ask Jesus if he were this figure. For, in a first-century Jewish context, it was widely believed that, in extraordinary circumstances, heavenly beings—including the God of Israel—could in fact appear on earth in human form. Consider the following examples from Jewish Scripture:

HEAVENLY "HUMANS" IN JEWISH SCRIPTURE

1. "The LORD" appears as a "man" to Abraham (Gen 18:1–33; cf. 19:1)
2. "God" appears as a "man" to Jacob (Gen 32:24–30)
3. The "commander" of God's army appears as "a man" to Joshua (Josh 5:13–15)
4. An "angel" appears as a "man" who looks like "a god" in the fiery furnace with Daniel and his companions (Dan 5:19–30)
5. "The LORD" will come and walk on the "earth" (Mic 1:2–4)[134]

131. Bultmann, *History of the Synoptic Tradition*, 23.

132. See Schröter, *Jesus of Nazareth*, 99–100; Hengel and Schwemer, *Jesus and Judaism*, 320–21; Puig i Tàrrech, *Jesus: A Biography*, 359; Allison, *Constructing Jesus*, 275; Keener, *Historical Jesus of the Gospels*, 170; Dunn, *Jesus Remembered*, 447, 450; Vermes, *Authentic Gospel of Jesus*, 199–200, 278–80; Theissen and Merz, *Historical Jesus*, 211; Meier, *A Marginal Jew*, 2:130, 136; Sanders, *Historical Figure of Jesus*, 167–68. See also Lohfink, *Jesus of Nazareth*, 313–14; Bond, *Historical Jesus*, 84–85, 108; Fredrisken, *Jesus of Nazareth*, 196, who appear to affirm its historicity but give no substantial discussion of why.

133. Casey, *Jesus of Nazareth*, 181.

134. See George Savran, *Encountering the Divine: Theophany in Biblical Narrative*, Journal for the Study of the Old Testament Supplement 420 (London: T&T Clark, 2005), for a full study.

To be sure, all of these passages are mysterious, and early Jewish interpreters seem to have been divided about whether it is "God" himself or just his "angel/s" who appear on earth (cf. Gen 18:1–2; 32:29 LXX; Wisdom of Solomon 10:12; Jubilees 16:1–4; Philo, *On Dreams* 1.171; *Flight* 208; Josephus, *Antiquities* 1.333, 196–200).[135] Either way, however, I know of no early Jewish interpreter who denies that these passages describe some kind of heavenly being appearing on earth.[136] Nor are such appearances confined to the ancient past, for the oracle from Micah cited above describes the future "descent of YHWH" from heaven to earth.[137] In fact, it is this very oracle that is alluded to in one early Jewish apocalypse which begins by declaring that "the eternal God" will one day "appear" on "earth" to carry out the final judgment (1 Enoch 1:3–4).[138] In light of such evidence, it *is quite plausible that an apocalyptic Jewish prophet like John the Baptist would entertain the possibility that Jesus of Nazareth was a heavenly being who had come down to earth in human form*. This is especially likely if Jesus was already known as a miracle worker, and if some of Jesus's Jewish contemporaries were speculating that he may in fact be "Elijah" come down from heaven to earth (Matt 16:14; Mark 8:28; Luke 9:19; cf. cf. 2 Kgs 2:1–12).[139]

Equally important: Jesus's act of answering John's question about his identity by alluding to certain oracles in the book of Isaiah (Matt 11:5; Luke 7:22; cf. Isa 26:19; 35:4–6; 61:1) is totally credible in a first-century Jewish context.[140] For in one of the Dead Sea Scrolls, the very same oracles alluded to by Jesus are used in a description of what will take place at the time of the messiah:

135. See James E. Bowley, "Abraham," and Roger Good, "Jacob," in Collins and Harlow, *Eerdmans Dictionary of Early Judaism*, 294–95, 781–82; James Kugel, *Traditions of the Bible: A Guide to the Bible as It Was at the Start of the Common Era* (Cambridge, MA: Harvard University Press, 1998), 384–87.

136. Given how much has been made out of John the Baptist's declaring himself unworthy to handle the "sandals" of "the one who is to come" (Matt 3:11; Mark 1:7; Luke 3:16; John 1:27), it may also be worth pointing out that Abraham provides "the LORD" (YHWH) with water to "wash" his "feet" (Gen 18:4–8; 19:1).

137. Francis I. Anderson and David Noel Freedman, *Micah*, Anchor Bible 24E (New York: Doubleday, 2000), 159 (slightly adapted).

138. See George W. E. Nickelsburg, *1 Enoch 1*, Hermeneia (Minneapolis: Fortress, 2001), 142–45.

139. Cf. Bond, *Historical Jesus*, 84.

140. See Hengel and Schwemer, *Jesus and Judaism*, 347; Schröter, *Jesus of Nazareth*, 99; Vermes, *Authentic Gospel of Jesus*, 200; Craig A. Evans, "Jesus and the Dead Sea Scrolls from Qumran Cave 4," in *Eschatology, Messianism, and the Dead Sea Scrolls*, ed. Craig A. Evans and Peter W. Flint (Grand Rapids: Eerdmans, 1997), 96–97.

> [For the heav]ens and the earth will listen to *his messiah*, [and all th]at is in them will not turn away from the precepts of the holy ones. Strengthen yourselves, you who are seeking the Lord, in his service! *Blank* Will you not in this encounter the Lord, all those who hope in their heart? For *the Lord* will consider the pious, and call the righteous by name, and his spirit will hover upon the poor, and he will renew the faithful with his strength. For he will honour the pious upon the throne of an eternal kingdom, *freeing prisoners, giving sight to the blind, straightening out the twis[ted.]* And for[e] ver shall I cling [to those who h]ope, and in his mercy [. . .] and the fru[it of. . .] . . . not be delayed. And *the Lord will perform marvellous acts such as have not existed, just as he sa[id,]* [for] *he will heal the badly wounded and will make the dead live, he will proclaim good news to the poor.* (4QMessianic Apocalypse [4Q521] 2 II, 1–13)[141]

Notice here that the scroll explicitly refers to the coming of God's "anointed one" or "messiah" (*mshykh*), who is depicted as having some kind of power over heaven and earth (4QMessianic Apocalypse [4Q521] 2 II, 1). Notice also that it clearly describes the fulfillment of several prophecies from Isaiah which say that, in the coming era, the "blind" will see, the "dead" will "live," and the "poor" will have good news preached to them (4QMessianic Apocalypse [4Q521] 2 II, 8, 12; cf. Isa 5:5; 42:7; 26:19; 61:1). With that said, the scroll never explicitly states that the messiah himself will carry out these miracles. To the contrary, it emphasizes that it is "the Lord" (*'dny*) who will perform these "marvelous acts" (4QMessianic Apocalypse [4Q521] 2 II, 11–12).[142] On this crucial point, several scholars agree:

> It is God who will heal the wounded, give life to the dead, and preach good news to the poor.[143]

> God himself appears as the actor from line 5 onward. . . . [In] 4Q521, God himself appears to be the proclaimer of the good news vis-à-vis the poor.[144]

141. In Florentino García Martínez and Eibert J. C. Tigchelaar, *The Dead Sea Scrolls Study Edition*, 2 vols. (Grand Rapids: Eerdmans, 2000), 2:1045 (adapted).

142. Hengel and Schwemer, *Jesus and Judaism*, 349. This is not to say that the messiah was not expected to perform miracles at all. Compare the first-century Jewish apocalypses 4 Ezra 13:50, which explicitly states the messiah will perform "very many wonders" after the inauguration of the eschatological kingdom. See Michael Edward Stone, *Fourth Ezra*, Hermeneia (Minneapolis: Fortress, 1990), 394, 406.

143. John J. Collins, *The Scepter and the Star: Messianism in Light of the Dead Sea Scrolls*, 2nd ed. (Grand Rapids: Eerdmans, 2016), 132.

144. Hengel and Schwemer, *Jesus and Judaism*, 349n79.

> [In 4Q521,] God himself is the one who saves.[145]

In other words, although the Dead Sea Scroll mentions the coming of the messiah, a solid case can be made that it identifies God as the one who gives sight to the blind, raises the dead, and proclaims good news to the poor.[146] Hence, when Jesus answers John's question about *his* identity by pointing to the miracles performed by *God* in Isaiah, his answer functions as a kind of riddle, one that implicitly identifies him with the God of Israel. However extraordinary this implication may seem, the parallels between Jesus's words and the Dead Sea Scrolls demonstrate beyond doubt that Jesus's answer to John is indeed credible in a first-century Jewish context. As Martin Hengel and Anna Maria Schwemer put it: Jesus's response "contains not only an implicit Christology but rather a Christology that is already explicit to some extent."[147]

Perhaps most striking of all, even Jesus's implicit claim to John the Baptist to be the one God of Israel come in person is contextually plausible within first-century Judaism. Although to my knowledge the point is universally overlooked in studies of Jesus and early Christology, there is positive evidence that the idea of the one God of Israel becoming human was *not* inconceivable within early Jewish monotheism. In the writings of Philo of Alexandria—a first-century contemporary of Jesus—there is an important passage in which Philo criticizes the Roman emperor Gaius Caligula for placing himself among "the gods" and demanding divine "worship."[148] In the context of Philo's polemic, he says the following remarkable words:

> Need we more than these proofs to teach us that *Gaius has no right to be likened to any of the gods or demigods*, for his nature, his substance, his purpose in life, is different than theirs? . . . *For he looked with disfavor on the Jews alone because they alone opposed him on principle, trained as they were we might say even from the cradle, by parents and tutors and instructors and by the far higher authority of the sacred laws and also the unwritten customs, to acknowledge one God who is the Father and Maker of the world.*

145. Becker, *Jesus of Nazareth*, 113.

146. See also Émile Puech, "Messianic Apocalypse," in *Encyclopedia of the Dead Sea Scrolls*, 2 vols., ed. Lawrence H. Schiffman and James C. VanderKam (Oxford: Oxford University Press, 2000), 1:543.

147. Hengel and Schwemer, *Jesus and Judaism*, 349.

148. On the divine claims of Caligula, see also Cassius Dio, *Roman History* 59.26, 28; cf. 51.20; Anthony A. Barrett, *Caligula: The Corruption of Power* (New Haven: Yale University Press, 1990), 140–53.

> For all others, men, women, cities, nations, countries, regions of the earth, I might almost say the whole inhabited world, groaning though they were at what was happening, flattered him all the same and magnified him out of all proportion and augmented his vanity. Some too even introduced into Italy the barbarian practice of prostrating themselves, a degradation of the high tradition of Roman freedom. One nation only, standing apart, the nation of the Jews, was suspected of intending opposition, since it was accustomed to accept death as willingly as if it were immortality, to save them from submitting to the destruction of any of their ancestral traditions, even the smallest. . . . But that displacement was nothing petty, but of the greatest of all that exists, when the created and corruptible nature of man was made to appear uncreated and incorruptible by a deification which our nation judged to be the most grievous impiety, *since God could sooner change into a human than a human into God.* (Philo of Alexandria, *Embassy to Gaius* 114–118)[149]

Notice here that when Philo says "God could sooner change into a human than a human into God" (*thatton gar an eis anthrōpon theon ē eis theon anthrōpon metabalein*), he is not speaking about just any deity. In context, he is specifically referring to "the one God" (*hena theon*) of the Jewish people, who are taught from youth to acknowledge him alone as "Father and Maker of the world" (*ton patera kai tou kosmou*). In other words, he is referring to the God of early Jewish monotheism. Notice also that Philo is not making this claim in the course of abstract theological speculation, but in the concrete imperial context of explaining why the Jewish people as a whole refuse to engage in the impiety of offering the emperor Caligula worship by "prostrating themselves" (*proskynēsis*) to him as if he were one of the "gods" (*theōn*) or "demigods" (*hēmitheōn*). In short: *in the context of an unequivocal confession of early Jewish monotheism and monolatry, Philo declares that it would be more likely for the one God to become a human being than for a human being to become God.*

Amazingly, Philo's momentous declaration that the God of Israel could possibly become a human being is not only ignored in major works on the historical Jesus; it is even ignored in major studies of Jewish monotheism and early Christology.[150] Nevertheless, it is extremely consequential. For if a first-

149. Loeb Classical Library translation adapted.

150. For example, Philo's statement that the one God could become human receives no mention in Kevin P. Sullivan, "Monotheism," in Gurtner and Stuckenbruck, *T&T Clark*

century Jewish monotheist like Philo could assert that the one God of Israel could become human, then it is contextually plausible for a first-century Jewish monotheist like Jesus of Nazareth to suggest that scriptural prophecies about the coming of God are (somehow) being fulfilled in his own person. Likewise, if Jesus's response to John the Baptist implies that Jesus is not merely human but also "a heavenly figure" come down to earth,[151] then this would provide a compelling explanation for why Jesus concludes with a beatitude for anyone who is not "scandalized by me" (Matt 11:6; Luke 7:23).[152] For in a first-century Jewish context, there would be nothing intrinsically scandalous about Jesus claiming to be the messiah. Nor would there be anything scandalous about healing the sick and raising the dead.[153] However, if Jesus claimed to be *a heavenly being* come down to earth—especially if he were claiming to be the God of Israel come in person—then this would *certainly* be scandalous. But, as the evidence from Philo demonstrates, scandalous is not the same thing as impossible.

Encyclopedia of Second Temple Judaism, 513–14; Peter Schäfer, *Two Gods in Heaven: Jewish Concepts of God in Antiquity*, trans. Allison Brown (Princeton: Princeton University Press, 2020); Matthew V. Novenson, ed., *Monotheism and Christology in Greco-Roman Antiquity*, Supplements to Novum Testamentum 180 (Leiden: Brill, 2020); Larry W. Hurtado, *One God, One Lord: Early Christian Devotion and Ancient Jewish Monotheism*, 3rd ed. (London: T&T Clark, 2015); Carey C. Newman, James R. Davila, Gladys S. Lews, eds., *The Jewish Roots of Christological Monotheism: Papers from the St. Andrews Conference on the Historical Origins of the Worship of Jesus* (repr., Waco, TX: Baylor University Press, 2017); E. P. Sanders, *Judaism: Practice and Belief, 63 BCE–66* CE (Minneapolis: Fortress, 2016). It is mentioned in passing by Bird, *Jesus the Eternal Son*, 57; James F. McGrath, *The Only True God: Early Christian Monotheism in Its Jewish Context* (Urbana: University of Illinois Press, 2009), 18; and J. Lionel North, "Jesus and God, Worship and Sacrifice," in *Early Jewish and Christian Monotheism*, ed. Loren T. Stuckenbruck and Wendy E. S. North, Journal for the Study of the New Testament Supplement Series 263 (London: T&T Clark, 2004), 188n5—but none of these discusses it (or its implications). Remarkably, even studies of Philo's reaction to Caligula's self-deification skip over Philo's claim that the one God could become a human being. See, e.g., Maren R. Niehoff, *Philo of Alexandria: An Intellectual Biography*, Anchor Yale Bible Reference Library (New Haven: Yale University Press, 2018), 63–68; Per Jarle Bekken, "Philo's Relevance of the Study of the New Testament," in *Reading Philo: A Handbook of Philo of Alexandria*, ed. Torrey Seland (Grand Rapids: Eerdmans, 2014), 252–55.

151. Cf. Lüdemann, *Jesus after Two Thousand Years*, 306.

152. Author's translation.

153. See Eric Eve, *The Jewish Context of Jesus' Miracles*, Library of New Testament Studies 172 (Sheffield: Sheffield Academic Press, 2002), for many examples of other miracle-workers.

Coherence: Roundabout Answers, Self-Centered Claims, and the Forerunner of God

The second major argument for the historicity of the exchange between John the Baptist and Jesus is from coherence with other evidence about Jesus, on several counts.

For one thing, Jesus's "roundabout" way of responding to John's direct question about his identity coheres perfectly with other evidence in which Jesus answers direct questions either by (1) posing a riddle, as with the question about fasting (Matt 9:14–17; Mark 2:18–22; Luke 5:33–39) or the question about taxes (Matt 22:15–22; Mark 12:13–17; Luke 20:20–26); (2) responding with a question, as with the question about John the Baptist's authority (Matt 21:23–27; Mark 11:27–33; Luke 20:1–8) and the question about divorce (Matt 19:1–19; Mark 10:1–12); or (3) alluding to Jewish Scripture, as with the question about why his disciples do not wash their hands (Matt 15:1–9; Mark 7:1–13) and the Sadducees' question about the resurrection (Matt 22:23–33; Mark 12:18–24; Luke 20:27–40).[154]

Moreover, the list of miracles to which Jesus points John is also perfectly congruent with abundant other evidence that Jesus was regarded by his Jewish contemporaries as "a doer of startling deeds" (Josephus, *Antiquities* 18.63) who was known for performing such extraordinary acts as healing the blind, making the lame walk and the deaf hear, cleansing lepers, and raising the dead:[155]

1. *Healing the blind*: two blind men (Matt 9:27–30), Bartimaeus (Matt 20:29–34; Mark 10:46–51; Luke 18:35–43), blind man at Bethsaida (Mark 8:22–26), the man born blind (John 9:1–41)
2. *Making the lame walk*: healing the paralytic (Matt 9:2–8; Mark 2:1–12; Luke 5:17–26), healing the lame in Galilee (Matt 15:30–31), healing the lame in the Jerusalem temple (Matt 21:14), the paralyzed man on the Sabbath (John 5:1–9)
3. *Making the deaf hear*: healing a deaf man (Mark 7:31–37), casting out a deaf and mute spirit (Mark 9:14–29)
4. *Healing lepers*: the cleansing of a leper (Matt 8:1–4; Mark 1:40–45; Luke 5:12–16), the healing of ten lepers (Luke 17:11–19)

154. Keener, *Historical Jesus of the Gospels*, 170.

155. Dunn, *Jesus Remembered*, 450. See also Bond, *Historical Jesus*, 102.

5. *Raising the dead*: the raising of Jairus's daughter (Matt 9:18–26; Mark 5:21–43; Luke 8:40–56), the raising of Lazarus (John 11:1–44).

Likewise, Jesus's description of his activity as preaching "good news" to the "poor" is congruent with other evidence in which he speaks as if he himself is the "anointed" figure of Isaiah who has been sent by God to "bring good news to the poor" (Luke 4:18, quoting Isa 61:1–2).[156]

Contrary to what is sometimes claimed, even Jesus's final beatitude for anyone who is not "scandalized" by him (Matt 11:6; Luke 7:23) coheres well with other evidence that Jesus was aware of the potentially "scandalous" character of his words.[157] It also fits with passages in which Jesus places *himself* at the center of his message. Take one prominent example:

> And I tell you, *everyone who acknowledges me* before others, the Son of Man also will acknowledge before the angels of God; but *whoever denies me* before others will be denied before the angels of God. (Luke 12:8–9)

> Everyone therefore *who acknowledges me* before others, I also will acknowledge before my Father in heaven; but *whoever denies me* before others, I also will deny before my Father in heaven. (Matt 10:32–33)

It is very difficult to reconcile this saying—which there are good reasons to think goes back to Jesus[158]—with the common assertion that "Jesus' preaching concerned God and God's kingly reign rather than himself."[159] To the contrary: Jesus speaks here "as though people's eternal destiny depended on their response to this activity and therefore to Jesus himself."[160]

Last, but not least, Jesus's implicitly affirmative response to John's question about whether he is "the one who is to come" (Matt 11:3; Luke 7:19) strongly coheres with other evidence in which Jesus identifies John as preparing the way for the coming of God. For example, when Jesus asks the Jewish crowds

156. Cf. Casey, *Jesus of Nazareth*, 182.

157. Dunn, *Jesus Remembered*, 450. Dunn lists the following examples: Mark 9:43, 45, 47//Matt 5:30, 29//Matt 18:8–9; Mark 9:42//Matt 18:6//Luke 17:2; Mark 14:27, 29//Matt 26:31, 33//Matt 17:27; 24:10; cf. Mark 6:3//Matt 13:57; Matt 15:12; John 6:61.

158. See Brian Han Gregg, *The Historical Jesus and the Final Judgment Sayings in Q*, Wissenschaftliche Untersuchungen zum Neuen Testament 2.207 (Tübingen: Mohr Siebeck, 2006), 161–90.

159. Bond, *Historical Jesus*, 110.

160. Bauckham, *Jesus*, 90.

who they think John is, Jesus explicitly identifies John as the figure whom the prophet Malachi had said would "prepare the way" for the coming of "the LORD" (YHWH) (Mal 3:1).[161] Consider the following:

> What then did you go out to see? A prophet? Yes, I tell you, and more than a prophet. *This is the one about whom it is written, "See, I am sending my messenger ahead of you*, who will prepare your way before you." (Matt 11:9–10)

> What then did you go out to see? A prophet? Yes, I tell you, and more than a prophet. *This is the one about whom it is written, "See, I am sending my messenger ahead of you*, who will prepare your way before you." (Luke 7:26–28)

Contrary to what is sometimes claimed, there is no reason to suggest that the oracle cited by Jesus is being used to describe John as the forerunner of "the coming Son of Man-Messiah."[162] Instead, as John Meier rightly points out: "in Malachi's text, 'before me' refers to Yhwh."[163] Indeed, when Jesus's description of John is interpreted in the light of Jewish Scripture, the clear implication is that Jesus is identifying John the Baptist as "the forerunner of God himself."[164] Seen in this light, Jesus's description of John as the forerunner of God is perfectly congruent with Jesus's affirmation that he is indeed the seemingly divine figure of "the one who is to come."[165]

161. In favor of the basic historicity of this designation, see Joel Marcus, *John the Baptist in History and Theology* (Columbia: University of South Carolina Press, 2018), 90, 210n47. Given everything we have seen so far in this study, contra Meier, *A Marginal Jew*, 2:141–42, the mere "transfer" of "OT references from Yahweh to Jesus" in this saying is not sufficient grounds to put it aside as "probably a Christian reflection added to an authentic logion of Jesus concerning the Baptist."

162. Contra Hengel and Schwemer, *Jesus and Judaism*, 321.

163. Meier, *A Marginal Jew*, 2:141 (adapted).

164. Grindheim, *God's Equal*, 59. For arguments favoring the historicity of this passage, see Brant Pitre, *Jesus, the Tribulation, and the End of the Exile: Restoration Eschatology and the Origin of the Atonement*, Wissenschaftliche Untersuchungen zum Neuen Testament 2.204 (Tübingen: Mohr Siebeck; Grand Rapids: Baker Academic, 2005), 192–97; Steven M. Bryan, *Jesus and Israel's Traditions of Judgment and Restoration*, Society for New Testament Studies Monograph Series 117 (Cambridge: Cambridge University Press, 2002), 98–101.

165. It is important to note here that it is precisely Jesus's implicit identification of John the Baptist as the forerunner of God that leads some historical Jesus scholars to reject this particular verse as unhistorical. See Dunn, *Jesus Remembered*, 451; Meier, *A Marginal Jew*, 2:141–42. However, given everything we have seen so far, this argument does not hold.

Consequences: Followers of John and the Divinity of "the One Who Is to Come"

A third argument in favor of the historicity of Jesus's answer to John the Baptist can be made from the plausibility of its effects in the early church.

For one thing, despite the continued existence of some followers of John the Baptist (cf. Acts 18:24–25; 19:1–7), the scripturally allusive and indirect character of Jesus's answer to John provides a more than ample explanation for why some followers of John the Baptist may not have accepted Jesus as the divine messiah.[166] After all, Jesus does not respond to John by explicitly declaring, "Yes, I am the messiah," much less, "Yes, I am God." Even apart from other historical factors (which are inaccessible to us), the indirect, almost cryptic character of Jesus's response easily explains why some of John the Baptist's followers may not become disciples of Jesus, while others—such as Peter and Andrew—did (cf. John 1:35–42).[167]

Moreover, if Jesus identified himself with the seemingly divine figure of "the one who is to come" (*ho erchomenos*) (Matt 11:3; Luke 7:19), then it would also provide a plausible explanation for why early Christian writers like the author of the Apocalypse of John use the same expression to refer to both Jesus and God. Consider the following:

> John to the seven churches that are in Asia:
>
> Grace to you and peace from *him who is and who was and who is to come*, and from the seven spirits who are before his throne, and *from Jesus Christ*, the faithful witness, the firstborn of the dead, and the ruler of the kings of the earth.
>
> To him who loves us and freed us from our sins by his blood, and made us to be a kingdom, priests serving his God and Father, to him be glory and dominion forever and ever. Amen.
>
> Look! He is coming with the clouds;
> every eye will see him,
> even those who pierced him;
> and on his account all the tribes of the earth will wail.
> So it is to be. Amen.

166. Contra Klausner, *Jesus of Nazareth*, 249.

167. See Meier, *A Marginal Jew*, 2:116–30, for an excellent discussion of Jesus and John's disciples.

> "I am the Alpha and the Omega," says *the Lord God, who is and who was and who is to come, the Almighty*. (Rev 1:4–8)

In this passage, the expression "he who is to come" (*ho erchomenos*) is used to describe both "Jesus Christ" (Rev 1:4–5) and "the Lord God" (*kyrios ho theos*) (Rev 1:8).[168] As David Aune puts it: "John's developing Christology is evident when the same divine names that he earlier ascribed to God are applied to his Christ."[169] How do we explain the origins of this divine Christology? One plausible explanation is that John the Baptist himself, in the context of his questioning Jesus, had already used the expression "the one who is to come" to refer to the coming of a mysterious figure who is (somehow) both human and divine.

Weighing the Arguments for and against Historicity

With all of this in mind, we can once again sum up by comparing the force of the arguments for and against the historical plausibility of Jesus's response to the question of John the Baptist about whether he was "the one who is to come."

In this case, one reason so few historical Jesus scholars raise objections to the historicity of the exchange between Jesus and John is perhaps because the arguments against its historical plausibility are fairly weak. For example, the argument that John's question must be unhistorical because he could not have believed that God or some other heavenly being could appear on earth in human form not only begs the very question under investigation; it is also demonstrably false. As we saw above, not only is Jewish Scripture replete with famous examples of God and other heavenly beings coming to earth in human form (Gen 18:1–33; 32:24–30; Josh 5:13–15; Dan 5:19–20), but Philo of Alexandria expressly states that it is *more* likely that God would become a human being than a human being would become God (Philo, *Embassy to Gaius* 118)! Moreover, the argument that the exchange between Jesus and John is historically doubtful because Jesus quotes the Jewish Scriptures and fails to mention his exorcisms is an inexcusable case of forgetting that Jesus was a Jew and of grasping at straws. Finally, the argument that if the exchange really did take

168. See Craig R. Koester, *Revelation*, Anchor Yale Bible 38A (New Haven: Yale University Press, 2014), 215.

169. David E. Aune, *Revelation*, 3 vols., Word Biblical Commentary 52a–c (Dallas: Word, 1997), 1:59.

place, then all of John's followers should have become believers in Jesus both fails to take seriously the vicissitudes of human history and assumes without reason that all of John's disciples were privy to the answer given by Jesus to John's question.

By contrast, the arguments in favor of historicity are quite strong. Perhaps the most striking of them all is the argument from contextual plausibility within Judaism, based on the remarkable parallels between the miracles listed by Jesus in his response to John's question about his identity (Matt 11:5; Luke 7:22) and the description of the miracles that God would perform in the eschatological age at the time of the coming of the messiah in the Dead Sea Scroll known as 4QMessianic Apocalypse (4Q521). When Jesus's response to John is interpreted in light of Jewish Scripture and the Dead Sea Scrolls, it strongly supports the conclusion that Jesus answered John's question about his identity by pointing to passages in Jewish Scripture that referred to the eschatological coming of a divine figure (cf. Isa 26:19–21; 35:4–6; cf. 61:1). In other words, Jesus seems to answer John's question about his identity by describing the advent of a divine messiah. This would certainly explain why elsewhere Jesus makes eschatological salvation dependent on whether someone acknowledges him or not (Luke 12:8–9; Matt 10:32–33), as well as why he concludes his exchange with John with a solemn beatitude for anyone who is not offended or scandalized by Jesus himself (Matt 11:6; Luke 7:23). It would also offer a reasonable point of origin for early Christian evidence in which Jesus is identified as the one "who is to come" (Rev 1:8).

If this is correct and the episode is historically veracious, then the exchange between Jesus and his apocalyptic predecessor, John the Baptist, provides us with important evidence that John the Baptist was expecting the coming of an eschatological figure who was somehow *both human and heavenly*. When asked by John whether he might be this coming one, Jesus used riddle-like allusions to the prophecies in Jewish Scripture to indicate that, in his words and actions, it was not only the long-awaited coming of the messiah that was taking place, but—even more—the long-awaited coming of God in person. In the words of Sigurd Grindheim:

> Jesus identifies his own miracles with these prophecies regarding God's own acts. He thereby implicitly places himself in the role of God. . . . In the historical context, Jesus' claim would be a claim to take God's place. . . . Jesus identifies his own presence with the presence of God, and his own acts with the eschatological acts of God.[170]

170. Grindheim, *God's Equal*, 52, 53, 59.

I think this is correct, though I would nuance it slightly: because Jesus refers not only to prophecies in Isaiah about the coming of God (Isa 26, 35, 40) but also about the coming of a messianic figure (Isa 61), it follows that he is identifying his preaching with that of the messiah *and* his miracles with the actions of God. In short, in his response to John the Baptist, Jesus uses the Jewish Scriptures—especially Isaiah—to point the Baptist to the apocalyptic secret of his divinity in a way that both conceals it from those who stay on the surface of his words and reveals it to those who know the Jewish Scriptures.

The Apocalyptic "Thunderbolt"

The third and final passage that demands our attention is one of the most explicitly apocalyptic sayings attributed to Jesus. It is also one of only two occasions in the Four Gospels in which Jesus explicitly speaks of something hidden being "revealed" (*apokalyptō*).[171] I am referring here to the logion that Karl von Hase once famously described as "a thunderbolt from the Johannine sky."[172] Ironically, however, the so-called Johannine thunderbolt is not actually *in* the Gospel of John,[173] but is only found in the Gospels of Matthew and Luke:

> At that time Jesus said, "I thank you, *Father, Lord of heaven and earth*, because you have *hidden* these things from the wise and the intelligent and have *revealed* them to infants; yes, Father, for such was your gracious will. *All things have been handed over to me by my Father; and no one knows the Son except the Father, and no one knows the Father except the Son and anyone to whom the Son chooses to reveal him.* (Matt 11:25–27)

> At that same hour Jesus rejoiced in the Holy Spirit and said, "I thank you, *Father, Lord of heaven and earth*, because you have *hidden* these things from the wise and the intelligent and have *revealed* them to infants; yes, Father,

171. See Brant Pitre, "The Historical Jesus and the Apocalyptic 'Thunderbolt' (Matt 11:25–27//Luke 10:21–22)," in *The Figure of Jesus in History and Theology: Essays in Honor of John Meier*, ed. Vincent T. M. Skemp and Kelley Coblentz Bautch, Catholic Biblical Quarterly Imprints 1 (Washington, DC: Catholic Biblical Association of America, 2020), 169–85. The other case of explicitly apocalyptic language is when Jesus says to Peter: "Flesh and blood has not revealed [*apekalypsen*] to you, but my Father in heaven" (Matt 16:17).

172. Karl von Hase, *Die Geschichte Jesu: Nach akademischen Vorlesungen*, 2nd ed. (Leipzig: Breitkopf & Härtel, 1876), 422.

173. Vermes, *Authentic Gospel of Jesus*, 229.

for such was your gracious will. *All things have been handed over to me by my Father; and no one knows who the Son is except the Father, or who the Father is except the Son and anyone to whom the Son chooses to reveal him."* (Luke 10:21–22)

In this instance, the similarity between the two versions is so close that the substance can be fairly easily summarized: (1) Jesus gives thanks to God "the Father" for having "hidden" certain realities from some and having "revealed" (*apekalypsas*) them to others. (2) Jesus then solemnly declares that "all things" have been "handed over" to him by the Father, and that (3) no one knows "the Son" except the Father, and (4) no one knows "the Father" except the Son and anyone to whom the Son chooses to "reveal" (*apokalypsai*) him. Let's take a few moments to interpret each of these aspects in a first-century Jewish context.

Jesus's Apocalyptic Thanksgiving to the Omnipotent Father

We begin with Jesus's act of giving thanks to the Father, as "Lord of heaven and earth," for "hiding" certain "things" from the wise and learned and "revealing" them to infants (Matt 11:25; Luke 10:21).

On the one hand, Jesus's act of addressing God in prayer as both "Father" and "Lord of heaven and earth" (Matt 11:25; Luke 10:21) is firmly rooted in Jewish Scripture and tradition.[174] For example, in the book of Psalms, king David is described as praying to God as "my Father" (Ps 89:26), while the prophet Isaiah is described as addressing "the LORD" as "our father" (Isa 63:16). Likewise, in the book of Tobit, the Israelite woman Edna prays that "the Lord of heaven" will grant Sarah joy (Tobit 7:17), while in the book of Judith, the Jewish heroine cries out to God in prayer: "Please, please, God of my father, God of the heritage of Israel, *Lord of heaven and earth*, *Creator of the waters*, King of all your creation, hear my prayer!" (Judith 9:12). Notice here that the expression "Lord of heaven and earth" is employed to emphasize "God's omnipotence" as creator.[175] In light of such parallels, Jesus clearly begins his prayer of thanksgiving in a thoroughly Jewish manner by addressing God both as Father and omnipotent creator.

174. See Schröter, *Jesus of Nazareth*, 134; Amy-Jill Levine, *The Misunderstood Jew: The Church and the Scandal of the Jewish Jesus* (San Francisco: HarperOne, 2007), 42–43; Flusser with Notley, *Sage from Galilee*, 100–101.

175. Carey A. Moore, *Judith*, Anchor Bible 40 (New York: Doubleday, 1985), 194.

At the same time, Jesus's prayer of thanksgiving to the Father for "hiding" (*kryptō*/*apokryptō*) certain realities from the wise and "revealing" (*apokalyptō*) them to infants (Matt 11:25; Luke 10:21) is also firmly rooted in early Jewish apocalypticism. Consider, for example, the prophet Daniel's strikingly similar prayer of thanksgiving:[176]

> *Then the mystery was revealed to Daniel in a vision of the night*, and Daniel blessed the God of heaven.
>
> Daniel said:
> "Blessed be the name of God from age to age . . .
> *he gives wisdom to the wise*
> *and knowledge to those who have understanding.*
> *He reveals deep and hidden things . . .*
> *To you, O God of my ancestors,*
> *I give thanks and praise,*
> *for you have given me wisdom and power,*
> *and have now revealed to me what we asked of you,*
> for you have revealed to us what the king ordered." (Dan 2:19–23)

The parallels between the Greek version of Daniel's prayer and Jesus's prayer are remarkable.[177] Just as the meaning of King Nebuchadnezzar's dream is hidden from the king and all of his "wise men" (Dan 2:12; cf. 2:1–11),[178] so too Jesus declares that the Father has "hidden" (*kryptō*) certain truths from the "wise" (*sophōn*) and the intelligent (Matt 11:25; Luke 10:21).[179] And just as Daniel gives thanks to God for having "reveal[ed]" the hidden mysteries of what will take place "in the latter days" (Dan 2:22, 28),[180] so too Jesus declares that the Father has "revealed" (*apokalyptō*) certain hidden truths to "infants" (Matt 11:25; Luke 10:21)—a scriptural image commonly used to describe the humble and righteous (cf. Ps 18:6 [19:6]; 114:6 [116:6]; 118:130 [119:13] LXX).[181] Finally, just as Daniel "gives thanks" (*exomologeomai*) to "The God of heaven" for what God has revealed to him (Dan 2:19, 23 LXX), so too Jesus "gives

176. See Collins, *Apocalyptic Imagination*, 107–43.

177. Contra Michael Wolter, *The Gospel according to Luke*, trans. Wayne Coppins and Christoph Heilig, 2 vols. (Waco, TX: Baylor University Press, 2017), 2:69.

178. MT *khakkim*; LXX *sophous*.

179. Dunn, *Jesus Remembered*, 712: "a familiar motif in Jewish wisdom and apocalyptic writing."

180. MT *gelah*; LXX *anakalytpōn*; Theod. *apokalyptōn*.

181. Davies and Allison, *Matthew*, 2:275.

thanks" (*exomologeō*) to his "Father" for revealing these hidden mysteries to the lowly (Matt 11:25; Luke 10:21). In short, Jesus's cry to the Father is an *apocalyptic prayer of thanksgiving* for the revelation of certain mysteries that are hidden from the wise and learned but revealed to the simple and humble.

Jesus Declares That Omnipotence Has Been Given to Him

The second feature of Jesus's prayer that needs to be unpacked is his solemn declaration that "all things" have been "handed over" to him by his "Father" (Matt 11:25; Luke 10:22). What would such a declaration have meant in a first-century Jewish context?

Many interpreters suggest that when Jesus speaks of "all things," he means "all knowledge."[182] According to this view, Jesus is referring by way of anticipation to the exclusive "knowledge" of the Father which the Son possesses (Matt 11:27; Luke 10:22). Others contend that when Jesus refers to "all things," he means "all power."[183] From this perspective, Jesus is declaring that the eschatological "plenitude of authority" has already been given to him by the heavenly Father.[184]

These two interpretations are not necessarily mutually exclusive.[185] Several considerations, however, seem to tip the scale in favor of the view that when Jesus refers to "all things" he primarily (if not exclusively) means "*all power*." For one thing, Jesus has just finished emphasizing the *omnipotence* of the Father as Creator by addressing him as "Lord of heaven and earth" (Matt 11:25; Luke 10:21). In context, therefore, the most immediate referent for "all things" is "heaven and earth"—that is, the cosmos. Moreover, in Jewish Scripture, the expression "all things" is a standard way of referring to all creation, as when the book of Psalms describes God as having put "all things"[186]—that is, all earthly creatures—"under" the dominion of "the son of man" (*ben ʾadam*)

182. E.g., Grindheim, *God's Equal*, 182; Keener, *Historical Jesus of the Gospels*, 273; Luz, *Matthew*, 2:166; Davies and Allison, *Matthew*, 2:279–80; Witherington, *Christology of Jesus*, 227; Fitzmyer, *Gospel according to Luke*, 2:874.

183. E.g., Dunn, *Jesus Remembered*, 720; Lüdemann, *Jesus after Two Thousand Years*, 331; Theissen and Merz, *Historical Jesus*, 554.

184. Dunn, *Jesus Remembered*, 720.

185. Aquila H. Lee, *From Messiah to Preexistent Son*, Wissenschaftliche Untersuchungen zum Neuen Testament 2.192 (Tübingen: Mohr Siebeck, 2005), 142–43.

186. MT *kol*; LXX *panta*.

(Ps 8:3–8).[187] Last, given Jesus's insistence that all things have been "handed over" to him *personally* ("to me") (Matt 11:25; Luke 10:22), it seems reasonable to suggest that he is not just referring to ordinary human dominion over creation but rather to the eschatological dominion given by God to the Danielic son of man:

> I saw *one like a son of man*
> coming with the clouds of heaven.
> And he came to the Ancient of Days
> and was presented before him.
> *To him was given dominion*
> *and glory and kingship,*
> *that all peoples, nations, and languages*
> *should serve him.*
> His dominion is an everlasting dominion
> that shall not pass away,
> and his kingship is one
> that shall never be destroyed. (Dan 7:13–14)

Remarkably, just as the book of Daniel says that dominion over all peoples will be "given" (LXX *didōmi*) to the "son of man" (LXX *huios anthrōpou*) by the Ancient of Days (Dan 7:13–14), so too Jesus declares all things have been "handed over" (*paradidōmi*) to him personally as "the Son" (*ho huios*) by God the Father (Matt 11:25; Luke 10:22). And though the book of Daniel itself does not explicitly identify the heavenly "son of man" as the royal son of God, as we will see momentarily, the earliest Jewish interpretations *do* in fact explicitly identify the Danielic "son of man" as the heavenly "son" of God (cf. 1 Enoch 48:2–7; 62:1–8; 4 Ezra 13:25–52). In light of such considerations, Gerd Theissen and Annette Merz conclude:

> The earthly Jesus already speaks of himself as son of God to whom everything has been given by the Father . . . [he is] omnipotent.[188]

> In this logion [Matt 11:27; Luke 10:22], the transference of divine omnipotence to Jesus is presupposed.[189]

187. NRSV, adapted.
188. Theissen and Merz, *Historical Jesus*, 98, 100.
189. Theissen and Merz, *Historical Jesus*, 555.

When seen in this light, Jesus's declaration seems to suggest that the eschatological omnipotence that Daniel prophesied would one day be given to the heavenly "son of man" by the Ancient of Days has *already* been handed over to Jesus by the heavenly Father.

The Hidden Identity of the Apocalyptic Son

The third aspect of the so-called thunderbolt that requires explanation is Jesus's striking declaration that "no one" knows "the Son" except "the Father" alone (Matt 11:27; Luke 10:22).[190] Since Jesus has just asserted that all things have been handed over to *him* by the Father, in context, "the Son" here clearly refers to himself. What would such a declaration have meant in a first-century Jewish context?

In order to answer this question, it is important to recall that in Jewish Scripture, the terminology of "son" (Hebrew *ben*; Greek *huios*) is used to refer to a variety of different kinds of divine sonship.[191] For our purposes, four in particular stand out:

Various Kinds of Divine Sonship

1. *Creaturely sonship*: human beings are children of God because God as creator is their "father" and creator (Deut 32:6–7)[192]
2. *Corporate sonship*: the chosen people of Israel as a whole are the "firstborn son" of God (Exod 4:22); they are "sons" of "God" (Deut 14:1)[193]
3. *Messianic sonship*: the "anointed" Davidic king is the "son" of God and

190. Despite the two slightly different forms—"no one recognizes the Son [*epiginōskei ton huion*] except the Father" (Matthew) vs. "no one knows who the Son is [*ginōskei tis estin ho huios*] except the Father" (Luke)—the basic substance is the same. See Frederick Danker, *A Greek-English Lexicon of the New Testament and Other Early Christian Literature*, 3rd ed. (Chicago: University of Chicago Press, 2000), 369. Danker states that in Matt 11:25, "know" (*epiginōskō*) has "essentially" the same meaning as "know" (*ginōskō*).

191. See Garrick V. Allen, Kai Akagi, Paul Sloan, and Madhavi Naveder, eds., *Son of God: Divine Sonship in Jewish and Christian Antiquity* (Winona Lake, IN: Eisenbrauns, 2019); Michael Peppard, *The Son of God in the Roman World: Divine Sonship in Its Social and Political Context* (Oxford: Oxford University Press, 2011); Adela Yarbro Collins and John J. Collins, *King and Messiah as Son of God: Divine, Human, and Angelic Messianic Figures in Biblical and Related Literature* (Grand Rapids: Eerdmans, 2008).

192. Roland de Vaux, *Ancient Israel: Its Life and Institutions* (repr., Grand Rapids: Eerdmans, 1997), 51–52 ("divine fatherhood" of God as "Master and Creator").

193. Propp, *Exodus*, 1:217 ("covenantal relationship").

"begotten" by him (Ps 2:2, 7; cf. 110:1–3); God is his "father," and the king is God's "son" (2 Sam 7:14)[194]

4. *Angelic sonship*: angelic/heavenly beings are "sons of God" (Job 1:6; 4QDeuteronomy^j [4QDeut^j] 32:8; Ps 89:6)[195]

To which of these kinds of divine sonship is Jesus referring when he declares that "no one" knows "the Son" except God the Father? Several options have been laid on the table of interpretation.

(1) Some suggest that Jesus is referring to ordinary *human sonship*. According to this view, Jesus is making "a general statement about human experience" by declaring that all human "sons" are not truly "known" by anyone except their human "fathers."[196] One problem with this interpretation is that it fails to take into account the apocalyptic context and absolute character of Jesus's declaration that he himself is "the Son" to whom "all things" have been given by the Father (cf. Matt 11:25; Luke 10:21). Another problem with this view is that it is based on a "truism" that is apparently untrue: in antiquity, men were ordinarily closer to their friends or spouses than to their human fathers.[197]

(2) Others argue that Jesus is referring to his *messianic sonship*. According to this view, Jesus is saying that no one except the Father knows that Jesus is the anointed "son" of God—that is, the Davidic king.[198] Though this suggestion is not without merit, it too faces a major obstacle. According to the evidence in the Gospels, on several occasions, other human beings and even unclean spirits *do* in fact recognize Jesus as the Messiah. For example: during his public ministry, the crowds wonder if Jesus could be "the son of David" (Matt 12:22–

194. Frank Lothar Hossfeld and Eric Zenger, *Psalms 3: A Commentary on Psalm 101–150*, trans. Linda M. Maloney, Hermeneia (Minneapolis: Fortress, 2011), 143; Mitchell Dahood, SJ, *Psalms*, 3 vols., Anchor Bible 16, 16A, 16B (New York: Doubleday, 1966–1970), 11 ("through adoption"); P. Kyle McCarter Jr., *II Samuel*, Anchor Bible 9 (New York: Doubleday, 1984), 207 ("formula of adoption").

195. Marvin H. Pope, *Job*, Anchor Bible 15 (New York: Doubleday, 1965), 9 ("lesser members of the ancient pagan pantheon who are retained in later monotheistic theology as angels"). See Martin Abegg Jr., Peter Flint, and Eugene Ulrich, *The Dead Sea Scrolls Bible* (San Francisco: HarperOne, 1999), 191, for an English translation of 4QDeut^j 32:8.

196. Hengel and Schwemer, *Jesus and Judaism*, 574–75. So too Flusser with Notley, *Sage from Galilee*, 101; Ben F. Meyer, *The Aims of Jesus* (London: SCM, 1979), 152; Jeremias, *Proclamation of Jesus*, 58, 60.

197. Keener, *Historical Jesus of the Gospels*, 274; Witherington, *Christology of Jesus*, 226–27.

198. J. Daniel Kirk, *A Man Attested by God: The Human Jesus of the Synoptic Gospels* (Grand Rapids: Eerdmans, 2016), 232–33, 242–43; Theissen and Merz, *Historical Jesus*, 555.

23); the blind recognize Jesus as "son of David" (Matt 20:29–34; Mark 10:46–52; Luke 18:35–43); and even the demons "know" that Jesus is the "Son of God" and "Messiah" (Mark 1:32–34; Luke 4:40).[199] Hence, in context, Jesus seems to be referring to something more than merely royal Davidic sonship.

(3) Still others suggest that Jesus is referring to his *unique sonship*. According to this view, Jesus is declaring himself to be (in some sense) the only son of God.[200] Consider the remarkable consistency with which scholars utilize the adjective "unique":

> The absolute term "the Son" shows . . . the position of the Son as the unique and necessary revealer of the Father.[201]

> What links [Jesus] with God, whom he calls his Father, is the bond of a unique sonship.[202]

> This saying is about the unique and unprecedented relationship between Jesus and God.[203]

This view is certainly correct, but it leaves an important question unanswered: *"unique" in what sense?* For example, if Jesus is merely referring to his status as an Israelite "son" of God (corporate sonship), then there is nothing unique about it (cf. Exod 4:22). Likewise, if Jesus is referring to his identity as the royal Davidic "son" of God (messianic sonship), this too is not unique. For Davidic sonship is dynastic: all anointed Davidic kings are "sons" of God (cf. 2 Sam 7:14; Ps 2:7; 89:26). Finally, even if Jesus were referring to his angelic sonship—that is, if he is implying that he is an angelic being—this too would

199. Cf. Kirk, *Man Attested by God*, 233, who admits that "other spiritual agents know that Jesus is the Christ" but insists nevertheless that "none of the data demands that the secret of Jesus's identity is that he is God, and all is well accounted for under the notion that Jesus's identity is well understood as messiah" (Kirk, 233). The latter is demonstrably false; the thunderbolt cannot be explained by merely messianic sonship.

200. Cf. Hengel and Schwemer, *Jesus and Judaism*, 411; Grindheim, *God's Equal*, 188; Lee, *From Messiah to Preexistent Son*, 143; Bruce D. Chilton, "(The) Son of (the) Man, and Jesus," in *Authenticating the Words of Jesus*, ed. Bruce Chilton and Craig A. Evans (Leiden: Brill, 1999), 285–86; James D. G. Dunn, *Christology in the Making: A New Testament Inquiry into the Origins of the Doctrine of the Incarnation*, 2nd ed. (Grand Rapids: Eerdmans, 1989), 28–29.

201. Casey, *Jesus of Nazareth*, 389–90.

202. Gnilka, *Jesus of Nazareth*, 263.

203. Witherington, *Christology of Jesus*, 227.

not be unique. For, as we saw above, Jewish Scripture describes angels collectively as "sons of God" (Job 1:6; Ps 89:6).

(4) In light of these difficulties, I would suggest that the best description of the kind of divine sonship to which Jesus is referring is *"apocalyptic" sonship*. This sonship is more than just unique; it is apocalyptic, because it is so hidden that it has to be "revealed" (*apokalyptō*) in order to even be known.[204] In the so-called thunderbolt, Jesus is speaking of a filial relation to God the Father that is different from and goes beyond creaturely, corporate, messianic, and even angelic divine sonship. He is declaring that his own divine sonship is so transcendent that it is "hidden" from everyone "except the Father" (Matt 11:27; Luke 10:22).

The Hidden Identity of the Apocalyptic Father

The final aspect of the so-called thunderbolt that deserves attention is Jesus's declaration that "no one" knows "the Father" except for "the Son" and "anyone" to whom the Son chooses to "reveal" (*apokalyptō*) the Father (Matt 11:27; Luke 10:22). Although what Jesus says about the Father tends to garner less attention than what he says about the Son, in some ways it is even more striking. For in it, Jesus denies that God the Father—that is, the God of Israel—is known by *anyone except Jesus himself* and those to whom Jesus chooses to reveal him. What might such words have meant in a first-century Jewish context?

In order to answer this question, it is important to recall that, just as there are various kinds of divine sonship in Jewish Scripture, so too are there various ways in which the terminology of "father" (Hebrew *'ab*; Greek *patēr*) is applied to God.[205] Consider, for example, the following examples:

VARIOUS KINDS OF DIVINE FATHERHOOD

1. *Creative fatherhood*: God is "father" of human beings because he "created" or "made" them (Deut 32:6)
2. *Providential fatherhood*: God is "father" of "orphans" and "widows" because he protects them and cares for them (Ps 68:5)
3. *Covenantal fatherhood*: God is "father" of the children of Abraham and

204. See Pitre, "Historical Jesus and the Apocalyptic 'Thunderbolt.'"

205. See David R. Tasker, *Ancient Near Easter Literature and the Hebrew Scriptures about the Fatherhood of God*, Studies in Biblical Literature 69 (New York: Peter Lang, 2004), for a full study.

Israel as a people because he has redeemed them (Isa 63:16); he is a merciful "father" to those who keep his "covenant" (Ps 103:8–18)

4. *Messianic fatherhood*: God is "father" of the anointed Davidic king because he adopts him as his "son" (2 Sam 7:14; Ps 89:26; cf. Ps 2:6–7; 110:3)

To which of these various kinds of divine fatherhood is Jesus referring when he declares that "no one" knows "the Father" except the Son? Once again, interpreters suggest a variety of proposals.

(1) Some suggest that Jesus is referring to the *creative* or *providential* fatherhood of God. According to this view, Jesus is declaring that no one can have "knowledge of God" apart from him.[206] The obvious problem with this suggestion is that Jewish Scripture clearly describes human beings (to say nothing of angelic figures) as able to know God as Creator (see Deut 32:6). In fact, one early Jewish writing declares in no uncertain terms that it is precisely "from the greatness and beauty of created things" that human beings are able to arrive at "a corresponding perception of their Creator" (Wisdom of Solomon 13:5).

(2) Others suggest that Jesus is referring to the *covenantal* fatherhood of God.[207] The problem with this suggestion is similar to that noted above: Jewish Scripture is quite clear that human beings—especially the people of Israel—are in fact able to know God as "father" and redeemer (see Isa 63:16). Indeed, the book of Deuteronomy explicitly states that Moses was able to "know" the God of Israel in a strikingly intimate manner (Exod 33:12; Deut 34:10–11).[208] Moreover, the book of Jeremiah states that, in the future age of salvation, every single member of the "new covenant" will be able to "know" God (Jer 31:31–34). From the vantage point of Jewish Scripture, the claim that no one "knows" the covenantal fatherhood of God is demonstrably false.

(3) Still other interpreters suggest that Jesus is referring to "a *messianic*, rather than divine" knowledge of God the Father.[209] According to this view, Jesus is declaring that he, as messiah, will be "specially taught by God."[210] In support of this view, one can point, for example, to one early Jewish text that

206. Casey, *Jesus of Nazareth*, 290; cf. also Aaron M. Gale, "The Gospel of Matthew," in Levine and Brettler, *Jewish Annotated New Testament*, 32: "Jesus claims a unique knowledge of the divine."

207. François Bovon, *Luke: A Commentary*, trans. Christine M. Thomas, Donald S. Deer, and James E. Crouch, 3 vols., Hermeneia (Minneapolis: Fortress, 2002–2013), 2:44.

208. Allison, *Constructing Jesus*, 226. See also Dale C. Allison, *The Intertextual Jesus: Scripture in Q* (Harrisburg, PA: Trinity Press International, 2000), 43–51.

209. Kirk, *Man Attested by God*, 233. So too Theissen and Merz, *Historical Jesus*, 554–55.

210. Kirk, *Man Attested by God*, 233.

describes the messianic "king" as being "taught by God" (Pss. Sol. 17:32). One problem with this view, however, is that it fails to take seriously the exclusive character of the knowledge of the Father to which Jesus lays claim. In context, Jesus does not just make a positive affirmation of his special wisdom or knowledge; he categorically denies such knowledge to anyone else. By contrast, the special knowledge attributed to the messiah in the Psalms of Solomon explicitly states that his knowledge is akin to that possessed by "the holy ones": "His words will be as the words of the holy ones" (Pss. Sol. 17:43).[211]

(4) In light of the difficulties faced by each of these interpretations, I would suggest that the best description of the kind of divine fatherhood to which Jesus is referring is *"apocalyptic" fatherhood*. This divine fatherhood is apocalyptic because it is so hidden that it has to be "revealed" (*apokalyptō*) by "the Son" in order to even be known (Matt 11:27; Luke 10:22). In the so-called thunderbolt, Jesus speaks of a divine paternity that is different from and goes beyond creative, providential, covenantal, and even messianic fatherhood. He also declares that the Son's exclusive ability to "know" the Father—a knowledge greater than that of Moses, Abraham, or David—is something that the Son can share with "anyone" to whom he chooses to reveal the Father (Matt 11:27; Luke 10:22).

The Thunderbolt and the Apocalyptic Secret of Jesus's Divinity

To sum up my interpretation so far: just as the prophet Daniel offers a prayer of thanksgiving to God for revealing the mystery of the kingdom of God to himself rather than the Babylonian wise men (Dan 2:1–9), so Jesus offers a prayer of thanksgiving to the Father for having "hidden" certain realities from "the wise and intelligent" and "revealed" them to the humble and childlike (Matt 11:25; Luke 10:21). And just as universal power over all nations and peoples is "given" by the Ancient of Days to the heavenly "son of man" (Dan 7:13–14), so too Jesus declares that "all things" have been "handed over" to him as "the Son" by God "the Father" (Matt 11:27; Luke 10:22). Finally, although Jewish Scripture makes it quite clear that angels, the Davidic king, the chosen people of Israel, and human beings in general can be described in various ways as "sons" of God (Deut 32:6–7; Exod 4:2; Job 1:6; Ps 2:7), Jesus declares that he possesses an identity as "the Son" which is known to God the Father alone.

211. In James H. Charlesworth, ed., *Old Testament Pseudepigrapha*, 2 vols., Anchor Bible Reference Library (New York: Doubleday, 1983, 1985), 2:639–70.

Likewise, despite the fact that Jewish Scripture makes quite clear that other human beings—Moses above all, could indeed possess "knowledge" of God as "Father" (cf. Exod 33:12; Deut 34:10)—Jesus declares that God is "the Father" in a way that is known to him and him alone as "the Son."

In light of such considerations, on the level of exegesis, a strong case can be made that, *in the so-called thunderbolt, Jesus is revealing the apocalyptic "secret" of his "divinity."*[212] Notably, other studies of this passage have come to similar conclusions:

> At the level of the tradition the speaker in [Luke 10] v. 21 is already a divine being.[213]

> Behind this probably stands the uniqueness of his relation to God and his special consciousness of his sonship (*Sohnesbewußtsein*), which could be designated as the "secret of his sonship" (*Sohnesgeheimnis*).[214]

> The saying in Lk. 10.22 par. shows that Jesus understood [his] sonship in a unique way. The Father's relationship to Jesus differed from his relationship to all other human beings. . . . In other words, Jesus was closer to the Father than everyone else, so close in fact that he belonged on the divine side of the divine-human divide.[215]

> Matt. 11:27; and Luke 10:22 quote Jesus as saying that the Son alone—not Abraham, not Moses, not David—knows the divine Father.[216]

I agree with this basic conclusion, but I would also stress that Jesus is not just speaking about *any* kind of divinity. Rather, he insists that he possesses a kind of divine sonship that *transcends* the divine sonship of Israel, the Davidic king, and even the angels themselves. Likewise, Jesus reveals that the hidden fatherhood of God is different from and goes beyond the creative, providential, covenantal, and adoptive fatherhood of God described in the Jewish Scriptures. In the apocalyptic thunderbolt, Jesus reveals that his true identity involves some

212. I owe this phrase to Kirk, *Man Attested by God*, 234.

213. Theissen and Merz, *Historical Jesus*, 100.

214. Hengel and Schwemer, *Jesus and Judaism*, 483. See also Peppard, *Son of God*, 13: "The secret of Jesus' identity was not his messiahship but his sonship; it is the *sonship* secret."

215. Grindheim, *God's Equal*, 188.

216. Dale C. Allison Jr., *The Historical Christ and the Theological Jesus* (Grand Rapids: Eerdmans, 2009), 80–81.

kind of hidden divine sonship and that the identity of God the Father involves some kind of hidden divine fatherhood.

Arguments against Historical Plausibility

When we turn from exegesis to the historicity of the so-called thunderbolt (Matt 11:25–27; Luke 10:21–22), we encounter a remarkable situation.[217] As we've already seen, the hypothesis that the historical Jesus was an apocalyptic prophet is widely accepted in contemporary research. On the other hand, despite the fact that the thunderbolt is arguably one of the most explicitly apocalyptic sayings attributed to Jesus, many books on the historical Jesus—even books on the "apocalyptic" Jesus!—do not even mention it, as if it did not exist.[218] Others mention it in passing, but without any substantial discussion of its meaning or historical plausibility.[219] Still others contend that while Jesus's initial prayer of thanksgiving to the Father may be historical (Matt 11:25; Luke 10:21), the declarations regarding the Father and the Son are a creation of the early church (Matt 11:26–27; Luke 10:22).[220] When arguments against its historical plausibility are given, three in particular stand out.

The first major argument against historicity is from contextual implausibility within early Judaism. According to this view, Jesus's identification of

217. See Pitre, "Historical Jesus and the Apocalyptic 'Thunderbolt,'" 169–85. Cf. Fitzmyer, *Gospel according to Luke*, 2:870: "There is probably no more disputed saying in the Synoptic tradition that this one, when the question of authenticity is raised."

218. For example, the thunderbolt is not mentioned or discussed in Schröter, *Jesus of Nazareth*; Lohfink, *Jesus of Nazareth*; Bauckham, *Jesus*; Levine, *Misunderstood Jew*; Fredriksen, *Jesus of Nazareth*; Ehrman, *Jesus: Apocalyptic Prophet*; Becker, *Jesus of Nazareth*; Sanders, *Historical Figure of Jesus*; Crossan, *Historical Jesus*; Sanders, *Jesus and Judaism*. Despite its obvious relevance to his topic, the saying likewise receives no mention in James H. Charlesworth, "Jesus' Concept of God and His Self-Understanding," in *Jesus within Judaism*, Anchor Bible Reference Library (New York: Doubleday, 1988), 131–64. Cf. Klausner, *Jesus of Nazareth*, 300, who briefly mentions the opening prayer of thanksgiving, but completely ignores Jesus's declarations about "the Father" and "the Son."

219. E.g., Ehrman, *How Jesus Became God*; Allison, *Constructing Jesus*, 226, 295; Johannes Weiss, *Jesus' Proclamation of the Kingdom of God*, trans. Richard Hyde Hiers and David Larrimore Holland (Philadelphia: Fortress, 1971 [1892 orig.]), 115–16. It worth noting here that, in the five volumes of John Meier's *A Marginal Jew*, the thunderbolt is mentioned only once in an endnote, as an example of the metaphor of "father, son" (cf. Meier, *A Marginal Jew*, 1:307).

220. Most famously, Bultmann, *History of the Synoptic Tradition*, 159–60.

himself as the unique "Son" of the Father who has been given power over "all things" (Matt 11:27; Luke 10:22) is simply too exalted to be plausible on the lips of a first-century Jewish monotheist. In the words of Gerd Lüdemann and Gerd Theissen with Annette Merz:

> At the level of the tradition the speaker in v. 21 [of Luke 10:21] is already a divine being. . . . The verse is inauthentic.[221]

> Post-Easter faith is introduced into pre-Easter life when in it Jesus is already proclaimed as "Son of God" . . . and is thought to be omnipotent (Matt. 11.27).[222]

Along similar lines, because Jesus accepted the Jewish Scriptures, in which the entire people of Israel—to say nothing of figures like Moses—could indeed "know" God (e.g., Deut 34:10), a saying in which Jesus declares that he alone "knows" God cannot be historical. In the words of Maurice Casey: "This view [expressed in Matt 11:25–27; Luke 10:21–22] does not have a satisfactory setting in the teaching of the historical Jesus, for it necessarily implies that Jews in the diaspora, and any other Jews who could not go and hear Jesus preach, did not know God."[223] In other words, because Jesus accepted the Jewish belief in one God, and because he accepted the Jewish Scripture as revealed by God, the implicit depiction of himself as "a divine being" who is "omnipotent" and the only one who truly "knows" God is historically implausible. For such reasons, several scholars have suggested that it is rather a product of a "Hellenistic" rather than Jewish milieu.[224]

The second major argument against historicity is from a lack of coherence with other evidence about Jesus. According to this view, Jesus's absolute use of "the Son" and "the Father," as well as his emphasis on the heavenly and hidden identity of the Father and the Son, is incompatible with other authentic teachings of Jesus. On this point, perhaps no scholar has been as insistent as Geza Vermes, who repeats this argument over the course of several decades of writing on Jesus.[225] Consider just one of his statements:

221. Lüdemann, *Jesus after Two Thousand Years*, 330, 331.

222. Theissen and Merz, *Historical Jesus*, 100.

223. Casey, *Jesus of Nazareth*, 390.

224. Vermes, *Authentic Gospel of Jesus*, 229; Bultmann, *History of the Synoptic Tradition*, 159–60.

225. See Vermes, *Authentic Gospel of Jesus*, 229; Geza Vermes, *The Religion of Jesus the Jew* (Minneapolis: Fortress, 1993), 162.

> In removing this hymn from the lips of Jesus and accrediting it instead to the primitive Church, contemporary exegetical skepticism joins forces for once with common sense; for no unbiased interpreter can fail to notice how discrepant these words are in both tone and content from the normal sayings of Jesus.[226]

In this view, both Jesus's "claim to unrestricted authority" in speaking of all things being handed over to him and the "absoluteness and exclusiveness" of his hidden relationship with the Father stand "in complete contrast" to how Jesus speaks about himself and God elsewhere in the Gospels.[227]

Third and finally, for many scholars, the so-called thunderbolt is also too similar to several sayings of Jesus in the Gospel of John, in which Jesus speaks of "the Son" and "the Father" (cf. John 3:35; 7:29; 10:15; 13:3). This similarity is the origin of Karl von Hase's now famous description of the passage as "a thunderbolt from the Johannine sky."[228] Of all the arguments against historicity, this one is by far the most decisive. Consider, for example, the following statements by major contributors to the quest for the historical Jesus.

> This verse is inauthentic. The Johannine terminology is not that of the historical Jesus.[229]

> The saying is untypical of the Synoptic tradition and has a distinctively Johannine ring.[230]

> We are faced here with a Synoptic section which most closely resembles the Fourth Gospel (see John 10:15; 17:25–26). Someone has recently, and perhaps not quite inappropriately, referred to it as a "Johannine thunderbolt." Not surprisingly, the extant formulation of Matthew 11:25–27 and Luke 10:21–22 has been declared by most New Testament critics as foreign to the ideology of Jesus.[231]

226. Vermes, *Jesus the Jew*, 201.

227. So Dunn, *Jesus Remembered*, 719; Funk, Hoover, and the Jesus Seminar, *Five Gospels*, 322; Günther Bornkamm, *Jesus of Nazareth*, trans. Irene McLuskey and Fraser McLuskey, with James M. Robinson (New York: Harper, 1960), 226.

228. Hase, *Die Geschichte Jesu*, 422.

229. Lüdemann, *Jesus after Two Thousand Years*, 331.

230. Dunn, *Jesus Remembered*, 718–19.

231. Vermes, *Authentic Gospel of Jesus*, 229.

According to this logic, although Jesus's declaration regarding the unique relationship between "the Father" and "the Son" is only present in material shared by the Gospels of Matthew and Luke (Matt 11:25–27; Luke 10:21–22)—often designated as "Q" material—its similarity to sayings of Jesus in the Gospel of John render its historical plausibility "indefensible."[232] In short, although the thunderbolt is only found in the Synoptic Gospels, it is simply *too Johannine* to be from Jesus himself.[233]

Context: The Scrolls, the "Son of God," and the Preexistent Messiah

Despite the widespread tendency of Jesus research to ignore the thunderbolt, there are in fact several important reasons to favor its historical plausibility. The first major argument is from contextual plausibility within Judaism, on several counts.

For one thing, Jesus's initial prayer of thanksgiving to God the Father for having "hidden" certain realities from the wise and having "revealed" them to the humble (Matt 11:25; Luke 10:21) fits quite squarely into an apocalyptic Jewish context, in which heavenly realities are often revealed to a seer or to a special group.[234] Compare, for example, the words of Jesus with an early Jewish prayer of thanksgiving from one of the Dead Sea Scrolls:

> *I give you thanks, Lord,* because you have lightened my face for your covenant and [. . .] I have looked for you. Like perfect dawn you have revealed yourself to me with perf[ect] light. . . . *Through me you have enlightened the face of the Many,* you have increased them, so that they are uncountable, *for you have shown me your wondrous mysteries.* (1QHodayoth[a] [1QH[a]] XII, 5–6, 27)[235]

Just as Jesus gives thanks to the Father for hiding certain truths from the wise and learned and revealing them to "little ones" (Matt 11:25; Luke 10:21), so too

232. Harnack, *Sayings of Jesus*, 302–3.

233. See also Casey, *Jesus of Nazareth*, 389–90; Funk and the Jesus Seminar, *Five Gospels*, 181–82.

234. See Keener, *Historical Jesus of the Gospels*, 544n80; Dunn, *Jesus Remembered*, 495; Flusser with Notley, *Sage from Galilee*, 101–3; Evans, *Jesus and His Contemporaries*, 287–88; James H. Charlesworth, "The Dead Sea Scrolls and the Historical Jesus," in *Jesus and the Dead Sea Scrolls*, Anchor Bible Reference Library (New York: Doubleday, 1992), 17. Compare Vermes, *Authentic Gospel of Jesus*, 228–29, who quietly admits this parallel, but does not allow it to influence his verdict against historicity.

235. García Martínez and Tigchelaar, *Dead Sea Scrolls Study Edition*, 1:168, 169.

the author of this scroll—widely regarded as the "Teacher of Righteousness"—gives "thanks" to God for having illuminated "the Many," a group which he elsewhere refers to as "the simple" (cf. 1QHodayoth[a] [1QH[a]] X, 9–10).[236] In light of such a parallel, it is abundantly clear that Jesus's prayer of thanksgiving is indeed "thoroughly Jewish."[237]

Along similar lines, Jesus's identification of himself as the divine "Son" who has special knowledge of God is also contextually plausible within a first-century Jewish context. Consider, for example, the following parallels, one from the Dead Sea Scrolls and the other from the Wisdom of Solomon:

> [And] YHWH [de]clares to you that "he will build you a house. I will raise up your seed after you and establish the *throne of his kingdom* [for ev]er. *I will be a father to him and he will be a son to me*" [2 Sam 7:12–14] This (refers to the) *"branch of David,"* who will arise with the Interpreter of the law who [will rise up] in Zi[on in] the [l]ast days, as it is written: "I will raise up the hut of David which has fallen" [Amos 9:11] (4QFlorilegium [4Q174] I, 10–13)[238]

> He professes to have *knowledge of God*,
> and *calls himself a child of the Lord.*
> He became to us a reproof of our thoughts;
> the very sight of him is a burden to us,
> because his manner of life is unlike that of others,
> and his ways are strange.
> We are considered by him as something base,
> and he avoids our ways as unclean;
> he calls the last end of the righteous happy,
> and *boasts that God is his father*. (Wis 2:13–16)

Once again, the parallels are strong. Just as Jesus speaks of himself as "the Son" of God "the Father" (Matt 11:27; Luke 10:22), so too the scroll speaks of the eschatological "branch of David"—that is, the messiah—as being the "son" of God his "father" (4QFlorilegium [4Q174] I, 11).[239] And just as Jesus declares that

236. See Émile Puech, "Hodayot," in Schiffman and VanderKam, *Encyclopedia of the Dead Sea Scrolls*, 1:365–68.

237. Dunn, *Jesus Remembered*, 721n32, 729.

238. García Martínez and Tigchelaar, *Dead Sea Scrolls Study Edition*, 1:353.

239. See Collins, *Scepter and the Star*, 171–90, for a full discussion.

as Son of "the Father" (*ho patēr*), he "knows" (*ginōskō/epiginōskō*) the Father in a unique way (Matt 11:27; Luke 10:22), so too Wisdom describes the mysterious "child" of God as possessing a special "knowledge of God" (*gnōsin theou*) and boasting that "God is his father" (*patera theon*) (Wisdom of Solomon 2:16).[240] In light of such parallels, it seems quite clear that the idea of a divine "Son" of "the Father" is completely credible in a first-century Jewish context.[241]

Finally, even Jesus's declaration of his identity as the hidden and heavenly Son of God is contextually plausible within the context of early Jewish apocalypticism. For the most ancient Jewish interpretations of the book of Daniel that we possess not only identify the Danielic "son of man" as the messiah (cf. Dan 7:13–14). They also describe him as a heavenly, preexistent son of God, whose identity has been hidden by God since the beginning of creation:

> And in that hour, *that son of man* was named in the presence of the Lord of Spirits;
> and his name, before the Head of Days.
> *Even before the sun and the constellations were created,*
> *before the stars of heaven were made,*
> his name was named before the Lord of Spirits. . . .
> All who dwell on the earth will fall down and worship before him,
> and they will glorify and bless and sing hymns to the name of the Lord of Spirits.
> *For this (reason) he was chosen and hidden in his presence,*
> *before the world was created and forever.*
> And the wisdom of the Lord of Spirits has revealed him to the holy and the righteous. (1 Enoch 48:2–7; cf. 62:1–8)[242]

> "As for your seeing *a man come up from the heart of the sea, this is he whom the Most High has been keeping for many ages*, who will himself deliver his creation. . . . And when these things come to pass and the signs occur which I showed you before, then *my son will be revealed, whom you saw as a man coming up from the sea*. . . . And Zion will come and be made manifest to all people, prepared and built, as you saw the mountain carved out without

240. Dunn, *Jesus Remembered*, 719, citing W. D. Davies's article "'Knowledge' in the Dead Sea Scrolls and Matt. 11.25–30," in *Christian Origins and Judaism* (London: DLT, 1962), 119–44.

241. Witherington, *Christology of Jesus*, 225.

242. Nickelsburg and VanderKam, *1 Enoch* 2, 166, 254.

> hands. . . . And then he will show them very many wonders. . . ." He [the angel] said to me [Ezra], "Just as no one can explore or know what is in the depths of the sea, *so no one on earth can see my Son or those who are with him*, except in the time of his day." (4 Ezra 13:25–26, 32, 36, 52)[243]

Notice here that in both early Jewish apocalypses, the eschatological redeemer is directly based on the "son of man" in the book of Daniel (cf. Dan 7:13–14).[244] Notice also that in both apocalypses, the Danielic son of man is explicitly identified as the "anointed one" and "the Messiah" (1 Enoch 48:10; 52:4; 4 Ezra 7:28–29).[245] In 4 Ezra, he is even explicitly identified by God as "my son" (*filius meus*) (4 Ezra 13:32, 37; cf. 13:52).[246] Perhaps most striking of all, in both apocalypses, the messiah is described as a *preexistent, heavenly being*.[247] Indeed, a case can be made that both texts bear witness to the early Jewish idea of "the heavenly existence" of "the hidden Son of Man" (cf. Isa 49:1–3).[248] Consider the following statements from experts in early Judaism:

> The Son of Man . . . is located in the heavenly sphere in the presence of the Lord of Spirits . . . he is not a man, at least not in the usual sense of the word, but is rather a heavenly being.[249]

> [1 Enoch] presume[s] the actual, hidden existence of the Son of Man in God's presence before creation.[250]

243. Translation in Charlesworth, *Old Testament Pseudepigrapha*, 1:552–53.

244. Nickelsburg and VanderKam, *1 Enoch 2*, 262; Stone, *Fourth Ezra*, 384.

245. Nickelsburg and VanderKam, *1 Enoch 2*, 168; Stone, *Fourth Ezra*, 401.

246. Stone, *Fourth Ezra*, 208.

247. See Nickelsburg and VanderKam, *1 Enoch 2*, 170 ("possessing a real preexistence"); Stone, *Fourth Ezra*, 385 ("the precreation of the Messiah"); Collins, *Apocalyptic Imagination*, 258 ("apparently preexistent"); Sigmund Mowinckel, *He That Cometh: The Messiah Concept in the Old Testament and Later Judaism*, trans. G. W. Anderson (Grand Rapids: Eerdmans, 2005), 305 ("the preexistent being, the Son of Man"). Even Joseph A. Fitzmyer, SJ, *The One Who Is to Come* (Grand Rapids: Eerdmans, 2007), 121, who is known for his caution in such matters, describes the Danielic son of man in 4 Ezra 13 as a "transcendent (= preexistent?) figure." For other early Jewish examples of preexistence, see 4 Ezra 13:26; 13:52; 14:9; 1 Enoch 48:2–3, 6; 62:7; 2 Baruch 29:3; 30:1.

248. Nickelsburg and VanderKam, *1 Enoch 2*, 173. See also Stone, *4 Ezra*, 406 ("the hiddenness of the Messiah").

249. Collins, *Apocalyptic Imagination*, 228, 230. See also Collins, *Scepter and the Star*, 204: "The apparition of the figure on the clouds in Daniel could easily suggest preexistence."

250. Nickelsburg and VanderKam, *1 Enoch 2*, 170.

> In 4 Ezra the "one like a man" is definitely the messiah. . . . Yet he also embodies many of the traits of the heavenly savior. He rises mysteriously from the sea and is apparently preexistent.[251]

> He is the Messiah whom the Most High has kept for many ages.[252]

> [4 Ezra describes] a transcendent hidden (=preexistent?) figure.[253]

If this is correct, and two early Jewish apocalypses depict the messianic son of man as a preexistent, heavenly being, then there is no reason to doubt that an apocalyptic Jewish prophet like Jesus of Nazareth could also describe himself as the heavenly, preexistent, and (heretofore) hidden "Son" of God "the Father." Indeed, if the apocalyptic Jesus saw himself as anything like the figures described in these early Jewish apocalypses, then it is quite plausible that he considered himself to be a "heavenly person."[254]

Indeed, it was precisely these early Jewish apocalypses that led Albert Schweitzer to modify his view regarding whether the historical Jesus could have believed himself to be a preexistent heavenly being. As I have shown elsewhere, in the first edition of *The Quest for the Historical Jesus* (1906) Schweitzer completely ignored Jesus's declaration regarding the hidden Son of God (Matt 11:25–27; Luke 10:21–22) and did not entertain the possibility that Jesus saw himself as anything more than the long-awaited Jewish messiah.[255] However, in the second edition of *The Quest* (1913), after taking a closer look at the relevant Jewish apocalyptic literature, Schweitzer admitted Jesus could well have regarded himself as preexistent:

> It is impossible to decide whether for Jesus the notion of *the pre-existence* of the ruler of the kingdom was exorbitant. It is given with the Danielic scheme and presupposed in the Similitudes of Enoch (62). Paul (Phil. 2.6) and the Apocalypse of Ezra (13.52) operate with it. So the presupposition is

251. Collins, *Apocalyptic Imagination*, 258.
252. Stone, *Fourth Ezra*, 401.
253. Fitzmyer, *One Who Is to Come*, 121.
254. Nickelsburg and VanderKam, *1 Enoch* 2, 170; Stone, *4 Ezra*, 385.
255. See Brant Pitre, "From Reimarus to Allison: The Quest for Jesus and the Christological 'Thunderbolt' (Matt 11:25–27//Luke 10:21–22)," in *"To Recover What Has Been Lost": Essays on Eschatology, Intertextuality, and Reception History in Honor of Dale C. Allison, Jr.*, ed. Tucker S. Ferda, Daniel Frayer-Griggs, Nathan C. Johnson, Supplements to Novum Testamentum 183 (Leiden: Brill, 2021), 373–404.

> that it had already been accepted by learned scribes at that time. We need to be careful about claiming that Jesus could not possibly have shared it because he regarded himself as the coming of Son of man. . . . *Thus it is possible, though not probable, that Jesus believed in his own pre-existence. The powerful hymn in Matt. 11.25–30 makes one think.* The words "All things have been given to me by my Father, and no one knows the son but the Father . . ." could have been spoken out of *a sense of pre-existence.*[256]

In this case, Schweitzer is right: if early Jewish apocalyptic writers could depict the messianic son of man in the book of Daniel as a preexistent, heavenly being, then there is no reason to deny that Jesus of Nazareth, as a first-century Jewish apocalyptic prophet, could also describe himself as the heavenly, hidden, and preexistent Son of God.[257]

Coherence with Other Evidence: The Father, the Son, and the Secret of Jesus's Identity

The second major argument for the historical plausibility of the so-called thunderbolt is from coherence with other evidence about Jesus, in several ways.[258]

For one thing, Jesus's prayer to God as "Father" (Matt 11:25; Luke 10:21) coheres remarkably well with the ample evidence that Jesus repeatedly referred to God as "father" (Matt 6:14–15; Mark 11:25), addressed God as "Father" in prayer (Matt 26:39, 42; Mark 14:36; Luke 22:42, 34, 46), and taught his disciples to pray to God as "our Father" (Matt 6:9–13; Luke 11:2–4).[259]

256. Albert Schweitzer, *The Quest of the Historical Jesus: First Complete Edition*, trans. W. Montgomery, J. R. Coates, Susan Cupitt, and John Bowden (Minneapolis: Fortress, 2001), 254–55.

257. Like Schweitzer, Oscar Cullman likewise thought the thunderbolt might support the conclusion that Jesus thought of himself as preexistent. See Oscar Cullman, *The Christology of the New Testament*, trans. Shirley C. Guthrie and Charles A. M. Hall, Library of Early Christology (Waco, TX: Baylor University Press, 2018), 288. I owe this reference to Simon J. Gathercole, *The Preexistent Son: Recovering the Christologies of Matthew, Mark, and Luke* (Grand Rapids: Eerdmans, 2006), 280.

258. Dunn, *Jesus Remembered*, 720.

259. Christine Gerber, "Jesus's Concept of God and the Meaning of the Father Metaphor," in *The Jesus Handbook*, ed. Jens Schröter and Christine Jacobi, trans. Robert L. Brawley (Grand Rapids: Eerdmans, 2022), 358–66 (especially 362); Lee, *From Messiah to Preexistent Son*, 139; Gnilka, *Jesus of Nazareth*, 262.

Likewise, his declaration that the Father has "hidden" certain truths from the wise and "revealed" them to the lowly (Matt 11:25; Luke 10:21) is congruent with other evidence in which Jesus speaks about the kingdom of God as a "mystery" that is hidden from outsiders but revealed to the disciples:[260]

> "To you it has been given to know *the secrets of the kingdom of heaven*, but to them it has not been given. . . . The reason I speak to them in parables is that 'seeing they *do not perceive*, and hearing they do not listen, *nor do they understand*.'" (Matt 13:11, 13)

> And he said to them, "*To you has been given the secret of the kingdom of God*, but for those outside, everything comes in parables; in order that
>
> > 'they may indeed look, but *not perceive*,
> > and may indeed listen, but *not understand*;
> > so that they may not turn again and be forgiven.'" (Mark 4:11–12)

> "To you it has been given *to know the mysteries of the kingdom of God*; but to others I speak in parables, so that
>
> > 'looking they may *not perceive*,
> > and listening they may *not understand*.'" (Luke 8:9–10)

In a similar vein, Jesus's declaration regarding the hidden identity of the Son (Matt 11:27; Luke 10:22) coheres strongly with the evidence that Jesus tended to demand secrecy about his identity from both humans and demons who realized who he was.[261] This tendency to secrecy on Jesus's part is known as the "messianic secret" (e.g., Mark 3:11–12).[262]

260. Vermes, *Authentic Gospel of Jesus*, 228 (recall here that Vermes accepts Jesus's prayer of thanksgiving as authentic); Keener, *Historical Jesus of the Gospels*, 544n80; Meyer, *Aims of Jesus*, 152. As James Dunn points out, Jesus's emphasis on the reciprocal "knowing" (*ginōskō*) of the Father and the Son (Luke 10:22) also coheres with Jesus's declaration in the Gospel of John: "just the Father knows [*ginōskei*] and I know [*ginōsko*] the Father" (John 10:15). See Dunn, *Jesus Remembered*, 719, citing C. H. Dodd, *Historical Tradition in the Fourth Gospel* (Cambridge: Cambridge University Press, 1963), 359–61.

261. Casey, *Jesus of Nazareth*, 390–91 (though he draws no historical conclusions from the point).

262. See Neil Elliot, "Messianic Secret," in *The Routledge Encyclopedia of the Historical Jesus*, ed. Craig A. Evans (New York: Routledge, 2010), 404–6. The phrase goes back to the

Significantly, even Jesus's description of himself as the unique "Son" of God coheres with other evidence in which Jesus presents himself as the unique "son" of God.[263] Particularly important in this regard are Jesus's implicit identification of himself as the unique "son" of God in the parable of the wicked tenants (Matt 21:33–46; Mark 12:1–12; Luke 20:9–19)[264] and his use of the absolute form of "the Son" and "the Father" in his statement about the Son's ignorance of the timing of the dissolution of heaven and earth (Matt 24:35–36; Mark 13:31–32).[265] In the parable, Jesus identifies himself as "'Son' of God in a final and unique sense."[266] In the saying about the end of time, Jesus uses the absolute forms of both expressions:

> Heaven and earth will pass away, but my words will not pass away. *But about that day and hour no one knows*, neither the angels of heaven, *nor the Son*, but only *the Father*. (Matt 24:35–36)

> Heaven and earth will pass away, but my words will not pass away. *But about that day or hour no one knows*, neither the angels in heaven, nor *the Son*, but only *the Father*. (Mark 13:31–32)

Note well that one does not have to go to the Gospel of John to find examples of Jesus's absolute use of the expressions "the Father" (*ho patēr*) or "the Son" (*ho huios*) (Matt 11:27; Luke 10:21). They are already present in the Synoptic tradition (Matt 24:36; Mark 13:32). In light of such evidence, there are solid reasons to accept that Jesus's reference to himself as "God's unique son" in the so-called thunderbolt is in fact historical.[267]

Consequences: The Apocalyptic Christ and the Preexistent Son

The third major argument for the historicity of the apocalyptic thunderbolt is that it provides a plausible origin for several effects that we see in the early church.

---

work of William Wrede, *The Messianic Secret*, trans. J. C. G. Greig (Cambridge: James Clarke, 1971 [orig. 1901]). See also Keener, *Historical Jesus of the Gospels*, 263–64.

263. See Witherington, *Christology of Jesus*, 224–25; Harvey, *Jesus and the Constraints of History*, 154–73.

264. Dunn, *Jesus Remembered*, 720–22; see Harvey, *Jesus and the Constraints of History*, 154–73.

265. Grindheim, *God's Equal*, 185–86; Keener, *Historical Jesus of the Gospels*, 274.

266. Casey, *Jesus of Nazareth*, 391.

267. Keener, *Historical Jesus of the Gospels*, 274.

On a very basic level, Jesus's addressing God as "Father" (*ho patēr*) in prayer (Matt 11:25; Luke 10:21), as well as his declaration regarding the unique nature of his own relationship with "the Father" (Matt 11:27; Luke 10:22), would provide a plausible origin for Paul's presumption that believers in both Asia Minor and Italy knew of the custom of addressing God in prayer as "Abba! Father!" (*Abba ho patēr*) (Gal 4:6; Rom 8:15).

More directly, Jesus's emphasis on the fact that the identity of both the Father and the Son has to be "revealed" (*apokalyptō*) in order to be known (Matt 11:27; Luke 10:22) would provide a remarkably compelling explanation for why Paul describes the divine sonship of Jesus as the result of a supernatural, apocalyptic revelation: [268]

> For I want you to know, brothers and sisters, that the gospel that was proclaimed by me is *not of human origin*; for I did not receive it from a human source, nor was I taught it, but *I received it through a revelation of Jesus Christ*. You have heard, no doubt, of my earlier life in Judaism. I was violently persecuting the church of God and was trying to destroy it. I advanced in Judaism beyond many among my people of the same age, for I was far more zealous for the traditions of my ancestors. But when *God, who had set me apart before I was born and called me through his grace, was pleased to reveal his Son to me*, so that I might proclaim him among the Gentiles, I did not confer with any human being, nor did I go up to Jerusalem to those who were already apostles before me, but I went away at once into Arabia, and afterwards I returned to Damascus. (Gal 1:11–17)

Just as Jesus declares "no one" can know the identity of the heavenly "Son" unless the Father "reveals" (*apokalyptō*) it to him or her (cf. Matt 11:25–26; Luke 10:21–22), so too Paul insists that it was "God" (rather than any human being) who "revealed" (*apokalyptō*) his "Son" to Paul, in a "revelation" (*apokalypsis*) of "Jesus Christ" (Gal 1:12). Seen in this light, a strong case can be made that *the apocalyptic Christology of Paul* is remarkably continuous with *the apocalyptic self-understanding of Jesus*.[269]

268. See Martinus C. de Boer, *Galatians: A Commentary*, New Testament Library (Louisville: Westminster John Knox, 2011), 77–79; J. Louis Martyn, *Galatians*, Anchor Yale Bible 33A (New Haven: Yale University Press, 1997), 144.

269. See Brant Pitre, Michael P. Barber, and John A. Kincaid, *Paul, a New Covenant Jew: Rethinking Pauline Theology* (Grand Rapids: Eerdmans, 2019), 95–128.

Finally, and perhaps most significant of all, if Jesus's declaration that the identity of "the Son," which is known only to "the Father" (Matt 11:27; Luke 10:22), does indeed refer to his heavenly, hidden, and preexistent divine sonship, then this would provide a compelling point of origin for the remarkably widespread descriptions of Jesus as the preexistent Son of God. Consider the following:

> In the beginning was the Word, and the Word was with God, and the Word was God. He was in the beginning with God. *All things came into being through him*, and without him not one thing came into being. (John 1:3)

> For God has done what the law, weakened by the flesh, could not do: by *sending his own Son in the likeness of sinful flesh*. (Rom 8:3)

> Christ Jesus . . . though he was in the form of God,
> did not regard equality with God
> as something to be exploited,
>   but emptied himself,
> taking the form of a slave,
> *being born in human likeness*.
> *And being found in human form*,
> he humbled himself
> and became obedient to the point of death—
> even death on a cross. (Phil 2:6–8)

> He is the image of the invisible God, the firstborn of all creation; for in him all things in heaven and on earth were created, things visible and invisible, whether thrones or dominions or rulers or powers—*all things have been created through him and for him. He himself is before all things*, and in him all things hold together. (Col 1:15–16)

> Long ago God spoke to our ancestors in many and various ways by the prophets, but in these last days he has spoken to us by *a Son*, whom he appointed heir of all things, *through whom he also created the worlds*. (Heb 1:1–3)

> See, I am coming soon. . . . I am *the Alpha* and the Omega, *the first* and the last, *the beginning* and the end. (Rev 22:12–13; cf. 1:17)

As multiple commentators have argued, these passages describe Jesus as the preexistent, divine Son of God, who is in some sense equal with God.[270] How does one explain such early and widespread affirmations of divine Christology? One plausible explanation is that if Jesus implicitly identified himself with the early Jewish idea of a heavenly, hidden, omnipotent Son of God—as in the so-called thunderbolt (Matt 11:25–27; Luke 10:21–22)—then it would account for the origins of the explicit, developed, and widespread belief in his preexistent divine Sonship in the early church.

Weighing the Arguments for and against Historical Plausibility

With all of this in mind, we can now evaluate the arguments for and against the historical plausibility of the so-called thunderbolt. When we do so, the weight of the evidence clearly tips the scales in favor of its substantial historicity.

The first reason for drawing such a conclusion is that each of the standard arguments against historicity is either fallacious or based on demonstrably anachronistic reasoning. For example, the claim that the thunderbolt cannot be historical because Jesus speaks about the Son as an omnipotent divine being is another example of begging the question. Along similar lines, the argument that Jesus's use of the absolute forms of "the Father" and "the Son" (Matt 11:25–27; Luke 10:21–22) are incompatible with other teachings of Jesus fails to take seriously other evidence in which Jesus does just that, whether in the parable of the wicked tenants (Matt 21:33–46; Mark 12:1–12; Luke 20:9–19), or in his eschatological teaching about the final day and hour (Matt 25:35–36; Mark 13:31–32). Most egregious of all, the argument that the thunderbolt is unhistorical because it is "too Johannine" may be the most blatant case of fallacious reasoning in the entire history of the quest for the historical Jesus. It should go without saying—but obviously, it has to be said—that if a passage does not even *occur* in the Gospel of John, it cannot be labeled "Johannine" and then dismissed as

270. See Ehrman, *How Jesus Became God*, 273; Yarbro Collins and Collins, *King and Messiah as Son of God*, 203; Pitre, Barber, and Kincaid, *Paul, a New Covenant Jew*, 102–6; Richard Bauckham, *Jesus and the God of Israel: God Crucified and Other Studies on the New Testament's Christology of Divine Identity* (Grand Rapids: Eerdmans, 2008), 197–210; Markus Barth and Helmut Blanke, *Colossians*, trans. Astrid B. Beck, Anchor Bible 34B (New York: Doubleday, 1994), 203; Harold W. Attridge, *Hebrews*, Hermeneia (Minneapolis: Fortress, 1989), 40; Craig R. Koester, *Revelation*, Anchor Yale Bible 38A (New Haven: Yale University Press, 2014), 854.

unhistorical because it contains "Johannine terminology."[271] Such wildly anachronistic argumentation is the very opposite of historical-critical reasoning and should be jettisoned once and for all from any future Jesus research.

By contrast, when the so-called thunderbolt is examined in light of a triple-context approach, multiple lines of arguments suggest (1) that the saying is contextually plausible in light of early Jewish apocalypses that appear to describe a heavenly or preexistent messianic figure (Dan 7:13–14; 1 Enoch 48:2–7; 62:1–8; 4 Ezra 13:25–52), (2) that it is coherent with other evidence that Jesus spoke to his disciples of apocalyptic "mysteries" that were revealed to them but concealed from others (Matt 13:11–13; Mark 4:11–12; Luke 8:9–10) and demanded secrecy regarding his identity during his public ministry (Mark 13:11–12), and (3) that it is a plausible point of origin for the apocalyptic Christology of the early church, in which Jesus is described as the preexistent and divine Son of God (John 1:3; Rom 8:3; Phil 2:6–8; Col 1:15–16; Heb 1:1–3; Rev 22:12–13). In light of such considerations, Joseph Fitzmyer writes:

> There is no firm basis for denying all connection of . . . [Luke 10:21–22] with the historical Jesus. He must have said or insinuated something similar to what is recorded here to give rise to the rapid conclusion, which emerged not long after his death, that he was indeed the Son of God (albeit not yet understood in the sense of Nicaea). Although I am inclined to regard the substance of these sayings as authentic, that substance should more likely be traced to an implicit christology expressed in Jesus' words and deeds in his earthly ministry.[272]

I agree, though I would put the point more strongly. If the so-called thunderbolt goes back to Jesus, and if he did in fact claim to be the hidden and omnipotent Son of God the heavenly Father, then one can rightly describe Jesus as speaking here of *the apocalyptic "secret" of his divinity.* It is this heavenly, unique, and utterly unknowable divine sonship that Günther Bornkamm once rightly referred to as "the secret of his being."[273]

Indeed, as we will see in the next chapter, it is precisely Jesus's claim to be the heavenly messiah and Son of God that will lead him to be accused of and eventually charged with the crime of blasphemy, which will lead directly to his crucifixion at the hands of the Roman authorities.

271. Lüdemann, *Jesus after Two Thousand Years*, 91.
272. Fitzmyer, *Gospel according to Luke*, 2:870 (emphasis added).
273. Bornkamm, *Jesus of Nazareth*, 178.

CHAPTER 5

Crucified for Blasphemy

> Pilate, upon hearing him accused by men of the highest standing amongst us . . . condemned him to be crucified.
>
> —Josephus[1]

> If [Jesus] made a strong personal claim which would be sufficient to lead to his execution, that fact would help account for several elements of his death and the rise of Christianity. The difficulty here is finding a sufficiently strong personal claim to account for execution.
>
> —E. P. Sanders[2]

> The one charge which is explicitly laid against Jesus in both the synoptics and John's gospel, [is] that of blasphemy.
>
> —Anthony E. Harvey[3]

The Criterion of Execution

Out of all the areas we have examined so far in which there is widespread agreement among scholars—Jesus's fame as a worker of miracles, his reputation as a teacher of parables, his identity as a Jewish apocalyptic prophet—none is so strong as the scholarly consensus regarding his crucifixion. Consider, for example, the following statements:

1. Josephus, *Antiquities* 18.63. In Jan Willem van Henten, "*Testimonium Flavianum*," in *From Paul to Josephus: Literary Receptions of Jesus in the First Century CE*, vol. 1 of *The Reception of Jesus in the First Three Centuries*, ed. Helen K. Bond (London: T&T Clark, 2020), 365–70 (here 366)

2. E. P. Sanders, *Jesus and Judaism* (Minneapolis: Fortress, 1985), 55.

3. A. E. Harvey, *Jesus and the Constraints of History* (Philadelphia: Westminster, 1982), 170.

> The crucifixion under Pontius Pilate . . . belongs to the most certain events of the activity of Jesus.[4]

> The one thing that we know for sure about the historical Jesus is that he died, and that he died in the most gruesome, cruel, and shameful of ways—on a Roman cross.[5]

> One of the clearest and most striking facts regarding Jesus is that he was executed as a messianic pretender.[6]

Notice here that even scholars who are ordinarily cautious about using the language of historical certainty do not hesitate to speak about "the historical fact" that Jesus was crucified.[7] Notice also that this historical confidence extends to the messianic claim implicit in the words of the Roman charge affixed to the cross of Jesus: "King of the Jews" (Matt 27:37; Mark 15:26; Luke 23:38; John 19:19). In short, if there is any event that historical Jesus scholars agree on almost to a person, it is that Jesus of Nazareth was crucified by the Roman authorities for a crime involving some kind of royal claim.

In light of this consensus, prominent contributors to the contemporary quest for Jesus also agree that if a scholarly reconstruction of the teachings and actions of Jesus is going to be historically plausible, then it must depict *a crucifiable Jesus*. John Meier takes this point as so axiomatic that he has developed what he calls a "criterion" of rejection and crucifixion:

> *The criterion of Jesus' rejection and execution* . . . directs our attention to the historical fact that Jesus met a violent end at the hands of Jewish and Roman officials and then asks us what historical words and deeds of Jesus can explain his trial and crucifixion as "King of the Jews." . . . *A Jesus whose words and deeds would not alienate people, especially powerful people, is not the historical Jesus.*[8]

4. Jens Schröter, *Jesus of Nazareth: Jew from Galilee, Savior of the World*, trans. Wayne Coppins and S. Brian Pounds (Waco, TX: Baylor University Press, 2014), 185.

5. Helen K. Bond, *The Historical Jesus: A Guide for the Perplexed* (London: T&T Clark, 2012), 152.

6. James D. G. Dunn, *Jesus Remembered*, vol. 1 of *Christianity in the Making* (Grand Rapids: Eerdmans, 2003), 628.

7. John P. Meier, *A Marginal Jew: Rethinking the Historical Jesus*, 5 vols., Anchor Yale Bible Reference Library (New Haven: Yale University Press, 1991–2016), 1:177 (emphasis added).

8. Meier, *A Marginal Jew*, 1:177 (emphasis added).

Meier even goes so far as to suggest that "in a sense, the whole portrait of Jesus . . . must be evaluated in the light of this criterion."[9] I wholeheartedly agree. If Jesus of Nazareth was simply a great moral teacher who never spoke or acted in ways that his contemporaries considered to be shocking, gravely offensive, or punishable by death, then he would never have ended up dead on a Roman cross. A non-offensive, non-crucifiable Jesus is not the historical Jesus.

The Problem of the Reason for Jesus's Crucifixion

With that said, when we turn to the question of *why* Jesus of Nazareth was crucified, we find ourselves in a very different situation. In stark contrast to the almost universal agreement *that* Jesus was crucified, there is remarkably little agreement among scholars about exactly *why* he was crucified. More troublesome, many of the historical explanations offered by scholars for why Jesus was rejected and crucified are not explicitly supported by first-century evidence. In order to see this clearly, consider the following list of proposals for why Jesus was rejected and crucified:

1. *False prophet*: because he was seen as a "false prophet"[10]
2. *Deceiver*: because he "led Israel astray"[11]
3. *Anti-Torah*: because of his "criticism of the Law"[12]
4. *Anti-temple*: because he spoke and acted "against the temple"[13]
5. *Messianic pretender*: because he was a "messianic pretender"[14]

9. Meier, *A Marginal Jew*, 5:17.

10. Martin Hengel and Anna Maria Schwemer, *Jesus and Judaism*, trans. Wayne Coppins (Waco, TX: Baylor University Press, 2019 [orig. 2007]), 634; Armand Puig i Tàrrech, *Jesus: A Biography*, trans. Jenny Read-Heimerdinger (Waco, TX: Baylor University Press, 2011), 512.

11. Bond, *Historical Jesus*, 157; N. T. Wright, *Jesus and the Victory of God*, vol. 2 of *Christian Origins and the Question of God* (Minneapolis: Fortress, 1996), 548–50.

12. Gerd Theissen and Annete Merz, *The Historical Jesus: A Comprehensive Guide*, trans. John Bowden (Minneapolis: Fortress, 1998), 464, who describe this "widespread theory" as the traditional view of "Protestant exegetes," citing Jürgen Roloff, *Neues Testament: Neukirchener Arbeitsbücher*, 4th ed. (Neukirchen-Vluyn: Neukirchener Verlag, 1985), 184, as an example. Theissen and Merz themselves do not accept this theory.

13. Schröter, *Jesus of Nazareth*, 190; Maurice Casey, *Jesus of Nazareth: An Independent Historian's Account of His Life and Teaching* (London: T&T Clark, 2010), 444; Dunn, *Jesus Remembered*, 631–32; Gerd Lüdemann, *Jesus after Two Thousand Years: What He Really Said and Did*, trans. John Bowden (London: SCM; Amherst: Prometheus Books, 2001), 102; E. P. Sanders, *The Historical Figure of Jesus* (London: Penguin, 1993), 272–73.

14. Paula Fredriksen, *Jesus of Nazareth, King of the Jews* (New York: Vintage Books, 1999),

The most striking feature of these hypotheses is that all but one of them have little or no explicit foundation in first-century evidence about the rejection and execution of Jesus. For example, (1) one searches the first-century gospels in vain for any evidence that Jesus was ever rejected as a "false prophet," much less that he was charged by the Jewish authorities with the capital crime of false prophecy (see Deut 13:1–5; 18:20–22).

(2) It is true the Gospel of John says that during the Feast of Tabernacles, some pilgrims said Jesus was "leading the people astray" (John 7:12; cf. 7:47). However, there is not a shred of first-century evidence that Jesus was ever charged by Jewish authorities with the biblical crime of "leading astray"—that is, of leading people to "serve other gods" (Deut 13:6–11). Indeed, it is only *after* his death that Jesus is reportedly referred to by the chief priests and Pharisees as an "impostor" or "deceiver" (*planos*) (Matt 27:63–64).

(3) There is ample evidence that Jesus came into conflict with some of his contemporaries over the interpretation of the Mosaic Torah, as in the Sabbath controversies.[15] However, "there is no evidence that Jesus opposed the Torah,"[16] and there is no historical basis whatsoever for the claim that Jesus was handed over by the Sanhedrin to the Romans for crucifixion because of any disregard for halakic aspects of the Mosaic Torah.[17]

(4) Even the common suggestion that Jesus was handed over to crucifixion because of his act of turning over the money changers' tables in the temple runs into serious problems. Although it is true that the Gospels say the chief priests and other Jerusalem leaders sought "to destroy him" in the wake of this incident (Mark 11:18; Luke 19:47), as we will see below, in the accounts of Jesus's hearing before the Sanhedrin, there is *no mention whatsoever of the temple incident*, and no evidence that he was charged with any crime as a result of his actions (see Matt 26:57–68; Mark 14:53–65; Luke 22:66–71). In

234; Bart D. Ehrman, *Jesus: Apocalyptic Prophet of the New Millennium* (Oxford: Oxford University Press, 1999), 217–23.

15. See Nina L. Collins, *Jesus, the Sabbath, and the Jewish Debate: Healing on the Sabbath in the 1st and 2nd Centuries CE*, Library of New Testament Studies 474 (London: Bloomsbury T&T Clark, 2014); Meier, *A Marginal Jew*, 4:235–341.

16. Thomas Kazen, "Jesus's Interpretation of the Torah," in *The Jesus Handbook*, ed. Jens Schröter and Christine Jacobi, trans. Robert L. Brawley (Grand Rapids: Eerdmans, 2022), 400–413 (here 413).

17. See William Loader, "Jesus and the Law," in *Handbook for the Study of the Historical Jesus*, 4 vols., ed. Tom Holmén and Stanley E. Porter (Leiden: Brill, 2011), 3:2745–72 (especially 2767–69).

the words of Jürgen Becker: "Relating Jesus' temple action to his death may be a popular thing to do today, but that connection is nowhere indicated by the sources."[18] Given the remarkably popular character of this particular explanation for Jesus's crucifixion, it is difficult to overemphasize the fact that there is no positive evidence Jesus was charged with any crime in relation to the temple incident.

Indeed, only (5) the claim that Jesus was executed as a "messianic pretender" has any explicit historical evidence in its favor. As I mentioned above, the *titulus* clearly shows that a royal claim played a key role in Jesus's execution by Rome (Matt 27:37; Mark 15:26; Luke 23:38; John 19:19). However, even this charge does not adequately explain why Jesus was handed over for execution by the Judean leaders in Jerusalem, since it was *not* a capital crime to claim to be the Jewish messiah.[19] After all, when the messiah finally came, if he did not claim to be the messiah, how would anyone know who he was? There is certainly no law in Jewish Scripture against claiming to be the heir to the Davidic throne—especially if one belongs to the Davidic family. As Armand Puig i Tàrrech states:

> From a Jewish point of view, Jesus' messianic pretensions *do not merit capital punishment*. . . . [N]ever in the history of the Jewish people had a messianic pretender, for the simple fact of being such, been accused of being an enemy of God's and sentenced to death.[20]

This point leaves us with a puzzling historical question. If there is no evidence that Jesus was handed over to the Romans for being a false prophet, or a deceiver, or anti-Torah, or anti-temple, or a mere messianic pretender, then *exactly what capital crime* was Jesus charged with? As we will see, the problem of providing a historical explanation for why Jesus was handed over to the Romans to be put to death is particularly difficult for those scholars who regard the accounts of his examination by the Sanhedrin and the charge of blasphemy as unhistorical.[21] Invariably, they are forced into the realm of speculation without positive evidence to support their claims.[22]

18. Jürgen Becker, *Jesus of Nazareth*, trans. James E. Crouch (New York: Walter de Gruyter, 1998), 332.

19. Theissen and Merz, *Historical Jesus*, 463–64.

20. Puig i Tàrrech, *Jesus: A Biography*, 507, 508 (emphasis added).

21. See Sanders, *Jesus and Judaism*, 300–301, who admits that if the blasphemy charge is unhistorical, then "we do not know" why Jesus was handed over for crucifixion.

22. See, for example, Fredriksen, *Jesus of Nazareth*, 234, who speculates that Jesus was

The Evidence: Multiple Accusations of Blasphemy

By contrast, in this chapter, I will argue that according to all of the first-century evidence we possess, the one charge brought against Jesus by the Judeans in Jerusalem was *the charge of blasphemy*. Moreover, as we will see, the final charge of blasphemy that led to Jesus's execution was *not the first time* he was accused of blasphemy during his public ministry. According to the first-century Gospels, Jesus was accused of blasphemy at least three times during his public ministry before ultimately being charged with the crime of blasphemy that led to his execution:

1. Jesus is accused of blasphemy while healing a paralytic in Galilee (Matt 9:2–8; Mark 2:1–12; Luke 5:18–26).
2. Jesus is accused of blasphemy in the Jerusalem temple during Tabernacles (John 8:58–59).
3. Jesus is accused of blasphemy in Solomon's portico during Hanukkah (John 10:30–33).
4. Jesus is charged with the crime of blasphemy by the Jerusalem Sanhedrin (Matt 26:63–66; Mark 14:61–64; cf. John 19:7).

We have already examined the accusation of blasphemy in Galilee in chapter 4. In this chapter, we will analyze the three episodes in which Jesus is accused of blasphemy in Jerusalem. As with the other evidence examined so far, we will attempt to interpret each episode in its first-century Jewish context before evaluating arguments for and against historicity using the triple-context approach of contextual plausibility, coherence with other evidence about Jesus, and consequences in the early church.

As we will see, contrary to what is often assumed, in each of these episodes, Jesus does claim to be divine, but in a very Jewish way—using riddles, questions, and allusions to Jewish Scripture that are meant to lead his audience to draw their own conclusions about his identity. Indeed, according to the extant evidence, the main reason Jesus is handed over by the Jerusalem leaders to the Roman authorities is because he is charged with making claims about his identity which, from their point of view, are considered to be blasphemy.

---

crucified "as a messianic pretender . . . not because Jesus thought he was messiah," but "because others"—that is, the Jerusalem crowds—"thought and proclaimed he was." This is an excellent example of a hypothesis that is right in what it affirms and wrong in what it denies.

They Picked Up Stones

The first episode in which Jesus is (implicitly) accused of blasphemy comes from the Gospel of John's account of the exchange between Jesus and some of his Jewish contemporaries in the Jerusalem temple during the Feast of Tabernacles:

> The Jews answered him, "Are we not right in saying that you are a Samaritan and have a demon?" Jesus answered, "I do not have a demon; but I honor my Father, and you dishonor me. Yet I do not seek my own glory; there is one who seeks it and he is the judge. Amen amen, I tell you, whoever keeps my word will never see death." The Jews said to him, "Now we know that you have a demon. Abraham died, and so did the prophets; yet you say, 'Whoever keeps my word will never taste death.' *Are you greater than our father Abraham, who died? The prophets also died. Who do you claim to be?*" Jesus answered, "If I glorify myself, my glory is nothing. It is my Father who glorifies me, he of whom you say, 'He is our God,' though you do not know him. But I know him; if I would say that I do not know him, I would be a liar like you. But I do know him and I keep his word. *Your ancestor Abraham rejoiced that he would see my day; he saw it and was glad.*" Then the Jews said to him, "You are not yet fifty years old, and have you seen Abraham?" Jesus said to them, "*Amen amen, I tell you, before Abraham was, I am.*" *So they picked up stones to throw at him*, but Jesus hid himself and went out of the temple. (John 8:48–59)[23]

Given the reluctance of many works on the historical Jesus to even discuss evidence in the Gospel of John, it is important to begin by emphasizing that I am *not* seeking the exact words of Jesus (the *ipsissima verba Iesu*). Instead, I am asking whether the *substance* of the account is historically plausible in Jesus's first-century Jewish context. With this point firmly in mind, the substance of the episode can be summarized as follows: (1) Jesus is accused by some of his Jewish contemporaries of being a demon-possessed Samaritan, to which he responds by denying he is possessed and by declaring that whoever follows his teaching will never die. (2) His interlocutors respond by asking whether Jesus thinks himself greater than Abraham and who exactly he claims to be, to which Jesus responds by declaring that he knows the Father in a way they do not and that Abraham himself rejoiced to "see" Jesus's day. (3) His interlocutors point out that Jesus is not even fifty years old and ask if he has "seen" Abraham,

23. NRSV, slightly adapted.

to which Jesus responds by solemnly declaring, "Before Abraham was, I am." (4) His audience responds by picking up stones in order to stone Jesus, but he slips away and leaves the temple. Before turning to questions of historicity, we will first attempt to interpret this episode in its first-century Jewish context.

The Judeans' Accusations and Jesus's Initial Response

In order to understand the initial accusation that Jesus is a demon-possessed Samaritan (John 8:48), it is important to begin by emphasizing that, despite the conventional identification of Jesus's interlocutors as "the Jews" (John 8:48), a strong case can be made that they should be identified as "the Judeans" (*hoi Ioudaioi*) (John 8:48, 52). That is, they are *southern Jews*, living in Jerusalem, who appear to harbor certain hostilities toward Jesus because he is a Galilean. Although scholars continue to debate the exact meaning of this expression throughout the Gospel of John,[24] here it seems to be used in a *geographical and genealogical* sense to differentiate between northern Jews of Galilean provenance and descent and southern Jews of Judean provenance and descent. Consider, for example, the way the expression is used in the introduction to Jesus's activity in Jerusalem during the Feast of Tabernacles:

> After this Jesus went about *in Galilee*. He would not go about in Judea [*Ioudaia*], because the Judeans [*hoi Ioudaioi*] sought to kill him. Now the Judeans' [*Ioudaiōn*] Feast of Tabernacles was at hand. (John 7:1–2)[25]

Once this geographical distinction between Jesus and his interlocutors is clear, their accusation of his being a demon-possessed Samaritan makes more sense. For the Jewish Scriptures identify the origin of the Samaritans with the king of Assyria's eighth-century resettlement of the northern kingdom with Gentiles (see 2 Kgs 17:24, 33–34). By the time of Jesus, the Samaritan people had come to accept the Mosaic Torah and to worship the one God of Israel, but there was still a great deal of animosity between them and their Jewish contempo-

24. See Adele Reinhartz, "The Jews of the Fourth Gospel," in *The Oxford Handbook of Johannine Studies*, ed. Judith M. Lieu and Martinus C. de Boer (Oxford: Oxford University Press, 2018), 121–37; Steve Mason, "Jews, Judaeans, Judaizing, Judaism: Problems of Categorization in Ancient History," *Journal for the Study of Judaism in the Persian, Hellenistic, and Roman Periods* 38 (2007): 457–512; Johannes Beutler, *Judaism and the Jews in the Gospel of John*, Subsidia Biblica 30 (Rome: Editrice Pontifico Instituto Biblico, 2006).

25. Author's translation.

raries, not least because the Samaritans rejected the Jerusalem temple (cf. John 4:20; Josephus, *Antiquities* 18.85–89).[26] The Samaritans were also apparently regarded as inclined to illicit practices like magic and syncretism.[27] Seen in this light, the Judeans' accusation poses the questions: Is Jesus the Galilean really a Jew, or is he actually "a Samaritan" of mixed descent (John 8:48)? And are his teachings true, or just the ravings of an evil spirit?

Jesus responds by both ignoring the charge of being a Samaritan and by insisting he is not possessed. Instead, he insists that he honors "the Father" (John 8:49) and then uses a double "amen" saying to solemnly declare that anyone who follows his teaching will "never see death" (John 8:51). Both these Semitic expressions can be found in the book of Psalms:

> *Who can live and never see death?*
> *Who can escape the power of Sheol?* . . .
> Remember, O Lord, how your servant is taunted;
> how I bear in my bosom the insults of the peoples . . .
> with which they taunted the *footsteps of your anointed.*
> Blessed be the Lord forever.
> *Amen and Amen.* (Ps 89:48, 50–52)

In context, the expression "never see death" simply means to "never die," and the double "amen" formula is a solemn expression used to confirm a statement that precedes (or follows) it (cf. Ps 41:13; 72:19).[28] Thus, Jesus is using the language of Jewish Scripture to solemnly confirm that whoever follows his teachings will be rescued from death and possess eternal life.[29]

The Question of Jesus's Identity and the Vision of Abraham

In response to Jesus's solemn declaration, the Judeans point out that even "Abraham" and "the prophets" died (John 8:52) and ask Jesus whether he thinks

26. See Reinhard Pummer, *The Samaritans: A Profile* (Grand Rapids: Eerdmans, 2016), 26–46.

27. Johannes Beutler, SJ, *A Commentary on the Gospel of John*, trans. Michael Tait (Grand Rapids: Eerdmans, 2013), 246.

28. Frank-Lothar Hossfeld and Erich Zenger, *Psalms 2*, trans. Linda M. Maloney, Hermeneia (Minneapolis: Fortress, 2005), 218, 412.

29. Raymond E. Brown, *The Gospel according to John*, 2 vols., Anchor Yale Bible Commentary 29–29A (New Haven: Yale University Press, 1966, 1970), 1:359.

himself "greater than our father Abraham" (John 8:53). They also ask him point blank: "Who do you claim to be?" (John 8:53). Jesus responds by declaring that he "knows" the Father in a way they do not (John 8:55) and by insisting that Abraham "saw" Jesus's day and was glad (John 8:56). In order to understand this exchange, a couple of points are important to keep in mind.

According to both Jewish Scripture and later Jewish traditions, Abraham and all of the prophets—with the obvious exception of Elijah (cf. 2 Kgs 2:1–12)—suffered the same fate as every other human being: death. Not only does Jewish Scripture say that Abraham "died in a good old age" (Gen 25:8), but later Jewish writings say the prophet Isaiah "died under Manasseh by being sawn in two," and the prophet Jeremiah "died" when he was "stoned by his people" (Lives of the Prophets 1:2; 2:1).[30] In light of such passages, Jesus seems to imply that he is greater than the patriarchs and prophets. Indeed, it is precisely Jesus's implicit claim of superiority that leads the Judeans to demand that he make an explicit statement about his identity: "Who do you claim to be?" (John 8:53).

In response, Jesus declares that Abraham rejoiced to "see" his "day" (John 8:56). Here it is not exactly clear what he is referring to. Some suggest that Jesus is alluding to the time Abraham "laughed" when God said he was going to have a son at a hundred years of age (Gen 17:7). Others suggest it was the joy he experienced at the birth of Isaac (cf. Gen 21:6).[31] Neither suggestion really does justice to Jesus's emphasis on the *vision* of Abraham and its orientation toward a *future* day. Hence, it seems more likely that Jesus is either referring to the revelation of the future given to Abram during his "deep sleep" (Gen 15:12–21) or to God's declaration that the "nations of the earth" would be "blessed" because Abraham was willing to sacrifice Isaac (Gen 22:13–19). All things considered, the latter option seems more likely, since Genesis emphasizes the faculty of sight in its description of the event:

> And Abraham *lifted up his eyes and saw a ram*, caught in a thicket by its horns. Abraham went and took the ram and offered it up as a burnt offering instead of his son. So Abraham called that place "*The Lord will see*"; as it is said to this day, "*On the mount, the Lord will be seen*." The angel of the Lord called to Abraham a second time from heaven, and said, "By myself

30. In James H. Charlesworth, ed., *Old Testament Pseudepigrapha*, 2 vols., Anchor Bible Reference Library (New York: Doubleday, 1983, 1985), 2:385, 386.

31. Beutler, *Commentary on the Gospel of John*, 247; Brown, *Gospel according to John*, 1:359.

> I have sworn, says the Lord: Because you have done this, and have not withheld your son, your only son, I will indeed bless you, and I will make your offspring as numerous as the stars of heaven and as the sand that is on the seashore. And your offspring shall possess the gate of their enemies, and by your offspring shall all the nations of the earth be blessed, because you have obeyed my voice." (Gen 22:13–17)[32]

Though many English translations have "the Lord will provide" and "on the mount of the Lord it shall be provided" (e.g., NRSV), the Hebrew text more likely means "the Lord will see" (*YHWH yireh*) and "on the mountain the Lord will be seen" (*behar YHWH yer'aeh*).[33] This is how the Greek Septuagint translated the Hebrew text: "The Lord saw" (*kyrios eiden*), and "On the mountain the Lord was seen" (*en tō orei kyrios ophthē*) (Gen 22:14 LXX).[34] When this emphasis on sight is combined with the language of "this day" (Gen 22:14),[35] it seems reasonable to conclude that Jesus is describing Abraham's mountaintop experience as a kind of apocalyptic vision in which the patriarch saw the future age of salvation, when all the nations of the earth would be blessed through his "offspring" (Gen 22:18).

Jesus Declares He Existed before Abraham

Again Jesus's interlocutors object, this time because he is not even "fifty years old"; how then can he have "seen Abraham" (John 8:47)? Jesus responds with an even more solemn declaration: "Amen, amen, I say to you, before Abraham was, I am" (*egō eimi*) (John 8:48). Here Jesus makes two momentous claims.

First, although the Pentateuch situates the life of Abraham only several generations after Noah and the flood (cf. Gen 11:27–32), Jesus claims that he existed before Abraham. Just as the book of Psalms describes God as the one who existed "before" the world was created (Ps 90:2),[36] so Jesus implies that

32. NRSV, adapted.

33. Cf. Claus Westermann, *Genesis 12–36: A Continental Commentary*, trans. John J. Scullion, SJ (Minneapolis: Fortress, 1995), 363: "YHWH appears," and "On the mountain, there is YHWH seen."

34. *A New English Translation of the Septuagint*, ed. Albert Pietersma and Benjamin G. Wright (Oxford: Oxford University Press, 2007), 19.

35. MT *yowm*; LXX *sēmeron*.

36. Brown, *Gospel according to John*, 1:360.

he too has existed since ancient times. On this point, scholars from a variety of perspectives agree:

> The "existence" of Jesus reaches back into the past prior to Abraham. A statement of preexistence is basically present here.[37]

> Jesus speaks of his pre-existence, his eternal being with God. . . . As the one who already "is" in the beginning (cf. Ex. 3.14), of course Jesus also "is" before Abraham.[38]

> Jesus speaks and acts as the revealer who is aware of his pre-existence (John 8.58).[39]

In other words, in response to a direct question about his age, Jesus not only affirms that he is very, very old; he also declares his eternal "preexistence."[40]

Jesus Refers to Himself Using the Divine "I Am"

Second, and even more shocking, Jesus responds to the question about his identity by taking the divine self-designation "I am" (*egō eimi*) as his own (John 8:58). As we have seen earlier, this expression is rooted in both the Torah and the Prophets:

> God said to Moses, "*I Am Who I Am*." He said further, "Thus you shall say to the Israelites, '*I Am* has sent me to you.'" God also said to Moses, "Thus you

37. Jörg Frey, *The Glory of the Crucified One: Christology and Theology in the Gospel of John*, trans. Wayne Coppins and Christoph Heilig (Waco, TX: Baylor University Press, 2018), 82.

38. Lüdemann, *Jesus of Nazareth*, 491 (Frank Schleritt).

39. Theissen and Merz, *Historical Jesus*, 36.

40. Adele Reinhartz, "The Gospel according to John," in *The Jewish Annotated New Testament*, ed. Amy-Jill Levine and Mark Zvi Brettler, 2nd ed. (Oxford: Oxford University Press, 2017), 196 ("perhaps also a claim to pre-existence"; Bart D. Ehrman, *How Jesus Became God: The Exaltation of a Jewish Preacher from Galilee* (San Francisco: HarperOne, 2014), 124; Maurice Casey, *Is John's Gospel True?* (London: Routledge, 1996), 32; C. K. Barrett, *The Gospel according to St. John*, 2nd ed. (Philadelphia: Westminster, 1978), 352. For a full study, see F. Kunath, *Dei Präexistenz Jesu im Johannesevangelium. Struktur und Theologie eines johanneischen Motivs*, Beihefte zur Zeitschrift für die neutestamentliche Wissenschaft 212 (Berlin: Walter de Gruyter, 2016).

shall say to the Israelites, 'The Lord, the God of your ancestors, the God of Abraham, the God of Isaac, and the God of Jacob, has sent me to you': This is my name forever, and this my title for all generations." (Exod 3:14–15)

I, I am the Lord,
and besides me there is no savior.
I declared and saved and proclaimed,
when there was no strange god among you;
and you are my witnesses, says the Lord.
I am God, and also henceforth *I am He*. (Isa 43:10; cf. 43:25)

In the book of Exodus, the absolute "I am"[41] is a divine self-designation, one that in context appears to function as another name for "the Lord God" (Exod 3:15).[42] This epithet also suggests that the God of Israel is an *eternal* being who has no beginning and no end; he simply "is."[43] Along similar lines, in the passages from Isaiah, the divine self-designation "I Am He"[44] functions as "a self-predication" of YHWH that echoes "the equally enigmatic *ʾehyeh* [I am]" revealed to Moses in the burning bush (Exod 3:14).[45]

In light of these passages in Jewish Scripture, commentators agree that when Jesus uses the absolute "I am" with reference to himself, he is using an allusive (but explosive) divine self-designation:

> *I am*, [is an] allusion to God's revelation to Moses at the burning bush (Ex 3.14).[46]
>
> Jesus tells his opponents, "Truly I tell you, before Abraham was, I am" (8:58). This particular phrase, "I am," rings a familiar chord to anyone acquainted with the Hebrew Bible. In the book of Exodus, in the story of the burning

41. MT *ʾehyeh*; LXX *ho ōn*.

42. MT *YHWH ʾelohim*; LXX *kyrios ho theos*. See William H. C. Propp, *Exodus*, 2 vols., Anchor Yale Bible 2–2A (New Haven: Yale University Press, 1999, 2006), 1:204–205, 223–25.

43. See James Kugel, *Traditions of the Bible: A Guide to the Bible as It Was at the Start of the Common Era* (Cambridge, MA: Harvard University Press, 1997), 516–17.

44. MT *ʾani hu'*; LXX *egō eimi*.

45. Joseph Blenkinsopp, *Isaiah*, Anchor Yale Bible 19–19B (New Haven: Yale University Press, 2000–2003), 2:224.

46. Adele Reinhartz, "The Gospel according to John," in Levine and Brettler, *Jewish Annotated New Testament*, 196.

> bush . . . , Moses asks God what his name is, and God tells him that his name is "I am." Jesus appears to be claiming not only to have existed before Abraham, but to have been given the name of God himself.[47]

> The "I am" statements are intended to recall Old Testament passages such as Exod. 3.14 . . . , in which the words "I am" are part of God's revelation of his name, and to hint thereby at Jesus' deity.[48]

These examples could easily be multiplied.[49] For our purposes here, the main point is that Jesus is doing more than just claiming to have "extrahuman status."[50] By using the divine "I am," *Jesus is claiming to be the same God who appeared to Moses on Mount Sinai.* As Rudolf Bultmann once put it: "the *egō* of eternity is to be heard in an historical person, who is not yet 50 years old."[51]

Stoning for Blasphemy and Jesus's Claim to Divinity

If there is any doubt about the divine implications of Jesus's self-designation, the way the Judeans respond to his words should lay it to rest: "So they took up stones to throw at him . . ." (John 8:59). Though no one explicitly states that Jesus has blasphemed, the move to stone him to death implies that the Judeans think he has committed it. For in the Pentateuch, stoning is the punishment for the crime of blasphemy:

> "*He who blasphemes the name of the* Lord *shall be put to death; all the congregation shall stone him*; the sojourner as well as the native, when he blasphemes the Name, shall be put to death" (Lev 24:16).

47. Ehrman, *How Jesus Became God*, 124; cf. 278–79.

48. Casey, *Jesus of Nazareth*, 519.

49. See Beutler, *Commentary on the Gospel of John*, 249; Marianne Meye Thompson, *John: A Commentary* (Louisville: Westminster John Knox, 2015), 197; Craig S. Keener, *The Gospel of John*, 2 vols. (Grand Rapids: Baker Academic, 2003), 1:768, 770; Catrin H. Williams, "'I Am' or 'I Am He': Self Declaratory Pronouncements in the Fourth Gospel and Rabbinic Tradition," in *Jesus in the Johannine Tradition*, ed. Robert T. Fortna and Tom Thatcher (Louisville: Westminster John Knox, 2001), 343–52.

50. Fredriksen, *Jesus of Nazareth*, 32–33.

51. Rudolf Bultmann, *The Gospel of John: A Commentary*, trans. G. R. Beasley-Murray (Philadelphia: Westminster, 1971), 328.

Commentators on Leviticus debate whether the word "blaspheme" (*naqab*) originally referred to the unlawful pronunciation of the divine name, the cursing of God, or both.[52] By the time of Jesus, however, the concept of blasphemy had expanded to include both the illicit pronunciation of God's name and any word or action of a human being that violated divine prerogatives.[53] Because Jesus uses the divine "I am" to refer to himself (John 8:58), he seems to his contemporaries to have transgressed on both counts.

In light of such observations, scholars from a variety of religious perspectives concur that the reason the Judeans pick up stones to execute Jesus is because they recognize he is claiming to be divine:

> Jesus appears to be claiming not only to have existed before Abraham, but to have been given the name of God himself. His Jewish opponents know exactly what he is saying. They immediately take up stones to stone him.[54]

> [Jesus] speaks openly and frankly of his own extrahuman status: "Before Abraham was, I am" ([John] 8:58).[55]

> The Jewish reaction of taking up stones to throw at him shows that they have interpreted his words as a claim to divinity.[56]

The most notable of these is from Raymond Brown's landmark commentary on the Gospel of John:

> *No clearer implication of divinity is found in the Gospel tradition, and "the Jews" recognize this implication. . . .* We are not certain what the legal definition of blasphemy was in Jesus' time; but in John's account the use of the divine name represented by *egō eimi* seems to be sufficient, for the Jews seek to carry out the command of Leviticus.[57]

52. Jacob Milgrom, *Leviticus 23–27*, Anchor Yale Bible 3B (New Haven: Yale University Press, 2001), 2109.

53. See Adela Yarbro Collins, "Blasphemy," in *The Eerdmans Dictionary of Early Judaism*, ed. John J. Collins and Daniel C. Harlow (Grand Rapids: Eerdmans, 2010), 445.

54. Ehrman, *How Jesus Became God*, 124.

55. Fredriksen, *Jesus of Nazareth*, 32–33.

56. Casey, *Is John's Gospel True?*, 32. See also Lüdemann, *Jesus after Two Thousand Years*, 491 (Frank Schleritt).

57. Brown, *The Gospel according to John*, 1:367 (emphasis added).

In short, when Jesus's words and his audience's response are interpreted in light of the Mosaic Torah, the most plausible interpretation is that his interlocutors move to stone Jesus to death because he is "claiming in fact to be God."[58] Not for the last time, Jesus is accused of blasphemy in the context of a question about his identity.

Arguments against Historical Plausibility

With these exegetical observations in mind, we can now raise the question of historical plausibility. What are the arguments for and against the historicity of Jesus claiming to have existed before Abraham, taking the divine "I am" as his own, and almost being stoned to death as a result (John 8:48–59)?

Given the widespread tendency to exclude the Gospel of John from the quest for the historical Jesus, it is perhaps unsurprising that the overwhelming majority of major works on Jesus simply ignore this episode, as if it did not exist.[59] This tendency is even found in studies explicitly devoted to the historical Jesus in the Gospel of John.[60] Apparently, if there is any episode that is a "no-go area" in the study of the historical Jesus, it is when Jesus declares "before Abraham was, I am" (John 8:58).[61] Some do mention it in passing, but

58. Ehrman, *How Jesus Became God*, 278–79.

59. For example, the evidence for Jesus's claim that he existed "before Abraham" receives no discussion in Hengel and Schwemer, *Jesus and Judaism*; Lohfink, *Jesus of Nazareth*; Puig i Tàrrech, *Jesus: A Biography*; Allison, *Constructing Jesus*; Keener, *Historical Jesus of the Gospels*; Vermes, *Authentic Gospel of Jesus*; Dunn, *Jesus Remembered*; Flusser with Notley, *Sage from Galilee*; Ehrman, *Jesus: Apocalyptic Prophet*; Fredriksen, *Jesus of Nazareth*; Becker, *Jesus of Nazareth*; Gnilka, *Jesus of Nazareth*; Sanders, *Historical Figure of Jesus*; Wright, *Jesus and the Victory of God*; Witherington, *Christology of Jesus*; Sanders, *Jesus and Judaism*; Vermes, *Jesus the Jew*; Jeremias, *Proclamation of Jesus*; Bornkamm, *Jesus of Nazareth*; Klausner, *Jesus of Nazareth*.

60. Remarkably, Jesus's claim to have existed before Abraham and his use of the divine "I am" receives no discussion in James H. Charlesworth, *Jesus as Mirrored in John: The Genius of the New Testament* (London: T&T Clark, 2019); Jörg Frey, *Theology and History in the Fourth Gospel: Tradition and Narration* (Waco, TX: Baylor University Press, 2018); Paul N. Anderson, Felix Just, SJ, and Tom Thatcher, eds., *Aspects of Historicity in the Fourth Gospel*, vol. 2 of *John, Jesus, and History* (Atlanta: Society of Biblical Literature, 2009); Paul N. Anderson, Felix Just, SJ, and Tom Thatcher, eds., *Glimpses of Jesus through the Johannine Lens*, vol. 3 of *John, Jesus, and History* (Atlanta: Society of Biblical Literature, 2016).

61. Cf. John A. T. Robinson, "The Last Tabu? The Self-Consciousness of Jesus," in *The Historical Jesus in Recent Research*, ed. James D. G. Dunn and Scot McKnight, Sources for Biblical and Theological Study 10 (Winona Lake, IN: Eisenbrauns, 2005), 553–66 (here 553).

without any discussion of whether or not it is historical.[62] Others explicitly deem the episode a creation of the early church.[63] Several reasons are given in favor of this negative verdict.

The first major argument against historicity is from contextual implausibility within early Judaism. According to this view, it is virtually inconceivable that a first-century Jew like Jesus would ever claim to be a divine being. As Bart Ehrman puts the point:

> Jesus is not claiming to be God the Father here. . . . But he is saying that he is equal with God and has been that way from before the world was created. These are amazingly exalted claims. But looked at from a historical perspective, they simply cannot be ascribed to the historical Jesus . . . they are not at all contextually credible. We have no record of any Palestinian Jew ever saying any such things about himself. These divine self-claims in John are part of John's distinctive theology; they are not part of the historical record of what Jesus actually said.[64]

In this view, because we have no record of any *other* first-century Jews besides Jesus making similar divine claims, the claims of preexistence and divinity ascribed to Jesus in his exchange with the Judeans in the temple must be unhistorical.

A second major reason for deeming the episode unhistorical is from a lack of coherence with other evidence about Jesus. In this view, Jesus's claim to have existed before Abraham and his use of the divine "I am" (John 8:48–59) cannot be reconciled with the evidence in the Synoptic Gospels that Jesus did not speak explicitly about his identity, and even forbade others to speak about it (e.g., Matt 8:4; 12:16; 16:20; Mark 1:34, 44–45; 3:11–12; 7:36–37; 8:30; 9:9; Luke 4:41; 5:14–15; 9:21).[65] In the words of Paula Fredriksen: "John's eloquent, talkative Jesus is under no such constraint [as in the Synoptics]. . . . He speaks openly and frankly of his own extrahuman status: 'Before Abraham was, I am' (8:58). . . . [T]his Jesus openly and from the beginning teaches his own elevated theological status."[66] In other words, the exchange between Jesus and the Judeans in the temple is at odds with the evidence that Jesus practiced some form

62. See Schröter, *Jesus of Nazareth*, 215; Theissen and Merz, *Historical Jesus*, 558.

63. See Robert W. Funk, Roy Hoover, and the Jesus Seminar, *The Five Gospels: The Search for the Authentic Words of Jesus* (New York: Macmillan, 1993), 430.

64. Ehrman, *How Jesus Became God*, 125.

65. Ehrman, *How Jesus Became God*, 125.

66. Fredriksen, *Jesus of Nazareth, King of the Jews*, 32–33.

of the "messianic secret."[67] For this reason alone, many would agree with James Charlesworth's sweeping conclusion: "Obviously, no historical person named Jesus of Nazareth went around Galilee making the Christological claims we find in John."[68]

The third and final argument against the historicity of Jesus's exchange with the Judeans in the temple is based on the assumption that Jesus never claimed to be more than merely human. According to this view, since we know in advance that Jesus made no claims to divinity during his lifetime, then any records of conflict over a divine claim on Jesus's part must be an anachronistic retrojection of the early church. As Maurice Casey writes:

> The Fourth Gospel's Jews, in open debate, have espoused the Johannine interpretation of Jesus' pre-existence as an indication of his deity, thereby indicating the setting of this interpretation of Jesus' pre-existence in the conflict between the Johannine community and the Jewish community, in Ephesus towards the end of the first century CE.[69]

In light of such reasoning, when it comes to the historicity of this episode, the verdict of the majority of contemporary Jesus research is straightforward: "none of the statements supposed to have been made by Jesus or the Jews in 8.30–59 was spoken during Jesus' lifetime."[70]

Context: Abraham's Vision, the Divine "I Am," and Stoning for Blasphemy

Despite the widespread tendency to ignore or reject this episode as unhistorical, when we apply a triple-context approach to Jesus's exchange with the Judeans in the temple (John 8:48–59), the first thing we discover is that several features of the episode are actually quite plausible within a first-century Jewish context.

For one thing, Jesus's assertion that "Abraham" had a vision of the future in which he "saw" all the way up to Jesus's own "day" (John 8:56) fits

67. Cf. Dale C. Allison, "Reflections on Matthew, John, and Jesus," in *Jesus Research: The Gospel of John in Historical Inquiry*, ed. James H. Charlesworth with Jolyon G. R. Pruszinski, Jewish and Christian Texts 26 (London: T&T Clark, 2019), 67–68; Charlesworth, *Jesus as Mirrored in John*, 145.

68. Charlesworth, *Jesus as Mirrored in John*, 145.

69. Casey, *Jesus of Nazareth*, 518.

70. Lüdemann, *Jesus after Two Thousand Years*, 492 (Frank Schleritt).

very well into an early Jewish context. For in the Second Temple period, there was a widespread tradition that Abraham had experienced visions in which he "foresaw the days of the Messiah."[71] Consider the following early Jewish texts:

> We [angels] came to Abraham. . . . *We blessed him and told him everything that had been commanded for him*: that . . . one of Isaac's sons would become a holy progeny. . . . Then we went on our way and told Sarah all that we had reported to him. *The two of them were extremely happy*. . . . He celebrated a joyful festival in this month—for seven days. . . . He was the first to celebrate *the Festival of Tabernacles* on the earth. (Jubilees 16:15–17, 19–21)[72]

> Then a voice came speaking to me twice, "Abraham, Abraham!" And I said, "Here I am." And he said, "Behold, *it is I*. Fear not, for I am Before-the-World and Mighty, the God who created previously, before the light of the age. . . . you shall set out for me the sacrifice which I have commanded you, in the place which I will show you on a high mountain. *And there I will show you the things which were made by the ages and by my word, and affirmed, created, and renewed*. (Apocalypse of Abraham 9:1–4, 8–9)[73]

> *To him [Abraham] only you [God] revealed the end of times*, secretly by night. (4 Ezra 3:14)[74]

These are striking parallels with Jesus's statements about Abraham. Just as the book of Jubilees says that angels revealed the future to Abraham so that he was "extremely happy" and celebrated the "feast of Tabernacles" (Jubilees 16:17, 21), so too Jesus—apparently during the Feast of Tabernacles—says that Abraham "rejoiced" to see Jesus's day and "was glad" (John 8:57; cf. 7:2, 37–44). Likewise, just as the Apocalypse of Abraham says that God "showed" Abraham a vision of the future "ages" when the world would be renewed (Apocalypse of Abraham 9:10; cf. Gen 15:17–20), so too Jesus describes Abraham's knowl-

71. Beutler, *Commentary on the Gospel of John*, 247. See Kugel, *Traditions of the Bible*, 299–301.

72. In James C. VanderKam, *Jubilees 1–21*, Hermeneia (Minneapolis: Fortress, 2018), 527.

73. In Charlesworth, *Old Testament Pseudepigrapha*, 1:693.

74. In Charlesworth, *Old Testament Pseudepigrapha*, 1:528. For further examples of this tradition, see also *Pseudo-Philo* 23:6–7; Philo, *Who Is Heir of Divine Things?* 258; 2 Baruch 4:1–6.

edge of the future as a vision in which he "saw" the future "day" of salvation (John 8:56–57). According to early Jewish tradition, Abraham was not just a patriarch; he was *an apocalyptic prophet* who experienced heavenly visions of "the end of times" (4 Ezra 3:14).

Even Jesus's startling declaration "Before Abraham was, I am" (John 8:56) is contextually credible in an early Jewish context. For one thing, if Jesus claimed to be the Danielic son of man (cf. Dan 7:13–14), then it is quite credible that he also claimed to be a preexistent, divine being. For as we have already seen, the "son of man" figure in the book of Daniel is described in some early Jewish apocalypses as a preexistent, heavenly messiah:

> *For from the beginning the Son of Man was hidden,*
> and the Most High preserved him in the presence of his might,
> and he revealed him to the chosen. (1 Enoch 62:8)[75]

> As for your seeing *a man come up from the heart of the sea, this is he whom the Most High has been keeping for many ages.* . . . When these things come to pass . . . , then *my son will be revealed, whom you saw as a man coming up from the sea.* (4 Ezra 13:25–26)[76]

In light of such evidence, experts in early Judaism have concluded that some apocalyptic Jews did indeed expect "the messiah" to be a "preexistent" and "heavenly being."[77] If this is true, then there is no reason Jesus could not make a similar claim for himself. Moreover, if Jesus did claim preexistence, then it is contextually plausible that he would do so by using the divine epithet "I am." For, in an early Jewish context, the divine "I am" that was revealed to Moses on Sinai (Exod 3:14–15; cf. Isa 43:10) had come to be connected with the name of the eternal God:

75. In George W. E. Nickelsburg and James C. VanderKam, *1 Enoch* 2, Hermeneia (Minneapolis: Fortress, 2012), 166, 254.

76. Charlesworth, *Old Testament Pseudepigrapha*, 1:552–53.

77. John J. Collins, *The Apocalyptic Imagination: An Introduction to Jewish Apocalyptic Literature*, 3rd ed. (Grand Rapids: Eerdmans, 2016), 228, 230, 258 ("apparently preexistent"); Nickelsburg and VanderKam, *1 Enoch* 2, 170 ("possessing a real preexistence"); Michael Stone, *Fourth Ezra*, Hermeneia (Minneapolis: Fortress, 1990), 385 ("the precreation of the Messiah"); Sigmund Mowinckel, *He That Cometh: The Messiah Concept in the Old Testament and Later Judaism*, trans. G. W. Anderson (repr., Grand Rapids: Eerdmans, 2005), 305 ("the preexistent being, the Son of Man"). Cf. Joseph A. Fitzmyer, SJ, *The One Who Is to Come* (Grand Rapids: Eerdmans, 2007), 121: a "transcendent (= preexistent?) figure."

> Moses . . . also besought him not to deny him knowledge of *his name. . . . Then God revealed to him his name*, which before then had not come to men's ears, and of which I am forbidden to speak. (Josephus, *Antiquities* 2.275–276)

> Then a voice came speaking to me twice, "Abraham, Abraham!" And I said, "Here I am." And he said, "*Behold, it is I.* Fear not, for *I am Before-the-World and Mighty*, before the light of the age." (Apoc. Ab. 9:1)[78]

In light of such evidence, it seems reasonable to conclude that when Jesus says "Before Abraham was, I am" (John 8:58), he is not just claiming to be any kind of divine being. Rather, he is claiming to be *the same God who appeared to Moses* and the other patriarchs in Jewish Scripture and tradition.

Now, if Jesus did indeed claim to exist before Abraham and take the divine "I am" as his own name, then it is eminently credible that some members of his Judean audience attempt to stone him for blasphemy. For one thing, stoning was not only the biblical penalty for blasphemy (cf. Lev 24:18). As Josephus shows, there is evidence that a stoning once took place during the feast of Passover in the temple itself:

> *Let him that blasphemes God be stoned*, then hung for a day; and buried ignominiously and in obscurity. (Josephus, *Antiquities* 4.202)

> At this time *there came round the festival . . . called Passover. . . .* Now the fomenters of disorder . . . stood together *in the temple* . . . and Archelaus, fearing that something dangerous might grow out of their fanaticism, sent a cohort of legionaries under a tribune to suppress the violence of the rebels. . . . By this act . . . the crowd were infuriated, and uttering cries and exhortations, *they rushed upon the soldiers and after surrounding them stoned most of them to death.* (Josephus, *Antiquities* 17.213–216)[79]

In light of such evidence, it seems clear that if the historical Jesus made claims about himself that were viewed as blasphemous while he was teaching in the Jerusalem temple during the Feast of Tabernacles, then it is perfectly plausible

78. Charlesworth, *Old Testament Pseudepigrapha*, 1:693.

79. For another spontaneous act of stoning in which Josephus himself barely escaped with his life, cf. Josephus, *Life* 300.

that some of his Jewish contemporaries would have "picked up stones" in order to put him to death (John 8:59; cf. Lev 24:16).[80]

Most significant of all, despite claims to the contrary, Jesus is *not* "the only Palestinian Jew" alleged to have made divine claims about himself.[81] According to Josephus, King Herod Agrippa—who lived at the same time as Jesus, and who was actually known for his "enthusiasm and zeal for Judaism"[82]—is described as publicly acting as if he were divine. Consider this remarkable account:

> After the completion of the third year of his reign over the whole of Judaea, Agrippa came to the city of Caesarea. . . . On the second day of the spectacles, clad in a garment woven completely of silver so that its texture was indeed wondrous, he entered the theatre at daybreak. There the theatre, illumined by the touch of the first rays of the sun, was wondrously radiant and by its glitter inspired fear and awe in those who gazed intently upon it. *Straightaway his flatterers raised their voices from various directions*—though hardly for his good—*addressing him as a god.* "May you be propitious to us," they added, "and *if we have hitherto feared you as a man, yet henceforth we agree that you are more than mortal in your being.*" The king did not rebuke them nor did he reject their flattery as impious. (Josephus, *Antiquities* 19.343–346)

Notice here that this is a *Jewish* king being treated as if he is a "god" (*theos*), even though he is just a "man" (*anthrōpos*). Notice also the reason Agrippa appears to have accepted worship as a god is because he was a *royal* figure.[83] To be sure, there is no evidence that Agrippa, like Jesus, took the divine "I am" as his own or claimed to be the same God who appeared to Moses. Nevertheless, the case of King Herod Agrippa's willingness to receive divine accolades shows that, however shocking it might have been for Jesus as a first-century Jew to speak and act if he were divine, it is neither implausible nor impossible.

80. Keener, *Gospel of John*, 2:772; Brown, *Gospel according to John*, 1:360.

81. Ehrman, *How Jesus Became God*, 125.

82. Adam Marshak, "Herodian Dynasty," in Collins and Harlow, *Eerdmans Dictionary of Early Judaism*, 738.

83. See Stewart Perowne, *The Later Herods: The Political Background of the New Testament* (Nashville: Abingdon, 1958), 81–82.

Coherence: The Preexistent Messiah and the Divine "I Am"

A second major argument in favor of the historicity of Jesus's exchange with the Judeans in the Jerusalem temple is from multiple points of coherence with other evidence about Jesus.

To begin with, that Jesus was accused by Judeans of being possessed by "a demon" (John 8:48) is quite congruent with evidence that he was accused of casting out demons by the power of "Beelzebul," the "prince of demons" (Matt 12:24–26; Mark 3:22–23; Luke 11:15–18). Likewise, Jesus's declaration that anyone who adheres to his "word" will "never see death" (John 8:51) fits well with other passages in which Jesus states that a person's ability to receive eschatological "life" is dependent on whether they will follow him and his "words" (Matt 16:24–25; Mark 9:34–38; Luke 9:23–26). Along similar lines, Jesus's declaration that the Judeans do not "know" God his "Father," but Jesus does "know" him (John 8:55) coheres perfectly with the apocalyptic thunderbolt in which he declares that "no one knows" God "the Father" except "the Son" (Matt 11:27; Luke 10:22).[84] Even Jesus's enigmatic declaration that the patriarch Abraham longed to "see" Jesus's "day" (John 8:56) finds a suggestive parallel in another passage in which Jesus declares to his disciples that many "prophets" and figures from of old "longed to see" what they see—that is, to see Jesus himself and the time of the kingdom—but "did not see it" (Matt 13:17; Luke 10:24).

Moreover, Jesus's act of declaring that he existed before Abraham and taking the divine "I am" as his own (John 8:48) also presents a strong case of coherence with other evidence in which Jesus uses the divine "I am" with reference to himself, such as in the account of him walking on the sea:

> But immediately Jesus spoke to them and said, "Take heart, *I am* [*egō eimi*]; do not be afraid." (Matt 14:27)
>
> But immediately he spoke to them and said, "Take heart, *I am* [*egō eimi*]; do not be afraid." (Mark 6:49–50)
>
> But he said to them, "*I am* [*egō eimi*]; do not be afraid." (John 6:20)[85]

In light of such parallels, the still popular assertion that Jesus makes "no such exalted claims" about himself or his divinity in the Synoptic Gospels is an idea

84. See chapter 4 for discussion.

85. I've adapted the NRSV here to bring out more clearly the parallels with John 8:58.

whose time for "mandatory retirement" has definitely come.[86] Whatever one thinks of its historicity, *Jesus clearly refers to his own preexistence by using the divine "I am"* (*egō eimi*) in *both the Gospel of John* (John 6:20; 8:58) *and the Synoptics* (Matt 14:27; Mark 6:50).

Last, but certainly not least, even the Judeans' response of picking up "stones" in order to execute Jesus for blasphemy (John 8:59) coheres well with the evidence that Jesus is accused of blasphemy when he declares the sins of the paralytic to be forgiven (Matt 9:2–8; Mark 2:3–12; Luke 5:18–26).[87]

In sum, despite the Johannine *style* of the account of the exchange between Jesus and the Judeans in the temple during Tabernacles (John 8:48–59), the *substance* coheres remarkably well with other data we possess about the kind of things Jesus was remembered as having done and said during his public ministry.

Consequences: Christological Monotheism and the Stonings of Jewish Christians

Finally, if Jesus did indeed claim to have existed before Abraham, and if he used the divine "I am" to identify himself, then this would provide a reasonable explanation for two notable features of practice and belief in the early church.

First, it would explain why some early believers in Jesus went on to continue to describe Jesus as an eternal being equal to the one creator God—a phenomenon some scholars refer to as "Christological monotheism."[88] Consider once again the parallels between the language used for the one God and the risen Christ in the book of Revelation:

86. Ehrman, *How Jesus Became God*, 125. Cf. Paula Fredriksen, "Mandatory Retirement: Ideas in the Study of Christian Origins Whose Time Has Come to Go," in *Israel's God and Rebecca's Children: Christology and Community in Early Judaism and Christianity: Essays in Honor of Larry W. Hurtado and Alan F. Segal*, ed. David B. Capes, April D. DeConick, Helen K. Bond, and Troy A. Miller (Waco, TX: Baylor University Press, 2007), 25–38.

87. See chapter 2 above.

88. E.g., Carey C. Newman, James R. Davila, and Gladys S. Lews, eds., *The Jewish Roots of Christological Monotheism: Papers from the St. Andrews Conference on the Historical Origins of the Worship of Jesus* (repr., Waco, TX: Baylor University Press, 2017); Crispin Fletcher-Louis, *Christological Origins: The Emerging Consensus and Beyond*, vol. 1 of *Jesus Monotheism* (Eugene, OR: Cascade, 2015), 24–25.

> [God:] "*I am* the Alpha and the Omega," says the Lord God, who is and who was and who is to come, the Almighty. (Rev 1:8)
>
> [Christ:] "*I am* the first and the last, the living one." (Rev 1:17)
>
> [God:] "*I am* the Alpha and the Omega, the beginning and the end." (Rev 21:6)
>
> [Christ:] "*I am* the Alpha and the Omega, the first and the last, the beginning and the end." (Rev 22:13)

Although these passages do not use the absolute form of "I am" (*egō eimi*) (cf. John 8:58), the repeated refrain of "I am" (*egō eimi*) does identify the risen Christ with the preexistent, eternal God.[89] How is this possible? One reasonable historical explanation is that during his lifetime, Jesus himself laid the foundations for later divine Christology when he claimed to have existed "before Abraham" and identified himself using the divine "I am" (John 8:58).

Moreover, if Jesus was indeed almost stoned to death for blasphemy during his public ministry in Jerusalem (John 8:59), this would provide a plausible explanation for the evidence that some early Jewish believers in Jesus were executed by stoning at the behest of the Jerusalem Sanhedrin.[90] According to the New Testament and Josephus, some of the first believers in Jesus to be martyred—Stephen of Jerusalem and James, the brother of Jesus—were executed by the same method with which Jesus was threatened:

> When they [the high priest and leaders in Jerusalem] heard these things, they became enraged and ground their teeth at Stephen. But filled with the Holy Spirit, he gazed into heaven and saw the glory of God and Jesus standing at the right hand of God. "Look," he said, "I see the heavens opened and the Son of Man standing at the right hand of God!" *But they covered their ears, and with a loud shout all rushed together against him. Then they*

89. See Craig R. Koester, *Revelation*, Anchor Yale Bible 38A (New Haven: Yale University Press, 2014), 854.

90. See Larry W. Hurtado, "Pre-70 C.E. Jewish Opposition to Christ Devotion," in his *Ancient Jewish Monotheism and Early Christian Jesus-Devotion: The Context and Character of Christological Faith* (Waco, TX: Baylor University Press, 2017), 185–208 (here 192–94). See also E. Hammel, "Jewish Activity against Christians in Palestine according to Acts," in *Palestinian Setting*, vol. 4 of *The Book of Acts in Its First-Century Setting*, ed. Richard Bauckham (Grand Rapids: Eerdmans, 1995), 357–63.

> *dragged him out of the city and began to stone him*; and the witnesses laid their coats at the feet of a young man named Saul. (Acts 7:54–58)

> The younger Ananus, who, as we have said, had been appointed to the high priesthood, was rash in his temper and unusually daring. He followed the school of the Sadducees, who are indeed more heartless than any of the other Jews, as I have already explained, when they sit in judgment. Possessed of such a character, Ananus thought that he had a favourable opportunity because Festus was dead and Albinus was still on the way. *And so he convened the judges of the Sanhedrin and brought before them a man named James, the brother of Jesus who was called the Christ, and certain others. He accused them of having transgressed the law and delivered them up to be stoned.* (Josephus, *Antiquities* 20.199–200)

In order to interpret these parallels correctly, it is important to recall that, according to the Pentateuch, a person could not be executed by stoning for just any crime. Here is the list of capital crimes for which the Mosaic Torah prescribes stoning:

1. Sacrificing children to Molech (Lev 20:2)
2. Being a medium or a wizard (Lev 20:27)
3. *Blasphemy* (Lev 24:13–23)
4. Violating the Sabbath (Num 15:32–36)
5. Secretly enticing others to worship false gods (Deut 13:6–11)
6. Worshiping false gods (Deut 17:2–7)
7. Stubborn rebellion against one's parents (Deut 21:18–21)
8. Loss of virginity by an unmarried young woman (Deut 22:20–21)
9. Adultery with a betrothed woman (Deut 22:23–27)

Since there is no evidence whatsoever that Stephen, James, or the other martyrs in Jerusalem had committed any of the other crimes listed above, the most plausible explanation is that they were stoned for blasphemy (cf. Eusebius, *Church History* 2.23.10–18).[91] Indeed, the fact that Stephen's executioners cover

91. See Sean McDowell, *The Fate of the Apostles: Examining the Martyrdom Accounts of the Closest Followers of Jesus* (London: Routledge, 2015), 115–34; Richard Bauckham, "James and the Jerusalem Community," in *Jewish Believers in Jesus: The Early Centuries*, ed. Oskar Skarsaune and Reidar Hvalvik (Peabody, MA: Hendrickson, 2007), 75–77; Bauckham, "For What Offence Was James Put to Death?," in *James the Just and Christian Origins*, ed. Bruce

"their ears" and drag him out of the city before stoning him (Acts 7:57–58) strongly suggests he is being stoned for blasphemy, since the Torah instructs the Israelites to take the blasphemer "outside the camp" (cf. Lev 24:14–16).[92] In light of such evidence, it seems clear that the best historical explanation for the eventual execution of both Stephen and James the Just as blasphemers by the Jerusalem Sanhedrin is that they were making divine claims about Jesus similar to those that Jesus himself had made—divine claims that almost got *him* stoned to death during his public ministry.

Weighing the Arguments for and against Historicity

Now that we have surveyed the major arguments for and against the historicity of this episode, we can step back and evaluate the strengths of the respective positions.

When we do so, we discover that the case against the historicity of Jesus's exchange with the Judeans in the temple during the Feast of Tabernacles (John 8:48–59) is much weaker than one might expect. For one thing, it seems quite clear that the primary reason most studies ignore the evidence that Jesus claimed to have existed before Abraham and used the divine "I am" to refer to himself is simply because the episode is found in the Gospel of John. But this prejudice against a first-century source is no kind of historical argument and is therefore of no weight whatsoever. Along similar lines, the argument that the episode must be unhistorical because "we have no record of any Palestinian Jew ever saying any such things about himself" is simply untrue.[93] We *do* in fact have records of at least *one* Palestinian Jew saying precisely these kinds of things about himself: Jesus of Nazareth. There is also solid evidence that King Herod Agrippa, who was of mixed Jewish descent and known for practicing Judaism, publicly acted as if he were a "god" and not a "man" during his lifetime (Josephus, *Antiquities* 19.343–346; Acts 20:21–23). Hence, the argument from contextual implausibility fails upon closer inspection. Last, it should go without saying (but nevertheless must be said) that the claim that the episode

Chilton and Craig A. Evans, Supplements to Novum Testamentum 98 (Leiden: Brill, 1999), 199–232.

92. Carl R. Holladay, *Acts: A Commentary*, New Testament Library (Louisville: Westminster John Knox, 2016), 176; Joseph A. Fitzmyer, *The Acts of the Apostles*, Anchor Yale Bible 31 (New Haven: Yale University Press, 1997), 393.

93. Ehrman, *How Jesus Became God*, 125.

must be unhistorical simply because in it Jesus claims to be a preexistent divine being is a textbook example of viciously circular reasoning.

As far as I can tell, the only apparently strong argument against historicity is from a lack of coherence with other evidence that Jesus was reticent to speak about his identity—the so-called messianic secret. But even this point loses its force when we recognize that even Jesus's declaration "Before Abraham was, I am" (John 8:58) is an enigmatic statement; it is *not* as explicit as simply saying "I am the God of Abraham." Indeed, the absence of a predicate coheres remarkably well with Jesus's characteristic tendency of making shocking but nevertheless enigmatic and riddle-like self-references elsewhere.

On the other hand, when the positive arguments from a triple-context perspective are given due weight, the results are remarkable. For one thing, Jesus's exchange with the Judeans is completely credible within an early Jewish context given the widespread evidence for the early Jewish tradition that Abraham had apocalyptic visions of the messianic age (Jubilees 16:15–17, 19–21; Apocalypse of Abraham 9:1–10; 4 Ezra 3:14) and the early Jewish evidence that the Danielic son of man was identified as a preexistent heavenly being (1 Enoch 62:8; 4 Ezra 13:25–26). It also passes the criterion of coherence with flying colors. For as we saw in chapter 3, this is not the only time Jesus uses the divine "I am" to refer to himself; he also does so in the account of him walking on the sea (Matt 14:27; Mark 6:50; John 6:20). Finally, the evidence that Jesus implied that he was a preexistent divine being and that his fellow Jews reacted by threatening to stone him to death provides a plausible explanation for the origins of early Christian belief in his preexistent divinity and equality with God (Rev 1:8, 17; 21:6; 22:13), as does the evidence that some believers living in Jerusalem such as Stephen and James the brother of Jesus were likewise stoned to death by the Jerusalem authorities for what appear to have been charges of blasphemy (Acts 7:54–58; Josephus, *Antiquities* 20.199–200).

In sum, despite widespread reluctance in contemporary Jesus research to even countenance the possibility that Jesus claimed to be preexistent and divine and was almost stoned to death as a result (John 8:48–59), there are actually no solid arguments against its historicity. As Raymond Brown writes in his magisterial commentary on John:

> It is difficult to avoid the impression created by all the Gospels that the Jewish authorities saw something blasphemous in Jesus' understanding of himself and his role. . . . We also mention the possibility that John is historically correct in showing that the Jewish authorities took umbrage at Jesus' claims long before that Sanhedrin trial when, on the night before

> Jesus' death, another *egō eimi* (Mark xiv 62) provoked the high priest to cry blasphemy and call for death.[94]

As we will see below, Brown is quite right to emphasize that Jesus was not handed over to the Romans because he was a "reformer" but because he was a blasphemer. He is also correct to point out that, according to the extant evidence, informal charges of blasphemy were levied against Jesus long before his final hearing before the Sanhedrin. In order to see this more clearly, however, we need to turn to another example.

You Make Yourself God

The next major episode in which Jesus is accused of blasphemy also takes place in the Jerusalem temple. This time, however, the setting is the winter feast of Hanukkah:

> *At that time the festival of the Dedication took place in Jerusalem.* It was winter, and Jesus was walking in the temple, in the portico of Solomon. So the Jews gathered around him and said to him, *"How long will you keep us in suspense? If you are the Messiah, tell us plainly."*
>
> Jesus answered, "I have told you, and you do not believe. The works that I do in my Father's name testify to me; but you do not believe, because you do not belong to my sheep. My sheep hear my voice. I know them, and they follow me. I give them eternal life, and they will never perish. No one will snatch them out of my hand. What my Father has given me is greater than all else, and no one can snatch it out of the Father's hand. *The Father and I are one."*
>
> *The Jews took up stones again to stone him.* Jesus replied, "I have shown you many good works from the Father. For which of these are you going to stone me?" The Jews answered, *"It is not for a good work that we are going to stone you, but for blasphemy, because you, though only a human being, are making yourself God."*
>
> Jesus answered, "Is it not written in your law,[95] 'I said, you are gods'? *If those to whom the word of God came were called 'gods'—and the scripture*

94. Brown, *Gospel according to John*, 1:368.

95. Although "your" (*hymōn*) is included in the NRSV, it is in fact missing from some of the most ancient manuscripts, including P[45], Codex Sinaiticus (1st hand), and Codex

> *cannot be annulled—can you say that the one whom the Father has sanctified and sent into the world is blaspheming because I said, 'I am God's Son'?* If I am not doing the works of my Father, then do not believe me. But if I do them, even though you do not believe me, believe the works, so that you may know and understand that the Father is in me and I am in the Father." *Then they tried to arrest him again*, but he escaped from their hands. (John 10:22–39)

Once again, the substance of this account can be summed up as follows: (1) While Jesus is in the Jerusalem temple during Hanukkah, he is asked by his Judean contemporaries to tell them plainly whether he is the messiah. (2) Jesus responds by pointing to his "works," describing himself as a shepherd with sheep, and declaring that he and "the Father" are "one." (3) His questioners respond by picking up rocks to stone him to death. (4) When Jesus asks them why, they respond by explaining that Jesus has committed blasphemy, because he, though merely "human," is making himself "God." (5) Jesus responds by pointing out that if even the Scriptures refer to human beings as "gods" (Ps 82:6), how can he be blaspheming for simply claiming to be God's "Son"? He again points them to his "works" and declares that the Father is "in" him and he is "in" the Father. (6) They respond by trying to arrest him, but he escapes. As with each of the other episodes we have examined herein, I will begin by attempting to interpret this evidence in its first-century Jewish context.

The Judeans, Solomon's Portico, and the Feast of Hanukkah

This episode begins by identifying the persons involved, the specific location, and the liturgical timing of the exchange.

As for the persons involved, as I noted above, the group referred to as "the Jews" (*hoi Ioudaioi*) (John 10:24, 31) likely refers to the *Judeans*—that is, southern Jews—who live in Jerusalem and who seem inclined to have doubts about Jesus the Galilean (cf. John 7:1–2).[96]

With regard to the location, Jesus again encounters his Judean critics in the Jerusalem temple, this time in "the portico of Solomon" (John 10:23).[97] As

Bezae. See Francis J. Moloney, SDB, *The Gospel of John*, Sacra Pagina 4 (Collegeville: Liturgical Press, 1998), 320.

96. See Reinhartz, "Jews of the Fourth Gospel," 121–37; Mason, "Jews, Judaeans, Judaizing, Judaism," 457–512; Beutler, *Judaism and the Jews*.

97. See Dan Bahat, "Jesus and the Herodian Temple Mount," in *Jesus and Archaeology*, ed. James H. Charlesworth (Grand Rapids: Eerdmans, 2006), 301–2; Lee I. Levine, *Jerusalem:*

Josephus tells us, this portico was a visually impressive eastern porch of the temple complex:

> King Solomon, the actual founder of the temple, having walled up the eastern side, a single portico was reared on this made ground; on its other sides the sanctuary remained exposed. . . . The porticoes, all in double rows, were supported by columns five and twenty cubits high—each a single block of the purest white marble—and ceiled with panels of cedar. The natural magnificence of these columns, their excellent polish and fine adjustment presented a striking spectacle. (Josephus, *War* 5.184–185, 190–191)[98]

Since Solomon's portico provided some protection from the elements, it would be a fitting place for Jesus to engage in teaching and dialogue within the temple complex.[99]

As for the timing of the encounter, "the festival of the Dedication" (John 10:22) is the Greek name for the feast of Hanukkah, a Jewish winter festival celebrating the rededication of the Jerusalem temple by Judas Maccabeus in 164 CE, after its altar had been desecrated by King Antiochus IV Epiphanes (cf. 1 Macc 1:49–59). According to the first book of Maccabees, it was an eight-day annual festival instituted to recall "the dedication of the altar" (1 Macc 4:54) and the celebration that accompanied it:

> So they celebrated the dedication of the altar for eight days, and joyfully offered burnt offerings; they offered a sacrifice of well-being and a thanksgiving offering. . . . Then Judas and his brothers and all the assembly of Israel determined that every year at that season the days of dedication of the altar should be observed with joy and gladness for eight days, beginning with the twenty-fifth day of the month of Chislev. (1 Macc 4:56, 59)

Apparently because the initial rededication of the temple also involved the replacement of the "lampstand" known as the menorah (1 Macc 4:49), by the time of Jesus, Hanukkah had also come to be known as the "festival of lights," and was a popular annual Jewish celebration (see Josephus, *Antiquities* 12.324–325).[100]

Portrait of the City in the Second Temple Period (538 B. C.E.–70 C.E.) (Philadelphia: Jewish Publication Society, 2002), 226–37.

98. Cf. Josephus, *Antiquities* 15.396–402; 20.221.

99. Cf. Brown, *Gospel according to John*, 1:405.

100. See Daniel K. Falk, "Festivals and Holy Days," in Collins and Harlow, *Eerdmans Dictionary of Early Judaism*, 644–45.

The Question of Jesus's Identity and the Messianic Secret

It is here that the Judeans, in Solomon's portico, during the feast of Hanukkah, ask Jesus a very direct question: "How long will you keep us in suspense? *If you are the Messiah, tell us plainly*" (John 10:24).

Notice here that his audience is asking Jesus about his identity: namely, whether or not he is "the messiah" (*ho christos*)—that is, the "anointed one," the Davidic king (cf. Ps 2:2; 89:51 LXX). Notice also that when the Judeans demand that Jesus answer their question "plainly" or "openly" (*parrēsia*), they clearly imply that, up to this point, he has *not* spoken explicitly about his identity.

This last point is extremely significant, for it provides clear evidence that *even in the Gospel of John, Jesus practices what has come to be known as the "messianic secret"*:

> Some of Jesus' teachings in the Fourth Gospel . . . [include] a form of the Messianic Secret. . . . Although John presents the Messianic Secret differently from Mark, he does have one.[101]

> The synoptic . . . presentation of Messiahship is governed by the theme of the messianic secret. . . . This theme is not absent from John; the Jews ask Jesus to tell them plainly whether he is the Christ (10.24). . . . The fact is that in John the Messiahship of Jesus is both hidden and revealed.[102]

> Neither here [in John] nor in the Synoptics, however, does Jesus answer without qualification a direct question about his messiahship.[103]

Even William Wrede, who authored the influential book entitled *The Messianic Secret* (1901), saw an example of this secret in Jesus's exchange with the Judeans during Hanukkah:

> The idea of the secret Christ—in the broadest sense—is not unknown to John. . . . The general idea seems to be fundamental, that during his earthly life Jesus proclaimed in a mysterious, allusive form the superhuman truth which he brought from heaven. . . . Jesus in some sense keeps his teaching

101. Keener, *Gospel of John*, 1:76, 824.
102. Barrett, *Gospel according to St John*, 71; cf. 378.
103. Brown, *Gospel according to John*, 1:406.

> hidden in John too, or else imparts it in a way which hinders his hearers from grasping it.[104]

Hence, rather than speaking "plainly" or "openly" (John 10:24), Jesus uses enigmatic forms of speech—such as riddles, parables, questions, and allusions—to speak about his identity. It is only when the Judeans demand that Jesus answer the question of his messianic identity plainly that he responds by making some of the most exalted self-claims found anywhere in the Gospels.

Jesus Implies That He Is the Messianic Shepherd King

Jesus responds to the Judeans' inquiry regarding his identity by first pointing them to the "works" he has already performed (John 10:25) and by declaring that the reason they do not believe his works is because they do not belong to his "sheep," to whom he shall give "eternal life" (John 10:26–27). With these words, Jesus implicitly affirms that he is indeed the *messianic shepherd* spoken of in the Prophets.[105]

In order to see this clearly, it is important to recall that in Jewish Scripture, King David himself begins his life as a "shepherd" (1 Sam 16:11; cf. 2 Sam 7:7) and is made "shepherd" and "ruler" of Israel (2 Sam 5:2). Moreover, when the Prophets speak about the future Davidic king, they describe the king as a "shepherd" and the people of Israel as "sheep" (cf. Jer 23:3–5).[106] Perhaps the clearest example of this is from the book of Ezekiel:

> I will set up over them *one shepherd, my servant David*, and *he shall feed them: he shall feed them and be their shepherd*. And I, the LORD, will be their God, and my servant David shall be prince among them; I, the LORD, have spoken. (Ezek 34:23–24)

104. William Wrede, *The Messianic Secret*, trans. J. C. G. Greig (Cambridge: James Clarke, 1971), 182, 201, 205.

105. Beutler, *Gospel of John*, 285; Richard B. Hays, *Echoes of Scripture in the Gospels* (Waco, TX: Baylor University Press, 2016), 294.

106. See Jack R. Lundbom, *Jeremiah 21–36*, Anchor Yale Bible 21B (New Haven: Yale University Press, 2004), 172.

This "single future Davidide" would later be known simply as "the messiah."[107] Hence, when these oracles from Jewish Scripture are taken into account, "the messianic implications of Jesus' claim to be shepherd" functions as an affirmative answer to the question of Jesus's messianic identity.[108] At the same time, Jesus does not give an entirely "unambiguous answer to their question"; he still does not explicitly say "'I am the Messiah.'"[109]

Jesus Declares That He and "the Father" Are "One"

After implying that he is the messianic shepherd of Israel, Jesus makes an even more staggering declaration: "I and the Father are one" (*egō kai ho patēr hen esmen*) (John 10:30).[110] In order to understand this saying in its Jewish context, three key points are necessary.

First, when Jesus refers to "the Father" (John 10:29–30), he is speaking about *the one God of Israel*, the sovereign creator of the world.[111] For example, the Pentateuch describes the creator God as "father" (Deut 32:6), while the Prophets use "father" to identify Israel's divine redeemer (Isa 63:16). In the book of Psalms, King David even addresses God as "my Father" in a strikingly "monotheistic" prayer that emphasizes God's "incomparability" by confessing that it is he who made "the heavens" and "the earth" and who is above all other "heavenly beings" (Ps 89:6, 11, 20, 26).[112]

Second, when Jesus declares that he and the Father are "one" (John 10:30), he is not simply saying that he "does just what God does."[113] He is also certainly *not* saying that "what goes for the Father, goes for me too"(!)—as claimed by the Jesus Seminar's remarkably infelicitous translation.[114] Rather, Jesus is drawing

107. Moshe Greenberg, *Ezekiel 21–37*, Anchor Yale Bible 22A (New Haven: Yale University Press, 1997), 702.

108. Brown, *Gospel according to John*, 1:406.

109. Barrett, *Gospel according to St John*, 378.

110. See Bruce M. Metzger, *A Textual Commentary on the Greek New Testament*, 2nd ed. (Stuttgart: Deutsche Bibelgesellschaft, 1994), 197–98, regarding the textual and grammatical issues with this verse.

111. For a full study, see David R. Tasker, *Ancient Near Eastern Literature and the Hebrew Scriptures about the Fatherhood of God*, Studies in Biblical Literature 69 (New York: Peter Lang, 2004), for a full study.

112. Hossfeld and Zenger, *Psalms 2*, 408.

113. Ernst Haenchen, *John*, trans. Robert W. Funk, 2 vols., Hermeneia (Minneapolis: Fortress, 1984), 2:50.

114. See Funk, Hoover, and the Jesus Seminar, *Five Gospels*, 435.

on the language of *the Shema*, the scriptural confession of faith in the unity of the God of Israel, and the foundation of early Jewish "monotheism":[115]

> Hear, O Israel: *The LORD our God, the LORD is one*. You shall love the LORD your God with all your heart, and with all your soul, and with all your might (Deut 6:4–5).[116]

In a first-century Jewish context, it seems reasonable to suggest that Jesus's declaration of being "one" (*hen*) with God the Father (John 10:30) would indeed call to mind "the basic confession of Judaism that affirmed God's unity."[117] This is especially true if, by the first century, it had already become customary to recite the Shema as a part of Jewish daily prayer.[118] If this is correct, then Jesus is answering the Judeans' question about his identity not only by implying that he is the messiah, but also by *identifying himself with the one God of Israel.*

Third and finally, by both distinguishing himself from the Father ("I and the Father are . . .") and insisting on their unity ("one") (John 10:30), Jesus does not claim to *be* the Father, but he does claim to be divine. On this crucial point, Jewish, Christian, and nonreligious scholars alike agree:

> [Jesus] speaks openly and frankly of his own extrahuman status: "Before Abraham was, I am" (8:58), and, yet more daringly, "I and the Father are one" (10:30).[119]

> Jesus is not claiming to be God the Father here, obviously. . . . But he is saying that he is equal with God. . . . the verb used is the plural *are*, not the singular *am*. Jesus does not say, "I am the Father" or "the Father and I am one." He says, "The Father and I *are* [plural] one."[120]

115. See Moshe Weinfeld, *Deuteronomy 1–11*, Anchor Bible 5 (New York: Doubleday, 1991), 337–38, on the "monotheistic" character of the Shema in the wider context of the Decalogue and Deut 10:17.

116. NRSV, alternate translation.

117. Keener, *Gospel of John*, 1:826.

118. See Kim Huat Tan, "Jesus and the Shema," in *Handbook for the Study of the Historical Jesus*, 4 vols., ed. Tom Holmén and Stanley E. Porter (Leiden: Brill, 2011), 3:2677–707; Armin Lange, "The Shema Israel in Second Temple Judaism," *Journal of Ancient Judaism* 1.2 (2010): 207–14; E. P. Sanders, *Judaism: Practice and Belief, 63 BCE–66 CE* (Minneapolis: Fortress, 2016), 338–39, 387–88.

119. Fredriksen, *Jesus of Nazareth, King of the Jews*, 32–33.

120. Ehrman, *How Jesus Became God*, 125, 312.

> In the pointed statement of John 10.30: "I and the Father are one (ἕν)." One must note that it is not "one person" (εἷς). . . . In the oneness with the Father ([John 10:30]), the "Son" of the Father is himself "God."[121]

> The evangelist does not put forward the view that Jesus is *identical* with God: Jesus and God are *one*, but not *one person* (cf. also 14.28: "The Father is greater than I").[122]

If these scholars are correct, then, in his exchange with the Judeans in the temple during Hanukkah, Jesus is making a divine claim that seeks to maintain both the distinction between himself and God the Father as well as the unity of the one God of the Shema.

Jesus Is Accused of "Blasphemy" for Making Himself "God"

In response to Jesus's momentous declaration, his audience picks up "stones" to stone him to death (John 10:31). When Jesus asks them why, they tell him that it is not because of anything he has done, but because of his divine claim: "because you, though only a human being [*anthrōpos*], are making yourself God [*theon*]" (John 10:33).

The Judeans' response shows that they see Jesus as having committed blasphemy; for the Mosaic penalty for blasphemy is execution by stoning (cf. Lev 24:17).[123] It is also evocative of passages in the Prophets which describe the divine claims of the pagan king of Babylon and the prince of Tyre:

> *You said in your heart,*
> "I will ascend to heaven;
> I will raise my throne
> above the stars of God . . .
> I will ascend to the tops of the clouds,
> *I will make myself like the Most High.*" (Isa 14:13–14)

> Thus says the Lord God:
> Because your heart is proud

121. Frey, *Glory of the Crucified*, 294n35, 302.
122. Lüdemann, *Jesus after Two Thousand Years*, 505 (Frank Schleritt).
123. Beutler, *Commentary on the Gospel of John*, 286.

> and *you have said, "I am a god;*
> I sit in the seat of the gods,
> in the heart of the seas,"
> *yet you are but a human, and no god.* (Ezek 28:1–2)[124]

Curiously, the remarkable parallels between these oracles and the accusation levied against Jesus often go unnoted.[125] Just as the prince of Tyre is a mere "human" who thinks himself a "god" (Ezek 28:1), so too the Judeans set the fact that Jesus is a "human being" (*anthrōpos*) against his speaking as if he is "God" (*theos*) (John 10:33).[126] And just as the gentile king in Isaiah is described as wanting to "make" himself like God (Isa 14:14), so too the Judeans accuse Jesus of "making" (*poeiō*) himself God (John 10:33).[127]

Hence, when both the words of Jesus and the response of the Judeans are interpreted in the light of Jewish Scripture, it seems indisputable that he is indeed claiming to be the one God. In the words of Maurice Casey:

> The classic declaration is "I and the Father are one" (10.30), a declaration so provocative that "the Jews" immediately take up stones to throw at Jesus. At 10.33, they give their reasons—"for blasphemy and because, although you're a man, you make yourself God." This reaction is as important as the sayings.[128]

This is absolutely correct. The reaction of the Judeans clinches the case for a divine self-claim on the lips of Jesus. It is the only way to explain the charge of blasphemy apart from the groundless suggestion the Judeans misunderstand what Jesus is saying.

Jesus Defends Himself Using Jewish Scripture

Finally, Jesus responds to the Judeans' accusation with a scriptural rejoinder. If Jewish Scripture (the "law") refers to mere human beings as "gods," then

124. NRSV, adapted.

125. See Lüdemann, *Jesus after Two Thousand Years*, 506 (Frank Schleritt).

126. Moshe Greenberg, *Ezekiel 21–37*, Anchor Bible 22A (New York: Doubleday, 1997), 573 (the text describes "self-deification").

127. Joseph Blenkinsopp, *Isaiah 1–39*, Anchor Bible 19 (New York: Doubleday, 2000), 288 ("the tyrant even aspires to replace the high god").

128. Casey, *Is John's Gospel True?*, 31.

how can the Judeans say that Jesus is "blaspheming" because he claims to be "God's Son" (John 10:36; cf. Ps 82:6)? He then points once more to "the works" he is doing, this time as evidence that the Father is "in" him and he is "in the Father" (John 10:38). This scriptural rejoinder and his insistence on "mutual indwelling" with the Father do nothing to bring down the temperature,[129] for the Judeans try to arrest him again, but he slips away (John 10:39).

In this response to the charge of blasphemy, Jesus alludes to one of the Psalms, which uses "gods" to refer to beings other than the Creator:

> I say, "*You are gods,*
> *sons of the Most High, all of you*;
> nevertheless, you shall die like mortals,
> and fall like any prince." (Ps 82:6)[130]

In its original context, this passage appears to describe a divine judgment scene in which "the God of Israel" announces "the death of *all* the gods"—that is, the lower "gods" who compose the "divine council" (Ps 82:1).[131] By the Second Temple period, however, its interpretation had expanded to include other beings referred to in Jewish Scripture as "gods" or "sons" of God, such as the angels (cf. Job 1:8), the leaders of Israel (cf. Exod 22:28 LXX), or the people of Israel at mount Sinai (cf. Exod 4:22).[132]

Jesus's response takes this psalm and applies it to the people of Israel—"those to whom the word of God came" (John 10:35)—using it to make an argument from the lesser to the greater. As C. K. Barrett puts it: "If Scripture can describe men by such a word, why should I not use it for myself?"[133] Jesus's appeal to Scripture, however, does not seem to allay his audience's objection that he is making blasphemous divine claims. As Raymond Brown incisively notes: "The Jews are not objecting that Jesus is raising himself to the level of a god in the sense in which the judges [of Israel] were gods; they are objecting that he is making himself God with a capital 'G.'"[134] If this is correct, then, once again, we have an episode in which Jesus is not merely claiming to be divine in the sense of "superhuman"; he is claiming to be divine *in the sense of being equal*

129. Barrett, *Gospel according to St John*, 386.

130. NRSV, adapted.

131. See Hossfeld and Zenger, *Psalms 2*, 334–35.

132. See Beutler, *Commentary on the Gospel of John*, 284; Jerome Neyrey, "I Said 'You Are Gods': Psalm 82,6 and John 10," *Journal of Biblical Literature* 108 (1989): 647–62.

133. Barret, *Gospel according to St John*, 385.

134. Brown, *Gospel according to John*, 409.

with the one God.[135] If this is correct, then the final response of Jesus's audience makes sense: despite his biblical appeal to Psalm 82, they still attempt to arrest him, but he escapes from their hands (John 10:39).

Arguments against Historical Plausibility

With all of this in mind, we can now ask the question: Is it historically plausible that Jesus of Nazareth claimed to be one with God the Father in the Jerusalem temple during the feast of Hanukkah and was almost stoned to death as a result (John 10:22–33)? What are the arguments for and against the historicity of this episode?

As with the accusation of blasphemy during the feast of Tabernacles (John 8:48–59), the vast majority of Jesus research simply ignores the evidence for this exchange between Jesus and the Judeans during Hanukkah.[136] Remarkably, even studies focused on the historical Jesus in the Gospel of John are at one in failing to mention the episode.[137] This is a truly gaping lacuna, which suggests once again that the divine self-claims made by Jesus in the Fourth

135. Cf. Ruben A. Bühner, *Messianic High Christology: New Testament Variants of Second Temple Judaism* (Waco, TX: Baylor University Press, 2021), 10–20.

136. For example, Jesus's claim to be one with the Father (John 10:30) receives no mention or discussion in Hengel and Schwemer, *Jesus and Judaism*; Schröter, *Jesus of Nazareth*; Puig i Tàrrech, *Jesus: A Biography*; Allison, *Constructing Jesus*; Keener, *Historical Jesus of the Gospels*; Vermes, *Authentic Gospel of Jesus*; Dunn, *Jesus Remembered*; Flusser with Notley, *Sage from Galilee*; Becker, *Jesus of Nazareth*; Gnilka, *Jesus of Nazareth*; Sanders, *Historical Figure of Jesus*; John Dominic Crossan, *The Historical Jesus: The Life of a Mediterranean Jewish Peasant* (San Francisco: HarperCollins, 1991); Wright, *Jesus and the Victory of God*; Witherington, *The Christology of Jesus*; Sanders, *Jesus and Judaism*; Ben F. Meyer, *The Aims of Jesus* (London: SCM, 1979); Geza Vermes, *Jesus the Jew: A Historian's Reading of the Gospels* (Philadelphia: Fortress, 1973); Joachim Jeremias, *The Proclamation of Jesus*, trans. John Bowden, New Testament Theology 1 (New York: Charles Scribner's Sons, 1971); Günther Bornkamm, *Jesus of Nazareth*, trans. Irene McLuskey and Fraser McLuskey, with James M. Robinson (New York: Harper, 1960); Joseph Klausner, *Jesus of Nazareth: His Life, Times, and Teaching* (New York: Macmillan, 1926).

137. For example, Jesus's claim to be one with the Father (John 10:30) receives no discussion in Charlesworth, *Jesus as Mirrored in John*; James H. Charlesworth and Jolyon G. R. Pruszinski, eds., *Jesus Research: The Gospel of John in Historical Inquiry*, Jewish and Christian Texts 26 (London: T&T Clark, 2019); Paul N. Anderson, Felix Just, SJ, and Tom Thatcher, eds., *Aspects of Historicity in the Fourth Gospel*, vol. 2 of *John, Jesus, and History* (Atlanta: Society of Biblical Literature, 2009); Anderson, Just, Thatcher, eds., *Glimpses of Jesus through the Johannine Lens*, vol. 3 of *John, Jesus, and History* (Atlanta: Society of Biblical Literature, 2016).

Gospel are still "no-go areas" for historical inquiry. Others simply assert without argumentation that it is unhistorical.[138] Still others explicitly reject it as a "literary fiction" and conclude that there is "no echo here of the authentic voice of Jesus."[139] When actual reasons are given against its historicity, three in particular stand out.

First there is the argument from contextual implausibility within Judaism. Geza Vermes puts this succinctly when he writes: "The blunt assertion of the Jesus of John that 'I and the Father are one' (10:30) is framed as an unequivocal affirmation of equality [with God]. It is very un-Jewish."[140] According to this view, it is inconceivable that a first-century monotheistic Jew like Jesus of Nazareth would ever dare affirm his equality with God by saying anything like "I and the Father are one" (John 10:30). Because the saying cannot be plausibly situated in the context of early Jewish monotheism, it must be unhistorical.

The second major argument against historicity is from a lack of coherence with other evidence about Jesus. According to this view, Jesus's unequivocal assertion of equality with the one God of Israel cannot be reconciled with passages in which he either refuses to speak about his identity or does not do so in an explicit way.[141] As Bart Ehrman puts the point:

> John says things about Jesus found nowhere else . . . only here does Jesus claim to be God (10:30). . . . These are powerful theological statements. But if they were actually said by Jesus, the historian might ask, why do they never occur in sources that were written earlier than John? Nothing like them can be found in Mark, Q, M, or L—let alone Paul or Josephus. As true as these statements about Jesus might be to the believer, it is difficult to think that they represent things he really said to his disciples.[142]

According to this view, it is not just that Jesus claims to be God that makes this episode suspect; it is that he does it so "daringly,"[143] in a way that simply cannot be reconciled with Synoptic evidence for Jesus's practice of the "messianic secret."[144]

138. Lohfink, *Jesus of Nazareth*, 325.

139. Lüdemann, *Jesus after Two Thousand Years*, 506 (Frank Schleritt); Funk, Hoover, and the Jesus Seminar, *Five Gospels*, 435.

140. Geza Vermes, *The Changing Faces of Jesus* (New York: Penguin Putnam, 2000), 51.

141. Casey, *Jesus of Nazareth*, 517.

142. Ehrman, *Jesus: Apocalyptic Prophet*, 88.

143. Fredriksen, *Jesus of Nazareth*, 32–33.

144. Frey, *Theology and History*, 14; cf. also Lohfink, *Jesus of Nazareth*, 325.

The third and final reason given against historicity comes from previous assumptions about Jesus and the practice and the belief of the early church. According to this view, since we know in advance that Jesus was only believed to be divine *after* the disciples' experience of his resurrection, any divine self-claims that take place during his public ministry are, by definition, unhistorical. So Gerd Lüdemann:

> Since Jesus did not understand himself as Son of God but was regarded as such by his adherents only as a consequence of his resurrection visions, [John 10:]34–36 cannot go back to him.[145]

Out of all the arguments given, this assumption that Jesus made no divine self-claims during his lifetime and was only believed to be equal with God in the post-Easter period seems to be one of the main reasons many conclude that the exchange between Jesus and the Judeans during the feast of Hanukkah is substantially unhistorical.

Context: Hanukkah, the Messianic Shepherd, and Early Jewish Monotheism

On the other hand, there are in fact several historical arguments to be made in favor of the historicity of the episode. The first is from several aspects of contextual plausibility within early Judaism.

To begin with, it is completely plausible that an exchange between Jesus and his Judean contemporaries could take place in Solomon's portico during the annual feast of Hanukkah (John 10:22–39). As Josephus tells us, the feast of Dedication was a popular festival in the first century: "[Judas Maccabee and his fellow-citizens] made a law that their descendants should celebrate the restoration of the temple service. *And from that time to the present we observe this festival,* which we call the festival of Lights" (Josephus, *Antiquities* 12.324–325). Moreover, as mentioned above, during the wintertime, "Solomon's portico was an ideal shelter from cold winter blasts."[146] Hence it would be a very plausible setting for Jesus to teach in during the winter season.

Jesus's implicit identification of himself as the shepherd messiah is also

145. Lüdemann, *Jesus after Two Thousand Years*, 506 (Frank Schleritt).

146. Charlesworth, *Jesus as Mirrored in John*, 152. See also Paul N. Anderson, "Aspects of Historicity in the Gospel of John," in Charlesworth, *Jesus and Archaeology*, 603; Brown, *Gospel according to John*, 1:405.

quite plausible. As we saw above, the prophets bear solid witness to the expectation of a future shepherd-king (Jer 23:3–6; Ezek 34:20–24). Early Jewish writings outside the Bible likewise use similar imagery to speak about the advent of the messiah:

> "*Strike the shepherd, and the flock may scatter . . .*" [Zech 13:7] Those who revere him are "*the poor ones of the flock*" [Zech 11:11]. These shall escape in the age of visitation; but those that remain shall be delivered up to the sword *when there comes the messiah of Aaron and Israel.* (Damascus Document[b] [CD[b]] XIX, 8–10)[147]

Insofar as this Dead Sea Scroll connects the deliverance of an eschatological "flock" with the advent of "the messiah" (*mshykh*),[148] it is contextually credible that Jesus would answer the question about whether he is "the Messiah" (*ho christos*) (John 10:24) by describing himself as a shepherd and his followers as "sheep" who will inherit "eternal life" (John 10:27–28).[149]

Most important of all, even the language of Jesus's divine claim is plausible within an early Jewish context. As we saw above, when Jesus declares himself to be "one" with the Father (John 10:30), he is alluding to the biblical confession of the "one" God in the Shema (cf. Deut 6:4–6).[150] As experts have shown, this emphasis on the "oneness" of God was a distinctive feature of early Judaism.[151] Consider, for example, the following descriptions of early Jewish belief in one God:

> [Eleazar] began first of all by demonstrating that *God is one*, that his power is shown in everything, every place being filled with his sovereignty. . . . *all the rest of mankind* ("except ourselves," as he said), *believe that there are many gods.* (Letter of Aristeas 132, 134)[152]

147. Florentino García Martínez and Eibert J. C. Tigchelaar, *The Dead Sea Scrolls Study Edition*, 2 vols. (Grand Rapids: Eerdmans, 2000), 1:577.

148. See Steven D. Fraade, *The Damascus Document*, Oxford Commentaries on the Dead Sea Scrolls (Oxford: Oxford University Press, 2022), 113–16; John J. Collins, *The Scepter and the Star: Messianism in Light of the Dead Sea Scrolls*, 2nd ed. (Grand Rapids: Eerdmans, 2010), 79–91.

149. Cf. C. T. R. Hayward, "'The Lord Is One': Reflections on the Theme of Unity in John's Gospel from a Jewish Perspective," in *Early Jewish and Christian Monotheism*, ed. Loren T. Stuckenbruck and Wendy E. S. North, Journal for the Study of the New Testament Supplement Series 263 (London: T&T Clark, 2004), 151–54.

150. MT *'ekhad*; LXX *heis*.

151. See Larry Hurtado, "Monotheism," in Collins and Harlow, *Eerdmans Dictionary of Early Judaism*, 962–63.

152. Charlesworth, *Old Testament Pseudepigrapha*, 2:21, 22.

> This is the first and most sacred of commandments, to acknowledge and honour one God [*hena . . . theon*] Who is above all, and let the idea that gods are many [*polytheos*] never even reach the ears of the man whose rule of life is to seek for truth. (Philo, *The Decalogue* 65)

> Our lawgiver . . . [placed] all sovereignty and authority in the hands of God. . . . *He represented Him as One* [*hena goun auton*], uncreated and immutable to all eternity. . . . We have but *one temple* for *the one God*. (Josephus, *Against Apion* 2.167, 193)

> The Egyptians worship many animals and monstrous images; *the Jews conceive of one God only* . . . that supreme and eternal being is to them incapable of representation and without end. (Tacitus, *Histories* 5.4)

Although contemporary scholars continue to debate how best to describe this feature of early Judaism, the fact that both Jewish and gentile writers explicitly speak of the Jewish belief in "the only God" (*ton monon theon*) or "the one God" (*henos theou*) and contrast it with gentile beliefs in "many gods" (*pollous theous*) supports the view that the terminology of "monotheism" or "henotheism," properly understood, is completely defensible.[153] For our purposes here, these texts show that when Jesus declares himself to be "one" with "the Father" (John 10:30), he is making a divine claim *in a way that upholds the common Jewish belief in the oneness of God*. As Jörg Frey rightly states:

> The oneness of Jesus and the Father is not the oneness of two gods, but still maintains a form of biblical monotheism . . .[154]

This maintenance of monotheism by Jesus would not, of course, prevent Jesus's Judean contemporaries from charging him with blasphemy. As we have

153. For critiques of the use of *monotheism*, see Peter Schäfer, *Two Gods in Heaven: Jewish Concepts of God in Antiquity* (Princeton: Princeton University Press, 2020), 1–15; R. L. W. Moberly, "How Appropriate is 'Monotheism' as a Category for Biblical Interpretation?," in Stuckenbruck and North, *Early Jewish and Christian Monotheism*, 216–43—neither of which (strangely) mentions any of the text listed above. For arguments in favor of continuing to speak of monotheism, see Kevin P. Sullivan, "Monotheism," in *Encyclopedia of Second Temple Judaism*, 2 vols., ed. Daniel M. Gurtner and Loren T. Stuckenbruck (London: T&T Clark, 2020), 2:513–15; Larry W. Hurtado, "First-Century Jewish Monotheism," in Hurtado, *Ancient Jewish Monotheism*, 115–35, esp. 123.

154. Frey, *Theology and History*, 25.

already seen, it was precisely Antiochus IV Epiphanes's claim to be "equal to God" (*isothea*) that led Second Temple Jews to describe him as a "blasphemer" (*blasphēmos*) (2 Macc 9:8, 12). Nevertheless, although Jesus's claim to be "one" with the Father would certainly be shocking and offensive within an early Jewish context (John 10:30), it would nonetheless be *comprehensible*. It is therefore contextually plausible. Indeed, one could even go so far as to say that if Jesus wanted to make a divine self-claim without undermining early Jewish belief in the unity of God, the most intelligible way for him to do so would be to use the language of the Shema itself to reveal the mystery of his divinity.

Coherence: Jesus's Works, the Shepherd Messiah, and Exalted Self-Claims

The second major argument in favor of historicity is from coherence with other evidence about Jesus in which he points to his works, implies that he is the messianic shepherd, and makes exalted claims about himself.

For example, just as Jesus responds to the Judeans' question about whether he is "the Messiah" by pointing them to his "works" (John 10:24), so too he responds to John the Baptist's question about whether he is "the one who is to come" by pointing John to his miraculous healings of the blind, the lame, the lepers, the deaf, and the dead (Matt 11:4–5; Luke 7:22). In both cases, Jesus does not explicitly answer the question about his identity, but maintains the "messianic secret" by answering the question in an oblique way.

Likewise, Jesus's implicit description of himself as the messianic shepherd whose followers are his "sheep" (John 10:25–28) is quite congruent with the evidence that on the night before he was crucified, he compared himself to the mysterious figure of the "shepherd" who is "struck" and whose "sheep" (i.e., his disciples) are "scattered" (Matt 26:30–32; Mark 14:26–28; cf. Zech 13:7).[155]

Even Jesus's declaration that he and "the Father" are "one" (John 10:30) coheres with other evidence in which Jesus both upholds the *oneness* of God and makes staggering claims about himself.[156] Consider, for example, his re-

155. Regarding the interpretation and historicity of this episode, see Brant Pitre, *Jesus, the Tribulation, and the End of the Exile: Restoration Eschatology and the Origin of the Atonement*, Wissenschaftliche Untersuchungen zum Neuen Testament 2.204 (Tübingen: Mohr Siebeck; Grand Rapids: Baker Academic, 2005), 455–78.

156. Cf. James D. G. Dunn, "Was Jesus a Monotheist? A Contribution to the Discussion

sponse to the rich man and his declaration that "all things" have been handed over to him by the Father:

> There is *only one* who is good. (Matt 19:17)

> No one is good but *the one God.* (Mark 10:18)

> No one is good but *the one God.* (Luke 18:19)[157]

> *All things have been handed over to me by my Father*; and no one knows the Son except the Father. (Matt 11:25)

> *All things have been handed over to me by my Father*; and no one knows who the Son is except the Father. (Luke 10:21)

As we saw in chapter 3, Jesus's declaration that there is only "one" (*heis*) who is good is *not* a denial of his divinity, but a riddle-like *mashal* inviting his questioner to recognize his equality with the "one" (*heis*) God of the Shema (Deut 6:4 LXX). As we saw in chapter 4, when Jesus says that "all things" (*panta*) have been delivered to him by the Father, he means "all creation" (cf. Ps 8:6–8). That is, he is claiming to be "omnipotent."[158] Taken together, these two claims cohere remarkably well with Jesus's declaration that he and the Father, although distinct, are indeed "one" (John 10:30).

Finally, but by no means least significantly, even the more explicit character of Jesus's declaration "I and the Father are one" (John 10:30) coheres well with other evidence in which Jesus speaks more explicitly about his divinity when he is questioned directly.[159] Compare the question put to him in Solomon's portico with the interrogation before the Sanhedrin:

> So the Jews gathered around him and said to him, "How long will you keep us in suspense? *If you are the Messiah, tell us plainly.*" (John 10:24)

---

of Christian Monotheism," in Stuckenbruck and North, *Early Jewish and Christian Monotheism*, 104–19.

157. I've adapted the NRSV here to bring out the echoes of the Shema; cf. Deut 6:4–5 LXX.

158. Theissen and Merz, *Historical Jesus*, 98, 100. Note well that Jesus does not say that "all things" have been handed over to "the Son," but to *him.* So much for the supposed lack of exalted self-claims in the Synoptic Gospels.

159. Brown, *Gospel according to John*, 1:405.

> The high priest said to him, "I put you under oath before the living God, *tell us if you are the Messiah,* the Son of God." (Matt 26:63)

> Again the high priest asked him, "*Are you the Messiah,* the Son of the Blessed One?" (Mark 14:61)

> They brought him to their council. They said, "*If you are the Messiah, tell us.*" (Luke 22:66–67)

We will examine Jesus's response to the Sanhedrin in the final section of this chapter. For now, the basic point is that just as Jesus only declares that he and the Father are "one" when the Judeans' demand that he "tell" them "plainly" who he is (John 10:24), so too Jesus will only explicitly declare his identity when the Jerusalem leaders ask him point blank who he claims to be. Likewise, just as the Judeans react to Jesus's more explicit declaration by accusing of him of "blasphemy" for making himself "God" (John 10:33), so too will Caiaphas and the Sanhedrin charge Jesus with the crime of "blasphemy" and thereby condemn him to death (Matt 26:65; Mark 14:64). In both cases, Jesus only makes a more explicit declaration about his identity in the context of his interlocutors' insistence that he reveal his identity. Hence, far from being incongruent, the account of the exchange in the temple during Hanukkah actually bears witness to Jesus's practice of the messianic secret, even in the Gospel of John.

Consequences: Jesus, God the Father, and Early Binitarian Monotheism

A final major argument in favor of historicity is from the plausibility of effects in the early church. It can be formulated as follows: if Jesus did indeed declare that he and "the Father" were "one" (John 10:30), then this would provide a reasonable point of origin for the early church's practice of *both* distinguishing Jesus from God the Father *and* speaking about Jesus as if he were equal with God. Consider the following passages from the Pauline, Johannine, and Petrine writings of the New Testament:

> Indeed, even though there may be so-called gods in heaven or on earth—as in fact there are many gods and many lords—yet for us there is *one God, the Father*, from whom are all things and for whom we exist, and *one Lord, Jesus Christ*, through whom are all things and through whom we exist. (1 Cor 8:5–6)

> In the beginning was the Word, and the Word was *with God*, and *the Word was God*. He was in the beginning with God. All things came into being through him, and without him not one thing came into being. . . . And the Word became flesh and lived among us, and we have seen his glory, the glory as of *a father's only son*, full of grace and truth. . . . No one has ever seen God. It is *God the only Son*, who is close to *the Father's* heart, who has made him known. (John 1:1–3, 14, 18)

> Simeon Peter, a servant and apostle of Jesus Christ, To those who have received a faith as precious as ours through the righteousness of *our God and Savior Jesus Christ*: May grace and peace be yours in abundance in the knowledge *of God* and *of Jesus our Lord*. (2 Pet 1:1–2)

In all three texts, the person of "Jesus Christ" is clearly distinguished from the person of the one "God" (*theos*), the Father (1 Cor 8:6; John 1:1, 17–18; 2 Pet 1:2). Grammatically speaking, they are different subjects. On the other hand, in all three texts Jesus is also identified as equal with God. For instance, Paul stunningly draws on the language of the Shema itself to identify Jesus as the "one Lord" of Israel, through whom the world was also created (1 Cor 8:6; cf. Deut 6:4).[160] Likewise, the Gospel of John explicitly states that "the Word" who became flesh "was God" (*theos ēn*) and that all creation was made through him (John 1:1–2). In other words, John describes Jesus as "divine"; he possesses "divinity"; he is "equal to [God]"; indeed, "he is God."[161] Finally, as commentators on 2 Peter widely agree, the use of a single article in the expression "our God and Savior Jesus Christ" (*tou theou hēmōn kai sōtēros Iēsou Christou*) identifies Jesus not only as Savior but also as "God" (*theos*) (2 Pet 1:1).[162]

160. See Brant Pitre, Michael P. Barber, and John A. Kincaid, *Paul, a New Covenant Jew: Rethinking Pauline Theology* (Grand Rapids: Eerdmans, 2019), 102–8; E. P. Sanders, *Paul: The Apostle's Life, Letters, and Thought* (Minneapolis: Fortress, 2017), 603; N. T. Wright, *Paul and the Faithfulness of God*, vol. 4 of *Christian Origins and the Question of God* (Minneapolis: Fortress, 2013), 661–70; Joseph A. Fitzmyer, *First Corinthians*, Anchor Yale Bible 32 (New Haven: Yale University Press, 2008), 342–43.

161. Frey, *Theology and History*, 38; Udo Schnelle, "The Person of Jesus Christ in the Gospel of John," in Lieu and Boer, *Oxford Handbook of Johannine Studies*, 312; Johannes Beutler, *Commentary on the Gospel of John*, 37.

162. See Jörg Frey, *The Letter of Jude and the Second Letter of Peter: A Theological Commentary*, trans. Kathleen Ess (Waco, TX: Baylor University Press, 2018), 252–53.

Taken together, this evidence has led some scholars to describe the shape of early Christian Christology as "binitarian,"[163] or as "binitarian monotheism."[164] Jörg Frey defines this expression as follows:

> On the one hand, it excludes the talk of two gods who stand alongside each other, and thus the mode of thinking of a ditheism or polytheism. On the other hand, a simple identification of Jesus with the one God is also exclusive. . . . the Son and the Father remain distinct "persons." . . . At the same time, they are most intimately related to each other through the "oneness" terminology.[165]

From a historical point of view, how do we explain the presence of this form of monotheism in the Pauline, Johannine, and Petrine streams of early Christian writings? As Larry Hurtado points out, "Jewish monotheism by itself is not an adequate explanation" for their view of God.[166] In light of everything we have seen so far, I submit that the best explanation for the origins of binitarian monotheism is that Jesus himself, during his public ministry, spoke as if he were both *distinct* from God the Father and yet in some sense *equal* to the one God of Israel. Indeed, this is precisely what he seems to be doing in Solomon's portico during Hanukkah when he says to the Judeans: "I and the Father are one" (John 10:30).

Weighing the Arguments for and against Historicity

Having completed our overview of the major reasons given for and against the historical veracity of Jesus claiming to be "one" with the Father in the Jerusalem temple and almost getting stoned to death as a result (John 10:22–33), we can now ask the question: Which arguments are stronger?

Once again, the fact that the evidence for this episode is ordinarily dismissed or ignored simply because it is only found in the Gospel of John is hardly a compelling historical argument. Likewise, the claim that the evidence must be a post-Easter creation of the early church because Jesus made no such

163. E.g., Larry Hurtado, "The Binitarian Shape of Early Christian Worship," in Hurtado, *Ancient Jewish Monotheism*, 324; Hurtado, *Lord Jesus Christ: Devotion to Jesus in Earliest Christianity* (Grand Rapids: Eerdmans, 2003), 42–52; Fitzmyer, *First Corinthians*, 343 ("a binitarian pattern of Christianity").

164. See Frey, *Glory of the Crucified*, 335–38.

165. Frey, *Glory of the Crucified*, 336.

166. Hurtado, *Lord Jesus Christ*, 51.

divine claims during his lifetime is another example of begging the very question under consideration. Once these two examples of specious reasoning are taken off the table, all that remains is the assertion that "I and the Father are one" (John 10:30) is too "un-Jewish" to be historical and the argument that the explicit character of Jesus's divine claim cannot be reconciled with the Synoptic evidence for the "messianic secret."[167]

At first glance these two claims seem to be reasonably compelling. They are certainly stronger than many of the other arguments against historicity we have repeatedly encountered in the course of this study. Nevertheless, upon closer inspection they simply do not stand up to critical scrutiny. For one thing, Jesus's declaration regarding his identity is actually remarkably congruent with the Synoptic evidence for the "messianic secret," since the episode begins with the Judeans demanding Jesus no longer keep them in "suspense" but tell them "plainly" whether or not he is "the Messiah" (John 10:24). Far from being in conflict with the messianic secret, Jesus's exchange during Hanukkah confirms it! Indeed, in context, the only reason Jesus gives such an explicit teaching about his identity is because his audience presses him to do so (John 10:25–30)—exactly what happens when he is brought before the Sanhedrin (cf. Matt 26:63; Mark 14:61; Luke 22:66–67). Moreover, far from being too "un-Jewish" to be historical, Jesus's declaration that he is "one" with God "the Father" echoes the language of perhaps the most familiar passage in all of Jewish Scripture: the Shema (Deut 6:4–6). If Jesus the Jew wanted to make a divine claim *without* violating the unity of God confessed in the Shema, then emphasizing his "oneness with the Father" would certainly be an intelligible (albeit provocative) way to do so.[168] Last, but certainly not least, if Jesus did indeed make such a claim in the presence of his Judean contemporaries while teaching in the Jerusalem temple during Hanukkah, it is completely credible that at least some of his audience would respond to such a claim by accusing Jesus of blasphemy and picking up stones in order to carry out the Mosaic law of execution (cf. Lev 24:17).

In short, despite the fact that Jesus's declaration of oneness with the Father and his subsequent brush with being stoned for blasphemy is almost universally ignored or rejected in contemporary Jesus research, I for one can see no compelling historical reasons for concluding that the substance of the episode does not go back to the historical Jesus. Perhaps such arguments exist, but they

167. Vermes, *Changing Faces of Jesus*, 51; Frey, *Theology and History*, 14.

168. Rudolf Schnackenburg, *The Gospel according to St. John*, trans. Kevin Smith, Cecily Hasting, Francis McDonagh, David Smith, Richard Foley, SJ, and G. A. Con, 3 vols. (New York: Herder & Herder/Crossroad, 1968–1982), 2:308.

do not appear in the pages of major contemporary works on the historical Jesus. Although the *style* of the account is certainly stamped with the hand of the author of John's Gospel, the *substance* is contextually plausible, coherent with other evidence about Jesus, and even provides a compelling point of origin for the christological monotheism of the early church.

The Charge of Blasphemy

The final episode in which Jesus is accused of blasphemy in the context of a question about his identity is, of course, the account of his interrogation and condemnation by the high priest Caiaphas and members of the Jerusalem Sanhedrin on the night before his execution:[169]

> Those who had arrested Jesus took him to Caiaphas the high priest, in whose house the scribes and the elders had gathered. *But Peter was following him at a distance, as far as the courtyard of the high priest; and going inside, he sat with the guards in order to see how this would end.* Now the chief priests and the whole council were looking for false testimony against Jesus so that they might put him to death, but they found none, though many false witnesses came forward. At last two came forward and said, "This fellow said, 'I am able to destroy the temple of God and to build it in three days.'" The high priest stood up and said, "Have you no answer? What is it that they testify against you?" But Jesus was silent. Then the high priest said to him, "I put you under oath before the living God, *tell us if you are the Messiah, the Son of God.*" Jesus said to him, "*You have said so. But I tell you,*
> *From now on you will see the Son of Man*
> *seated at the right hand of Power*
> *and coming on the clouds of heaven.*"
> Then the high priest tore his clothes and said, "*He has blasphemed!* Why do we still need witnesses? *You have now heard his blasphemy.* What is your verdict?" They answered, "*He deserves death.*" Then they spat in his face and

169. See Hengel and Schwemer, *Jesus and Judaism*, 628–29; Dunn, *Jesus Remembered*, 630; for problems with the conventional description of Jesus's interrogation as a full-scale "trial," see Raymond E. Brown, *The Death of the Messiah: From Gethsemane to the Grave: A Commentary on the Passion Narratives in the Four Gospels*, Anchor Yale Bible Reference Library (New Haven: Yale University Press, 1994), 1:423–26.

> struck him; and some slapped him, saying, "Prophesy to us, you Messiah! Who is it that struck you?" *Now Peter was sitting outside in the courtyard.* (Matt 26:57–66)

> They took Jesus to the high priest; and all the chief priests, the elders, and the scribes were assembled. *Peter had followed him at a distance, right into the courtyard of the high priest*; and he was sitting with the guards, warming himself at the fire. Now the chief priests and the whole council were looking for testimony against Jesus to put him to death; but they found none. For many gave false testimony against him, and their testimony did not agree. Some stood up and gave false testimony against him, saying, "We heard him say, 'I will destroy this temple that is made with hands, and in three days I will build another, not made with hands.'" But even on this point their testimony did not agree. Then the high priest stood up before them and asked Jesus, "Have you no answer? What is it that they testify against you?" But he was silent and did not answer. Again the high priest asked him, "*Are you the Messiah, the Son of the Blessed One?*" [6]Jesus said, "*I am; and*
>
> *'you will see the Son of Man*
> *seated at the right hand of the Power,'*
> *and 'coming with the clouds of heaven.'"*
>
> Then the high priest tore his clothes and said, "Why do we still need witnesses? *You have heard his blasphemy!* What is your decision?" *All of them condemned him as deserving death.* Some began to spit on him, to blindfold him, and to strike him, saying to him, "Prophesy!" The guards also took him over and beat him. While *Peter was below in the courtyard*, one of the servant-girls of the high priest came by. When she saw Peter warming himself, she stared at him and said, "You also were with Jesus, the man from Nazareth." But he denied it, saying, "I do not know or understand what you are talking about." *And he went out into the forecourt.* (Mark 14:53–64)

The amount of ink that has been spilled over the evidence that Jesus was examined and condemned by the Jerusalem Sanhedrin is virtually incalculable.[170]

170. For full studies with bibliography, see David W. Chapman and Eckhard J. Schnabel, *The Trial and Crucifixion of Jesus: Texts and Commentary*, Wissenschaftliche Untersuchungen zum Neuen Testament 344 (Tübingen: Mohr Siebeck, 2015); Helen K. Bond, *Pontius Pilate in History and Interpretation*, Society for New Testament Studies Monograph Series 100 (Cambridge: Cambridge University Press, 1998); Brown, *Death of the Messiah*, 1:315–562; Paul Winter, *On the Trial of Jesus*, rev. and ed. T. A. Burkill and Geza Vermes, 2nd ed. (Berlin:

For our purposes here, the basic substance of the accounts can be summarized as follows: (1) On the night before his crucifixion, Jesus is brought to the house of the Jewish high priest Caiaphas to be examined by the Jerusalem Sanhedrin, while Simon Peter stays in the courtyard. (2) During the questioning, some testify that Jesus claimed he would destroy the Jerusalem temple and rebuild it in three days, but no charge is made involving the temple. (3) Caiaphas asks Jesus directly whether he is the messiah and Son of God, and Jesus responds affirmatively. (4) In the context of answering the question about his identity, Jesus alludes to the heavenly king in Psalm 110 and the heavenly "son of man" in Daniel 7. (5) In response, Caiaphas tears his garments, accuses Jesus of blasphemy, and invites the Sanhedrin to make a decision. The Jerusalem Sanhedrin condemns Jesus to death for the crime of blasphemy. As with each of the episodes we have analyzed so far, before we can take up questions of historical plausibility, we must first attempt to interpret this data in its first-century context.

Jesus Is Examined by the High Priest Caiaphas and the Jerusalem Sanhedrin

The episode begins with Jesus being brought under arrest to the house of Caiaphas "the high priest" to be examined by him and the Jerusalem "council" (*synedrion*) (Matt 26:57–59; Mark 14:53–55; see also Luke 22:54). Notably, Simon Peter is also described as having followed Jesus and being present in "the courtyard" (*aulē*) of Caiaphas's house during the examination (Matt 26:58, 69; Mark 14:54, 66; cf. Luke 22:55). In order to understand this initial description, a few points of historical background are necessary.

First, the Gospels identify the leading figure in Jesus's examination as Caiaphas, who other sources tell us was appointed by Roman authorities to the office of Jewish high priest.[171] According to Josephus, Caiaphas himself was one of the sons of the high priest Annas and had been appointed around the same time Pontius Pilate became procurator of Judea (see *Antiquities* 18.33–35). On this basis, historians ordinarily date the active high priesthood of Caiaphas to between the years 18 and 36/37 CE.[172] According

Walter de Gruyter, 1974); David Catchpole, *The Trial of Jesus: A Study in the Gospels and Jewish Historiography from 1770 to the Present Day* (Leiden: Brill, 1971).

171. See Adele Reinhartz, *Caiaphas: The High Priest* (Minneapolis: Fortress, 2013).

172. See James C. VanderKam, *From Joseph to Caiaphas: High Priests after the Exile* (Minneapolis: Fortress; Assen: Van Gorcum, 2004), 426–36.

to Josephus, after a remarkably long time in office, Caiaphas was eventually deposed by Vitellius, the Roman governor of Syria, and his brother Jonathan (also the son of Annas) was appointed in Caiaphas's stead (Josephus, *Antiquities* 18.95).

Second, in addition to the high priest, the Gospels also describe Jesus as standing before the "council" or "Sanhedrin" (*synedrion*) (Matt 26:59; Mark 14:55). This expression refers to those Jewish leaders who "together" (*syn*) sit on the "seat" (*hedra*) of judgment.[173] There is evidence that by the first century, there were in fact "five sanhedrins" (*pente synedria*) located in the cities of Jerusalem, Gadara, Amathus, Jericho, and Sepphoris; however, "the Sanhedrin at Jerusalem" was the supreme council (Josephus, *Antiquities* 14.91; *Life* 62). It was composed of the high priest and a group of elders, who worked in concert with the Roman authorities in certain matters of governance, especially the trials and punishments of Jewish offenders.[174] For example, Josephus describes the Sanhedrin's role in the condemnation of one of the sons of Herod Antipater as follows:

> Our Law . . . forbids us to slay a man, even an evildoer, unless he has first been condemned by the Sanhedrin to suffer this fate. (Josephus, *Antiquities* 14.167)

As we will see below, during the Roman period, restrictions seem to have been imposed on the Sanhedrin's ability to punish offenders with death without Roman approval (cf. John 18:31).

Third, the Gospels specify that the location of Jesus's interrogation was the house of Caiaphas. This is clear from the fact that Peter is described as having followed Jesus into the "courtyard" or "palace" (*aulē*) of "the high priest" (Matt 26:58; Mark 14:54; cf. Luke 22:54). Here the Gospels appear to be referring to the palace built by the high priest John Hyrcanus in Jerusalem sometime in the second century BCE, which had long functioned as the official residence of high priests. According to Josephus:

173. See Kenneth D. Litwak, "Sanhedrin," in *T&T Clark Encyclopedia of Second Temple Judaism*, ed. Daniel M. Gurtner and Loren T. Stuckenbruck, 2 vols. (London: T&T Clark, 2020), 706–8; Craig A. Evans, "Sanhedrin," in Collins and Harlow, *Eerdmans Dictionary of Early Judaism*, 1193–94; Sanders, *Judaism: Practice and Belief*, 742–57.

174. Cf. Gnilka, *Jesus of Nazareth*, 293, who notes that according to the Mishnah, only twenty-three members of the seventy-one-member Jerusalem Sanhedrin were required for a valid resolution to be carried out (m. Sanhedrin 4:1).

> One of the priests, Hyrcanus, the first of many by that name, had constructed a large house near the temple and lived there most of the time. . . . His sons and their children also followed the same practice. When Herod became king, he made lavish repairs to this building, which was conveniently situated, and, being a friend of Antony, he called it Antonia. (Josephus, *Antiquities* 18.91–95)

As Josephus says elsewhere, the high priestly palace was located "near the Temple," apparently on the western hill of Jerusalem, in the upper city, near the palaces of Herod Agrippa and Berenice (Josephus, *Antiquities* 18.91; *War* 2.426).[175] Although contemporary archaeologists continue to debate the exact location of Caiaphas's house, for our purposes here, the main point is that it was *not* a small home but a palatial residence, including a courtyard where many people could be gathered.[176] Moreover, the ordinary gathering place for the Jerusalem Sanhedrin was not the high priest's house but the so-called council-chamber (*bouleutērion*) (Josephus, *War* 5.144; 6.354), which appears to have been located where the old city wall joined the western wall of the temple and thus outside the temple proper.[177]

Jesus Is Not Charged with Anything Involving the Jerusalem Temple

Once the participants in and location of Jesus's interrogation are clear, the next thing that needs to be stressed is that while Jesus is accused by some unnamed witnesses of having threatened to "destroy" the Jerusalem temple and "build" it again, *no actual charge is levied against him involving the Jerusalem temple* (Matt 26:61–63; Mark 14:58–59).

In order to grasp the significance of this point, it is important to recall that the Mosaic Torah repeatedly emphasizes that no one can be legally charged with a capital crime apart from the explicit testimony of two or three witnesses: "On the evidence of two or three witnesses the death sentence shall

175. Shimon Gibson, *The Final Days of Jesus: The Archaeological Evidence* (San Francisco: HarperOne, 2009), 81–106 (here 82).

176. See Jürgen K. Zangenberg, "Jerusalem and Judea as a Sphere of Activity," in Schröter and Jacobi, *The Jesus Handbook*, 233–40 (here 238); Helen K. Bond, *Caiaphas: Friend of Rome and Judge of Jesus?* (Louisville: Westminster John Knox, 2004), 154–59; Levine, *Jerusalem*, 326–27. According to Gibson, *Final Days of Jesus*, 82, both Annas and Caiaphas dwelt in the same residence.

177. See Brown, *Death of the Messiah*, 1:348–50.

be executed; a person must not be put to death on the evidence of only one witness" (Deut 17:6; cf. 19:14; Num 35:30). Hence, while some unnamed figures do testify that Jesus threatened to destroy and rebuild the temple, for some reason—either because their testimonies do not agree (Mark 14:59) or because Jesus refuses to answer their claims (Matt 26:62–63)—their claims do not actually lead to any charge. As a result, contrary to what is often asserted, "the key charge brought against Jesus" is *not* "that he had threatened to destroy the Temple."[178] According to the Gospels, Jesus is never actually charged by the high priest or Sanhedrin with any crime involving the Jerusalem temple.

Jesus Answers Caiaphas's Messianic Question in the Affirmative

In the wake of the abortive attempt to bring a charge against Jesus, the high priest Caiaphas intervenes and asks him point blank whether or not he is "the Messiah" (*ho christos*) and "Son" (*huios*) of God (Matt 26:63; Mark 14:61). Jesus responds to Caiaphas's question about his identity—*not* his "authority"[179]—in the affirmative, whether by saying "I am" (Mark 14:62) or "You have said so" (Matt 26:64).[180] In order to properly understand Caiaphas's question and Jesus's response, two key points are necessary.

First, when Caiaphas asks Jesus whether he is "the Messiah" and "Son" of God (Matt 26:63; Mark 14:62), he is asking whether Jesus is the *anointed Davidic king* of ancient Jewish expectation. In Jewish Scripture, both epithets are used to describe the Davidic king and his relationship to the God of Israel:[181]

178. So Dunn, *Jesus Remembered*, 631; Brown, *The Death of the Messiah*, 1:460: "Something done and/or said by Jesus prognostic of the Temple/sanctuary destruction was *at least a partial cause* of the Sanhedrin decision that led to his death" (emphasis added). The reason Brown must add the qualification is because the Gospels say no such thing.

179. Contra Lohfink, *Jesus of Nazareth*, 274.

180. See Brown, *Death of the Messiah*, 1:488–93. Curiously, this is perhaps the one case in which many scholars choose the Matthean version ("You have said so") over the Markan version ("I am") as more original, even though the text-critical evidence for "you have said so" in Mark 14:62 is so weak that it is not even discussed in Bruce M. Metzger, *Textual Commentary*. Cf. Joel Marcus, *Mark*, 2 vols., Anchor Yale Bible 27–27A (New Haven: Yale University Press, 2000, 2009), 2:1105–6.

181. See Shirley Lucass, *The Concept of the Messiah in the Scriptures of Judaism and Christianity*, Library of Second Temple Studies 78 (London: Bloomsbury, 2011), 66–157.

> *Moreover the* L*ORD declares to you [David] that the* L*ORD will make you a house.* When your days are fulfilled and you lie down with your ancestors, I will raise up your offspring after you, who shall come forth from your body, and I will establish his kingdom. He shall build a house for my name, and I will establish the throne of his kingdom forever. *I will be a father to him, and he shall be a son to me.* (2 Sam 7:11–14)

> The kings of the earth set themselves,
> and the rulers take counsel together,
> against the LORD and *his anointed*, saying,
> "I have set *my king* on Zion, my holy hill."
> I will tell of the decree of the Lord:
> He said to me, "*You are my son*;
> *today I have begotten you*." (Ps 2:2, 6–7)

In the first text, the Davidic king is being described as "the son of Yhwh."[182] In a similar vein, the psalm is a kind of "messianic hymn" depicting the birth or enthronement of a Davidic king.[183] Given our interest in Jesus's divine self-claims, it is also worth noting that this and other enthronement psalms seem to depict the Davidic king as a *superhuman* figure. As John Collins puts it: "The king is still subject to the Most High, but he is as an *elohim* [god], *not just a man*" (cf. Ps 45:6; Isa 9:6–7).[184] Hence, in context, Caiaphas's use of the phrase clearly refers primarily to the Davidic messiah of early Jewish expectation, who following Jewish Scripture, can be described as "son of God" (2 Sam 7:14; Ps 2:7).[185]

Second, in both accounts of Jesus's nighttime examination, he responds to Caiaphas's question in the affirmative: either by explicitly stating "I am" (Mark 14:62) or with the more riddle-like affirmation "You have said so" (Matt 26:64). Though some suggest that the latter is a negative response,[186] most scholars agree that it is an affirmation emphasizing that the person asking the question

182. P. Kyle McCarter Jr., *2 Samuel*, Anchor Yale Bible 9 (New Haven: Yale University Press, 1984), 207.

183. See Adela Yarbro Collins and John J. Collins, *King and Messiah as Son of God: Divine, Human, and Angelic Messianic Figures in Biblical and Related Literature* (Grand Rapids: Eerdmans, 2008), 10–15; Lucas, *Concept of the Messiah*, 72–73.

184. Yarbro Collins and Collins, *King and Messiah*, 15 (emphasis added).

185. Allison, *Constructing Jesus*, 287.

186. See Vermes, *Jesus the Jew*, 148–49, citing a latter rabbinic expression in t. Kelim Bava Qamma 1:6. Significantly, the exact meaning of the rabbinic expression is itself doubtful.

has spoken the truth—as in the contemporary English expression "You said it." Compare similar rhetorical affirmatives attributed to Jesus elsewhere:

> The Son of Man goes as it is written of him, but woe to that one by whom the Son of Man is betrayed! It would have been better for that one not to have been born." Judas, who betrayed him, said, "Surely not I, Rabbi?" He replied, "*You have said so.*" (Matt 26:24–25)

> Now Jesus stood before the governor; and the governor asked him, "Are you the King of the Jews?" Jesus said, "*You say so.*" (Matt 27:11)

In light of such parallels, Ulrich Luz rightly concludes: "In both places it is clear that Jesus affirms the content of the question posed to him. In all three texts, however, one can also see a distance between Jesus and the questioners to which Jesus' 'you said it' calls attention."[187] Hence, whatever the exact form of Jesus's response to Caiaphas, the substance is indeed an affirmation, in the presence of the high priest and the Jerusalem Sanhedrin, that Jesus thinks he is the long-awaited Davidic messiah and the Son of God.

Jesus Identifies Himself as the Heavenly Messiah of Psalm 110 and Daniel 7

With that said, Jesus's response to Caiaphas goes *beyond* mere affirmation and also implicitly identifies himself with two figures in Jewish Scripture: the king who sits at the "right hand" of God in heaven (Ps 110:1–2) and the heavenly "son of man" who comes on "the clouds" (Dan 7:14; cf. Matt 26:64; Mark 14:62).[188] In order to feel the full force of these implicit self-designations, it is important to recall two key points.

First, as we saw in chapter 4, the royal figure in Psalm 110 is not merely described as a priest and king. He is also described as the divine son of God, who shares God's own throne in heaven:

187. See Ulrich Luz, *Matthew: A Commentary*, trans. James E. Crouch, 3 vols., Hermeneia (Minneapolis: Fortress, 2001–2007), 3:429. See also Adela Yarbro Collins, *Mark: A Commentary*, Hermeneia (Minneapolis: Fortress, 2007), 704; Brown, *Death of the Messiah*, 1:491: "*Su eipas* is not a negative . . . *Su eipas* is a qualified affirmative: There is truth in what the high priest has said, but he must take responsibility for the way he interprets it and the use he plans to make of it."

188. Sven-Olav Black, "The Trials of Jesus," in Schröter and Jacobi, *The Jesus Handbook*, 474–81 (here 477); Allison, *Constructing Jesus*, 230; Dunn, *Jesus Remembered*, 749–50.

> *The* Lord *says to my Lord,*
> *"Sit at my right hand,*
> until I make your enemies your footstool."
> The Lord sends out from Zion
> your mighty scepter.
> "Rule in the midst of your foes.
> Yours is princely power in the day of your birth, in holy splendor;
> *From the womb of the dawn*, like the dew, *I have begotten you*."
> (Ps 110:1–14)[189]

As commentators point out, the image of the king sitting at the "right hand" of God implies that he is (somehow) equal with "the Lord" (YHWH), and the imagery of his being "begotten" before the dawn of creation implies his divine status:

> "I have borne/begotten you" [Ps 110:3] . . . proclaims the enthronement as divine begetting or birth from the dawn.[190]

> A seated position at the right hand of a deity implies co-regency with him. . . . The imagery of the quoted portion of the psalm, then, implies that "my lord" stands in a position of near-equality with God.[191]

If this is correct, then Jesus answers Caiaphas's question about his identity by "appropriat[ing] for himself" one of the clearest descriptions of a heavenly king anywhere in Jewish Scripture.[192] Hence, by quoting Psalm 110, Jesus implies that he is not merely the human descendent of David; he is also the super-Davidic son of God who sits at God's right hand as God's equal.

Second, as we also discussed earlier, the heavenly figure in Daniel 7 is not just the fifth king in a series of kings, the one who would rule over the kingdom of God.[193] He is also described as a *heavenly being* who acts *like God himself* by riding on the "clouds" of heaven and receiving human worship:

189. NRSV, adapted.

190. Frank Lothar Hossfeld and Eric Zenger, *Psalms 3*, trans. Linda M. Maloney, Hermeneia (Minneapolis: Fortress, 2011), 142.

191. Marcus, *Mark*, 2:850–51.

192. Allison, *Constructing Jesus*, 230.

193. See Pitre, *Jesus, the Tribulation*, 53–55. See also John J. Collins, *Daniel: A Commentary*, Hermeneia (Minneapolis: Fortress, 1993), 294–313, for a full discussion of the sequence of kings and kingdoms.

> *I saw one like a son of man*
> *coming with the clouds of heaven.*
> And he came to the Ancient of Days
> and was presented before him.
> *To him was given dominion*
> *and glory and kingdom,*
> that all peoples, nations, and languages
> should *serve him*. (Dan 7:13–14)[194]

Notice here that in Jewish Scripture, coming with the "clouds" is something done by "the Deity" (cf. Exod 19:9; 34:5; Num 11:25; Isa 19:1; Ps 104:3).[195] Indeed, the act of "riding clouds" is "beyond human ability."[196] Notice also the expression "one *like* a son of man" (Dan 7:13), implies that the figure *appears* to be merely "human," but is in fact "a heavenly being" (Dan 7:13; cf. 8:15; 10:5, 16, 18; 12:6–7).[197] Finally, though the point is sometimes overlooked, after the Danielic "son of man" is presented to "the Ancient of Days" (Dan 7:13), all peoples are said to "serve"[198] him (Dan 7:14). Significantly, the same verb is used elsewhere to describe how Daniel and his Jewish companions refused to "serve"[199] any *god* except their own "God" (Dan 3:28 MT; Dan 3:95 LXX). In other words, the heavenly son of man receives the cultic "service" or "worship" elsewhere offered only to a deity (cf. Dan 3:12, 14, 18). In light of such observations, it is reasonable to conclude that the son of man in the book of Daniel is a "divine being."[200] In the words of Daniel Boyarin:

> What this text [Daniel 7] projects is a second divine figure to whom will be given eternal dominion of the entire world. . . . In other words, a simile, *a God who looks like a human being* (literally Son of Man) has become the name for that God, who is now called "Son of Man," a reference to his human-appearing divinity.[201]

194. NRSV, adapted.
195. Collins, *Daniel*, 311.
196. Allison, *Constructing Jesus*, 296.
197. Theissen and Merz, *Historical Jesus*, 553.
198. MT *pelakh*; LXX *latreuō*.
199. MT *pelakh*; LXX *latreuō*.
200. Markus Zehnder, "Why the Danielic 'Son of Man' Is a Divine Being," *Bulletin of Biblical Research* 24.3 (2014): 331–47.
201. Daniel Boyarin, *The Jewish Gospels: The Story of the Jewish Christ* (New York: New Press, 2012), 32–33 (emphasis added).

In short, in his answer to Caiaphas, Jesus is not just affirming that he is the messiah; he is also claiming to be *the divine son of God*, a "celestial figure" who will sit at God's right hand (Ps 110:1–3) and the heavenly son of man, who will one day receive the kind of "worship" due to God alone (Dan 7:13–14).[202]

Jesus Is Condemned to Death for Blasphemy against God

Should there be any doubt that Jesus is claiming to be a divine messiah, we need only turn to the reaction of Caiaphas and the Sanhedrin for confirmation. For one thing, Caiaphas responds to Jesus's declaration by tearing his garments and explicitly accusing Jesus of "blasphemy" (*blasphēmia*) (Matt 26:65; Mark 14:63–64). Moreover, when Caiaphas asks the rest of the Sanhedrin for their decision, they too condemn Jesus as deserving "death" (Matt 26:65–66; Mark 14:64).

In order to understand this response, it is important to recall that a person could be accused of the crime of blasphemy for either illicitly pronouncing the divine name (cf. Lev 24:17; Philo, *Life of Moses* 2.206; Josephus, *Antiquities* 4.202) or for offending God by making divine self-claims (cf. 2 Macc 9:12, 28; Philo, *Embassy to Gaius* 45.367; *On Dreams* 2.130–132).[203] Since there is no evidence that Jesus pronounces the divine name during his examination,[204] some suggest that, "technically, Jesus does not blaspheme" and that the Sanhedrin is being depicted as falsely accusing Jesus with a "trumped up" verdict.[205] Others suggest that Jesus is regarded as having insulted the high priest Caiaphas (rather than God) (cf. Exod 22:27).[206] Both proposals fail to take seriously

202. Puig i Tàrrech, *Jesus: A Biography*, 514.

203. See Yarbro Collins, "Blasphemy," 445; Craig A. Evans, *Jesus and His Contemporaries: Comparative Studies* (Leiden: Brill, 2001), 407–34.

204. Brown, *Death of the Messiah*, 1:522–23.

205. See Aaron M. Gale, "Matthew," in Levine and Brettler, *Jewish Annotated New Testament*, 61; Lawrence M. Wills, "The Gospel of Mark," in Levine and Brettler, *Jewish Annotated New Testament*, 102. In support of his view, Gale cites the later mishnaic law that "the blasphemer is not culpable unless he pronounces the Name itself" (m. Sanhedrin 7:5). However, this view does not take into account the evidence from the Second Temple (cited above) that a person could also be accused of blasphemy for making divine claims. For the later law, see Herbert Danby, *The Mishnah* (Oxford: Oxford University Press, 1933), 392.

206. For a summary of this position, see Darrell L. Bock, "Blasphemy and the Jewish Examination of Jesus," in *Key Events in the Life of the Historical Jesus*, ed. Darrell L. Bock and Robert L. Webb, Wissenschaftliche Untersuchungen zum Neuen Testament 247 (Tübingen:

the divine implications of Jesus's allusions to Psalm 110 and Daniel 7, as well as Caiaphas's act of tearing his garments. According to Jewish Scripture, the tearing of one's garments is not just a sign of grief (Gen 37:29–35; 2 Sam 11:1–11; 2 Kgs 6:30); it is also a way of expressing horror at blasphemy against God. Consider the following passages:

> Thus says the king of Assyria: . . . "Do not listen to Hezekiah when he misleads you by saying, 'The Lord will deliver us. . . . *Who among all the gods of the countries have delivered their countries out of my hand, that the Lord should deliver Jerusalem out of my hand?*'" . . . Then Eliakim son of Hilkiah, who was in charge of the palace, and Shebna the secretary, and Joah son of Asaph, the recorder, came to Hezekiah *with their clothes torn* and told him the words of the Rabshakeh. When King Hezekiah heard it, *he tore his clothes*. (2 Kgs 18:31–32, 35; 19:1)

> When the king of Israel read the letter, *he tore his clothes* and said, "*Am I God*, to give death or life, that this man sends word to me to cure a man of his leprosy?" (2 Kgs 5:7)

In both instances, the tearing of the garments signifies that a human being committed blasphemy "against YHWH," either by claiming to be more powerful than "the Lord" (like the king of Assyria) or by attributing an exclusively divine power to a mere human being (like the king of Aram).[207] In a similar way, the fact that Caiaphas tears his garments demonstrates that "blasphemy against God"—rather than himself—"is the issue."[208] This is especially true when we recall that Caiaphas is high priest. As E. P. Sanders points out: "For the high priest to tear his clothing was the most extreme sign of mourning, since the Bible forbids him to tear his garments, or even to dishevel his hair (Lev 21.10). Caiaphas' transgression of the law showed horror."[209] Such horror is easily explained if Jesus is claiming to be a heavenly messiah who is somehow equal with God.

Mohr Siebeck, 2009), 622–25. It is worth noting that when one Eleazar insulted the high priest John Hyrcanus, he was punished by a whipping, not by death (Josephus, *Antiquities* 13.293–296).

207. See Mordechai Cogan and Hayim Tadmor, *II Kings*, Anchor Yale Bible 11 (New Haven: Yale University Press, 1988), 233.

208. Luz, *Matthew*, 3:431.

209. Sanders, *Historical Figure of Jesus*, 271.

Jesus Is Making a Divine Claim

In short, according to the Gospels, the principal reason Jesus is rejected and handed over for execution by the Jerusalem Sanhedrin is not because of what he says about the temple, but because of *what he claims about himself*. On this point, Jewish, Christian, and nonreligious scholars alike agree:

> In the mouths of Jesus' opponents, blasphemy is a charge leveled against Jesus for claiming to be God.[210]

> Jesus is accused of blasphemy not because he spoke against God or for having pronounced his name but for having made himself equal to him. . . . Jesus is a "blasphemer" because he claims prerogatives that are divine. . . . This is the conclusion reached by the majority of the leaders . . . , and this becomes the reason for having Jesus killed.[211]

> The one like a man who sits upon the throne of God's glory, the sublime eschatological judge, is the highest conception of the Redeemer ever developed by ancient Judaism . . . a human being who is divine.[212]

> The high priest understands Jesus' claim as Mark wants him to: Jesus is not simply the Messiah—this would have been an indifferent matter in Judaism—he is rather the supernatural son of God and in fact like God.[213]

> Jesus is being accused of arrogantly claiming for himself what belongs to God and thus insulting God. . . . the blasphemy they have heard is . . . Jesus' clear "I am" to being the Messiah, the Son of the Blessed, and his self-identification as the exalted Son of Man sitting at the right hand of Power and coming on the clouds to judge—the christological claims.[214]

In other words, according to the evidence in the Gospels, *Jesus is accused of blasphemy by the Jerusalem Sanhedrin in the context of a question about his identity*. That is the reason Jesus is rejected by Caiaphas and the Jerusalem

210. J. R. Daniel Kirk, *A Man Attested by God: The Human Jesus of the Synoptic Gospels* (Grand Rapids: Eerdmans, 2016), 330.

211. Puig i Tàrrech, *Jesus: A Biography*, 516–17.

212. Flusser with Notley, *Sage from Galilee*, 115–16.

213. Lüdemann, *Jesus after Two Thousand Years*, 102.

214. Brown, *Death of the Messiah*, 1:523.

leaders, and that is the reason he is handed over to Pontius Pilate to be executed. No other reason is given, and no other charge is recorded. Jesus was rejected and executed for making claims about himself that were viewed as blasphemy against the one God of Israel.[215]

With all of this in mind, we can now ask the historical question: What are the principal arguments for and against the historical plausibility of Jesus being condemned to death for blasphemy during an interrogation by the high priest Caiaphas and the Jerusalem Sanhedrin on the night before he was crucified by Pontius Pilate?

Arguments against Historical Plausibility

When we turn from the exegesis of this episode to the question of its historicity, we discover that many major works on the historical Jesus conclude that the evidence in question is substantially unhistorical.[216] Indeed, the view that the accounts have "no historical value"[217] is so widespread that one full-length study of the origins of belief in Jesus's divinity does not even *mention* the evidence that Jesus was condemned to death for blasphemy![218] One would think such a datum would merit some discussion. In any case, most of the arguments against historicity are from contextual implausibility within Judaism. Four in particular stand out.

The first major argument against historicity is from the apparent lack of eyewitnesses to the exchange between Jesus, Caiaphas, and the Sanhedrin. According to this view, even if the high priest and the Jerusalem Sanhedrin

215. See also Bühner, *Messianic High Christology*, 65–75.

216. See Schröter, *Jesus of Nazareth*, 174 (accounts "almost certainly" reflect "a later view"); Bond, *Historical Jesus*, 157 (reflects "Jewish allegations against Christians in the late first century rather than something from the lifetime of Jesus"); Lüdemann, *Jesus after Two Thousand Years*, 101 (examination "cannot be regarded as an historical account"); Flusser, *Sage from Galilee*, 138–39 ("Jesus' condemnation to death by the Jewish supreme court" is "a product of Mark's literary creativity"); Fredriksen, *Jesus of Nazareth*, 221 (the gospel account "beggars belief"); Becker, *Jesus of Nazareth*, 348 (the scene has "no historical value"); Theissen and Merz, *Historical Jesus*, 464 (the trial presupposes the "post-Easter confession of Jesus"); Funk, Hoover, and the Jesus Seminar, *Five Gospels*, 121 ("the account of the Judean trial was mostly a fabrication of the Christian imagination"); Vermes, *Jesus the Jew*, 3 ("historically more than dubious"); Bornkamm, *Jesus of Nazareth*, 163–64 ("the story arouses critical doubts"). The fullest case against historicity remains P. Winter, *On the Trial*, 27–130.

217. Becker, *Jesus of Nazareth*, 348.

218. See Ehrman, *How Jesus Became God*.

did question Jesus on the night before he was executed, there is no way of knowing what Jesus was asked or how he responded since no followers of Jesus were present:

> Unfortunately, we have no reliable way of knowing what happened when Jesus appeared before Caiaphas. In part we are hampered by our sources: according to the accounts themselves, the only persons present were Jesus, who was to be executed the next morning, and the Jewish rulers. Where, then, did our sources get their information? There wasn't a court stenographer whose records could be consulted.[219]

For many scholars, this single argument from a lack of eyewitnesses is sufficient to demonstrate that the entire account must be a fabrication of the early church.[220] As the members of the Jesus Seminar assert: "Even if Jesus was tried by Judean authorities, his followers were certainly not present. Statements made in the absence of those providing testimony are not historically verifiable."[221]

The second prominent argument against historicity is from the timing of Jesus's interrogation. According to this view, it is highly implausible—if not impossible—that the Jewish high priest and the Jerusalem Sanhedrin would gather during the feast of Passover to examine someone charged with a capital crime. For later rabbinic law in the Mishnah clearly states that trials were not permitted on or immediately before a feast day:

> Trials may not be held on the eve of a Sabbath or on the eve of a Festival-day. (m. Sanhedrin 4:1)[222]

> None may sit in judgement . . . on a Festival day. (m. Betzah 5:2)[223]

For many, the argument from the implausibility of Jesus being interrogated by the Sanhedrin during the feast of Passover appears to be the principal reason they conclude that "the historicity of this Sanhedrin trial" is "highly questionable,"[224]

219. Ehrman, *Jesus: Apocalyptic Prophet*, 220.
220. See Casey, *Jesus of Nazareth*, 441; Sanders, *Jesus and Judaism*, 298.
221. Funk, Hoover, and the Jesus Seminar, *Five Gospels*, 122.
222. Danby, *Mishnah*, 387.
223. Danby, *Mishnah*, 187.
224. Gale, "Gospel according to Matthew," 61.

if not entirely unhistorical.[225] Bart Ehrman sums up this position well when he writes: "As scholars have long noted, the trial appears to be illegal on a large number of counts, when judged by the later descriptions in the Mishnah of how the Sanhedrin was to function. There could not be trials at night, for example, or on a festival; and a capital offense required two separate hearings."[226] In other words, if later rabbinic law forbidding trials on feast days was in force at the time of Jesus and followed by the Jerusalem Sanhedrin, then it is "hard to imagine" anything like what the Gospels describe taking place, and the historicity of the entire account is called into question.[227]

The third major argument against historicity is from the implausibility of both the charge of blasphemy and the manner of Jesus's execution. According to this view, it is not credible that Jesus would be accused of blasphemy simply for affirming that he was the messiah. For in a first-century Jewish context, *it was not blasphemy to claim to be the messiah.* As Paula Fredriksen puts it:

> Reflected on critically and historically, Mark's presentation [of Jesus's examination by the Sanhedrin] grows increasingly unlikely. Take the climax of the Jewish hearing. Even if the high priest had reason to ask Jesus if he were the messiah . . . , and even if Jesus (for some reason) had said "Yes," the claim itself would not count as blasphemy. We have ample record in Josephus of other messianic figures in the period leading up to and including the revolt; later, we have the example of Bar Kokba. History had falsified these men's claims, but nowhere are the claims themselves seen as blasphemous.[228]

Since it was not blasphemy to claim to be the messiah in a first-century Jewish context, some conclude that the gospel accounts of Jesus's condemnation are highly unlikely.[229] This seems especially true given the fact that Jewish Scripture specifies stoning as the punishment for blasphemy (Lev 24:16), but there is no evidence that Jesus was stoned. In this view, "Jesus was not stoned; and so blasphemy was not the charge."[230]

225. See Vermes, *Authentic Gospel of Jesus*, 193; Becker, *Jesus of Nazareth*, 347; Sanders, *Jesus and Judaism*, 298; Bultmann, *History of the Synoptic Tradition*, 270.

226. Ehrman, *Jesus: Apocalyptic Prophet*, 221.

227. Fredriksen, *Jesus of Nazareth*, 223; Ehrman, *Jesus of Nazareth: Apocalyptic Prophet*, 221.

228. Fredriksen, *Jesus of Nazareth*, 222–23.

229. E.g., Sanders, *Jesus and Judaism*, 298.

230. Brown, *Death of the Messiah*, 1:532, summarizing this common objection to historicity.

Other arguments against historicity could be marshaled, but these four seem to be the primary reasons given by those who conclude that the evidence for Jesus's interrogation and condemnation by the Jerusalem Sanhedrin is an unhistorical creation of the early church. Gerd Lüdemann even goes so far as to say that "the historical value of the pericope is nil."[231] Indeed, if a trial during Passover was impossible, the claims attributed to Jesus are not actually blasphemous, and there were no eyewitnesses to report what happened anyway, then it seems reasonable to conclude that the accounts of Jesus before the Sanhedrin are largely fictional.

Context: The Presence of Eyewitnesses, Festival Executions, and Death for Blasphemy

Despite widespread doubts about Jesus being condemned to death for blasphemy, a significant number of scholars do in fact argue for the historicity of Jesus's interrogation and condemnation by Caiaphas and the Sanhedrin.[232] The first major argument in favor of historicity is from contextual plausibility within Judaism, on several fronts.

First and foremost: contrary to what is often claimed, there is in fact positive evidence for the presence of eyewitnesses to Jesus's exchange with Caiaphas and the Sanhedrin. Indeed, even a cursory reading of the gospel accounts shows that at least one disciple of Jesus—Simon Peter—is actually said to have been present *inside* the house of Caiaphas while Jesus is being questioned.[233] Since the point is so often overlooked or underemphasized, I will quote the evidence here:

> Those who had arrested Jesus took him to Caiaphas the high priest, *in whose house* the scribes and the elders had gathered. *But Peter was following him*

231. Lüdemann, *Jesus after Two Thousand Years*, 102.

232. See Eckhard J. Schnabel, *Jesus in Jerusalem: The Last Days* (Grand Rapids: Eerdmans, 2018), 242–65; Hengel and Schwemer, *Jesus and Judaism*, 625–34; Lohfink, *Jesus of Nazareth*, 272–74; Puig i Tàrrech, *Jesus: A Biography*, 500–514; Bock, "Blasphemy and the Jewish Examination," 589–667; Casey, *Jesus of Nazareth*, 440–45; Keener, *Historical Jesus of the Gospels*, 313–17; Dunn, *Jesus Remembered*, 628–34; Vermes, *Gospel of Jesus*, 192–93; Harvey, *Jesus and the Constraints of History*, 32, 136, 170–73. Although dated, Josef Blinzler, *The Trial of Jesus*, trans. Isabel McHugh and Florence McHugh (Westminster, MD: Newman, 1959), remains an erudite study.

233. See Brown, *Death of the Messiah*, 1:593–95.

> *at a distance, as far as the courtyard of the high priest*; and *going inside*, he sat with the guards in order to see how this would end. (Matt 26:57–58)

> They took Jesus to the high priest; and all the chief priests, the elders, and the scribes were assembled. *Peter had followed him at a distance, right into the courtyard of the high priest*; and he was sitting with the guards, warming himself at the fire. (Mark 14:53–54)

> Then they seized him and led him away, bringing him into the high priest's house. But Peter was following at a distance. *When they had kindled a fire in the middle of the courtyard and sat down together, Peter sat among them. . . .* The Lord turned *and looked at Peter*. (Luke 22:54–55, 61)

Notice here that Peter not only follows Jesus into the "courtyard" of Caiaphas's house; he is also clearly described as being in close proximity to Jesus. Peter sits among the "guards" to "see" the proceedings (Matt 26:58), and is even in visual proximity to Jesus himself (Luke 22:61).[234] As Ulrich Luz points out, Peter is "as close as possible to the event in the Sanhedrin," so that he can indeed be described as "an eyewitness."[235] In light of such evidence, other scholars contend that the common assertion that there are no eyewitnesses to the examination of Jesus is simply false. In the words of James Dunn and Joseph Klausner:

> The oft repeated comment that there were no later Christian witnesses present is rather facile.[236]

> But who was present during the trial and heard what the witnesses said, the challenge of the High Priest and Jesus' answer? According to all three Synoptists it was Simon Peter . . . who came into the court of the High Priest together with the guards and sat with the attendants, warming himself by the fire.[237]

I agree, though I would add that the Gospel of John also testifies to the presence of an unnamed disciple who reportedly gained Peter access to the high-priestly courtyard (John 18:15–16). Moreover, it is at least possible (though

234. Fitzmyer, *Gospel according to Luke*, 2:1465 (Jesus is "somewhere in the courtyard").
235. Luz, *Matthew*, 3:424.
236. Dunn, *Jesus Remembered*, 631n88.
237. Klausner, *Jesus of Nazareth*, 344.

not demonstrable), that other members of the Jerusalem Sanhedrin—such as Joseph of Arimathea or Nicodemus, who are reportedly sympathizers of Jesus (cf. Mark 14:43; John 19:39)—may also have been present.[238] That the presence of such eyewitnesses is historically plausible finds support in the fact that Josephus tells us that he once received reliable information from an eyewitness who was present at a secret session of the Jerusalem Sanhedrin in which the high priest Annas decided to have Josephus put to death.[239] Consider the following account:

> On hearing this speech of Annas, Simon implored the embassy to keep to themselves and not divulge what had passed at the conference. . . . [Finally,] as the result of bribery, Annas and his party agreed to expel me from Galilee. . . . They had orders, in the event of my volunteering to lay down my arms to send me alive to Jerusalem, but if I offered any resistance to kill me. . . . My information reached me in a letter from my father, *to whom the news was confided by Jesus, son of Gamalas, an intimate friend of mine, who had been present at the council.* (Josephus, *Life* 195, 196, 202, 204)[240]

The parallels between the two gatherings of the Sanhedrin regarding Jesus and Josephus are striking: both are led by the Jewish high priest and Jerusalem Sanhedrin; both are rushed because of expediency; both verdicts are done in secret so as to avoid resistance and possible turmoil; both involve the testimony of multiple witnesses; and both end in a sentence of death. Now, if Josephus could discover what took place during a secret meeting of the high priest and the Sanhedrin at which he was *not* present, then it is even more plausible that the early followers of Jesus could discover what took place during a meeting of Caiaphas and the Sanhedrin at which Simon Peter *was* present. As Sven-Olav Back has argued, "If Jesus was indeed sentenced for blasphemy, Caiaphas and the other members of the Sanhedrin would not have had any reason to conceal the matter. On the contrary, it would have been in their interest to inform the public about what had taken place during the trial."[241]

Second, as I have argued elsewhere in much greater detail, the timing of Jesus's condemnation by the Jerusalem Sanhedrin during the feast of Pass-

238. See Hengel and Schwemer, *Jesus and Judaism*, 633; Casey, *Jesus of Nazareth*, 442.
239. See Keener, *Historical Jesus of the Gospels*, 316.
240. Loeb Classical Library translation adapted.
241. Back, "The Trials of Jesus," 478.

over is also quite plausible within an ancient Jewish context.[242] For one thing, though later rabbinic literature does forbid local trials by *local* sanhedrins to be carried out on Jewish feast days (m. Betzah 5:2), the same rabbinic law actually *requires* criminals charged with capital crimes to be brought to the *Jerusalem* Sanhedrin and executed during the annual Jewish festivals.[243] Consider the following (widely ignored) passage from the Tosefta:

> A rebellious and incorrigible son, a defiant elder, *one who leads people astray to worship idols*, one who leads a town to apostasy, *a false prophet*, and perjured witnesses—they do not kill them immediately. *But they bring them up to the court in Jerusalem and keep them until the festival*, and *then they put them to death on the festival*, as it is said, "And all the peoples shall hear and fear, and no more do presumptuously" (Deut 17:13). The words of Rabbi 'Aquiba. (t. Sanhedrin 11:7)[244]

My point in citing this text is not to insist that these later rabbinic laws were being observed by the Jerusalem Sanhedrin in the first century. I doubt that they were—especially if the Sanhedrin was led by Sadducees at the time of Jesus's crucifixion.[245] The point is rather to show that those who cite rabbinic law from centuries after Jesus as decisive proof that Jesus was not tried and executed during Passover by the Jerusalem Sanhedrin are ignoring a devastating piece of counter-evidence.[246] This failure is especially egregious when we realize that the same rabbinic treatise allows for the ordinary rules of a trial to be set aside in certain especially grave cases (t. Sanhedrin 10:11).[247] The appeal to later rabbinic law is even more problematic when we realize that we have first-century evidence for the arrest and condemnation of other Jewish figures *during Jewish festivals*. Indeed, Josephus himself tells us that another first-century Jew named Jesus (the son of Ananias) was arrested by the Jerusalem

242. For a full-length case for the crucifixion of Jesus during the feast of Passover, see Brant Pitre, *Jesus and the Last Supper* (Grand Rapids: Eerdmans, 2015), 251–373.

243. Pitre, *Jesus and the Last Supper*, 300–304.

244. Jacob Neusner, *The Tosefta*, 2 vols. (Peabody, MA: Hendrickson, 2002), 2:1183.

245. See Brown, *Death of the Messiah*, 1:350–57, 361, 421: "There is little or no solid evidence that mishnaic rules governed Sanhedrin proceedings in this period." Cf. Josephus, *War* 2.7.10; *Antiquities* 20.91, who identifies the high priests Ananias and Ananus II as Sadducees.

246. See Hengel and Schwemer, *Jesus and Judaism*, 626–27; Lohfink, *Jesus of Nazareth*, 272–73; Keener, *Historical Jesus of the Gospels*, 314; Blinzler, *Trial of Jesus*, 86–89, 117–21; Klausner, *Jesus of Nazareth*, 337.

247. Cf. Theissen and Merz, *Historical Jesus*, 463.

leaders during an annual Jewish festival and then handed over to the Roman Procurator to be scourged:

> Four years before the war, when the city was enjoying profound peace and prosperity, *there came to the feast at which it is the custom of all Jews to erect tabernacles to God, one Jesus, son of Ananias, a rude peasant, who, standing in the temple, suddenly began to cry out,* "A voice from the east, a voice from the west, a voice from the four winds; a voice against Jerusalem and the sanctuary, a voice against the bridegroom and the bride, a voice against all the people." Day and night he went about all the alleys with this cry on his lips. *Some of the leading citizens, incensed at these ill-omened words, arrested the fellow and severely chastised him.* But he, without a word on his own behalf or for the private ear of those who smote him, only continued his cries as before. *Thereupon, the magistrates, supposing, as was indeed the case, that the man was under some supernatural impulse, brought him before the Roman governor; there, although flayed to the bone with scourges,* he neither sued for mercy nor shed a tear, but, merely introducing the most mournful of variations into his ejaculation, responded to each stroke with "Woe to Jerusalem!" When Albinus, the governor, asked him who and whence he was and why he uttered these cries, he answered him never a word, but unceasingly reiterated his dirge over the city, until Albinus pronounced him a maniac and let him go. . . . *His cries were loudest at the festivals.* (Josephus, *War* 6.300–307)

The parallels between Jesus of Nazareth and Jesus the son of Ananias are remarkable: both are arrested by the Jewish leaders in Jerusalem during an annual festival; both are interrogated "first by the Jewish authorities, and then by the Romans";[248] and both are punished with Roman scourging. The key difference, of course, is that Jesus the son of Ananias merely speaks against the temple and is not condemned to death,[249] whereas Jesus of Nazareth is charged with "blasphemy" and handed over for execution (cf. Lev 24:17). In light of a closer study of the evidence from Josephus, E. P. Sanders ultimately changed his mind about the plausibility of the gospel accounts and wrote:

> The synoptic descriptions of the high priest and his council agree 100 per cent with Josephus' descriptions of how Jerusalem was governed when it

248. Sanders, *Historical Figure of Jesus*, 267.

249. Cf. Hengel and Schwemer, *Jesus and Judaism*, 611–12.

> was part of a Roman province. . . . The theory advanced here—that Caiaphas had Jesus arrested because of his responsibility to put down trouble-makers, especially during festivals—corresponds perfectly with all the evidence. . . . He sent armed guards to arrest Jesus, he gave him a hearing, and he recommended execution to Pilate, who promptly complied. That is the way the gospels describe the events, and that is the way things really happened, as the numerous stories in Josephus prove.[250]

In short: if Jesus the son of Ananias was arrested and interrogated by the Jewish authorities during the Feast of Tabernacles and then handed over to the Procurator Albinus for punishment, then Jesus of Nazareth could also be arrested and interrogated by the Jewish authorities during the feast of Passover and handed over to the procurator Pontius Pilate for punishment. As Sanders rightly argues, far from being implausible, the gospel accounts "correspond perfectly" with what we know about first-century coordination between the Jerusalem Sanhedrin and the local Roman government.[251]

Another major argument from contextual plausibility is based on the fact that while it was certainly not blasphemy for a Jew to claim to be the messiah, Jesus does *more* than merely affirm his messianic identity. Jesus claims to be the *heavenly* "Son of Man" who will sit at God's "right hand" on the heavenly throne and comes on "the clouds" like God himself (Matt 26:64; Mark 14:62; Luke 22:69; cf. 1 Enoch 62:2–3, 5–7). In other words, Jesus claims to be "the divine Son of Man."[252] Now, if Jesus made such a divine self-claim, then it is eminently credible that Caiaphas and the Sanhedrin would charge him with blasphemy and condemn him to death. For in a first-century Jewish context, the fate of blasphemers was not just execution, but even cru-

250. Sanders, *Historical Figure of Jesus*, 269. See also Sanders, *Judaism: Practice and Belief*, 766–67: "The high priest ordered Jesus' arrest, he hastily convened a court, he interrogated the prisoner, he took the extreme step of rending his garments while declaring Jesus guilty, and he achieved the desired result (Mark 14.53–64; similarly Matthew and Luke). Scholars have labored endlessly over the trial scene because it does not agree with Mishnah *Sanhedrin*. The gospel accounts [of Jesus's trial] do present problems, but disagreement with the Mishnah is not one of them. . . . The system as the gospels describe it corresponds to what we see in Josephus. The trial of Jesus agrees very well with his stories of how things happened." Before publishing his massive study of early Judaism, Sanders was much more skeptical about the trial. For his earlier position, see Sanders, *Jesus and Judaism*, 298.

251. Cf. Casey, *Jesus of Nazareth*, 441; Dunn, *Jesus Remembered*, 30; Gnilka, *Jesus of Nazareth*, 287.

252. Boyarin, *Jewish Gospels*, 56.

cifixion.[253] Consider, once again, Josephus's description of the fate of those who blaspheme God:

> Let him that blasphemes God [*blasphēmēsas theon*] be stoned, *then hung for a day*; and buried ignominiously and in obscurity. (Josephus, *Antiquities* 4.202)[254]

In light of such evidence, if Jesus did indeed lay claim to "divinity" or "divine dignity" in the presence of Caiaphas and the Sanhedrin, then it is completely credible that the Jerusalem leaders would react by charging him with blasphemy and handing him over to the Romans to be crucified.[255]

Given everything we know about the political context of the time, it is also contextually plausible that Caiaphas and the Sanhedrin would not carry out the execution themselves.[256] For one thing, in the early first century, the official legal power to "inflict capital punishment," known as the *ius gladii*, did not belong to the Sanhedrin; it had been entrusted by Caesar to the Judean "procurator" (Josephus, *War* 2.117; cf. John 18:31).[257] Moreover, when Caiaphas and the Sanhedrin hand Jesus over to Pilate, they apparently focus on the *royal* dimension of Jesus's claim—"We found this man . . . saying that he himself is *Christ a king*" (Luke 23:1). That is why Pilate affixes the *titulus* "King of the Jews" to the cross (Matt 27:11, 37; Mark 15:2, 26; Luke 23:38; John 19:19).[258] As Sven-Olav Black rightly points out: "If Jesus did affirm the question regarding his messianic claim ('I am'), this would explain why he was accused and condemned as 'the King of the Jews' in the Roman trial, which was to follow."[259]

In this way, Caiaphas and the Sanhedrin both secure Jesus's execution on the grounds of sedition while simultaneously avoiding getting themselves

253. See Chapman and Schnabel, *Trial and Crucifixion of Jesus*, 102–3.

254. Loeb Classical Library translation adapted. For discussion of this text, see Darrell L. Bock, *Blasphemy and Exaltation in Judaism: The Charge against Jesus in Mark 14:53–65*, Wissenschaftliche Untersuchungen zum Neuen Testament 2.106 (Tübingen: Mohr Siebeck, 1998), 54–55.

255. Boyarin, *Jewish Gospels*, 138; Theissen and Merz, *Historical Jesus*, 464.

256. Chapman and Schnabel, *Trial and Crucifixion of Jesus*, 30.

257. Puig i Tàrrech, *Jesus: A Biography*, 560; Brown, *Death of the Messiah*, 1:364–71; A. N. Sherwin-White, *Roman Society and Roman Law in the New Testament* (Oxford: Oxford University Press, 1963), 35–38.

258. See Bond, *Pontius Pilate in History*, for a full study of Pilate's role in the Roman execution of Jesus.

259. Black, "The Trials of Jesus," 474.

into trouble by authorizing the stoning of Jesus in Jerusalem right under the nose of Pilate during Passover. Indeed, should there be any doubt that Pilate would execute a Jew for such a charge, consider the often-overlooked evidence that, not long after the time of Jesus, the Roman procurator Cumanus executed a Roman soldier for the crime of blasphemy at the behest of the Jewish people:

> After the sacking of the villages, one of the soldiers, who had found a copy of the laws of Moses that was kept in the villages, fetched it out where all could see and tore it in two while he uttered blasphemies and railed violently. *The Jews, on learning of this, collected in large numbers, went down to Caesarea, where Cumanus [the Procurator] happened to be, and besought him to avenge not them but God, whose laws had been subjected to outrage.* For, they said, they could not endure to live, since their ancestral code was thus wantonly insulted. *Cumanus, alarmed at the thought of a fresh revolution of the masses, after taking counsel with his friends, beheaded the soldier who had outraged the laws* and thus prevented the uprising when it was on the verge of breaking out a second time. (Josephus, *Antiquities* 20.115–117)

The upshot of this parallel is simple but momentous: if a Roman soldier could be beheaded by the procurator Cumanus because the Jewish people accused him of "blaspheming" (*blasphēmōn*) against the God of Israel, then it is completely plausible that a Jew from Nazareth such as Jesus could be crucified by the procurator Pontius Pilate because the Jerusalem Sanhedrin charged him with the crime of "blasphemy" (Matt 26:65; Mark 14:63–64). This is especially true if Jesus's crime included the arguably seditious identification of himself as messianic "king of the Jews."[260] The plausibility also increases if Pontius Pilate, like Cumanus after him, was concerned about uprisings from the crowds during the Jewish festival of Passover (cf. Matt 27:24; Acts 12:4). In light of such evidence, the old argument that the Romans would never have executed Jesus simply because he had offended Jewish religious sensibilities needs to be dispensed with once and for all. History shows that Romans and non-Romans alike could be put to death for insulting the God of Israel.

260. See Bock, *Blasphemy and Exaltation*, 58n54.

Coherence: The Sanhedrin, the Divine Son of Man, and the Charge of Blasphemy

The second major argument in favor of the historicity of the charge of blasphemy is from coherence with other evidence about Jesus, in several key ways.

Although the fact often goes unnoted, the evidence that Jesus was condemned by Caiaphas and other Jewish leaders in Jerusalem before being handed over to Pontius Pilate (Matt 26:57–27:2; Mark 14:53–15:1; Luke 22:66–23:5; John 19:12–28) coheres perfectly with evidence from Josephus himself that Jesus was accused by Jewish leaders of some crime and handed over to Pontius Pilate to be put to death.[261] Consider, once again, the famous *Testimonium Flavianum*:

> About this time, there lived Jesus, a wise man. . . . Pilate, *upon hearing him accused by men of the highest standing amongst us*, . . . condemned him to be crucified. (Josephus, *Antiquities* 18.63–64)

Though Josephus does not tell us what crime Jesus was charged with, recent studies of this passage hold that there are good grounds for affirming the authenticity of Josephus's claim that Jesus was "accused" (*epitetimēkotos*) by Jewish leaders before being crucified by Pilate.[262] If this is correct, then the condemnation of Jesus by Jewish leaders in Jerusalem before his crucifixion at the hands of Pontius is one of the strongest cases of coherence anywhere in the Gospels, and the condemnation of Jesus (as well as his execution) should be regarded as one of the most secure facts we possess about him.

Jesus's affirmative answer to the Sanhedrin's question about his messianic identity (Matt 26:64; Mark 14:62; Luke 22:70) also coheres well with other evidence that Jesus saw himself as the heavenly "son of man" and as the divine "Son of God."[263] For example, as I argued in chapter 4, Jesus refers to himself as both the human and heavenly "Son of Man," who has authority on earth to forgive sins (Matt 9:2–7; Mark 2:1–12; Luke 5:17–26). Moreover, as we also saw in chapter 4, when Jesus makes his apocalyptic declaration that "all things" have been handed over to him by "the Father," he is not just

261. See Steve Mason, "Jewish Sources: Flavius Josephus," in Schröter and Jacobi, *The Jesus Handbook*, 160–66, for an up-to-date discussion.

262. See van Henten, "*Testimonium Flavianum*," 365–70; Meier, *A Marginal Jew*, 1:59–66.

263. See Lohfink, *Jesus of Nazareth*, 275.

claiming to be the royal messiah, but the hidden and heavenly "Son" of God (Matt 11:25; Luke 10:21–22). Finally, as I mentioned in chapter 1, in light of such evidence, there is a growing agreement in contemporary Jesus research that the historical Jesus thought he was indeed the messiah and spoke and acted accordingly.[264] If this is correct, then the depiction of Jesus affirming his messianic identity in the presence of Caiaphas and the Sanhedrin is both coherent and credible.

In addition, Jesus's use of Psalm 110 and Daniel 7 to declare his heavenly identity also coheres perfectly well with other evidence in which he identifies the messiah with the divine son of Psalm 110 and with the heavenly figure who comes riding on the clouds in Daniel 7. Think here of Jesus's riddle of the "Messiah" as David's "Lord" (Matt 22:41–46; Mark 12:35–37; Luke 20:41–43), which we examined in chapter 3, as well as Jesus's declaration regarding the final coming of the son of man:

> They will see *"the Son of Man coming on the clouds of heaven" with power and great glory*. (Matt 24:30)
>
> Then they will see *"the Son of Man coming in clouds" with great power and glory*. (Mark 13:26)
>
> And then they will see *"the Son of Man coming in a cloud" with power and great glory*. (Luke 21:27)

As I have argued elsewhere, there are compelling reasons for concluding this oracle about the eschatological coming of the son of man on the "clouds" goes back to the historical Jesus, who identified himself with this figure.[265] If this is correct, then it is quite plausible to suggest that Jesus likewise implicitly identified himself as the heavenly son of man from the book of Daniel during his questioning by Caiaphas and the Sanhedrin.

264. See Ehrman, *How Jesus Became God*, 118–19; Hengel and Schwemer, *Jesus and Judaism*, xix; Lohfink, *Jesus of Nazareth*, 314; Casey, *Jesus of Nazareth*, 399; Puig i Tàrrech, *Jesus: A Biography*, 449; Meier, "From Elijah-Like Prophet to Royal Davidic Messiah," in *Jesus: A Colloquium in the Holy Land*, ed. Doris Donnely (New York: Continuum, 2001), 48, 71; Flusser with Notley, *Sage from Galilee*, 115; Sanders, *Historical Figure of Jesus*, 248.

265. See Pitre, *Jesus, the Tribulation*, 292–379. See also Larry W. Hurtado and Paul W. Owen, *"Who Is This Son of Man?" The Latest Scholarship on a Puzzling Expression of the Historical Jesus*, Library of New Testament Studies 390 (London: T&T Clark, 2011).

Perhaps most importantly for the purposes of this chapter, the Synoptic evidence that Jesus was charged with the capital crime "blasphemy" in the context of a question about his identity (Matt 26:65–66; Mark 14:63–64) coheres perfectly with evidence in the Gospel of John that Jesus was handed over to the Romans by the Jerusalem leaders for the crime of blasphemous self-claims:

> When the chief priests and the police saw him, they shouted, "Crucify him! Crucify him!" Pilate said to them, "Take him yourselves and crucify him; for I find no case against him." The Jews answered him, "*We have a law, and according to that law he ought to die, because he has claimed to be the Son of God.*" (John 19:6–7)

The "law" to which the Judeans are referring here is the Mosaic law against blasphemy (cf. Lev 24:16).[266] And as I've already shown, by the time of Jesus, the idea of blasphemy included both the abuse of God's name and humans who made divine claims. In light of such evidence, Armand Puig i Tàrrech rightly concludes:

> This accusation of blasphemy should not be seen as breaking the Law on pronouncing the Lord's name, which is prohibited by Judaism, or cursing God, but, as R. E. Brown states, in the sense of claiming for oneself what belongs to God. Jesus was seen to have blasphemed because, arrogantly and presumptuously, he saw himself as "equal with God."[267]

If this is correct—and I think it is—then we find ourselves in the rather remarkable situation in which *none* of the first-century gospels testify that Jesus was charged with speaking against the temple (even though this is the dominant hypothesis) and *all four* agree that Jesus was accused of blasphemy. In short, all of the historical evidence we possess leads to the conclusion that, in the final analysis, the principal reason Jesus was rejected by the Jerusalem authorities and handed for execution to the Romans is because he claimed to be a divine messiah.

266. Reinhartz, "Gospel according to John," 214; Brown, *Death of the Messiah*, 1:829; Lüdemann, *Jesus after Two Thousand Years*, 566.

267. Puig i Tàrrech, *Jesus: A Biography*, 514–15.

Consequences: Psalm 110, the Divine Son of Man, and Martyrdoms for Blasphemy

The last major argument in favor of the historicity of Jesus's condemnation for blasphemy by Caiaphas and the Jerusalem Sanhedrin is from the plausibility of its effects in the early church, in three key ways.

First, if Jesus implicitly identified himself with the divine son of Psalm 110 who would sit at "the right hand" of God (Matt 26:64; Mark 14:62; Luke 22:69), then it would provide a reasonable explanation for why Psalm 110 would go on to become the most frequently cited passage from Jewish Scripture in the entire New Testament.[268] Since I've already mentioned this above, here we will take just a few examples:

> *Being therefore exalted at the right hand of God*, and having received from the Father the promise of the Holy Spirit, he [Jesus] has poured out this that you both see and hear. For David did not ascend into the heavens, but he himself says,
>
> "*The Lord said to my Lord,*
> *'Sit at my right hand,*
> *until I make your enemies your footstool.'*
>
> Therefore let the entire house of Israel know with certainty that *God has made him both Lord and Messiah*, this Jesus whom you crucified." (Acts 2:33–35)

> In these last days he has spoken to us by a Son, whom he appointed heir of all things, *through whom he also created the worlds*. . . . When he had made purification for sins, *he sat down at the right hand of the Majesty on high*, having become as much superior to angels as the name he has inherited is more excellent than theirs. . . . But to which of the angels has he ever said,
>
> "*Sit at my right hand*
> *until I make your enemies a footstool for your feet*"? (Heb 1:2–4, 14)

268. See Aquila H. Lee, *From Messiah to Preexistent Son: Jesus' Self-Consciousness and Early Christian Exegesis of Messianic Psalms*, Wissenschaftliche Untersuchungen zum Neuen Testament 2.192 (Tübingen: Mohr Siebeck, 2005), 202–39; as well as the studies of Hengel, *Studies in Early Christology*, 118–225; and David M. Hay, *Glory at the Right Hand: Psalm 110 in Early Christianity*, Society of Biblical Literature Monograph Series 18 (Nashville: Abingdon, 1973).

> *Jesus Christ* . . . has gone into heaven and *is at the right hand of God*, with angels, authorities, and powers made subject to him. (1 Pet 3:21–22)

Notice here that Jesus's exaltation to the "right hand" of God (Ps 110:1) is directly tied to the fact that he is both "Christ" (*christos*) and "Lord" (*kyrios*) (Acts 2:36). In other words, he is "the equal of YHWH of the OT."[269] Notice also that being at the right hand of God means that Jesus is "superior" (*kreittōn*) to "angels" (Heb 1:4) and above angelic "authorities and powers" (1 Pet 3:22).[270] Hence, these texts bear witness to a *super-angelic divine Christology*, in which the divinity of Jesus exceeds the heavenly nature of angelic beings.[271] Finally, note that whereas Jesus says nothing explicit about his future resurrection or ascension when he quotes Psalm 110, early Christian writers apply Psalm 110 to the resurrection and ascension of Christ in an explicitly post-Easter context. The most plausible explanation of this difference is that the early church made explicit what was only implicit in the teachings of Jesus.

Second, if Jesus implicitly identified himself with the heavenly "son of man" in Daniel 7 (Matt 26:64; Mark 14:62; Luke 22:69), then it would likewise explain the explicit identification of Jesus with the Danielic "son of man." Consider, for example, the vision of the risen Christ in the Apocalypse of John:

> Then I turned to see whose voice it was that spoke to me, and on turning I saw seven golden lampstands, and in the midst of the lampstands I saw *one like the Son of Man*, clothed with a long robe and with a golden sash across his chest. *His head and his hair were white as white wool, white as snow*; his eyes were like a flame of fire, his feet were like burnished bronze, refined as in a furnace, and his voice was like the sound of many waters. In his right hand he held seven stars, and from his mouth came a sharp, two-edged sword, and his face was like the sun shining with full force. When I saw him, I fell at his feet as though dead. But he placed his right hand on me, saying, "Do not be afraid; *I am the first and the last, and the living one. I was dead, and see, I am alive forever and ever*; and I have the keys of Death and of Hades." (Rev 1:12–18)

269. Joseph A. Fitzmyer, *The Acts of the Apostles*, Anchor Yale Bible 31 (New York: Doubleday, 1997), 260.

270. E.g., Harold W. Attridge, *Hebrews*, Hermeneia (Minneapolis: Fortress, 1989), 40 (the verse reflects "a high or pre-existence christology"); Paul J. Achtemeier, *1 Peter*, Hermeneia (Minneapolis: Fortress, 1996), 274 (the exalted Christ is "Lord of the cosmos").

271. See Bühner, *Messianic High Christology*, 178–81.

Here Jesus is clearly identified with the Danielic "one like a Son of Man" (Rev 1:13; cf. Dan 7:13–14), but in an explicitly post-Easter context (cf. Rev 1:18). Jesus is also identified both as a human being who "died" (Rev 1:18; cf. 1:5) and a divine being whose "head" and "hair" are "white" like the heavenly "Ancient of Days" (Rev 1:14; cf. Dan 7:9). He is even described as an eternal being who is "the first and the last" (Rev 1:17) in a way that "implies some kind of equal status for God and Jesus Christ."[272] Indeed, this divine epithet is taken directly from one the most monotheistic passages in all of Jewish Scripture: "I am the first and I am the last; besides me there is no god" (Isa 44:6). In other words, in the book of Revelation, the figure of the divine "Son of Man" is "fused with that of God" while still "retaining a monotheistic perspective."[273]

Finally, if Jesus was indeed condemned to death by the Jerusalem Sanhedrin for claiming to be the heavenly "Son of Man" (Matt 26:64; Mark 14:62; Luke 22:69), it would provide a plausible explanation for the evidence that two of the earliest martyrs in the Jerusalem church—Stephen and James—were likewise executed for identifying Jesus as the heavenly "Son of Man."[274] Consider the following two accounts:

> When they [the high priest and the Sanhedrin] heard these things [that Stephen said], they became enraged and ground their teeth at Stephen. But filled with the Holy Spirit, he gazed into heaven and saw the glory of God and Jesus standing at the right hand of God. "Look," he said, "*I see the heavens opened and the Son of Man standing at the right hand of God!*" *But they covered their ears*, and with a loud shout all rushed together against him. *Then they dragged him out of the city and began to stone him*; and the witnesses laid their coats at the feet of a young man named Saul. (Acts 7:54–58; cf. 6:12; 7:1)

> [James] answered with a loud voice, "*Why do you ask me concerning the Son of Man? He is sitting in heaven on the right hand of the great power, and he will come on the clouds of heaven.*" . . . Then again the same Scribes and Pharisees said to one another, "We did wrong to provide Jesus with such testimony, but let us go up and throw him down that they may be afraid

272. David Aune, "Stories of Jesus in the Apocalypse of John," in *Contours of Christology in the New Testament*, ed. Richard N. Longenecker (Grand Rapids: Eerdmans, 2005), 312.

273. Koester, *Revelation*, 854.

274. See Hengel and Schwemer, *Jesus and Judaism*, 94; Flusser, *Sage from Galilee*, 138; Sanders, *Historical Figure of Jesus*, 267.

> and not believe him." And they cried out saying, "Oh, oh, even the just one [James] erred." . . . *So they went up and threw down the Just, and they said to one another, "Let us stone James the Just," and they began to stone him since the fall had not killed him.* (Hegesippus, in Eusebius, *Church History* 2.23.13–16)[275]

As I argued earlier, in the case of Stephen's execution, the charge of blasphemy is clear from the fact that his executioners stop "their ears" when they hear him say he sees "the Son of Man" standing in heaven at "the right of hand of God" (Acts 7:57).[276] It also seems to be why they drag him "out of the city" before stoning him (Acts 7:58; cf. Lev 24:17).[277] As we also saw above, Josephus himself gives us reason to believe that James was stoned to death at the behest of the Jerusalem Sanhedrin, likely because he too was charged with blasphemy (Josephus, *Antiquities* 20.199–200).[278] For our purposes here, the account of Hegesippus quoted above is noteworthy because in it, James is likewise put to death for describing Jesus as the heavenly "Son of Man" who sits on "the right hand of the great power" and will come on "the clouds of heaven" (Eusebius, *Church History* 2.23.13; cf. Dan 7:13–14). Although Hegesippus's account is too late to be given much historical weight, taken together, the cumulative evidence from Acts, Josephus, and Eusebius at the very least suggests that both Stephen and James were put to death in Jerusalem at the instigation of the high priest and the Sanhedrin for making blasphemous claims about Jesus.[279]

275. Translation from the Loeb Classical Library edition.

276. See Fitzmyer, *Acts of the Apostles*, 393.

277. Carl R. Holladay, *Acts: A Commentary*, New Testament Library (Louisville: Westminster John Knox, 2016), 176.

278. See Bauckham, "For What Offence?," 199–232.

279. The key difference, of course, between the execution of Jesus and the executions of Stephen and James is that Jesus is crucified by the Romans, whereas Stephen and James are stoned to death at the behest of the Sanhedrin. However, this difference is easily explained: as Josephus himself tell us, the reason the high priest Ananus and the Sanhedrin were able to execute James by stoning without suffering repercussions from the Roman authorities is because Ananus took the opportunity to convene "the Sanhedrin" to take up the case because the former Procurator Festus "was dead" and the new Procurator, Albinus, "was still on the way" (Josephus, *Antiquities* 2.200). See VanderKam, *From Joshua to Caiaphas*, 476–77. In fact, some have suggested that Stephen himself may likewise have been stoned to death during the "interregnum" after Pontius Pilate was ordered to return to Rome by Vitellius, governor of Syria (cf. Josephus, *Antiquities* 18.4.89). See Fitzmyer, *Acts of the Apostles*, 391.

Weighing the Arguments for and against Historicity

Now that we have surveyed the major arguments for and against the historical veracity of Jesus being interrogated by the Jerusalem Sanhedrin and condemned to death for blasphemy, we can take one last step back from the details in an attempt to weigh the merits of the respective positions. When we do so, it seems clear to me that the arguments in favor of substantial historicity are far stronger than the arguments against it.

For one thing, as we saw above, the now-standard claim that we have no access to the substance of the exchange between Jesus and the Sanhedrin because there is no evidence that any of his disciples were present is simply false. Not only do the gospel accounts explicitly state that Simon Peter was in the courtyard of Caiaphas's house during the interrogation (Matt 26:57–58; Mark 14:53–54; Luke 22:54–55, 61); it also strains historical credulity to posit that none of the members of the Sanhedrin (to say nothing of the guards and servants standing by) would have said anything to anyone about what was said during the examination or why Jesus was handed over to the Romans for execution. The argument from the lack of eyewitnesses is a bad argument, and it is a wonder that it continues to be deployed in otherwise serious works of scholarship. Along similar lines, the equally popular claim that it would have been illegal and therefore impossible for Caiaphas to gather the Sanhedrin for an interrogation during Passover is likewise demonstrably false. Not only is it based on a highly dubious (and highly anachronistic) assumption that later rabbinic laws were strictly followed by the largely Sadducean Sanhedrin of the first century, but the very rabbinic laws to which scholars appeal to make such a claim—for there is no first-century evidence to support it—also requires that capital cases be carried out during the annual pilgrimage festivals by the Jerusalem Sanhedrin so that pilgrims could witness the fate of those guilty of crimes worthy of death (cf. Deut 17:13; t. Sanhedrin 11:7; m. Sanhedrin 10:4). Last, but certainly not least, the argument that the verdict of blasphemy must be unhistorical because it was not blasphemy to claim to be the messianic Son of God completely fails to take into account the fact that Jesus goes beyond merely answering Caiaphas's messianic question in the affirmative. Jesus also identifies himself with the divine Son of God in Psalm 110 and the heavenly son of man in Daniel 7, thereby making an implicitly superhuman claim. As Sven-Olav Black states: "Alluding to Ps. 110:1 and Dan. 7:13, Jesus made a self-claim that was *far too high*; he portrayed himself as being too close to God."[280]

280. Black, "Trials of Jesus," 478.

Indeed, such problematic (though popular) claims completely fall apart in the face of the contextual credibility of Jesus being arrested during a festival by the Jerusalem Sanhedrin—much like Jesus the son of Ananias (Josephus, *War* 6.300–307)—or handed over to be executed for blasphemy to the Roman procurator—not unlike a certain Roman soldier who was put to death by Pilate's successor (Josephus, *Antiquities* 20.115–117). They are all but demolished by the explicit testimony of Josephus that Jesus of Nazareth was in fact both "accused" and "condemned" by the leading men of Jerusalem before being handed over to Pilate for crucifixion (Josephus, *Antiquities* 18.63). And the argument from coherence with other evidence about Jesus could not be stronger. According to both the Synoptics and John, though the Roman charge against Jesus was that of making himself a king (Matt 27:37; Mark 15:26; Luke 23:38; John 19:19), the reason he was condemned by the Jewish Sanhedrin and then handed over to Pilate for punishment was because he was regarded as guilty of blasphemy (Matt 26:65–66; Mark 14:63–64; John 19:6–7). Indeed, as far as the historical sources go, there is no evidence for any other charge against Jesus by the Sanhedrin. When this powerful case for contextual plausibility and coherence is coupled with the fact that the earliest Christology in the church was a divine Christology that confessed the risen and ascended Jesus to be sitting at the right hand of God (Acts 2:33–35; Heb 1:2–3, 14; 1 Pet 3:21–22), and the earliest followers of Jesus who were martyred were likely stoned to death for blasphemy (Acts 7:54–58; Josephus, *Antiquities* 20.199–200; Hegesippus, in Eusebius, *Church History* 2.23.2), one could reasonably argue that the accounts of Jesus's interrogation and condemnation by the Sanhedrin present a stronger case for historical plausibility than almost any other episode examined in this study.

As E. P. Sanders once wrote (though he did not mean it in quite the same way I do): "*I do not doubt that Jesus died for his self-claim.*"[281] Nor do I. But in his first-century Jewish context, the only "self-claim" for which a person could be licitly condemned to death by the Sanhedrin and handed over to the Romans for execution was the claim that he was a divine messiah. And that, according to all of the extant evidence, is precisely what happened to Jesus of Nazareth. Jesus was crucified for blasphemy.

281. E. P. Sanders, *Jewish Law between Jesus and the Mishnah: Five Studies* (London: SCM; Harrisburg: Trinity Press International, 1990), 67 (emphasis added).

CHAPTER 6

Implications

> The maxim, familiar to critical scholars, that Jesus proclaimed not himself but the kingdom corresponds not to the Jesus tradition as we know it, but only to that tradition after scholars have excised large portions of it.
>
> —Dale C. Allison Jr.[1]

> It has proved difficult to do justice to the question posed by Joseph Klausner: how was it that Jesus lived totally within Judaism, and yet was the origin of a movement that separated from Judaism, since *ex nihilo nihil fit*, nothing comes from nothing, or, more idiomatically, where there is smoke there is fire.
>
> —E. P. Sanders[2]

Ex Nihilo Nihil Fit

In the preceding pages, I have argued that there are compelling reasons for thinking that Jesus of Nazareth was a Jewish apocalyptic prophet, wonder-worker, and teacher of parables who also spoke and acted as if he were a divine messiah. In particular, I argued that it was Jesus's divine claims that led him to be accused of blasphemy on several occasions during his public ministry and then eventually to be condemned to death for the same charge. As we saw over the course of our study, there are at least twelve episodes in the first-century Gospels in which Jesus speaks and acts as if he is more than merely human. By way of summary, here are the key episodes from the Gospels we have examined herein, along with important passages from the Jewish Scriptures that help clarify in what sense Jesus is speaking or acting as if he is divine:

1. Dale C. Allison Jr., *Constructing Jesus: Memory, Imagination, and History* (Grand Rapids: Baker Academic, 2010), 226–27.

2. E. P. Sanders, *Jesus and Judaism* (Minneapolis: Fortress, 1985), 3.

Evidence from Gospels	*Jewish Scriptures*
1. Stilling the storm (Matt 8:23–27; Mark 4:35–41; Luke 8:22–25)	Lord of wind and sea (Ps 104:1–7; 107:23–30)
2. Walking on the sea (Matt 14:22–27; Mark 6:45–52; John 6:16–21)	Creator God ("I am") (Job 9:8; Exod 3:14)
3. The transfiguration (Matt 17:1–9; Mark 9:2–9; Luke 9:28–36)	God of Mount Sinai (Ex 33:18–23; 1 Kgs 19:9–14)
4. More than father or mother (Matt 10:37; Luke 14:25–27)	God of the Decalogue (Exod 20:12; Deut 5:16)
5. No one is good but God (Matt 19:16–22; Mark 10:17–22; Luke 18:18–23)	One God of the Shema (Deut 6:4–6)
6. Riddle of David's lord (Matt 22:41–46; Mark 12:35–37; Luke 20:41–43)	Divine "Lord" of David (Ps 110:1–4)
7. Healing of the paralytic (Matt 9:2–7; Mark 2:1–2; Luke 5:17–26)	Heavenly son of man (Dan 7:13–14; Isa 43:25)
8. Answer to John the Baptist (Matt 11:2–6; Luke 7:18–23)	Divine messiah (Isa 35:4–6; 40:9–10; 61:1)
9. Apocalyptic "thunderbolt" (Matt 11:25–27; Luke 10:21–22)	Hidden, unique Son of God (Ps 2:7; Dan 7:13–14)
10. Before Abraham was, I am (John 8:48–59)	Preexistent Creator ("I am") (Exod 3:14; Isa 43:10–13)
11. I and the Father are one (John 10:22–33)	One God of the Shema (Deut 6:4–6)
12. Condemned for blasphemy (Matt 26:57–66; Mark 14:53–64; John 19:7)	Heavenly son of man Coequal with God (Dan 7:13–14; Ps 110:1; cf. Lev 24:17)

It is worth emphasizing that these are not necessarily the only episodes in which Jesus speaks or acts as if he is divine. According Kurt Aland's widely used Gospel synopsis, there are some 365 identifiable pericopes in the four first-century gospels; herein I have examined only twelve of them.[3] With that said, when each of these twelve episodes is evaluated from a triple-context approach to historicity, there are strong reasons to conclude that the historical Jesus used riddles, questions, and, above all, allusions to the Jewish Scriptures to both reveal and conceal the apocalyptic secret of his identity as the heavenly son of man, the divine messiah, and omnipotent Son of God. Indeed, on more than one occasion, Jesus did not just claim to be *any* heavenly being—such as an angel or other divine agent. Rather, he spoke and acted as if he were coequal with the one God of early Jewish monotheism who had appeared to Moses on Mount Sinai, especially by referring to himself with the divine self-designation "I am." Indeed, because of his both shocking and riddle-like divine self-claims, Jesus was accused of blasphemy on more than one occasion during his public ministry. Finally, according to both Synoptic and Johannine evidence, during Jesus's last days in Jerusalem, it was precisely his claim to be a divine messiah—and not his words or actions regarding the Jerusalem temple—that led him to be charged with the capital crime of blasphemy against God and condemned to death by Caiaphas and the Jerusalem Sanhedrin. Jesus was then handed over to the Roman authorities to be executed by Pontius Pilate for claiming to be "king of the Jews"—a charge that flowed directly from (but only partially reflected) his divine messianic claims.

If this overall hypothesis is correct, then it should go without saying that the now long-standing tradition of asserting that there is "no evidence whatever" that Jesus "spoke or acted as if he believed himself to be 'a god' or 'divine'" needs to be left behind as the outdated relic that it is.[4] Even if readers disagree with my interpretation or historical evaluation of one or more episodes treated herein (as some no doubt will), the fact remains that there *is* evidence—and a substantial amount of it—that Jesus spoke and acted as if he were more than merely human. Hence, the categorical manner in which some blithely assert that "Jesus did not declare himself to be God"[5] should be recognized for what it is: a misleading oversimplification that does not take seriously the ample evidence that Jesus was an apocalyptic Jewish prophet who used parables, questions, and allusions to Jewish Scripture to both conceal and reveal the secret of his heavenly sonship and divine messiahship.

3. See Kurt Aland, ed., *Synopsis Quattuor Evangeliorum*, 15th rev. ed. (Stuttgart: Deutsche Bibelgesellschaft, 1996).

4. A. E. Harvey, *Jesus and the Constraints of History* (Philadelphia: Westminster, 1982), 168.

5. Bart D. Ehrman, *How Jesus Became God: The Exaltation of a Jewish Preacher from Galilee* (San Francisco: HarperOne, 2014), 6.

Moreover, the widespread assumption (often formulated as an assertion) that Jesus is a merely human figure in the Synoptic Gospels also needs to be abandoned once and for all as demonstrably false.[6] As I have shown in the preceding chapters, there are at least twelve key episodes in the first-century gospels in which Jesus speaks and acts as if he is more than merely human. Significantly, *ten of these twelve episodes*—that is, the vast majority of the evidence—*are from the Synoptic Gospels*. Only two of the twelve I have examined herein are exclusively found in the Gospel of John. Hence, even if we did not have the Gospel of John, there would still be abundant evidence in the Synoptic Gospels that Jesus of Nazareth spoke and acted as if he were both human and divine.

Last, but certainly not least, the hypothesis that Jesus spoke and acted as if he were divine during his lifetime also has enormous implications for the development of christological belief in the early church. As the words of E. P. Sanders quoted at the beginning of this chapter testify, when it comes to the aftermath of Jesus's life, contemporary scholarship has had a difficult time doing justice to Joseph Klausner's historical principle of *ex nihilo nihil fit* ("nothing comes from nothing"). In particular, it has struggled to explain "how Jesus lived totally within Judaism, and yet was the origin of a movement that separated from Judaism."[7] In this concluding chapter, I would like to briefly suggest that my hypothesis that Jesus spoke and acted as if he were a divine messiah does not labor under the same difficulties. It does justice to Klausner's dictum in three areas:

1. The origin of early divine Christology
2. The so-called parting of the ways
3. The monotheistic features of later christological doctrine

It should go without saying that I do not have the space to explore any of these topics in any depth. Entire monographs have been written on each of them. In what follows, I simply want to trace out a few suggestions about the relationship between Jesus's own claims about his identity and early divine Christology.

6. See especially J. R. Daniel Kirk, *A Man Attested by God: The Human Face of Jesus in the Synoptic Gospels* (Grand Rapids: Eerdmans, 2016), whose insightful case for the full humanity of Jesus in the Synoptic Gospels suffers from the pervasive weakness of being right in what it affirms (that Jesus is depicted as fully human) and wrong in what it denies (that Jesus is not depicted as divine).

7. Sanders, *Jesus and Judaism*, 3.

Early Divine Christology

The first implication of our study impacts the current debate over the origins of early high Christology. If the historical Jesus claimed to be a divine messiah and was rejected and condemned to death as a result, then this would provide a compelling explanation for why the earliest Christology was high Christology—that is, a Christology in which Jesus is a divine being who becomes human. In other words, *the "smoke" of early divine Christology originated in the "fire" of Jesus's own divine messianism.*

The Problem of Early Divine Christology

As we saw in chapter 1, the problem of early high Christology flows from the paradoxical character of the current scholarly landscape. On the one hand, the vast majority of historical Jesus scholars do not believe that Jesus of Nazareth spoke or acted as if he were anything more than merely human and that his disciples did not believe that he was divine (in any sense) during his lifetime.[8] On the other hand, a growing number of New Testament scholars agree that the earliest Christology after the death of Jesus was high Christology, in which Jesus was believed to be divine in some sense.[9]

In the face of this paradox, the question arises: If Jesus did not speak and act as if he were divine during his lifetime, how did he come to regarded as divine so quickly after his death? With his characteristic clarity of expression, Bart Ehrman puts the problem well when he writes:

> How did an apocalyptic prophet from the backwaters of rural Galilee, crucified for crimes against the state, come to be thought of as equal to the One God Almighty, maker of all things? How did Jesus—in the minds and hearts of his later followers—come to be God?[10]

8. See Ehrman, *How Jesus Became God*, 127–28; Maurice Casey, *Jesus of Nazareth: An Independent Historian's Account of His Life and Teaching* (London: T&T Clark, 2010), 399, 506; James D. G. Dunn, *Jesus Remembered*, vol. 1 of *Christianity in the Making* (Grand Rapids: Eerdmans, 2003), 761–62.

9. See Ehrman, *How Jesus Became God*, 3; Dale C. Allison Jr., *Constructing Jesus: Memory, Imagination, and History* (Grand Rapids: Baker Academic, 2010), 304; Richard Bauckham, *Jesus and the God of Israel* (Grand Rapids: Eerdmans, 2008), ix–x; Larry Hurtado, *Lord Jesus Christ: Devotion to Jesus in Earliest Christianity* (Grand Rapids: Eerdmans, 2003), 650.

10. Ehrman, *How Jesus Became God*, 45.

As one might expect, a fairly diverse set of answers to this question has been given. For example, some contend that divine Christology originated with the influx and influence of gentile believers late in the first century, who divinized Jesus in ways reflective of the polytheism of Greco-Roman culture.[11] Others propose that fully divine Christology originated in the late first-century with the Gospel of John and that early Jewish views of divine agents laid the groundwork for the gradual unfolding of belief in his divinity.[12] Still others argue that divine Christology originated with the teachings of Paul of Tarsus and his description of Jesus as a preexistent divine being who became human.[13] Finally, a growing number of scholars contend that divine Christology originated shortly after Jesus's death, when his followers began to have experiences of Jesus as risen from the dead and exalted into heaven. These experiences led his followers to regard Jesus as divine and to begin giving cultic devotion to him.[14] This is not the place to review or critique these complex, variegated, and sometimes overlapping theories. I simply want to point out that the one thing they all have in common is the assumption that Jesus himself did not claim to be a divine messiah during his public ministry; nor did his disciples believe he was divine during his lifetime.

11. See P. Maurice Casey, *From Jewish Prophet to Gentile God: The Origins and Development of New Testament Christology* (Cambridge: James Clarke; Louisville: Westminster/John Knox, 1991), 176–77; Wilhelm Bousset, *Kyrios Christos: A History of Belief in Christ from the Beginnings of Christianity to Irenaeus*, trans. John E. Steely (Waco, TX: Baylor University Press, 2013 [orig. 1931]).

12. See James D. G. Dunn, "The Making of Christology—Evolution or Unfolding?," in *Jesus of Nazareth, Lord and Christ: Essays on the Historical Jesus and New Testament Christology*, ed. Joel B. Green and Max Turner (Grand Rapids: Eerdmans, 1994), 437–52. See James D. G. Dunn, *Christology in the Making: A New Testament Inquiry into the Origins of the Doctrine of the Incarnation*, 2nd ed. (Grand Rapids: Eerdmans, 1989), for the classic articulation of his overall position.

13. See Paula Fredriksen, "How High Can Early High Christology Be?," in *Monotheism and Christology in Greco-Roman Antiquity*, ed. Matthew V. Novenson, Supplements to Novum Testamentum 180 (Leiden: Brill, 2020), 317; Paula Fredriksen, *Paul: The Pagan's Apostle* (New Haven: Yale University Press, 2017), 137–41.

14. See Ehrman, *How Jesus Became God*, 204–46; Michael Peppard, *The Son of God in the Roman World: Divine Sonship in its Social and Political Context* (Oxford: Oxford University Press, 2011), 9–30; Larry W. Hurtado, *How on Earth Did Jesus Become a God? Historical Questions about Earliest Devotion to Jesus* (Grand Rapids: Eerdmans, 2005), 13–30; Hurtado, *Lord Jesus Christ*, 53–78; Hurtado, *One God, One Lord: Early Christian Devotion and Ancient Jewish Monotheism*, 3rd ed. (London: T&T Clark, 2015), 122–28. It is worth noting Ehrman and Peppard single out the work of Raymond E. Brown as a key influence for their understanding of the origin and development of Christology. See Raymond E. Brown, *The Birth of the Messiah*, rev. ed. (New York: Doubleday, 1993), 29–32.

It is precisely the assumption that Jesus never claimed to be divine that this study has called into question. For if the historical Jesus did indeed speak and act as if he was a divine messiah during his public ministry, and if he was accused of blasphemy on more than one occasion as a result, and if he ultimately "died for his self-claim,"[15] then every one of the early high Christology hypotheses listed above would be fundamentally flawed and in need of serious revision. For they all fail to reckon with the possibility that the earliest "high Christology" has its roots in the divine messianism of the historical Jesus. I am not, of course, the first to propose such a hypothesis.[16] But I am, as far as I know, the first to mount a comprehensive study of the evidence in all four first-century gospels and to use a triple-context approach to evaluate the potential historicity of the relevant data. When the evidence for Jesus's divine self-claims is interpreted in its first-century Jewish context and the arguments both for and against the historicity of each episode are weighed on the scales, it seems to me that a compelling case can be made that this hypothesis makes the best sense of the most evidence.

The Insufficiency of the Resurrection

With that said, I would like to take a moment to say a brief word about what is perhaps the most influential explanation for the origins of early high Christology in the field of contemporary Jesus research. I am speaking here of the theory that Jesus only begins to be regarded as divine *after* his death, on the basis of the resurrection appearances (whether veridical or not) experienced by his followers. Consider, for example, the words of Gerd Theissen and Annette Merz:

> Jesus was "divinized" only on the basis of the Easter experience. . . . Our conclusion must be that the acclamation of Jesus as "Kyrios" was the most

15. E. P. Sanders, *Jewish Law between Jesus and the Mishnah: Five Studies* (London: SCM; Harrisburg, PA: Trinity Press International, 1990), 67. It should be noted that Sanders immediately goes on to shift the locus of the charge of blasphemy from Jesus's self-claim to his action in the temple.

16. See, e.g., Andrew Ter Ern Loke, *The Origin of Divine Christology*, Society for New Testament Studies Monograph Series 169 (Cambridge: Cambridge University Press, 2017), 153–74; Sigurd Grindheim, *God's Equal: What Can We Know about Jesus' Self-Understanding in the Synoptic Gospels?*, Library of New Testament Studies 446 (London: T&T Clark, 2011); Peter Stuhlmacher, "The Messianic Son of Man: Jesus' Claim to Deity," in *The Historical Jesus in Recent Research*, ed. James D. G. Dunn and Scot McKnight, Sources for Biblical and Theological Study 10 (Winona Lake, IN: Eisenbrauns, 2005), 325–44.

> far-reaching innovation after Easter. The Risen Christ was worshipped alongside God. . . . He participated in divine power. But above all, from now on he was called on and worshipped as a divine being.[17]

Notice here that Theissen and Merz insist that it was only on the basis of the resurrection experiences that Jesus's followers divinized him and that this process of deification did not take place until after his death. Hence, according to this view, the sole genesis of early high Christology is the Easter experience.

At first glance, this might seem to be a compelling hypothesis. After all, it is certainly true that if Jesus had been crucified and *never* seen alive again by any of his Jewish followers, it is extremely unlikely that any of them would have ever come to regard him as divine. In other words, the experience of Jesus's resurrection is a necessary condition for the continued belief in Jesus's divinity. It is also quite true that the first-century accounts of the resurrection appearances—however one explains them historically—do indeed suggest that these encounters led some of Jesus's disciples to worship him as if he were more than merely human (Matt 28:9, 16–18; Luke 24:50–53; cf. John 20:26–28). It seems indisputable that it is the experience of encountering the risen Jesus which leads some of the women who followed him and the eleven disciples to "worship" (*proskyneō*) Jesus as if he were divine (Matt 28:17; Luke 24:52) and to confess him as both "Lord" (*ho kyrios*) and "God" (*ho theos*) (John 20:28).[18] For many scholars, it is precisely this kind of evidence that leads them to describe the "divinization" of Jesus specifically as a "post-Easter" development that not only took place in the wake of the resurrection appearances but was

17. Theissen and Merz, *Historical Jesus*, 464, 560.

18. See Christopher Bryan, *The Resurrection of the Messiah* (Oxford: Oxford University Press, 2011), 295n3 ("*this* worship, which was and is proper toward none by the God of Israel [Isa 45:21–24], was and is properly offered to Jesus" [cf. 95]); Ulrich Luz, *Matthew: A Commentary*, trans. James E. Crouch, 3 vols., Hermeneia (Minneapolis: Fortress, 2001–2007), 3:622 ("Obeisance, *proskynesis*, is the attitude that is fitting toward rulers. With Jesus this attitude includes worship"); François Bovon, *Luke: A Commentary*, trans. Christine M. Thomas, Donald S. Deer, and James E. Crouch, 3 vols., Hermeneia (Minneapolis: Fortress, 2002–2013), 412 ("Jesus has crossed the barrier that separates human beings from God. After the resurrection, he can receive divine honors"); Jörg Frey, *The Glory of the Crucified One: Christology and Theology in the Gospel of John*, trans. Wayne Coppins and Christoph Heilig (Waco, TX: Baylor University Press, 2018), 302 (Jesus is "explicitly designated as θεός" in "the highest confession in the whole Gospel"); Hurtado, *Lord Jesus Christ*, 338 (in Matt 28:18, the "worship" of his disciples indicates Jesus's "transcendent status and power"), 345 (in Luke 24:52, the disciples give "the full reverence given to a figure of divine status/significance"), 637 (in John 20:28, Jesus is "worthy of the sort of reverence otherwise reserved for God").

also the exclusive result of these appearances. Indeed, some even argue that Jesus, on the analogy of the Roman imperial cult, could "only" be divinized "after his death and apotheosis."[19] Finally, it is also certainly true that belief in the ascension of Jesus into heaven after his resurrection played a central role in early divine Christology. As we saw above, over and over again, the description of the Davidic king who is exalted to sit at the "right hand" of God in heaven (Ps 110:1–4) repeatedly figures in early Christian writings that depict Jesus as the divine Son of God.[20]

At the same time, however, the idea that it was the resurrection *alone* that led Jesus's first Jewish followers to believe he was divine has serious drawbacks. As Pheme Perkins has argued, when we consider the idea of bodily resurrection "as it is understood by Jews of the first century C.E.," it cannot in fact "bear the weight of generating christological claims for Jesus of Nazareth without some antecedent beliefs about his unusual or unique relationship with God."[21] For one thing, although it is true that ancient pagan beliefs about mythical figures from the distant past, such as Asclepius, Heracles, or Romulus, sometimes connect their "corporeal immortalization" with their deification and worship, there is no evidence to support the claim that the disciples of Jesus—who were all Jews—would have regarded the resurrection of a recently crucified Jewish teacher as sufficient grounds for divinizing him and prostrating themselves before him as if he were divine.[22] To the contrary, we possess ample evidence that other first-century Jewish figures—such as John the Baptist (Matt 14:1–2; Mark 6:14–16; Luke 9:7–9), Jairus's daughter (Matt 9:18–26; Mark 5:21–43; Luke 9:40–56), the widow of Nain's son (Luke 7:11–17), and Lazarus of Bethany (John 11:1–45; 12:9–11)—were believed to have been raised from the dead. Nevertheless, there is zero evidence that any of their Jewish contemporaries ever thought to deify or worship any of these figures as a result. Why not? How is the risen Jesus different from the (reputedly) risen John the Baptist, or the

19. Bovon, *Luke*, 3:412, following S. R. F. Price, *Rituals and Power: The Roman Imperial Cult in Asia Minor* (Cambridge: Cambridge University Press, 1998), 75.

20. See M. David Litwa, *Iesous Deus: The Early Christian Depiction of Jesus as a Mediterranean God* (Minneapolis: Fortress, 2014), 173–79; Timo Eskola, *Messiah and Throne: Jewish Merkabah Mysticism and Early Christian Exaltation Discourse*, Wissenschaftliche Untersuchungen zum Neuen Testament 2.142 (Tübingen: Mohr Siebeck, 2001), 158–390; Martin Hengel, *Studies in Early Christology* (Edinburgh: T&T Clark, 1995), 119–225.

21. Pheme Perkins, "Resurrection and Christology: Are They Related?," in *Israel's God and Rebecca's Children: Christology and Community in Early Judaism and Christianity; Essays in Honor of Larry W. Hurtado and Alan F. Segal*, ed. David B. Capes, April D. DeConick, Helen K. Bond, and Troy A. Miller (Waco, TX: Baylor University Press, 2007), 67–75 (here 67).

22. Cf. Litwa, *Iesous Deus*, 141–79.

risen Lazarus? One key difference is that Jesus of Nazareth is the only first-century Jew we know of who spoke and acted as if he were a heavenly being *long before his death*. As Martin Hengel states:

> The origin of christology appears unthinkable without the assumption of a messianic claim of Jesus. Christology cannot be based alone on the resurrection appearances.[23]

Hengel is right, though I think his point can be strengthened by emphasizing that in order for someone to experience bodily resurrection from the dead, that person has to *die* first. And I for one can think of no early Jewish evidence that a heavenly being even *could* die—to say nothing of the one God of Israel experiencing human death. In other words, the bodily resurrection of Jesus from the dead is a *necessary* but not a *sufficient* condition for explaining the origin of his earliest followers' belief in his divinity.

In sum, I would contend that, when all of the relevant evidence is taken into account, it seems certain that during Jesus's lifetime, some of his contemporaries believed he was divine in some sense. Otherwise it is virtually impossible to explain why his followers thought he was divine after he had died. It is implausible to suggest that they started thinking him divine only after they were convinced that he had been raised from the dead, for the simple reason that, as far as we know, there were no Jews in the Second Temple period who believed that mere resurrection from the dead would make anyone equal with God. In no extant Jewish writing—whether the Scriptures of Israel or other, extrabiblical writings—is the bodily resurrection of the dead a sign that those who have been raised are equal with the one God and worthy of divine worship. Instead, *the most probable explanation for why Jesus's earliest followers spoke and acted as if he was divine after his death is because Jesus himself spoke and acted as if he was divine while he was still alive*. On its own, the mere experience of the resurrection is insufficient to explain the genesis of early divine Christology. Once again, Klausner was right: when it comes to early belief in the divinity of Jesus, *ex nihilo nihil fit*.

The Parting of the Ways

The second important implication of this study impacts the current debate over the so-called parting of the ways between Jews and Gentiles who believed in Jesus

23. Hengel, *Studies in Early Christology*, 217 (emphasis added).

as messiah and Son of God and other Jews who did not accept such claims.[24] It can be formulated as follows: if the historical Jesus not only claimed to be the messiah but also spoke and acted as if he were equal with the one God of Israel, this would provide a compelling explanation for certain conflicts between early Jewish believers in Jesus and their contemporaries, especially the stonings of Jewish believers in Jesus by the Jerusalem Sanhedrin, and the eventual separation of the early churches from the wider network of Jewish synagogues. In this case, the "smoke" of early martyrdoms of some Jewish believers in Jesus may have originated in the "fire" of Jesus's own seemingly blasphemous divine claims.

The Problem of the "Parting of the Ways"

Recent decades have seen a virtual explosion of scholarship on the "parting of the ways" between the first-century communities that would later go on to be known as "Christianity" and "Judaism."[25] In contrast to older treatments of the question, more recent scholarship has emphasized that the process of separation (or "partition") was much longer, more complex, and more variegated than has tended to be thought. Nevertheless, at the end of the day, the central questions remain: How did Jesus the Jew give rise to a movement that ultimately came to be separated from the Jewish synagogues in which it had come to birth? Why did the majority of believers in Jesus in the first several centuries eventually end up separated from the majority of members of the wider Jewish community?

As one can imagine, a variety of explanations have been given—too many to treat here in any depth. To take just a few examples: some suggest that the partition began with the apostle Paul's mission to the gentiles, which led to conflicts with Jewish believers in Jesus as well as the wider Jewish community.[26] Others contend that the parting of the ways can be located between the 60s and 90s of the first century CE, when persecutions by the Roman author-

24. As far as I can tell, the expression "parting of the ways" seems to have been coined by James Parkes in *The Conflict of the Church and the Synagogue: A Study in the Origins of Antisemitism* (New York: Jewish Publication Society, 1934), 71–120.

25. For collections of essays by major scholars, see Hershel Shanks, *Partings: How Judaism and Christianity Became Two* (Washington, DC: Biblical Archaeology Society, 2013); and James D. G. Dunn, ed., *Jews and Christians: The Parting of the Ways, A.D. 70 to 135* (Grand Rapids: Eerdmans, 1992).

26. See Gerd Lüdemann, *Paul: The Founder of Christianity* (London: SCM; Amherst, NY: Prometheus, 2002), 213–26.

ities served to exacerbate tensions and foster divisions between Jewish and gentile Christian communities.[27] Many scholars locate the definitive parting of the ways in the early second century CE, in the wake of the second Jewish revolt against Rome (132–135 CE) and rising polemics between ethnically Jewish communities and gentile Christian churches, as reflected in the writings of Ignatius of Antioch and Justin Martyr.[28] More recent scholarship has pushed the point of division even later, highlighting evidence that Jewish believers in Jesus not only continued to exist, but to frequent synagogues (and be rebuked by their gentile Christian bishops for doing so!) well into the fourth and fifth centuries.[29] Last, some have even called into question whether there ever even *was* a "parting of the ways," contending that the "paradigm of separation" between "Judaism" and "Christianity" should be abandoned altogether.[30]

It is beyond the scope of this project to adjudicate between these various hypotheses. For our purposes here, what is significant is the insistence by some contributors to this discussion that early divine Christology played *little or no role* in the conflicts between early Jewish believers in Jesus and their Jewish contemporaries who did not believe in his messiahship or divinity. Consider, for example, the conclusion of James Dunn, after decades of research and writing on the topic:

> The principal "other" for early Christianity was early Judaism, and the principal "other" for early Judaism was early Christianity. . . . [S]omewhat surprisingly, the developing christology within the great church was not such a dividing line initially as it became later [in the second century CE].[31]

27. See Mariusz Rosik, *Church and Synagogue (30–313 AD): Parting of the Ways*, European Studies in Theology, Philosophy, and History of Religions 20 (Berlin: Peter Lang, 2019), 470; Margaret H. Williams, "Jews and Christians at Rome: An Early Parting of the Ways," in Shanks, *Partings*, 151–78; James D. G. Dunn, *The Partings of the Ways between Christianity and Judaism and Their Significance for the Character of Christianity*, 2nd ed. (London: SCM, 2006 [orig. 1991]), 312–19.

28. See Shaye J. D. Cohen, "In Between: Jewish-Christians and the Curse of the Heretics," in Shanks, *Partings*, 207–36; Thomas A. Robinson, *Ignatius of Antioch and the Parting of the Ways: Early Jewish-Christian Relations* (Peabody, MA: Hendrickson, 2009).

29. See Oskar Skarsaune and Reidar Hvalvik, eds., *Jewish Believers in Jesus: The Early Centuries* (Peabody, MA: Hendrickson, 2007); Daniel Boyarin, *Border Lines: The Partition of Judaeo-Christianity* (Philadelphia: University of Pennsylvania Press, 2004).

30. See Paula Fredriksen, "What 'Parting of the Ways'? Jews, Gentiles, and the Ancient Mediterranean City," in *The Ways That Never Parted: Jews and Christians in Late Antiquity and the Early Middle Ages*, ed. Adam H. Becker and Annette Yoshiko Reed (Minneapolis: Fortress, 2007), 35–64; James H. Charlesworth, "Did They Ever Part?," in Shanks, *Partings*, 281–300.

31. James D. G. Dunn, *Neither Jew nor Greek: A Contested Identity*, vol. 3 of *Christianity in the Making* (Grand Rapids: Eerdmans, 2015), 671–72 (emphasis added).

In other words, according to Dunn, it was not primarily early beliefs about the identity of Jesus that led to divisions between "early Judaism" and "early Christianity." Indeed, one searches in vain through the pages of the massive body of literature on the "parting of ways" cited above for any extensive discussion about the role played in the division between early Judaism and early Christianity by the belief that Jesus was divine and equal with the one God.[32]

The Stonings of Early Jewish Believers in Jesus

One problem with this lack of focus on early Christian belief in the divinity of Jesus is that it fails to do justice to the evidence we surveyed above that some of the earliest Jewish followers of Jesus were subject to execution by stoning for the same kind of accusation as Jesus: that of blasphemy. As the contemporary Jewish scholar Claudia Setzer has pointed out, the earliest Jewish opposition to belief in Jesus seems to have revolved around the early church's christological claims.[33] Since I have already examined some of this material in chapter 5, here I will briefly look at three key examples:

Stoned for Blasphemy	*Leaders Involved*	*Chronology*
1. Stoning of Stephen in Jerusalem (Acts 7:55–58)	High Priest Caiaphas and Sanhedrin	ca. 36–37 CE
2. Stoning of Paul in Lystra	Jews from Antioch and Iconium (Acts 14:19; cf. 2 Cor 11:25)	ca. 45–49 CE
3. Stoning of James and other Jewish believers in Jerusalem (Josephus, *Antiquities* 20.200; Hegesippus, in Eusebius, *Church History* 2.23.13–16)	High Priest Ananus and Sanhedrin	ca. 62 CE

32. One important exception is Michael F. Bird, "Jesus and the 'Partings of the Ways,'" in *Handbook for the Study of the Historical Jesus*, ed. Tom Holmén and Stanley E. Porter, 4 vols. (Leiden: Brill, 2011), 2:1183–1215.

33. See Claudia Setzer, "You Invent a Christ," *USQR* 44 (1991): 315–28.

In these accounts, the charge of blasphemy is implied by the fact that both Stephen and Paul are both dragged "out of the city" to be executed (Acts 7:58; 14:19), in keeping with the Levitical legislation that the blasphemer be taken "outside the camp" to be stoned (Lev 24:13–17).[34] The implication of blasphemy is also evident in that both Stephen and James are only stoned to death after they profess to see "the Son of Man" in heaven at the "right hand" of God (Acts 7:56; Eusebius, *Church History* 2.23.13). Notice here that the stonings of Stephen, James, and the other Jerusalem believers in Jesus are *not* cases of mob violence, but the result of a "judicial sentence" sanctioned by the high priests Caiaphas and Ananus II, as well as the Jerusalem Sanhedrin.[35] It is also worth noting that the stonings of Stephen and Paul take place well before there is any evidence of conflict between believers in Jesus and Jewish leadership over other distinctively Jewish issues—such as circumcision or food laws—that would occupy the Council of Jerusalem (ca. 49 CE). Instead, in all three of these cases, the execution (or, in Paul's case, attempted execution) by stoning appears to have been carried out because Jewish believers in Jesus were viewed by either the Jerusalem Sanhedrin or the leaders in the diaspora as guilty of the capital crime of blasphemy.[36]

In short, according to the evidence in Paul, Acts, and Josephus, conflicts between Jews who believed in Jesus and Jewish leaders who did not were already underway in the 30s, 40s, and early 60s of the first century. Now, if executions can be taken as an index of conflict—and if they cannot, what else can?—then the division between followers of Jesus and the wider network of Jewish synagogues seems to reach all the way back to a mere *three or four years* after the crucifixion of Jesus. Given the fact that Jesus himself was rejected by

34. Carl R. Holladay, *Acts: A Commentary*, New Testament Library (Louisville: Westminster John Knox, 2016), 176.

35. Richard Bauckham, "For What Offence Was James Put to Death?," in *James the Just and Christian Origins*, ed. Bruce Chilton and Craig A. Evans, Supplements to Novum Testamentum 98 (Leiden: Brill, 1999), 219. Contrast this with the mob stonings recorded in Josephus, *Antiquities* 16.394; 14.22–24 (Honi the Circle-Drawer); and *War* 2.445 (Judas the Galilean), in which the condemned are not brought outside the city before execution.

36. This is especially likely when we recall that, according to the book of Acts, it was precisely Paul's Christology—i.e., his public confession of Jesus as "the Son of God" and "Christ" in the synagogue at Damascus—that led to the initial plots by synagogue officials to execute him (cf. Acts 9:19–23). See chapter 5, and Larry W. Hurtado, "Pre-70 C.E. Jewish Opposition to Christ Devotion," in his *Ancient Jewish Monotheism and Early Christian Jesus-Devotion: The Context and Character of Christological Faith* (Waco, TX: Baylor University Press, 2017), 185–208 (here 200–207).

the Jerusalem Sanhedrin for blasphemy, one could even say that this intra-Jewish conflict had its origins with the claims made by Jesus himself.

If this is correct, then a strong case can be made that many of the common explanations for the causes and chronology of the so-called parting of the ways are inadequate. Indeed, many works on the "parting of the ways" pay little or no attention to the evidence that Stephen, James, and other Jewish believers in Jesus were executed for the crime of blasphemy. Remarkably, one recent full-length study of "the history of martyrdom in the first and second centuries" contains chapters on martyrdoms in Asia Minor, Rome, Gaul, North Africa, and Alexandria—but *no* discussion of the first-century martyrdoms of Jewish Christians in Jerusalem.[37] This is, to say the least, a major omission. Others recognize that the execution of Stephen marked "the beginning of a clear parting of the ways" but say nothing about the fact that Stephen appears to have been executed for blasphemy.[38] Still others claim that "we have absolutely no information" about why James was executed by the Jerusalem Sanhedrin, as if Hegesippus's account of James's execution for blasphemy did not exist.[39] Even Pauline scholars who are very interested in his Jewish identity do not provide compelling explanations for why, as a Jew, Paul was not only beaten "five times" in Jewish synagogues, but also "stoned"—a sentence that strongly suggests that the leaders who instigated the stoning viewed Paul as guilty of blasphemy (2 Cor 11:25; cf. Acts 14:19).[40] By contrast, all of this evidence is easily explained if the "parting of the ways" first began to take place when Jesus of Nazareth himself stood before the high priest Caiaphas and the Jerusalem Sanhedrin and declared that he was the heavenly son of man who would sit at God's "right hand" as an equal.

37. See Candida R. Moss, *Ancient Christian Martyrdom: Diverse Practices, Theologies, and Traditions*, Anchor Yale Bible Reference Library (New Haven: Yale University Press, 2012).

38. Dunn, *Partings of the Ways*, 94–95.

39. Paula Fredriksen, *When Christians Were Jews: The First Generation* (New Haven: Yale University Press, 2018), 179–80.

40. Cf. Fredriksen, *Paul*, 87, 127, who assumes (without argumentation) that the stoning of Paul was "presumably by a crowd action" and suggests (unconvincingly) that it was "Paul's pursuit" of "synagogue-affiliated pagans" that led to his "repeatedly receiving disciplinary lashing." Given the severity of the punishment of forty lashes minus one—from which the condemned person sometimes died—is Paul's evangelization of god-fearing gentiles really a sufficient explanation? Cf. Deut 25:1–3; Josephus, *Antiquities* 4.238, 248; m. Makkot 3:1–14.

CHAPTER 6

The Long Road to Nicaea

The final implication of our study impacts the current discussion of the development of christological doctrine in the first centuries of early Christianity. If the historical Jesus used questions, riddles, and allusions to Jewish Scripture in order to reveal his identity as the divine messiah, then this would provide a plausible explanation for why it took his followers and later believers several centuries of debate and development to explain *how* Jesus could be both truly human and truly divine.

In particular, if Jesus revealed his divine messiahship using key monotheistic passages in Jewish Scripture—such as the divine "I am" (Exod 3:14) and the Shema (Deut 6:4–6)—then it is especially plausible that it would take the early church some time to figure out how to define the doctrine of Jesus's divinity without abandoning the early Jewish confession of faith in one God. In fact, such a formal definition of christological doctrine did not take place until some three centuries after the life of Jesus himself, in 325 CE, during the first "ecumenical" (or "empire-wide") council at Nicaea.

The Problem of the "Time Lag" Between Jesus and Nicaea

One reason it is important to spell out this implication is because some have argued that if Jesus really did claim to be a divine messiah, then there would have been no need for the complex christological developments that took place in the second, third, and fourth centuries and culminated in the first ecumenical council of Nicaea in 325 CE. In her essay "How High Can Early High Christology Be?," Paula Fredriksen states:

> One last historical problem with early very high Christology: it renders the next several centuries of theological development all but incomprehensible. . . . Why indeed did the Arian controversy even happen at all, if the radical identification of Jesus with God had already debuted back in the mid-first century? Why, if Paul provides the Christological Big Bang, do we have this big lag?[41]

According to Fredriksen, if believers had "radically" identified Jesus "with God"—to say nothing of Jesus himself doing so—then the next several centu-

41. Fredriksen, "How High?," 317 (cf. 295).

ries of heated christological debate should not have been necessary, since the full divinity of Christ would have already been "articulated and proclaimed in Jerusalem, at Easter, among Jews, following the initial Big Bang of Jesus' resurrection."[42]

At first glance, this seems like a compelling point. For one thing, given the centrality of the divinity of Christ in subsequent Christian doctrine and discourse, it does seem rather puzzling that it took the apostolic churches some three hundred years to clarify the meaning of such a central claim. Moreover, it seems true that if Jesus himself had simply, directly, and unambiguously declared "I am God," or "I am the eternal Son of the Father," then it seems likely that the Arian controversy would never have taken place (though such a claim cannot, of course, be proven). Finally, there is no doubt that the emergence of the philosophical terminology and concepts of "substance" (*ousia*), "person" (*hypostasis*), and "consubstantial" (*homoousios*) that later found their way into the Nicene Creed were complex developments that took time.[43] Nevertheless, there are several major problems with the claim that the time "lag" between Jesus and Nicaea means that Jesus was not "radically identified with God" from the very beginning.

The Council of Nicaea Was Not about Whether Jesus Was "God"

For one thing, even a cursory reading of the texts of the Council of Nicaea reveals that the primary question being addressed was *not* whether Jesus could be "radically identified with God."[44] As Lewis Ayres points out in his recent study of Nicaea, "we should avoid thinking of these controversies as focusing on the status of Christ as 'divine' or 'not divine.'"[45] Indeed, none of the major figures at Nicaea—including Arius—doubted that Jesus was divine or that he could be referred to as "God." In fact, long before the council, Arius himself is on record as describing the Son as the "only-begotten God" (*theos*).[46]

42. Fredriksen, "How High?," 295.

43. The complexity of the issues involved is on full display in R. P. C. Hanson, *The Search for the Christian Doctrine of God: The Arian Controversy, 318–81* (London: T&T Clark, 1988), which spends nine hundred pages (!) on a mere sixty-odd years of the controversy.

44. Fredriksen, "How High?," 317.

45. Lewis Ayres, *Nicaea and Its Legacy: An Approach to Fourth Century Trinitarian Theology* (Oxford: Oxford University Press, 2004), 3.

46. Arius of Alexandria, *Thalia*, cited in Athanasius, *On the Synods of Arminum and Seleucia* 15.2.24, in *A New Eusebius: Documents Illustrating the History of the Church to*

Instead, the driving force behind the council was a set of *complex christological questions* that cannot be reduced to the mere issue of whether Jesus was God. This is especially clear if one examines the four anathemas (enumerated below) that were originally promulgated along with the Nicene profession of faith which later came to be known as the "creed":

> We believe in one God, the Father almighty,
> maker of all things both visible and invisible.
> And in one Lord Jesus Christ, the Son of God,
> the Only-Begotten, begotten from the Father,
> that is, from the substance of the Father,
> God from God, light from light, true God from true God,
> begotten not made, consubstantial with the Father,
> through whom all things were made,
> both those in heaven and those on earth;
> for us humans and for our salvation he came down and became incarnate, became human, suffered, and rose up on the third day,
> ascended into the heavens, is coming to judge the living and the dead.
> And in the Holy Spirit.
> *But those who say [1] "there was a time when he was not,"*
> *and [2] "before he was begotten he was not,"*
> *and that [3] "he came to be from things that were not,"*
> *or [4] from another hypostasis or substance,*
> *[5] affirming that the Son of God is subject to change or alteration—these the catholic and apostolic church anathematizes.*
>
> (Council of Nicaea, Profession of the 318 Fathers)[47]

Note well that there is not a single anathema against "those who say that Jesus is not God" or "those who say the Son is not divine." The reason for this is simple: both the followers of Athanasius and the followers of Arius affirmed the divinity of Jesus Christ. That was not the issue that led to the Council of Nicaea.[48] Instead, as the language of the anathemas makes clear, the bishops at

---

AD 337, ed. J. Stevenson, rev. W. H. C. Frend (Grand Rapids: Baker Academic, 2013), 374–75. On the theology of Arius, see Rowan Williams, *Arius: Heresy and Tradition*, rev. ed. (Grand Rapids: Eerdmans, 2001), 95–116.

47. Norman P. Tanner, SJ, ed., *Decrees of the Ecumenical Councils*, trans. Norman P. Tanner, SJ, 2 vols. (London: Sheed & Ward; Washington, DC: Georgetown University Press, 1990), 1:5 (translation adapted).

48. Cf. Michael F. Bird, *Jesus among the Gods: Early Christology in the Greco-Roman*

Nicaea were wrestling with other, far more complex christological questions, to which the words of Jesus and the writings of the New Testament do not provide unambiguous answers, questions such as:

1. Was there a time when the Son did not exist?
2. Did the Son exist before he was begotten by the Father?
3. Did the Son come to be from things that were not?
4. Did the Son come from another hypostasis or substance than that of the Father?
5. Is the Son subject to change or alteration?

In short, Paula Fredriksen's argument that if Jesus had been "radically identified with God" from the very beginning then the Arian controversy would never have happened is a misleading oversimplification of the actual christological questions at the heart of the Arian controversy and the Council of Nicaea to which it led. Hence, any appeal to a supposed time "lag" between Jesus and Nicaea is a bad argument against early divine Christology, one based on a caricature of the Arian controversy and an inattentive reading of the decrees of Nicaea. When the actual christological and trinitarian issues driving the council are compared with the New Testament writings, it is not at all surprising that it took several centuries of doctrinal development to get them (somewhat) sorted out.[49]

Early Christology Was Also Very Low Christology

The argument from the supposed time "lag" between the life of Jesus and the council of Nicaea also fails to do justice to the evidence that *the earliest Chris-*

World (Waco, TX: Baylor University Press, 2022): "The church's contentious debates across the second to fourth centuries were not about the fact of Christ's divinity, whether or not he was God; rather, the torrid debates were concerned with the quest for a scripturally sound and philosophically coherent account of Christ as divine beside God the Father." On the developments leading up to Nicaea, see especially Khaled Anatolios, *Retrieving Nicaea: The Development and Meaning of Trinitarian Doctrine* (Grand Rapids: Baker Academic, 2011), 51–31; Ayres, *Nicaea and Its Legacy*, 11–40; John Behr, *The Nicene Faith*, part 1, The Formation of Christian Theology 2 (Crestwood, NY: St. Vladimir's Seminary Press, 2004), 61–161.

49. I say "somewhat" because, as is well known, the Council of Nicaea did *not* settle the Arian controversy, but was followed by several further centuries of christological debate and development, which eventually culminated in the Council of Chalcedon (451 CE). See Ayres, *Nicaea and Its Legacy*, 85–272; Frances M. Young, with Andrew Teal, *From Nicaea to Chalcedon: A Guide to Its Literature and Background*, 2nd ed. (Grand Rapids: Baker Academic, 2010).

tology was not only a very high Christology (in which Jesus is truly divine); it was also a very low Christology (in which Jesus is truly human).[50]

As we saw above, on multiple occasions, when Jesus speaks or acts as if he is divine, he does so in such a way that also makes clear that he is truly human. The most obvious example of this is Jesus's repeated use of "the Son of Man" (*ho huios tou anthrōpou*) to refer to himself. "Son of Man" not only identifies Jesus as the *heavenly* being of Daniel's apocalyptic vision (Dan 7:13–14), but also as a "human being" (*anthrōpos*) (Matt 9:6; Mark 2:10; Luke 5:24). Likewise, when Jesus responds to John the Baptist's question about his identity (Matt 11:4–5; Luke 7:18–23), he identifies himself not only with the one "God" who is to come (Isa 35:4–6; 40:9–10), but also with the human figure who is "anointed" to preach "good news" to the poor (Isa 61:1). Finally, as we saw above, when Jesus poses his riddle about "the Messiah," he does not deny that the messiah is David's "son" (i.e., human); he only insists that he is also the super-Davidic "lord" (*kyrios*) (i.e., divine) (Mark 12:35–37). Even the account of Jesus's walking on the sea and declaring "I am" begins with him going away by himself "to pray" to God like any other human being (Mark 6:46). In light of such evidence, John Meier makes the following important point:

> When it comes to understanding NT christology, it is best to recite this mantra: in the beginning was the grab bag. The next couple of centuries would be taken up sorting out the grab bag. *Many early Christians were quite content to make both "low" and "high" affirmations about Jesus*, with no great concern about consistency, systematization, or synthesis.[51]

In other words, the earliest Christology was *theanthropic Christology*: it not only radically identified Jesus with God (Greek *theos*); it also radically identified him with human beings (Greek *anthrōpos*). Indeed, this radical identification with human beings is one reason I have argued throughout this book that Jesus did not just claim to be "divine" *simpliciter*, but rather that he claimed to be the *divine messiah*. A divine messiah is, by definition, also human, since the messiah is the anointed human heir to the Davidic kingdom (cf. 2 Sam 7:14). In my view, the phrase *divine Christology* is also helpful, be-

50. Cf. Fredriksen, "How High?," 317.

51. John P. Meier, *A Marginal Jew: Rethinking the Historical Jesus*, 5 vols., Anchor Yale Bible Reference Library (New Haven: Yale University Press, 1991–2016), 2:919 (emphasis added).

cause it gives due emphasis to both the divinity and humanity of the "messiah" (Greek *christos*).[52]

With this in mind, we can turn back to the Council of Nicaea and see somewhat more clearly that the Nicene Creed likewise affirms both a very high Christology and a very low Christology. As is widely known, the high Christology of the creed is most evident it in its description of Jesus as "true God from true God" (*theon alēthinon ek theou alēthinou*), "begotten, not made" (*gennēthenta ou poiēthenta*), and "consubstantial with the Father" (*homoousion tō patri*).[53] However, the low Christology of Nicaea is equally clear in the articles regarding the incarnation, suffering, and resurrection of Jesus:

> We believe . . .
> in one Lord, Jesus Christ, the Son of God . . .
> [who] came down and *became incarnate,*
> *became human, suffered, and rose up on the third day,*
> ascended into the heavens, is coming to judge the living and the dead.
> (Council of Nicaea, Profession of the 318 Fathers)[54]

So much attention is paid to the Nicene profession of Jesus as *homousious* with the Father that it can be easy to overlook the fact that the creed is equally emphatic that he "became incarnate" (*sarkōthenta*), "became human" (*enanthrōpēsanta*), and was so truly human that he "suffered" (*pathonta*) and "rose up" (*anastanta*) from the dead. Indeed, it is precisely these claims—that Jesus really took human flesh, really was a human being, really suffered, and really rose from the dead—that were disputed by some early Christians known as "docetists." This movement took its name from the claim that Jesus only "appeared" (*dokeō*) to be human but was in fact only divine.[55] By confessing that Jesus truly became incarnate, became human, and suffered, the Council of Nicaea rejected Docetism and combined its confession of Jesus's divinity with an equally firm confession of his humanity.

52. For recent use of this terminology, see Nick Brennan, *Divine Christology in the Epistle to the Hebrews*, Library of New Testament Studies (London: T&T Clark, 2023); Loke, *Origin of Divine Christology*; Chris Tilling, *Paul's Divine Christology* (Grand Rapids: Eerdmans, 2015).

53. Tanner, *Decrees of the Ecumenical Councils*, 1:5.

54. Tanner, *Decrees of the Ecumenical Councils*, 1:5.

55. See Joseph Verheyden, Reimund Bieringer, Jens Schröter, and Ines Jäger, eds., *Docetism in the Early Church*, Wissenschaftliche Untersuchungen zum Neuen Testament 399 (Tübingen: Mohr Siebeck, 2018).

Once again, it is precisely Jesus's paradoxical affirmation of his divinity and humanity that makes the several centuries of christological debate and development that led up to the council of Nicaea quite comprehensible. If Jesus had only claimed to be human or only claimed to be divine, such a long process of debate would have been unnecessary. As Adela Yarbro Collins points out:

> This recognition of ambiguity . . . is supported by the christological controversies of the fourth century. If the texts of the New Testament had been unambiguous, there would have been fewer disagreements about what the texts meant.[56]

When we take the ambiguity of New Testament Christology seriously, there is nothing at all implausible about it taking several generations for early Christian writers to develop the language and concepts to explain how it is that Jesus could be both fully divine (without abandoning or reducing his humanity) and fully human (without abandoning or reducing his divinity).

The Monotheism of Jesus and the Faith of Nicaea

Finally, the argument from the supposed "time lag" between the life of Jesus and the Council of Nicaea also fails to do justice to both the *monotheistic* character of the language of Nicaea and the fact that when Jesus speaks or acts as if he is divine, he often alludes to key passages in Jewish Scripture that affirm *the oneness of God*.

As we saw above, on more than one occasion, Jesus takes the absolute form of the divine name "I am" as his own (Matt 14:27; Mark 6:50; John 6:20; 8:58). Jesus's use of the absolute "I am" is not only an allusion to the divine name revealed to Moses on Mount Sinai (cf. Exod 3:14); it also echoes one of the most explicitly "monotheistic" passages in all of Jewish Scripture (cf. Isa 43:10–11).[57] Likewise, when Jesus declares "I and the Father are one" and is almost stoned to death by his Judean contemporaries (John 10:30–31), he is likewise alluding to the Shema, the biblical profession that "the LORD God" is "one" (cf. Deut 6:4–5). At the same time, however, Jesus also clearly

56. Adela Yarbro Collins, "How on Earth Did Jesus Become a God? A Reply," in Capes, DeConick, Bond, and Miller, *Israel's God and Rebecca's Children*, 64.

57. See Yarbro Collins, "How on Earth?," 64–65.

distinguishes himself as the "Son of God" from God "the Father." He not only does this when he declares "I and the Father *are* [pl.] one" (John 10:30), but also when he declares that "all things" have been "handed over to me" by the "Father" (Matt 11:25; Luke 10:21). *In other words, by alluding to explicitly monotheistic passages in Jewish Scripture, Jesus is not just claiming to be any divine being; he is claiming to be the one God of Israel.* Hence, when Jesus also distinguishes himself from God by claiming to be the divine "Son" of "the Father," he does so without abandoning the early Jewish confession of faith in one God. Later in the first century, the apostle Paul would do something very similar, when he used the language of the Shema to insist both that there is "one God, the Father" *and* "one Lord, Jesus Christ" through whom "all things" were made (1 Cor 8:5–6).

It is precisely this tension between the affirmation of the oneness of God and the divinity of Jesus that is present in the very first lines of the Nicene Creed. To be sure, many studies of the Council of Nicaea focus primarily on its philosophical and patristic background.[58] However, it is also important to emphasize that the opening language of the Nicene Creed is not drawn from the writings of Plato but from the writings of Paul, who is himself quoting the Jewish Scriptures:[59]

> We believe in *one God* [*hena theon*], the Father almighty,
> maker of all things visible and invisible.
> And in *one Lord* [*hena kyrion*], Jesus Christ, the son of God,
> the only-begotten who is begotten from the Father.
> (Council of Nicaea, Profession of the 318 Fathers)[60]

> Although there may be so-called gods in heaven or on earth—as indeed there are many "gods" and many "lords"—yet for us there is *one God* [*heis theos*], *the Father*, from whom are all things and for whom we exist, and *one Lord* [*heis kyrios*], *Jesus Christ*, through whom are all things and through whom we exist. (1 Cor 8:5–6)

58. See Behr, *Nicene Faith*, 150–61. For a helpful critique of an approach to Nicaea that focuses only on its philosophical roots and downplays the role of Scripture, see Michael F. Bird, *Jesus the Eternal Son: Answering Adoptionist Christology* (Grand Rapids: Eerdmans, 2017), 67–73.

59. J. N. D. Kelly, *Early Christian Creeds*, 3rd ed. (London: Routledge, 1972), 25, recognizes that the first line of the creed is "based upon the Jewish *Shema*."

60. Tanner, *Decrees of the Ecumenical Councils*, 1:5.

> Hear O Israel: *the* Lord [*kyrios*] our *God* [*ho theos*], *the* Lord *is one* [*kyrios heis estin*]. And you shall love *the* Lord *your God* [*kyrion ton theon sou*] with all your heart, with all your soul, and with all your strength. (Deut 6:4–5 LXX)

Now, if both Jesus of Nazareth and the early church insisted on claiming both that God was "one" and that Jesus himself was divine yet distinct from God the Father, then it is completely unsurprising that it would take several generations for Christian writers and thinkers to acquire and develop the philosophical terminology necessary to explain, in a precise manner, exactly *how* Jesus could be fully divine without transgressing the boundaries of ancient Jewish belief in one God.[61]

In fact, one could make the case that argument from a time "lag" between Jesus and Nicaea could actually be turned on its head. If Jesus of Nazareth *never* claimed to be the one God, then the early church could easily have divinized him in such a way that he was simply set up as a second deity, without any recourse to the language of the Shema or any concern for the constraints of early Jewish monotheism. This would be especially likely if the church eventually began to flourish (as it did) in a predominantly gentile context. But it was precisely the early church's concern to stay faithful to the early Jewish monotheism of Jesus and his first followers that necessitated the long, complex, and controverted process of christological debate and development that would eventually culminate in the Council of Nicaea. If Jesus had merely claimed to be a superhuman being or a divine king like some of the Roman emperors, there would likely have been no need for such a debate.[62] But one reason Nicaea was necessary was because it took centuries for early Christians to think through how Jesus could be fully divine while still preserving the monotheistic professions of Jewish Scripture (Deut 6:4–6; Isa 43:10) and Jesus himself (Matt 19:17; Mark 10:17; Luke 18:20).

In sum, from a historical point of view, the best explanation for why the earliest Christology was a divine Christology is because Jesus himself spoke and acted as if he were a divine messiah. Likewise, the best explanation for

61. For an excellent example of a study that takes seriously the role of Jewish Scripture in the development of early christological and Trinitarian doctrine, see Matthew W. Bates, *The Birth of the Trinity: Jesus, God, and Spirit in New Testament and Early Christian Interpretations of the Old Testament* (Oxford: Oxford University Press, 2015).

62. Cf. Bruce W. Winter, *Divine Honours for the Caesars: The First Christians' Responses* (Grand Rapids: Eerdmans, 2015); Ittai Gradel, *Emperor Worship and Roman Religion* (Oxford: Oxford University Press, 2002).

why the first opposition to Jewish followers of Jesus came from Jerusalem leaders who believed they were blaspheming is because Jesus himself said and did things that were regarded as blasphemous by some of his contemporaries. Finally, the best explanation for why the early church took several centuries to debate and discuss how Jesus could be both the divine messiah and yet somehow distinct from "the one God, the Father almighty," is because Jesus himself had spoken and acted as if he were divine without abandoning early Jewish monotheism. In other words, when it comes to Joseph Klausner's principle of *ex nihilo nihil fit*, it seems reasonable to conclude that that the "smoke" of early divine Christology originated in the "fire" of Jesus's own divine claims; the "smoke" of early Jewish Christian martyrdoms originated in the "fire" of Jesus's seemingly "blasphemous" self-designations; and even the "smoke" of Nicaea's emphatically monotheistic Christology—after a long, long road of doctrinal development—had its ultimate origin in the divine messianism of the man from Nazareth.

Acknowledgments

Acknowledgments such as these often begin by stating when an author began his or her research into the subject, but in this case, I cannot. The truth is I have been pondering the question of who Jesus of Nazareth claimed to be for almost thirty years, ever since I first picked up volume 1 of John Meier's *A Marginal Jew: Rethinking the Historical Jesus* and began reading it.[1] At the time, I was an undergraduate student pursuing a degree in English literature. However, once I turned to volume 2—*Mentor, Message, and Miracles*, which is still my favorite in the series—I was hooked. As a result, I added a major in religious studies to my curriculum and decided then and there that I would pursue a PhD in New Testament with the goal of becoming a historical Jesus scholar. Over the years, as I watched Meier's work on Jesus progress, I ended up having the privilege of studying under him during my doctoral research at the University of Notre Dame. At the time, Meier was finishing volume 3 (*Companion and Competitors*) and beginning volume 4 (*Law and Love*).

Though I read and learned from each of Meier's volumes, I have to confess that I was most excited about the proposed final volume, in which Meier promised he would at last address one of the "four enigmas": the enigma of Jesus's "self-designation."[2] When I was honored by an invitation to contribute to Meier's *Festschrift* celebrating his seventy-fifth birthday, I published the results of my own research on the so-called Johannine "thunderbolt" (Matt 11:25–27//Luke 10:21–22) but expressed my hope that I would soon be able to read Meier's own treatment of this important pericope in volume 6.[3] Sadly, that day never came. On October 18,

1. See John P. Meier, *A Marginal Jew: Rethinking the Historical Jesus*, 5 vols., Anchor Yale Bible Reference Library (New Haven: Yale University Press, 1991–2016).

2. Cf. Meier, *A Marginal Jew*, 5:2.

3. See Brant Pitre, "The Historical Jesus and the Apocalyptic 'Thunderbolt' (Matt 11:25–27//Luke 10:21–22)," in *The Figure of Jesus in History and Theology: Essays in Honor of John Meier*, ed. Vincent T. M. Skemp and Kelley Coblentz Bautch, Catholic Biblical Quarterly Imprints 1 (Washington, DC: Catholic Biblical Association of America, 2020), 169–85.

2022, John Meier passed away. To my knowledge, volume 6 of *A Marginal Jew* is and will remain unfinished. It therefore seemed fitting that I honor him by dedicating this volume to his memory. For I would not have even entered this field of research if it wasn't for my early encounter with Meier's extraordinarily thorough, brilliantly written, and incomparably learned scholarship. I have no doubt that he would find many flaws in my book (any doctoral student who ever received a term paper back from Meier did so with fear and trembling; he was a staunch critic), but I also hope he might be somewhat proud of a former student who will never match his learning but who has tried to build on his legacy by continuing to contribute to the quest for Jesus.

I would also like to thank my colleagues at the Augustine Institute Graduate School of Theology. The last six years of work on this project simply would not have been possible without the generous support of Timothy Gray, its president. Thank you, Tim, for always giving me time and resources to pursue my research and writing. I also want to express my thanks to colleagues and friends who read the manuscript and offered their critiques and suggestions, especially Michael P. Barber, Matthew Levering, Curtis Mitch, and John Sehorn. Michael above all spent countless hours reading, critiquing, and debating the contents of this volume with me; words cannot express how grateful I am to him for his friendship and his feedback over all these many years (especially when we disagree!). I'm also deeply grateful to Dale Allison, whose learning is surpassed only by his kindness, and who graciously took time to read the manuscript in its entirety and to share his thoughts and suggestions with me.

Finally, I want to thank everyone on the wonderful publishing team at Eerdmans, especially James Ernest, Trevor Thompson, and Jenny Hoffman, and Eerdmans's excellent anonymous external reviewer, whose close reading and helpful suggestions greatly improved the quality of the manuscript. This is my third book with Eerdmans, and I continue to be amazed by and grateful for your professionalism and commitment to excellence in publications.

Of course, whatever errors and weaknesses remain are mine alone, but as the years pass I become more and more aware of how no scholarship—at least, no *good* scholarship—is ever written in isolation. It takes colleagues, friends, and other collaborators to bring such a work to completion. I for one am truly grateful for all those who have helped me in this endeavor to shed fresh light on the historical Jesus and the origins of divine Christology.

August 6, 2023
Feast of the Transfiguration

Bibliography

Abegg, Martin, Jr., Peter Flint, and Eugene Ulrich. *The Dead Sea Scrolls Bible*. San Francisco: HarperOne, 1999.

Achtemeier, Paul J. *1 Peter*. Hermeneia. Minneapolis: Fortress, 1996.

Allen, Garrick V., Kai Akagi, Paul Sloan, and Madhavi Naveder, eds. *Son of God: Divine Sonship in Jewish and Christian Antiquity*. Winona Lake, IN: Eisenbrauns, 2019.

Allison, Dale C., Jr. *Constructing Jesus: Memory, Imagination, and History*. Grand Rapids: Baker Academic, 2010.

———. *A Critical and Exegetical Commentary on the Epistle of James*. International Critical Commentaries. London: Bloomsbury, 2013.

———. *The Historical Christ and the Theological Jesus*. Grand Rapids: Eerdmans, 2009.

———. *The Intertextual Jesus: Scripture in Q*. Harrisburg, PA: Trinity Press International, 2000.

———. *Jesus of Nazareth: Millenarian Prophet*. Minneapolis: Fortress, 1998.

———. "Reflections on Matthew, John, and Jesus." Pages 47–68 in *Jesus Research: The Gospel of John in Historical Inquiry*. Edited by James H. Charlesworth with Jolyon G. R. Pruszinski. Jewish and Christian Texts 26. London: T&T Clark, 2019.

Allison, Dale C., Jr., Marcus J. Borg, John Dominic Crossan, and Stephen J. Patterson. *The Apocalyptic Jesus: A Debate*. Edited by Robert J. Miller. Santa Rosa: Polebridge, 2001.

Anatolios, Khaled. *Retrieving Nicaea: The Development and Meaning of Trinitarian Doctrine*. Grand Rapids: Baker Academic, 2011.

Anderson, Francis I., and David Noel Freedman. *Micah*. Anchor Bible 24E. New York: Doubleday, 2000.

Anderson, Paul N. "Aspects of Historicity in the Gospel of John." Pages 587–618 in *Jesus and Archaeology*. Edited by James H. Charlesworth. Grand Rapids: Eerdmans, 2006.

———. *The Fourth Gospel and the Quest for Jesus: Modern Foundations Reconsidered*. Library of New Testament Studies 321. New York: T&T Clark, 2006.

———. "Why the Gospel of John Is Fundamental to Jesus Research." Pages 7–46 in *Jesus Research: The Gospel of John in Historical Inquiry*. Edited by James H. Charlesworth and Jolyon G. R. Pruszinski. Jewish and Christian Texts 26. London: T&T Clark, 2019.

Anderson, Paul N., Felix Just, SJ, and Tom Thatcher, eds. *John, Jesus, and History*. 3 vols. Atlanta: Society of Biblical Literature, 2007–2016.

Aran Murphy, Francesca, ed. *The Oxford Handbook of Christology*. Oxford: Oxford University Press, 2015.

Arrian. *History of Alexander and Indica 1*. Translated by P. A. Brunt. Loeb Classical Library 236. Cambridge, MA: Harvard University Press, 1976.

———. *History of Alexander and Indica* 2. Translated by P. A. Brunt. Loeb Classical Library 269. Cambridge, MA: Harvard University Press, 1983.

Attridge, Harold W. *Hebrews: A Commentary*. Hermeneia. Minneapolis: Fortress, 1989.

———. "John and Other Gospels." Pages 44–62 in *The Oxford Handbook of Johannine Studies*. Edited by Judith M. Lieu and Martinus C. de Boer. Oxford: Oxford University Press, 2018.

———. "Some Methodological Considerations Regarding John, Jesus, and History." Pages 71–84 in *Jesus Research: The Gospel of John in Historical Inquiry*. Edited by James H. Charlesworth and Jolyon G. R. Pruszinski. Jewish and Christian Texts 26. London: T&T Clark, 2019.

Aune, David E. *Revelation*. 3 vols. Word Biblical Commentary 52a–c. Dallas: Word, 1997.

———. "Stories of Jesus in the Apocalypse of John." Pages 292–319 in *Contours of Christology in the New Testament*. Edited by Richard N. Longenecker. Grand Rapids: Eerdmans, 2005.

Aus, Roger David. *The Stilling of the Storm: Studies in Early Palestinian Judaic Traditions*. Binghamton, NY: Binghamton University, 2000.

Ayres, Lewis. *Nicaea and Its Legacy: An Approach to Fourth Century Trinitarian Theology*. Oxford: Oxford University Press, 2004.

Backhaus, Knut. "Jesus and John the Baptizer." Pages 241–48 in *The Jesus Handbook*. Edited by Jens Schröter and Christine Jacobi. Translated by Robert L. Brawley. Grand Rapids: Eerdmans, 2022.

Bahat, Dan. "Jesus and the Herodian Temple Mount." Pages 300–308 in *Jesus and*

Archaeology. Edited by James H. Charlesworth. Grand Rapids: Eerdmans, 2006.

Barker, James W. *John's Use of Matthew*. Minneapolis: Fortress, 2015.

Barrett, Anthony A. *Caligula: The Abuse of Power*. 2nd ed. London: Routledge, 2015.

———. *Caligula: The Corruption of Power*. New Haven: Yale University Press, 1990.

Barrett, C. K. *The Gospel according to St. John*. 2nd ed. Philadelphia: Westminster, 1978.

Barth, Markus, and Helmut Blanke. *Colossians*. Anchor Bible 34B. Translated by Astrid B. Beck. New York: Doubleday, 1994.

Bates, Matthew W. *The Birth of the Trinity: Jesus, God, and Spirit in New Testament and Early Christian Interpretations of the Old Testament*. Oxford: Oxford University Press, 2015.

Bauckham, Richard. "For What Offence Was James Put to Death?" Pages 199–232 in *James the Just and Christian Origins*. Edited by Bruce Chilton and Craig A. Evans. Supplements to Novum Testamentum 98. Leiden: Brill, 1999.

———. "James and the Jerusalem Community." Pages 55–95 in *Jewish Believers in Jesus: The Early Centuries*. Edited by Oskar Skarsaune and Reidar Hvalvik. Peabody, MA: Hendrickson, 2007.

———. *Jesus and the Eyewitnesses: The Gospels as Eyewitness Testimony*. 2nd ed. Grand Rapids: Eerdmans, 2017.

———. *Jesus and the God of Israel: God Crucified and Other Studies on the New Testament's Christology of Divine Identity*. Grand Rapids: Eerdmans, 2008.

———. *Jesus: A Very Short Introduction*. Oxford: Oxford University Press, 2011.

Becker, Eve-Marie, Helen K. Bond, and Catrin H. Williams, eds. *John's Transformation of Mark*. London: T&T Clark, 2021.

Becker, Jürgen. *Jesus of Nazareth*. Translated by James E. Crouch. New York: Walter de Gruyter, 1998.

Behr, John. *The Nicene Faith*. Part 1. The Formation of Christian Theology 2. Crestwood, NY: St. Vladimir's Seminary Press, 2004.

Bekken, Per Jarle. "Philo's Relevance of the Study of the New Testament." Pages 226–67 in *Reading Philo: A Handbook of Philo of Alexandria*. Edited by Torrey Seland. Grand Rapids: Eerdmans, 2014.

Beutler, Johannes, SJ. *A Commentary on the Gospel of John*. Translated by Michael Tait. Grand Rapids: Eerdmans, 2017.

———. *Judaism and the Jews in the Gospel of John*. Subsidia Biblica 30. Rome: Editrice Pontifico Instituto Biblico, 2006.

Bird, Michael F. *Are You the One Who Is to Come? The Historical Jesus and the Messianic Question*. Grand Rapids: Baker Academic, 2009.

———. *The Gospel of the Lord: How the Early Church Wrote the Story of Jesus*. Grand Rapids: Eerdmans, 2014.

———. *Jesus among the Gods: Early Christology in the Greco-Roman World*. Waco, TX: Baylor University Press, 2022.

———. "Jesus and the 'Partings of the Ways.'" Pages 1183–215 in vol. 1 of *Handbook for the Study of the Historical Jesus*. Edited by Tom Holmén and Stanley E. Porter. 4 vols. Leiden: Brill, 2011.

———. *Jesus the Eternal Son: Answering Adoptionist Christology*. Grand Rapids: Eerdmans, 2017.

Black, Sven-Olav. "The Trials of Jesus." Pages 474–81 in *The Jesus Handbook*. Edited by Jens Schröter and Christine Jacobi. Translated by Robert L. Brawley. Grand Rapids: Eerdmans, 2022.

Blenkinsopp, Joseph. *Isaiah*. 3 vols. Anchor Yale Bible 19, 19A, 19B. New Haven: Yale University Press, 2000–2003.

Blinzler, Josef. *The Trial of Jesus*. Translated by Isabel McHugh and Florence McHugh. Westminster, MD: Newman, 1959.

Bock, Darrell L. *Blasphemy and Exaltation in Judaism: The Charge against Jesus in Mark 14:53–65*. Wissenschaftliche Untersuchungen zum Neuen Testament 2.106. Tübingen: Mohr Siebeck, 1998.

———. "Blasphemy and the Jewish Examination of Jesus." Pages 589–667 in *Key Events in the Life of the Historical Jesus*. Edited by Darrell L. Bock and Robert L. Webb. Wissenschaftliche Untersuchungen zum Neuen Testament 247. Tübingen: Mohr Siebeck, 2009.

Bock, Darrell L., and Robert L. Webb, eds. *Key Events in the Life of the Historical Jesus*. Wissenschaftliche Untersuchungen zum Neuen Testament 247. Tübingen: Mohr Siebeck; Grand Rapids: Eerdmans, 2009.

Boer, Martinus C. de. *Galatians: A Commentary*. New Testament Library. Louisville: Westminster John Knox, 2011.

Bond, Helen K. *Caiaphas: Friend of Rome and Judge of Jesus?* Louisville: Westminster John Knox, 2004.

———. *The Historical Jesus: A Guide for the Perplexed*. London: T&T Clark, 2012.

———. *Pontius Pilate in History and Interpretation*. Society for New Testament Studies Monograph Series 100. Cambridge: Cambridge University Press, 1998.

Bornkamm, Günther. *Jesus of Nazareth*. Translated by Irene McLuskey and Fraser McLuskey, with James M. Robinson. New York: Harper, 1960.

Bousset, Wilhelm. *Kyrios Christos: A History of Belief in Christ from the Beginnings of Christianity to Irenaeus*. Translated by John E. Steely. Waco, TX: Baylor University Press, 2013 (orig. 1931).

Bovon, François. *Luke: A Commentary*. 3 vols. Translated by Christine M. Thomas, Donald S. Deer, and James E. Crouch. Hermeneia. Minneapolis: Fortress, 2002–2013.

Boyarin, Daniel. *Border Lines: The Partition of Judaeo-Christianity*. Philadelphia: University of Pennsylvania Press, 2004.

———. *The Jewish Gospels: The Story of the Jewish Christ*. New York: The New Press, 2012.

Brennan, Nick. *Divine Christology in the Epistle to the Hebrews*. Library of New Testament Studies. London: T&T Clark, 2023.

Broadhead, Edwin K. "Implicit Christology and the Historical Jesus." Pages 1169–82 in vol. 2 of *Handbook for the Study of the Historical Jesus*. Edited by Tom Holmén and Stanley E. Porter. 4 vols. Leiden: Brill, 2011.

Brown, Raymond E. *The Birth of the Messiah*. Rev. ed. Anchor Yale Bible Reference Library. New Haven: Yale University Press, 1993.

———. *The Death of the Messiah: From Gethsemane to the Grave: A Commentary on the Passion Narratives in the Four Gospels*. Anchor Yale Bible Reference Library. New Haven: Yale University Press, 1994.

———. *The Gospel according to John*. 2 vols. Anchor Yale Bible Commentary 29–29A. New Haven: Yale University Press, 1966–1970.

Bryan, Christopher. *The Resurrection of the Messiah*. Oxford: Oxford University Press, 2011.

Bryan, Steven M. *Jesus and Israel's Traditions of Judgment and Restoration*. Society for New Testament Studies Monograph Series 117. Cambridge: Cambridge University Press, 2002.

Bühner, Ruben A. *Messianic High Christology: New Testament Variants of Second Temple Judaism*. Waco, TX: Baylor University Press, 2021.

Bultmann, Rudolf. *The Gospel of John: A Commentary*. Translated by G. R. Beasley-Murray. Philadelphia: Westminster, 1971.

———. *History of the Synoptic Tradition*. Rev. ed. Translated by John Marsh. Oxford: Basil Blackwell, 1963.

———. *Jesus and the Word*. Translated by Louise Pettibone Smith and Erminie Huntress Lantero. New York: Charles Scribner's Sons, 1934.

Burkett, Delbert. *The Son of Man Debate: A History and Evaluation*. Society for New Testament Studies Monograph Series 107. Cambridge: Cambridge University Press, 2007.

Burkitt, F. C. "The Hebrew Papyrus of the Ten Commandments." *Jewish Quarterly Review* 15 (1903): 392–40.

Burridge, Richard A. *What Are the Gospels? A Comparison with Graeco-Roman Biography*. 25th anniv. ed. Waco, TX: Baylor University Press, 2018.

Cargill, Robert R. *Melchizedek, King of Sodom: How Scribes Invented the Biblical Priest-King*. Oxford: Oxford University Press, 2019.

Casey, P. Maurice. *From Jewish Prophet to Gentile God: The Origins and Development of New Testament Christology*. Cambridge: James Clarke; Louisville: Westminster/John Knox, 1991.

———. *Jesus of Nazareth: An Independent Historian's Account of His Life and Teaching*. London: T&T Clark, 2010.

Catchpole, David. *The Trial of Jesus: A Study in the Gospels and Jewish Historiography from 1770 to the Present Day*. Leiden: Brill, 1971.

Chapman, David W., and Eckhard J. Schnabel. *The Trial and Crucifixion of Jesus: Texts and Commentary*. Wissenschaftliche Untersuchungen zum Neuen Testament 344. Tübingen: Mohr Siebeck, 2015.

Charlesworth, James H. "Did They Ever Part?" Pages 281–300 in *Partings: How Judaism and Christianity Became Two*. Edited by Hershel Shanks. Washington, DC: Biblical Archaeology Society, 2013.

———. *Jesus and the Dead Sea Scrolls*. Anchor Bible Reference Library. New York: Doubleday, 1992.

———. *Jesus as Mirrored in John: The Genius in the New Testament*. London: T&T Clark, 2019.

———. *Jesus within Judaism*. Anchor Bible Reference Library. New York: Doubleday, 1988.

———, ed. *Old Testament Pseudepigrapha*. 2 vols. Anchor Bible Reference Library. New York: Doubleday, 1983, 1985.

Charlesworth, James H., and Jolyon G. R. Pruszinski, eds. *Jesus Research: The Gospel of John in Historical Inquiry*. Jewish and Christian Texts 26. London: T&T Clark, 2019.

Charlesworth, James H., Brian Rhea, and Petr Pokorny, eds. *Jesus Research: New Methodologies and Perceptions: The Second Princeton-Prague Symposium on Jesus Research*. Grand Rapids: Eerdmans, 2014.

Chester, Andrew. "High Christology—Whence, When, and Why?" *Early Christianity* 2 (2011): 22–50.

———. *Messiah and Exaltation: Jewish Messianic and Visionary Traditions and New Testament Christology*. Wissenschaftliche Untersuchungen zum Neuen Testament 207. Tübingen: Mohr Siebeck, 2007.

Chilton, Bruce. *The Herods: Murder, Politics, and the Art of Succession*. Minneapolis: Fortress, 2021.

———. "(The) Son of (the) Man, and Jesus." Pages 259–87 in *Authenticating the Words of Jesus*. Edited Bruce Chilton and Craig A. Evans. Leiden: Brill, 1999.

Cogan, Mordechai. *1 Kings*. Anchor Yale Bible 10A. New Haven: Yale University Press, 2001.

Cogan, Mordechai, and Hayim Tadmor. *2 Kings*. Anchor Yale Bible 11. New Haven: Yale University Press, 1988.

Cohen, Shaye J. D. "In Between: Jewish-Christians and the Curse of the Heretics." Pages 207–36 in *Partings: How Judaism and Christianity Became Two*. Edited by Hershel Shanks. Washington, DC: Biblical Archaeology Society, 2013.

Collins, John J. *The Apocalyptic Imagination: An Introduction to Jewish Apocalyptic Literature*. 3rd ed. Grand Rapids: Eerdmans, 2016.

———. *Daniel: A Commentary*. Hermeneia. Minneapolis: Fortress, 1993.

———, ed. *The Oxford Handbook of Apocalyptic Literature*. Oxford: Oxford University Press, 2014.

———. "Powers in Heaven: God, Gods, and Angels in the Dead Sea Scrolls." Pages 9–28 in *Religion in the Dead Sea Scrolls*. Edited by John J. Collins and Robert A. Kugler. Grand Rapids: Eerdmans, 2000.

———. *The Scepter and the Star: Messianism in Light of the Dead Sea Scrolls*. 2nd ed. Grand Rapids: Eerdmans, 2010.

———. "The Son of Man in Ancient Judaism." Pages 1545–68 in vol. 2 of *Handbook for the Study of the Historical Jesus*. Edited by Tom Holmén and Stanley E. Porter. 4 vols. Leiden: Brill, 2011.

Collins, Nina L. *Jesus, the Sabbath, and the Jewish Debate: Healing on the Sabbath in the 1st and 2nd Centuries CE*. Library of New Testament Studies 474. London: Bloomsbury T&T Clark, 2014.

Compton, Jared. *Psalm 110 and the Logic of Hebrews*. Library of New Testament Studies 537. London: T&T Clark, 2012.

Corley, Kathleen E. *Women and the Historical Jesus: Feminist Myths of Christian Origins*. Santa Rose: Polebridge, 2002.

Cotter, Wendy, CSJ. *Miracles in Greco-Roman Antiquity: A Sourcebook*. London: Routledge, 1999.

Crossan, John Dominic, and Jonathan L. Reed. *Excavating Jesus: Beneath the Stones, Behind the Texts*. San Francisco: HarperCollins, 2001.

———. *The Historical Jesus: The Life of a Mediterranean Jewish Peasant*. San Francisco: HarperCollins, 1991.

Crossley, James. "The Nature Miracles as Pure Myth." Pages 86–106 in *The Nature Miracles of Jesus: Problems, Perspectives, and Prospects*. Edited by Graham H. Twelftree. Eugene, OR: Cascade, 2017.

Dahood, Mitchell, SJ. *Psalms*. 3 vols. Anchor Bible 16, 16A, 16B. New York: Doubleday, 1966–1970.

Danker, Frederick. *A Greek-English Lexicon of the New Testament and Other Early Christian Literature*. 3rd ed. Chicago: University of Chicago Press 2000.

Davies, W. D. "'Knowledge' in the Dead Sea Scrolls and Matt. 11.25–30." Pages 119–44 in *Christian Origins and Judaism*. London: DLT, 1962.

Davies, W. D., and Dale C. Allison, Jr. *A Critical and Exegetical Commentary on the Gospel according to Saint Matthew*. 3 vols. International Critical Commentaries. Edinburgh: T&T Clark, 1988–1997.

Dio Chrysostom. *Discourses 1–11*. Translated by J. W. Cohoon. Loeb Classical Library 257. Cambridge, MA: Harvard University Press, 1932.

Dodd, C. H. *Historical Tradition in the Fourth Gospel*. Cambridge: Cambridge University Press, 1963.

———. *The Parables of the Kingdom*. Rev. ed. New York: Charles Scribner's Sons, 1961.

Doran, Robert. "Antiochus IV Epiphanes." Pages 338–39 in *Eerdmans Dictionary of Early Judaism*. Edited by John J. Collins and Daniel C. Harlow. Grand Rapids: Eerdmans, 2010.

Dunn, James D. G. *Beginning from Jerusalem*. Vol. 2 of *Christianity in the Making*. Grand Rapids: Eerdmans, 2009.

———. *Christology in the Making: A New Testament Inquiry into the Origins of the Doctrine of the Incarnation*. 2nd ed. Grand Rapids: Eerdmans, 1989.

———. *Jesus Remembered*. Vol. 1 of *Christianity in the Making*. Grand Rapids: Eerdmans, 2003.

———, ed. *Jews and Christians: The Parting of the Ways, A. D. 70 to 135*. Grand Rapids: Eerdmans, 1992.

———. "John and the Historical Jesus: A Response." Pages 493–505 in *Glimpses of Jesus Through the Johannine Lens*. Edited by Paul N. Anderson, Felix Just, SJ, and Tom Thatcher. Vol. 3 of *John, Jesus, and History*. Atlanta: Society of Biblical Literature, 2016.

———. "The Making of Christology—Evolution or Unfolding?" Pages 437–52 in *Jesus of Nazareth, Lord and Christ: Essays on the Historical Jesus and New Testament Christology*. Edited by Joel B. Green and Max Turner. Grand Rapids: Eerdmans, 1994.

———. *Neither Jew nor Greek: A Contested Identity*. Vol. 3 of *Christianity in the Making*. Grand Rapids: Eerdmans, 2015.

———. *The Partings of the Ways between Christianity and Judaism and Their Significance for the Character of Christianity*. 2nd ed. London: SCM, 2006 [orig. 1991].

———. "Was Jesus a Monotheist? A Contribution to the Discussion of Christian Monotheism." Pages 104–19 in *Early Jewish and Christian Monotheism*. Edited by Loren T. Stuckenbruck and Wendy E. S. North. Journal for the Study of the New Testament Supplement Series 263. London: T&T Clark, 2004.

Ehrman, Bart D. *Forgery and Counterforgery: The Use of Literary Deceit in Early Christian Polemics*. Oxford: Oxford University Press, 2013.

———. *How Jesus Became God: The Exaltation of a Jewish Preacher from Galilee*. San Francisco: HarperOne, 2014.

———. *Jesus: Apocalyptic Prophet of the New Millennium*. Oxford: Oxford University Press, 1999.

Eidinow, Esther, and Julia Kindt, eds. *The Oxford Handbook of Ancient Greek Religion*. Oxford: Oxford University Press, 2015.

Elledge, C. D. *Resurrection of the Dead in Early Judaism*. Oxford: Oxford University Press, 2017.

Elliot, Neil. "Messianic Secret." Pages 404–6 in *The Routledge Encyclopedia of the Historical Jesus*. Edited by Craig A. Evans. New York: Routledge, 2010.

Eshel, Esther. "The Identification of the 'Speaker' in the Self-Glorification Hymn." Pages 619–35 in *The Provo International Conference on the Dead Sea Scrolls*. Studies on the Texts of the Desert of Judah 30. Leiden: Brill, 1999.

Eskola, Timo. *Messiah and Throne: Jewish Merkabah Mysticism and Early Christian Exaltation Discourse*. Wissenschaftliche Untersuchungen zum Neuen Testament 2.142. Tübingen: Mohr Siebeck, 2001.

Eusebius. *Ecclesiastical History, Books 1–5*. Translated by Kirsopp Lake. Loeb Classical Library 153. Cambridge, MA: Harvard University Press, 1926.

Evans, Craig A. *Jesus and His Contemporaries: Comparative Studies*. Arbeiten zur Geschichte des antiken Judentums und des Urchristentums 25. Leiden: Brill, 1995.

———. "Jesus and the Dead Sea Scrolls from Qumran Cave 4." Pages 91–100 in *Eschatology, Messianism, and the Dead Sea Scrolls*. Edited by Craig A. Evans and Peter W. Flint. Grand Rapids: Eerdmans, 1997.

———. "Sanhedrin." Pages 1193–94 in *Eerdmans Dictionary of Early Judaism*. Edited by John J. Collins and Daniel C. Harlow. Grand Rapids: Eerdmans, 2010.

Eve, Eric. *Behind the Gospels: Understanding the Oral Tradition*. Minneapolis: Fortress, 2014.

———. "The Growth of the Nature Miracles." Pages 66–85 in *The Nature Miracles of Jesus: Problems, Perspectives, and Prospects*. Edited by Graham H. Twelftree. Eugene, OR: Cascade, 2017.

———. *The Jewish Context of Jesus' Miracles*. Library of New Testament Studies 172. Sheffield: Sheffield Academic Press, 2002.

———. *Writing the Gospels: Composition and Memory*. London: SPCK, 2016.

Falk, Daniel K. "Festivals and Holy Days." Pages 636–45 in *The Eerdmans Dictionary of Early Judaism*. Edited by John J. Collins and Daniel C. Harlow. Grand Rapids: Eerdmans, 2010.

———. "Moses." Pages 967–70 in *The Eerdmans Dictionary of Early Judaism*. Edited by John J. Collins and Daniel C. Harlow. Grand Rapids: Eerdmans, 2010.

Fine, Steven. "Death, Burial, and Afterlife." Pages 440–62 in *The Oxford Handbook of Jewish Daily Life in Roman Palestine*. Edited by Catherine Hezser. Oxford: Oxford University Press, 2010.

Fitzmyer, Joseph A. *The Acts of the Apostles*. Anchor Yale Bible 31. New Haven: Yale University Press, 1997.

———. *First Corinthians*. Anchor Yale Bible 32. New Haven: Yale University Press, 2008.

———. *The Gospel according to Luke*. 2 vols. Anchor Yale Bible 28–28A. New Haven: Yale University Press, 1983–1985.

———. *The One Who Is to Come*. Grand Rapids: Eerdmans, 2007.

Fletcher-Louis, Crispin. "Jesus and Apocalypticism." Pages 2877–909 in vol. 3 of *Handbook for the Study of the Historical Jesus*. Edited by Tom Holmén and Stanley E. Porter. 4 vols. Leiden: Brill, 2011.

———. *Jesus Monotheism*. Vol. 1 of *Christological Origins: The Emerging Consensus and Beyond*. Eugene, OR: Cascade, 2015.

———. "Jewish Apocalyptic and Apocalypticism." Pages 1569–607 in vol. 2 of *Handbook for the Study of the Historical Jesus*. Edited by Tom Holmén and Stanley E. Porter. 4 vols. Leiden: Brill, 2011.

Flusser, David, with R. Steven Notley. *The Sage from Galilee: Rediscovering Jesus' Genius*. Grand Rapids: Eerdmans, 2007.

———. "The Ten Commandments and the New Testament." Pages 219–46 in *The Ten Commandments in History and Tradition*. Edited by Ben-Zion Segal. Translated by Gershon Levi. Jerusalem: Magnes, 1990.

Foster, Paul. "Memory, Orality, and the Fourth Gospel: Three Dead Ends in Historical Jesus Research." *Journal for the Study of the Historical Jesus* 10 (2012): 191–227.

Foster, Paul A. Gregory, J. S. Kloppenborg, and J. Verheyden, eds. *New Studies in the Synoptic Problem: Oxford Conference, April 2008; Essays in Honor of Christopher M. Tuckett*. Bibliotheca Ephemeridum Theologicarum Lovaniensium 239. Leuven: Peeters, 2011.

Fox, Michael V. *Proverbs 1–9*. Anchor Yale Bible 18A. New Haven: Yale University Press, 2000.

———. *Proverbs 10–31*. Anchor Yale Bible 18B. New Haven: Yale University Press, 2009.

Fraade, Steven D. *The Damascus Document*. Oxford Commentaries on the Dead Sea Scrolls. Oxford: Oxford University Press, 2022.

Fredricksmeyer, A. E. "Alexander's Religion and Divinity." Pages 253–78 in *Brill's Companion to Alexander the Great*. Edited by Joseph Roisman. Leiden: Brill, 2003.

Fredriksen, Paula. "How High Can Early High Christology Be?" Pages 293–319 in *Monotheism and Christology in Greco-Roman Antiquity*. Edited by Matthew V. Novenson. Supplements to Novum Testamentum 180. Leiden: Brill, 2020.

———. "Mandatory Retirement: Ideas in the Study of Christian Origins Whose Time Has Come to Go." Pages 25–38 in *Israel's God and Rebecca's Children: Christology and Community in Early Judaism and Christianity: Essays in Honor of Larry W. Hurtado and Alan F. Segal*. Edited by David B. Capes, April D. DeConick, Helen K. Bond, and Troy A. Miller. Waco, TX: Baylor University Press, 2007.

———. *Paul: The Pagan's Apostle*. New Haven: Yale University Press, 2017.

———. "What 'Parting of the Ways'? Jews, Gentiles, and the Ancient Mediterranean City." Pages 35–64 in *The Ways That Never Parted: Jews and Christians in Late Antiquity and the Early Middle Ages*. Edited by Adam H. Becker and Annette Yoshiko Reed. Minneapolis: Fortress, 2007.

———. *When Christians Were Jews: The First Generation*. New Haven: Yale University Press, 2018.

Freedman, David Noel. "Yhwh." Pages 501–11 in vol. 5 of *Theological Dictionary of the Old Testament*. Edited by G. J. Botterweck et al. 15 vols. Grand Rapids: Eerdmans, 1974–2006.

Freund, A. "The Decalogue in Early Judaism and Christianity." Pages 124–41 in *The Function of Scripture in Early Judaism and Christian Tradition*. Edited by Craig A. Evans and James A. Sanders. Sheffield: Sheffield Academic Press, 1998.

Frey, Jörg. "Die Apokalyptik als Herausforderung der neutestamentlichen Wissenschaft. Zum Problem: Jesus und die Apokalyptik." Pages 23–94 in *Apokalyptik als Herausforderung neutestamentlicher Theologie*. Edited by Michael Becker and Markus Öhler. Wissenschaftliche Untersuchungen zum Neuen Testament 2.214. Tübingen: Mohr Siebeck, 2006.

———. *The Glory of the Crucified One: Christology and Theology in the Gospel of John*. Translated by Wayne Coppins and Christoph Heilig. Waco, TX: Baylor University Press, 2018.

———. "The Gospel of John as a Historical Source." Pages 138–40 in *The Jesus Handbook*. Edited by Jens Schröter and Christine Jacobi. Translated by Robert L. Brawley. Grand Rapids: Eerdmans, 2022.

———. *The Letter of Jude and the Second Letter of Peter: A Theological Commentary*. Translated by Kathleen Ess. Waco, TX: Baylor University Press, 2018.

———. *Theology and History in the Fourth Gospel: Tradition and Narration*. Waco, TX: Baylor University Press, 2018.

Freyne, Sean. *Jesus, a Jewish Galilean: A New Reading of the Jesus-Story*. Repr., London: T&T Clark, 2005.

Funk, Robert W., Roy Hoover, and the Jesus Seminar. *The Five Gospels: The Search for the Authentic Words of Jesus*. New York: Macmillan, 1993.

Funk, Robert W., and the Jesus Seminar. *The Acts of Jesus: The Search for the Authentic Deeds of Jesus*. San Francisco: HarperSanFrancisco/Polebridge, 1998.

Gale, Aaron M. "The Gospel according to Matthew." Pages 9–66 in *The Jewish Annotated New Testament*. Edited by Amy-Jill Levine and Marc Zvi Brettler. 2nd ed. Oxford: Oxford University Press, 2017.

García Martínez, Florentino. *Qumranica Minora II*. Studies in the Texts of the Desert of Judea 64. Leiden: Brill, 2007.

García Martínez, Florentino, and Eibert J. C. Tigchelaar. *The Dead Sea Scrolls Study Edition*. 2 vols. Grand Rapids: Eerdmans, 2000.

Gathercole, Simon J. *The Preexistent Son: Recovering the Christologies of Matthew, Mark, and Luke*. Grand Rapids: Eerdmans, 2006.

Gerber, Christine. "Jesus's Concept of God and the Meaning of the Father Metaphor." Pages 358–66 in *The Jesus Handbook*. Edited by Jens Schröter and Christine Jacobi. Translated by Robert L. Brawley. Grand Rapids: Eerdmans, 2022.

Gibson, Shimon. *The Final Days of Jesus: The Archaeological Evidence*. San Francisco: HarperOne, 2009.

Gnilka, Joachim. *Jesus of Nazareth. Message and History*. Translated by Siegfried S. Schatzmann. Peabody, MA: Hendrickson, 1997.

Goldstein, Jonathan A. *2 Maccabees*. Anchor Yale Bible 41A. New Haven: Yale University Press, 1983.

Goodacre, Mark. *The Case against Q: Studies in Markan Priority and the Synoptic Problem*. Harrisburg: Trinity Press International, 2002.

Gradel, Ittai. *Emperor Worship and Roman Religion*. Oxford: Oxford University Press, 2002.

Gray, Rebecca. *Prophetic Figures in Late Second Temple Jewish Palestine: The Evidence from Josephus*. Oxford: Oxford University Press, 1993.

Green, Gene L. *Jude and 2 Peter*. Baker Exegetical Commentary on the New Testament. Grand Rapids: Baker Academic, 2008.

Green, Peter. *Alexander of Macedon, 356–323 B.C.: A Historical Biography*. Berkeley: University of California Press, 2013.

Greenberg, Moshe. *Ezekiel 21–37*. Anchor Yale Bible 22A. New Haven: Yale University Press, 1997.

Gregg, Brian Han. *The Historical Jesus and the Final Judgment Sayings in Q*. Wissenschaftliche Untersuchungen zum Neuen Testament 2.207. Tübingen: Mohr Siebeck, 2006.

Grindheim, Sigurd. *God's Equal: What Can We Know about Jesus' Self-Understanding in the Synoptic Gospels?* Library of New Testament Studies 446. London: T&T Clark, 2011.

Hägerland, Tobias. *Jesus and the Forgiveness of Sins: An Aspect of His Prophetic Mission*. Society for New Testament Studies Monograph Series 150. Cambridge: Cambridge University Press, 2012.

Hamerton-Kelly, R. G. *Pre-existence, Wisdom, and the Son of Man*. Society for New Testament Studies Monograph Series 21. Cambridge: Cambridge University Press, 1973.

Hammel, E. "Jewish Activity against Christians in Palestine according to Acts." Pages 357–63 in *Palestinian Setting*, vol. 4 of *The Book of Acts in Its First-Century Setting*. Edited by Richard Bauckham. Grand Rapids: Eerdmans, 1995.

Hanson, R. P. C. *The Search for the Christian Doctrine of God: The Arian Controversy, 318–81*. London: T&T Clark, 1988.

Harnack, Adolf von. *What Is Christianity?* Translated by Thomas Bailey Saunders. Philadelphia: Fortress, 1986 (orig. 1901).

Harrington, Hannah K. "Sin." Pages 1230–31 in *The Eerdmans Dictionary of Early Judaism*. Edited by John J. Collins and Daniel C. Harlow. Grand Rapids: Eerdmans, 2010.

Hartman, Louis F., and Alexander A. DiLella. *The Book of Daniel*. Anchor Bible 23. New York: Doubleday, 1978.

Harvey, A. E. *Jesus and the Constraints of History*. Philadelphia: Westminster, 1982.

Hase, Karl von. *Die Geschichte Jesu: Nach akademischen Vorlesungen*. 2nd ed. Leipzig: Breitkopf & Härtel, 1876.

Hay, David M. *Glory at the Right Hand: Psalm 110 in Early Christianity*. Society of Biblical Literature Monograph Series 18. Nashville: Abingdon, 1973.

Hays, Richard B. *Echoes of Scripture in the Gospels*. Waco, TX: Baylor University Press, 2016.

———. *Reading Backwards: Figural Christology and the Fourfold Gospel Witness.* Waco, TX: Baylor University Press, 2014.

Hayward, C. T. R. "'The Lord Is One': Reflections on the Theme of Unity in John's Gospel from a Jewish Perspective." Pages 138–54 in *Early Jewish and Christian Monotheism.* Edited by Loren T. Stuckenbruck and Wendy E. S. North. Journal for the Study of the New Testament Supplement Series 263. London: T&T Clark, 2004.

Hengel, Martin. *Between Jesus and Paul: Studies in the Earliest History of Christianity.* Translated by John Bowden. Philadelphia: Fortress, 1983.

———. *The Charismatic Leader and His Followers.* Translated by James Greig. New York: Crossroad, 1981.

———. *Judaism and Hellenism: Studies in Their Encounter in Palestine During the Early Hellenistic Period.* Translated by John Bowden. 2 vols. Philadelphia: Fortress, 1974.

———. *The Son of God: The Origin of Christology and the History of Jewish-Hellenistic Religion.* Philadelphia: Fortress, 1976.

———. *Studies in Early Christology.* Edinburgh: T&T Clark, 1995.

Hengel, Martin, and Anna Maria Schwemer. *Jesus and Judaism.* Translated by Wayne Coppins. Waco, TX: Baylor University Press, 2019.

Henten, Jan Willem van. "*Testimonium Flavianum.*" Pages 365–70 in *From Paul to Josephus: Literary Receptions of Jesus in the First Century CE.* Vol. 1 of *The Reception of Jesus in the First Three Centuries.* Edited by Helen K. Bond. London: T&T Clark, 2020.

Herz, Peter. "Emperors: Caring for the Empire and Their Successors." Pages 304–16 in *A Companion to Roman Religion.* Oxford: Wiley-Blackwell, 2011.

Hiebert, Theodore. "Theophany in the Old Testament." Pages 505–11 in vol. 6 of *The Anchor Bible Dictionary.* Edited by David Noel Freedman. 6 vols. New York: Doubleday, 1992.

Holladay, Carl R. *Acts: A Commentary.* New Testament Library. Louisville: Westminster John Knox, 2016.

Holmén, Tom. "Doubts about Double Dissimilarity: Restructuring the Main Criterion of Jesus-of-History Research." Pages 47–80 in *Authenticating the Words of Jesus.* Edited by Bruce Chilton and Craig A. Evans. Leiden: Brill, 1999.

———. "An Introduction to the Continuum Approach." Pages 1–16 in *Jesus from Judaism to Christianity: Continuum Approaches to the Historical Jesus.* Edited by Tom Holmén. Library of New Testament Studies 352. London: T&T Clark, 2007.

Holmén, Tom, and Stanley E. Porter, eds. *Handbook for Handbook for the Study of the Historical Jesus*. Edited by Tom Holmén and Stanley E. Porter. 4 vols. Leiden: Brill, 2011.

Hossfeld, Frank Lothar, and Erich Zenger. *Psalms 2*. Translated by Linda M. Maloney. Hermeneia. Minneapolis: Fortress, 2005.

———. *Psalms 3*. Translated by Linda M. Maloney. Hermeneia. Minneapolis: Fortress, 2011.

Hultgren, Arland J. "The Message of Jesus II: Parables." Pages 2549–71 in vol. 3 of *Handbook for the Study of the Historical Jesus*. Edited by Tom Holmén and Stanley E. Porter. 4 vols. Leiden: Brill, 2011.

———. *The Parables of Jesus: A Commentary*. Grand Rapids: Eerdmans, 2000.

Hume, David. *An Enquiry Concerning Human Understanding: And Other Writings*. Edited by Stephen Buckle. Cambridge: Cambridge University Press, 2007.

Hurtado, Larry W. *Ancient Jewish Monotheism and Early Christian Jesus-Devotion: The Context and Character of Christological Faith*. Waco, TX: Baylor University Press, 2017.

———. "The Binitarian Shape of Early Christian Worship." Pages 301–26 in Larry Hurtado, *Ancient Jewish Monotheism and Early Christian Jesus-Devotion: The Context and Character of Christological Faith*. Waco, TX: Baylor University Press, 2017.

———. *How on Earth Did Jesus Become a God? Historical Questions about Earliest Devotion to Jesus*. Grand Rapids: Eerdmans, 2005.

———. *Lord Jesus Christ: Devotion to Jesus in Earliest Christianity*. Grand Rapids: Eerdmans, 2003.

———. "Monotheism." Pages 962–66 in *The Eerdmans Dictionary of Early Judaism*. Edited by John J. Collins and Daniel C. Harlow. Grand Rapids: Eerdmans, 2010.

———. *One God, One Lord: Early Christian Devotion and Ancient Jewish Monotheism*. 3rd ed. London: T&T Clark, 2015.

Hurtado, Larry W., and Paul L. Owen, eds. *"Who Is This Son of Man?" The Latest Scholarship on a Puzzling Expression of the Historical Jesus*. Library of New Testament Studies 390. London: Bloomsbury T&T Clark, 2011.

Jacobson, A. D. "Jesus against the Family: The Dissolution of Family Ties in the Gospel Tradition." Pages 189–218 in *From Quest to Q: Festschrift for James M. Robinson*. Edited by J. M. Asgeirsson et al. Bibliotheca Ephemeridum Theologicarum Lovaniensium 146. Leuven: Leuven University Press, 2000.

Jeremias, Joachim. *The Parables of Jesus*. 2nd rev. ed. Upper Saddle River, NJ: Prentice Hall, 1972.

———. *The Proclamation of Jesus*. Translated by John Bowden. New Testament Theology 1. New York: Charles Scribner's Sons, 1971.

Johannson, Daniel. "Who Can Forgive Sins but God Alone? Human and Angelic Agents, and Divine Forgiveness in Early Judaism." *Journal for the Study of the New Testament* 33 (2011): 351–74.

Josephus. *Jewish Antiquities, Books I–III*. Translated by H. St. J. Thackeray. Loeb Classical Library 242. Cambridge, MA: Harvard University Press, 1930.

———. *Jewish Antiquities, Books IV–VI*. Translated by H. St. J. Thackeray and Ralph Marcus. Loeb Classical Library 490. Cambridge, MA: Harvard University Press, 1934.

———. *Jewish Antiquities, Books IX–XI*. Translated by Ralph Marcus. Loeb Classical Library 326. Cambridge, MA: Harvard University Press, 1937.

———. *Jewish Antiquities, Books XII–XIII*. Translated by Ralph Marcus. Loeb Classical Library 365. Cambridge, MA: Harvard University Press, 1933.

———. *Jewish Antiquities, Books XVI–XVII*. Translated by Ralph Marcus and Allen Wikgren. Loeb Classical Library 410. Cambridge, MA: Harvard University Press, 1969.

———. *Jewish Antiquities, Books XVIII–XIX*. Translated by Louis H. Feldman. Loeb Classical Library 433. Cambridge: Harvard University Press, 1965.

———. *Jewish Antiquities, Book XX, General Index*. Translated by L. H. Feldman. Loeb Classical Library 456. Cambridge, MA: Harvard University Press, 1965.

———. *The Jewish War, Books I–II*. Translated by H. St. J. Thackeray. Loeb Classical Library 203. Cambridge, MA: Harvard University Press, 1927.

———. *The Jewish War, Books V–VII*. Translated by H. St. J. Thackeray. Loeb Classical Library 210. Cambridge, MA: Harvard University Press, 1928.

———. *The Life, Against Apion*. Translated by H. St. J. Thackeray. Loeb Classical Library 186. Cambridge, MA: Harvard University Press, 1926.

Joynes, Christine E. "Elijah." Pages 577–78 in *The Eerdmans Dictionary of Early Judaism*. Edited by John J. Collins and Daniel C. Harlow. Grand Rapids: Eerdmans, 2010.

Jülicher, Adolf. *Die Gleichnisreden Jesu*. 2nd ed. 2 vols. Tübingen: J. C. B. Mohr (Paul Siebeck), 1899.

Käsemann, Ernst. "The Disciples of John the Baptist in Ephesus." Pages 136–48 in *Essays on New Testament Themes*. Studies in Biblical Theology 41. London: SCM, 1964.

Kazen, Thomas. "Jesus's Interpretation of the Torah." Pages 400–413 in *The Jesus Handbook*. Edited by Jens Schröter and Christine Jacobi. Translated by Robert L. Brawley. Grand Rapids: Eerdmans, 2022.

Keel, Othmar. *The Symbolism of the Biblical World: Ancient Near Eastern Iconography and the Book of Psalms*. Translated by Timothy J. Hallett. Winona Lake, IN: Eisenbrauns, 1997.

Keener, Craig S. *Christobiography: Memory, History, and the Reliability of the Gospels*. Grand Rapids: Eerdmans, 2019.

———. *The Gospel of John*. 2 vols. Grand Rapids: Baker Academic, 2003.

———. *The Historical Jesus of the Gospels*. Grand Rapids: Eerdmans, 2009.

Keith, Chris. "The Indebtedness of the Criteria Approach to Form Criticism and Recent Attempts to Rehabilitate the Search for an Authentic Jesus." Pages 25–48 in *Jesus, Criteria, and the Demise of Authenticity*. Edited by Chris Keith and Anthony Le Donne. London: T&T Clark, 2012.

———. *Jesus' Literacy: Scribal Culture and the Teacher from Galilee*. Library of New Testament Studies 413; Library of Historical Jesus Studies 8. London: Bloomsbury T&T Clark, 2011.

———. "Scribes and Scribalism." Pages 712–13 in *T&T Clark Encyclopedia of Second Temple Judaism*. Edited by Daniel M. Gurtner and Loren T. Stuckenbruck. 2 vols. London: T&T Clark, 2020.

Kelly, J. N. D. *Early Christian Creeds*. 3rd ed. London: Routledge, 1972.

Kirk, Alan. *Memory and the Jesus Tradition*. The Reception of Jesus in the First Three Centuries 2. London: T&T Clark, 2018.

Kirk, J. Daniel. *A Man Attested by God: The Human Jesus of the Synoptic Gospels*. Grand Rapids: Eerdmans, 2016.

Klausner, Joseph. *Jesus of Nazareth: His Life, Times, and Teaching*. Translated by Herbert Danby. New York: Macmillan, 1926.

Koester, Craig R. *Revelation*. Anchor Yale Bible 38A. New Haven: Yale University Press, 2014.

Kokkinos, Nick. *The Herodian Dynasty: Origins, Role in Society, and Eclipse*. London: Spinck, 2010.

Kollmann, Bernd. "Resuscitations of the Dead and Nature Miracles." Pages 315–22 in *The Jesus Handbook*. Edited by Jens Schröter and Christine Jacobi. Translated by Robert L. Brawley. Grand Rapids: Eerdmans, 2022.

Konradt, Matthias. *The Gospel according to Matthew: A Commentary*. Translated by M. Eugene Boring. Waco, TX: Baylor University Press, 2020.

Kreplin, Matthias. "The Self-Understanding of Jesus." Pages 1169–82 in vol. 2 of *Handbook for Handbook for the Study of the Historical Jesus*. Edited by Tom Holmén and Stanley E. Porter. 4 vols. Leiden: Brill, 2011.

Kugel, James. *Traditions of the Bible: A Guide to the Bible as It Was at the Start of the Common Era*. Cambridge, MA: Harvard University Press, 1997.

Kunath, F. *Dei Präexistenz Jesu im Johannesevangelium. Struktur und Theologie eines johanneischen Motivs*. Beihefte zur Zeitschrift für die neutestamentliche Wissenschaft 212. Berlin: Walter de Gruyter, 2016.

Laato, Antii. *A Star Is Rising: The Historical Development of the Old Testament*

Royal Ideology and the Rise of the Jewish Messianic Expectations. Atlanta: Scholars Press, 1997.

Lange, Armin. "The Shema Israel in Second Temple Judaism." *Journal of Ancient Judaism* 1.2 (2010): 207–14.

Le Donne, Anthony. "The Criterion of Coherence: Its Development, Inevitability, and Historiographical Limitations." Pages 95–114 in *Jesus, Criteria, and the Demise of Authenticity*. Edited by Chris Keith and Anthony Le Donne. London: T&T Clark, 2012.

———. *The Historiographical Jesus: Memory, Typology, and the Son of David*. Waco, TX: Baylor University Press, 2009.

Lee, Aquila H. *From Messiah to Preexistent Son*. Wissenschaftliche Untersuchungen zum Neuen Testament 2.192. Tübingen: Mohr Siebeck, 2005.

Lesses, Rebecca. "Supernatural Beings." Pages 682–88 in *The Jewish Annotated New Testament*. Edited by Amy-Jill Levine and Mark Zvi Brettler. 2nd ed. Oxford: Oxford University Press, 2017.

Levenson, David B. "Messianic Movements." Pages 622–28 in *The Jewish Annotated New Testament*. Edited by Amy-Jill Levine and Marc Zvi Brettler. 2nd ed. Oxford: Oxford University Press, 2017.

Levine, Amy-Jill. "The Gospel according to Luke." Pages 106–67 in *The Jewish Annotated New Testament*. Edited by Amy-Jill Levine and Mark Zvi-Brettler. 2nd ed. Oxford: Oxford University Press, 2017.

———. *The Misunderstood Jew: The Church and the Scandal of the Jewish Jesus*. San Francisco: HarperOne, 2007.

———. *Short Stories by Jesus: The Enigmatic Parables of a Controversial Rabbi*. San Francisco: HarperOne, 2014.

Levine, Lee I. *Jerusalem: Portrait of the City in the Second Temple Period (538 B.C.E.–70 C.E.)*. Philadelphia: Jewish Publication Society, 2002.

Litwa, David M. *How the Gospels Became History: Jesus and Mediterranean Myths*. New Haven: Yale University Press, 2019.

———. *Iesous Deus: The Early Christian Depiction of Jesus as a Mediterranean God*. Minneapolis: Fortress, 2014.

Litwak, Kenneth D. "Sanhedrin." Pages 706–8 in *T&T Clark Encyclopedia of Second Temple Judaism*. Edited by Daniel M. Gurtner and Loren T. Stuckenbruck. 2 vols. London: T&T Clark, 2020.

Loader, William. "Jesus and the Law." Pages 2745–72 in vol. 3 of *Handbook for the Study of the Historical Jesus*. Edited by Tom Holmén and Stanley E. Porter. 4 vols. Leiden: Brill, 2011.

Lohfink, Gerhard. *The Forty Parables of Jesus*. Translated by Linda M. Maloney. Collegeville: Liturgical Press, 2021.

———. *Jesus of Nazareth: What He Wanted, Who He Was*. Translated by Linda M. Maloney. Collegeville: Liturgical Press, 2012.

Lohmeyer, Ernst. "Die Verklärung Jesu nach dem Markus-Evangelium." *Zeitschrift für die Neutestamentliche Wissenschaft* 21 (1922): 185–215.

Loke, Andrew Ter Ern. *The Origin of Divine Christology*. Society for New Testament Studies Monograph Series 169. Cambridge: Cambridge University Press, 2017.

Loos, Hendrik van der. *The Miracles of Jesus*. Supplements to Novum Testamentum 9. Leiden: Brill, 1965.

Lucass, Shirley. *The Concept of the Messiah in the Scriptures of Judaism and Christianity*. Library of Second Temple Studies 78. London: Bloomsbury, 2011.

Lüdemann, Gerd. *Jesus after Two Thousand Years. What He Really Said and Did*. Translated by John Bowden. London: SCM; Amherst: Prometheus Books, 2001.

———. *Paul: The Founder of Christianity*. London: SCM; Amherst, NY: Prometheus, 2002.

Lundbom, Jack R. *Jeremiah 21–36*. Anchor Yale Bible 21B. New Haven: Yale University Press, 2004.

Luz, Ulrich. *Matthew: A Commentary*. Translated by James E. Crouch. 3 vols. Hermeneia. Minneapolis: Fortress, 2001–2007.

Madden, Patrick J. *Jesus' Walking on the Sea*. Beiheft zur Zeitschrift für die neutestamentliche Wissenschaft 81. Berlin: Walter de Gruyter, 1997.

Magness, Jodi. *The Archaeology of the Holy Land: From the Destruction of Solomon's Temple to the Muslim Conquest*. Cambridge: Cambridge University Press, 2012.

Malina, Bruce J. "Assessing the Historicity of Jesus' Walking on the Sea." Pages 351–71 in *Authenticating the Activities of Jesus*. Edited by Bruce Chilton and Craig A. Evans. Leiden: Brill, 1999.

Manns, Frédéric. "Mount Tabor." Pages 167–77 in *Jesus and Archaeology*. Edited by James H. Charlesworth. Grand Rapids: Eerdmans, 2006.

Manson, T. W. *The Sayings of Jesus*. London: SCM, 1949.

Marcus, Joel. *John the Baptist in History and Theology*. Columbia: University of South Carolina Press, 2018.

———. *Mark*. 2 vols. Anchor Yale Bible 27–27A. New Haven: Yale University Press, 2000–2009.

Marshak, Adam. "Herodian Dynasty." Pages 735–39 in *The Eerdmans Dictionary of Early Judaism*. Edited by John J. Collins and Daniel C. Harlow. Grand Rapids: Eerdmans, 2010.

Marshall, I. Howard. "The Christology of Luke's Gospel and Acts." Pages 122–47 in

Contours of Christology in the New Testament. Edited by Richard N. Longenecker. Grand Rapids: Eerdmans, 2005.

Martyn, J. Louis. *Galatians*. Anchor Bible 33A. New York: Doubleday, 1997.

Mason, Steve. "Jewish Sources: Flavius Josephus." Pages 160–66 in *The Jesus Handbook*. Edited by Jens Schröter and Christine Jacobi. Translated by Robert L. Brawley. Grand Rapids: Eerdmans, 2022.

———. "Jews, Judaeans, Judaizing, Judaism: Problems of Categorization in Ancient History." *Journal for the Study of Judaism in the Persian, Hellenistic, and Roman Periods* 38 (2007): 457–512.

McCarter, P. Kyle, Jr. *2 Samuel*. Anchor Yale Bible 9. New Haven: Yale University Press, 1984.

McDonough, Sean M. *Christ as Creator: Origins of a New Testament Doctrine*. Oxford: Oxford University Press, 2009.

McDowell, Sean. *The Fate of the Apostles: Examining the Martyrdom Accounts of the Closest Followers of Jesus*. London: Routledge, 2015.

McGrath, James F. *The Only True God: Early Christian Monotheism in Its Jewish Context*. Urbana: University of Illinois Press, 2009.

McKnight, Scot, and Joseph B. Modica, eds. *Who Do My Opponents Say That I Am? An Investigation of the Accusations against Jesus*. Library of New Testament Studies 327. London: T&T Clark, 2008.

Meier, John P. "Basic Methodology in the Quest for the Historical Jesus." Pages 291–331 in vol. 1 of *Handbook for the Study of the Historical Jesus*. Edited by Tom Holmén and Stanley E. Porter. 4 vols. Leiden: Brill, 2011.

———. "From Elijah-Like Prophet to Royal Davidic Messiah." Pages 45–83 in *Jesus: A Colloquium in the Holy Land*. Edited by Doris Donnely. New York: Continuum, 2001.

———. *A Marginal Jew: Rethinking the Historical Jesus*. 5 vols. Anchor Yale Bible Reference Library. New Haven: Yale University Press, 1991–2016.

Metzger, Bruce M. *A Textual Commentary on the Greek New Testament*. 2nd ed. Stuttgart: Deutsche Bibelgesellschaft, 1994.

Meyer, Ben F. *The Aims of Jesus*. London: SCM, 1979.

Milgrom, Jacob. *Leviticus*. 3 vols. Anchor Yale Bible 3, 3A, 3B. New Haven: Yale University Press, 1991–2001.

Mittag, Peter Franz. *Antiochos IV. Epiphanes: Eine politische Biographie. Klio*. Beiträge zur Alten Geschichte Beihefte, Neue Folge 11. Berlin: Akademie Verlag, 2006.

Moberly, R. W. L. "How Appropriate Is 'Monotheism' as a Category for Biblical Interpretation?" Pages 216–34 in *Early Jewish and Christian Monotheism*. Edited by Loren T. Stuckenbruck and Wendy E. S. North. London: T&T Clark, 2004.

Moloney, Francis J., SDB. *The Apocalypse of John: A Commentary*. Grand Rapids: Baker Academic, 2020.

———. *The Gospel of John*. Sacra Pagina 4. Collegeville: Liturgical Press, 1998.

Moore, Carey A. *Judith*. Anchor Bible 40. New York: Doubleday, 1985.

Moss, Candida R. *Ancient Christian Martyrdom: Diverse Practices, Theologies, and Traditions*. Anchor Yale Bible Reference Library. New Haven: Yale University Press, 2012.

Mowinckel, Sigmund. *He That Cometh: The Messiah Concept in the Old Testament and Later Judaism*. Translated by G. W. Anderson. Repr., Grand Rapids: Eerdmans, 2005.

Murphy, Frederick J. *Apocalypticism in the Bible and Its World: A Comprehensive Introduction*. Grand Rapids: Baker Academic, 2012.

Murphy-O'Connor, Jerome. *The Holy Land: An Oxford Archaeological Guide*. 5th ed. Oxford: Oxford University Press, 2008.

———. "What Really Happened at the Transfiguration?" *Bible Review* 3 (1987): 8–21.

Naiden, F. S. *Soldier, Priest, and God: A Life of Alexander the Great*. Oxford: Oxford University Press, 2019.

Najman, Hindy. "Decalogue." Pages 526–28 in *The Eerdmans Dictionary of Early Judaism*. Edited by John J. Collins and Daniel C. Harlow. Grand Rapids: Eerdmans, 2010.

Neusner, Jacob. *A Rabbi Talks with Jesus*. New York: Doubleday, 1993.

———. *A Rabbi Talks with Jesus*. Rev. ed. Montreal: McGill-Queen's University Press, 2000.

———. *The Tosefta*. 2 vols. Peabody, MA: Hendrickson, 2002.

Newman, Carey C., James R. Davila, and Gladys S. Lews, eds. *The Jewish Roots of Christological Monotheism: Papers from the St. Andrews Conference on the Historical Origins of the Worship of Jesus*. Repr., Waco, TX: Baylor University Press, 2017.

Newman, Judith H. "Psalms, Book of." Pages 1105–7 in *The Eerdmans Dictionary of Early Judaism*. Edited by John J. Collins and Daniel C. Harlow. Grand Rapids: Eerdmans, 2010.

Newsom, Carol A. "The Book of Job." Pages 319–637 in vol. 4 of *The New Interpreter's Bible*. Nashville: Abingdon, 1996.

———, with Brennan W. Breed. *Daniel: A Commentary*. Louisville: Westminster John Knox, 2014.

Neyrey, Jerome. "I Said 'You Are Gods': Psalm 82,6 and John 10." *Journal of Biblical Literature* 108 (1989): 647–62.

Nickelsburg, George W. E. *1 Enoch 1*. Hermeneia. Minneapolis: Fortress, 2001.

———. *Resurrection, Immortality, and Eternal Life in Intertestamental Judaism and Early Christianity*. Expanded ed. Harvard Theological Studies 56. Cambridge, MA: Harvard University Press, 2006.

Nickelsburg, George W. E., and James C. VanderKam. *1 Enoch* 2. Hermeneia. Minneapolis: Fortress, 2012.

Niehoff, Maren R. *Philo of Alexandria: An Intellectual Biography*. Anchor Yale Bible Reference Library. New Haven: Yale University Press, 2018.

North, J. Lionel. "Jesus and Worship, God and Sacrifice." Pages 186–202 in *Early Jewish and Christian Monotheism*. Edited by Loren T. Stuckenbruck and Wendy E. S. North. Journal for the Study of the New Testament Supplement Series 263. London: T&T Clark, 2004.

Novenson, Matthew V. "Did Paul Abandon Either Judaism or Monotheism?" Pages 239–59 in *The New Cambridge Companion to St. Paul*. Edited by Bruce W. Longenecker. Cambridge: Cambridge University Press, 2020.

———. *The Grammar of Messianism: An Ancient Jewish Political Idiom and Its Users*. Oxford: Oxford University Press, 2017.

———. "Messiah." Pages 492–94 in *T&T Clark Encyclopedia of Second Temple Judaism*. Edited by Daniel M. Gurtner and Loren T. Stuckenbruck. 2 vols. London: T&T Clark, 2020.

———. *Monotheism and Christology in Greco-Roman Antiquity*. Supplements to Novum Testamentum 180. Leiden: Brill, 2020.

O'Collins, Gerald, SJ. *Christology: A Biblical, Historical, and Systematic Study of Jesus*. 2nd ed. Oxford: Oxford University Press, 2009.

Oegema, Gerbern S. *The Anointed and His People: Messianic Expectations from the Maccabees to Bar Kochba*. Journal for the Study of the Pseudepigrapha Supplement Series 27. Sheffield: Sheffield Academic Press, 1998.

Osiek, Carolyn, and David L. Balch. *Families in the New Testament World: Households and House Churches*. Louisville: Westminster John Knox, 1997.

Oswalt, J. N. *The Book of Isaiah*. 2 vols. New International Commentary on the Old Testament. Grand Rapids: Eerdmans, 1986–1998.

Owen, Paul, and David Shepherd. "Speaking Up for Qumran, Dalman, and the Son of Man: Was *Bar Enasha* a Common Term for 'Man' in the Time of Jesus?" *Journal for the Study of the New Testament* 81 (2001): 81–22.

Parkes, James. *The Conflict of the Church and the Synagogue: A Study in the Origins of Antisemitism*. New York: Jewish Publication Society, 1934

Paulus, Heinrich Eberhard Gottlob. *Philologisch-kritische und historische Commentar über die drey ersten Evangelien*. 4 vols. Lübeck: Bohn, 1800–1808.

Peppard, Michael. *The Son of God in the Roman World: Divine Sonship in Its Social and Political Context*. Oxford: Oxford University Press, 2011.

Perkins, Pheme. "Resurrection and Christology: Are They Related?" Pages 67–75 in *Israel's God and Rebecca's Children: Christology and Community in Early Judaism and Christianity: Essays in Honor of Larry W. Hurtado and Alan F. Segal*. Edited by David B. Capes, April D. DeConick, Helen K. Bond, and Troy A. Miller. Waco, TX: Baylor University Press, 2007.

Perowne, Stewart. *The Later Herods: The Political Background of the New Testament*. Nashville: Abingdon, 1958.

Pervo, Richard I. *Acts*. Hermeneia. Minneapolis: Fortress, 2009.

Pfremmer De Long, Kindalee. "Angels and Visions in Luke-Acts." Pages 79–107 in *The Jewish Apocalyptic Tradition and the Shaping of New Testament Thought*. Edited by Benjamin E. Reynolds and Loren T. Stuckenbruck. Minneapolis: Fortress, 2017.

Philo. *Volumes I–X, Supplements I–II*. Translated and edited by F. H. Colson, G. H. Whitaker, and R. Marcus. Loeb Classical Library. Cambridge, MA: Harvard University Press, 1929–1953.

Pietersma, Albert, and Benjamin G. Wright, eds. *A New English Translation of the Septuagint*. Oxford: Oxford University Press, 2007.

Pitre, Brant. "From Reimarus to Allison: The Quest for Jesus and the Christological 'Thunderbolt' (Matt 11:25–27//Luke 10:21–22)." Pages 373–404 in *"To Recover What Has Been Lost": Essays on Eschatology, Intertextuality, and Reception History in Honor of Dale C. Allison, Jr.* Edited by Tucker S. Ferda, Daniel Frayer-Griggs, and Nathan C. Johnson. Supplements to Novum Testamentum 183. Leiden: Brill, 2021.

———. "The Historical Jesus and the Apocalyptic 'Thunderbolt' (Matt 11:25–27// Luke 10:21–22)." Pages 169–85 in *The Figure of Jesus in History and Theology: Essays in Honor of John Meier*. Edited by Vincent T. M. Skemp and Kelley Coblentz Bautch. Catholic Biblical Quarterly Imprints 1. Washington, DC: Catholic Biblical Association of America, 2020.

———. *Jesus, the Tribulation, and the End of the Exile: Restoration Eschatology and the Origin of the Atonement*. Wissenschaftliche Untersuchungen zum Neuen Testament 2.204. Tübingen: Mohr Siebeck; Grand Rapids: Baker Academic, 2005.

———. *Jesus and the Last Supper*. Grand Rapids: Eerdmans, 2015.

Pitre, Brant, Michael P. Barber, and John A. Kincaid. *Paul, a New Covenant Jew: Rethinking Pauline Theology*. Grand Rapids: Eerdmans, 2019.

Plutarch. *Hellenistic Lives, Including Alexander the Great*. Translated by Robin Waterfield. Oxford: Oxford University Press, 2016.

———. *Lives, Demosthenes and Cicero, Alexander and Caesar*. Translated by Bernadotte Perrin. Loeb Classical Library 99. Cambridge, MA: Harvard University Press, 1919.

Pomykala, Kenneth E. "Messianism." Pages 938–42 in *The Eerdmans Dictionary of Early Judaism*. Edited by John J. Collins and Daniel C. Harlow. Grand Rapids: Eerdmans, 2010.

Pope, Marvin H. *Job*. Anchor Bible 15. New York: Doubleday, 1965.

Porter, Stanley E. *The Criteria for Authenticity in Historical-Jesus Research: Previous Discussion and New Proposals*. Library of New Testament Studies 191. London: T&T Clark, 2004.

Price, S. R. F. *Rituals and Power: The Roman Imperial Cult in Asia Minor*. Cambridge: Cambridge University Press, 1998.

Propp, William H. C. *Exodus*. 2 vols. Anchor Yale Bible 2–2A. New Haven: Yale University Press, 1999–2006.

Puech, Émile. "Hodayot." Pages 365–68 in vol. 1 of *Encyclopedia of the Dead Sea Scrolls*. Edited by Lawrence H. Schiffman and James C. VanderKam. 2 vols. Oxford: Oxford University Press, 2000.

———. "Messianic Apocalypse." Pages 543–44 in vol. 1 of *Encyclopedia of the Dead Sea Scrolls*. Edited by Lawrence H. Schiffman and James C. VanderKam. 2 vols. Oxford: Oxford University Press, 2002.

Puig i Tàrrech, Armand. *Jesus: A Biography*. Translated by Jenny Read-Heimerdinger. Waco, TX: Baylor University Press, 2011.

Pummer, Reinhard. *The Samaritans: A Profile*. Grand Rapids: Eerdmans, 2016.

Quintus Curtius. *History of Alexander*. Vol. 2, *Books 6–10*. Translated by J. C. Rolfe. Loeb Classical Library 369. Cambridge, MA: Harvard University Press, 1946.

Rainbow, Paul. "Melchizedek as a Messiah at Qumran." *Bulletin of Biblical Research* 7 (1997): 179–94.

Raphael, Rebecca. "Sickness and Disease." Pages 1228–30 in *The Eerdmans Dictionary of Early Judaism*. Edited by John J. Collins and Daniel C. Harlow. Grand Rapids: Eerdmans, 2010.

Rashkover, Randi. "Christology." Pages 754–56 in *The Jewish Annotated New Testament*. Edited by Amy-Jill Levine and Marc Zvi Brettler. 2nd ed. Oxford: Oxford University Press, 2017.

Regev, Eyal. "2 Maccabees." Pages 251–88 in *The Jewish Annotated Apocrypha*. Edited by Jonathan Klawans and Lawrence M. Wills. Oxford: Oxford University Press, 2020.

Reid, Barbara E. *The Transfiguration: A Source- and Redaction-Critical Study of Luke 9:28–36*. Paris: Gabalda, 1993.

Reimarus, Herman Samuel. *Fragments*. Edited by Charles H. Talbert. Translated by Ralph Fraser. Philadelphia: Fortress, 1970 (orig. 1774–1778).

Reinhartz, Adele. "The Gospel according to John." Pages 168–218 in *The Jewish Annotated New Testament*. Edited by Amy-Jill Levine and Marc Zvi Brettler. 2nd ed. Oxford: Oxford University Press, 2017.

———. "The Jews of the Fourth Gospel." Pages 121–37 in *The Oxford Handbook of Johannine Studies*. Edited by Judith M. Lieu and Martinus C. de Boer. Oxford: Oxford University Press, 2018.

Reiser, Marius. *Jesus and Judgment: The Eschatological Proclamation in Its Jewish Context*. Translated by Linda M. Maloney. Minneapolis: Fortress, 1997.

Renan, Ernest. *The Life of Jesus*. London: Watts & Co., 1935 (orig. 1863).

Reynolds, Benjamin E., and Loren T. Stuckenbruck, eds. *The Jewish Apocalyptic Tradition and the Shaping of New Testament Thought*. Minneapolis: Fortress, 2017.

Robinson, John A. T. "The Last Tabu? The Self-Consciousness of Jesus." Pages 553–66 in *The Historical Jesus in Recent Research*. Edited by James D. G. Dunn and Scot McKnight. Sources for Biblical and Theological Study 10. Winona Lake, IN: Eisenbrauns, 2005.

Robinson, Thomas A. *Ignatius of Antioch and the Parting of the Ways: Early Jewish-Christian Relations*. Peabody, MA: Hendrickson, 2009.

Rodriguez, Rafael. "The Embarrassing Truth about Jesus: The Criterion of Embarrassment and the Failure of Historical Authenticity." Pages 132–51 in *Jesus, Criteria, and the Demise of Authenticity*. Edited by Chris Keith and Anthony Le Donne. London: T&T Clark, 2012.

Roloff, Jürgen. *Neues Testament: Neukirchener Arbeitsbücher*. 4th ed. Neukirchen-Vluyn: Neukirchener Verlag, 1985.

Romm, James. *Alexander the Great: Selections from Arrian, Diodorus, Plutarch, and Quintus Curtius*. Indianapolis: Hackett, 2005.

Rosik, Mariusz. *Church and Synagogue (30–313 AD): Parting of the Ways*. European Studies in Theology, Philosophy, and History of Religions 20. Berlin: Peter Lang, 2019.

Rothstein, David. "Phylacteries and Mezuzoth." Pages 1086–88 in *The Eerdmans Dictionary of Early Judaism*. Edited by John J. Collins and Daniel C. Harlow. Grand Rapids: Eerdmans, 2010.

Rowland, Christopher, and Christopher R. A. Morray-Jones. *The Mystery of God: Early Jewish Mysticism and the New Testament*. Compendia Rerum Iudaicarum ad Novum Testamentum 12. Leiden: Brill, 2009.

Rüpke, Jörg, ed. *A Companion to Roman Religion*. Oxford: Wiley-Blackwell, 2011.

Ryan, Jordan. "The Historian's Craft and the Future of Historical Jesus Research:

Engaging Brant Pitre's *Jesus and the Last Supper* as a Work of History." *Journal for the Study of the Historical Jesus* 15 (2017): 60–87.

Sanders, E. P. *The Historical Figure of Jesus*. London: Penguin, 1993.

———. *Jesus and Judaism*. Minneapolis: Fortress, 1985.

———. *Jewish Law between Jesus and the Mishnah: Five Studies*. London: SCM; Harrisburg, PA: Trinity Press International, 1990.

———. *Jewish Law from Jesus to the Mishnah: Five Studies*. London: SCM; Harrisburg, PA: Trinity Press International, 1990.

———. *Judaism: Practice and Belief 63 BCE–66 CE*. Minneapolis: Fortress, 2016.

———. *Paul: The Apostle's Life, Letters, and Thought*. Minneapolis: Fortress, 2017.

Sanders, E. P., and Margaret Davies. *Studying the Synoptic Gospels*. London: SCM; Philadelphia: Trinity Press International, 1989.

Savran, Gene L. *Encountering the Divine: Theophany in Biblical Narrative*. Journal for the Study of the Old Testament Supplement 420. London: T&T Clark, 2005.

Schäfer, Peter. *Two Gods in Heaven: Jewish Concepts of God in Antiquity*. Translated by Allison Brown. Princeton: Princeton University Press, 2020.

Schams, Christine. *Jewish Scribes in the Second Temple Period*. Library of Hebrew Bible/Old Testament Studies 291. Sheffield: Sheffield Academic Press, 1998.

Schaper, Joachim. *Eschatology in the Greek Psalter*. Wissenschaftliche Untersuchungen zum Neuen Testament 2.76. *Tübingen: Mohr Siebeck, 1995*.

Schnabel, Eckhard J. *Jesus in Jerusalem: The Last Days*. Grand Rapids: Eerdmans, 2018.

Schnackenburg, Rudolf. *The Gospel according to St. John*. Translated by Kevin Smith, Cecily Hasting, Francis McDonagh, David Smith, Richard Foley, SJ, and G. A. Con. 3 vols. New York: Herder & Herder/Crossroad, 1968–1982.

———. *The Gospel of Matthew*. Translated by Robert R. Barr. Grand Rapids: Eerdmans, 2002.

Schnelle, Udo. "The Person of Jesus Christ in the Gospel of John." Pages 311–30 in *The Oxford Handbook of Johannine Studies*. Edited by Judith M. Lieu and Martinus C. de Boer. Oxford: Oxford University Press, 2018.

Schröter, Jens. *Jesus of Nazareth: Jew from Galilee, Savior of the World*. Translated by Wayne Coppins and S. Brian Pounds. Waco, TX: Baylor University Press, 2014.

Schwartz, Daniel R. *Agrippa I: The Last King of Judaea*. Texte und Studien zum Antiken Judentum 23. Tübingen: Mohr Siebeck, 1990.

Schweitzer, Albert. *The Quest of the Historical Jesus: A Critical Study of Its Progress from Reimarus to Wrede*. Translated by William Montgomery. Rev. ed. New York: Macmillan, 1968.

Setzer, Claudia. "You Invent a Christ." *Union Seminary Quarterly Review* 44 (1991): 315–28.

Shanks, Hershel, ed. *Partings: How Judaism and Christianity Became Two*. Washington, DC: Biblical Archaeology Society, 2013.

Sherwin-White, A. N. *Roman Society and Roman Law in the New Testament*. Oxford: Oxford University Press, 1963.

Siculus, Diodorus. *Library of History, Books 16.66–17*. Translated by C. Bradford Welles. Loeb Classical Library 422. Cambridge, MA: Harvard University Press, 1963.

Skarsaune, Oskar, and Reidar Hvalvik, eds. *Jewish Believers in Jesus: The Early Centuries*. Peabody, MA: Hendrickson, 2007.

Smith, Dwight Moody. "Jesus Tradition in the Gospel of John." Pages 1997–2040 in vol. 3 of *Handbook for the Study of the Historical Jesus*. Edited by Tom Holmén and Stanley E. Porter. 4 vols. Leiden: Brill, 2011.

———. *John among the Gospels*. 2nd ed. Columbia: University of South Carolina Press, 2001.

Snodgrass, Klyne R. *Stories with Intent: A Comprehensive Guide to the Parables of Jesus*. 2nd ed. Grand Rapids: Eerdmans, 2018.

Stanton, Graham. *The Gospels and Jesus*. 2nd ed. Oxford: Oxford University Press, 2002.

Stauffer, E. "Jesus, Geschichte und Verküdigung." *Aufstieg und Niedergang der Römischen Welt* 25.1:3–130. Part 2, *Principat*, 25.1. Edited by H. Temporini and W. Haase. New York: Walter de Gruyter, 1989.

Steudel, Annette. "Melchizedek." Pages 535–36 in vol. 2 of *Encyclopedia of the Dead Sea Scrolls*. Edited by Lawrence H. Schiffman and James C. VanderKam. 2 vols. Oxford: Oxford University Press, 2000.

Stevenson, Angus J., ed. *Shorter Oxford English Dictionary*. 2 vols. Oxford: Oxford University Press, 2007.

Stevenson, J., ed. *A New Eusebius: Documents Illustrating the History of the Church to AD 337*. Revised by W. H. C. Frend. Grand Rapids: Baker Academic, 2013.

Stone, Michael E. "Apocalyptic Literature." Pages 383–441 in *Jewish Writings of the Second Temple Period: Apocrypha, Pseudepigrapha, Qumran Sectarian Writings, Philo, Josephus*. Edited by Michael E. Stone. Compendia Rerum Iudaicarum ad Novum Testamentum 2. Assen: Van Gorcum, 1984.

———. *Fourth Ezra*. Hermeneia. Minneapolis: Fortress, 1990.

Strauss, David Friedrich. *The Life of Jesus Critically Examined*. Translated by George Eliot. Philadelphia: Fortress, 1972 (orig. 1835–1836).

Stuhlmacher, Peter. "The Messianic Son of Man: Jesus' Claim to Deity." Pages 325–44 *The Historical Jesus in Recent Research*. Edited by James D. G. Dunn and Scot McKnight. Sources for Biblical and Theological Study 10. Winona Lake, IN: Eisenbrauns, 2005.

Suetonius. *Volume 1*. Translated by J. C. Rolfe. Loeb Classical Library 31. Cambridge, MA: Harvard University Press, 1998.

Sullivan, Kevin P. "Monotheism." Pages 513–15 in vol. 2 of *Encyclopedia of Second Temple Judaism*. Edited by Daniel M. Gurtner and Loren T. Stuckenbruck. London: T&T Clark, 2020.

Tacitus. *Histories, Books 4–5, Annals, Books 1–3*. Translated by Clifford H. Moore and John Jackson. Loeb Classical Library 249. Cambridge, MA: Harvard University Press, 1931.

Tan, Kim Huat. "Jesus and the Shema." Pages 2677–707 in vol. 3 of *Handbook for the Study of the Historical Jesus*. Edited by Tom Holmén and Stanley E. Porter. 4 vols. Leiden: Brill, 2011.

Tanner, Norman P., SJ, ed. *Decrees of the Ecumenical Councils*. 2 vols. London: Sheed & Ward; Washington, DC: Georgetown University Press, 1990.

Tasker, David R. *Ancient Near Easter Literature and the Hebrew Scriptures about the Fatherhood of God*. Studies in Biblical Literature 69. New York: Peter Lang, 2004.

Temporini, Hildegard, and Wolfgang Haase, eds. *Aufstieg und Niedergang der römischen Welt: Geschichte und Kultur Roms im Spiegel der neueren Forschung*. Part 2, *Principat*. Berlin: Walter de Gruyter, 1972–.

Thatcher, Tom. *Jesus the Riddler: The Power of Ambiguity in the Gospels*. Louisville: Westminster John Knox, 2006.

Theissen, Gerd, and Annette Merz. *The Historical Jesus: A Comprehensive Guide*. Translated by John Bowden. Minneapolis: Fortress, 1998.

Thompson, Marianne Meye. *John: A Commentary*. Louisville: Westminster John Knox, 2015.

Tilling, Chris. *Paul's Divine Christology*. Grand Rapids: Eerdmans, 2015.

Toit, David du. "The Third Quest for the Historical Jesus." Pages 93–108 in *The Jesus Handbook*. Edited by Jens Schröter and Christine Jacobi. Translated by Robert L. Brawley. Grand Rapids: Eerdmans, 2022.

Twelftree, Graham H. "The Message of Jesus I: Miracles, Continuing Controversies." Pages 2517–48 in vol. 3 of *Handbook for the Study of the Historical Jesus*. Edited by Tom Holmén and Stanley E. Porter. 4 vols. Leiden: Brill, 2011.

———. *The Miracles of Jesus: A Historical and Theological Study*. Downers Grove: IVP Academic, 1999.

———, ed. *The Nature Miracles of Jesus: Problems, Perspectives, and Prospects*. Eugene, OR: Cascade, 2017.

VanderKam, James C. *From Joseph to Caiaphas: High Priests after the Exile*. Minneapolis: Fortress; Assen: Van Gorcum, 2004.

———. *Jubilees: A Commentary*. 2 vols. Hermeneia. Minneapolis: Fortress, 2018.

Vaux, Roland de. *Ancient Israel: Its Life and Institutions*. Repr., Grand Rapids: Eerdmans, 1997.

Verheyden, Joseph, Reimund Bieringer, Jens Schröter, and Ines Jäger, eds. *Docetism in the Early Church*. Wissenschaftliche Untersuchungen zum Neuen Testament 399. Tübingen: Mohr Siebeck, 2018.

Vermes, Geza. *The Authentic Gospel of Jesus*. London: Penguin, 2003

———. *The Changing Faces of Jesus*. New York: Penguin Putnam, 2000.

———. *Christian Beginnings: From Nazareth to Nicaea*. New Haven: Yale University Press, 2013.

———. *Jesus the Jew: A Historian's Reading of the Gospels*. Philadelphia: Fortress, 1973.

———. *The Religion of Jesus the Jew*. Minneapolis: Fortress, 1993.

Viviano, Benedict T. "Eschatology and the Quest for the Historical Jesus." Pages 73–90 in *The Oxford Handbook of Eschatology*. Oxford: Oxford University Press, 2008.

Wachsmann, Shelley. *The Sea of Galilee Boat*. College Station: Texas A&M University Press, 2000.

Webb, Robert L. "The Historical Enterprise and Historical Jesus Research." Pages 54–75 in *Key Events in the Life of the Historical Jesus*. Edited by Darrell L. Bock and Robert L. Webb. Wissenschaftliche Untersuchungen zum Neuen Testament 247. Tübingen: Mohr Siebeck, 2009.

———. *John the Baptizer and Prophet: A Socio-Historical Study*. Journal for the Study of the New Testament Supplement Series 62. Sheffield: JSOT Press, 1991.

Weinfeld, Moshe. *Deuteronomy 1–11*. Anchor Bible 5. New York: Doubleday, 1991.

Weiss, Johannes. *Jesus' Proclamation of the Kingdom of God*. Translated by Richard Hyde Hiers and David Larrimore Holland. Philadelphia: Fortress, 1971 (orig. 1892).

Westermann, Claus. *Genesis 12–36: A Continental Commentary*. Translated by John J. Scullion, SJ. Minneapolis: Fortress, 1995.

Wevers, J. W. *Notes on the Greek Text of Exodus*. Septuagint and Cognate Studies 30. Atlanta: Scholars Press, 1990.

Whealey, Alice. "The *Testimonium Flavianum*." Pages 345–55 in *A Companion to Josephus*. Edited by Honora Howell Chapman and Zuleika Rodgers. London: Wiley Blackwell, 2016.

Williams, Catrin H. *I Am He: The Interpretation of 'Anî Hû' in Jewish and Early*

Christian Literature. Wissenschaftliche Untersuchungen zum Neuen Testament 113. Tübingen: Mohr Siebeck, 2000.

———. "'I Am' or 'I Am He': Self Declaratory Pronouncements in the Fourth Gospel and Rabbinic Tradition." Pages 343–52 in *Jesus in the Johannine Tradition*. Edited by Robert T. Fortna and Tom Thatcher. Louisville: Westminster John Knox, 2001.

Williams, Margaret H. "Jews and Christians at Rome: An Early Parting of the Ways." Pages 151–78 in *Partings: How Judaism and Christianity Became Two*. Edited by Hershel Shanks. Washington, DC: Biblical Archaeology Society, 2013.

Williams, Rowan. *Arius: Heresy and Tradition*. Rev. ed. Grand Rapids: Eerdmans, 2001.

Wills, Lawrence M. "The Gospel according to Mark." Pages 67–106 in *The Jewish Annotated New Testament*. Edited by Amy-Jill Levine and Mark Zvi Brettler. 2nd ed. Oxford: Oxford University Press, 2017.

Winter, Bruce W. *Divine Honours for the Caesars: The First Christians' Responses*. Grand Rapids: Eerdmans, 2015.

Winter, Dagmar. "Saving the Quest for Authenticity from the Criterion of Dissimilarity: History and Plausibility." Pages 115–31 in *Jesus, Criteria, and the Demise of Authenticity*. Edited by Chris Keith and Anthony Le Donne. London: T&T Clark, 2012.

Winter, Paul. *On the Trial of Jesus*. Revised and edited by T. A. Burkill and Geza Vermes. 2nd ed. Berlin: Walter de Gruyter, 1974.

Winterling, Aloys. *Caligula: A Biography*. Translated by Deborah Lucas Schneider, Glenn W. Most, and Paul Psoinos. Berkeley: University of California Press, 2011.

Wise, Michael O., Martin G. Abegg Jr., and Edward M. Cook. *The Dead Sea Scrolls: A New Translation*. Rev. ed. San Francisco: HarperOne, 2005.

Witherington, Ben, III. *The Christology of Jesus*. Minneapolis: Fortress, 1990.

Wolter, Michael. *The Gospel according to Luke*. Translated by Wayne Coppins and Christoph Heilig. 2 vols. Waco, TX: Baylor University Press, 2017.

———. "Jesus as a Teller of Parables: On Jesus' Self-Interpretation in His Parables." Pages 123–39 in *Jesus Research: An International Perspective, The First Princeton-Prague Symposium on Jesus Research*. Edited by James H. Charlesworth and Petr Pokorny. Grand Rapids: Eerdmans, 2009.

———. "Jesus's Understanding of Himself." Pages 422–29 in *The Jesus Handbook*. Edited by Jens Schröter and Christine Jacobi. Translated by Robert L. Brawley. Grand Rapids: Eerdmans, 2022.

Worthington, Ian. *Alexander the Great: Man and God*. Harlow: Longman Pearson, 2004.

Wrede, William. *The Messianic Secret*. Translated by J. C. G. Greig. Cambridge: James Clarke, 1971 (orig. 1901).

Wright, N. T. *Jesus and the Victory of God*. Vol. 2 of *Christian Origins and the Question of God*. Minneapolis: Fortress, 1996.

———. *Paul and the Faithfulness of God*. Vol. 4 of *Christian Origins and the Question of God*. Minneapolis: Fortress, 2013.

Yarbro Collins, Adela. "Blasphemy." Page 445 in *The Eerdmans Dictionary of Early Judaism*. Edited by John J. Collins and Daniel C. Harlow. Grand Rapids: Eerdmans, 2010.

———. "How on Earth Did Jesus Become a God? A Reply." Pages 55–66 in *Israel's God and Rebecca's Children: Christology and Community in Early Judaism and Christianity: Essays in Honor of Larry W. Hurtado and Alan F. Segal*. Edited by David B. Capes, April D. DeConick, Helen K. Bond, and Troy A. Miller. Waco, TX: Baylor University Press, 2007.

———. *Mark: A Commentary*. Hermeneia. Minneapolis: Fortress, 2007.

Yarbro Collins, Adela, and John J. Collins. *King and Messiah as Son of God: Divine, Human, and Angelic Messianic Figures in Biblical and Related Literature*. Grand Rapids: Eerdmans, 2008.

Young, Frances M., with Andrew Teal. *From Nicaea to Chalcedon: A Guide to Its Literature and Background*. 2nd ed. Grand Rapids: Baker Academic, 2010.

Zangenberg, Jürgen K. "Jerusalem and Judea as a Sphere of Activity." Pages 233–40 in *The Jesus Handbook*. Edited by Jens Schröter and Christine Jacobi. Translated by Robert L. Brawley. Grand Rapids: Eerdmans, 2022.

Zehnder, Markus. "Why the Danielic 'Son of Man' Is a Divine Being." *Bulletin of Biblical Research* 24.3 (2014): 331–47.

Zimmerman, Johannes. *Messianische Texte as Qumran*. Wissenschaftliche Untersuchungen zum Neuen Testament 2.104. Tübingen: Mohr Siebeck, 1998.

Zimmerman, Ruben. "Re-counting the Impossible." Pages 107–27 in *The Nature Miracles of Jesus: Problems, Perspectives, and Prospects*. Edited by Graham H. Twelftree. Eugene, OR: Cascade, 2017.

Index of Authors

Index of Subjects

Index of Scripture and Other Ancient Sources

New Testament

Matthew

Luke